Intermediate
Microeconomics

Intermediate Microeconomics

A Modern Approach

Hal R. Varian

University of Michigan

W. W. Norton & Company • New York • London

To Carol

Copyright © 1987 by Hal R. Varian

All rights reserved
Printed in the United States of America

FIRST EDITION

Library of Congress Cataloging-in-Publication Data
Varian, Hal R.
  Intermediate microeconomics.
  Includes index.
  1. Microeconomics. I. Title.
HB172.V34   1986   338.5   86-21785

ISBN 0-393-95554-0

W. W. Norton & Company, Inc., 500 Fifth Avenue, New York, N.Y. 10110
W. W. Norton Ltd., 37 Great Russell Street, London WC1B 3NU

4 5 6 7 8 9 0

CONTENTS

3 Preferences

4 Utility

5 Choice

6 Demand

7 Revealed Preference

8 Slutsky Equation

9 Buying and Selling

10 Labor Supply

11 Intertemporal Choice

12 Asset Markets

13 Uncertainty

14 Risky Assets

15 Consumer's Surplus

16 Market Demand

17 Equilibrium

18 Technology

19 Profit Maximization

20 Cost Minimization

21 Cost Curves

22 Firm Supply

23 Industry Supply

24 Markets

25 Monopoly

26 Oligopoly

27 Game Theory

28 Exchange

29 Production

30 Welfare

31 Externalities

32 Public Goods

Mathematical Appendix

PREFACE

I wrote this book for the usual reason: I couldn't find an existing book that I liked. If you're like me, you've probably received half a dozen textbooks from publishers in the last few years. These books seem to have everything: color, boxes, examples, test banks, etc. There's only one thing that they lack: content.

After students have used one of these books, they probably have mastered a number of new terms, and have likely understood a few diagrams, but they are often incapable of solving simple problems such as how a competitive market with linear demand and supply curves reacts to a tax, or what happens to the equilibrium price in a Cournot industry as more firms enter.

The fault is not with the students. Most intermediate microeconomics books simply don't give them the analytic tools to examine such problems. There are plenty of graphs, and plenty of "real world" illustrations, but there is almost nothing that exhibits the ability of microeconomic analysis to solve quantitative problems.

My aim in this book is to offer a deep enough understanding of the analytic methods of microeconomics so that students will be able to apply these tools on their own, and not just passively absorb the pre-digested cases described in the text. I have found that the best way to do this is to emphasize the fundamental conceptual foundations of microeconomics and provide concrete examples of their application, rather than to attempt to provide an encyclopedia of terminology and anecdote.

A challenge in pursuing this analytic approach arises from the lack of mathematical prerequisites for intermediate microeconomics courses at many colleges and universities. The lack of calculus and problem solving experience in general makes it difficult to present some of the analytical methods of economics. However, it is not impossible. One can go a long way with just a few simple facts about linear demand functions and supply functions, and some elementary algebra. It is perfectly possible to be analytical without being excessively mathematical.

The distinction is worth emphasizing. An analytical approach to economics is one that uses rigorous, logical reasoning. This does not necessarily imply the use of advanced mathematical methods. The language of mathematics certainly aids in helping to ensure a rigorous analysis, and is undoubtedly the best way to proceed when possible, but it may not be appropriate for all students.

Many undergraduate majors in economics are students who *should* know calculus, but don't—at least, not very well. For this reason I have kept calculus out of the main body of the text. However, I have provided complete calculus appendices to many of the chapters. This means that the calculus methods are there for the students who can handle them, but do not pose a barrier to understanding for the others.

I think that this approach manages to convey the idea that calculus is not just a footnote to the argument of the text, but is instead a deeper way to examine the same sorts of issues that one can also examine verbally and graphically. Many arguments are much simpler with a little mathematics, and all economics students should learn that. In many cases I've found that with a little motivation, and a few nice economic examples, students become quite enthusiastic about looking at things from an analytic perspective.

There are several other innovations in this text. First, the chapters are generally very short. I've tried to make most of them roughly "lecture size" so that they can be read at one sitting. I have followed the standard order of first discussing consumer theory and then producer theory, but I've spent a bit more time on consumer theory than is normally the case. This is not because I think that consumer theory is necessarily the most important part of microeconomics; rather, I have found that this is the material that students find the most mysterious, so I wanted to provide more detailed analysis of it.

Second, I've tried to put in a lot of examples of how to use the theory described here. In most books, students look at a lot of diagrams of shifting curves, but they don't see much algebra, or much calculation of any sort for that matter. But it is the algebra that is used to solve problems in practice. Graphs can provide insight, but the real power of economic analysis comes in calculating quantitative answers to economic problems. Every economics student should be able to translate an economic story into an equation or a numerical example, but all too often the development of this skill is neglected. For this reason I have also provided a workbook that I feel is an integral accompaniment to this book. The workbook was written with my colleague Theodore Bergstrom, and we have put a lot of effort into generating interesting and instructive problems. We think that the workbook provides an important aid to the student for the study of microeconomics.

Third, I believe that the treatment of the topics in this book is more accurate than is usually the case in intermediate micro texts. It is true that I've sometimes chosen special cases to analyze when the general case is too difficult, but I've tried to be honest about that when I did it. In general, I've tried to spell out every step of each argument in detail. I believe that the discussion I've provided is not only more complete and more accurate than usual, but this attention to detail also makes the arguments easier to understand than the loose discussion presented in many other books.

There is probably more material in this book than can be comfortably taught in one semester, so it is worthwhile picking and choosing carefully the material that you want to examine in depth. I suspect that only a minority of users of this book will study the sections on uncertainty, for example. But I wanted an accurate treatment of the topic, precisely for that minority. There are some people who want to discuss this material in undergraduate courses, and it is helpful to them to have a textbook discussion available. It is my feeling that a textbook should provide a solid reference for the course—a place that students can go to see material spelled out in detail. But a textbook is no substitute for well-designed lectures and a carefully chosen syllabus.

The Production of the Book

You may be interested to know how this book was produced, as the methods were somewhat novel. The entire book was typeset by the author on a personal computer using TEX, the wonderful typesetting system designed by Donald Knuth. TEX gives the author an extraordinary control over the structure and appearance of a document, and is especially convenient for text involving mathematics.

I used Finalword I and II on an IBM XT and a Zenith Z241 to enter the text and then used PCTEX from Personal TEX, Inc. and MicroTEX from Addison-Wesley to typeset the material. The rough diagrams for the preliminary editions were prepared on a Macintosh using MacDraw. These were then redrawn and improved by a professional artist for the final version.

I used DVILaser from Textset, Inc. to prepare the TEX output for printing on an Apple LaserWriter printer. This provided an exact proof copy which could be class tested and critiqued. After several months of polishing, the final version of the manuscript was run through an Autologic APS 5 phototypesetter to typeset the TEX output.

The book design was by Nancy Dale Muldoon, with some modifications by Roy Tedoff and the author. Nancy Palmquist was the manuscript editor and Drake McFeely coordinated the whole effort in his capacity as editor.

I wrote all of the TEX macros for the book design myself, but I learned some tricks from Gary Grosso, of Textset, and Bob Blue, from the University of Michigan Computing Center. Kari Gluski and Gary Gray helped create the TEX Font Metric files for the Athena font used for section headings and other display material.

Acknowledgments

Several people contributed to this project. First, I must thank my research assistants, John Miller and Debra Holt. John provided many comments, suggestions, and exercises based on early drafts of this text, and made a significant contribution to the coherence of the final product. Debra did a careful proofreading and consistency check during the final stages, and helped in preparing the index.

Several of my colleagues at Michigan used the text on an experimental basis in the winter term of 1986, among them Mark Bagnoli, John Cross, and Steve Salant. Jonathan Hoag (Bowling Green State University), Allen Jacobs (M.I.T.), Hal White (University of California at San Diego), and Gary Yohe (Wesleyan University) used the text at their schools. Ken Binmore (London School of Economics), Larry Chenault (Miami University) and John McMillan (University of Western Ontario) prepared review comments. I want to thank all of these people—and especially their students!—for the valuable help they provided.

Ann Arbor
June 1986

1

THE MARKET

The conventional first chapter of a microeconomics book is a discussion of the "scope and methods" of economics. Although this material can be very interesting, it hardly seems appropriate to *begin* your study of economics with such material. It is hard to appreciate such a discussion until you have seen some examples of economic analysis in action.

So instead, we will begin this book with an *example* of economic analysis. In this chapter we will examine a model of a particular market, the market for apartments. Along the way we will introduce several new ideas and tools of economics. Don't worry if it all goes by rather quickly. This chapter is meant only to provide a quick overview of how these ideas can be used. Later on we will study them in substantially more detail.

1.1 Constructing a Model

Economics proceeds by developing **models** of social phenomena. By a model we mean a simplified representation of reality. The emphasis here is on the word "simple." Think about how useless a map on a one-to-one scale would be. The same is true of an economic model that attempts to describe every aspect of reality. A model's power stems from the elimination of irrelevant detail, thereby allowing the economist to focus on the essential features of the economic reality he or she is attempting to understand.

Here we are interested in what determines the price of apartments, so we want to have a simplified description of the apartment market. There is a certain art to choosing the right simplifications in building a model. In general we want to adopt the simplest model that is capable of describing the economic situation we are examining. We can then add complications one at a time, allowing the model to become more complex and, we hope, more realistic.

The particular example we want to consider is the market for apartments in a medium-size midwestern college town. In this town there are two sorts of apartments. There are some that are adjacent to the university, and others that are farther away. The adjacent apartments are generally considered to be more desirable by students, since they allow easier access to the university. The apartments that are farther away necessitate taking a bus, or a long, cold bicycle ride, so most students would prefer a nearby apartment ... if they can afford one.

We will think of the apartments as being located in two large circles surrounding the university. The adjacent apartments are in the inner circle, while the rest are located in the outer circle. We will focus exclusively on the market for apartments in the inner circle. The outer circle should be interpreted as where people can go who don't find one of the closer apartments. We'll suppose that there are many apartments available in the outer ring, and their price is fixed at some known level. We'll be concerned solely with the determination of the price of the inner-ring apartments and who gets to live there.

An economist would describe the distinction between the prices of the two kinds of apartments in this model by saying that the price of the outer-ring apartments is an **exogenous variable**, while the price of the inner-ring apartments is an **endogenous variable**. This means that the price of the outer-ring apartments is taken as predetermined by factors not discussed in this particular model, while the price of the inner-ring apartments is determined by forces described in the model.

The first simplification that we'll make in our model is that all apartments are identical in every respect except for location. Thus it will make sense to speak of "the price" of apartments, without worrying about whether the apartments are one bedroom, or two bedroom, or have a terrace, or whatever.

But what determines this price? What determines who will live in the inner-ring apartments and who will live farther out? What can be said about the desirability of different economic mechanisms for allocating apartments? What concepts can we use to judge the merit of different assignments of apartments to individuals? These are all questions that we want our model to address.

1.2 Optimization and Equilibrium

Whenever we try to explain the behavior of human beings we need to have some kind of organizing principle; that is, some terms in which behavior can be described. The two principles we will use here are very simple.

The optimization principle: People try to choose the best patterns of consumption that they can afford.

The equilibrium principle: Prices adjust until the amount that people demand of something is equal to the amount that is supplied.

Let us consider these two principles. The first is *almost* tautological. If people are free to choose their actions, it is reasonable to assume that they try to choose things they want rather than things they don't want. Of course there are exceptions to this general principle, but they typically lie outside the domain of economic behavior.

The second notion is a bit more problematic. It is at least conceivable that at any given time peoples' demands and supplies are not compatible, and hence something must be changing. These changes may take a long time to work themselves out, and, even worse, they may induce other changes that might "destabilize" the whole system.

This kind of thing can happen ... but it usually doesn't. In the case of apartments, we typically see a fairly stable rental price from month to month. It is this *equilibrium* price that we are interested in, not in how the − market gets to this equilibrium or how it might change over long periods of time.

How do we use these two principles to determine the answers to the questions we raised above? It is time to introduce some economic concepts.

1.3 The Demand Curve

Suppose that we consider all of the possible renters of the apartments and ask each of them the maximum amount that he or she would be willing to pay to rent one of the apartments.

Let's start at the top. There must be someone who is willing to pay the highest price. Perhaps this person has a lot of money, perhaps he is very lazy and doesn't want to walk far ... or whatever. Suppose that this person is willing to pay $500 a month for an apartment.

If there is only one person who is willing to pay $500 a month to rent an apartment, then if the price for apartments were $500 a month, exactly one apartment would be rented—to the one person who was willing to pay that price.

Suppose that the next highest price that anyone is willing to pay is $490. Then if the market price were $499, there would still be only one apartment rented: the person who was *willing* to pay $500 would rent an apartment, but the person who was willing to pay $490 wouldn't. And so it goes. Only one apartment would be rented if the price were $498, $497, $496, and so on ... until we reach a price of $490. At that price, exactly two apartments would be rented: one to the $500 person and one to the $490 person.

Similarly, two apartments would be rented until we reach the maximum price that the person with the *third* highest price would be willing to pay, and so on.

The maximum willingness to pay of a given person is often called his or her **reservation price**. The reservation price is the highest price that a given person will accept and still purchase the good. In other words, a person's reservation price is the price at which he or she is just indifferent between purchasing or not purchasing the good. In our example, if a person has a reservation price p it means that he or she would be just indifferent between living in the inner ring and paying a price p, and living in the outer ring.

Thus the number of apartments that will be rented at a given price p^* will just be the number of people who have a reservation price greater than or equal to p^*. For if the market price is p^*, then everyone who is willing to pay at least p^* for an apartment will want an apartment in the inner ring, and everyone who is not willing to pay p^* will prefer to live in the outer ring.

We can plot these reservation prices in a diagram as in Figure 1.1. Here the price is depicted on the vertical axis and the number of people who are willing to pay that price or more is depicted on the horizontal axis.

Another way to view Figure 1.1 is to think of it as measuring how many people would want to rent apartments at any particular price. Such a curve is an example of a **demand curve**—a curve that relates the quantity demanded to price. When the market price is above $500, zero apartments will be rented. When the price is between $500 and $490, one apartment will be rented. When it is between $490 and the third highest reservation price, two apartments will be rented, and so on. The demand curve describes the quantity demanded at each of the possible prices.

The demand curve for apartments slopes down: as the price of apartments decreases more people will be willing to rent apartments. If there are a large number of people and their reservation prices differ only slightly from person to person, it is reasonable to think of the demand curve as sloping smoothly downward, as in Figure 1.2. The curve in Figure 1.2 is what the demand curve in Figure 1.1 would look like if there were many people who want to rent the apartments. The "jumps" shown in Figure 1.1 are now so small relative to the size of the market that we can safely ignore them in drawing the market demand curve.

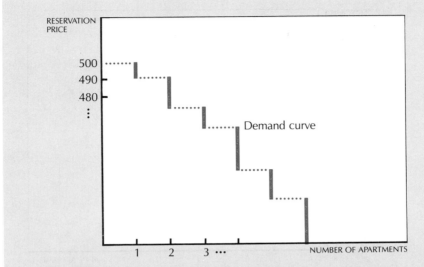

The demand curve for apartments. The vertical axis measures the market price and the horizontal axis measures how many apartments will be rented at each price.

Figure
1.1

1.4 The Supply Curve

We now have a nice graphical representation of demand behavior, so let us turn to supply behavior. Here we have to think about the nature of the market we are examining. The situation we will consider is where there are many independent landlords who are each out to rent their apartments for the highest price the market will bear. We will refer to this as the case of a **competitive market**. Other sorts of market arrangements are certainly possible, and we will examine a few later.

For now, let's consider the case where there are many landlords who all operate independently. It is clear that if all landlords are trying to do the best they can and the renters are fully informed about the prices the landlords charge, then the equilibrium price of all apartments in the inner ring must be the same. The argument is not difficult. Suppose instead that there is some high price, p_h, and some low price, p_l, being charged for apartments. The people who are renting their apartments for a high price could go to a low price landlord and offer to rent his apartment for some price between p_h and p_l. A transaction at such a price would make both the renters and the landlord better off. To the extent that all parties are seeking to further their own interests and are aware of the alternative prices being charged, a situation with different prices being charged for the same good cannot persist in equilibrium.

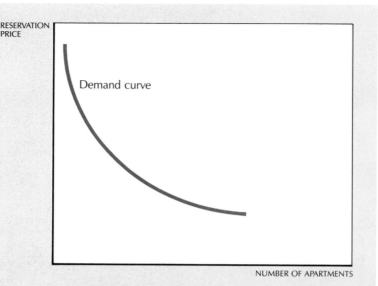

RESERVATION PRICE

Demand curve

NUMBER OF APARTMENTS

Figure
1.2
Demand curve for apartments with many demanders.
Because of the large number of demanders, the jumps between
prices will be small, and the demand curve will have the conventional smooth shape.

But what will this single equilibrium price be? Let us go through the
same sort of exercise that we considered in our construction of the demand
curve: we will pick a price and ask how many apartments will be supplied
at that price.

The answer depends to some degree on the time frame in which we are
examining the market. If we are considering a time frame of several years,
so that new construction can take place, the number of apartments will
certainly respond to the price that is charged. But in the "short run"—
within a given year, say—the number of apartments is more or less fixed.
If we consider only this short-run case, the supply of apartments will be
constant at some predetermined level.

The **supply curve** in this market is depicted in Figure 1.3 as a vertical
line. Whatever price is being charged, the same number of apartments will
be rented, namely, all the apartments that are available at that time.

1.5 Market Equilibrium

We now have a way of representing the demand and the supply side of the
apartment market. Let us put them together and ask what the equilibrium
behavior of the market is. We do this by drawing both the demand and
the supply curve on the same graph in Figure 1.4.

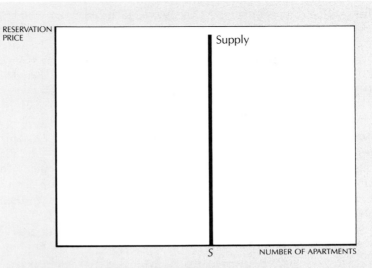

Short-run supply curve. The supply of apartments is fixed in the short run.

Figure
1.3

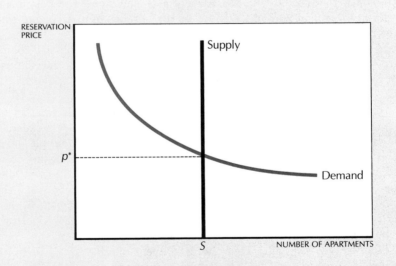

Equilibrium in the apartment market. The equilibrium price is determined by the intersection of the supply and demand curves.

Figure
1.4

In this graph we have used p^* to denote the price where the quantity of apartments demanded equals the quantity supplied. This is the **equilib-**

rium price of apartments. At this price, each consumer who is willing to pay at least p^* is able to find an apartment to rent, and each landlord will be able to rent his apartment at the going market price. Neither the consumers nor the landlords have any reason to change their behavior. This is why we refer to this as an *equilibrium*: no change in behavior will be observed.

To better understand this point, let us consider what would happen at a price other than p^*. For example, consider some price $p < p^*$ where demand is greater than supply. Can this price persist? At this price at least some of the landlords will have more renters than they can handle. There will be lines of people hoping to get an apartment at that price; there are more people who are willing to pay the price p than there are apartments. Certainly some of the landlords would find it in their interest to raise the price of the apartments they are offering.

Similarly, suppose that the price of apartments is some p greater than p^*. Then some of the apartments will be vacant: there are fewer people who are willing to pay p than there are apartments. Some of the landlords are now in danger of getting no rent at all for their apartments. Thus they will have an incentive to lower their price in order to attract more renters.

If the price is above p^* there are too few renters; if it is below p^* there are too many renters. Only at the price of p^* is the number of people who are willing to rent at that price equal to the number of apartments available for rent. Only at that price does demand equal supply.

At the price p^* the landlords' and the renters' behaviors are compatible in the sense that the number of apartments demanded by the renters at p^* is equal to the number of apartments supplied by the landlords. This is the equilibrium price in the market for apartments.

Once we've determined the market price for the close-in apartments, we can ask who ends up getting these apartments, and who is exiled to the farther away apartments. In our model there is a very simple answer to this question: in the market equilibrium everyone who is willing to pay p^* or more gets an apartment in the inner ring, and everyone who is willing to pay less than p^* gets one in the outer ring. The person who has a reservation price of p^* is just indifferent between taking an apartment in the inner ring and taking one in the outer ring. The rest of the people in the inner ring are getting their apartments at less than the maximum they would be willing to pay for them. Thus the assignment of apartments to apartment dwellers is determined by their willingness to pay.

1.6 Comparative Statics

Now that we have an economic model of the apartment market, we can begin to use it to analyze the behavior of the equilibrium price. We can ask how the price of apartments changes when various aspects of the market change. This kind of an exercise is known as **comparative statics**, since it involves comparing two "static" equilibria, without particularly worrying about how the market moves from one equilibrium to another.

The movement from one equilibrium to another can take a substantial amount of time, and questions about how such movement takes place can be very interesting and important. But we must walk before we can run, so we will ignore such dynamic questions for now. Comparative statics analysis is only concerned with comparing equilibria, and there will be enough questions to answer in this framework for the present.

Let's start with a simple case. Suppose that the supply of apartments were increased, as in Figure 1.5. It is easy to see from the diagram that the equilibrium price will fall: the intersection of demand and supply occurs at a lower price. Similarly, if the supply of apartments were reduced the equilibrium price would rise.

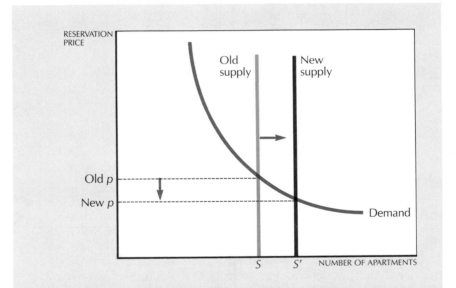

Increasing the supply of apartments.   As the supply of apartments increases, the equilibrium price decreases.

Figure
1.5

Let's try a more complicated—and more interesting—example. Suppose that a developer decides to turn several of the apartments into condominiums. What will happen to the price of the remaining apartments?

Your first guess is probably that the price of apartments will go up, since the supply has been reduced. But this isn't necessarily right. It is true that the supply of apartments to rent has been reduced. But the *demand for apartments* has been reduced as well, since some of the people who were renting apartments may decide to purchase the new condominiums.

It is natural to assume that the condominium purchasers come from those who already live in the inner-ring of apartments—those people who are willing to pay more than p^* for an apartment. Suppose, for example, that the demanders with the 10 highest reservation prices decide to buy condos rather than rent apartments. Then the new demand curve is just the old demand curve with 10 fewer demanders at each price. Since there are also 10 fewer apartments to rent, the new equilibrium price is just what it was before, and exactly the same people end up living in the inner-ring apartments. This situation is depicted in Figure 1.6. Both the demand curve and the supply curve shift left by 10 apartments, and the equilibrium price remains unchanged.

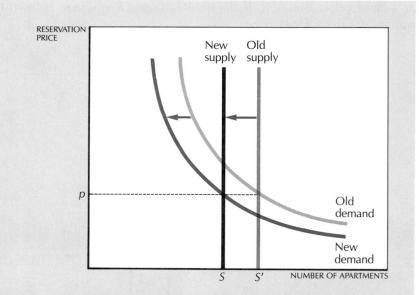

Figure 1.6

Effect of creating condominiums. If demand and supply both shift left by the same amount the equilibrium price is unchanged.

Most people find this result surprising. They tend to just see the reduction in the supply of apartments, and don't think about the reduction in demand. The case we've considered is an extreme one: *all* of the condo purchasers were former apartment dwellers. But the other case—where none of the condo purchasers were apartment dwellers—is even more extreme.

The model, simple though it is, has led us to an important insight. If we want to determine how conversion to condominiums will affect the apartment market, we have to consider not only the effect on the supply of apartments but also the effect on the demand for apartments.

Let's consider another example of a surprising comparative statics analysis: the effect of an apartment tax. Suppose that the city council decides that there should be a tax on apartments of $50 a year. Thus each landlord will have to pay $50 a year to the city for each apartment that he owns. What will this do to the price of apartments?

Most people would think that at least some of the tax would get passed along to apartment renters. But, rather surprisingly, that is not the case. In fact, the equilibrium price of apartments will remain unchanged!

In order to verify this, we have to ask what happens to the demand curve and the supply curve. The supply curve doesn't change—there are just as many apartments after the tax as before the tax. And the demand curve doesn't change either, since the number of apartments that will be rented at each different price will be the same as well. If neither the demand curve nor the supply curve shifts, the price can't change as a result of the tax.

Here is a way to think about the effect of this tax. Before the tax is imposed, each landlord is charging the highest price that he can get that will keep his apartments occupied. The equilibrium price p^* is the highest price that can be charged that is compatible with all of the apartments being rented. After the tax is imposed can the landlords raise their prices to compensate for the tax? The answer is no: if they could raise the price and keep their apartments occupied, they would have already done so. If they were charging the maximum price that the market could bear, the landlords couldn't raise their prices any more: none of the tax can get passed along to the renters. The landlords have to pay the entire amount of the tax.

This analysis depends critically on the assumption that the supply of apartments remains fixed. If the number of apartments can vary as the tax changes, then the price paid by the renters will typically change. We'll examine this kind of behavior later on, after we've built up some more powerful tools for analyzing such problems.

1.7 Other Ways to Allocate Apartments

In the last section we described the equilibrium for apartments in a competitive market. But competitive markets are only one way to allocate resources. Let us consider a few other ways. Some of these ways to allocate apartments may sound rather strange, but each will illustrate a worthwhile point.

The Discriminating Monopolist

First, let us consider a situation where there is one dominant landlord who owns all of the apartments. Or, alternatively, we could think of a number of individual landlords getting together and coordinating their actions to act as one. A situation where a market is dominated by a single seller of a product is known as the case of **monopoly**.

In renting the apartments the landlord could decide to auction them off one by one to the highest bidders. Since this means that different people would end up paying different prices for apartments, we will call this the case of the **discriminating monopolist**. Let us suppose for simplicity that the discriminating monopolist knows each person's reservation price for apartments. (This is not terribly realistic, but it will serve to illustrate an important point.)

This means he would rent the first apartment to the fellow who would pay the most for it, in this case $500. The next apartment would go for $490 and so on as we moved down the demand curve. Each apartment would be rented to the person who was willing to pay the most for it.

Here is the interesting feature of the discriminating monopolist: *exactly the same people will get the apartments as in the case of the market solution*, namely, everyone who valued an apartment at more than p^*. The last person to rent an apartment pays the price p^*—the same as the equilibrium price in a competitive market. The discriminating monopolist's attempt to maximize his own profits leads to the same allocation of apartments as the supply and demand mechanism of the competitive market. The amount the people *pay* is different, but who gets the apartments is the same. It turns out that this is no accident, but we'll have to wait until later to explain the reason.

The Ordinary Monopolist

We assumed that the discriminating monopolist was able to rent each apartment at a different price. But what if he were forced to rent all apartments at the same price? In this case the monopolist faces a tradeoff: if he chooses a low price he will rent more apartments, but he may end up making less money than if he sets a higher price.

Let us use $D(p)$ to represent the demand function—the number of apartments demanded at price p. Then if the monopolist sets a price p, he will rent $D(p)$ apartments, and thus receive a revenue of $pD(p)$. The revenue that the monopolist receives can be thought of as the area of a box: the height of the box is the price p and the width of the box is the number of apartments $D(p)$. Thus the product of the height and the width—the area of the box—represents the revenue the monopolist receives. This is the box depicted in Figure 1.7.

If the monopolist has no costs associated with renting an apartment, he would want to choose a price that maximized his rental income—that is, choose a price that had the largest associated revenue box. The largest revenue box in Figure 1.7 occurs at the price $\hat{p}$.

In this case the monopolist will find it in his interest *not* to rent all of the apartments. In fact this will generally be the case for a monopolist. The

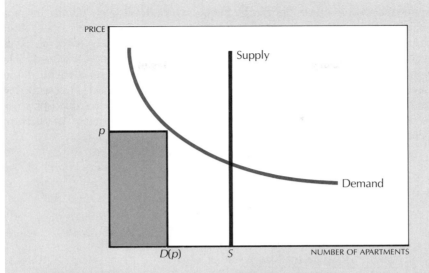

Revenue box. The revenue received by the monopolist is just the price times the quantity, which can be interpreted as the area of the box illustrated.

Figure 1.7

monopolist will want to restrict the output available in order to maximize his profit. This means that the monopolist will generally want to charge a price that is higher than the equilibrium price in a competitive market, p^*. In the case of the ordinary monopolist, fewer apartments will be rented and each apartment will be rented at a higher price than in the competitive market.

Rent Control

A third and final case that we will discuss will be the case of rent control. Suppose that the city decides to impose a maximum rent that can be charged for apartments, say p_{max}. We suppose that the price p_{max} is less than the equilibrium price in the competitive market, p^*. If this is so we would have a situation of **excess demand**: there are more people who are willing to rent apartments at p_{max} than there are apartments available. Who will end up with the apartments?

The theory that we have described up until now doesn't have an answer to this question. We can describe what will happen when supply equals demand, but we don't have enough detail in the model to describe what will happen if supply doesn't equal demand. The answer to who gets the apartments under rent control depends on who has the most time to spend looking around, who knows the current tenants, etc. All of these things are outside the scope of the simple model we've developed. It may be that exactly the same people get the apartments under rent control as under the competitive market. But that is an extremely unlikely outcome. It is much more likely that some of the formerly outer-ring people will end up in some of the inner-ring apartments and thus displace the people who would have been living there under the market system. So under rent control the same number of apartments will be rented at the rent–controlled price as were rented under the competitive price: they'll just be rented to different people.

1.8 Which Way Is Best?

We've now described four possible ways of allocating apartments to people:

- The competitive market.
- A discriminating monopolist.
- An ordinary monopolist.
- Rent control.

These are four different economic institutions for allocating apartments. Each method will result in different people getting apartments and in different prices being charged for apartments. We might well ask which economic institution is best. But first we have to define "best." What criteria might we use to compare these ways of allocating apartments?

One thing we can do is to look at the economic positions of the people involved. It is pretty obvious that the owners of the apartments end up with the most money if they can act as a discriminating monopolist: this would generate the most revenues for the apartment owner(s). Similarly the rent-control solution is probably the worst situation for the apartment owners.

What about the renters? They are probably worse off on average in the case of a discriminating monopolist—most of them would be paying a higher price than they would under the other ways of allocating apartments. Are the consumers better off in the case of rent control? Some of them are: the consumers *who end up getting the apartments* are better off than they would be under the market solution. But the ones who didn't get the apartments are *worse off* than they would be under the market solution.

What we need here is a way to look at the economic position of all the parties involved—all the renters *and* all the landlords. How can we examine the desirability of different ways to allocate apartments, taking everybody into account? What can be used as a criterion for a "good" way to allocate apartments taking into account *all* of the parties involved?

1.9 Pareto Efficiency

One useful criterion for comparing the outcomes of different economic institutions is a concept known as Pareto efficiency or economic efficiency.[1] In our context, a way of allocating apartments to the renters is **Pareto efficient** if there is no alternative allocation that leaves everyone at least as well off and makes some people strictly better off. If a situation is *not* Pareto efficient, it means that there is some way to make somebody better off without hurting anyone else.

An economic institution that yields a Pareto inefficient allocation has the undesirable feature that it results in a situation where there is some way to make somebody better off without hurting anyone else. There may be other positive things about the allocation, but the fact that it is Pareto inefficient is certainly one strike against it. If there is a way to make someone better off without hurting anyone else, why not do it?

The idea of Pareto efficiency is an important one in economics and we will examine it in some detail later on. It has many subtle implications that we will have to investigate more slowly, but we can get an inkling of what is involved even now.

Here is a useful way to think about the idea of Pareto efficiency. Suppose that we assigned the renters to the inner- and outer-ring apartments randomly, but then allowed them to rent their apartments to each other. Some people who really wanted to live close in might, through bad luck, end up with an outer-ring apartment. But then they could sublet an inner-ring apartment from someone who was assigned to such an apartment but who didn't value it as highly as the other person. If individuals were assigned randomly to apartments, there would generally be some who would want to trade apartments, if they were sufficiently compensated for doing so.

For example, suppose that person A is assigned an apartment in the inner ring that he feels is worth $200, and person B is assigned an apartment in the outer ring. Suppose further that person B would be willing to pay $300 for A's apartment. Then there is a definite "gain from trade" if these two agents swap apartments and arrange a side payment from B to A of some amount of money between $200 and $300. The exact amount of the transaction isn't important. What is important is that the people who are willing to pay the most for the apartments get them—otherwise, there would be an incentive for someone who attached a low value to an inner-ring apartment to make a trade with someone who placed a high value on an inner-ring apartment.

Suppose that we think of all voluntary trades as being carried out so

---

[1] Pareto efficiency is named after the nineteenth-century economist and sociologist Vilfredo Pareto (1848–1923) who was one of the first to examine the implications of this idea.

that all gains from trade are exhausted. The resulting allocation must be Pareto efficient. If not, there would be some trade that would make two people better off without hurting anyone else—but this would contradict the assumption that all voluntary trades had been carried out. An allocation in which all voluntary trades have been carried out is a Pareto efficient allocation.

1.10 Comparing Ways to Allocate Apartments

The trading process we've described above is so general that you wouldn't think that anything much could be said about its outcome. But there is one very interesting point that can be made. Let us ask who will end up with apartments in an allocation where all of the gains from trade have been exhausted.

To see the answer, just note that anyone who has an apartment in the inner-ring must have a higher reservation price than anyone who has an apartment in the outer ring—otherwise, they could make a trade and make both people better off. Thus if there are S apartments to be rented, then the S people with the highest reservation prices end up getting apartments in the inner ring. This allocation is Pareto efficient—anything else is not, since any other assignment of apartments to people would allow for some trade that would make at least two of the people better off without hurting anyone else.

Let us try to apply this criterion of Pareto efficiency to the outcomes of the various resource allocation devices mentioned above. Let's start with the market mechanism. It is easy to see that the market mechanism assigns the people with the S highest reservation prices to the inner ring—namely, those people who are willing to pay more than the equilibrium price, p^*, for their apartments. Thus there are no further gains from trade to be had, once the apartments have been rented in a competitive market. The outcome of the competitive market is Pareto efficient.

What about the discriminating monopolist? Is that arrangement Pareto efficient? The easy way to see the answer is to simply observe that exactly the same people get an apartment using the discriminating monopolist to allocate apartments as get apartments if a competitive market operates: everyone who is willing to pay more than p^* for an apartment. Thus the discriminating monopolist generates a Pareto efficient outcome as well.

Although both the competitive market and the discriminating monopolist generate Pareto efficient outcomes in the sense that there will be no further trades desired, they can result in quite different distributions of income. Certainly the consumers are much worse off under the discriminating monopolist than under the competitive market, and the landlord(s) are much better off. In general Pareto efficiency doesn't have much to say about distribution of the gains from trade. It is only concerned with the *efficiency* of the trade: whether all of the possible trades have been made.

What about the ordinary monopolist who is constrained to charge just one price? It turns out that this situation is not Pareto efficient. All we have to do to verify this is to note that, since all the apartments will not in general be rented by the monopolist, he can increase his profits by renting an apartment to someone who doesn't have one at *any* positive price. There is some price at which both the monopolist and the renter must be better off. As long as the monopolist doesn't change the price that anybody else pays, the other renters are just as well off as they were before. Thus we have found a Pareto improvement—a way to make two parties better off without making anyone else worse off.

The final case is that of rent control. This also turns out not to be Pareto efficient. The argument here rests on the fact that an arbitrary assignment of renters to apartments will generally involve someone living in the inner ring (say Mr. In) who is willing to pay less for an apartment than someone living in the outer ring (say Ms. Out). Suppose that Mr. In's reservation price is $300 and Ms. Out's reservation price is $500.

We need to find a Pareto improvement—a way to make Mr. In and Ms. Out better off without hurting anyone else. But there is an easy way to do this: just let Mr. In sublet his apartment to Ms. Out. It is worth $500 to Ms. Out to live close to the university, but it is only worth $300 to Mr. In. If Ms. Out pays Mr. In $400, say, and trades apartments, they will both be better off: Ms. Out will get an apartment that she values at more than $400, and Mr. In will get $400 that he values more than an inner-ring apartment.

This example shows that the rent-controlled market will generally not result in a Pareto efficient allocation, since there will still be some trades that could be carried out after the market has operated. As long as some people get inner-ring apartments who value them less highly than people who don't get them, there will be gains to be had from trade.

1.11 Equilibrium in the Long Run

We have analyzed the equilibrium pricing of apartments in the **short run**— when there is a fixed supply of apartments. But in the **long run** the supply of apartments can change. Just as the demand curve measures the number of apartments that will be demanded at different prices, the supply curve measures the number of apartments that will be supplied at different prices. The final determination of the market price for apartments will depend on the interaction of supply and demand.

And what is it that determines the supply behavior? In general, the number of new apartments that will be supplied by the private market will depend on how profitable it is to provide apartments, which depends, in part, on the price that landlords can charge for apartments. In order to analyze the behavior of the apartment market in the long run, we have to examine the behavior of suppliers as well as demanders, a task we will eventually undertake.

When supply is variable, we can ask questions not only about who gets the apartments, but about how many will be provided by various types of market institutions. Will a monopolist supply more or fewer apartments than a competitive market? Will rent control increase or decrease the equilibrium number of apartments? Which institutions will provide a Pareto efficient number of apartments? In order to answer these and similar questions we must develop more systematic and powerful tools for economic analysis.

Summary

1. Economics proceeds by making models of social phenomena, which are simplified representations of reality.

2. In this task, economists are guided by the optimization principle, which states that people typically try to choose what's best for them, and the equilibrium principle, which says that prices will adjust until demand and supply are equal.

3. The demand curve measures how much people wish to demand at each price, and the supply curve measures how much people wish to supply at each price. An equilibrium price is one where the amount demanded equals the amount supplied.

4. The study of how the equilibrium price and quantity change when the underlying conditions change is known as comparative statics.

5. An economic situation is Pareto efficient if there is no way to make some group of people better off without making some other group of people worse off. The concept of Pareto efficiency can be used to evaluate different ways of allocating resources.

Review Questions

1. Suppose that there were 25 people who had a reservation price of $500, and the 26th person had a reservation price of $200. What would the demand curve look like?

2. In the above example, what would the equilibrium price be if there were 24 apartments to rent? What if there were 26 apartments to rent? What if there were 25 apartments to rent?

3. If people have different reservation prices, why does the market demand curve slope down?

4. In the text we assumed that the condominium purchasers came from the inner-ring people—people who were already renting apartments. What would happen to the price of inner-ring apartments if all of the condominium purchasers came from the outer-ring people—the people who were not currently renting apartments in the inner ring?

5. Suppose now that the condominium purchasers were all inner-ring people, but that each condominium was constructed from 2 apartments. What would happen to the price of apartments?

6. What do you suppose the effect of a tax would be on the number of apartments that would be built in the long run?

7. If the demand curve for apartments is given by $D(p) = 100 - 2p$, what price would maximize the monopolist's revenue? How many apartments would be rented at this price? (This question is most easily solved using simple calculus.)

8. Suppose the demand curve is the same as in the above example. What price would the monopolist set if he had 60 apartments? How many would he rent? What price would he set if he had 40 apartments? How many would he rent? (To solve this problem, you need to use the answer to the problem above.)

9. If our model of rent control allowed for unrestricted subletting, who would end up getting apartments in the inner circle? Would the outcome be Pareto efficient?

2

BUDGET CONSTRAINT

The economic theory of the consumer is very simple: economists assume that consumers choose the best bundle of goods they can afford. To give content to this theory, we have to describe more precisely what we mean by "best" and what we mean by "can afford." In this chapter we will examine how to describe what a consumer can afford; the next chapter will focus on the concept of how the consumer determines what is best. We will then be able to undertake a detailed study of the implications of this simple model of consumer behavior.

2.1 The Budget Constraint

We begin by examining the concept of the **budget constraint**. Suppose that there is some set of goods from which the consumer can choose. In real life there are many goods to consume, but for our purposes it is convenient to consider only the case of two goods, since we can then depict the consumer's choice problem graphically.

We will indicate the consumer's **consumption bundle** by (x_1, x_2). This is simply a list of two numbers that tells us how much the consumer is choosing to consume of good 1, x_1, and how much the consumer is choosing to consume of good 2, x_2. Sometimes it is convenient to denote the consumer's bundle by a single symbol like X, where X is simply an abbreviation for the list of two numbers (x_1, x_2).

We suppose that we can observe the prices of the two goods, (p_1, p_2), and the amount of money the consumer has to spend, m. Then the **budget constraint** of the consumer can be written as

$$p_1 x_1 + p_2 x_2 \leq m. \tag{2.1}$$

Here $p_1 x_1$ is the amount of money the consumer is spending on good 1 and $p_2 x_2$ is the amount of money the consumer is spending on good 2. The budget constraint of the consumer requires that the amount of money spent on the two goods is no more than the total amount the consumer has to spend. The consumer's *affordable* consumption bundles are those that don't cost any more than m. We call this set of affordable consumption bundles at prices (p_1, p_2) and income m the **budget set** of the consumer.

2.2 Two Goods Are Often Enough

The two-good assumption is more general than you might think at first, since we can often interpret one of the goods as representing everything else the consumer might want to consume.

For example, if we are interested in studying a consumer's demand for milk, we might let x_1 measure his or her consumption of milk in quarts per month. We can then let x_2 stand for everything else the consumer might want to consume other than milk.

When we adopt this interpretation, it is convenient to think of good 2 as being the dollars that the consumer can use to spend on other goods. Under this interpretation the price of good 2 will automatically be 1, since the price of one dollar is one dollar. Thus the budget constraint will take the form

$$p_1 x_1 + x_2 \leq m. \tag{2.2}$$

This expression simply says that the amount of money spent on good 1, $p_1 x_1$, plus the amount of money spent on all other goods, x_2, must be no more than the total amount of money the consumer has to spend, m.

We say that good 2 represents a **composite good** that stands for everything else that the consumer might want to consume other than good 1. Such a composite good is invariably measured in dollars to be spent on goods other than good 1. As far as the algebraic form of the budget constraint is concerned, equation (2.2) is just a special case of the formula given in equation (2.1), with $p_2 = 1$, so everything that we have to say about the budget constraint in general will hold under the composite good interpretation.

2.3 Properties of the Budget Set

The **budget line** is the set of bundles that cost exactly m:

$$p_1 x_1 + p_2 x_2 = m. \tag{2.3}$$

These are the bundles of goods that just exhaust the consumer's income.

The budget set is depicted in Figure 2.1. The heavy line is the budget line—the bundles that cost exactly m—and the bundles below this line are those that cost strictly less than m.

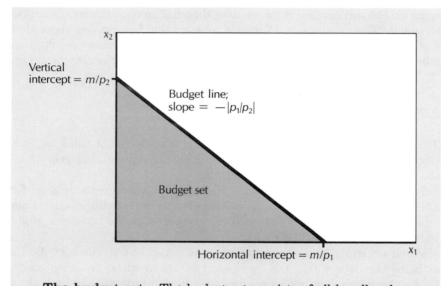

Figure
2.1
The budget set. The budget set consists of all bundles that are affordable at the given prices and income.

We can rearrange the budget line in equation (2.3) to give us the formula

$$x_2 = \frac{m}{p_2} - \frac{p_1}{p_2} x_1. \tag{2.4}$$

This is the formula for a straight line with a vertical intercept of m/p_2 and a slope of $-p_1/p_2$. The formula tells us how many units of good 2 the consumer needs to consume in order to just satisfy the budget constraint if she is consuming x_1 units of good 1.

Here is an easy way to draw a budget line given prices (p_1, p_2) and income m. Just ask yourself how much of good 2 the consumer could buy if she spent all of her money on good 2. The answer is of course m/p_2. Then ask how much of good 1 the consumer could buy if she spent all of her money on good 1. The answer is m/p_1. Thus the horizontal and vertical intercepts measure how much the consumer could get if she spent all of her money on goods 1 and 2, respectively. In order to depict the budget line just plot these two points on the appropriate axes of the graph and connect them with a straight line.

The slope of the budget line has a nice economic interpretation. It measures the rate at which the market is willing to "substitute" good 1 for good 2. Suppose for example that the consumer is going to increase her consumption of good 1 by Δx_1.[1] How much will her consumption of good 2 have to change in order to satisfy her budget constraint? Let us use Δx_2 to indicate her change in the consumption of good 2.

Now note that if she satisfies her budget constraint before and after making the change she must satisfy

$$p_1 x_1 + p_2 x_2 = m$$

and

$$p_1(x_1 + \Delta x_1) + p_2(x_2 + \Delta x_2) = m.$$

Subtracting the first equation from the second gives

$$p_1 \Delta x_1 + p_2 \Delta x_2 = 0.$$

This says that the total value of the change in her consumption must be zero. Solving for $\Delta x_2 / \Delta x_1$, the rate at which good 2 can be substituted for good 1 while still satisfying the budget constraint, gives

$$\frac{\Delta x_2}{\Delta x_1} = -\frac{p_1}{p_2}.$$

This is just the slope of the budget line. The negative sign is there since Δx_1 and Δx_2 must always have opposite signs. If you consume more of good 1, you have to consume less of good 2 and vice versa if you continue to satisfy the budget constraint.

Economists sometimes say that the slope of the budget line measures the **opportunity cost** of consuming good 1. In order to consume more of good 1 you have to give up some consumption of good 2. Giving up the opportunity to consume good 2 is the true economic cost of more good 1 consumption; and that cost is measured by the slope of the budget line.

---

[1] The Greek letter Δ, delta, is pronounced "del-ta". The notation Δx_1 means the change in good 1. For more on changes and rates of changes, see the Mathematical Appendix.

2.4 How the Budget Line Changes

When prices and incomes change, the set of goods that a consumer can afford changes as well. How do these changes affect the budget set?

Let us first consider changes in income. It is easy to see from equation (2.4) that an increase in income will increase the vertical intercept and not affect the slope of the line. Thus an increase in income will result in a *parallel shift outward* of the budget line as in Figure 2.2. Similarly, a decrease in income will cause a parallel shift inward.

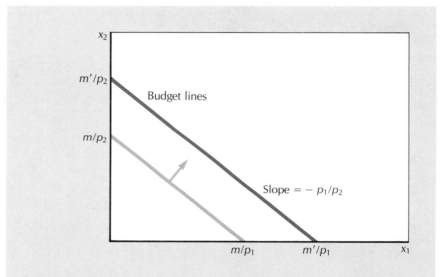

Figure 2.2

Increasing income. An increase in income causes a parallel shift outward of the budget line.

What about changes in prices? Let us first consider increasing price 1 while holding price 2 and income fixed. According to equation (2.4), increasing p_1 will not change the vertical intercept, but it will make the budget line steeper since p_1/p_2 will become larger.

Another way to see how the budget line changes is to use the trick described earlier for drawing the budget line. If you are spending all of your money on good 2, then increasing the price of good 1 doesn't change the maximum amount of good 2 you could buy—thus the vertical intercept of the budget line doesn't change. But if you are spending all of your money on good 1, and good 1 becomes more expensive, then your consumption of good 1 must decrease. Thus the horizontal intercept of

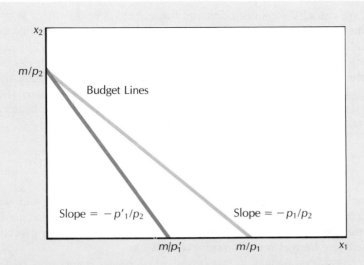

Increasing price.   If good 1 becomes more expensive, the budget line becomes steeper.

Figure
2.3

the budget line must shift inward, resulting in the tilt depicted in Figure 2.3.

What happens to the budget line when we change the prices of good 1 and good 2 at the same time? Suppose for example that we double the prices of both goods 1 and 2. In this case both the horizontal and the vertical intercepts shift inward by a factor of one-half and therefore the budget line shifts inward by one-half as well. Multiplying both prices by two is just like dividing income by 2.

We can also see this algebraically. Suppose our original budget line is

$$p_1 x_1 + p_2 x_2 = m.$$

Now suppose that both prices become t times as large. Multiplying both prices by t yields

$$t p_1 x_1 + t p_2 x_2 = m.$$

But this equation is the same as

$$p_1 x_1 + p_2 x_2 = \frac{m}{t}.$$

Thus multiplying both prices by a constant amount t is just like dividing income by the same constant t. It follows that if we multiply both prices by t *and* we multiply income by t, then the budget line won't change at all.

We can also consider price and income changes together. What happens if both prices go up and income goes down? Think about what happens to the horizontal and vertical intercepts. If m decreases and p_1 and p_2 both increase, then the intercepts m/p_1 and m/p_2 must both decrease. This means that the budget line will shift inward. What about the slope of the budget line? If price 2 increases more than price 1, so that $-p_1/p_2$ decreases (in absolute value), then the budget line will be flatter; if price 2 increases less than price 1, the budget line will be steeper.

2.5 The Numeraire

The budget line is defined by two prices and one income, but one of these variables is redundant. We could peg one of the prices, or the income, to some fixed value, and adjust the other variable so as to describe exactly the same budget set. Thus the budget line

$$p_1 x_1 + p_2 x_2 = m$$

is exactly the same budget line as

$$\frac{p_1}{p_2} x_1 + x_2 = \frac{m}{p_2}$$

or

$$\frac{p_1}{m} x_1 + \frac{p_2}{m} x_2 = 1$$

since the first budget line results from dividing everything by p_2 and the second budget line results from dividing everything by m. In the first case, we have pegged $p_2 = 1$, and in the second case, we have pegged $m = 1$. Pegging the price of one of the goods or income to 1 and adjusting the other price and income appropriately doesn't change the budget set at all.

When we set one of the prices equal to 1, as we did above, we often refer to that price as the **numeraire** price. The numeraire price is the price relative to which we are measuring the other price and income. It will occasionally be convenient to think of one of the goods as being a numeraire good, since there will then be one less price to worry about.

2.6 Taxes, Subsidies, and Rationing

Economic policy often uses tools that affect a consumer's budget constraint, such as taxes. For example, if the government imposes a **quantity tax**, this means that the consumer has to pay a certain amount to the government for each unit of the good he purchases. In the U.S., for example, we pay about 15 cents a gallon as a federal gasoline tax.

How does a quantity tax affect the budget line of a consumer? From the viewpoint of the consumer the tax is just like a higher price. Thus a quantity tax of t dollars per unit of good 1 simply changes the price of good 1 from p_1 to $p_1 + t$. As we've seen above, this implies that the budget line must get steeper.

Another kind of tax is a **value** tax. As the name implies this is a tax on the value—the price—of a good, rather than the quantity purchased of a good. A value tax is usually expressed in percentage terms. Most states in the U.S. have sales taxes. If the sales tax is 6 percent, then a good that is priced at \$1 will actually sell for \$1.06. (Value taxes are also known as **ad valorem** taxes.)

If good 1 has a price of p_1 but is subject to a sales tax at rate τ, then the actual price facing the consumer is $(1 + \tau)p_1$.[2] The consumer has to pay p_1 to the supplier and τp_1 to the government for each unit of the good so the total cost of the good to the consumer is $(1 + \tau)p_1$.

A **subsidy** is the opposite of a tax. In the case of a **quantity subsidy**, the government *gives* an amount to the consumer that depends on the amount of the good purchased. If, for example, the consumption of milk were subsidized, the government would pay some amount of money to each consumer of milk depending on the amount that consumer purchased. If the subsidy is s dollars per unit of consumption of good 1, then from the viewpoint of the consumer, the price of good 1 would be $p_1 - s$. This would therefore make the budget line flatter.

Similarly an ad valorem subsidy is a subsidy based on the price of the good being subsidized. If the government will give you back \$1 for every \$2 you donate to charity, then your donations to charity are being subsidized at a rate of 50 percent. In general, if the price of good 1 is p_1 and good 1 is subject to an ad valorem subsidy of rate σ then the actual price of good 1 facing the consumer is $(1 - \sigma)p_1$.

You can see that taxes and subsidies affect prices in exactly the same way except for the algebraic sign: a tax increases the price to the consumer, and a subsidy decreases it.

Another kind of tax or subsidy that the government might use is a **lump sum** tax or subsidy. In the case of a tax, this means that the government takes away some fixed amount of money, regardless of the individual's behavior. Thus a lump sum tax means that the budget line of a consumer will shift inward because his money income has been reduced. Similarly, a lump sum subsidy means that the budget line will shift outward. Quantity taxes and value taxes tilt the budget line one way or the other depending on which good is being taxed, but a lump sum tax shifts the budget line inward.

Governments also sometimes impose *rationing* constraints. This means

---

[2] The Greek letter τ, tau, rhymes with "wow."

that the amount of consumption of some good is fixed to be no larger than some amount. For example, during World War II the U.S. government rationed certain foods like butter and meat.

Suppose, for example, that good 1 were rationed so that no more than $\overline{x}_1$ could be consumed by a given consumer. Then the budget set of the consumer would look like that depicted in Figure 2.4: it would be the old budget set with a piece lopped off. The lopped off piece consists of all the consumption bundles that are affordable but have $x_1 > \overline{x}_1$.

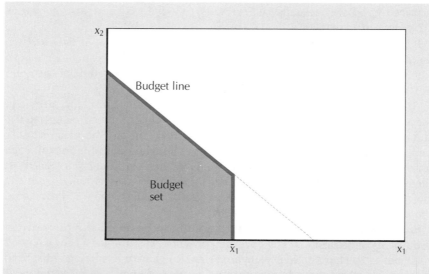

Figure
2.4
Budget set with rationing. If good 1 is rationed, the section of the budget set beyond the rationed quantity will be lopped off.

Sometimes taxes, subsidies, and rationing are combined. For example, we could consider a situation where a consumer could consume good 1 at a price of p_1 up to some level $\overline{x}_1$, and then had to pay a tax t on all consumption in excess of $\overline{x}_1$. The budget set for this consumer is depicted in Figure 2.5. Here the budget line has a slope of $-p_1/p_2$ to the left of $\overline{x}_1$, and a slope of $-(p_1 + t)/p_2$ to the right of $\overline{x}_1$.

EXAMPLE: The Food Stamp Program

Since the Food Stamp Act of 1964 the U.S. federal government has provided a subsidy on food for poor people. The details of this program have been

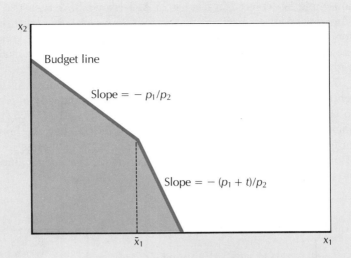

Taxing consumption greater than $\bar{x}_1$. In this budget set the consumer must pay a tax only on the consumption of good 1 that is in excess of $\bar{x}_1$, so the budget line becomes steeper to the right of $\bar{x}_1$.

Figure
2.5

adjusted several times. Here we will describe the economic effects of one of these adjustments.

Before 1979, households who met certain eligibility requirements were allowed to purchase food stamps, which could then be used to purchase food at retail outlets. In January 1975, for example, a family of four could receive a maximum monthly allotment of $153 in food coupons by participating in the program.

The price of these coupons to the household depended on the household income. A family of four with an adjusted monthly income of $300 paid $83 for the full monthly allotment of food stamps. If a family of four had a monthly income of $100, the cost for the full monthly allotment would have been $25.[3]

The pre–1979 Food Stamp program was an ad valorem subsidy on food. The rate at which food was subsidized depended on the household income. The family of four that was charged $83 for their allotment paid $1 to receive $1.84 worth of food (1.84 equals 153 divided by 83). Similarly, the household that paid $25 was paying $1 to receive $6.12 worth of food (6.12 equals 153 divided by 25).

The way that the Food Stamp program affected the budget set of a

---

[3] These figures are taken from Kenneth Clarkson, *Food Stamps and Nutrition*, American Enterprise Institute, 1975.

household is depicted in Figure 2.6A. Here we have measured the amount of money spent on food on the horizontal axis and expenditures on all other goods on the vertical axis. Since we are measuring each good in terms of the money spent on it, the "price" of each good is automatically 1, and the budget line will therefore have a slope of −1.

If the household is allowed to buy $153 of food stamps for $25, then this represents roughly an 84 percent (= 1 − 25/153) subsidy of food purchases, so the budget line will have a slope of roughly −.16 (= 25/153) until the household has spent $153 on food. Each dollar that the household spent on food up to $153 would only cost it about 16 cents less in consumption of other goods. After spending $153 on food, the budget line would again have a slope of −1.

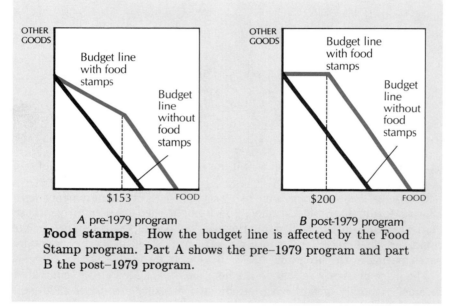

Figure
2.6

A pre-1979 program   *B* post-1979 program

Food stamps. How the budget line is affected by the Food Stamp program. Part A shows the pre–1979 program and part B the post–1979 program.

These effects lead to the kind of "kink" depicted in Figure 2.6. Households with higher incomes had to pay more for their allotment of food stamps. Thus the slope of the budget line would become steeper as household income increased.

In 1979 the Food Stamp program was modified. Instead of requiring that households purchase food stamps, they are now simply given to qualified households. Figure 2.6B shows how this affects the budget set.

Suppose that a household now receives a grant of $200 of food stamps a month. Then this means that the household can consume $200 more food per month, regardless of how much it is spending on other goods, which implies that the budget line will shift to the right by $200. The slope will not change: $1 less spent on food would mean $1 more to spend on other things. But since the household cannot legally sell food stamps, the maximum amount that it can spend on other goods does not change. The Food Stamp program is effectively a lump sum subsidy, except for the fact that the food stamps can't be sold.

2.7 Budget Line Changes

In the next chapter we will analyze how the consumer chooses an optimal consumption bundle from his or her budget set. But we can already state some observations here that follow from what we have learned about the movements of the budget line.

First, we can observe that since the budget set doesn't change when we multiply all prices and income by a positive number, the optimal choice of the consumer from the budget set can't change either. Without even analyzing the choice process itself, we have derived an important conclusion: a perfectly balanced inflation—one in which all prices and all incomes rise at the same rate—doesn't change anybody's budget set, and thus cannot change anybody's optimal choice.

Second, we can make some statements about how well-off the consumer can be at different prices and incomes. Suppose that the consumer's income increases and all prices remain the same. We know that this represents a parallel shift outward of the budget line. Thus every bundle the consumer was consuming at the lower income is also a possible choice at the higher income. But then the consumer must be at least as well-off at the higher income as at the lower income—since he or she has all the choices available before plus some more. Similarly, if one price declines and all others stay the same, the consumer must be at least as well-off. This simple observation will be of considerable use later on.

Summary

1. The budget set consists of all bundles of goods that the consumer can afford at given prices and income. We will typically assume that there are only two goods, but this assumption is more general than it seems.

2. The budget line is written as $p_1 x_1 + p_2 x_2 = m$. It has a slope of $-p_1/p_2$, a vertical intercept of m/p_2, and a horizontal intercept of m/p_1.

3. Increasing income shifts the budget line outward. Increasing the price of good 1 makes the budget line steeper. Increasing the price of good 2 makes the budget line flatter.

4. Taxes, subsidies, and rationing change the slope and position of the budget line by changing the prices perceived by the consumer.

Review Questions

1. Originally the consumer faces the budget line $p_1 x_1 + p_2 x_2 = m$. Then the price of good 1 doubles, the price of good 2 becomes 8 times larger, and income becomes 4 times larger. Write down an equation for the new budget line in terms of the original prices and income.

2. What happens to the budget line if the price of good 2 increases, but the price of good 1 and income remain constant?

3. If the price of good 1 doubles and the price of good 2 triples does the budget line become flatter or steeper?

4. What is the definition of a numeraire good?

5. Suppose that the government puts a tax of 15 cents a gallon on gasoline, and then later decides to put a subsidy on gasoline at a rate of 7 cents a gallon. What net tax is this combination equivalent to?

6. Suppose that a budget equation is given by $p_1 x_1 + p_2 x_2 = m$. The government decides to impose a lump sum tax of u, a quantity tax on good 1 of t, and a subsidy on good 2 of s. What is the formula for the new budget line?

7. If the income of the consumer increases, and one of the prices decreases at the same time, will the consumer necessarily be at least as well-off?

3

PREFERENCES

We saw in Chapter 2 that the economic model of consumer behavior is very simple: it says that people choose the best things they can afford. The last chapter was devoted to clarifying the meaning of "can afford," and this chapter will be devoted to clarifying the economic concept of "best things."

We call the objects of consumer choice **consumption bundles**. This is a complete list of the goods and services that are involved in the choice problem that we are investigating. The word "complete" deserves emphasis: when you analyze a consumer choice problem, make sure that you include all of the appropriate goods in the definition of the consumption bundle.

If we are analyzing consumer choice at the broadest level, we would want not only a complete list of the goods that a consumer might consume, but also a description of when, where, and under what circumstances they would become available. After all, people care about how much food they will have tomorrow as well as how much food they have today. A raft in the middle of the Atlantic Ocean is very different than a raft in the middle of the Sahara Desert. And an umbrella when it is raining is quite a different good than an umbrella on a sunny day. It is often useful to think of the "same" good available in different locations or circumstances as a different good, since the consumer may value the good differently in those situations.

However, when we limit our attention to a simple choice problem, the relevant goods are usually pretty obvious. We'll often adopt the idea described earlier of using just two goods and calling one of them "all other goods" so that we can focus on the tradeoff between one good and everything else. In this way we can consider consumption choices involving many goods and still use two-dimensional diagrams.

So let us take our consumption bundle to consist of two goods, and let x_1 denote the amount of one good, and x_2 the amount of the other. The complete consumption bundle is therefore denoted by (x_1, x_2). As noted before, we will occasionally abbreviate this consumption bundle by X.

3.1 Consumer Preferences

We will suppose that given any two consumption bundles, (x_1, x_2) and (y_1, y_2), the consumer can rank them as to their desirability. That is, the consumer can determine that one of the consumption bundles is strictly better than the other, or decide that she is indifferent between the two bundles.

We will use the symbol $\succ$ to mean that one bundle is **strictly preferred** to another, so that $(x_1, x_2) \succ (y_1, y_2)$ should be interpreted as saying that the consumer **strictly prefers** (x_1, x_2) to (y_1, y_2), in the sense that she definitely wants the x-bundle rather than the y-bundle. This preference relation is meant to be an operational notion. If the consumer prefers one bundle to another, it means that he or she would choose one over the other, given the opportunity. Thus the idea of preference is based on the consumer's *behavior*. In order to tell whether one bundle is preferred to another, we see how the consumer behaves in choice situations involving the two bundles. If she always chooses (x_1, x_2) when (y_1, y_2) is available, then it is natural to say that this consumer prefers (x_1, x_2) to (y_1, y_2).

If the consumer is **indifferent** between two bundles of goods, we use the symbol $\sim$ and write $(x_1, x_2) \sim (y_1, y_2)$. Indifference means that the consumer would be just as satisfied, according to her own preferences, consuming the bundle (x_1, x_2) as she would be consuming the other bundle, (y_1, y_2).

If the consumer prefers or is indifferent between the two bundles we say that she **weakly prefers** (x_1, x_2) to (y_1, y_2) and write $(x_1, x_2) \succeq (y_1, y_2)$.

These relations of strict preference, weak preference, and indifference are not independent concepts; the relations are themselves related! For example, if $(x_1, x_2) \succeq (y_1, y_2)$ and $(y_1, y_2) \succeq (x_1, x_2)$ we can conclude that $(x_1, x_2) \sim (y_1, y_2)$. That is, if the consumer thinks that (x_1, x_2) is at least as good as (y_1, y_2), *and* that (y_1, y_2) is at least as good as (x_1, x_2), then the consumer must be indifferent between the two bundles of goods.

Similarly, if $(x_1, x_2) \succeq (y_1, y_2)$ but we know that it is *not* the case that $(x_1, x_2) \sim (y_1, y_2)$, we can conclude that we must have $(x_1, x_2) \succ (y_1, y_2)$. This just says that if the consumer thinks that (x_1, x_2) is at least as good as (y_1, y_2), and she is not indifferent between the two bundles, then it must be that she thinks that (x_1, x_2) is strictly better than (y_1, y_2).

3.2 Assumptions about Preferences

Economists usually make some assumptions about the "consistency" of consumers' preferences. For example, it seems unreasonable—not to say contradictory—to have a situation where $(x_1, x_2) \succ (y_1, y_2)$ and, at the same time, $(y_1, y_2) \succ (x_1, x_2)$. For this would mean that the consumer strictly prefers the x-bundle to the y-bundle ... and vice–versa.

So we usually make some assumptions about how the preference relations work. Some of the assumptions about preferences are so fundamental that we can refer to them as "axioms" of consumer theory. Here are three such axioms about consumer preferences.

Complete. We assume that any two bundles can be compared. That is, given any x-bundle and any y-bundle, we assume that $(x_1, x_2) \succeq (y_1, y_2)$, or $(y_1, y_2) \succeq (x_1, x_2)$, or both, in which case the consumer is indifferent between the two bundles.

Reflexive. We assume that any bundle is at least as good as itself: $(x_1, x_2) \succeq (x_1, x_2)$.

Transitive. If $(x_1, x_2) \succeq (y_1, y_2)$ and $(y_1, y_2) \succeq (z_1, z_2)$ then we assume that $(x_1, x_2) \succeq (z_1, z_2)$. In other words, if the consumer thinks that X is at least as good as Y and that Y is at least as good as Z, then the consumer thinks that X is at least as good as Z.

The first axiom, completeness, is hardly objectionable, at least for the kinds of choices economists generally examine. To say that any two bundles can be compared is simply to say that given any two bundles the consumer is able to make a choice. One might imagine extreme situations involving life or death choices where ranking the alternatives might be difficult, or even impossible, but these choices are, for the most part, outside the domain of economic analysis.

The second axiom, reflexivity, is trivial. Any bundle is certainly at least as good as an identical bundle. Parents of small children may occasionally observe behavior that violates this assumption, but it seems plausible for most adult behavior.

The third axiom, transitivity, is more problematic. It isn't clear that transitivity of preferences is *necessarily* a property that preferences would have to have. The assumption that preferences are transitive doesn't seem compelling on grounds of pure logic alone. In fact it's not. Transitivity is a hypothesis about peoples' choice behavior, not a statement of pure logic. Whether it is a basic fact of logic or not isn't the point: it is whether or not it is a reasonably accurate description of how people behave that matters.

What would you think about a person who said that he preferred a bundle X to Y, and preferred Y to Z, but then also said that he preferred Z to X? This would certainly be taken as evidence of peculiar behavior.

More importantly, how would this consumer behave if faced with choices among the three bundles X, Y, and Z? If we asked him to choose his most preferred bundle, he would have quite a problem, for whatever bundle he chose, there would always be one that was preferred to it. If we are to have a theory where people are making "best" choices, preferences must satisfy the transitivity axiom or something very much like it. If preferences were not transitive there could well be a set of bundles for which there is no best choice.

3.3 Indifference Curves

It turns out that the whole theory of consumer choice can be formulated in terms of preferences that satisfy the three axioms described above, plus a few more technical assumptions. However, we will find it convenient to describe preferences graphically using a construction known as **indifference curves**.

Consider Figure 3.1 where we have illustrated two axes representing a consumer's consumption of goods 1 and 2. Let us pick a certain consumption bundle (x_1, x_2) and shade in all of the consumption bundles that are weakly preferred to (x_1, x_2). This is called the **weakly preferred set**. The bundles on the boundary of this set—the bundles for which the consumer is just indifferent to (x_1, x_2)—form the **indifference curve**.

We can draw an indifference curve through any consumption bundle we want. The indifference curve through a consumption bundle consists of all bundles of goods that leave the consumer indifferent to the given bundle.

One problem with using indifference curves to describe preferences is that they only show you the bundles that the consumer perceives as being indifferent to each other—they don't show you which bundles are better and which bundles are worse. It is sometimes useful to draw small arrows on the indifference curves to indicate the direction of the preferred bundles. We won't do this in every case, but we will do it in a few of the examples where confusion might arise.

If we make no further assumptions about preferences, indifference curves can take very peculiar shapes indeed. But even at this level of generality, we can state an important principle about indifference curves: *indifference curves representing distinct levels of preference cannot cross.*

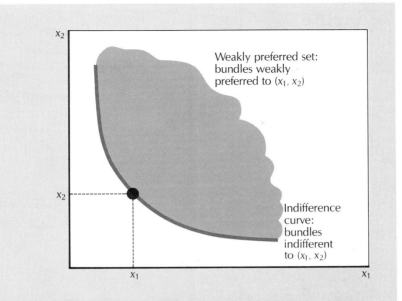

Weakly preferred set. The shaded area consists of all bundles that are at least as good as the bundle (x_1, x_2).

Figure 3.1

That is, the situation depicted in Figure 3.2 cannot represent two distinct indifference curves if the preferences satisfy the properties listed above. Let's prove this.

Pick three bundles of goods, X, Y, and Z, such that X lies only on one indifference curve, Y lies only on the other indifference curve, and Z lies at the intersection of the indifference curves. By assumption the indifference curves represent distinct levels of preference, so one of the bundles, say X, is strictly preferred to the other bundle, Y. By the definition of indifference curves, we know that $X \sim Z$ and $Z \sim Y$. From the axiom of transitivity, we can conclude that $X \sim Y$. But this contradicts the assumption that $X \succ Y$. This contradiction establishes the result—indifference curves representing distinct levels of preference cannot cross.

What other properties do indifference curves have? In the abstract, the answer is: not many. Indifference curves are a way to describe preferences. Nearly any "reasonable" preferences that you can think of can be depicted by indifference curves. The trick is to learn what kinds of preferences give rise to what shapes of indifference curves.

3.4 Examples of Preferences

Let's try to relate preferences to indifference curves via some examples. We'll describe some preferences and then see what the indifference curves look like that represent them.

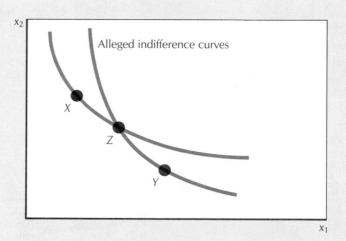

Figure
3.2

Indifference curves cannot cross. If they did, X, Y, and Z would all have to be indifferent to each other, and thus could not lie on distinct indifference curves.

There is a general procedure for constructing indifference curves given a "verbal" description of the preferences. First plop your pencil down on the graph at some consumption bundle (x_1, x_2). Now think about giving a little more of good 1, Δx_1, to the consumer, moving him to $(x_1 + \Delta x_1, x_2)$. Now ask yourself how would you have to *change* the consumption of x_2 to make the consumer indifferent to the original consumption point? Call this change Δx_2. Ask yourself the question "for a given change in good 1, how does good 2 have to change to make the consumer just indifferent between $(x_1 + \Delta x_1, x_2 + \Delta x_2)$ and (x_1, x_2)?" Once you have determined this movement at one consumption bundle you have drawn a piece of the indifference curve. Now try it at another bundle, and so on, until you develop a clear picture of the overall shape of the indifference curves.

Perfect Substitutes

Two goods are **perfect substitutes** if the consumer doesn't care how much he has of one or the other, but only about the total amount of the two goods. Suppose, for example, we are considering a choice between red pencils and blue pencils, and the consumer involved likes pencils, but doesn't care about color at all. Pick a consumption bundle, say $(10, 10)$. Then for this consumer, any other consumption bundle that has 20 pencils in it is just as good as $(10, 10)$. Mathematically speaking, any consumption bundle (x_1, x_2) such that $x_1 + x_2 = 20$ will be on this consumer's indifference curve through $(10, 10)$. Thus the indifference curves for this consumer are all parallel straight lines with a slope of -1, as depicted in Figure 3.3. Bundles with more total pencils are preferred to bundles with fewer total pencils, so the direction of increasing preference is up and to the right, as illustrated in Figure 3.3.

How does this work in terms of general procedure for drawing indifference curves? If we are at $(10, 10)$ and we increase the amount of the first good by one unit to 11, how much do we have to change the second good to get back to the original indifference curve? The answer is clearly that we have to decrease the second good by 1 unit. Thus the indifference curve through $(10, 10)$ has a slope of -1. The same procedure can be carried out at any bundle of goods with the same results—in this case all the indifference curves have a constant slope of -1.

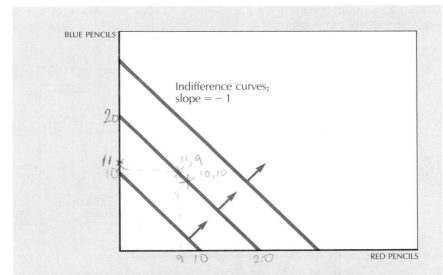

Perfect substitutes. The consumer only cares about the total number of pencils, not about their colors. Thus the indifference curves are straight lines with a slope of -1.

Figure 3.3

The important fact about perfect substitutes is that the indifference curves have a *constant* slope. In fact some economists define perfect substitutes to be goods where the consumer is willing to substitute one for the other at a constant rate, not necessarily 1 for 1. Suppose, for example, that we considered a consumer's preferences between red pencils, and *pairs* of blue pencils. The slopes of the indifference curves for these two goods would have a slope of -2, since the consumer would be willing to give up two red pencils to get one more pair of blue pencils.

Perfect Complements

Perfect complements are goods that are always consumed together in fixed proportions. In some sense the goods "complement" each other. A nice example is that of right shoes and left shoes. The consumer likes shoes, but always wears right and left shoes together. Having only one out of a pair of shoes doesn't do the consumer a bit of good.

Let us draw the indifference curves for perfect complements. Suppose we pick the consumption bundle $(10, 10)$. Now add 1 more right shoe so we have $(11, 10)$. By assumption this leaves the consumer indifferent to the original position: the extra shoe doesn't do him any good. The same thing happens if we have add left shoes, so that the consumer is also indifferent between $(10, 11)$ and $(10, 10)$.

Thus the indifference curves are L–shaped, with the vertex of the L occurring where the number of left shoes equals the number of right shoes as in Figure 3.4.

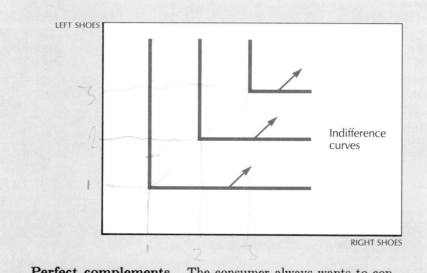

Figure 3.4

Perfect complements. The consumer always wants to consume the goods in fixed proportions to each other. Thus the indifference curves are L-shaped.

Increasing both the number of left shoes and the number of right shoes at the same time will move the consumer to a more preferred position, so the direction of increasing preference is again up and to the right, as illustrated in the diagram.

The important thing about perfect complements is that the consumer prefers to consume the goods in fixed proportions, not necessarily that the proportion is one to one. If a consumer always drinks two teaspoons of sugar in her cup of tea, and doesn't use sugar for anything else, then the indifference curves will still be L–shaped. In this case the corners of the L will occur at (2 teaspoons sugar, 1 cup tea), (4 teaspoons sugar, 2 cups tea) and so on, rather than at (1 right shoe, 1 left shoe), (2 right shoes, 2 left shoes), etc.

Bads

A **bad** is a commodity that the consumer doesn't like. For example, suppose that the commodities in question are now pepperoni and anchovies— and the consumer loves pepperoni but dislikes anchovies. But let us suppose there is some tradeoff possible between pepperoni and anchovies. That is, there would be some amount of pepperoni on a pizza that would compensate the consumer for having to consume a given amount of anchovies. How could we represent these preferences using indifference curves?

Pick a bundle (x_1, x_2) consisting of some pepperoni and some anchovies. If we give the consumer more anchovies what do we have to do with the pepperoni to keep him on the same indifference curve? Clearly, we have to give him some extra pepperoni to compensate him for having to put up with the anchovies. Thus this consumer must have indifference curves that slope up and to the right as depicted in Figure 3.5.

The direction of increasing preference is down and to the right—that is, towards the direction of decreased anchovy consumption and increased pepperoni consumption, just as the arrows in the diagram illustrate.

Neutrals

A good is a **neutral good** if the consumer doesn't care about it one way or the other. What if a consumer is just neutral about anchovies?[1] In this case his indifference curves will be vertical lines as depicted in Figure 3.6. He only cares about the amount of pepperoni he has, and doesn't care at all about how many anchovies he has. The more pepperoni the better, but adding more anchovies doesn't affect him one way or the other.

Satiation

We sometimes want to consider a situation involving **satiation**, where there is some overall best bundle for the consumer, and the "closer" he is

---

[1] Is anybody neutral about anchovies?

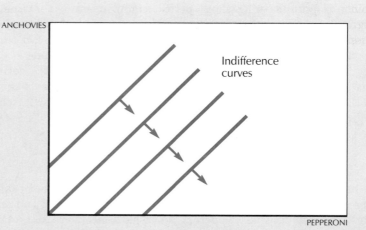

Figure
3.5 **Bads.** Here anchovies are a "bad" and pepperoni is a "good" for this consumer. Thus the indifference curves have a positive slope.

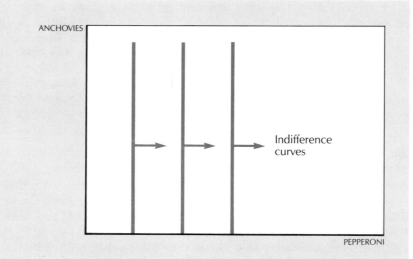

Figure
3.6 **A neutral good.** The consumer likes pepperoni, but is neutral about anchovies, so the indifference curves are vertical lines.

to that best bundle, the better off he is, in terms of his own preferences. For example, suppose that the consumer has some most preferred bundle of goods $(\overline{x}_1, \overline{x}_2)$, and the further away he is from that bundle the worse off he is. In this case we say that $(\overline{x}_1, \overline{x}_2)$ is a **satiation** point, or a **bliss** point. The indifference curves for the consumer look like those depicted in Figure 3.7. The best point is $(\overline{x}_1, \overline{x}_2)$ and points further away from this bliss point lie on "lower" indifference curves.

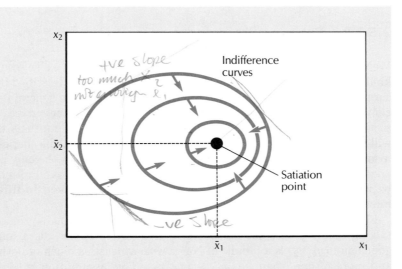

Satiated preferences. The bundle $(\overline{x}_1, \overline{x}_2)$ is the satiation point or bliss point, and the indifference curves surround this point.

Figure
3.7

In this case the indifference curves have a negative slope when the consumer has "too little" or "too much" of both goods, and a positive slope when he has "too much" of one of the goods. When he has too much of one of the goods, it becomes a bad—reducing the consumption of the bad good moves him closer to his "bliss point." If he has too much of both goods, they both are bads, so reducing the consumption of each moves him closer to the bliss point.

Suppose, for example, that the two goods are chocolate cake and ice cream. There might well be some optimal amount of chocolate cake and ice cream that you would want to eat per week. Any less than that amount would make you worse off, but any more than that amount would also make you worse off.

If you think about it, most goods are like chocolate cake and ice cream in this respect—you can have too much of nearly anything. But people would generally not voluntarily *choose* to have too much of the goods they consume. Why would you choose to have more than you want of something? Thus the interesting region from the viewpoint of economic choice is where you have *less* than you want of most goods. The choices that people actually care about are choices of this sort, and these are the choices with which we will be concerned.

3.5 Well-Behaved Preferences

We've now seen some examples of indifference curves. As we've seen, many kinds of preferences, reasonable or unreasonable, can be described by these simple diagrams. But if we want to describe preferences in general it will be convenient to focus on a few general shapes of indifference curves. In this section we will describe some more general sorts of assumptions that we will make about preferences and their implications about the shapes of the associated indifference curves. These assumptions are not the only possible ones; in some situations you might want to use different assumptions. But we will take them as the defining features for **well-behaved indifference curves**.

First we will typically assume that more is better, that is, that we are talking about *goods*, not bads. More precisely, if (x_1, x_2) is a bundle of goods and (y_1, y_2) is a bundle of goods with at least as much of both goods and more of one, then $(y_1, y_2) \succ (x_1, x_2)$. This assumption is sometimes called **monotonicity** of preferences. As we suggested in our discussion of satiation, more is better would probably only hold up to a point. Thus the assumption of monotonicity is saying only that we are going to examine situations *before* that point is reached—before any satiation sets in—while more *still is* better.

What does monotonicity imply about the shape of indifference curves? It implies that they have a *negative* slope. Consider Figure 3.8. If we start at a bundle (x_1, x_2) and move anywhere up and to the right, we must be moving to a preferred position. If we move down and to the left we must be moving to a worse position. So if we are moving to an *indifferent* position, we must be moving either left and up or right and down: the indifference curve must have a negative slope.

Second, we are going to assume that averages are preferred to extremes. That is, if we take two bundles of goods (x_1, x_2) and (y_1, y_2) on the same indifference curve and take a weighted average of the two bundles such as

$$(\frac{1}{2}x_1 + \frac{1}{2}y_1, \frac{1}{2}x_2 + \frac{1}{2}y_2)$$

then the average bundle will be at least as good as or strictly preferred to each of the two extreme bundles. This weighted average bundle has the average amount of good 1 and the average amount of good 2 that is present in the two bundles. It therefore lies halfway along the straight line connecting the x–bundle and the y–bundle.

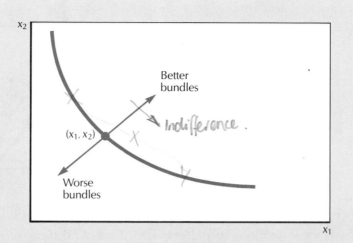

Monotonic preferences.   More of both goods is a better bundle for this consumer; less of both goods represents a worse bundle.

Figure 3.8

Actually, we're going to assume this for any weight t between 0 and 1, not just $1/2$. Thus we are assuming that if $(x_1, x_2) \sim (y_1, y_2)$ then

$$(tx_1 + (1 - t)y_1, tx_2 + (1 - t)y_2) \succeq (x_1, x_2)$$

for any t such that $0 \leq t \leq 1$. This weighted average of the two bundles gives t times as much weight to the x-bundle as to the y-bundle. Therefore, the distance from the x-bundle to the average bundle is just a fraction t of the distance from the y-bundle to the x-bundle, along the straight line connecting the two bundles.

What does this assumption about preferences mean geometrically? It means that the set of bundles weakly preferred to (x_1, x_2) is a **convex set**. For suppose that (y_1, y_2) and (x_1, x_2) are indifferent bundles. Then, if averages are preferred to extremes, all of the weighted averages of (x_1, x_2) and (y_1, y_2) are weakly preferred to (x_1, x_2) and (y_1, y_2). A convex set has the property that if you take *any* two points in the set and draw the line segment connecting those two points, that line segment lies entirely in the set.

Figure 3.9A depicts an example of convex preferences, while Figures 3.9B and 3.9C show two examples of nonconvex preferences. Figure 3.9C presents preferences that are so nonconvex that we might want to call them "concave preferences."

Can you think of preferences that are not convex? One possibility might be something like my preferences for ice cream and olives. I like ice cream

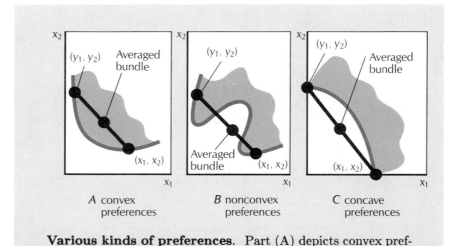

Figure 3.9

Various kinds of preferences. Part (A) depicts convex preferences, part (B) depicts nonconvex preferences, and part (C) depicts "concave" preferences.

and I like olives ... but I don't like to have them together! In considering my consumption in the next hour, I might be indifferent between consuming 8 ounces of ice cream and 2 ounces of olives, or 8 ounces of olives and 2 ounces of ice cream. But either one of these bundles would be better than consuming 5 ounces of each! These are the kind of preferences depicted in Figure 3.9C.

Why do we want to assume that well-behaved preferences are convex? Because, for the most part, goods are consumed together. The kinds of preferences depicted in Figures 3.9B and 3.9C imply that the consumer would prefer to specialize, at least to some degree, and consume only one of the goods. However, the normal case is where the consumer would want to trade some of one good for the other, and end up consuming some of each, rather than specializing in consuming only one of the two goods.

In fact, if we look at my preferences for *monthly* consumption of ice cream and olives, rather than my immediate consumption, they would tend to look much more like Figure 3.9A than Figure 3.9C. Each month I would prefer having some ice cream and some olives—albeit at different times—to specializing in consuming either one for the entire month.

Finally, one extension of the assumption of convexity is the assumption of **strict convexity.** This means that the weighted average of two indifferent bundles is *strictly* preferred to the two extreme bundles. Strictly convex preferences have indifference curves without flat spots; they are strictly rotund, like those depicted in Figure 3.9A.

3.6 The Marginal Rate of Substitution

We will often find it useful to refer to the slope of an indifference curve at a particular point. This idea is so useful that it even has a name: the slope of an indifference curve is known as the **marginal rate of substitution (MRS)**. The name comes from the fact that the marginal rate of substitution measures the rate at which the consumer is just willing to substitute one good for the other.

Suppose that we take a little of good 1, Δx_1, away from the consumer. Then we give him Δx_2, an amount that is just sufficient to put him back on his indifference curve, so that he is just as well off after this substitution of x_2 for x_1 as he was before. We think of the ratio $\Delta x_2 / \Delta x_1$ as being the *rate* at which the consumer is willing to substitute good 2 for good 1.

Now think of Δx_1 as being a very small change—a marginal change. Then the rate $\Delta x_2 / \Delta x_1$ measures the *marginal* rate of substitution of good 2 for good 1. As Δx_1 gets small, $\Delta x_2 / \Delta x_1$ approaches the slope of the indifference curve, as can be seen in Figure 3.10.

When we write the ratio $\Delta x_2 / \Delta x_1$, we will always think of both the numerator and the denominator as being small numbers—as describing

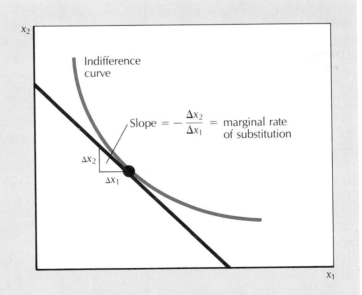

The marginal rate of substitution (MRS). The marginal rate of substitution measures the slope of the indifference curve.

Figure
3.10

marginal changes from the original consumption bundle. Thus the ratio defining the marginal rate of substitution will always describe the slope of the indifference curve: the rate at which the consumer is just willing to substitute a little more consumption of good 2 for a little less consumption of good 1.

The marginal rate of substitution measures an interesting aspect of the consumer's behavior. Suppose that the consumer has well-behaved preferences, that is, preferences which are monotonic and convex, and he is currently consuming some bundle (x_1, x_2). We now will offer him a trade: he can exchange good 1 for 2, or good 2 for 1, in any amount at a "rate of exchange" of E.

That is, if the consumer gives up Δx_1 units of good 1, he can get $E\Delta x_1$ units of good 2 in exchange. Or, conversely, if he gives up Δx_2 units of good 2, he can get $\Delta x_2/E$ units of good 1. Geometrically, we are offering the consumer an opportunity to move to any point along a line with slope $-E$ that passes through (x_1, x_2), as depicted in Figure 3.11. Moving up and to the left from (x_1, x_2) involves exchanging good 1 for good 2, and moving down and to the right involves exchanging good 2 for good 1. In either movement, the exchange rate is E. Since exchange always involves giving up one good in exchange for another, the exchange *rate E* corresponds to a *slope* of $-E$.

We can now ask what would the rate of exchange have to be in order for the consumer to want to stay put at (x_1, x_2)? To answer this question, we simply note that any time the exchange line *crosses* the indifference curve, there will be some points on that line that are preferred to (x_1, x_2)—that lie above the indifference curve. Thus, if there is to be no movement from (x_1, x_2), the exchange line must be tangent to the indifference curve. That is, the slope of the exchange line, $-E$, must be the slope of the indifference curve at (x_1, x_2). At any other rate of exchange, the exchange line would cut the indifference curve and thus allow the consumer to move to a more preferred point.

Thus the slope of the indifference curve, the marginal rate of substitution, measures the rate at which the consumer is just on the margin of trading or not trading. At any rate of exchange other than the marginal rate of substitution, the consumer would want to trade off one good for the other. But if the rate of exchange equals the marginal rate of substitution, the consumer wants to stay put.

3.7 Other Interpretations of the MRS

We have said that the MRS measures the rate at which the consumer is just on the margin of being willing to substitute good 1 for good 2. We could also say that the consumer is just on the margin of being willing to "pay" some of good 1 in order to buy some more of good 2. So sometimes

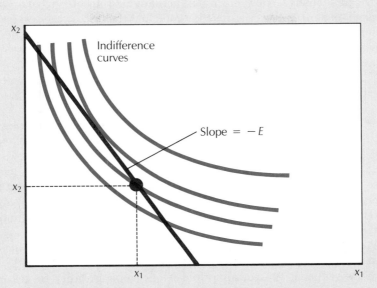

x_2

Indifference
curves

Slope $= -E$

x_2

x_1 x_1

Trading at an exchange rate. Here we are allowing the consumer to trade the goods at an exchange rate E, which implies the consumer can move along a line with slope $-E$.

Figure
3.11

you hear people say that the slope of the indifference curve measures the **marginal willingness to pay**.

If good 2 represents the consumption of "all other goods," and it is measured in dollars that you can spend on other goods, then the marginal willingness to pay interpretation is very natural. The marginal rate of substitution of good 2 for good 1 is how many dollars you would just be willing to give up spending on other goods in order to consume a little bit more of good 1. Thus the marginal rate of substitution measures the marginal willingness to give up dollars in order to consume a marginal amount more of good 1. But giving up those dollars is just like paying dollars in order to consume a little more of good 1.

If you use the marginal willingness to pay interpretation of the MRS, you should be careful to emphasize both the "marginal" and the "willingness." The MRS measures the amount of good 2 that one is *willing* to pay for a *marginal* amount of extra consumption of good 1. How much you actually *have* to pay for some given amount of extra consumption may be different than the amount you are willing to pay. How much you have to pay will depend on the price of the good in question. How much you are willing to pay doesn't depend on the price—it is determined by your preferences.

Similarly, how much you may be willing to pay for a large change in consumption may be different than how much you are willing to pay for a marginal change. How much you actually end up buying of a good will depend on your preferences for that good and the prices that you face. How much you would be willing to pay for a small amount extra of the good is a feature only of your preferences.

3.8 Behavior of the Marginal Rate of Substitution

It is sometimes useful to describe the shapes of indifference curves by describing the behavior of the marginal rate of substitution. For example, the "perfect substitutes" indifference curves are characterized by the fact that the marginal rate of substitution is constant at −1. The "neutrals" case is characterized by the fact that the marginal rate of substitution is everywhere infinite. The preferences for "perfect complements" are characterized by the fact that the MRS is either 0 or infinity, and nothing in between.

We've already pointed out that the assumption of monotonicity implies that indifference curves must have a negative slope, so the MRS always involves reducing the consumption of one good in order to get more of another for monotonic preferences.

The case of convex indifference curves exhibits yet another kind of behavior for the MRS. For convex indifference curves, the marginal rate of substitution—the slope of the indifference curve—decreases as we increase x_1. Thus the indifference curves exhibit a **diminishing marginal rate of substitution**. This means that the rate at which a person is just willing to trade x_1 for x_2 decreases as we increase the amount of x_1. Stated in this way, convexity of indifference curves seems very natural: it says that the more you have of one good, the more willing you are to give some of it up in exchange for the other good. (But remember the ice cream and olives example—for some pairs of goods this assumption might not hold!)

Summary

1. Economists assume that a consumer can rank various consumption possibilities. The way in which the consumer ranks the consumption bundles describes the consumer's preferences.

2. Indifference curves can be used to depict different kinds of preferences.

3. Well-behaved preferences are monotonic (meaning more is better) and convex (meaning averages are preferred to extremes).

4. The marginal rate of substitution measures the slope of the indifference curve. This can be interpreted as how much the consumer is willing to give up of good 2 to acquire more of good 1.

Review Questions

1. If we observe a consumer choosing (x_1, x_2) when (y_1, y_2) is available one time, are we justified in concluding that $(x_1, x_2) \succ (y_1, y_2)$?

2. Consider a group of people A, B, C, ... and the relation "at least as tall as," as in "A is at least as tall as B." Is this relation transitive? Is it complete?

3. Take the same group of people and consider the relation "strictly taller than." Is this relation transitive? Is it reflexive? Is it complete?

4. A college football coach says that given any two linemen A and B, he always prefers the one who is bigger and faster. Is this preference relation transitive? Is it complete?

5. Can an indifference curve cross itself? For example, could Figure 3.2 depict a single indifference curve?

6. Could Figure 3.2 be a single indifference curve if preferences are monotonic?

7. If both pepperoni and anchovies are bads, will the indifference curve have a positive or a negative slope?

8. Explain why convex preferences means that "averages are preferred to extremes."

9. What is your marginal rate of substitution of $1 bills for $5 bills?

10. If good 1 is a "neutral," what is its marginal rate of substitution for good 2?

11. Think of some other goods for which your preferences might be concave.

4

UTILITY

In Victorian days, philosophers and economists talked blithely of "utility" as an indicator of a person's overall well-being. Utility was thought of as a numeric measure of a person's happiness. Given this idea, it was natural to think of consumers as making choices so as to maximize their utility, that is, to make themselves as happy as possible.

The trouble is that these classical economists never really described how we were to measure utility. How are we supposed to quantify the "amount" of utility associated with different choices? Is one person's utility the same as another's? What would it mean to say that an extra candy bar would give me twice as much utility as an extra carrot? Does the concept of utility have any independent meaning other than its being what people maximize?

Because of these conceptual problems, economists have abandoned the old-fashioned view of utility as being a measure of happiness. Instead, the theory of consumer behavior has been reformulated entirely in terms of **consumer preferences**, and utility is seen only as a *way to describe preferences*.

Economists gradually came to recognize that all that mattered about utility as far as choice behavior was concerned was whether one bundle had a higher utility than another—how much higher didn't really matter. Originally, preferences were defined in terms of utility: to say a bundle (x_1, x_2) was preferred to a bundle (y_1, y_2) meant that the x-bundle had a higher utility than the y-bundle. But now we tend to think of things the other way around. The *preferences* of the consumer are the fundamental description useful for analyzing choice, and utility is simply a way of describing preferences.

A **utility function** is a way of assigning a number to every possible consumption bundle such that more-preferred bundles get assigned larger numbers than less-preferred bundles. That is, a bundle (x_1, x_2) is preferred to a bundle (y_1, y_2) if and only if the utility of (x_1, x_2) is larger than the utility of (y_1, y_2): in symbols, $(x_1, x_2) \succ (y_1, y_2)$ if and only if $u(x_1, x_2) > u(y_1, y_2)$.

The only property of a utility assignment that is important is how it *orders* the bundles of goods. The magnitude of the utility function is only important insofar as it *ranks* the different consumption bundles; the size of the utility difference between any two consumption bundles doesn't matter. Because of this emphasis on ordering bundles of goods, this kind of utility is referred to as **ordinal utility**.

Consider for example Table 4.1, where we have illustrated several different ways of assigning utilities to three bundles of goods, all of which order the bundles in the same way. In this example, the consumer prefers A to B and B to C. All of the ways indicated are valid utility functions that describe the same preferences because they all have the property that A is assigned a higher number than B, which in turn is assigned a higher number than C.

Different ways to assign utilities.

Bundle	U_1	U_2	U_3
A	3	17	-1
B	2	10	-2
C	1	.002	-3

Table 4.1

Since only the ranking of the bundles matters, there can be no unique way to assign utilities to bundles of goods. If we can find one way to assign utility numbers to bundles of goods, we can find an infinite number of ways to do it. If $u(x_1, x_2)$ represents a way to assign utility numbers to the bundles (x_1, x_2), then multiplying $u(x_1, x_2)$ by 2 (or any other positive number) is just as good a way to assign utilities.

Multiplication by 2 is an example of a **monotonic transformation**. A monotonic transformation is a way of transforming one set of numbers into another set of numbers in a way that preserves the order of the numbers.

We typically represent a monotonic transformation by a function $f(u)$ that transforms each number u into some other number $f(u)$, in a way that preserves the order of the numbers in the sense that $u_1 > u_2$ implies $f(u_1) > f(u_2)$. A monotonic transformation and a monotonic function are essentially the same thing.

Examples of monotonic transformations are multiplication by a positive number (e.g., $f(u) = 3u$), adding any number (e.g., $f(u) = u + 17$), raising u to an odd power (e.g., $f(u) = u^3$), and so on.[1]

The rate of change of $f(u)$ as u changes can be measured by looking at the change in f between two values of u, divided by the change in u:

$$\frac{\Delta f}{\Delta u} = \frac{f(u_2) - f(u_1)}{u_2 - u_1}.$$

For a monotonic transformation, $f(u_2) - f(u_1)$ always has the same sign as $u_2 - u_1$. Thus a monotonic function always has a positive rate of change. This means that the graph of a monotonic function will always have a positive slope, as depicted in Figure 4.1A.

If $f(u)$ is *any* monotonic transformation of utility function that represents some preferences $\succeq$, then $f(u(x_1, x_2))$ is also a utility function that represents those same preferences.

Why? The argument is given in the following three statements:

1. To say that $u(x_1, x_2)$ represents the preferences $\succeq$ means that $u(x_1, x_2) > u(y_1, y_2)$ if and only if $(x_1, x_2) \succ (y_1, y_2)$.
2. But if $f(u)$ is a monotonic transformation, then $u(x_1, x_2) > u(y_1, y_2)$ if and only if $f(u(x_1, x_2)) > f(u(y_1, y_2))$.
3. Therefore, $f(u(x_1, x_2)) > f(u(y_1, y_2))$ if and only if $(x_1, x_2) \succ (y_1, y_2)$, so the function $f(u)$ represents the preferences $\succeq$ in the same way as the original utility function $u(x_1, x_2)$.

We summarize this discussion by stating the following principle: *a monotonic transformation of a utility function is a utility function that represents the same preferences as the original utility function.*

Geometrically, a utility function is a way to label indifference curves. Since every bundle on an indifference curve must get the same utility, a utility function is a way of assigning numbers to the different indifference

---

[1] What we are calling a "monotonic transformation" is, strictly speaking, called a "positive monotonic transformation," in order to distinguish it from a "negative monotonic transformation," which is one that *reverses* the order of the numbers. Monotonic transformations are sometimes called "monotonous transformations," which seems unfair, since they can actually be quite interesting.

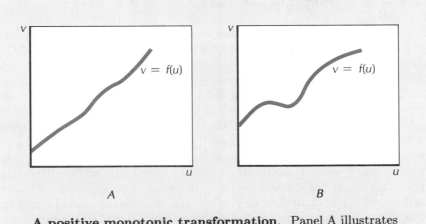

A positive monotonic transformation. Panel A illustrates a monotonic function—one that is always increasing. Panel B illustrates a function that is *not* monotonic, since it sometimes increases and sometimes decreases.

Figure
4.1

curves in a way that higher indifference curves get assigned larger numbers. Seen from this point of view a monotonic transformation is just a relabeling of indifference curves. As long as indifference curves containing more preferred bundles get a larger label than indifference curves containing less preferred bundles, the labeling will represent the same preferences.

4.1 Cardinal Utility

There are some theories of utility that attach a significance to the magnitude of utility. These are known as **cardinal utility theories.** In a theory of cardinal utility, the size of the utility difference between two bundles of goods is supposed to have some sort of significance.

We know how to tell whether a given person prefers one bundle of goods to another: we simply offer him or her a choice between the two bundles and see which one is chosen. Thus we know how to assign an ordinal utility to the two bundles of goods: we just assign a higher utility to the chosen bundle than to the rejected bundle. Any assignment that does this will be a utility function. Thus we have an operational criterion for determining whether one bundle has a higher utility than another bundle for some individual.

But how do we tell if a person likes one bundle twice as much as another? How could you even tell if *you* like one bundle twice as much as another?

One could propose various definitions for this kind of assignment: I like one bundle twice as much as another if I am willing to pay twice as much for it. Or, I like one bundle twice as much as another if I am willing to run twice as far to get it, or to wait twice as long, or to gamble for it at twice the odds.

There is nothing wrong with any of these definitions; each one would give rise to a way of assigning utility levels in which the magnitude of the numbers assigned had some operational significance. But there isn't much right about them either. Although each of them is a possible interpretation of what it means to want one thing twice as much as another, none of them appears to be an especially compelling interpretation of that statement.

Even if we did find a way of assigning utility magnitudes that seemed to be especially compelling, what good would it do us in describing choice behavior? To tell whether one bundle or another will be chosen, we only have to know which is preferred—which has the larger utility. Knowing how much larger doesn't add anything to our description of choice. Since cardinal utility isn't needed to describe choice behavior and there is no compelling way to assign cardinal utilities anyway, we will stick with a purely ordinal utility framework.

4.2 Constructing a Utility Function

But are we assured that there is any way to assign ordinal utilities? Given a preference ordering can we always find a utility function that will order bundles of goods in the same way as those preferences? Is there a utility function that describes any reasonable preference ordering?

Not every kind of preferences can be represented by a utility function. For example, suppose that someone had intransitive preferences so that $A \succ B \succ C \succ A$. Then a utility function for these preferences would have to consist of numbers $u(A)$, $u(B)$, and $u(C)$ such that $u(A) > u(B) > u(C) > u(A)$. But this is impossible.

However, if we rule out perverse cases like intransitive preferences, it turns out that we will typically be able to find a utility function to represent preferences. We will illustrate one construction here, and another one in Chapter 15.

Suppose that we are given an indifference map as in Figure 4.2. We know that a utility function is a way to label the indifference curves such that higher indifference curves get larger numbers. How can we do this?

One easy way is to draw the diagonal line illustrated and label each indifference curve with its distance from the origin, measured along the line.

How do we know that this is a utility function? It is not hard to see that if preferences are monotonic then the line through the origin must intersect every indifference curve exactly once. Thus every bundle is getting a label, and those bundles on higher indifference curves are getting larger labels— and that's all it takes to be a utility function.

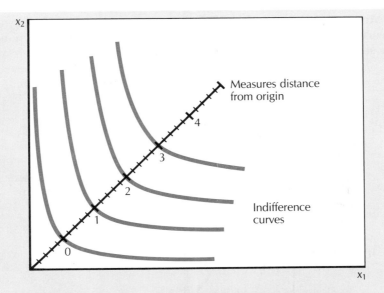

Measures distance
from origin

Indifference
curves

Constructing a utility function from indifference curves.
Draw a diagonal line and label each indifference curve with how
far it is from the origin measured along the line.

Figure
4.2

This gives us one way to find a labeling of indifference curves, at least as
long as preferences are monotonic. This won't always be the most natural
way in any given case, but at least it shows that the idea of an ordinal utility
function is pretty general: nearly any kind of "reasonable" preferences can
be represented by a utility function.

4.3 Some Examples of Utility Functions

In Chapter 3 we described some examples of preferences and the indifference curves that represented them. We can also represent these preferences
by utility functions. If you are given a utility function, $u(x_1, x_2)$, it is relatively easy to draw the indifference curves: you just plot all the points
(x_1, x_2) such that $u(x_1, x_2)$ equals a constant. In mathematics, the set of
all (x_1, x_2) such that $u(x_1, x_2)$ equals a constant is called a **level set**. For
each different value of the constant, you get a different indifference curve.

EXAMPLE: Indifference Curves from Utility

Suppose that the utility function is given by: $u(x_1, x_2) = x_1 x_2$. What do
the indifference curves look like?

We know that a typical indifference curve is just the set of all x_1 and x_2 such that $k = x_1 x_2$ for some constant k. Solving for x_2 as a function of x_1, we see that a typical indifference curve has the formula:

$$x_2 = \frac{k}{x_1}.$$

This curve is depicted in Figure 4.3 for $k = 1, 2, 3 \ldots$

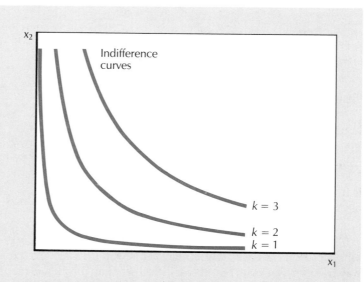

<table>
<tr><td>Figure
4.3</td><td>**Indifference curves.** The indifference curves $k = x_1 x_2$ for different values of k.</td></tr>
</table>

Let's consider another example. Suppose that we were given a utility function $v(x_1, x_2) = x_1^2 x_2^2$. What do its indifference curves look like? By the standard rules of algebra we known that:

$$v(x_1, x_2) = x_1^2 x_2^2 = (x_1 x_2)^2 = u(x_1, x_2)^2.$$

Thus the utility function v is just the square of the utility function u. For positive numbers $a > b$ if and only if $a^2 > b^2$, so $v(x_1, x_2)$ is a monotonic transformation of the previous utility function, $u(x_1, x_2)$. This means that the utility function $v(x_1, x_2) = x_1^2 x_2^2$ has to have exactly the same shaped indifference curves as those depicted in Figure 4.3. The labeling of the indifference curves will be different—the labels that were $1, 2, 3, \ldots$ will now be $1, 4, 9, \ldots$—but the set of bundles that has $v(x_1, x_2) = 9$ is exactly the same as the set of bundles that has $u(x_1, x_2) = 3$. Thus $v(x_1, x_2)$ describes exactly the same preferences as $u(x_1, x_2)$ since it *orders* all of the bundles in the same way.

Going the other direction—finding a utility function that represents some indifference curves—is somewhat more difficult. There are two ways to proceed. The first way is mathematical. Given the indifference curves, we want to find a function that is constant along each indifference curve and that assigns higher values to higher indifference curves.

The second way is a bit more intuitive. Given a description of the preferences, we try to think about what the consumer is trying to maximize—what combination of the goods describes the choice behavior of the consumer. This may seem a little vague at the moment, but it will be more meaningful after we discuss a few examples.

Perfect Substitutes

Remember the red pencil and blue pencil example? All that mattered to the consumer was the total number of pencils. Thus it is natural to measure utility by the total number of pencils. Therefore we provisionally pick the utility function $u(x_1, x_2) = x_1 + x_2$. Does this work? Just ask two things: is it constant along the indifference curves? Does it assign a higher label to more preferred bundles? The answer to both questions is yes, so we have a utility function.

Of course, this isn't the only utility function that we could use. We could also use the *square* of the number of pencils. Thus the utility function $v(x_1, x_2) = (x_1 + x_2)^2 = x_1^2 + 2x_1x_2 + x_2^2$ will also represent the perfect substitutes preferences, as would any other monotonic transformation of $u(x_1, x_2)$.

Perfect Complements

This is the left shoe–right shoe case. In these preferences the consumer only cares about the number of *pairs* of shoes he has, so it is natural to choose the number of pairs of shoes as the utility function. The number of complete pairs of shoes that you have is the *minimum* of the number of right shoes you have, x_1, and the number of left shoes you have, x_2. Thus the utility function for perfect complements takes the form $u(x_1, x_2) = \min\{x_1, x_2\}$.

To verify that this choice actually works, pick a bundle of goods such as $(10, 10)$. If we add one more unit of good 1 we get $(11, 10)$, which should leave us on the same indifference curve. Does it? Yes, since $\min\{10, 10\} = \min\{11, 10\} = 10$.

So $u(x_1, x_2) = \min\{x_1, x_2\}$ is a possible utility function to describe perfect complements. As usual, any monotonic transformation would be suitable as well.

Quasilinear Preferences

Here's a kind of preferences we haven't seen before. Suppose that a consumer has indifference curves that are vertical translates of each other, as in Figure 4.4. This means that all of the indifference curves are just vertically "shifted" versions of one indifference curve. It follows that the equation for an indifference curve takes the form $x_2 = k - v(x_1)$ where k is a different constant for each indifference curve. This equation says that the height of each indifference curve is some function of x_1, $-v(x_1)$, plus a constant k. Higher values of k give higher indifference curves. (The minus sign is only a convention; we'll see why it is convenient below.)

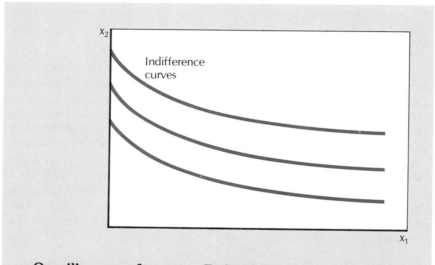

Figure 4.4

Quasilinear preferences. Each indifference curve is a vertically shifted version of a single indifference curve.

The natural way to label indifference curves here is with k—roughly speaking, the height of the indifference curve along the vertical axis. Solving for k and setting it equal to utility, we have

$$u(x_1, x_2) = k = v(x_1) + x_2.$$

In this case the utility function is linear in good 2, but nonlinear in good 1; hence the name **quasilinear utility**, meaning "partly linear" utility. Specific examples of quasilinear utility would be $u(x_1, x_2) = \sqrt{x_1} + x_2$, or $u(x_1, x_2) = \ln x_1 + x_2$. Quasilinear utility functions are not particularly realistic, but they are very easy to work with, as we'll see in several examples later on in the book.

Cobb-Douglas Preferences

Another commonly used utility function is the **Cobb-Douglas** utility function

$$u(x_1, x_2) = x_1^a x_2^{1-a}$$

where a is a number satisfying $0 < a < 1$.[2]

The Cobb-Douglas utility function is not terribly realistic, but it will be useful in several examples. The preferences represented by the Cobb-Douglas utility function have the general shape depicted in Figure 4.5.

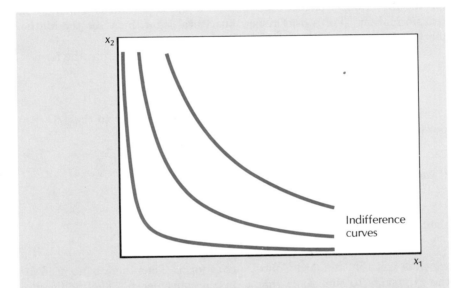

x_2

Indifference
curves

x_1

Cobb-Douglas indifference curves. This is an example of the shape of indifference curves that arise from a Cobb-Douglas utility function.

Figure
4.5

Note that Cobb-Douglas indifference curves look just like the nice convex monotonic indifference curves that we referred to as well-behaved indifference curves in Chapter 3. Cobb-Douglas preferences are the standard example of indifference curves that look well-behaved, and in fact the formula describing them is about the simplest algebraic expression that generates

---

[2] Paul Douglas was a twentieth-century economist at the University of Chicago who later became a U.S. senator. Charles Cobb was a mathematician at Amherst College. The Cobb-Douglas functional form was originally used to study production behavior.

well-behaved preferences. We'll find Cobb-Douglas preferences quite useful to present algebraic examples of the economic ideas we'll study later.

Of course a monotonic transformation of the Cobb-Douglas utility function will represent exactly the same preferences, and it is useful to see a couple of examples of these transformations.

First, if we take the natural log of utility, the product of the terms will become a sum so that we have

$$v(x_1, x_2) = \ln(x_1^a x_2^{1-a}) = a \ln x_1 + (1-a) \ln x_2.$$

The indifference curves for this utility function will look just like the ones for the first Cobb-Douglas function, since the logarithm is a monotonic transformation. (For a brief review of natural logarithms, see the Mathematical Appendix at the end of the book.)

For the second example, suppose that a utility function has the form

$$v(x_1, x_2) = x_1^b x_2^c$$

where b and c are positive numbers. Then raising utility to the $1/(b+c)$ power, we have

$$x_1^{\frac{b}{b+c}} x_2^{\frac{c}{b+c}}.$$

If we define

$$a = \frac{b}{b+c}$$

then this becomes

$$v(x_1, x_2) = x_1^a x_2^{1-a}$$

which is just the standard Cobb-Douglas form. Thus there is no need for the exponents to sum to 1; that is just a convenience. The indifference curves will look the same no matter what the sum of the exponents.

The Cobb-Douglas utility function can be expressed in a variety of ways; you should learn to recognize them, as this family of preferences is very useful for examples.

4.4 Marginal Utility

Consider a consumer who is consuming some bundle of goods (x_1, x_2). How does this consumer's utility change as we give him or her a little more of good 1? This rate of change is called the **marginal utility** with respect to good 1. We write it as MU_1 and think of it as being a ratio

$$MU_1 = \frac{\Delta U}{\Delta x_1} = \frac{u(x_1 + \Delta x_1, x_2) - u(x_1, x_2)}{\Delta x_1}$$

that measures the rate of change in utility (ΔU) associated with a small change in the amount of good 1 (Δx_1). Note that the amount of good 2 is held fixed in this calculation.

This definition implies that to calculate the change in utility associated with a small change in consumption of good 1, we can just multiply the change in consumption by the marginal utility of the good:

$$\Delta U = MU_1 \Delta x_1.$$

The marginal utility with respect to good 2 is defined in a similar manner:

$$MU_2 = \frac{\Delta U}{\Delta x_2} = \frac{u(x_1, x_2 + \Delta x_2) - u(x_1, x_2)}{\Delta x_2}.$$

Note that when we compute the marginal utility with respect to good 2 we keep the amount of good 1 constant. We can calculate the change in utility associated with a change in the consumption of good 2 by the formula

$$\Delta U = MU_2 \Delta x_2.$$

It is important to realize that the magnitude of marginal utility depends on the magnitude of utility. Thus it depends on the particular way that we choose to measure utility. If we multiplied utility by 2 then marginal utility would also be multiplied by 2. We would still have a perfectly valid utility function in that it would represent the same preferences, but it would just be scaled differently.

This means that marginal utility itself has no behavioral content. How can we calculate marginal utility from a consumer's choice behavior? We can't. Choice behavior only reveals information about the way a consumer *ranks* different bundles of goods. Marginal utility depends on the particular utility function that we use to reflect the preference ordering and its magnitude has no particular significance. However, it turns out that marginal utility can be used to calculate something that does have behavioral content, as we will see in the next section.

4.5 Marginal Utility and MRS

A utility function $u(x_1, x_2)$ can be used to measure the marginal rate of substitution defined in Chapter 3. Recall that the marginal rate of substitution measures the slope of the indifference curve at a given bundle of goods; it can be interpreted as the rate at which a consumer is just willing to substitute good 2 for good 1.

This interpretation gives us a simple way to calculate the marginal rate of substitution. Consider a change in the consumption of each good

$(\Delta x_1, \Delta x_2)$ that keeps utility constant—that is, a change in consumption that moves us along the indifference curve. Then we must have

$$MU_1 \Delta x_1 + MU_2 \Delta x_2 = \Delta U = 0.$$

Solving for the slope of the indifference curve we have

$$\text{MRS} = \frac{\Delta x_2}{\Delta x_1} = -\frac{MU_1}{MU_2}. \qquad (4.1)$$

(Note that we have 2 over 1 on the left-hand side of the equation and 1 over 2 on the right-hand side. Don't get confused!)

The algebraic sign of the MRS is negative, since if you get more of good 1 you have to get *less* of good 2 in order to keep the same level of utility. However, it gets very tedious to keep track of that pesky minus sign, so economists typically refer to the MRS by its absolute value—that is, as a positive number. We'll follow this convention as long as no confusion will result.

Now here is the interesting thing about the MRS calculation: the marginal rate of substitution can be measured by observing people's actual behavior—we find that rate of exchange where they are just willing to stay put, as described in Chapter 3. Thus there is a specific value of the marginal rate of substitution at any given consumption bundle.

The utility function, and therefore the marginal utility function, is not uniquely determined. Any monotonic transformation of a utility function leaves you with another equally valid utility function. Thus, if we multiply utility by 2, for example, the marginal utility is multiplied by 2. Thus the magnitude of the marginal utility function depends on the choice of utility function, which is arbitrary. It doesn't depend on behavior alone; instead it depends on the utility function that we use to describe behavior.

But the *ratio* of marginal utilities gives us an observable magnitude—namely the marginal rate of substitution. The ratio of marginal utilities is independent of the particular transformation of the utility function you choose to use. Look at what happens if you multiply utility by 2. The marginal rate of substitution becomes

$$\text{MRS} = -\frac{2MU_1}{2MU_2}.$$

The 2s just cancel out, so the MRS remains the same.

The some sort of thing occurs when we take any monotonic transformation of a utility function. Taking a monotonic transformation is just relabeling the indifference curves, and the calculation for the marginal rate of substitution given above is concerned with moving along a given indifference curve. Even though the marginal utilities are changed by monotonic transformations, the *ratio* of marginal utilities is independent of the particular way chosen to represent the preferences.

4.6 Utility for Commuting

Utility functions are basically ways of describing choice behavior: if a bundle of goods X is chosen when a bundle of goods Y is available, then X must have a higher utility than Y. By examining choices consumers make we can estimate a utility function to describe their behavior.

This idea has been widely applied in the field of transportation economics to study consumers' commuting behavior. In most large cities commuters have a choice between taking public transit or driving to work. Each of these alternatives can be thought of as representing a bundle of different characteristics: travel time, waiting time, out-of-pocket costs, comfort, convenience, and so on. We could let x_1 be the amount of travel time involved in each kind of transportation, x_2 the amount of waiting time for each kind, and so on.

If $(x_1, x_2, \ldots, x_n)$ represents the values of n different characteristics of driving, say, and $(y_1, y_2, \ldots, y_n)$ represents the values of taking the bus, we can consider a model where the consumer decides to drive or take the bus depending on whether he prefers one bundle of characteristics to the other.

More specifically, let us suppose that the average consumer's preferences for characteristics can be represented by a utility function of the form

$$U(x_1, x_2, \ldots, x_n) = \beta_1 x_1 + \beta_2 x_2 + \ldots + \beta_n x_n$$

where the coefficients β_1, β_2, and so on are unknown parameters. Any monotonic transformation of this utility function would describe the choice behavior equally well of course, but the linear form is especially easy to work with from a statistical point of view.

Suppose now that we observe a number of similar consumers making choices between driving and taking the bus based on the particular pattern of commute times, costs, etc. that they face. There are statistical techniques that can be used to find the values of the coefficients β_i for $i = 1, \ldots n$ that best fit the observed pattern of choices by a set of consumers. These statistical techniques give a way to estimate the utility function for different transportation modes.

One study reports a utility function that had the form[3]

$$U = -0.147TW - 0.0411TT - 2.24C + 3.78A/W - 2.91R - 2.36Z$$

where

TW = total walking time to and from bus or car

---

[3] See Thomas Domenich and Daniel McFadden, *Urban Travel Demand* (North–Holland Publishing Company, 1975).

TT = total time of trip in minutes
C = total cost of trip in dollars
A/W = autos per worker in the household
R = race of the household (0 if black, 1 if white)
Z = 1 if white-collar worker, 0 if blue-collar.

This utility function correctly described the choice between auto and bus transport for 93 percent of the households in McFadden's study.

The coefficients in this equation describe the weight that an average household places on the various characteristics; that is, the marginal utility of each characteristic. The *ratio* of one coefficient to another measures the marginal rate of substitution between one characteristic and another. For example, the ratio of the marginal utility of walking time to the marginal utility of total time indicates that walking time is viewed as being roughly 3 times as onerous as travel time by the average consumer. In other words, the consumer would be willing to substitute 3 minutes of additional travel time to save 1 minute of walking time.

Similarly, the ratio of cost to travel time indicates the average consumer's tradeoff between these two variables. In this study, the average commuter valued a minute of commute time at $0.0411/2.24 = 0.0183$ dollars per minute, which is $1.10 per hour. For comparison, the hourly wage for the average commuter in the sample when the study was done was about $2.85 an hour.

Such estimated utility functions can be very valuable for determining whether or not it is worthwhile to make some change in the public transportation system. For example, in the above utility function one of the significant factors explaining mode choice is the time involved in taking the trip. The city transit authority can, at some cost, add more buses to reduce this travel time. But will the number of extra riders warrant the increased expense?

Given a utility function and a sample of consumers we can forecast which consumers will drive and which consumers will choose to take the bus. This will give us some idea as to whether the revenue will be sufficient to cover the extra cost.

Furthermore, we can use the marginal rate of substitution to estimate the *value* that each consumer places on the reduced travel time. We saw above that in McFadden's study the average commuter in 1967 valued commute time at a rate of $1.10 per hour. Thus the commuter should be willing to pay about $0.37 to cut 20 minutes from his or her trip. This number gives us a measure of the dollar benefit of providing more timely bus service. This benefit must be compared to the cost to determine if such a provision is worthwhile. Having a quantitative measure of benefit will certainly be helpful in making a rational decision about transport policy.

Summary

1. A utility function is simply a way to represent or summarize a preference ordering. The numerical magnitudes of utility levels have no intrinsic meaning.

2. Thus, given any one utility function, any monotonic transformation of it will represent the same preferences.

3. The marginal rate of substitution can be calculated from the utility function via the formula $MRS = \Delta x_2/\Delta x_1 = -MU_1/MU_2$.

Review Questions

1. The text said that raising a number to an odd power was a monotonic transformation. What about raising a number to an even power? Is this a monotonic transformation? (Hint: consider the case $f(u) = u^2$.)

2. Which of the following are monotonic transformations? (1) $u = 2v - 13$; (2) $u = -1/v^2$; (3) $u = 1/v^2$; (4) $u = \ln v$; (5) $u = -e^{-x}$; (6) $u = v^2$; (7) $u = v^2$ for $v > 0$; (8) $u = v^2$ for $v < 0$.

3. We claimed in the text that if preferences were monotonic then a diagonal line through the origin would intersect each indifference curve exactly once. Can you prove this rigorously? (Hint: what would happen if it intersected some indifference curve twice?)

4. What kind of preferences are represented by a utility function of the form $u(x_1, x_2) = \sqrt{x_1 + x_2}$? What about the utility function $v(x_1, x_2) = 13x_1 + 13x_2$?

5. What kind of preferences are represented by a utility function of the form $u(x_1, x_2) = x_1 + \sqrt{x_2}$? Is the utility function $v(x_1, x_2) = x_1^2 + 2x_1\sqrt{x_2} + x_2$ a monotonic transformation of $u(x_1, x_2)$?

6. Consider the utility function $u(x_1, x_2) = \sqrt{x_1 x_2}$. What kind of preferences does it represent? Is the function $v(x_1, x_2) = x_1^2 x_2$ a monotonic transformation of $u(x_1, x_2)$? Is the function $w(x_1, x_2) = x_1^2 x_2^2$ a monotonic transformation of $u(x_1, x_2)$?

7. Can you explain why taking a monotonic transformation of a utility function doesn't change the marginal rate of substitution?

APPENDIX

First, let us clarify what is meant by "marginal utility." As elsewhere in economics, "marginal" just means a derivative. So the marginal utility of good 1 is just

$$MU_1 = \lim_{\Delta x_1 \to 0} \frac{u(x_1 + \Delta x_1, x_2) - u(x_1, x_2)}{\Delta x_1} = \frac{\partial u(x_1, x_2)}{\partial x_1}.$$

Note that we have used the *partial* derivative here, since the marginal utility of good 1 is computed holding good 2 fixed.

Now we can rephrase the derivation of the marginal rate of substitution in the text using calculus. We'll do it two ways, the first using differentials, and the second using implicit functions.

For the first method, we consider making a change (dx_1, dx_2) that keeps utility constant. So we want

$$du = \frac{\partial u(x_1, x_2)}{\partial x_1} dx_1 + \frac{\partial u(x_1, x_2)}{\partial x_2} dx_2 = 0.$$

The first term measures the increase in utility from the small change dx_1, and the second term measures the increase in utility from the small change dx_2. We want to pick these changes so that the total change in utility, du, is zero. Solving for dx_2/dx_1 gives us

$$\frac{dx_2}{dx_1} = -\frac{\partial u(x_1, x_2)/\partial x_1}{\partial u(x_1, x_2)/\partial x_2},$$

which is just the calculus analog of equation (4.1) in the text.

As for the second method, we now think of the indifference curve as being described by a function $x_2(x_1)$. That is, for each value of x_1, the function $x_2(x_1)$ tells us how much x_2 we need to get on that specific indifference curve. Thus the function $x_2(x_1)$ has to satisfy the identity

$$u(x_1, x_2(x_1)) \equiv k$$

where k is the utility label of the indifference curve in question.

We can differentiate both sides of this identity with respect to x_1 to get

$$\frac{\partial u(x_1, x_2)}{\partial x_1} + \frac{\partial u(x_1, x_2)}{\partial x_2} \frac{\partial x_2(x_1)}{\partial x_1} = 0.$$

Notice that x_1 occurs in two places in this identity, so changing x_1 will change the function in two ways, and we have to take the derivative at each place that x_1 appears.

We then solve this equation for $\partial x_2(x_1)/\partial x_1$ to find

$$\frac{\partial x_2(x_1)}{\partial x_1} = -\frac{\partial u(x_1, x_2)/\partial x_1}{\partial u(x_1, x_2)/\partial x_2},$$

just as we had before.

The implicit function method is a little more rigorous, but the differential method is more direct, as long as you don't do something silly.

Suppose that we take a monotonic transformation of a utility function, say, $v(x_1, x_2) = f(u(x_1, x_2))$. Let's calculate the MRS for this utility function. Using the chain rule

$$\text{MRS} = -\frac{\partial v/\partial x_1}{\partial v/\partial x_2} = -\frac{\partial f/\partial u \; \partial u/\partial x_1}{\partial f/\partial u \; \partial u/\partial x_2}$$

$$= -\frac{\partial u/\partial x_1}{\partial u/\partial x_2}$$

since the $\partial f/\partial u$ term cancels out from both the numerator and denominator. This shows that the MRS is independent of the utility representation.

This gives a useful way to recognize preferences that are represented by different utility functions: given two utility functions, just compute the marginal rates of substitution and see if they are the same. If they are, then the two utility functions have the same indifference curves. If the direction of increasing preference is the same for each utility function, then the underlying preferences must be the same.

EXAMPLE: Cobb-Douglas Preferences

The marginal rate of substitution for Cobb-Douglas preferences is easy to calculate using the formula derived above.

If we choose the log representation where

$$u(x_1, x_2) = a \ln x_1 + (1 - a) \ln x_2$$

then we have

$$\text{MRS} = -\frac{\partial u(x_1, x_2)/\partial x_1}{\partial u(x_1, x_2)/\partial x_2}$$

$$= -\frac{a/x_1}{(1 - a)/x_2}$$

$$= -\frac{ax_2}{(1 - a)x_1}.$$

What if we choose the exponent representation where

$$u(x_1, x_2) = x_1^a x_2^{1-a}?$$

Then we have

$$\text{MRS} = -\frac{\partial u(x_1, x_2)/\partial x_1}{\partial u(x_1, x_2)/\partial x_2}$$

$$= -\frac{ax_1^{a-1} x_2^{1-a}}{(1 - a)x_1^a x_2^{-a}}$$

$$= -\frac{ax_2}{(1 - a)x_1}$$

which is the same as we had before. Of course you knew all along that a monotonic transformation couldn't change the marginal rate of substitution!

5

CHOICE

In this chapter we will put together the budget set and the theory of preferences in order to examine the optimal choice of consumers. We said earlier that the economic model of consumer choice is that people choose the best bundle they can afford. We can now rephrase this in terms that sound more professional by saying that "consumers choose the most preferred bundle from their budget sets."

5.1 Optimal Choice

A typical case is illustrated in Figure 5.1. Here we have drawn the budget set and several of the consumer's indifference curves on the same diagram. We want to find the bundle in the budget set that is on the highest indifference curve. Since preferences are well behaved, so that more is preferred to less, we can restrict our attention to bundles of goods that lie *on* the budget line, and not worry about those *beneath* the budget line.

Now simply start at the right-hand corner of the budget line and move to the left. As we move along the budget line we note that we are moving to higher and higher indifference curves. We stop when we get to the highest indifference curve that just touches the budget line. In the diagram, the bundle of goods that is associated with the highest indifference curve that just touches the budget line is labeled (x_1^*, x_2^*).

The choice (x_1^*, x_2^*) is an **optimal choice** for the consumer. The set of bundles that she prefers to (x_1^*, x_2^*)—the set of bundles *above* her indifference curve—doesn't intersect the bundles she can afford—the bundles *beneath* her budget line. Thus the bundle (x_1^*, x_2^*) is the best bundle that the consumer can afford.

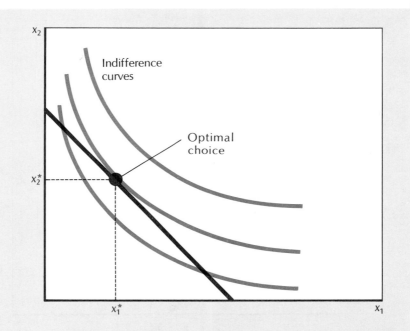

Optimal choice. The optimal consumption position is where the indifference curve is tangent to the budget line.

Figure
5.1

Note an important feature of this optimal bundle: at this choice, the indifference curve is *tangent* to the budget line. If you think about it a moment you'll see that this has to be the case: if the indifference curve weren't tangent it would cross the budget line, and if it crossed the budget line, there would be some nearby point on the budget line that lies above the indifference curve—which means that we couldn't have started at an optimal bundle.

Does this tangency condition really *have* to hold at an optimal choice? Well, it doesn't hold in *all* cases, but it does hold for most interesting cases.

What is always true is that at the optimal point the indifference curve can't cross the budget line. So when does "not crossing" imply tangent? Let's look at the exceptions first.

First, the indifference curve might not have a tangent, as in Figure 5.2. Here the indifference curve has a kink at the optimal choice, and a tangent just isn't defined, since the mathematical definition of a tangent requires that there be a unique tangent line at each point. This case is more of a nuisance than anything else.

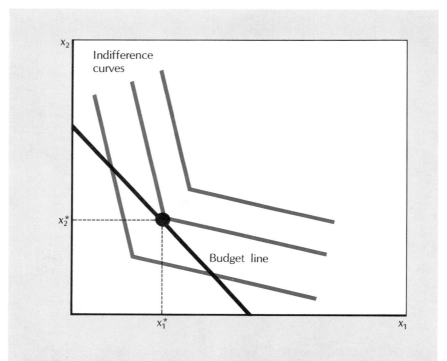

Figure 5.2

Kinky tastes. An optimal consumption point where the indifference curve doesn't have a tangent.

The second exception is more interesting. Suppose that the optimal point occurs where the consumption of some good is zero as in Figure 5.3. Then the slope of the indifference curve and the slope of the budget line are different, but the indifference curve still doesn't *cross* the budget line. We say that Figure 5.3 represents a **boundary** optimum, while a case like Figure 5.1 represents an **interior** optimum.

If we are willing to rule out "kinky tastes" we can forget about the example given in Figure 5.2.[1] And if we are willing to restrict ourselves only to *interior* optima, we can rule out the other example. If we have an interior optimum with smooth indifference curves, the slope of the indifference curve and the slope of the budget line must be the same ... because if they were different the indifference curve would cross the budget line, and we couldn't be at the optimal point.

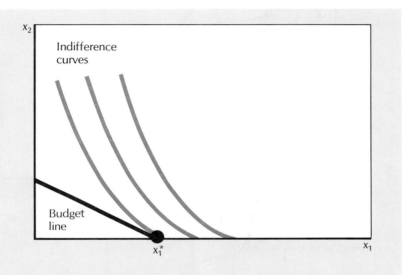

Boundary optimum. The optimal consumption involves consuming 0 units of good 2. The indifference curve is not tangent to the budget line.

Figure
5.3

We've found a necessary condition that the optimal choice must satisfy. If the optimal choice involves consuming some of both goods—so that it is an interior optimum—then necessarily the indifference curve will be tangent to the budget line. But is the tangency condition a *sufficient* condition for a bundle to be optimal? If we find a bundle where the indifference curve is tangent to the budget line can we be sure we have an optimal choice?

Look at Figure 5.4. Here we have three bundles where the tangency condition is satisfied, all of them interior, but only two of them are optimal. So in general, the tangency condition is only a necessary condition for optimality, not a sufficient condition.

However, there is one important case where it is sufficient: the case of convex preferences. In the case of convex preferences, any point that

---

[1] Otherwise, this book might get an R rating.

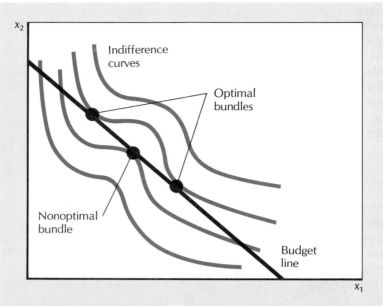

Figure
5.4

More than one tangency. Here there are three tangencies, but only two optimal points, so the tangency condition is necessary but not sufficient.

satisfies the tangency condition must be an optimal point. This is clear geometrically: since convex indifference curves must curve away from the budget line, they can't bend back to touch it again.

Figure 5.4 also shows us that in general there may be more than one optimal bundle that satisfies the MRS condition. However, again convexity implies a restriction. If the indifference curves are *strictly* convex—they don't have any flat spots—then there will be only one optimal choice on each budget line. Although this can be shown mathematically, it is also quite plausible from looking at the figure.

The condition that the marginal rate of substitution must equal the slope of the budget line at an interior optimum is obvious graphically, but what does it mean economically? Recall that one of our interpretations of the marginal rate of substitution was that it was that rate of exchange at which the consumer was just willing to stay put. Well, the market is offering a rate of exchange to the consumer of $-p_1/p_2$—if you give up one unit of good 1, you can buy p_1/p_2 units of good 2. If the consumer is at a consumption bundle where he or she is willing to stay put, it must be one where the marginal rate of substitution is equal to the price ratio:

$$\text{MRS} = \frac{p_1}{p_2}.$$

Another way to think about this is to imagine what would happen if the marginal rate of substitution were different from the price ratio. Suppose, for example, that the MRS is $\Delta x_2 / \Delta x_1 = 1/2$ and the price ratio is $1/1$. Then this means the consumer is just willing to give up 2 units of good 1 in order to get 1 unit of good 2—but the market is willing to exchange them on a 1 to 1 basis. Thus the consumer would certainly be willing to give up some of good 1 in order to purchase a little more of good 2. Whenever the marginal rate of substitution is different from the price ratio the consumer cannot be at his or her optimal choice.

5.2 Consumer Demand

The optimal choice of goods 1 and 2 at some set of prices and income is called the consumer's **demanded bundle**. In general when prices and income change, the consumer's optimal choice will change. The **demand function** is the function that relates the optimal choice—the quantities demanded—to the different values of prices and incomes.

We will write the demand functions as depending on both prices and income: $x_1(p_1, p_2, m)$ and $x_2(p_1, p_2, m)$. For each different set of prices and income, there will be a different combination of goods that is the optimal choice of the consumer. Different preferences will lead to different demand functions; we'll see some examples shortly. Our major goal in the next few chapters is to study the behavior of these demand functions—how the optimal choices change as prices and income change.

5.3 Some Examples

Let us apply the model of consumer choice we have developed to the examples of preferences described in Chapter 3. The basic procedure will be the same for each example: plot the indifference curves and budget line and find the point where the highest indifference curve touches the budget line.

Perfect Substitutes

The case of perfect substitutes is illustrated in Figure 5.5. We have three possible cases. If $p_2 > p_1$ then the slope of the budget line is flatter than the slope of the indifference curves. In this case, the optimal bundle is where the consumer spends all of his or her money on good 1. If $p_1 > p_2$ then the consumer purchases only good 2. Finally if $p_1 = p_2$ there is a whole range of optimal choices—any amount of goods 1 and 2 that satisfies the budget constraint is optimal in this case. Thus the demand function for good 1 will be

$$x_1 = \begin{cases} m/p_1 & \text{when } p_1 < p_2; \\ \text{any number between 0 and } m/p1 & \text{when } p_1 = p_2; \\ 0 & \text{when } p_1 > p_2. \end{cases}$$

Are these results consistent with common sense? All they say is that if two goods are perfect substitutes, then a consumer will purchase the cheaper one. If both goods have the same price, then the consumer doesn't care which one he or she purchases.

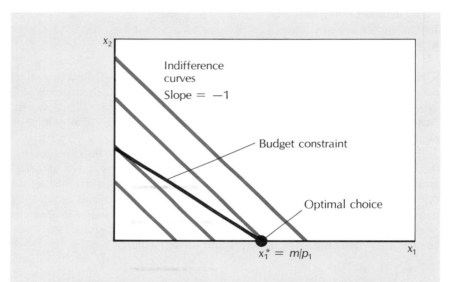

Figure 5.5

Optimal choice with perfect substitutes. If the goods are perfect substitutes, the optimal choice will usually be on the boundary.

Perfect Complements

The case of perfect complements is illustrated in Figure 5.6. Note that the optimal choice must always lie on the diagonal, where the consumer is purchasing equal amounts of both goods, no matter what the prices are. In terms of our example, this says that people with two feet buy shoes in pairs.[2]

Let us solve for the optimal choice algebraically. We know that this consumer is purchasing the same amount of good 1 and good 2, no matter

---

[2] Don't worry, we'll get some more exciting results later on.

what the prices. Let this amount be denoted by x. Then we have to satisfy the budget constraint

$$p_1 x + p_2 x = m.$$

Solving for x gives us the optimal choices of goods 1 and 2:

$$x_1 = x_2 = x = \frac{m}{p_1 + p_2}.$$

The demand function for the optimal choice here is quite intuitive. Since the two goods are always consumed together, it is just as if the consumer were spending all of her money on a single good that had a price of $p_1 + p_2$.

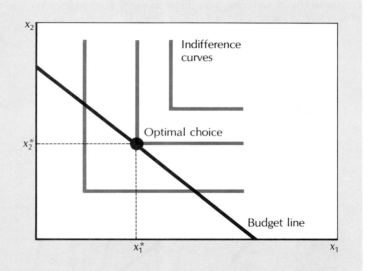

Optimal choice with perfect complements. If the goods are perfect complements, the quantities demanded will always lie on the diagonal since the optimal choice occurs where x_1 equals x_2.

Figure
5.6

Neutrals and Bads

In the case of a neutral good the consumer spends all of her money on the good she likes and doesn't purchase any of the neutral good. The same thing happens if one commodity is a bad. Thus, if commodity 1 is a good and commodity 2 is a bad, then the demand functions will be

$$x_1 = \frac{m}{p_1}$$
$$x_2 = 0.$$

Concave Preferences

Consider the situation illustrated in Figure 5.7. Is X the optimal choice? No! The optimal choice for these preferences is always going to be a boundary choice, like the bundle Z. Think of what nonconvex preferences mean. If you have money to purchase ice cream and olives, and you don't like to consume them together, you'll spend all of your money on one or the other.

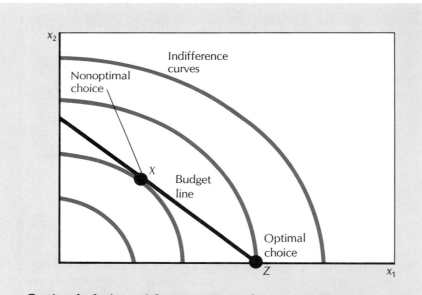

Figure
5.7 **Optimal choice with concave preferences.** The optimal choice is the boundary point, Z, not the interior tangency point, X, because Z lies on a higher indifference curve.

Cobb-Douglas Preferences

Suppose that the utility function is of the Cobb-Douglas form, $u(x_1, x_2) = x_1^a x_2^{1-a}$. In the Appendix to this chapter we use calculus to derive the optimal choices for this utility function. They turn out to be

$$x_1 = \frac{am}{p_1}$$
$$x_2 = \frac{(1-a)m}{p_2}.$$

These demand functions are often useful in algebraic examples, so you should probably memorize them.

The Cobb-Douglas preferences have a convenient property. Consider the fraction of his income that a Cobb-Douglas consumer spends on good 1. If he consumes x_1 units of good 1, this costs him $p_1 x_1$, so this represents a fraction $p_1 x_1/m$ of total income. Substituting the demand function for x_1 we have

$$\frac{p_1 x_1}{m} = \frac{p_1}{m}\frac{am}{p_1} = a.$$

Similarly the fraction of his income that the consumer spends on good 2 is $(1-a)$.

Thus the Cobb-Douglas consumer always spends a fixed fraction of his income on each good. The size of the fraction is determined by the exponent in the Cobb-Douglas function. Although this is not a particularly realistic assumption, it does simplify calculations in exercises and examples.

5.4 Implications of the MRS Condition

The examples above show that there are a variety of cases that can arise in dealing with consumer demand. However, the standard case is the one with a nice interior solution where the marginal rate of substitution equals the price ratio. But why is that interesting? Why should you care about this implication of optimizing behavior? Although this fact has several important implications, let us consider just one here.

In well-organized markets, it is typical that everyone faces roughly the same prices for goods. Take, for example, two goods like butter and milk. If everyone faces the same prices for butter and milk, and everyone is optimizing, and everyone is at an interior solution ... then everyone must have the same marginal rate of substitution for butter and milk.

This follows directly from the analysis given above. The market is offering everyone the same rate of exchange for butter and milk, and everyone is adjusting their consumption of the goods until their own "internal" marginal valuation of the two goods equals the market's "external" valuation of the two goods.

Now the interesting thing about this statement is that it is independent of income and tastes. People may value their *total* consumption of the two goods very differently. Some people may be consuming a lot of butter and a little milk, and some may be doing the reverse. Some wealthy people may be consuming a lot of milk and a lot of butter while other people may be consuming just a little of each good. But everyone who is consuming the two goods must have the same marginal rate of substitution. Everyone who is consuming the goods must agree on how much one is worth in terms of the other: how much of one they would be willing to sacrifice to get some more of the other.

The fact that price ratios measure marginal rates of substitution is very important, for it means that we have a way to value possible changes in consumption bundles. Suppose, for example, that the price of milk is $1 a quart and the price of butter is $2 a pound. Then the marginal rate of substitution for all people who consume milk and butter must be 2: they have to have 2 quarts of milk to compensate them for giving up 1 pound of butter. Or conversely, they have to have 1 pound of butter to make it worth their while to give up 2 quarts of milk. Hence everyone who is consuming both goods will value a marginal chance in consumption in the same way.

Now suppose that an inventor discovers a new way of turning milk into butter: for every 3 quarts of milk poured into this machine, you get out 1 pound of butter, and no other useful byproducts. Question: is there a market for this device? Answer: the venture capitalists won't beat a path to his door, that's for sure. For everyone is already operating at a point where they are just willing to trade 2 quarts of milk for 1 pound of butter; why would they be willing to substitute 3 quarts of milk for 1 pound of butter? The answer is they wouldn't; this invention isn't worth anything.

But what would happen if he got it to run in reverse so he could dump in a pound of butter get out 3 quarts of milk? Is there a market for this device? Answer: Yes! The market prices of milk and butter tell us that people are just barely willing to trade one pound of butter for 2 quarts of milk. So getting 3 quarts of milk for a pound of butter is a better deal than is currently being offered in the marketplace. Sign me up for a 1000 shares! (And several pounds of butter.)

The market prices show that the first machine is unprofitable: it produces $2 of butter by using $3 of milk. The fact that it is unprofitable is just another way of saying that people value the inputs more than the outputs. The second machine produces $3 worth of milk by using only $2 worth of butter. This machine is profitable because people value the outputs more than the inputs.

The point is that, since prices measure the rate at which people are just willing to substitute one good for another, they can be used to value policy proposals that involve making changes in consumption. The fact that prices are not arbitrary numbers but reflect how people value things on the margin is one of the most fundamental and important ideas in economics.

5.5 Choosing Taxes

Even the small bit of consumer theory we have discussed so far can be used to derive interesting and important conclusions. Here is a nice example describing a choice between two types of taxes. We saw that a **quantity tax** is a tax on the amount consumed of a good, like a gasoline tax of 15 cents per gallon. An **income tax** is just a tax on income. If the government wants to raise a certain amount of revenue, is it better to raise it via a quantity tax or an income tax? Let's apply what we've learned to answer this question.

First we analyze the imposition of a quantity tax. Suppose that the original budget constraint is

$$p_1 x_1 + p_2 x_2 = m.$$

What is the budget constraint if we tax the consumption of good 1 at a rate of t? The answer is simple. From the viewpoint of the consumer it is just as if the price of good 1 has increased by an amount t. Thus the new budget constraint is

$$(p_1 + t)x_1 + p_2 x_2 = m. \tag{5.1}$$

Therefore a quantity tax on a good increases the price perceived by the consumer. Figure 5.8 gives an example of how that price change might affect demand. At this stage, we don't know for certain whether this tax will increase or decrease the consumption of good 1, although the presumption is that it will decrease it. Whichever is the case, we do know that the optimal choice, (x_1^*, x_2^*), must satisfy the budget constraint

$$(p_1 + t)x_1^* + p_2 x_2^* = m. \tag{5.2}$$

The revenue raised by this tax is $R^* = t x_1^*$.

Let's now consider an income tax that raises the same amount of revenue. The form of this budget constraint would be

$$p_1 x_1 + p_2 x_2 = m - R^*$$

or, substituting for R^*,

$$p_1 x_1 + p_2 x_2 = m - t x_1^*.$$

Where does this budget line go in Figure 5.8?

It is easy to see that is has the same slope as the original budget line, $-p_1/p_2$, but the problem is to determine its location. As it turns out, the budget line with the income tax must pass through the point (x_1^*, x_2^*). The way to check this is to plug (x_1^*, x_2^*) into the income tax budget constraint and see if it is satisfied.

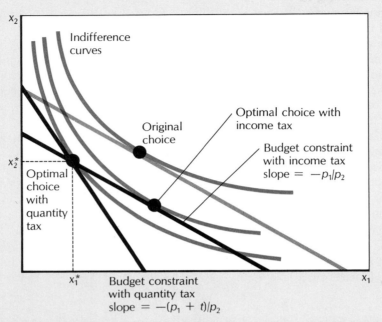

Figure 5.8

Income tax versus a quantity tax. Here we consider a quantity tax that raises revenue R^*, and an income tax that raises the same revenue. The consumer will be better off under the income tax, since he can choose a point on a higher indifference curve.

Is it true that

$$p_1 x_1^* + p_2 x_2^* = m - t x_1^*?$$

Yes it is, since this is just a rearrangement of equation (5.2), which we know to be true.

This establishes that (x_1^*, x_2^*) lies on the income tax budget line: it is an *affordable* choice for the consumer. But is it an optimal choice? It is easy to see that the answer is no. At (x_1^*, x_2^*) the marginal rate of substitution is $-(p_1 + t)/p_2$. But the income tax allows us to trade at a rate of exchange of $-p_1/p_2$. Thus the budget line cuts the indifference curve at (x_1^*, x_2^*), which implies that there will be some point on the budget line that will be preferred to (x_1^*, x_2^*).

Therefore the income tax is definitely superior to the quantity tax in the sense that you can raise the same amount of revenue from a consumer and still leave him or her better off under the income tax than under the quantity tax.

This is a nice result, and worth remembering, but it is also worthwhile understanding its limitations. First, it only applies to one consumer. The argument shows that for any given consumer there is an income tax that will raise as much money from that consumer as a quantity tax and leave him or her better off. But the amount of that income tax will typically differ from person to person. So a *uniform* income tax for all consumers is not necessarily better than a *uniform* quantity tax for all consumers. (Think about a case where some consumer doesn't consume any of good 2—this person would certainly prefer the quantity tax to a uniform income tax.)

Second, we have assumed that when we impose the tax on income the consumer's income doesn't change. We have assumed that the income tax is basically a lump sum tax—one that just changes the amount of money a consumer has to spend, but doesn't affect any choices he has to make. This is an unlikely assumption. If income is earned by the consumer, we might expect that taxing it will discourage earning income, so that after tax income might fall by even more than the amount taken by the tax.

Third, we have totally left out the supply response to the tax. We've shown how demand responds to the tax change, but supply will respond too, and a complete analysis would take those changes into account as well.

Summary

1. The optimal choice of the consumer is that bundle in the consumer's budget set that lies on the highest indifference curve.

2. Typically the optimal bundle will be characterized by the condition that the slope of the indifference curve (the marginal rate of substitution) will equal the slope of the budget line.

3. If everyone faces the same prices for the two goods, then everyone will have the same marginal rate of substitution, and will thus be willing to trade off the two goods in the same way.

Review Questions

1. If two goods are perfect substitutes, what is the demand function for good 2?

2. Suppose that indifference curves are described by straight lines with a slope of $-b$. Given arbitrary prices and money income p_1, p_2, and m, what will the consumer's optimal choices look like?

3. Suppose that a consumer always consumes 2 spoons of sugar with each cup of coffee. If the price of sugar is p_1 per spoonful and the price of coffee

is p_2 per cup and the consumer has m dollars to spend on coffee and sugar, how much will he or she want to purchase?

4. Suppose that you have highly nonconvex preferences for ice cream and olives, like those given in the text, and that you face prices p_1, p_2 and have m dollars to spend. List the choices for the optimal consumption bundles.

5. If a consumer has a utility function $u(x_1, x_2) = x_1 x_2^4$, what fraction of her income will she spend on good 2?

6. For what kind of preferences will the consumer be just as well-off facing a quantity tax as an income tax?

APPENDIX

It is very useful to be able to solve the preference maximization problem and get algebraic examples of actual demand functions. We did this in the body of the text for easy cases like perfect substitutes and perfect complements, and in this Appendix we'll see how to do it in more general cases.

First, we will generally want to represent the consumer's preferences by a utility function $u(x_1, x_2)$. We've seen in Chapter 4 that this is not a very restrictive assumption; most well-behaved preferences can be described by a utility function.

The first thing to observe is that we already *know* how to solve the optimal choice problem. We just have to put together the facts that we learned in the last three chapters. We know from this chapter that an optimal choice (x_1, x_2) must satisfy the condition

$$\text{MRS}(x_1, x_2) = \frac{p_1}{p_2} \tag{5.3}$$

and we saw in the Appendix to Chapter 4 that the MRS can be expressed as the ratio of derivatives of the utility function. Making this substitution we have

$$\frac{\partial u(x_1, x_2)/\partial x_1}{\partial u(x_1, x_2)/\partial x_2} = \frac{p_1}{p_2}. \tag{5.4}$$

From Chapter 2 we know that the optimal choice must also satisfy the budget constraint

$$p_1 x_1 + p_2 x_2 = m. \tag{5.5}$$

This gives us two equations—the MRS condition and the budget constraint—and two unknowns, x_1 and x_2. All we have to do is to solve these two equations to find the optimal choices of x_1 and x_2 as a function of the prices and income. There are a number of ways to solve two equations in two unknowns. One way that always works, although it might not always be the simplest, is to solve the budget constraint for one of the choices, and then substitute that into the MRS condition.

Rewriting the budget constraint, we have

$$x_2 = \frac{m}{p_2} - \frac{p_1}{p_2}x_1 \qquad (5.6)$$

and substituting this into Equation 5.4 we get

$$\frac{\partial u(x_1, m/p_2 - (p_1/p_2)x_1)/\partial x_1}{\partial u(x_1, m/p_2 - (p_1/p_2)x_1)/\partial x_2} = \frac{p_1}{p_2}.$$

This rather formidable looking expression has only one unknown variable, x_1, and it can typically be solved for x_1 in terms of (p_1, p_2, m). Then the budget constraint yields the solution for x_2 as a function of prices and income.

We can also derive the solution to the utility maximization problem in a more systematic way, using calculus conditions for maximization. To do this, we first pose the utility maximization problem as a constrained maximization problem:

$$\max_{x_1, x_2} u(x_1, x_2)$$

such that $p_1 x_1 + p_2 x_2 = m$.

This problem asks that we choose values of x_1 and x_2 that do two things: first, they have to satisfy the constraint, and second, they give a larger value for $u(x_1, x_2)$ than any other values of x_1 and x_2 that satisfy the constraint.

There are two useful ways to solve this kind of problem. The first way is simply to solve the constraint for one of the variables in terms of the other and then substitute it into the objective function.

For example, for any given value of x_1, the amount of x_2 that we need to satisfy the budget constraint is given by the linear function

$$x_2(x_1) = \frac{m}{p_2} - \frac{p_1}{p_2}x_1. \qquad (5.7)$$

Now substitute $x_2(x_1)$ for x_2 in the utility function to get the *unconstrained* maximization problem

$$\max_{x_1} u(x_1, m/p_2 - (p_1/p_2)x_1).$$

This is an unconstrained maximization problem in x_1 alone, since we have used the function $x_2(x_1)$ to ensure that the value of x_2 will always satisfy the budget constraint, whatever the value of x_1 is.

We can solve this kind of problem just by differentiating with respect to x_1 and setting the result equal to zero in the usual way. This procedure will give us a first-order condition of the form

$$\frac{\partial u(x_1, x_2(x_1))}{\partial x_1} + \frac{\partial u(x_1, x_2(x_1))}{\partial x_2}\frac{dx_2}{dx_1} = 0. \qquad (5.8)$$

Here the first term is the direct effect of how increasing x_1 increases utility. The second term consists of two parts: the rate of increase of utility as x_2 increases,

$\partial u/\partial x_2$, times dx_2/dx_1, the rate of increase of x_2 as x_1 increases in order to continue to satisfy the budget equation. We can differentiate (5.7) to calculate this latter derivative

$$\frac{dx_2}{dx_1} = -\frac{p_1}{p_2}.$$

Substituting this into (5.8) gives us

$$\frac{\partial u(x_1^*, x_2^*))/\partial x_1}{\partial u(x_1^*, x_2^*))/\partial x_2} = \frac{p_1}{p_2},$$

which just says that the marginal rate of substitution between x_1 and x_2 must equal the price ratio at the optimal choice (x_1^*, x_2^*). This is exactly the condition we derived above: the slope of the indifference curve must equal the slope of the budget line. Of course the optimal choice must also satisfy the budget constraint $p_1 x_1^* + p_2 x_2^* = m$, which again gives us two equations in two unknowns.

The second way that these problems can be solved is through the use of **Lagrange multipliers**. This method starts by defining an auxiliary function known as the *Lagrangian*:

$$L = u(x_1, x_2) - \lambda(p_1 x_1 + p_2 x_2 - m).$$

The new variable λ is called a **Lagrange multiplier** since it is multiplied by the constraint. Then Lagrange's theorem says that an optimal choice (x_1^*, x_2^*) must satisfy the three first-order conditions

$$\frac{\partial L}{\partial x_1} = \frac{\partial u(x_1^*, x_2^*)}{\partial x_1} - \lambda p_1 = 0$$

$$\frac{\partial L}{\partial x_2} = \frac{\partial u(x_1^*, x_2^*)}{\partial x_2} - \lambda p_2 = 0$$

$$\frac{\partial L}{\partial \lambda} = p_1 x_1^* + p_2 x_2^* - m = 0.$$

There are several interesting things about these three equations. First, note that they are simply the derivatives of the Lagrangian with respect to x_1, x_2, and λ, each set equal to zero. The last derivative, with respect to λ, is just the budget constraint. Second, we now have three equations for the three unknowns, x_1, x_2, and λ. We have a hope of solving for x_1 and x_2 in terms of p_1, p_2, and m.

Lagrange's theorem is proved in any advanced calculus book. It is used quite extensively in advanced economics courses, but for our purposes we only need to know the statement of the theorem and how to use it.

In our particular case, it is worthwhile noting that if we divide the first condition by the second one, we get

$$\frac{\partial u(x_1^*, x_2^*)/\partial x_1}{\partial u(x_1^*, x_2^*)/\partial x_2} = \frac{p_1}{p_2}$$

which simply says the MRS must equal the price ratio, just as before. The budget constraint gives us the other equation, so we are back to two equations in two unknowns.

EXAMPLE: Cobb-Douglas Demand Functions

In Chapter 4 we introduced the **Cobb-Douglas utility function:**

$$u(x_1, x_2) = x_1^a x_2^{1-a}.$$

Since utility functions are only defined up to a monotonic transformation, it is convenient to take logs of this expression and work with

$$\ln u(x_1, x_2) = a \ln x_1 + (1 - a) \ln x_2.$$

Let's find the demand functions for x_1 and x_2 for the Cobb-Douglas utility function. The problem we want to solve is

$$\max_{x_1, x_2} a \ln x_1 + (1 - a) \ln x_2$$

such that $p_1 x_1 + p_2 x_2 = m.$

There are at least three ways to solve this problem. One way is just to write down the MRS condition and the budget constraint. Using the expression for the MRS derived in Chapter 4, we have

$$\frac{ax_2}{(1 - a)x_1} = \frac{p_1}{p_2}$$

$$p_1 x_1 + p_2 x_2 = m.$$

These are two equations in two unknowns that can be solved for the optimal choice of x_1 and x_2. One way to solve them is to substitute the second into the first to get

$$\frac{a(m/p_2 - x_1 p_1/p_2)}{(1 - a)x_1} = \frac{p_1}{p_2}.$$

Cross multiplying gives

$$a(m - x_1 p_1) = (1 - a)p_1 x_1.$$

Canceling $-ap_1 x_1$ from each side and rearranging gives

$$am = p_1 x_1$$

or

$$x_1 = \frac{am}{p_1}.$$

This is the demand function for x_1. To find the demand function for x_2, substitute into the budget constraint to get

$$x_2 = \frac{m}{p_2} - \frac{p_1}{p_2}\frac{am}{p_1}$$

$$= \frac{(1 - a)m}{p_2}.$$

The second way is to substitute the budget constraint into the maximization problem at the beginning. If we do this, our problem becomes

$$\max_{x_1} a \ln x_1 + (1 - a) \ln(m/p_2 - x_1 p_1/p_2).$$

The first-order condition for this problem is

$$\frac{a}{x_1} - (1 - a) \frac{p_2}{m - p_1 x_1} \frac{p_1}{p_2} = 0.$$

A little algebra—which you should do!—gives us the solution

$$x_1 = \frac{am}{p_1}.$$

Substitute this back into the budget constraint $x_2 = m/p_2 - x_1 p_1/p_2$ to get

$$x_2 = \frac{(1 - a)m}{p_2}.$$

These are the demand functions for the two goods, which, happily, are the same as those derived earlier by the other method.

Now for Lagrange's method. Set up the Lagrangian

$$L = a \ln x_1 + (1 - a) \ln x_2 - \lambda(p_1 x_1 + p_2 x_2 - m)$$

and differentiate to get the three first-order conditions

$$\frac{\partial L}{\partial x_1} = \frac{a}{x_1} - \lambda p_1 = 0$$

$$\frac{\partial L}{\partial x_2} = \frac{1 - a}{x_2} - \lambda p_2 = 0$$

$$\frac{\partial L}{\partial \lambda} = p_1 x_1 + p_2 x_2 - m = 0.$$

Now the trick is to solve them! The best way to proceed is to first solve for λ and then for x_1 and x_2. So we rearrange and cross multiply the first two equations to get

$$a = \lambda p_1 x_1$$

$$1 - a = \lambda p_2 x_2.$$

These equations are just asking to be added together:

$$1 = \lambda(p_1 x_1 + p_2 x_2) = \lambda m$$

which gives us

$$\lambda = \frac{1}{m}.$$

Substitute this back into the first two equations and solve for x_1 and x_2 to get

$$x_1 = \frac{am}{p_1}$$

$$x_2 = \frac{(1 - a)m}{p_2}$$

just as before.

6

DEMAND

In the last chapter we presented the basic model of consumer choice: how maximizing utility subject to a budget constraint would yield optimal choices. We saw that the optimal choices of the consumer would depend on the consumer's income and the prices of the goods, and we worked a few examples to see what the optimal choices would be for some simple kinds of preferences.

The consumer's **demand functions** give the optimal amounts of each of the goods as a function of the prices and income faced by the consumer. We write the demand functions as

$$x_1 = x_1(p_1, p_2, m)$$
$$x_2 = x_2(p_1, p_2, m).$$

The left-hand side of each equation stands for the quantity demanded. The right-hand side of each equation is the function that relates the prices and income to that quantity.

In this chapter we will examine how the demand for a good changes as prices and income change. Studying how a choice responds to changes in the economic environment is known as **comparative statics**, which we first described in Chapter 1. "Comparative" means that we want to compare two situations: before and after the change in the economic environment. "Statics" means that we are not concerned with any adjustment process that may be involved in moving from one choice to another; rather we will only examine the final equilibrium choice.

In the case of the consumer, there are only two things in our model that affect the optimal choice: prices and income. The comparative statics questions in consumer theory therefore involve investigating how demand changes when prices and income change.

6.1 Normal and Inferior Goods

We start by considering how a consumer's demand for a good changes as his income changes. We want to know how the optimal choice at one income compares to the optimal choice at another level of income. During this exercise, we will hold the prices fixed, and examine only the change in demand due to the income change.

We know how an increase in money income affects the budget line when prices are fixed—it shifts it outward in a parallel fashion. So how does this affect demand?

We would normally think that the demand for each good would increase when income increases, as shown in Figure 6.1. Economists, with a singular lack of imagination, call such goods **normal** goods. If good 1 is a normal good, then the demand for it increases when income increases, and decreases when income decreases. For a normal good the quantity demanded always changes in the same way that income changes:

$$\frac{\Delta x_1}{\Delta m} > 0.$$

If something is called normal, you can be sure that there must be a *possibility* of being abnormal. And indeed there is. Figure 6.2 presents an example of nice, well-behaved indifference curves where an increase of income results in a *reduction* in the consumption of one of the goods. Such a good is called an **inferior** good. This may be "abnormal," but when you think about it, inferior goods aren't all that unusual. There are many goods for which demand decreases as income increases; examples might include gruel, bologna, shacks, or nearly any kind of low-quality good.

Whether a good is inferior or not depends on the income level that we are examining. It might very well be that very poor people consume more bologna as their income increases. But after a point, the consumption of bologna would probably decline as income increased. Since in real life the consumption of goods can increase or decrease when income increases, it is comforting to know that economic theory allows for both possibilities.

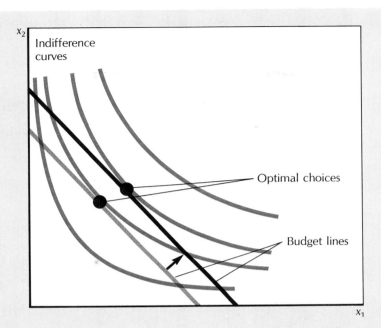

x_2

Indifference
curves

Optimal choices

Budget lines

x_1

Normal goods. The demand for both goods increases when income increases, so both goods are normal goods.

Figure
6.1

6.2 Income Offer Curves and Engel Curves

We can connect together the demanded bundles that we get as we slide the budget line outward in a parallel manner to construct the **income offer curves.** This curve just illustrates the bundles of goods that are demanded at the different levels of income, as depicted in Figure 6.3. The income offer curve is also known as **income expansion paths.** If both goods are normal goods, then the income expansion path will have a positive slope, as depicted in Figure 6.3.

For each level of income, m, there will be some optimal choice for each of the goods. Let us focus on good 1, and consider the optimal choice at each set of prices and income, $x_1(p_1, p_2, m)$. This is just the demand function for good 1. If we hold the prices of goods 1 and 2 fixed and look at how demand changes as we change income, we generate a curve known as the **Engel curve.** The Engel curve is a picture of how demand changes as income changes, with all prices being held constant. For an example of an Engel curve, see Figure 6.3B.

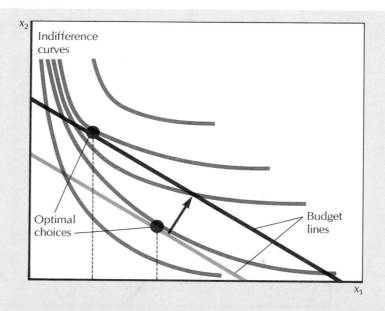

Figure 6.2

An inferior good. Good 1 is an inferior good, which means that the demand for it decreases when income increases.

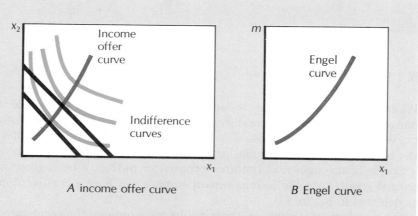

A income offer curve   *B Engel curve*

Figure 6.3

How demand changes as income changes. (A) The income offer curve (or income expansion path) depicts the optimal choice at different levels of income, but constant prices. (B) When we plot the optimal choice of good 1 against income, m, we get the Engel curve.

6.3 Some Examples

Let's consider some of the preferences that we examined in Chapter 5 and see what their income offer curves and Engel curves look like.

Perfect Substitutes

The case of perfect substitutes is depicted in Figure 6.4. If $p_1 < p_2$, so that the consumer is specializing in consuming good 1, then increasing income means that he will increase his consumption of good 1. Thus the income offer curve is the horizontal axis, as shown in Figure 6.4A.

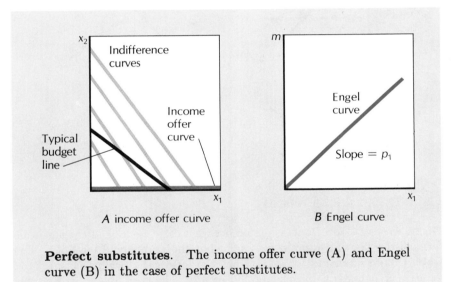

Perfect substitutes. The income offer curve (A) and Engel curve (B) in the case of perfect substitutes.

Figure
6.4

Since the demand for good 1 is $x_1 = m/p_1$ in this case, the Engel curve will be a straight line with a slope of p_1, as depicted in Figure 6.4B. (Since m is on the vertical axis, and x_1 on the horizontal axis, we can write $m = p_1 x_1$, which makes it clear that the slope is p_1.)

Perfect Complements

The demand behavior for perfect complements is shown in Figure 6.5. Since the consumer will always consume the same amount of each good, no matter what, the income offer curve is the diagonal line through the origin as depicted in Figure 6.5A. We have seen that the demand for good 1 is $x_1 = m/(p_1 + p_2)$, so the Engel curve is a straight line with a slope of $p_1 + p_2$ as shown in Figure 6.5B.

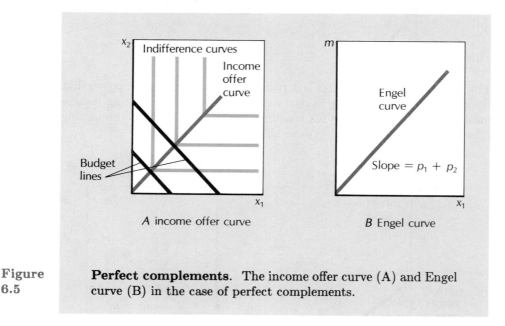

A income offer curve

B Engel curve

Figure
6.5

Perfect complements. The income offer curve (A) and Engel curve (B) in the case of perfect complements.

Cobb-Douglas Preferences

For the case of Cobb-Douglas preferences it is easier to look at the algebraic form of the demand functions to see what the graphs will look like. The Cobb-Douglas demand for good 1 has the form $x_1 = am/p_1$. For a fixed value of p_1, this is a *linear* function of m. Thus doubling m will double demand, tripling m will triple demand, and so on. In fact, multiplying m by any positive number t will just multiply demand by the same amount.

The demand for good 2 is $x_2 = (1-a)m/p_2$ and this is also clearly linear. The fact that the demand functions for both goods are linear functions of income means that the income expansion paths will be straight lines through the origin, as depicted in Figure 6.6A. The Engel curve for good 1 will be a straight line with a slope of p_1/a, as depicted in Figure 6.6B.

Homothetic Preferences

All of the income offer curves and Engel curves that we have seen up to now have been straightforward—in fact they've been straight lines! This has

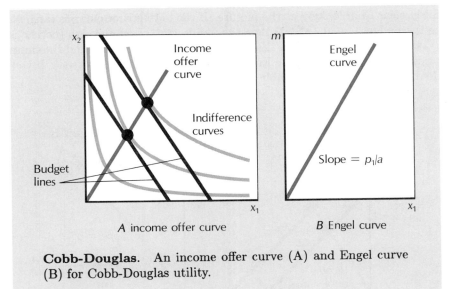

A income offer curve   B Engel curve

Cobb-Douglas. An income offer curve (A) and Engel curve (B) for Cobb-Douglas utility.

Figure
6.6

happened because our examples have been so simple. Real Engel curves do not have to be straight lines. In general when income goes up the demand for a good could increase more or less rapidly than income increases. If the demand for a good goes up by a greater proportion than income, we say that it is a **luxury good**, and if it goes up by a lesser proportion than income we say that it is a **necessary good.**

The dividing line is the case where the demand for a good goes up by the same proportion as income. This is what happened in the three cases we examined above. What aspect of the consumer's preferences leads to this behavior?

Suppose that the consumer's preferences only depend on the *ratio* of good 1 to good 2. This means that if the consumer prefers (x_1, x_2) to (y_1, y_2), then she automatically prefers $(2x_1, 2x_2)$ to $(2y_1, 2y_2)$, $(3x_1, 3x_2)$ to $(3y_1, 3y_2)$, and so on, since the ratio of good 1 to good 2 is the same for all of these bundles. In fact, the consumer prefers (tx_1, tx_2) to (ty_1, ty_2) for any positive value of t. Preferences that have this property are known as **homothetic preferences.** It is not hard to show that the three examples of preferences given above—perfect substitutes, perfect complements, and Cobb-Douglas—are all homothetic preferences.

If the consumer has homothetic preferences then the income offer curves are all straight lines through the origin, as shown in Figure 6.7. More specifically, if preferences are homothetic, it means that when income is scaled up or down by any fraction t, the demanded bundle scales up or down by the same fraction. This can be established rigorously, but it is fairly clear from looking at the picture. If the indifference curve is tangent to the budget line at (x_1^*, x_2^*) then the indifference curve through (tx_1^*, tx_2^*) is tangent to the budget line that has t times as much income and the same prices. This implies that the Engel curves are straight lines as well. If you double income, you just double the demand for each good.

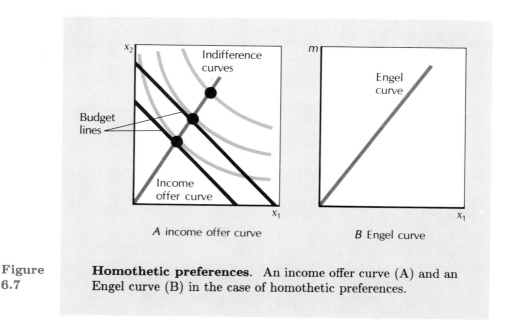

Homothetic preferences. An income offer curve (A) and an Engel curve (B) in the case of homothetic preferences.

Figure
6.7

Homothetic preferences are very convenient since the income effects are so simple. Unfortunately, homothetic preferences aren't very realistic for the same reason! But they will often be of use in our examples.

Quasilinear Preferences

Another kind of preferences that generates a special form of income offer curves and Engel curves is the case of quasilinear preferences. Recall the definition of quasilinear preferences given in Chapter 4. This is the case where all indifference curves are "shifted" versions of one indifference curve as in Figure 6.8. Equivalently, the utility function for these preferences takes the form $u(x_1, x_2) = v(x_1) + x_2$. What happens if we shift the budget line outward? In this case, if an indifference curve is tangent to the budget line at a bundle (x_1^*, x_2^*), then another indifference curve must also be tangent at $(x_1^*, x_2^* + k)$ for any constant k. Increasing income doesn't change the demand for good 1 at all, and all the extra income goes entirely to the consumption of good 2. If preferences are quasilinear we sometimes say that there is a "zero income effect" for good 1. Thus the Engel curve is a vertical line—as you change income, the demand for good 1 remains constant.

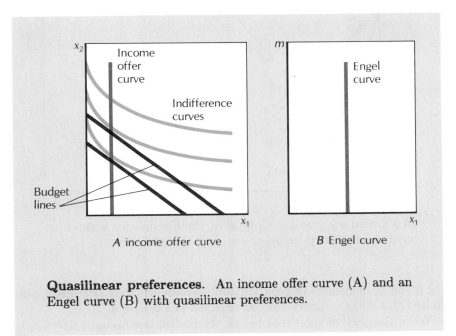

A income offer curve   *B Engel curve*

Quasilinear preferences. An income offer curve (A) and an Engel curve (B) with quasilinear preferences.

Figure
6.8

What would be a real life situation where this kind of thing might occur? Suppose good 1 is pencils and good 2 is money to spend on other goods. When my income goes up, I don't buy any extra pencils—all of my extra income is spent on other goods. Other examples of this sort might be salt or toothpaste. When we are examining a choice between all other goods and some single good that isn't a very large part of the consumer's budget, the quasilinear assumption may well be plausible.

6.4 Ordinary Goods and Giffen Goods

Let us now consider price changes. Suppose that we decrease the price of good 1 and hold the price of good 2 and money income fixed. Then what can happen to the quantity demanded of good 1? Intuition tells us that

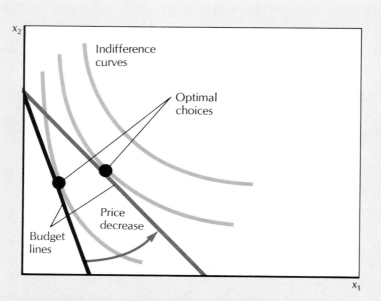

Figure
6.9

An ordinary good. Ordinarily, the demand for a good increases when its price decreases, as is the case here.

the quantity demanded of good 1 should increase when its price decreases. Indeed this is the ordinary case, as depicted in Figure 6.9.

When the price of good 1 decreases, the budget line becomes flatter. Or said another way, the vertical intercept is fixed and the horizontal intercept moves to the right. In Figure 6.9, the optimal choice of good 1 moves to the right as well: the quantity demanded of good 1 has increased.

But we might wonder whether this always happens this way. Is it always the case that no matter what kind of preferences the consumer has the demand for a good must increase when its price goes down?

As it turns out, the answer is no. It is logically possible to find well-behaved preferences for which a decrease in the price of good 1 leads to a reduction in the demand for good 1. Such a good is called a **Giffen good**, after the nineteenth-century economist who first noted the possibility. An example is illustrated in Figure 6.10.

What is going on here in economic terms? What kind of preferences might give rise to the peculiar behavior depicted in Figure 6.10? Suppose that the two goods that you are consuming are gruel and milk, and that you are currently consuming 7 bowls of gruel and 7 cups of milk a week. Now the price of gruel declines. If you consume the same 7 bowls of gruel a week, you will have money left over with which you can purchase more milk. In fact, with the extra money you have saved because of the lower

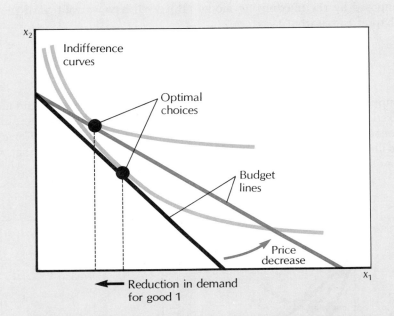

A Giffen good. Good 1 is a Giffen good, since the demand for it decreases when its price decreases.

Figure
6.10

price of gruel, you may decide to consume even more milk and reduce your consumption of gruel. The reduction in the price of gruel has freed up some extra money to be spent on other things—but one thing you might want to do with it is reduce your consumption of gruel! Thus the price change is to some extent *like* an income change. Even though *money* income remains constant, a change in the price of a good will change purchasing power, and thereby change demand.

So the Giffen good is not implausible purely on logical grounds, although Giffen goods are unlikely to be encountered in real world behavior. Most goods are ordinary goods—when their price increases, the demand for them declines. We'll see why this is the ordinary situation a little later.

Incidentally, it is no accident that we used gruel as an example of both an inferior good and a Giffen good. It turns out that there is an intimate relationship between the two which we will explore shortly.

But for now, our exploration of consumer theory may leave you with the impression that nearly anything can happen: if income increases the demand for a good can go up or down, and if price increases the demand can go up or down. Is consumer theory compatible with *any* kind of behavior? Or are there some kinds of behavior that the economic model of consumer behavior rules out? It turns out that there *are* restrictions on behavior

imposed by the maximizing model. But we'll have to wait until the next
chapter to see what they are.

6.5 The Offer Curve and the Demand Curve

Suppose that we let the price of good 1 change while we hold p_2 and income
fixed. Geometrically this involves pivoting the budget line. We can think of
connecting together the optimal points to construct the **price offer curve**
as illustrated in Figure 6.11A. This curve represents the bundles that would
be demanded at different prices for good 1.

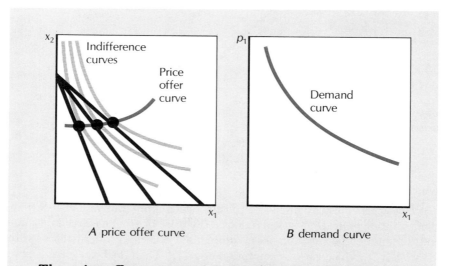

A price offer curve   B demand curve

Figure 6.11 **The price offer curve and demand curve.** Panel (A) contains a price offer curve, which depicts the optimal choices as
the price of good 1 changes. Panel (B) contains the associated
demand curve, which depicts a plot of the optimal choice of
good 1 as a function of its price.

We can depict this same information in a different way. Again, hold the
price of good 2 and money income fixed and for each different value of p_1
plot the optimal level of consumption of good 1. The result is the **demand
curve** depicted in Figure 6.11B. The demand curve is a plot of the demand
function $x_1(p_1, p_2, m)$, holding p_2 and m fixed at some predetermined values.

Ordinarily, when the price of a good increases, the demand for that
good will decrease. Thus the price and quantity of a good will move in

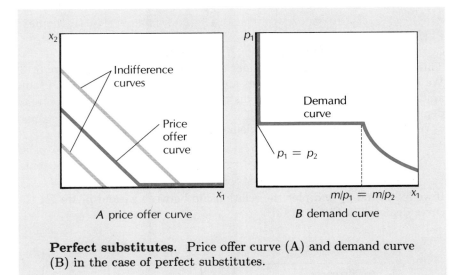

A price offer curve   B demand curve

Perfect substitutes. Price offer curve (A) and demand curve (B) in the case of perfect substitutes.

Figure 6.12

opposite directions, which means that the demand curve will typically have a negative slope. In terms of rates of change, we would normally have

$$\frac{\Delta x_1}{\Delta p_1} < 0$$

which simply says that demand curves usually have a negative slope.

However, we have also seen that in the case of Giffen goods, the demand for a good may decrease when its price decreases. Thus it is possible, but not likely, to have a demand curve with a positive slope.

6.6 Some Examples

Let's look at a few examples of demand curves, using the preferences that we discussed in Chapter 3.

Perfect Substitutes

The offer curve and demand curve for perfect substitutes—the red pencils–blue pencils case—are illustrated in Figure 6.12. As we saw in Chapter 5, the demand for good 1 is 0 when $p_1 > p_2$, any amount on the budget line when $p_1 = p_2$, and m/p_1 when $p_1 < p_2$. The offer curve traces out these possibilities.

In order to find the demand curve, we fix the price of good 2 and graph the demand for good 1 versus the price of good 1 to get the shape depicted in Figure 6.12.

Perfect Complements

This case—the right shoes–left shoes example—is depicted in Figure 6.13. We know that whatever the prices are, a consumer will demand the same amount of goods 1 and 2. Thus his offer curve will be a diagonal line as depicted in Figure 6.13A.

We saw in Chapter 5 that the demand for good 1 is given by

$$x_1 = \frac{m}{p_1 + p_2}.$$

If we fix m and p_2 and plot the relationship between x_1 and p_1 we get the curve depicted in Figure 6.13B.

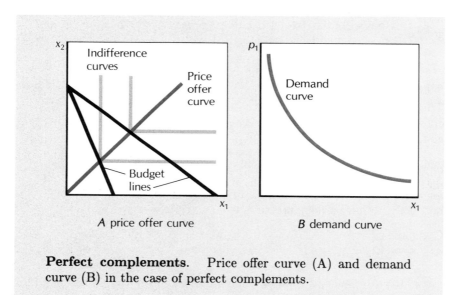

A price offer curve

B demand curve

Figure 6.13 **Perfect complements.** Price offer curve (A) and demand curve (B) in the case of perfect complements.

6.7 Substitutes and Complements

We have already used the terms substitutes and complements, but it is now appropriate to give a formal definition. Since we have seen *perfect* substitutes and *perfect* complements several times already, it seems reasonable to look at the imperfect case.

Let's think about substitutes first. We said that red pencils and blue pencils might be thought of as perfect substitutes, at least for someone who didn't care about color. But what about pencils and pens? This is a case of "imperfect" substitutes. That is, pens and pencils are, to some degree, a substitute for each other, although they aren't as perfect a substitute for each other as red pencils and blue pencils.

Similarly, we said that right shoes and left shoes were perfect complements. But what about a pair of shoes and a pair of socks? Right shoes and left shoes are nearly always consumed together, and shoes and socks are *usually* consumed together. Complementary goods are those like shoes and socks that tend to be consumed together, albeit not always.

Now that we've discussed the basic idea of complements and substitutes, we can give a precise economic definition. Recall that the demand function for good 1, say, will typically be a function of the price of both good 1 and good 2, so we write $x_2(p_1, p_2, m)$. We can ask how the demand for good 1 changes as the price of good 2 changes: does it go up or down?

If the demand for good 1 goes up when the price of good 2 goes up, then we say that good 1 is a **substitute** for good 2. In terms of rates of change, good 1 is a substitute for good 2 if

$$\frac{\Delta x_1}{\Delta p_2} > 0.$$

The idea is that when good 2 gets more expensive the consumer switches to consuming good 1: the consumer *substitutes* away from the more expensive good to the less expensive good.

On the other hand if the demand for good 1 goes down when the price of good 2 goes up, we say that good 1 is a **complement** to good 2. This means that

$$\frac{\Delta x_1}{\Delta p_2} < 0.$$

Complements are goods that are consumed together, like coffee and sugar, so when the price of one good rises, the consumption of both goods will tend to decrease.

The cases of perfect substitutes and perfect complements illustrate these points nicely. Note that $\Delta x_1 / \Delta p_2$ is positive (or zero) in the case of perfect substitutes, and that $\Delta x_1 / \Delta p_2$ is negative in the case of perfect complements.

A couple of warnings are in order about these concepts. First, the two-good case is rather special when it comes to complements and substitutes. Since income is being held fixed, if you spend more money on good 1, you'll have to spend less on good 2. This puts some restrictions on the kinds of behavior that are possible. When there are more than two goods, these restrictions are not so much of a problem.

Second, although the definition of substitutes and complements in terms of consumer demand behavior seems sensible, there are some difficulties with the definitions in more general environments. For example, if we use the above definitions in a situation involving more than two goods, it is perfectly possible that good 1 may be a substitute for good 3, but good 3 may be a complement for good 1. Because of this peculiar feature, more advanced treatments typically use a somewhat different definition of substitutes and complements. The definitions given above describe concepts known as **gross substitutes** and **gross complements**; they will be sufficient for our needs.

6.8 The Inverse Demand Curve

If we hold p_2 and m fixed and plot p_1 against x_1 we get the **demand curve**. As suggested above, we typically think that the demand curve slopes downwards, so that higher prices lead to less demand, although the Giffen example shows that it could be otherwise.

As long as we do have a downward sloping demand curve, as is usual, it is meaningful to speak of the **inverse demand curve**. The inverse demand curve is the demand curve viewing price as a function of quantity. That is, for each level of demand for good 1 the inverse demand curve measures what the price of good 1 would have to be in order for the consumer to choose that level of consumption. So the inverse demand curve measures the same relationship as the direct demand curve, but just from another point of view. Figure 6.14 depicts the inverse demand curve—or the direct demand curve, depending on your point of view.

Recall, for example, the Cobb-Douglas demand for good 1, $x_1 = am/p_1$. We could just as well write the relationship between price and quantity as $p_1 = am/x_1$. The first representation is the direct demand function; the second is the inverse demand function.

The inverse demand function has a useful economic interpretation. Recall that as long as both goods are being consumed in positive amounts, the optimal choice must satisfy the condition that the marginal rate of substitution equals the price ratio:

$$\text{MRS} = \frac{p_1}{p_2}.$$

This says that at the optimal level of demand for good 1, for example, we must have

$$p_1 = p_2\text{MRS}. \tag{6.1}$$

Thus, at the optimal level of demand for good 1, the price of good 1 is proportional to the marginal rate of substitution between good 1 and good 2.

Suppose for simplicity that the price of good 2 is 1. Then equation (6.1) tells us that at the optimal level of demand, the price of good 1 is exactly the marginal rate of substitution: how much the consumer is willing to give up of good 2 in order to get a little more of good 1. In this case the inverse demand curve is simply measuring the MRS. For any optimal level of x_1 the inverse demand curve tells how much of good 2 the consumer would want to have to compensate him for a small reduction in good 1. Or, turning this around, the inverse demand curve measures how much the consumer would be willing to sacrifice of good 2 to make him just indifferent to having a little more of good 1.

If we think of good 2 as being money to spend on other goods then we can think of the marginal rate of substitution as being how many dollars the individual would be willing to give up to have a little more of good 1. We suggested earlier that in this case, we can think of the marginal rate of substitution as measuring the marginal willingness to pay. Since the price of good 1 is just the MRS in this case, this means that the price of good 1 itself is measuring the marginal willingness to pay.

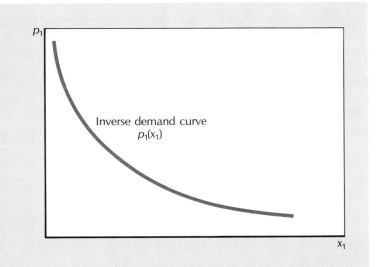

Inverse demand curve. If you view the demand curve as measuring price as a function of quantity, you have an inverse demand curve.

Figure 6.14

At each quantity x_1, the inverse demand curve is measuring how many dollars the consumer is willing to give up for a little more of good 1; or, said another way, how many dollars the consumer was willing to give up for the last unit purchased of good 1. For a small enough amount of good 1, they come down to the same thing.

Looked at in this way, the downward sloping inverse demand curve has a new meaning. When x_1 is very small, the consumer is willing to give up a lot of money—that is, a lot of other goods, to acquire a little bit more of good 1. As x_1 is larger, the consumer is willing to give up less money, on the margin, to acquire a little more of good 1. Thus the marginal willingness to pay, in the sense of the marginal willingness to sacrifice good 2 for good 1, is decreasing as we increase the consumption of good 1.

6.9 Elasticity

We have seen several expressions for rates of change in this chapter: how demand changes as income changes, how demand changes as price changes, and so on. These rates of change measure the "responsiveness" of demand to prices and income. If demand changes a lot when income changes, so that $\Delta x_1 / \Delta m$ is large, then the demand for good 1 is very responsive to income.

However, the *magnitude* of the rates of change may not be very meaningful. For the rate of change in demand as you change income, say, depends on the units of measurement. If we measured the amount of a good in pints we would get 8 times the "response" to an income change as if we measured it in gallons!

A better measure of responsiveness is to use the *percent* change in demand divided by the *percent* change in income. This measure is given by

$$\eta_1 = \frac{\Delta x_1 / x_1}{\Delta m / m}$$

and is known as the **income elasticity of demand** of good 1.[1] The analogous expression for good 2 is

$$\eta_2 = \frac{\Delta x_2 / x_2}{\Delta m / m}.$$

The income elasticity of demand is independent of the units in which demand is measured, and is thus a more meaningful measure of the responsiveness of demand to income changes. Income elasticity simply measures the percentage change in demand when income changes by a small percent. Roughly speaking, if income changes by 1 percent, and the income elasticity of demand is η, then the quantity of the good demanded will change by η percent.

We can apply simple algebra to the definition of income elasticity to get equivalent definitions:

$$\eta_1 = \frac{\Delta x_1}{\Delta m} \frac{m}{x_1}$$

$$\eta_2 = \frac{\Delta x_2}{\Delta m} \frac{m}{x_2}.$$

[1] The Greek letter η, eta, is pronounced "ate-uh."

These are in fact the form in which income elasticities are most often seen: the rate of change of demand as income changes times the ratio of income to demand.

Similar remarks apply to price changes. We have mentioned the "rate of change of demand as price changes." The sign of such a rate may be of interest, but the magnitude is not very meaningful since it will depend on the units in which things are measured.

For this reason, we define the **own price elasticity of demand for good 1** to be the percent change in demand in good 1 divided by the percent change in the price of good 1:[2]

$$\epsilon_{11} = \frac{\Delta x_1/x_1}{\Delta p_1/p_1}.$$

The **cross price elasticity of demand for good 1** is defined to be the percent change in demand for good 1 divided by the percent change in the price of good 2. In symbols this is

$$\epsilon_{12} = \frac{\Delta x_1/x_1}{\Delta p_2/p_2}.$$

Again, we can use simple algebra to get the equivalent definitions:

$$\epsilon_{11} = \frac{\Delta x_1}{\Delta p_1}\frac{p_1}{x_1}$$

$$\epsilon_{12} = \frac{\Delta x_1}{\Delta p_2}\frac{p_2}{x_1}.$$

Thus the own price elasticity of demand is just the rate of change of demand with respect to price multiplied by the ratio of price to demand. If the price of good 1 changes by 1 percent, and the elasticity of demand is ϵ_{11}, then the demand for good 1 will change by roughly ϵ_{11} percent.

Note that the own price elasticity will typically be a negative number—since the demand will typically change opposite the direction of price. The cross price elasticity can be of either sign, depending on whether the goods are complements or substitutes.

Optional   ## 6.10 The Elasticity Identities

The elasticity measures of responsiveness of demand to income and prices defined above are very useful in describing consumer behavior. It turns out that there are certain relationships that must hold among these elasticities.

[2] The Greek letter ϵ, epsilon, is pronounced "eps-i-lon."

These relationships all come from the fact that the consumer must satisfy his or her budget constraint no matter what the prices and income, so we will refer to them as **the elasticity identities**.

We start by considering the demands for goods 1 and 2 as functions of the prices and income:

$$x_1 = x_1(p_1, p_2, m)$$
$$x_2 = x_2(p_1, p_2, m).$$

We know that these choices must satisfy the budget constraint for *all* values of prices and income so we have

$$p_1 x_1(p_1, p_2, m) + p_2 x_2(p_1, p_2, m) \equiv m. \tag{6.2}$$

The symbol $\equiv$ is the *identity* symbol. It means that the left-hand side of this expression is equal to the right-hand side for *all* values of prices and incomes. An **equation**, on the other hand, need only hold for some values of the variables.

The budget identity follows from the definition of the optimal choices $x_1(p_1, p_2, m)$ and $x_2(p_1, p_2, m)$. Whatever prices and income the consumer faces, he must choose a bundle of goods that satisfies his budget constraint.

This simple budget identity has some interesting consequences. For example, suppose that we increase income but hold prices fixed. How will the choices respond? From equation (6.2), the budget identity, we have

$$p_1 \Delta x_1 + p_2 \Delta x_2 = \Delta m. \tag{6.3}$$

This identity implies, for example, that if income goes up ($\Delta m > 0$) then the demand for at least one of the goods has to go up as well.

If we divide equation (6.3) through by Δm we have

$$p_1 \frac{\Delta x_1}{\Delta m} + p_2 \frac{\Delta x_2}{\Delta m} = 1. \tag{6.4}$$

This equation says that the weighted sum of the rate of change of the demands must be 1, where the weights are given by the prices.

The terms $\Delta x_1 / \Delta m$ and $\Delta x_2 / \Delta m$ measure the responsiveness of demand to changes in income. But, as we've seen, these aren't very good measures of responsiveness, since they depend on the units of measurement. Let us convert these into elasticity measures.

To do this, we take equation (6.4) and transform it as follows:

$$\frac{p_1 x_1}{m} \frac{\Delta x_1}{\Delta m} \frac{m}{x_1} + \frac{p_2 x_2}{m} \frac{\Delta x_2}{\Delta m} \frac{m}{x_2} = 1. \tag{6.5}$$

All we've done is multiply the first term by $(x_1 m / x_1 m) = 1$ and the second term by $(x_2 m / x_2 m) = 1$.

Now define the **budget share of good 1** to be the fraction of income spent on good 1, and similarly for good 2:

$$s_1 = \frac{p_1 x_1}{m}$$
$$s_2 = \frac{p_2 x_2}{m}.$$

Using these definitions and the definitions of η_1 and η_2 given in the last section, equation (6.5) becomes

$$s_1 \eta_1 + s_2 \eta_2 = 1. \tag{6.6}$$

This says that the average income elasticity is 1—where the weights in the average are the income shares of each good. If income increases by 10 percent, the (weighted) average increase in demand for each good is 10 percent.

We can make similar calculations for changes in prices. Suppose, for example, that the price of good 1 changes, but the price of good 2 and income remain fixed. We must satisfy the budget constraint before and after this change, so

$$p_1 x_1 + p_2 x_2 = m$$
$$(p_1 + \Delta p_1)(x_1 + \Delta x_1) + p_2(x_2 + \Delta x_2) = m.$$

Multiplying out the second equation gives

$$p_1 x_1 + p_1 \Delta x_1 + x_1 \Delta p_1 + \Delta p_1 \Delta x_1 + p_2 x_2 + p_2 \Delta x_2 = m.$$

Subtracting the first equation from this yields

$$p_1 \Delta x_1 + x_1 \Delta p_1 + \Delta p_1 \Delta x_1 + p_2 \Delta x_2 = 0.$$

Dividing through by Δp_1 we get

$$p_1 \frac{\Delta x_1}{\Delta p_1} + x_1 + \Delta x_1 + p_2 \frac{\Delta x_2}{\Delta p_1} = 0.$$

Suppose now that we have a very small change in price, so that the change in demand is correspondingly small. Then the Δx_1 term will drop out of the above expression and we will have

$$p_1 \frac{\Delta x_1}{\Delta p_1} + p_2 \frac{\Delta x_2}{\Delta p_1} = -x_1. \tag{6.7}$$

In this expression, $\Delta x_1 / \Delta p_1$ and $\Delta x_2 / \Delta p_1$ measure how responsive the demands for goods 1 and 2 are to changes in price 1. But they suffer from the same problem as the income measures given above: the measures depend on the units that we measure things in. So, let us adopt the same solution that we used before: use the elasticity measures of responsiveness.

Using these definitions, we can multiply each term in equation (6.7) by (p_1/m), and then multiply the first term by x_1/x_1 and the second term by x_2/x_2. The result of these operations is

$$\frac{p_1 x_1}{m} \frac{\Delta x_1}{\Delta p_1} \frac{p_1}{x_1} + \frac{p_2 x_2}{m} \frac{\Delta x_2}{\Delta p_1} \frac{p_1}{x_2} = -\frac{p_1 x_1}{m}. \tag{6.8}$$

Using the budget share notation defined above this becomes

$$s_1 \epsilon_{11} + s_2 \epsilon_{21} = -s_1. \tag{6.9}$$

Thus the average percentage response in the demand for all goods to a price increase is negative, where the weights in the average are given by the budget shares.

When the price of a good increases it is natural to think that the demand for that good will drop, so the first term in equation (6.9) will typically be negative. But the demand for the other good might well rise. Equation (6.9) tells us that the weighted sum of these two changes must be negative—the demand for the second good can't rise too much.

Equations (6.6) and (6.9) are the budget identities. They follow entirely from the fact that the optimal choices have to satisfy the budget identity. They are useful in that they give some restrictions on the way in which the various elasticities must fit together.

Summary

1. The consumer's demand function for a good will depend on the prices and income.

2. A normal good is one for which the demand increases when income increases. An inferior good is one for which the demand decreases when income increases.

3. An ordinary good is one for which the demand decreases when its price increases. A Giffen good is one for which the demand increases when its price increases.

4. If the demand for good 1 increases when the price of good 2 increases, then good 1 is a substitute for good 2. If the demand for good 1 decreases in this situation, then it is a complement for good 2.

5. The inverse demand curve measures the price at which a given quantity will be demanded.

6. The income elasticity of demand is the percent change in demand divided by the percent change in income. The own price elasticity of demand is the percent change in demand divided by the percent change in price.

Review Questions

1. If the consumer is consuming exactly two goods, and she is always spending all of her money, can both of them be inferior goods?

2. Show that perfect substitutes are an example of homothetic preferences.

3. Show that Cobb-Douglas preferences are homothetic preferences.

4. The income offer curve is to the Engel curve as the price offer curve is to ...?

5. What is the demand function for concave preferences? Calculate it and draw the offer curve and demand curve.

6. What is the form of the inverse demand function for good 1 in the case of perfect complements?

7. What is the own price elasticity of the Cobb-Douglas demand function? What is the cross price elasticity?

8. Suppose that only two goods are being consumed. The consumer is spending 40 percent of her income on good 1 and 60 percent on good 2. The income elasticity of good 1 is .8. What is the income elasticity of good 2?

9. Suppose that the consumer is spending half of her income on good 1 and half on good 2. The own price elasticity of good 1 is $-.3$ and the cross price elasticity of good 2 is $+.5$. Is this possible?

APPENDIX

The calculus definition of income elasticity is just what you'd think; replace the Δ's by derivatives:

$$\eta_1 = \frac{\partial x_1}{\partial m}\frac{m}{x_1}$$

$$\eta_2 = \frac{\partial x_2}{\partial m}\frac{m}{x_2}.$$

If we differentiate the budget identity with respect to m, we find:

$$p_1 \frac{\partial x_1}{\partial m} + p_2 \frac{\partial x_2}{\partial m} = 1$$

which can be transformed into

$$\frac{p_1 x_1}{m} \frac{\partial x_1}{\partial m} \frac{m}{x_1} + \frac{p_2 x_2}{m} \frac{\partial x_2}{\partial m} \frac{m}{x_2} = 1$$

$$s_1 \eta_1 + s_2 \eta_2 = 1.$$

We can do the same sort of thing with the price elasticity. The definitions of own and cross price elasticity are

$$\epsilon_{11} = \frac{\partial x_1}{\partial p_1} \frac{p_1}{x_1}$$

$$\epsilon_{21} = \frac{\partial x_2}{\partial p_1} \frac{p_1}{x_2}.$$

Differentiating the budget identity with respect to p_1 gives

$$x_1 + p_1 \frac{\partial x_1}{\partial p_1} + p_2 \frac{\partial x_2}{\partial p_1} = 0$$

and making the same transformations as those used to derive equation (6.9) gives

$$\frac{p_1 x_1}{m} \frac{\partial x_1}{\partial p_1} \frac{p_1}{x_1} + \frac{p_2 x_2}{m} \frac{\partial x_2}{\partial p_1} \frac{p_1}{x_2} = -\frac{p_1 x_1}{m}.$$

Applying the definitions of elasticity and budget share we get the same equation we had in the text:

$$s_1 \epsilon_{11} + s_2 \epsilon_{21} = -s_1.$$

EXAMPLE: Quasilinear preferences.

If preferences take a special form, this will mean that the demand functions that come from those preferences will take a special form. In Chapter 4 we described quasilinear preferences. These preferences involve indifference curves that are all parallel to each other and can be represented by a utility function of the form

$$u(x_1, x_2) = v(x_1) + x_2.$$

The maximization problem for a utility function like this is

$$\max_{x_1, x_2} v(x_1) + x_2$$

$$\text{s.t. } p_1 x_1 + p_2 x_2 = m.$$

Solving the budget constraint for x_2 as a function of x_1 and substituting into the objective function we have

$$\max_{x_1} v(x_1) + m/p_2 - p_1 x_1/p_2.$$

Differentiating gives us the first-order condition

$$v'(x_1^*) = \frac{p_1}{p_2}.$$

This demand function has the interesting feature that the demand for good 1 must be independent of income—just as we saw using indifference curves. The inverse demand curve is given by

$$p_1(x_1) = v'(x_1)p_2.$$

That is, the inverse demand function for good 1 is the derivative of the utility function times p_2. Once we have the demand function for good 1, the demand function for good 2 comes from the budget constraint.

For example, let us calculate the demand functions for the utility function

$$u(x_1, x_2) = \ln x_1 + x_2.$$

Applying the first-order condition gives

$$\frac{1}{x_1} = \frac{p_1}{p_2}$$

so the direct demand function for good 1 is

$$x_1 = \frac{p_2}{p_1}$$

and the indirect demand function is

$$p_1(x_1) = \frac{p_2}{x_1}.$$

The direct demand function for good 2 comes from substituting $x_1 = p_2/p_1$ into the budget constraint:

$$x_2 = \frac{m}{p_2} - 1.$$

A warning is in order concerning these demand functions. Note that the demand for good 1 is independent of income in this example. This is a general feature of a quasilinear utility function—the demand for good 1 remains constant as income changes. However, this is only true for some values of income. A demand function can't literally be independent of income for *all* values of income; after all, when income is zero, all demands are zero. The quasilinear demand function derived above is only relevant when a positive amount of each good is being consumed. For low levels of income, demands take a somewhat different form. See Hal R. Varian, *Microeconomic Analysis*, 2nd edition (New York: Norton, 1984), Chapter 7.

7

REVEALED PREFERENCE

In Chapter 6 we saw how we can use information about the consumer's preferences and budget constraint to determine his or her demand. In this chapter we reverse this process and show how we can use information about the consumer's demand to discover information about his or her preferences. Up until now, we were thinking about what preferences could tell us about people's behavior. But in real life, preferences are not directly observable: we have to discover peoples' preferences from observing their behavior. In this chapter we'll develop some tools to do this.

When we talk of determining peoples' preferences from observing their behavior, we have to assume that the preferences will remain unchanged while we observe the behavior. Over very long time spans, this is not very reasonable. But for the monthly or quarterly time spans that economists usually deal with, it seems unlikely that a particular consumer's tastes would change radically. Thus we will adopt a maintained hypothesis that the consumer's preferences are stable over the time period for which we observe his or her choice behavior.

7.1 The Idea of Revealed Preference

Before we begin this investigation, let's adopt the convention that in this chapter, the underlying preferences—whatever they may be—are known to be strictly convex. Thus there will be a *unique* demanded bundle at each budget. This assumption is not necessary for the theory of revealed preference, but the exposition will be simpler with it.

Consider Figure 7.1, where we have depicted a consumer's demanded bundle (x_1, x_2) and another arbitrary bundle (y_1, y_2) that is beneath the consumer's budget line. Suppose that we are willing to postulate that this consumer is an optimizing consumer of the sort we have been studying. What can we say about the consumer's preferences between these two bundles of goods?

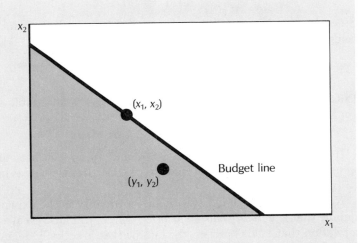

Revealed preference. The bundle (x_1, x_2) that the consumer chooses is revealed preferred to the bundle (y_1, y_2), a bundle that he could have chosen.

Figure 7.1

Well, the bundle (y_1, y_2) is certainly an affordable purchase at the given budget—the consumer could have bought it if he or she wanted to, and even had money left over. Since (x_1, x_2) is the *optimal* bundle, it must be better than anything else that the consumer could afford. Hence, in particular it must be better than (y_1, y_2).

The same argument holds for any bundle on or underneath the budget line other than the demanded bundle. Since it *could* have been bought at the given budget but wasn't, then what *was* bought must be better. Here is where we use the assumption that there is a *unique* demanded bundle for each budget. If preferences are not strictly convex, so that indifference curves have flat spots, it may be that some bundles that are *on* the budget line might be just as good as the demanded bundle. This complication can be handled without too much difficulty, but it is easier to just assume it away.

In Figure 7.1 all of the bundles in the shaded area underneath the budget line are revealed worse than the demanded bundle (x_1, x_2). This is because they could have been chosen, but were rejected in favor of (x_1, x_2). We will now translate this geometric discussion of revealed preference into algebra.

Let (x_1, x_2) be the bundle purchased at prices (p_1, p_2) when the consumer has income m. What does it mean to say that (y_1, y_2) is affordable at those prices and income? It simply means that (y_1, y_2) satisfies the budget constraint

$$p_1 y_1 + p_2 y_2 \leq m.$$

Since (x_1, x_2) is actually bought at the given budget, it must satisfy the budget constraint with equality

$$p_1 x_1 + p_2 x_2 = m.$$

Putting these two equations together, (y_1, y_2) is affordable at the budget (p_1, p_2, m) means:

$$p_1 x_1 + p_2 x_2 \geq p_1 y_1 + p_2 y_2.$$

If the above inequality is satisfied and (y_1, y_2) is actually a different bundle than (x_1, x_2), we say that (x_1, x_2) is **directly revealed preferred** to (y_1, y_2).

Note that the left-hand side of this inequality is the expenditure on the bundle that is *actually chosen* at prices (p_1, p_2). Thus revealed preference is a relation that holds between the bundle that is actually demanded at some budget and the bundles that *could have been* demanded at that budget.

The term "revealed preference" is actually a bit misleading. It does not inherently have anything to do with preferences, although we've see above that if the consumer is making optimal choices, the two ideas are closely related. Instead of saying "X is revealed preferred to Y," it would be better to say "X is chosen over Y." When we say that X is revealed preferred to Y, all we are claiming is that X is chosen when Y could have been chosen; that is, that $p_1 x_1 + p_2 x_2 \geq p_1 y_1 + p_2 y_2$.

7.2 From Revealed Preference to Preference

We can summarize the above section very simply. It follows from our model of consumer behavior—that people are choosing the best things they can afford—that the choices they make are preferred to the choices that they could have made. Or, in the terminology of the last section, if (x_1, x_2) is *directly revealed preferred* to (y_1, y_2) then (x_1, x_2) is in fact *preferred* to (y_1, y_2). Stated more formally:

The Principle of Revealed Preference.   *Let (x_1, x_2) be the chosen bundle when prices are (p_1, p_2), and let (y_1, y_2) be some other bundle such that $p_1 x_1 + p_2 x_2 \geq p_1 y_1 + p_2 y_2$. Then if the consumer is choosing the most preferred bundle he can afford, we must have $(x_1, x_2) \succ (y_1, y_2)$.*

When you first encounter this principle, it may seem circular. If X is revealed preferred to Y, doesn't that automatically mean that X is preferred to Y? The answer is no. Revealed preferred just means that X was chosen when Y was affordable; preference means that the consumer ranks X ahead of Y. If the consumer chooses the best bundles he can afford then revealed preference implies preference, but that is a consequence of the model of behavior, not the definitions of the terms.

This is why it would be better to say that one bundle is "chosen over" another, as suggested above. Then we would state the principle of revealed preference by saying: "If a bundle X is chosen over a bundle Y, then X must be preferred to Y." In this statement it is clear how the model of behavior allows us to use observed choices to infer something about the underlying preferences.

Whatever terminology you use, the essential point is clear: if we observe that one bundle is chosen when another one is affordable, then we have learned something about the preferences between the two bundles: namely, that the first is preferred to the second.

Now suppose that we happen to know that (y_1, y_2) is a demanded bundle at prices (q_1, q_2) and that (y_1, y_2) is itself revealed preferred to some other bundle (z_1, z_2). That is,

$$q_1 y_1 + q_2 y_2 \geq q_1 z_1 + q_2 z_2.$$

Then we know that $x \succ y$, and that $y \succ z$. From the transitivity assumption we can conclude that $x \succ z$.

This argument is illustrated in Figure 7.2. Revealed preference and transitivity tell us that (x_1, x_2) must be better than (z_1, z_2) for the consumer who made the illustrated choices.

It is natural to say that in this case (x_1, x_2) is **indirectly revealed preferred** to (z_1, z_2). Of course the "chain" of observed choices may be longer than just three: if bundle A is directly revealed preferred to B, and B to C, and C to D . . . all the way to M, say, then bundle A is still indirectly revealed preferred to M. The chain of direct comparisons can be of any length.

If a bundle is either directly or indirectly revealed preferred to another bundle, we will say that the first bundle is **revealed preferred** to the

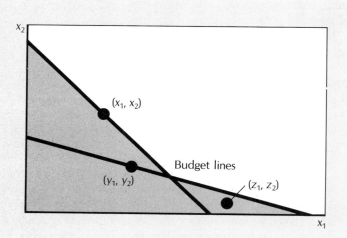

Figure
7.2

Indirect revealed preference. The bundle (x_1, x_2) is indirectly revealed preferred to the bundle (z_1, z_2).

second. The idea of revealed preference is simple, but it is surprisingly powerful. Just looking at a consumer's choices can give us a lot of information about the underlying preferences. Consider, for example, Figure 7.2. Here we have several observations on demanded bundles at different budgets. We can conclude from these observations that since (x_1, x_2) is revealed preferred, either directly or indirectly, to all of the bundles in the shaded area, (x_1, x_2) is in fact *preferred* to those bundles by the consumer who made these choices. Another way to say this is to note that the true indifference curve through (x_1, x_2), whatever it is, must lie above the shaded region.

7.3 Recovering Preferences

By observing choices made by the consumer, we can learn about his or her preferences. As we observe more and more choices, we can get a better and better estimate of what the consumer's preferences are like.

Such information about preferences can be very important in making policy decisions. Most economic policy involves trading off some kinds of goods for others: if we put a tax on shoes and subsidize clothing, we'll probably end up having more clothes and fewer shoes. In order to evaluate the desirability of such a policy, it is important to have some idea of what consumer preferences between clothes and shoes look like. By examining consumer choices, we can extract such information through the use of revealed preference and related techniques.

If we are willing to add more assumptions about consumer preferences, we can get more precise estimates about the shape of indifference curves. For example, suppose we observe two bundles Y and Z that are revealed preferred to X, as in Figure 7.3, and that we are willing to postulate preferences are convex. Then we know that all of the weighted averages of Y and Z are preferred to X as well. If we are willing to assume that preferences are monotonic, then all the bundles that have more of both goods than X, Y, and Z—or any of their weighted averages—are also preferred to X.

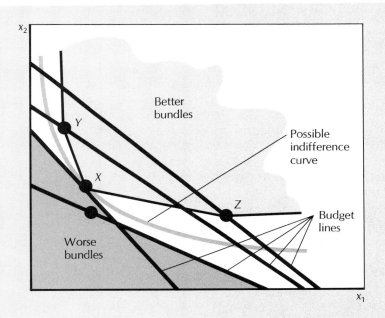

Trapping the indifference curve. The upper shaded area consists of bundles preferred to X, and the lower shaded area consists of bundles revealed worse than X. The indifference curve through X must lie somewhere in the region between the two shaded areas.

Figure 7.3

Thus, in Figure 7.3, we can conclude that all of the bundles in the upper shaded area are better than (x_1, x_2), and that all of the bundles in the lower shaded area are worse than (x_1, x_2), according to the preferences of the consumer who made the choices. The true indifference curve through (x_1, x_2) must lie somewhere between the two shaded sets. We've managed to trap the indifference curve quite tightly simply by an intelligent application of the idea of revealed preference and a few simple assumptions about preferences.

7.4 The Weak Axiom of Revealed Preference

All of the above is supposing that the consumer *has* preferences, and that she is always choosing the best bundle of goods she can afford. If the consumer is not behaving this way, the "estimates" of the indifference curves that we constructed above have no meaning. The question naturally arises: how can we tell if the consumer is following the maximizing model? Or, to turn it around: what kind of observation would lead us to conclude that the consumer was *not* maximizing?

Consider the situation illustrated in Figure 7.4. Could both of these choices be generated by a maximizing consumer? According to the logic of revealed preference, Figure 7.4 allows us to conclude two things: (1) (x_1, x_2) is preferred to (y_1, y_2); and (2) (y_1, y_2) is preferred to (x_1, x_2). This is clearly absurd. In Figure 7.4 the consumer has apparently chosen (x_1, x_2) when she could have chosen (y_1, y_2), indicating that (x_1, x_2) was preferred to (y_1, y_2), but then she chose (y_1, y_2) when she could have chosen (x_1, x_2)—indicating the opposite!

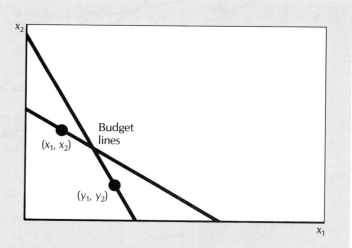

Figure 7.4   **Violation of the Weak Axiom of Revealed Preference.** A consumer who chooses both (x_1, x_2) and (y_1, y_2) violates the Weak Axiom of Revealed Preference.

Clearly, this consumer cannot be a maximizing consumer. Either the consumer is not choosing the best bundle she can afford, or there is some other aspect of the choice problem that has changed that we have not observed. Perhaps the consumer's tastes, or some other aspect of her economic environment, have changed. In any event, a violation of this sort is not consistent with the model of consumer choice in an unchanged environment.

The theory of consumer choice implies that such observations will not occur. If the consumers are choosing the best things they can afford, then things that are affordable, but not chosen, must be worse that what is chosen. Economists have formulated this simple point in a basic axiom of consumer theory:

Weak Axiom of Revealed Preference (WARP). *If (x_1, x_2) is directly revealed preferred to (y_1, y_2), and the two bundles are not the same, then it cannot happen that (y_1, y_2) is directly revealed preferred to (x_1, x_2).*

In other words, if a bundle (x_1, x_2) is purchased at prices (p_1, p_2), and a different bundle (y_1, y_2) is purchased at prices (q_1, q_2), then if

$$p_1 x_1 + p_2 x_2 \geq p_1 y_1 + p_2 y_2$$

it must *not* the case that

$$q_1 y_1 + q_2 y_2 \geq q_1 x_1 + q_2 x_2.$$

In English: if the y-bundle is affordable when the x-bundle is purchased, then when the y-bundle is purchased, the x-bundle must not be affordable.

The consumer in Figure 7.4 has *violated* WARP. Thus we know that this consumer's behavior could not have been maximizing behavior.[1]

There is no set of indifference curves that could be drawn in Figure 7.4 that could make both bundles maximizing bundles. On the other hand the consumer in Figure 7.5 satisfies WARP. Here it is possible to find indifference curves for which his behavior is optimal behavior. One possible choice of indifference curves is illustrated.

Optional   ## 7.5 Checking WARP

It is important to understand that WARP is a condition that must be satisfied by a consumer who is always choosing the best things he or she can afford. The Weak Axiom of Revealed Preference is a logical implication of

---

[1] Could we say his behavior is WARPed? Well, we could, but not in polite company.

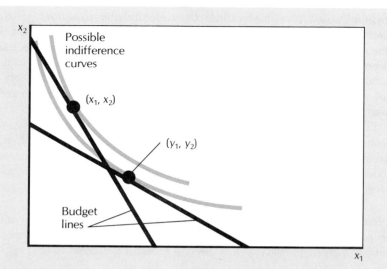

Figure
7.5

Satisfying WARP. Consumer choices that satisfy the Weak Axiom of Revealed Preference and some possible indifference curves.

that model, and can therefore be used to check whether or not a particular consumer, or an economic entity that we might want to model as a consumer, is consistent with our economic model.

Let's consider how we would go about systematically testing WARP in practice. Suppose that we observe several choices of bundles of goods at different prices. Let us use (p_1^t, p_2^t) to denote the tth observation of prices and (x_1^t, x_2^t) to denote the tth observation of choices. To use a specific example, let's take the data in Table 7.1.

Table
7.1

Some consumption data.

Observation	p_1	p_2	x_1	x_2
1	1	2	1	2
2	2	1	2	1
3	1	1	2	2

Given these data, we can compute how much it would cost the consumer to purchase each bundle of goods at each different set of prices, as we've done in Table 7.2. You should check a few entries of this table to see where they come from. For example, the entry in row 3, column 1 measures how much money the consumer would have to spend at the third set of prices to purchase the first bundle of goods.

Cost of each bundle at each set of prices.

Table 7.2

		Bundles		
		1	2	3
Prices	1	5	4*	6
	2	4*	5	6
	3	3*	3*	4

The diagonal terms in Table 7.2 measure how much money the consumer is spending at each choice. The entries in each row measure how much she would have spent if she purchased a different bundle. Thus we can see whether bundle 3, say, is revealed preferred to bundle 1, by seeing if the entry in row 3, column 1 (how much the consumer would have to spend at the third set of prices to purchase the first bundle) is less than the entry in row 3, column 3 (how much the consumer actually spent at the third set of prices to purchase the third bundle). In this particular case, bundle 1 was affordable when bundle 3 was purchased, which means that bundle 3 is revealed preferred to bundle 1. Thus we put a star in row 3, column 1 of the table.

From a mathematical point of view, we simply put a star in the entry in row s, column t if the number in that entry is less than the number in row s, column s.

In terms of this table, a violation of WARP is two observations t and s such that row t and column s contains a star *and* row s and column t contains a star. We can now use a computer (or a research assistant) to check and see whether there are any pairs of observations like these in the observed choices. If there are, the choices are inconsistent with the economic theory of the consumer. Either the theory is wrong for this particular consumer, or something else has changed in the consumer's environment that we have not controlled for. Thus the Weak Axiom of Revealed Preference gives us an easily checkable condition for whether some observed choices are consistent with the economic theory of the consumer.

In Table 7.2 we observe that row 1, column 2 contains a star and row 2, column 1 contains a star. This means that observation 2 could have been chosen when the consumer actually chose observation 1 and vice versa. This is a violation of the Weak Axiom of Revealed Preference. We can conclude that the data depicted in Tables 7.1 and 7.2 could not be generated by a consumer with stable preferences who was always choosing the best things he or she could afford.

7.6 The Strong Axiom of Revealed Preference

The Weak Axiom of Revealed Preference described in the last section gives us an observable condition that must be satisfied by all optimizing consumers. But there is a stronger condition that is sometimes useful.

We have already noted that if a bundle of goods X is revealed preferred to a bundle Y, and Y is in turn revealed preferred to a bundle Z then X must in fact be preferred to Z. If the consumer has consistent preferences, then we should never observe a sequence of choices that would reveal that Z was preferred to X.

The Weak Axiom of Revealed Preference required that if X is *directly* revealed preferred to Y then we should never observe Y being *directly* revealed preferred to X. The **Strong Axiom of Revealed Preference** requires that the same sort of condition hold for *indirect* revealed preference. More formally, we have:

Strong Axiom of Revealed Preference (SARP). *If (x_1, x_2) is revealed preferred to (y_1, y_2) (either directly or indirectly) and (y_1, y_2) is different from (x_1, x_2), then (y_1, y_2) cannot be directly or indirectly revealed preferred to (x_1, x_2).*

It is clear that if the observed behavior is optimizing behavior then it must satisfy the Strong Axiom. For if the consumer is optimizing and (x_1, x_2) is revealed preferred to (y_1, y_2), either directly or indirectly, then it must be the case that $(x_1, x_2) \succ (y_1, y_2)$. So having (x_1, x_2) revealed preferred to (y_1, y_2) *and* (y_1, y_2) revealed preferred to (x_1, x_2) would imply that $(x_1, x_2) \succ (y_1, y_2)$ *and* $(y_1, y_2) \succ (x_1, x_2)$ which is a contradiction. We can conclude that either the consumer must not be optimizing, or some other aspect of the consumer's environment—such as tastes, other prices, etc.—must have changed.

Thus SARP is a *necessary* implication of optimizing behavior: if a consumer is always choosing the best things that he can afford, then his observed behavior must satisfy SARP. What is more surprising is that any behavior satisfying the Strong Axiom can be thought of as being generated by optimizing behavior in the following sense: if the observed choices satisfy SARP, we can always find nice well-behaved preferences that *could have* generated the observed choices. In this sense SARP is a *sufficient* condition for optimizing behavior: if the observed choices satisfy SARP, then it is always possible to find preferences for which the observed behavior is optimizing behavior. The proof of this claim is unfortunately beyond the scope of this book, but appreciation of its importance is not.

What it means is that SARP gives us *all* of the restrictions on behavior imposed by the model of the optimizing consumer. For if the observed choices satisfy SARP we can "construct" preferences that could have generated these choices. Thus SARP is both a necessary and a sufficient condition for observed choices to be compatible with the economic model of consumer choice.

Does this prove that the constructed preferences actually generated the observed choices? Of course not. As with any scientific statement, we can only show that observed behavior is not inconsistent with the statement. We can't prove that the economic model is correct; we can just determine the implications of that model and see if observed choices are consistent with those implications.

Optional ## 7.7 How to Check SARP

Let us suppose that we have a table like the one described in Table 7.2 that has a star in row t and column s if observation t is directly revealed preferred to observation s. How can we use this table to check SARP?

The easiest way is first to transform the table. An example is given in Table 7.3. This is a table just like Table 7.2, but using a different set of numbers. Here the stars indicate direct revealed preference. The star in parentheses will be explained below.

How to check SARP.   Table 7.3

		Bundles		
		1	2	3
Prices	1	20	10*	22$^{(*)}$
	2	21	20	15*
	3	12	15	10

Now we systematically look through the entries of the table and see if there are any *chains* of observations that make some bundle indirectly revealed preferred to that one. For example, bundle 1 is directly revealed preferred to bundle 2 since there is a star in row 1, column 2. And bundle 2 is directly revealed preferred to bundle 3, since there is a star in row 2, column 3. Therefore bundle 1 is *indirectly* revealed preferred to bundle 3, and we indicate this by putting a star (in parentheses) in row 1, column 3.

In general, if we have many observations, we will have to look for chains of arbitrary length to see if one observation is indirectly revealed preferred to another. Although it may not be exactly obvious how to do this, it turns out that there are simple computer programs that can calculate the indirect revealed preference relation from the table describing the direct revealed preference relation. The computer can put a star in location st of the table if observation s is revealed preferred to observation t by any chain of other observations.

Once we have done this calculation, we can easily test for SARP. We just see if there is a situation where there is a star in entry ts *and* also a star in entry st. If so, we have found a situation where observation t is revealed preferred to observation s, either directly or indirectly, and, at the same time, observation s is revealed preferred to observation t. This is a violation of the Strong Axiom of Revealed Preference.

On the other hand, if we do not find such violations, then we know that the observations we have made are consistent with the economic theory of the consumer. These observations could have been made by an optimizing consumer with well-behaved preferences. Thus we have a completely operational test for whether or not a particular consumer is acting in a way consistent with economic theory.

This is important, since we can model several kinds of economic units as behaving like consumers. Think, for example, of a household consisting of several people. Will its consumption choices maximize "household utility"? If we have some data on household consumption choices, we can use the Strong Axiom of Revealed Preference to see. Another economic unit that we might think of as acting like a consumer is a nonprofit organization like a hospital or a university. Do universities maximize a utility function in making their economic choices? If we have a list of the economic choices that a university makes when faced with different prices, we can, in principle, answer this kind of question.

7.8 Index Numbers

Suppose that we examine the consumption bundles of a consumer at two different times. At time t prices are (p_1^t, p_2^t) and the consumer chooses (x_1^t, x_2^t). At some other time s, the prices are (p_1^s, p_2^s) and the consumer's choice is (x_1^s, x_2^s). We might want to ask how the "average" consumption of the consumer has changed.

If we let w_1 and w_2 be some "weights" that go into making an average, then we can look at the following kind of quantity index:

$$I_q = \frac{w_1 x_1^t + w_2 x_2^t}{w_1 x_1^s + w_2 x_2^s}.$$

If I_q is greater than 1 we can say that the "average" consumption has gone up in the movement from s to t, and if I_q is less than 1 we can say that the "average" consumption has gone down.

The question is, what do we use for the weights? A natural choice is to use the prices of the goods in question, since they measure in some sense the relative importance of the two goods. But there are two sets of prices here; which should we use?

If we use the s period prices for the weights, we have something called a **Laspeyres** index, and if we use the t period prices, we have something called a **Paasche** index. Both of these indices answer the question of what has happened to "average" consumption, but they just use different weights in the averaging process.

Substituting the t period prices for the weights, we see that the **Paasche quantity index** is given by

$$P_q = \frac{p_1^t x_1^t + p_2^t x_2^t}{p_1^t x_1^s + p_2^t x_2^s}$$

and substituting the s period prices shows that the **Laspeyres quantity index** is given by

$$L_q = \frac{p_1^s x_1^t + p_2^s x_2^t}{p_1^s x_1^s + p_2^s x_2^s}.$$

It turns out that the magnitude of the Laspeyres and Paasche indices can tell us something quite interesting about the consumer's welfare. Suppose that we have a situation where the Paasche quantity index is greater than 1:

$$P_q = \frac{p_1^t x_1^t + p_2^t x_2^t}{p_1^t x_1^s + p_2^t x_2^s} > 1.$$

What can we conclude about how well-off the consumer is at time t as compared to his situation at time s?

The answer is provided by revealed preference. Just cross multiply this inequality to give

$$p_1^t x_1^t + p_2^t x_2^t > p_1^t x_1^s + p_2^t x_2^s$$

which immediately shows that the consumer must be better off at t than at s, since he could have consumed the s consumption bundle in the t situation but chose not to do so.

What if the Paasche index is *less* than 1? Then we would have

$$p_1^t x_1^t + p_2^t x_2^t < p_1^t x_1^s + p_2^t x_2^s$$

which says that when the consumer chose the t bundle, the s bundle was not affordable. But that doesn't say anything about the consumer's ranking of the bundles. Just because something costs more than you can afford doesn't mean that you prefer it to what you're consuming now.

What about the Laspeyres index? It works in a similar way. Suppose that the Laspeyres index is *less* than 1:

$$L_q = \frac{p_1^s x_1^t + p_2^s x_2^t}{p_1^s x_1^s + p_2^s x_2^s} < 1.$$

Cross multiplying yields

$$p_1^s x_1^s + p_2^s x_2^s > p_1^s x_1^t + p_2^s x_2^t$$

which says that the s bundle is revealed preferred to the t bundle. Thus the consumer is better off at s than at t.

7.9 Price Indices

Price indices work in much the same way. In general, a price index will be a weighted average of prices:

$$I_p = \frac{p_1^t w_1 + p_2^t w_2}{p_1^s w_1 + p_2^s w_2}.$$

In this case it is natural to choose the quantities as the weights for computing the averages. We get two different indices, depending on our choice of weights. If we choose the t period quantities for weights, we get the **Paasche price index**:

$$P_p = \frac{p_1^t x_1^t + p_2^t x_2^t}{p_1^s x_1^t + p_2^s x_2^t}$$

and if we choose the s period quantities we get the **Laspeyres price index**:

$$L_p = \frac{p_1^t x_1^s + p_2^t x_2^s}{p_1^s x_1^s + p_2^s x_2^s}.$$

Suppose that the Paasche price index is less than 1; what does revealed preference have to say about the welfare situation of the consumer in periods t and s?

Revealed preference doesn't say anything at all. The problem is that there are now different prices in the numerator and the denominator of the fractions defining the indices, so the revealed preference comparison can't be made.

Let's define a new index of the change in total expenditure by

$$M = \frac{p_1^t x_1^t + p_2^t x_2^t}{p_1^s x_1^s + p_2^s x_2^s}.$$

This is the ratio of total expenditure in period t to the total expenditure in period s.

Now suppose that you are told that the Paasche price index was greater than M. This means that

$$P_p = \frac{p_1^t x_1^t + p_2^t x_2^t}{p_1^s x_1^t + p_2^s x_2^t} > \frac{p_1^t x_1^t + p_2^t x_2^t}{p_1^s x_1^s + p_2^s x_2^s}.$$

Canceling the numerators from each side of this expression and cross multiplying, we have

$$p_1^s x_1^s + p_2^s x_2^s > p_1^s x_1^t + p_2^s x_2^t.$$

This This statement says that the bundle chosen at year s is revealed preferred to the bundle chosen at year t. This analysis implies that if the Paasche price index is greater than the expenditure index, then the consumer must be better off in year s than in year t.

This is quite intuitive. After all, if prices rise by more than income rises in the movement from s to t, we would expect that would tend to make the consumer worse off. The revealed preference analysis given above confirms this intuition.

A similar statement can be made for the Laspeyres price index. If the Laspeyres price index is less than M, then the consumer must be better off in year t than in year s. Again, this simply confirms the intuitive idea that if prices rise less than income, the consumer would become better off. In the case of price indices, what matters is not whether the index is greater or less than one, but whether it is greater or less than the expenditure index.

EXAMPLE: Indexing Social Security Payments

Many elderly people have Social Security payments as their sole source of income. Because of this, there have been attempts to adjust Social Security payments in a way that will keep purchasing power constant even when prices change. Since the amount of payments will then depend on the movement of some price index or cost-of-living index, this kind of scheme is referred to as **indexing**.

One indexing proposal goes as follows. In some year t, the base year, economists measure the average consumption bundle of senior citizens. In each subsequent year the Social Security system adjusts payments so that the "purchasing power" of the average senior citizen remains constant in the sense that the average Social Security recipient is just able to afford the consumption bundle available in year t, as depicted in Figure 7.6.

One curious result of this indexing scheme is that the average senior citizen will almost always be better off than he or she was in the base year t. Suppose that year t is chosen as the base year for the price index. Then the bundle (x_1^t, x_2^t) is the optimal bundle at the prices (p_1^t, p_2^t). This means that the budget line at prices (p_1^t, p_2^t) must be tangent to the indifference curve through (x_1^t, x_2^t).

Now suppose that prices change. To be specific, suppose that prices increase so that the budget line, in the absence of Social Security, would shift inward and tilt. The inward shift is due to the increase in prices; the tilt is due to the change in relative prices. The indexing program would then increase the Social Security payment so as to make the original bundle

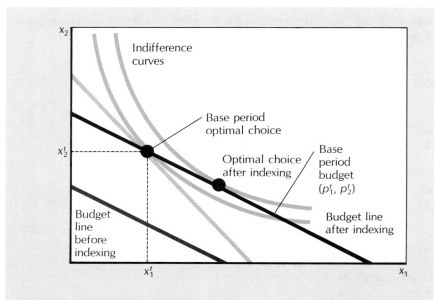

Figure
7.6

Social Security.   Changing prices will typically make the
consumer better off than in the base year.

(x_1^t, x_2^t) affordable at the new prices. But this means that the budget line
would cut the indifference curve, and there would be some other bundle
on the budget line that would be strictly preferred to (x_1^t, x_2^t). Thus the
consumer would typically be able to choose a better bundle than he or she
chose in the base year.

Summary

1. If one bundle is chosen when another could have been chosen, we say
that the first bundle is revealed preferred to the second.

2. If the consumer is always choosing the most preferred bundles he or she
can afford, this means that the chosen bundles must be preferred to the
bundles that were affordable but weren't chosen.

3. Observing the choices of consumers can allow us to "recover" or estimate the preferences that lie behind those choices. The more choices we
observe, the more precisely we can estimate the underlying preferences that
generated those choices.

4. The Weak Axiom of Revealed Preference (WARP) and the Strong Axiom of Revealed Preference (SARP) are necessary conditions that consumer

choices have to obey if they are to be consistent with the economic model of optimizing choice.

Review Questions

1. When prices are $(p_1, p_2) = (1, 2)$ a consumer demands $(x_1, x_2) = (1, 2)$ and when prices are $(q_1, q_2) = (2, 1)$ the consumer demands $(y_1, y_2) = (2, 1)$. Is this behavior consistent with the model of maximizing behavior?

2. When prices are $(p_1, p_2) = (2, 1)$ a consumer demands $(x_1, x_2) = (1, 2)$ and when prices are $(q_1, q_2) = (1, 2)$ the consumer demands $(y_1, y_2) = (2, 1)$. Is this behavior consistent with the model of maximizing behavior?

3. In the preceding exercise, which bundle is preferred by the consumer, the x-bundle or the y-bundle?

4. We saw that the Social Security adjustment for changing prices would typically make recipients at least as well-off as they were at the base year. What kind of price changes would leave them just as well-off, no matter what kind of preferences they had?

5. In the same framework as the above question, what kind of preferences would leave the consumer just as well-off as he was in the base year, for *all* price changes?

8

SLUTSKY EQUATION

Economists often are concerned with how a consumer's behavior changes in response to changes in the economic environment. The case we want to consider in this chapter is how a consumer's choice of a good responds to changes in its price. It is natural to think that when the price of a good rises the demand for it will fall. However, as we saw in Chapter 6 it is possible to construct examples where the optimal demand for a good *decreases* when its price falls. A good that has this property is called a **Giffen good**.

Giffen goods are pretty peculiar, and are primarily a theoretical curiosity, but there are other situations where changes in prices might have "perverse" effects that, on reflection, turn out to be not so unreasonable. For example, we normally think that if people get a higher wage they will work more. But what if your wage went from $10 an hour to $1000 an hour? Would you really work more? Might you not decide to work fewer hours and use some of the money you've earned to do other things? What if your wage were $1,000,000 an hour? Wouldn't you work less?

For another example, think of what happens to your demand for apples when the price goes up. You would probably consume fewer apples. But how about a family who grew apples to sell? If the price of apples went up, their income might go up so much that they would feel that they could now afford to consume more of their own apples. For the consumers in this family, an increase in the price of apples might well lead to an increase in the consumption of apples.

What is going on here? How is it that changes in price can have these ambiguous effects on demand? In this chapter and the next we'll try to sort out these effects.

8.1 The Substitution Effect

When the price of a good changes, there are two sorts of effects: the rate at which you can exchange one good for another changes, and the total purchasing power of your income is altered. If, for example, the price of good 1 becomes cheaper, it means that you have to give up less of good 2 to purchase good 1. The change in the price of good 1 has changed the rate at which the market allows you to "substitute" good 2 for good 1. The trade-off between the two goods that the market presents the consumer has changed.

At the same time, if the price of good 1 becomes cheaper it means that your money income will buy more of good 1. The purchasing power of your money has gone up; although the number of dollars you have is the same, the amount that they will buy has increased.

The first part—the change in demand due to the change in the rate of exchange between the two goods—is called the **substitution effect**. The second effect—the change in demand due to having more purchasing power—is called the **income effect.** These are only rough definitions of the two effects. In order to give a more precise definition we have to consider the two effects in greater detail.

The way that we will do this is to break the price movement into two steps: first we will let the *relative* prices change and adjust money income so as to hold purchasing power constant, then we will let purchasing power adjust while holding the relative prices constant.

This is best explained by referring to Figure 8.1. Here we have a situation where the price of good 1 has declined. This means that the budget line rotates around the vertical intercept m/p_2 and becomes flatter. We can break this movement of the budget line up into two steps: first *pivot* the budget line around the *original* demanded bundle, and then *shift* the pivoted line out to the *new* demanded bundle.

This "pivot–shift" operation gives us a convenient way to decompose the change in demand into two pieces. The first step—the pivot—is a movement where the slope of the budget line changes while its purchasing power stays constant, while the second step is a movement where the slope stays constant and the purchasing power changes. This decomposition is only a hypothetical construction—the consumer simply observes a change in price and chooses a new bundle of goods in response. But in analyzing how the consumer's choice changes, it is useful to think of the budget line

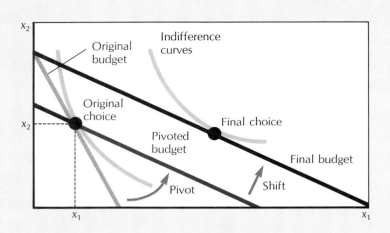

Figure
8.1

Pivot and shift. When the price of good 1 changes and income stays fixed, the budget line pivots around the vertical axis. We will view this adjustment as occurring in two stages: first pivot the budget line around the *original* choice, and then shift this line outward to the new demanded bundle.

changing in two stages—first the pivot, then the shift.

What are the economic meanings of the pivoted and the shifted budget lines? Let us first consider the pivoted line. Here we have a budget line with the same slope and thus the same relative prices as the final budget line. However, the money income associated with this budget line is different since the vertical intercept is different. Since the original consumption bundle (x_1, x_2) lies on the pivoted budget line, that consumption bundle is just affordable. In this sense, the purchasing power of the consumer has remained constant in the sense that the original bundle of goods is just affordable at the new pivoted line.

Let us calculate how much we have to adjust money income so as to keep the old bundle just affordable. Let m' be the amount of money income that will just make the original consumption bundle affordable; this will be the amount of money income associated with the pivoted budget line. Since (x_1, x_2) is affordable at both (p_1, p_2, m) and (p'_1, p_2, m'), we have

$$m' = p'_1 x_1 + p_2 x_2$$
$$m = p_1 x_1 + p_2 x_2.$$

Subtracting the second equation from the first gives

$$m' - m = x_1[p'_1 - p_1].$$

This equation says that the change in money income necessary to make the old bundle affordable at the new prices is just the original amount of consumption of good 1 times the change in prices.

Letting $\Delta p_1 = p'_1 - p_1$ represent the change in price 1, and $\Delta m = m' - m$ represent the change in income necessary to make the old bundle just affordable, we have

$$\Delta m = x_1 \Delta p_1. \tag{8.1}$$

Note that the change in income and the change in price will always move in the same direction: if the price goes up, then we have to raise income to keep the same bundle affordable.

Let's use some actual numbers. Suppose that the consumer is originally consuming 20 candy bars a week, and that candy bars cost 50 cents a piece. If the price of candy bars goes up by 10 cents—so that $\Delta p_1 = .60 - .50 = .10$—how much would income have to change to make the old consumption bundle affordable?

We can apply the formula given above. If the consumer had \$2.00 more income, he would just be able to consume the same number of candy bars, namely, 20. In terms of the formula:

$$\Delta m = \Delta p_1 \times x_1 = .10 \times 20 = \$2.00.$$

Now we have a formula for the pivoted budget line: it is just the budget line at the new price with income changed by Δm. Note that if the price of good 1 goes down, then the adjustment in income will be negative. When a price goes down, a consumer's purchasing power goes up, so we will have to decrease the consumer's income in order to keep purchasing power fixed. Similarly, when a price goes up, purchasing power goes down, so the change in income necessary to keep purchasing power constant must be positive.

Although (x_1, x_2) is still affordable, it is not generally the optimal purchase at the pivoted budget line. In Figure 8.2 we have denoted the optimal purchase on the pivoted budget line by Y. This bundle of goods is the optimal bundle of goods when we change the price and then adjust dollar income so as to keep the old bundle of goods just affordable. The movement from X to Y is known as the **substitution effect**. It indicates how the consumer "substitutes" one good for the other when a price changes but purchasing power remains constant.

More precisely, the substitution effect, Δx_1^s, is the change in the demand for good 1 when the price of good 1 changes to p'_1 and, at the same time, money income changes to m':

$$\Delta x_1^s = x_1(p'_1, m') - x_1(p_1, m).$$

In order to determine the substitution effect, we must use the consumer's demand function to calculate the optimal choices at (p'_1, m') and (p_1, m). The change in the demand for good 1 may be large or small, depending

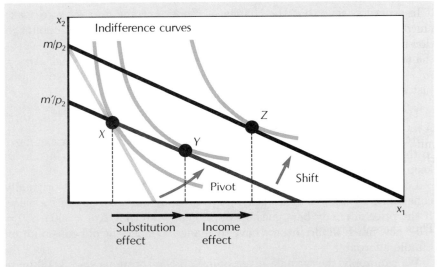

Figure
8.2 **Substitution effect and income effect.** The pivot gives the substitution effect and the shift gives the income effect.

on the shape of the consumer's indifference curves. But given the demand function, it is easy to just plug in the numbers to calculate the substitution effect. (Of course the demand for good 1 may well depend on the price of good 2; but the price of good 2 is being held constant during this exercise, so we've left it out of the demand function so as not to clutter the notation.)

The substitution effect is sometimes called the change in **compensated demand.** The idea is that the consumer is being compensated for a price rise by having enough income given back to him to purchase his old bundle. Of course if the price goes down he is "compensated" by having money taken away from him. We'll generally stick with the "substitution" terminology, for consistency, but the "compensation" terminology is also widely used.

EXAMPLE: Calculating the Substitution Effect

Suppose that the consumer has a demand function for milk of the form

$$x_1 = 10 + \frac{m}{10p_1}.$$

Originally his income is $120 per week and the price of milk is $3 per quart. Thus his demand for milk will be $10 + 120/(10 \times 3) = 14$ quarts per week.

Now suppose that the price of milk falls to $2 per quart. Then his demand at this new price will be $10 + 120/(10 \times 2) = 16$ quarts of milk per week. The *total* change in demand is $+2$ quarts a week.

In order to calculate the substitution effect, we must first calculate how much income would have to change in order to make the original consumption of milk just affordable when the price of milk is \$2 a quart. We apply the formula (8.1):

$$\Delta m = x_1 \Delta p_1 = 14 \times (2 - 3) = -\$14.$$

Thus the level of income necessary to keep purchasing power constant is $m' = m + \Delta m = 120 - 14 = 106$. What is the consumer's demand for milk at the new price, \$2 per quart, and this level of income? Just plug the numbers into the demand function to find

$$x_1(p'_1, m') = x_1(2, 106) = 10 + \frac{106}{10 \times 2} = 15.3.$$

Thus the substitution effect is

$$\Delta x_1^s = x_1(2, 106) - x_1(3, 120) = 15.3 - 14 = 1.3.$$

8.2 The Income Effect

We turn now to the second stage of the price adjustment—the shift movement. This is also easy to interpret economically. We know that a parallel shift of the budget line is the movement that occurs when income changes while relative prices remain constant. Thus the second stage of the price adjustment is called the **income effect**. We simply increase the consumer's income from m' to m, keeping the prices constant at (p'_1, p_2). In Figure 8.2 this change moves us from the point (y_1, y_2) to (z_1, z_2). It is natural to call this last movement the income effect since all we are doing is changing income while holding the prices constant.

More precisely, the income effect, Δx_1^n, is the change in the demand for good 1 when we change income from m' to m, holding the price of good 1 fixed at p'_1:

$$\Delta x_1^n = x_1(p'_1, m) - x_1(p'_1, m').$$

We have already considered the income effect earlier in section 6.1. There we saw that the income effect can operate either way: it will tend to increase or decrease the demand for good 1 depending on whether we have a normal good or an inferior good.

When the price of a good decreases, we need to decrease income in order to keep purchasing power constant. If the good is a normal good, then this decrease in income will lead to a decrease in demand. If the good is an inferior good, then the decrease in income will lead to an increase in demand.

EXAMPLE: Calculating the Income Effect

In the example given earlier in this chapter we saw that

$$x_1(p_1', m) = x_1(2, 120) = 16$$
$$x_1(p_1', m') = x_1(2, 106) = 15.3.$$

Thus the income effect for this problem is

$$\Delta x_1^n = x_1(2, 120) - x_1(2, 106) = 16 - 15.3 = 0.7.$$

Since milk is a normal good for this consumer, the demand for milk increases when income increases.

8.3 Sign of the Substitution Effect

We have seen above that the income effect can be positive or negative, depending on whether the good is a normal good or an inferior good. What about the substitution effect? If the price of a good goes down, as in Figure 8.2, then the change in the demand for the good due to the substitution effect *must* be nonnegative. That is, if $p_1 > p_1'$, then we *must* have $x_1(p_1', m') \geq x_1(p_1, m)$, so that $\Delta x_1^s \geq 0$.

The proof of this goes as follows. Consider the points on the pivoted budget line in Figure 8.2 where the amount of good 1 consumed is less than at the bundle X. These bundles were all affordable at the old prices (p_1, p_2) but they weren't purchased. Instead the bundle X was purchased. If the consumer is always choosing the best bundle he can afford, then X must be preferred to all of the bundles on the part of the pivoted line that lies inside the original budget set.

This means that the optimal choice on the pivoted budget line must not be one of the bundles that lies underneath the original budget line. The optimal choice on the pivoted line would have to be either X or some point to the right of X. But this means that the new optimal choice must involve consuming at least as much of good 1 as originally, just as we wanted to show. In the case illustrated in Figure 8.2, the optimal choice at the pivoted budget line is the bundle Y, which certainly involves consuming more of good 1 than at the original consumption point, X.

The substitution effect always moves opposite to the price movement. We say that *the substitution effect is negative*, since the change in demand due to the substitution effect is opposite to the change in price: if the price moves up, the demand for the good due to the substitution effect decreases.

8.4 The Total Change in Demand

The total change in demand, Δx_1, is the change in demand due to the change in price, holding income constant:

$$\Delta x_1 = x_1(p_1', m) - x_1(p_1, m).$$

We have seen above how this change can be broken up into two changes: the substitution effect and the income effect. In terms of the symbols defined above,

$$\Delta x_1 = \Delta x_1^s + \Delta x_1^n$$
$$x_1(p_1', m) - x_1(p_1, m) = [x_1(p_1', m') - x_1(p_1, m)]$$
$$+ [x_1(p_1', m) - x_1(p_1', m')].$$

In words this equation says that the total change in demand equals the substitution effect plus the income effect. This equation is called the **Slutsky identity**.[1] Note that it is an identity: it is true for all values of p_1, p_1', m, and m'. The first and fourth terms on the right-hand side cancel out, so the right-hand side is *identically* equal to the left-hand side.

The content of the Slutsky identity is not just the algebraic identity—that is a mathematical triviality. The content comes in the interpretation of the two terms on the right-hand side: the substitution effect and the income effect. In particular, we can use what we know about the signs of the income and substitution effects to determine the sign of the total effect.

While the substitution effect must always be negative—opposite the change in the price—the income effect can go either way. Thus the total effect may be positive or negative. However, if we have a normal good then the substitution effect and the income effect work in the same direction. An increase in price means that demand will go down due to the substitution effect. If the price goes up, that is like a decrease in income, which, for a normal good, means a decrease in demand. Both effects reinforce each other. In terms of our notation, the change in demand due to a price increase for a normal good means that

$$\Delta x_1 = \Delta x_1^s + \Delta x_1^n$$
$$(-) \quad (-) \quad (-) \quad.$$

(The minus signs beneath each term indicate that each term in this expression is negative.)

Note carefully the sign on the income effect. Since we are considering

[1] Named for Eugene Slutsky (1880–1948) a Russian economist who investigated demand theory.

a situation where the price rises, this implies a decrease in purchasing power—for a normal good this will imply a decrease in demand.

On the other hand, if we have an inferior good, it might happen that the income effect outweighs the substitution effect so that the total change in demand associated with a price increase is actually positive. This would be a case where

$$\Delta x_1 = \Delta x_1^s + \Delta x_1^n$$
$$(?) \quad (-) \quad (+)$$

If the second term on the right-hand side—the income effect—is large enough, the total change in demand could be positive. This would mean that an increase in price could result in an *increase* in demand. This is the perverse Giffen case described earlier: the increase in price has reduced the consumer's purchasing power so much that he has increased his consumption of the inferior good.

But the Slutsky identity shows that this kind of perverse effect can only occur for inferior goods: if a good is a normal good, then the income and substitution effects reinforce each other, so that the total change in demand is always in the "right" direction.

Thus a Giffen good must be an inferior good. But an inferior good is not necessarily a Giffen good: the income effect not only has to be of the "wrong" sign, it also has to be large enough to outweigh the "right" sign of the substitution effect. This is why Giffen goods are so rarely observed in real life: they would not only have to be inferior goods, but they would have to be *very* inferior.

This is illustrated graphically in Figure 8.3. Here we illustrate the usual pivot–shift operation to find the substitution effect and the income effect. In both cases, good 1 is an inferior good and the income effect is therefore negative. In Figure 8.3A, the income effect is large enough to outweigh the substitution effect and produce a Giffen good. In Figure 8.3B, the income effect is smaller, and thus good 1 responds in the ordinary way to the change in its price.

8.5 Rates of Change

We have seen that the income and substitution effects can be described graphically as a combination of pivots and shifts, or they can be described algebraically in the Slutsky identity

$$\Delta x_1 = \Delta x_1^s + \Delta x_1^n$$

which simply says that the total change in demand is the substitution effect plus the income effect. The Slutsky identity here is stated in terms of absolute changes, but it is more common to express it in terms of *rates* of change.

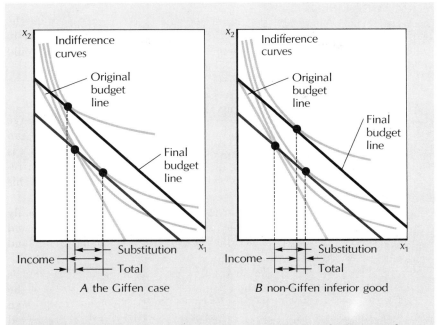

Inferior goods. Case (A) shows a good that is inferior enough to cause the Giffen case. Case (B) shows a good that is inferior, but the effect is not strong enough to create a Giffen good.

Figure
8.3

When we express the Slutsky identity in terms of rates of change it turns out to be convenient to define Δx_1^m to be the *negative* of the income effect:

$$\Delta x_1^m = x_1(p_1', m') - x_1(p_1', m) = -\Delta x_1^n.$$

Given this definition, the Slutsky identity becomes

$$\Delta x_1 = \Delta x_1^s - \Delta x_1^m.$$

If we divide each side of the identity by Δp_1, we have

$$\frac{\Delta x_1}{\Delta p_1} = \frac{\Delta x_1^s}{\Delta p_1} - \frac{\Delta x_1^m}{\Delta p_1}. \tag{8.2}$$

The first term on the right-hand side is the rate of change of demand when price changes and income is adjusted so as to keep the old bundle affordable—the substitution effect. Let's work on the second term. Since we have an income change in the numerator, it would be nice to get an income change in the denominator.

Remember that the income change, Δm, and the price change, Δp_1, are related by the formula

$$\Delta m = x_1 \Delta p_1.$$

Solving for Δp_1 we find

$$\Delta p_1 = \frac{\Delta m}{x_1}.$$

Now substitute this expression into the last term in (8.2) to get our final formula:

$$\frac{\Delta x_1}{\Delta p_1} = \frac{\Delta x_1^s}{\Delta p_1} - \frac{\Delta x_1^m}{\Delta m} x_1.$$

This is the Slutsky identity in terms of rates of change. We can interpret each term as follows:

$$\frac{\Delta x_1}{\Delta p_1} = \frac{x_1(p_1', m) - x_1(p_1, m)}{\Delta p_1}$$

is the rate of change in demand as price changes, holding income fixed;

$$\frac{\Delta x_1^s}{\Delta p_1} = \frac{x_1(p_1', m') - x_1(p_1, m)}{\Delta p_1}$$

is the rate of change in demand as the price changes, adjusting income so as to keep the old bundle just affordable, that is, the substitution effect; and

$$\frac{\Delta x_1^m}{\Delta m} x_1 = \frac{x_1(p_1', m') - x_1(p_1', m)}{m' - m} x_1$$

is the rate of change of demand holding prices fixed and adjusting income, that is, the income effect.

The income effect is itself composed of two pieces: how demand changes as income changes, times the original level of demand. When the price changes by Δp_1, the change in demand due to the income effect is

$$\Delta x_1^m = \frac{x_1(p_1', m') - x_1(p_1', m)}{\Delta m} x_1 \Delta p_1.$$

But this last term, $x_1 \Delta p_1$, is just the change in income necessary to keep the old bundle, Δm, feasible so the change in demand due to the income effect reduces to

$$\Delta x_1^m = \frac{x_1(p_1', m') - x_1(p_1', m)}{\Delta m} \Delta m$$

just as we had before.

8.6 The Law of Demand

In Chapter 5 we voiced some concerns over the fact that consumer theory seemed to have no particular content: demand could go up or down when a price increased, and demand could go up or down when income increased. If a theory doesn't restrict observed behavior in *some* fashion it isn't much of a theory. A model that is consistent with all behavior has no real content.

However, we know that consumer theory does have some content—we've seen that choices generated by an optimizing consumer must satisfy the Strong Axiom of Revealed Preference. Furthermore, we've seen that any price change can be decomposed into two changes: a substitution effect that is sure to be negative—opposite the direction of the price change— and an income effect whose sign depends on whether the good is a normal good or an inferior good.

Although consumer theory doesn't restrict how demand changes when price changes, or how demand changes when income changes, it does restrict how these two kinds of changes interact. In particular, we have:

The Law of Demand.   *If the demand for a good increases when income increases, then the demand for that good must decrease when its price increases.*

This follows directly from the Slutsky equation: if the demand increases when income increases, we have a normal good. And if we have a normal good, then the substitution effect and the income effect reinforce each other, and an increase in price will unambiguously reduce demand.

8.7 Examples of Income and Substitution Effects

Let's now consider some examples of price changes for particular kinds of preferences and decompose the demand changes into the income and the substitution effects.

We start with the case of perfect complements. The Slutsky decomposition is illustrated in Figure 8.4. When we pivot the budget line around the chosen point, the optimal choice at the new budget line is the same as at the old one—this means that the substitution effect is zero. The change in demand is due entirely to the income effect.

What about the case of perfect substitutes, illustrated in Figure 8.5? Here when we tilt the budget line, the demand bundle jumps from the vertical axis to the horizontal axis. There is no shifting left to do! The entire change in demand is due to the substitution effect.

As a third example, let us consider the case of quasilinear preferences. This situation is somewhat peculiar. We have already seen that a shift

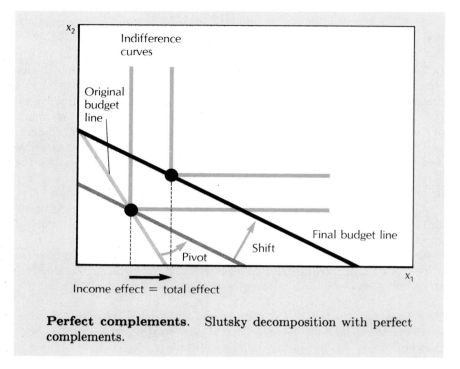

Figure 8.4

Perfect complements. Slutsky decomposition with perfect complements.

in income causes no change in demand for good 1 when preferences are quasilinear. This means that the entire change in demand is due to the substitution effect, and that the income effect is zero, as illustrated in Figure 8.6.

Optional

8.8 Slutsky Identity in Terms of Elasticity

The Slutsky identity is most commonly stated in terms of rates of change. But it is also sometimes seen expressed in elasticity terms. To convert the rates of change to elasticities, we first multiply both sides of the Slutsky equation by (p_1/x_1):

$$\frac{\Delta x_1}{\Delta p_1}\frac{p_1}{x_1} = \frac{\Delta x_1^s}{\Delta p_1}\frac{p_1}{x_1} - \frac{\Delta x_1^m}{\Delta m}x_1\frac{p_1}{x_1}$$

$$\epsilon_{11} = \epsilon_{11}^s - p_1\frac{\Delta x_1^m}{\Delta m}.$$

Here ϵ_{11} is the elasticity of the demand for good 1 with respect to its price, holding income fixed, and ϵ_{11}^s is the elasticity of good 1 with respect to its price, allowing income to adjust to keep the old bundle feasible—the **substitution elasticity**. (The substitution elasticity is sometimes called the **compensated elasticity**.)

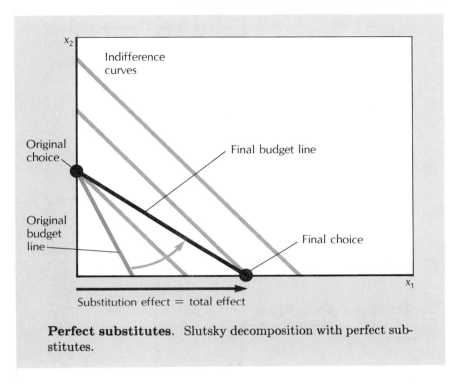

Perfect substitutes. Slutsky decomposition with perfect substitutes.

Figure
8.5

We can multiply the last term in this expression by $x_1 m / x_1 m = 1$ to get

$$p_1 \frac{\Delta x_1^m}{\Delta m} = \frac{p_1 x_1}{m} \frac{\Delta x_1^m}{\Delta m} \frac{m}{x_1}$$

$$= s_1 \eta_1$$

where s_1 is the share of good 1 in total expenditure $(p_1 x_1/m)$ and η_1 is the income elasticity of demand. Substituting this back into the previous formula, we have the final expression for the Slutsky equation in elasticity terms:

$$\epsilon_{11} = \epsilon_{11}^s - s_1 \eta_1.$$

EXAMPLE: Rebating a Tax

In 1974 the Organization of Petroleum Exporting Countries (OPEC) instituted an oil embargo against the United States. OPEC was able to stop oil shipments to U.S. ports for several weeks. The vulnerability of the U.S. to such disruptions was very disturbing to Congress and the president, and there were many plans proposed to reduce the U.S.'s dependence on foreign oil.

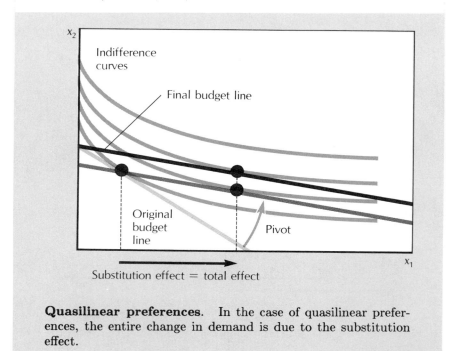

Figure
8.6   **Quasilinear preferences**.   In the case of quasilinear preferences, the entire change in demand is due to the substitution
effect.

One such plan involved increasing the gasoline tax. Increasing the cost
of gasoline to the consumers would make them reduce their consumption
of gasoline, and the reduced demand for gasoline would in turn reduce the
demand for foreign oil.

But a straight increase in the tax on gasoline would hit consumers where
it hurts—in the pocketbook—and by itself such a plan would be politically
infeasible. So it was suggested that the revenues raised from consumers by
this tax would be returned to the consumers in the form of direct money
payments, or via the reduction of some other tax.

Critics of this proposal argued that paying the revenue raised by the tax
back to the consumers would have no effect on demand since they could
just use the rebated money to purchase more gasoline. What does economic
analysis say about this plan?

Let us suppose, for simplicity, that the tax on gasoline would end up
being passed along entirely to the consumers of gasoline so that the price
of gasoline will go up by exactly the amount of the tax. (In general, only
part of the tax would be passed along, but we will ignore that complication
here.) Suppose that the tax would raise the price of gasoline from p to
$p' = p+t$ and the average consumer would respond by reducing his demand
from x to x'. The average consumer is paying t dollars more for gasoline,
and he is consuming x' gallons of gasoline after the tax is imposed, so the

amount of revenue raised by the tax from the average consumer would be

$$R = tx' = (p' - p)x'.$$

Note that the revenue raised by the tax will depend on how much gasoline the consumer *ends up* consuming, x', not how much he was initially consuming, x.

If we let y be the expenditure on all other goods, and set its price to be 1, then the original budget constraint is

$$px + y = m \qquad (8.3)$$

and the budget constraint in the presence of the tax–rebate plan is

$$(p + t)x' + y' = m + tx'. \qquad (8.4)$$

In budget constraint (8.4) the average consumer is choosing the left-hand side variables—the consumption of each good—but the right-hand side—his income and the rebate from the government—are taken as fixed. The rebate depends on what all consumers do, not what the average consumer does. In this case, the rebate turns out to be the taxes collected from the average consumer—but that's because he is average, not because of any causal connection.

If we cancel tx' from each side of equation (8.4) we have

$$px' + y' = m.$$

Thus (x', y') is a bundle that was affordable under the original budget constraint and rejected in favor of (x, y). Thus it must be that (x, y) is preferred to (x', y'): the consumers are made worse off by this plan. Perhaps that is why it was never put into effect!

The equilibrium with a rebated tax is depicted in Figure 8.7. The tax makes good 1 more expensive, and the rebate increases money income. The original bundle is no longer affordable, and the consumer is definitely made worse off. The consumer's choice under the tax–rebate plan involves consuming less gasoline, and more of "all other goods."

What can we say about the amount of consumption of gasoline? The average consumer could afford his old consumption of gasoline, but because of the tax, gasoline is now more expensive. In general, the consumer would choose to consume less of it.

8.9 Another Substitution Effect

The substitution effect is the name that economists give to the change in demand when prices change but a consumer's purchasing power is held

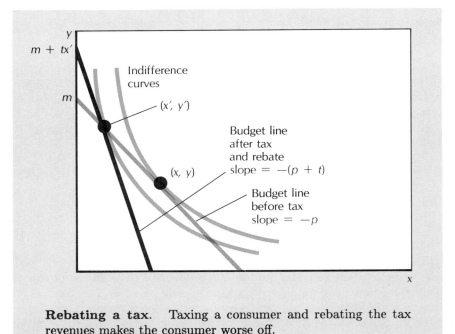

Figure
8.7

Rebating a tax. Taxing a consumer and rebating the tax revenues makes the consumer worse off.

constant, so that the original bundle remains affordable. At least this is *one* definition of the substitution effect. There is another definition that is also useful.

The definition we have studied above is called the **Slutsky substitution effect**. The definition we will describe in this section is called the **Hicks substitution effect**.[2]

Suppose that instead of pivoting the budget line around the original consumption bundle, we now *roll* the budget line around the indifference curve through the original consumption bundle, as depicted in Figure 8.8. In this way we present the consumer with a new budget line that has the same relative prices as the final budget line, but has different income. The purchasing power he has under this budget line will no longer be sufficient to purchase his original bundle of goods—but it will be sufficient to purchase a bundle that is just *indifferent* to his original bundle.

Thus the Hicks substitution effect keeps *utility* constant rather than keeping purchasing power constant. The Slutsky substitution effect gives the consumer just enough money to get back to his old level of consumption, while the Hicks substitution effect gives the consumer just enough money to get back to his old indifference curve. Despite this difference in defini-

---

[2] The concept is named for Sir John Hicks, an English recipient of the Nobel Prize in Economics.

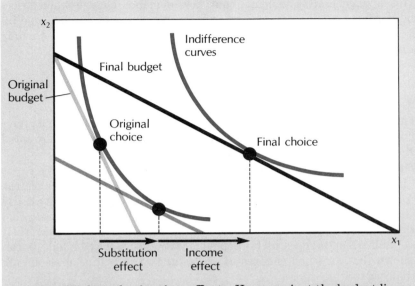

The Hicks substitution effect. Here we pivot the budget line around the indifference curve rather than around the original choice.

Figure 8.8

tion, it turns out that the Hicks substitution effect must be negative—in the sense that it is in a direction opposite that of the price change—just like the Slutsky substitution effect.

The proof is again by revealed preference. Let (x_1, x_2) be a demanded bundle at some prices (p_1, p_2) and let (y_1, y_2) be a demanded bundle at some other prices (q_1, q_2). Suppose that income is such that (x_1, x_2) is indifferent to (y_1, y_2). Since (x_1, x_2) is indifferent to (y_1, y_2) neither one can be revealed preferred to the other.

Using the definition of revealed preference, this means that the following two inequalities are *not* true:

$$p_1 x_1 + p_2 x_2 > p_1 y_1 + p_2 y_2$$

$$q_1 y_1 + q_2 y_2 > q_1 x_1 + q_2 x_2.$$

It follows that these inequalities *are* true:

$$p_1 x_1 + p_2 x_2 \leq p_1 y_1 + p_2 y_2$$

$$q_1 y_1 + q_2 y_2 \leq q_1 x_1 + q_2 x_2.$$

Adding these inequalities together and rearranging we have

$$(q_1 - p_1)(y_1 - x_1) + (q_2 - p_2)(y_2 - x_2) \leq 0.$$

This is a general statement about how demands change when prices change if income is adjusted so as to keep the consumer on the same indifference curve. In the particular case we are concerned with, we are only changing the first price. Therefore $q_2 = p_2$ and we are left with

$$(q_1 - p_1)(y_1 - x_1) \leq 0.$$

This equation says that the change in the quantity demanded must have the opposite sign from that of the price change, which is what we wanted to show.

The total change in demand is still equal to the substitution effect plus the income effect—but now it is the Hicks substitution effect. Since the Hicks substitution effect is also negative, the Slutsky equation takes exactly the same form as we had earlier, and has exactly the same interpretation. Both the Slutsky and Hicks definitions of the substitution effect have their place, and which is more useful depends on the problem at hand. It can be shown that for small changes in price, the two substitution effects are virtually identical.

Summary

1. When the price of a good decreases, there will be two effects on consumption. The change in relative prices makes the consumer want to consume more of the cheaper good. The increase in purchasing power due to the lower price may increase or decrease consumption, depending on whether the good is a normal good or an inferior good.

2. The change in demand due to the change in relative prices is called the substitution effect; the change due to the change in purchasing power is called the income effect.

3. The substitution effect is how demand changes when prices change and purchasing power is held constant, in the sense that the original bundle remains affordable. To hold real purchasing power constant, money income will have to change. The necessary change in money income is given by $\Delta m = x_1 \Delta p_1$.

4. The Slutsky equation says that the total change in demand is the sum of the substitution effect and the income effect.

5. The Law of Demand says that normal goods must have downward sloping demand curves.

Review Questions

1. Suppose that preferences are concave. Is it still the case that the substitution effect is negative?

2. Suppose that Fred's income elasticity of demand for soft drinks is 1, and that he spends 5 percent of his income on soft drinks. His price elasticity of demand for soft drinks is $-.2$. What is his substitution price elasticity?

3. In the case of the gasoline tax, what would happen if the rebate to the consumers were based on their original consumption of gasoline, x, rather than their final consumption of gasoline, x'?

4. In the case described in the previous question, would the government be paying out more or less than it received in tax revenues?

5. In this case would the consumers be better off or worse off if the tax with rebate based on original consumption were in effect?

APPENDIX

Let us derive the Slutsky equation using calculus. Consider the Slutsky definition of the substitution effect, in which the income is adjusted so as to give the consumer just enough to buy the original consumption bundle, which we will now denote by $(\bar{x}_1, \bar{x}_2)$. If the prices are (p_1, p_2), then the consumer's actual choice with this adjustment will depend on (p_1, p_2) and $(\bar{x}_1, \bar{x}_2)$. Let's call this relationship the **Slutsky demand function** for good 1, and write it as $x_1^s(p_1, p_2, \bar{x}_1, \bar{x}_2)$.

Suppose the original demanded bundle is $(\bar{x}_1, \bar{x}_2)$ at prices $(\bar{p}_1, \bar{p}_2)$ and income $\bar{m}$. The Slutsky demand function tells us what the consumer would demand facing some different prices (p_1, p_2) and having income $p_1 \bar{x}_1 + p_2 \bar{x}_2$. Thus the Slutsky demand function at $(p_1, p_2, \bar{x}_1, \bar{x}_2)$ is the ordinary demand at (p_1, p_2) and income $p_1 \bar{x}_1 + p_2 \bar{x}_2$. That is:

$$x_1^s(p_1, p_2, \bar{x}_1, \bar{x}_2) \equiv x_1(p_1, p_2, p_1 \bar{x}_1 + p_2 \bar{x}_2).$$

This equation says that the Slutsky demand at prices (p_1, p_2) is that amount that the consumer would demand if he had enough income to purchase his original bundle of goods $(\bar{x}_1, \bar{x}_2)$. This is just the definition of the Slutsky demand function.

Differentiating this identity, we have

$$\frac{\partial x_1^s(p_1, p_2, \bar{x}_1, \bar{x}_2)}{\partial p_1} = \frac{\partial x_1(p_1, p_2, \bar{m})}{\partial p_1} + \frac{\partial x_1(p_1, p_2, \bar{m})}{\partial m} \bar{x}_1.$$

Rearranging we have

$$\frac{\partial x_1(p_1,p_2,\overline{m})}{\partial p_1} = \frac{\partial x_1^s(p_1,p_2,\overline{x}_1,\overline{x}_2)}{\partial p_1} - \frac{\partial x_1(p_1,p_2,\overline{m})}{\partial m}\overline{x}_1.$$

Note the use of the chain rule in this calculation.

This is a derivative form of the Slutsky equation. It says that the total effect of a price change is composed of a substitution effect (where income is adjusted to keep the bundle $(\overline{x}_1,\overline{x}_2)$ feasible), and an income effect. We know from the text that the substitution effect is negative, and the sign of the income effect depends on whether the good in question is inferior or not. As you can see, this is just the form of the Slutsky equation considered in the text, except we have replaced the Δ's with derivative signs.

What about the Hicks substitution effect? It is also possible to define a Slutsky equation for it. We let $x_1^h(p_1,p_2,\overline{u})$ be the *Hicksian* demand function, which measures how much the consumer demands of good 1 at prices (p_1,p_2) if income is adjusted to keep the level of *utility* constant at the original level $\overline{u}$. It turns out that in this case the Slutsky equation takes the form

$$\frac{\partial x_1(p_1,p_2,m)}{\partial p_1} = \frac{\partial x_1^h(p_1,p_2,\overline{u})}{\partial p_1} - \frac{\partial x_1(p_1,p_2,m)}{\partial m}\overline{x}_1.$$

The proof of this equation hinges on the fact that

$$\frac{\partial x_1^h(p_1,p_2,\overline{u})}{\partial p_1} = \frac{\partial x_1^s(p_1,p_2,\overline{x}_1,\overline{x}_2)}{\partial p_1}$$

for infinitesimal changes in price. That is, for derivative size changes in price, the Slutsky substitution and the Hicks substitution effect are the same. The proof of this is not terribly difficult, but it involves some concepts that are beyond the scope of this book. A relatively simple proof is given in Hal R. Varian, *Microeconomic Analysis*, 2nd edition (New York: Norton, 1984), Chapter 3.

EXAMPLE: Rebating a Small Tax

We can use the calculus version of the Slutsky equation to see how consumption choices would react to a small change in a tax when the tax revenues are rebated to the consumers.

Assume, as before, that the tax causes the price to rise by the full amount of the tax. Let x be the amount of gasoline, p its original price, and t the amount of the tax. Then the change in consumption will be given by

$$dx = \frac{\partial x}{\partial p}t + \frac{\partial x}{\partial m}tx.$$

The first term measures how demand responds to the price change times the amount of the price change—which gives us the price effect of the tax. The second terms tells us how demand responds to a change in income times the amount that income has changed—income has gone up by the amount of the tax revenues rebated to the consumer.

Now use Slutsky's equation to expand the first term on the right-hand side to get the substitution and income effects of the price change itself:

$$dx = \frac{\partial x^s}{\partial p}t - \frac{\partial x}{\partial m}tx + \frac{\partial x}{\partial m}tx = \frac{\partial x^s}{\partial p}t.$$

The income effect cancels out, and all that is left is the pure substitution effect. Imposing a small tax and rebating the revenues of the tax is just like imposing a price change and adjusting income so that the old consumption bundle is feasible—as long as the tax is small enough so that the derivative approximation is valid.

9

BUYING AND SELLING

In the simple model of the consumer that we considered in the previous chapters, the income of the consumer was given. In reality people earn their income by selling things that they own: products that they have produced, assets that they have accumulated, or, most commonly, their own labor. In this chapter we will examine how the earlier model must be modified so as to describe this kind of behavior.

9.1 Net and Gross Demands

As before, we will limit ourselves to the two-good model. We now suppose that the consumer starts off with an **endowment** of the two goods, which we will denote by (ω_1, ω_2).[1] This is how much of the two goods the consumer has *before* he enters the market. Think of a farmer who goes to market with ω_1 units of carrots and ω_2 units of potatoes. The farmer inspects the prices available at the market and decides how much he wants to buy and sell of the two goods.

---

[1] The Greek letter ω, omega, is pronounced "o–may–gah."

Let us make a distinction here between the consumer's **gross demands** and his **net demands**. The gross demand for a good is the amount of the good that the consumer actually ends up consuming: how much of each of the goods he or she takes home from the market. The net demand for a good is the *difference* between what the consumer ends up with (the gross demand) and the initial endowment of goods. The net demand for a good is simply the amount bought or sold of the good.

If we let (x_1, x_2) be the gross demands, then $(x_1 - \omega_1, x_2 - \omega_2)$ are the net demands. Note that while the gross demands are typically positive numbers, the net demands may be positive or negative. If the net demand for good 1 is negative, it means that the consumer wants to consume less of good 1 than she has; that is, she wants to *supply* good 1 to the market. A negative net demand is simply an amount supplied.

For purposes of economic analysis, the gross demands are the more important, since that is what the consumer is ultimately concerned with. But the net demands are what are actually exhibited in the market and thus are closer to what the layman means by demand or supply.

9.2 The Budget Constraint

The first thing we should do is consider the form of the budget constraint. What constrains the consumer's final consumption? It must be the case that the value of the bundle of goods that she goes home with must be equal to the value of the bundle of goods that she came with. Or, algebraically:

$$p_1 x_1 + p_2 x_2 = p_1 \omega_1 + p_2 \omega_2.$$

We could just as well express this budget line in terms of net demands as

$$p_1(x_1 - \omega_1) + p_2(x_2 - \omega_2) = 0.$$

If $(x_1 - \omega_1)$ is positive we say that the consumer is a **net buyer** or **net demander** of good 1; if it is negative we say that she is a **net seller** or **net supplier**. Then the above equation says that the value of what the consumer buys must equal the value of what she sells, which seems sensible enough.

We could also express the budget line when the endowment is present in a form similar to the way we described it before. Now it takes two equations:

$$p_1 x_1 + p_2 x_2 = m$$
$$m = p_1 \omega_1 + p_2 \omega_2.$$

Once the prices are fixed, the value of the endowment, and hence the consumer's money income, is fixed.

What does the budget line look like graphically? When we fix the prices, money income is fixed, and we have a budget equation just like we had before. Thus the slope must be given by $-p_1/p_2$, just as before, so the only problem is to determine the location of the line.

The location of the line can be determined by the following simple observation: the endowment bundle is always on the budget line. That is, one value of (x_1, x_2) that satisfies the budget line is $x_1 = \omega_1$ and $x_2 = \omega_2$. The endowment is always just affordable, since the amount you have to spend is precisely the value of the endowment.

Putting these facts together shows that the budget line has a slope of $-p_1/p_2$ and passes through the endowment point. This is depicted in Figure 9.1.

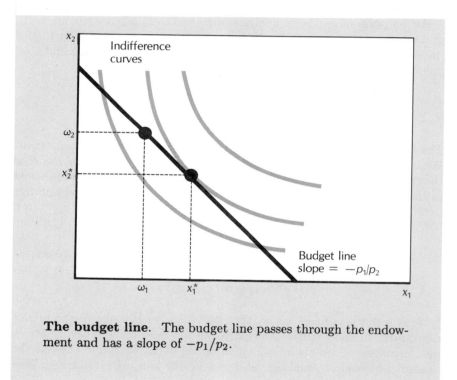

Figure 9.1

The budget line. The budget line passes through the endowment and has a slope of $-p_1/p_2$.

Given this budget constraint, the consumer can choose the optimal consumption bundle just as before. In Figure 9.1 we have shown an example of an optimal consumption bundle (x_1^*, x_2^*). Just as before, it will satisfy the optimality condition that the marginal rate of substitution is equal to the price ratio.

In this particular case, $x_1^* > \omega_1$ and $x_2^* < \omega_2$ so the consumer is a net buyer of good 1 and a net seller of good 2. The net demands are simply the net amounts that the consumer buys or sells of the two goods. In general the consumer may decide to be either a buyer or a seller depending on the relative prices of the two goods.

9.3 Changing the Endowment

In our previous analysis of choice we examined how the optimal consumption changed as the money income changed while the prices remained fixed. We can do a similar analysis here by asking how the optimal consumption changes as the *endowment* changes while the prices remain fixed.

For example, suppose that the endowment changes from (ω_1, ω_2) to some other value (ω_1', ω_2') such that

$$p_1\omega_1 + p_2\omega_2 > p_1\omega_1' + p_2\omega_2'.$$

This inequality means that the new endowment (ω_1', ω_2') is worth less than the old endowment—the money income that the consumer could achieve by selling her endowment is less.

This is depicted graphically in Figure 9.2A: the budget line shifts inward. Since this is exactly the same as a reduction in money income, we can conclude the same two things that we concluded in our examination of that case. First, the consumer is definitely worse off with the endowment (ω_1', ω_2') than she was with the old endowment, since her consumption possibilities have been reduced. Second, her demand for each good will change according to whether that good is a normal good or an inferior good.

For example, if good 1 is a normal good, and the consumer's endowment changes in a way that reduces its value, we can conclude that the consumer's demand for good 1 will decrease.

The case where the value of the endowment increases is depicted in Figure 9.2B. Following the above argument we conclude that if the budget line shifts outward in a parallel way, the consumer must be made better off. Algebraically, if the endowment changes from (ω_1, ω_2) to (ω_1', ω_2') and $p_1\omega_1 + p_2\omega_2 < p_1\omega_1' + p_2\omega_2'$, then the consumer's new budget set must contain her old budget set. This in turn implies that the optimal choice of the consumer with the new budget set must be preferred to the optimal choice given the old endowment.

It is worthwhile pondering this point a moment. In Chapter 7 we argued that just because a consumption bundle had a higher cost than another didn't mean that it would be preferred to the other bundle. But that only holds for a bundle that must be *consumed*. If a consumer can sell a bundle of goods on a free market at constant prices, then she will always prefer a higher valued bundle to a lower valued bundle, simply because a

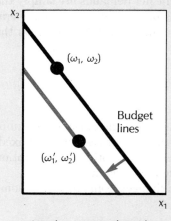
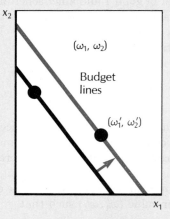

A a decrease in the value of the endowment

B an increase in the value of the endowment

Figure
9.2

Changes in the value of the endowment. In case A the value of the endowment decreases, and in case B it increases.

higher valued bundle gives her more income, and thus more consumption possibilities. Therefore an *endowment* that has a higher value will always be preferred to an endowment with a lower value. This simple observation will turn out to have some important implications later on.

There's one more case to consider: what happens if $p_1\omega_1 + p_2\omega_2 = p_1\omega_1' + p_2\omega_2'$? Then the budget set doesn't change at all: the consumer is just as well-off with (ω_1, ω_2) as with (ω_1', ω_2'), and her optimal choice should be exactly the same. The endowment has just shifted along the original budget line.

9.4 Price Changes

Earlier, when we examined how demand changed when price changed, we conducted our investigation under the hypothesis that money income remained constant. Now, when money income is determined by the value of the endowment, such a hypothesis is unreasonable: if the value of a good you are selling changes, your money income will certainly change. Thus in the case where the consumer has an endowment, changing prices automatically implies changing income.

Let us first think about this geometrically. If the price of good 1 decreases, we know that the budget line becomes flatter. Since the endowment bundle is always affordable, this means that the budget line must pivot around the endowment, as depicted in Figure 9.3.

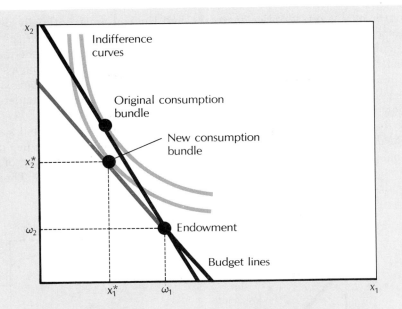

Decreasing the price of good 1. Lowering the price of good 1 makes the budget line pivot around the endowment. If the consumer remains a supplier she must be worse off.

Figure 9.3

In this case, the consumer is initially a seller of good 1, and remains a seller of good 1 even after the price has *declined*. What can we say about this consumer's welfare? In the case depicted, the consumer is on a lower indifference curve after the price change than before, but will this be true in general? The answer comes from applying the principle of revealed preference.

If the consumer remains a supplier, then her new consumption bundle must be on the blue part of the new budget line. But this part of the new budget line is inside the original budget set: all of these choices were open to the consumer before the price changed. Therefore, by revealed preference, all of these choices are worse than the original consumption bundle. We can therefore conclude that if the price of a good that a consumer is selling goes down, and the consumer decides to remain a seller, then the consumer's welfare must have declined.

What if the price of a good that the consumer is selling decreases and the consumer decides to switch to being a buyer of that good? In this case, the consumer may be better off or she may be worse off—there is no way to tell.

Let us now turn to the situation where the consumer is a net buyer of a good. In this case everything neatly turns around: if the consumer is a net buyer of a good, its price *increases*, and the consumer optimally decides to remain a buyer, then she must definitely be worse off. But if the price increase leads her to become a seller, it could go either way—she may be better off, or she may be worse off. These observations follow from a simple application of revealed preference just like the cases described above, but it is good practice for you to draw a graph just to make sure you understand how this works.

Revealed preference also allows us to make some interesting points about the decision of whether to remain a buyer or to become a seller when prices change. Suppose, as in Figure 9.4, that the consumer is a net buyer of good 1, and consider what happens if the price of good 1 *decreases*. Then the budget line becomes flatter as in Figure 9.4.

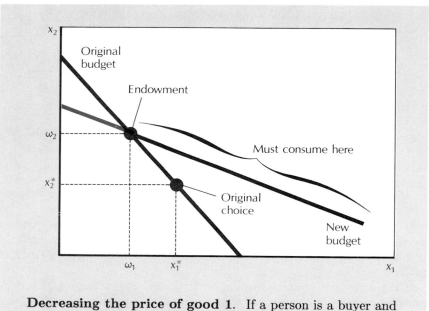

Figure 9.4

Decreasing the price of good 1. If a person is a buyer and the price of what she is buying decreases, she remains a buyer.

As usual we don't know for certain whether the consumer will buy more or less of good 1—it depends on her tastes. However, we can say something for sure: *the consumer will continue to be a net buyer of good 1—she will not switch to being a seller.*

How do we know this? Well, consider what would happen if the consumer did switch. Then she would be consuming somewhere on the blue part of the new budget line in Figure 9.4. But those consumption bundles were feasible for her when she faced the original budget line, and she rejected them in favor of (x_1^*, x_2^*). So (x_1^*, x_2^*) must be better than any of those points. And under the *new* budget line, (x_1^*, x_2^*) is a feasible consumption bundle. So whatever she consumes under the new budget line, it must be better than (x_1^*, x_2^*)—and thus better than any points on the bold part of the new budget line. This implies that her consumption of x_1 must be to the right of her endowment point—that is, she must remain a net demander of good 1.

Again, this kind of observation applies equally well to a person who is a net seller of a good: if the price of what she is selling goes *up*, she will not switch to being a net buyer. We can't tell for sure if the consumer will consume more or less of the good she is selling—but we know that she will keep selling it if the price goes up.

9.5 Offer Curves and Demand Curves

Recall from Chapter 6 that offer curves depict those combinations of both goods that may be demanded by a consumer, and that demand curves depict the relationship between the price and the quantity demanded of some good. Exactly the same constructions work when the consumer has an endowment of both goods.

Consider, for example, Figure 9.5, which illustrates the offer curve and demand curve for a consumer. The offer curve will always pass through the endowment, because at some price the endowment will be a demanded bundle; that is, at some prices the consumer will optimally choose not to trade.

As we've seen, the consumer may decide to be a buyer of good 1 for some prices and a seller of good 1 for other prices. Thus the offer curve will generally pass to the left and to the right of the endowment point.

The demand curve illustrated in Figure 9.5 is the gross demand curve—it measures the total amount the consumer chooses to consume of good 1. We have illustrated the net demand curve in Figure 9.6.

Note that the net demand for good 1 will typically be negative for some prices. This will be when the price of good 1 becomes so high that the consumer chooses to become a seller of good 1. At some price the consumer switches between being a net demander to being a net supplier of good 1.

It is conventional to plot the supply curve in the positive orthant, although it actually makes more sense to think of supply as just a negative demand. We'll bow to tradition here and plot the net supply curve in the normal way—as a positive amount, as in Figure 9.6.

Algebraically the net demand for good 1, $d_1(p_1, p_2)$, is the difference between the gross demand $x_1(p_1, p_2)$ and the endowment of good 1, when this difference is positive; that is, when the consumer wants more of the good than he or she has:

$$d_1(p_1, p_2) = \begin{cases} x_1(p_1, p_2) - \omega_1 & \text{if this is positive;} \\ 0 & \text{otherwise.} \end{cases}$$

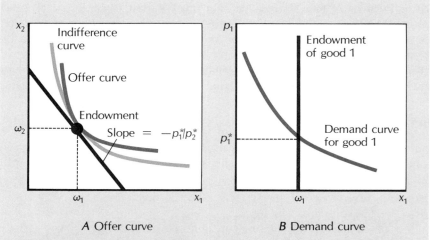

Figure 9.5

The offer curve and the demand curve. These are two ways of depicting the relationship between the demanded bundle and the prices when an endowment is present.

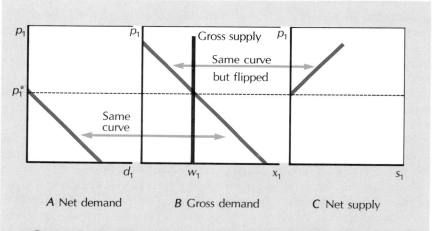

Figure 9.6

Gross demand, net demand, and net supply. Using the gross demand and net demand to depict the demand and supply behavior.

The net supply curve is the difference between how much the consumer has of good 1 and how much he or she wants when *this* difference is positive:

$$s_1(p_1, p_2) = \begin{cases} \omega_1 - x_1(p_1, p_2) & \text{if this is positive;} \\ 0 & \text{otherwise.} \end{cases}$$

Everything that we've established about the properties of demand behavior applies directly to the supply behavior of a consumer—because supply is just negative demand. If the *gross* demand curve is always downward sloping, then the net demand curve will be downward sloping and the supply curve will be upward sloping. Think about it: if an increase in the price makes the net demand more negative, then the net supply will be more positive.

9.6 The Slutsky Equation Revisited

The above applications of revealed preference are handy, but they don't really answer the main question: how does the demand for a good react to a change in its price? We saw in Chapter 8 that if money income was held constant, and the good was a normal good, then a reduction in its price must lead to an increase in demand.

The catch is the phrase "money income was held constant." The case we are examining here necessarily involves a change in money income, since the value of the endowment will necessarily change when a price changes.

In Chapter 8 we described the Slutsky equation that decomposed the change in demand due to a price change into a substitution effect and an income effect. The income effect was due to the change in purchasing power when prices change. But now, purchasing power has two reasons to change when a price changes. The first is the one involved in the definition of the Slutsky equation: when a price falls, for example, you can buy just as much of a good as you were consuming before and have some extra money left over. Let us refer to this as the **ordinary income effect.** But the second effect is new. When the price of a good changes, it changes the value of your endowment, and thus changes your money income. For example, if you are a net supplier of a good, then a fall in its price will reduce your money income directly since you won't be able to sell your endowment for as much money as you could before. We will have the same effects that we had before, plus an extra income effect from the influence of the prices on the value of the endowment bundle. We'll call this the **endowment income effect.**

In the earlier form of the Slutsky equation, the amount of money income you had was fixed. Now we have to worry about how your money income changes as the value of your endowment changes. Thus, when we calculate the effect of a change in price on demand, the Slutsky equation will take the form:

total change in demand = change due to substitution effect + change in demand due to ordinary income effect + change in demand due to endowment income effect.

The first two effects are familiar. As before, let us use Δx_1 to stand for the total change in demand, Δx_1^s to stand for the change in demand due to the substitution effect, and Δx_1^m to stand for the change in demand due to the ordinary income effect. Then we can substitute these terms into the above "verbal equation" to get the Slutsky equation in terms of rates of change:

$$\frac{\Delta x_1}{\Delta p_1} = \frac{\Delta x_1^s}{\Delta p_1} - x_1 \frac{\Delta x_1^m}{\Delta m} + \text{endowment income effect.} \qquad (9.1)$$

What will the last term look like? We'll derive an explicit expression below, but let us first think about what is involved. When the price of the endowment changes, money income will change, and this change in money income will induce a change in demand. Thus the endowment income effect will consist of two terms:

endowment income effect = change in demand when income changes
$\times$ the change in income when price changes. $\qquad (9.2)$

Let's look at the second effect first. Since income is defined to be

$$m = p_1 \omega_1 + p_2 \omega_2$$

we have

$$\frac{\Delta m}{\Delta p_1} = \omega_1.$$

This tells us how money income changes when the price of good 1 changes: if you have 10 units of good 1 to sell, and its price goes up by a dollar, your money income will go up by 10 dollars.

The first term in equation (9.2) is just how demand changes when income changes. We already have an expression for this: it is $\Delta x_1^m / \Delta m$: the change in demand divided by the change in income. Thus the endowment income effect is given by

$$\text{endowment income effect} = \frac{\Delta x_1^m}{\Delta m} \frac{\Delta m}{\Delta p_1} = \frac{\Delta x_1^m}{\Delta m} \omega_1. \qquad (9.3)$$

Inserting equation (9.3) into equation (9.1) we get the final form of the Slutsky equation:

$$\frac{\Delta x_1}{\Delta p_1} = \frac{\Delta x_1^s}{\Delta p_1} + (\omega_1 - x_1) \frac{\Delta x_1^m}{\Delta m}.$$

This equation can be used to answer the question posed above. We know that the sign of the substitution effect is always negative—opposite the direction of the change in price. Let us suppose that the good is a normal good so that $\Delta x_1^m / \Delta m > 0$. Then the sign of the combined income effect depends on whether the person is a net demander or a net supplier of the good in question. If the person is a net demander of a normal good, and its price increases, then the consumer will necessarily buy less of it. If the consumer is a net supplier of a normal good, then the sign of the total effect is ambiguous: it depends on the magnitude of the (positive) combined income effect as compared to the magnitude of the (negative) substitution effect.

As before, each of these changes can be depicted graphically, although the graph gets rather messy. Refer to Figure 9.7, which depicts the Slutsky decomposition of a price change. The total change in the demand for good 1 is indicated by the movement from A to C. This is the sum of three separate movements: the substitution effect, which is the movement from A to B, and two income effects. The ordinary income effect, which is the movement from B to D, is the change in demand *holding money income fixed*—that is, the same income effect that we examined in Chapter 8. But since the value of the endowment changes when prices change, there is now an extra income effect: because of the change in the value of the endowment, money income changes. This change in money income shifts the budget line back inward so that it passes through the endowment bundle. The change in demand from D to C measures this endowment income effect.

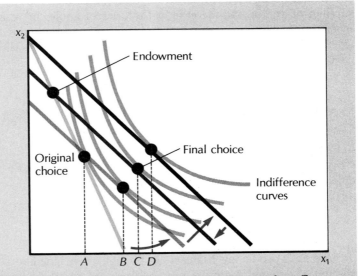

The Slutsky equation revisited. Breaking up the effect of the price change into the substitution effect (A to B), the ordinary income effect (B to D), and the endowment income effect (D to C).

Figure 9.7

9.7 Use of the Slutsky Equation

Suppose that we have a consumer who sells apples and oranges that he grows on a few trees in his backyard, like the consumer we described at the beginning of Chapter 8. We said there that if the price of apples increased then this consumer might actually consume more of them. Using the Slutsky equation derived in this chapter, it is not hard to see why. If we let x_a stand for the consumer's demand for apples, and let p_a be the price of apples, then we know that

$$\underset{(-)}{\frac{\Delta x_a}{\Delta p_a}} = \underset{(+)}{\frac{\Delta x_a^s}{\Delta p_a}} + \underset{(+)}{(\omega_a - x_a)\frac{\Delta x_a^m}{\Delta m}}.$$

This says that the total change in the demand for apples when the price of apples changes is the substitution effect plus the income effect. The substitution effect works in the right direction—increasing the price decreases the demand for apples. But if apples are a normal good for this consumer, the income effect works in the wrong direction. Since the consumer is a net supplier of apples, the increase in the price of apples increases his money income so much that he wants to consume more of them due to the income effect. If the latter term is strong enough to outweigh the substitution effect, we can easily get the "perverse" result.

EXAMPLE: Calculating the Endowment Income Effect

Let's try a little numerical example. Suppose that a dairy farmer produces 40 quarts of milk a week. Initially the price of milk is $3 a quart. His demand function for milk, for his own consumption, is

$$x_1 = 10 + \frac{m}{10p_1}.$$

Since he is producing 40 quarts at $3 a quart, his income is $120 a week. His initial demand for milk is therefore $x_1 = 14$. Now suppose that the price of milk changes to $2 a quart. His money income will then change to $m' = 2 \times 40 = \$80$, and his demand will be $x_1' = 10 + 80/20 = 14$.

If his money income had remained fixed at $m = \$120$, he would have purchased $x_1 = 10 + 120/10 \times 2 = 16$ quarts of milk at this price. Thus the endowment income effect—the change in his demand due to the change in the value of his endowment—is -2.0. The substitution effect and the ordinary income effect for this problem were calculated in Chapter 8.

Summary

1. Consumers earn income by selling their endowment of goods.

2. The gross demand for a good is the amount that the consumer ends up consuming. The net demand for a good is the amount the consumer buys. Thus the net demand is the difference between the gross demand and the endowment.

3. The budget constraint has a slope of $-p_1/p_2$ and passes through the endowment bundle.

4. When a price changes, the value of what the consumer has to sell will change and thereby generate an extra income effect in the Slutsky equation.

Review Questions

1. If a consumer's net demands are $(5, -3)$ and her endowment is $(4, 4)$, what are her gross demands?

2. The prices are $(p_1, p_2) = (2, 3)$ and the consumer is currently consuming $(x_1, x_2) = (4, 4)$. There is a perfect market for the two goods in which they can be bought and sold costlessly. Will the consumer necessarily prefer consuming the bundle $(y_1, y_2) = (3, 5)$? Will she necessarily prefer having the bundle (y_1, y_2)?

3. The prices are $(p_1, p_2) = (2, 3)$ and the consumer is currently consuming $(x_1, x_2) = (4, 4)$. Now the prices change to $(q_1, q_2) = (2, 4)$. Could the consumer be better off under these new prices?

4. The U.S. currently imports about half of the petroleum that it uses. The rest of its needs are met from domestic production. Could the price of oil rise so much that the U.S. would be made better off?

APPENDIX

The derivation of the Slutsky equation in the text contained one bit of hand waving. When we considered how changing the monetary value of the endowment affects demand, we said that it was equal to $\Delta x_1^m/\Delta m$. In our old version of the Slutsky equation this was the rate of change in demand when income changed so as to keep the original consumption bundle affordable. But that will not necessarily be equal to the rate of change of demand when the value of the endowment changes. Let's examine this point in a little more detail.

Let the price of good 1 change from p_1 to p_1', and use m'' to denote the new money income at the price p_1' due to the change in the value of the endowment. Suppose that the price of good 2 remains fixed so we can omit it as an argument of the demand function.

By definition of m'', we know

$$m'' - m = \Delta p_1 \omega_1.$$

Note that it is identically true that

$$\frac{x_1(p_1', m'') - x_1(p_1, m)}{\Delta p_1} =$$

$$+ \frac{x_1(p_1', m') - x_1(p_1, m)}{\Delta p_1} \quad \text{(substitution effect)}$$

$$- \frac{x_1(p_1', m') - x_1(p_1', m)}{\Delta p_1} \quad \text{(ordinary income effect)}$$

$$+ \frac{x_1(p_1', m'') - x_1(p_1', m)}{\Delta p_1} \quad \text{(endowment income effect)}.$$

(Just cancel out identical terms with opposite signs on the right-hand side.)

By definition of the ordinary income effect

$$\Delta p_1 = \frac{m' - m}{x_1}$$

and by definition of the endowment income effect

$$\Delta p_1 = \frac{m'' - m}{\omega_1}.$$

Making these replacements gives us a Slutsky equation of the form

$$\frac{x_1(p_1', m'') - x_1(p_1, m)}{\Delta p_1} =$$

$$+ \frac{x_1(p_1', m') - x_1(p_1, m)}{\Delta p_1} \quad \text{(substitution effect)}$$

$$- \frac{x_1(p_1', m') - x_1(p_1', m)}{m' - m} x_1 \quad \text{(ordinary income effect)}$$

$$+ \frac{x_1(p_1', m'') - x_1(p_1', m)}{m'' - m} \omega_1 \quad \text{(endowment income effect)}.$$

Writing this in terms of Δ's, we have

$$\frac{\Delta x_1}{\Delta p_1} = \frac{\Delta x_1^s}{\Delta p_1} - \frac{\Delta x_1^m}{\Delta m} x_1 + \frac{\Delta x_1^w}{\Delta m} \omega_1.$$

The only new term here is the last one. It tells how the demand for good 1 changes as income changes, times the *endowment* of good 1. This is precisely the endowment income effect.

Suppose that we are considering a very small price change, and thus a small associated income change. Then the fractions in the two income effects will be virtually the same, since the *rate* of change of good 1 when income changes from m to m' should be about the same as when income changes from m to m''. For such small changes we can collect terms and write the last two terms—the income effects—as

$$\frac{\Delta x_1^m}{\Delta m}(\omega_1 - x_1)$$

which yields a Slutsky equation of the same form as that derived earlier:

$$\frac{\Delta x_1^t}{\Delta p_1} = \frac{\Delta x_1^s}{\Delta p_1} + (\omega_1 - x_1)\frac{\Delta x_1^m}{\Delta m}.$$

If we want to express the Slutsky equation in calculus terms, we can just take limits in this expression. Or, if you prefer, we can calculate the correct equation directly, just by taking partial derivatives. Let $x_1(p_1, m(p_1))$ be the demand function for good 1 where we hold price 2 fixed and recognize that money income depends on the price of good 1 via the relationship $m(p_1) = p_1\omega_1 + p_2\omega_2$. Then we can write

$$\frac{dx_1(p_1, m(p_1))}{dp_1} = \frac{\partial x_1(p_1, m)}{\partial p_1} + \frac{\partial x_1(p_1, m)}{\partial m}\frac{dm(p_1)}{dp_1}.$$

By the definition of $m(p_1)$ we know how income changes when price changes:

$$\frac{\partial m(p_1)}{\partial p_1} = \omega_1 \tag{9.4}$$

and by the Slutsky equation we know how demand changes when price changes, holding money income fixed:

$$\frac{\partial x_1(p_1, m)}{\partial p_1} = \frac{\partial x_1^s(p_1)}{\partial p_1} - \frac{\partial x(p_1, m)}{\partial m}x_1. \tag{9.5}$$

Inserting equation (9.5) into equation (9.4) we have

$$\frac{dx_1(p_1, m(p_1))}{dp_1} = \frac{\partial x_1^s(p_1)}{\partial p_1} + \frac{\partial x(p_1, m)}{\partial m}(\omega_1 - x_1)$$

which is the form of the Slutsky equation that we want.

LABOR SUPPLY

In this chapter we will study an application of consumer theory to a specific choice problem, that of labor supply. As usual we will make some simplifying assumptions: that there are only two goods, consumption and labor, and in particular that there is only one kind of labor. Even in such a simple model there are some significant insights to be had from applying the economic theory of the consumer.

10.1 The Budget Constraint

Let us suppose that the consumer initially has some money income M that she receives whether she works or not. This might be income from investments or from relatives, for example. We call this amount the consumer's **nonlabor income**. (The consumer could have zero nonlabor income, but we want to allow for the possibility that it is positive.)

Let us use C to indicate the amount of consumption the consumer has, and use p to denote the price of consumption. Then letting w be the wage rate, and L the amount of labor supplied, we have the budget constraint:

$$pC = M + wL.$$

This says that the value of what the consumer consumes must be equal to her nonlabor income plus her labor income.

Let us try to compare the above formulation to the previous examples of budget constraints. The major difference is that we have something that the consumer is choosing—labor supply—on the right-hand side of the equation. We can easily transpose it to the left-hand side to get

$$pC - wL = M.$$

This is better, but we have a minus sign where we normally have a plus sign. How can we remedy this? Let us suppose that there is some maximum amount of labor supply possible—24 hours a day, 7 days a week, or whatever is compatible with the units of measurement we are using. Let $\overline{L}$ denote this amount of labor time. Then adding $w\overline{L}$ to each side and rearranging we have

$$pC + w(\overline{L} - L) = M + w\overline{L}.$$

Let us define $\overline{C} = M/p$. This is the amount of consumption that the consumer could have if she didn't work at all. That is, $\overline{C}$ is her endowment of consumption, so we write

$$pC + w(\overline{L} - L) = p\overline{C} + w\overline{L}.$$

Now we have an equation very much like those we've seen before. We have two choice variables on the left-hand side, and two endowment variables on the right-hand side. The variable $\overline{L} - L$ can be interpreted as the amount of "leisure"—that is, time that isn't labor time. Let us use the variable R (for relaxation!) to denote leisure, so that $R = \overline{L} - L$. Then the total amount of time you have available for leisure is $\overline{R} = \overline{L}$ and the budget constraint becomes

$$pC + wR = p\overline{C} + w\overline{R}.$$

The above equation is formally identical to the very first budget constraint that we wrote in this chapter. However, it has a much more interesting interpretation. It says that the value of a consumer's consumption plus her leisure has to equal the value of her endowment of consumption and her endowment of time, valued at her wage rate. The wage rate is not only the price of labor, it is also the price of *leisure*.

After all, if your wage rate is $10 an hour and you decide to consume an extra hour's leisure, how much does it cost you? The answer is that it costs you $10 in forgone income—that's the price of that extra hour's consumption of leisure. Economists sometimes say that the wage rate is the **opportunity cost** of leisure.

The right-hand side of this budget constraint is sometimes called the consumer's **full income** or **implicit income**. It measures the value of what the consumer owns—her endowment of consumption goods, if any, and her endowment of her own time. This is to be distinguished from the consumer's **measured income**, which is simply the income she receives from selling off some of her time.

The nice thing about this budget constraint is that it is just like the ones we've seen before. It passes through the endowment point $(\overline{L}, \overline{C})$ and has a slope of $-w/p$. The endowment would be what the consumer would get if she did not engage in market trade at all, and the slope of the budget line tells us the rate at which the market will exchange one good for another.

The optimal choice occurs where the marginal rate of substitution—the tradeoff between consumption and leisure—equals w/p, the **real wage**. The value of the extra consumption to the consumer from working a little more just has to be equal to the value of the lost leisure that it takes to generate that consumption. The real wage is the amount of consumption that the consumer can purchase if she gives up an hour of leisure.

This is depicted in Figure 10.1. We measure the demand for leisure from left to right, and the supply of labor from right to left.

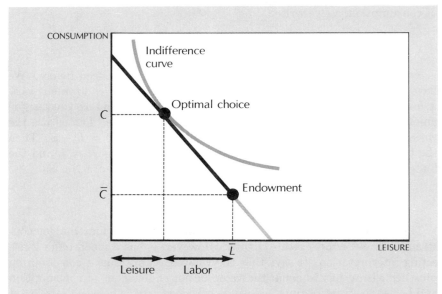

Figure 10.1   **Labor supply.** The optimal choice describes the demand for leisure measured from the origin to the right, and the supply of labor measured from the endowment to the left.

10.2 Comparative Statics of Labor Supply

First let us consider how a consumer's labor supply changes as money income changes with the price and wage held fixed. If you won the state lottery and got a big injection of money income, what would happen to your supply of labor? What would happen to your demand for leisure?

For most people, the supply of labor would drop when their money income increased. In other words, leisure is probably a normal good for most people: when their money income rises, people choose to consume more leisure. There seems to be a fair amount of evidence for this observation, so we will adopt it as a maintained hypothesis: we will assume that leisure is a normal good.

What does this imply about the response of the consumer's labor supply to changes in the wage rate? The above considerations lead us to pose this in terms of the demand for leisure.

When the wage rate increases, leisure becomes more expensive, which by itself leads people to want less of it (the substitution effect). Since leisure is a normal good, we would then predict that an increase in the wage rate would necessarily lead to a decrease in the demand for leisure—that is, an increase in the supply of labor. This follows from the Slutsky equation given in Chapter 8. A normal good must have a negative sloped demand curve. If leisure is a normal good, then the supply curve of labor must be positively sloped.

But there is a problem with this analysis. First, at an intuitive level, it does not seem reasonable that increasing the wage would *always* result in a increased supply of labor. If my wage becomes very high, I might well "spend" the extra income in consuming leisure. How can we reconcile this apparently plausible behavior with the economic theory given above?

If the theory gives the wrong answer, it is probably because we've misapplied the theory. And indeed in this case we have. The Slutsky example described earlier gave the change in demand *holding money income constant*. But if the wage rate changes then money income must change as well. The change in demand resulting from a change in money income is an extra income effect—the endowment income effect. It occurs on top of the ordinary income effect.

If we apply the *appropriate* version of the Slutsky equation given in Chapter 9 we get the following expression:

$$\frac{\Delta R}{\Delta w} = \text{substitution effect} + (\overline{R} - R)\,\frac{\Delta R}{\Delta m}.$$
$$\quad\quad\quad\quad\quad (-)\quad\quad\quad\quad (+)\quad (+)$$

In this expression the substitution effect is definitely negative, as it always is, and $\Delta R/\Delta m$ is positive since we are assuming leisure is a normal good. But $(\overline{R} - R)$ is positive as well, so the sign of the whole expression can go either way. Unlike the usual case of consumer demand, the demand for leisure will have an ambiguous sign, even if leisure is a normal good. As the wage rate increases, people may work more or less.

Why does this ambiguity arise? When the wage rate increases, the substitution effect says work more in order to substitute consumption for leisure. But when the wage rate increases, the value of the endowment goes up as well. This is just like extra income, which may very well be consumed in taking extra leisure. Which is the more important effect is an empirical matter and cannot be decided by theory alone. We have to look at people's actual labor supply decisions to determine which effect dominates.

The case where an increase in the wage rate results in a decrease in the supply of labor is known as the case of a **backwards-bending labor supply curve.** The Slutsky equation tells us that this effect is more likely to occur the larger is $(\overline{R} - R)$, that is, the larger is the supply of labor. When $\overline{R} = R$, the consumer is consuming only leisure, so an increase in the wage will result in a pure substitution effect and thus an increase in the supply of labor. But as the labor supply increases, each increase in the wage gives the consumer additional income for all the hours he is working, so that after some point he may well decide to use this extra income to "purchase" additional leisure—that is, to *reduce* his supply of labor.

EXAMPLE: Overtime and the Supply of Labor

Consider a worker who has chosen to supply a certain amount of labor L^* when faced with the wage rate w as depicted in Figure 10.2. Now suppose that the firm offers him a higher wage, $w' > w$, for extra time that he chooses to work. Such a payment is known as an **overtime wage.**

In terms of Figure 10.2, this means that the slope of the budget line will be steeper for labor supplied in excess of L^*. But then we know that the worker will optimally choose to supply more labor, by the usual sort of revealed preference argument: the choices involving working less than L^* were available before the overtime was offered and were rejected.

Note that we get an unambiguous increase in labor supply with an overtime wage, whereas just offering a higher wage for all hours worked has an ambiguous effect—as discussed above, labor supply may increase or it may decrease. The reason is that the response to an overtime wage is essentially a pure substitution effect—the change in the optimal choice resulting from *pivoting* the budget line around the chosen point. Overtime gives a higher payment for the *extra* hours worked, whereas a straight increase in the wage gives a higher payment for *all* hours worked. Thus a straight-wage increase involves both a substitution and an income effect while an overtime-wage increase results in a pure substitution effect. An example of this is shown in Figure 10.2. There an increase in the straight wage results in a *decrease* in

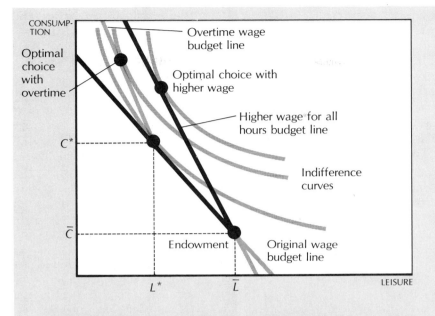

Overtime versus an ordinary wage increase. An increase in the overtime wage definitely increases the supply of labor, while an increase in the straight wage could decrease the supply of labor.

Figure 10.2

labor supply, while an increase in the overtime wage results in an increase in labor supply.

10.3 Taxes and Labor Supply

We can apply the tax analysis of Chapter 5 to the analysis of labor supply, and get the same sort of diagram that we examined there. Putting a tax on labor makes leisure less expensive. This might be expected to discourage labor supply, but, as we've seen above, this cannot be guaranteed. However, there is a new feature that arises naturally in the analysis of taxes and labor supply, namely, the effect of **nonlinear taxation.**

In most countries, the largest amount of government tax revenue is gathered from taxing income, and the largest component of income is labor income. Typically, the amount of income tax you pay depends on the amount of income you earn.

Suppose that the tax you owe if you have income m is given by some function $T(m)$. Consider a consumer currently earning some income m and paying some taxes T. Let the consumer's income change to $m + \Delta m$ which makes his taxes change to $T + \Delta T$. Then the consumer's **marginal tax rate** is defined to be $\Delta T / \Delta m$: the extra taxes that he pays per dollar of extra income.

It is the *marginal* tax rate that is appropriate for determining the labor supply decision. This is because the consumer's decision of whether or not to work an extra hour depends on how much after-tax money he or she will get to spend on consumption. And that depends on the taxes on the *extra* income from working that *extra* hour, not on the total amount of taxes that are paid on the total income.

We say that an income tax system is **progressive** if the marginal tax rate is rising, and **regressive** if the marginal tax rate is falling. A progressive marginal tax rate means that each extra hour of labor buys less and less after-tax income, and therefore less and less additional consumption. A regressive tax works the other way: each extra dollar is taxed less heavily. (There are other definitions of progressive and regressive tax systems, but this is the most convenient one for our purposes.)

A progressive tax structure yields a budget set like that shown in Figure 10.3. Each extra hour of labor brings less and less additional consumption, so the line segments making up the budget set are getting flatter and flatter as we move from right to left. The kinks in the budget line are where the consumer's tax bracket changes—where his marginal tax rate changes.

The optimal consumption point occurs where the marginal rate of substitution between consumption and leisure equals the slope of the budget line. The slope of the budget line measures how much extra consumption the consumer can get by giving up a little more leisure. If the consumer's optimum occurs when he faces a tax bracket of t, say, then working an extra hour, ΔL, will bring him extra money income of $w\Delta L$.

But he'll have to pay $tw\Delta L$ of this extra income as extra tax. Therefore the amount that he gets to keep from working ΔL hours more is $(1 - t)w\Delta L$. We call $(1 - t)w$ the **after-tax wage**. The slope of the budget line in the presence of taxed labor is then given by $-(1 - t)w/p$. Thus it is the after-tax wage that is relevant for determining the supply of labor, where the after-tax wage is computed using the appropriate *marginal* tax rate.

What does a budget constraint associated with a regressive tax look like? Here the tax rate declines as income decreases, so that each additional dollar buys more and more consumption. A nice example of this is the welfare system in many states. If a person is unemployed, he will receive a certain amount of money income, M, from the state welfare system. If he is able to find a job and earn some labor income, he will be eligible for a smaller level of welfare payments.

For example, suppose that a welfare recipient finds a job for $5 an hour, but each extra dollar that he earns results in a 40 percent reduction in his welfare payments. Then for each hour he works, he earns $5, but

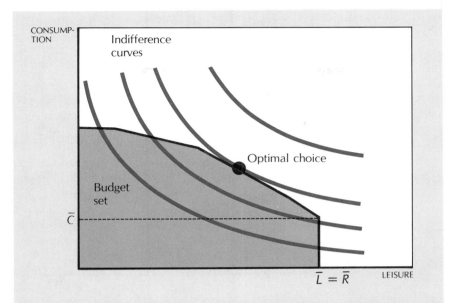

A budget set generated by a progressive tax. The budget
set bends at the points where the individual's marginal tax rate
changes.

Figure
10.3

he has to give up .4 × 5 = $2 of his welfare payments. Thus his net
wage—how much extra income he gets for each extra hour worked—is only
$5 − $2 = $3 an hour. In this case the initial segment of the budget line
is relatively flat: the extra consumption bought by extra labor is not very
large.

If the welfare recipient is able to earn enough money to get off of welfare,
he then gets to keep all of the $5 wage, so the slope of his budget constraint
will be −5/p. But if he is able to work even more, he has to start paying
income tax, and this will make the budget line flatter. The net shape might
be something like that depicted in Figure 10.4. Note that the budget set
is *not* convex.

The indifference curves illustrated in Figure 10.4 show a situation where
there are two optimal supplies of labor: either supply a little labor and
have a small amount of consumption, or supply a lot of labor and have
a larger amount of consumption. Both prospects are equally valued by
the consumer—they are on the same indifference curve. It is clear that
this kind of behavior can easily arise when budget sets have the kind of
nonconvex shape implied by a regressive tax system. A welfare recipient
who prefers to consume more leisure is not acting in an irrational way—he
or she may simply be making a rational economic choice in the face of a
very high marginal tax rate.

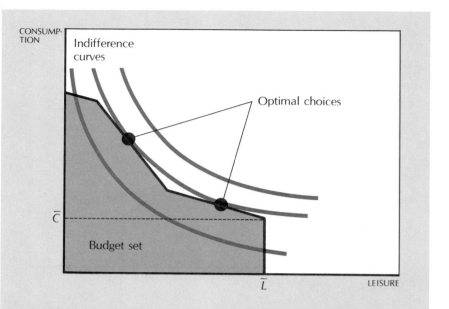

Figure 10.4

The budget set generated by a regressive tax. Increasing the supply of labor (moving left from the endowment) at first gives only a small increase in consumption due to the high marginal tax rate. But as income increases, the marginal tax rate falls, so the extra consumption for an extra hour's labor increases.

EXAMPLE: A Lump Sum Tax Versus a Wage Tax

Suppose that the government is considering two ways to raise revenue. The first way is by using a proportional wage tax. The second is by requiring everyone to pay a fixed, lump sum amount to the government, independent of how much they work. This latter kind of tax is known as a **lump sum tax** or a **head tax.**

The impact of these two kinds of tax on labor supply is depicted in Figure 10.5. The wage tax will make the budget line flatter. Although the effect on labor supply is theoretically ambiguous it is likely that the supply of labor would decrease, as shown in Figure 10.5A.

The effect of the lump sum tax is shown in Figure 10.5B. A lump sum tax is a parallel shift inward of the budget line. If leisure is a normal good, then the demand for leisure will fall. This means that the supply of labor must rise. Thus a lump sum tax will *increase* the supply of labor, while a proportional wage tax would probably *decrease* the supply of labor.

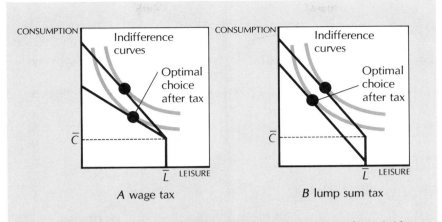

A wage tax versus a lump-sum tax. A wage tax (panel A) would probably decrease the supply of labor while a lump-sum tax (panel B) would probably increase the supply of labor.

Figure
10.5

Summary

1. The budget constraint for the consumption–labor decision can be arranged to look like those encountered in earlier chapters.

2. How labor supply responds to a change in the wage rate is the sum of a substitution effect and an income effect, but is theoretically ambiguous, even in the case where leisure is a normal good.

3. An overtime wage must increase the supply of labor since it gives rise to a pure substitution effect.

4. The marginal tax rate is the crucial variable for determining labor supply behavior.

Review Questions

1. Suppose by some miracle the number of hours in the day increased from 24 to 30 hours (with luck this would happen shortly before exam week). How would this affect the budget constraint?

2. If leisure is an inferior good, what can you say about the slope of the labor supply curve?

3. In order to have a backwards bending labor supply curve what must be true about the demand for leisure? Should it be a normal good or an inferior good?

11

INTERTEMPORAL CHOICE

In this chapter we continue our examination of consumer behavior by considering the choices involved in saving and consuming over time. Choices of consumption over time are known as **intertemporal choices.**

11.1 The Budget Constraint

Let us imagine a consumer who chooses how much of some good to consume in each of two time periods. We will usually want to think of this good as being a composite commodity, as described in Chapter 2, but you can think of it as being a specific commodity if you wish. We denote the amount of consumption in each period by (c_1, c_2), and suppose that the prices of consumption in each period are constant at 1. The amount of money the consumer will have in each period is denoted by (m_1, m_2).

Suppose initially that the only way the consumer has of transferring money from period 1 to period 2 is by saving it without earning interest. Furthermore let us assume for the moment that he has no possibility of

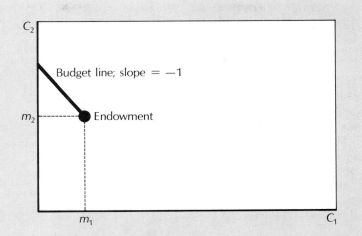

Budget constraint. This is the budget constraint when the
rate of interest is zero and no borrowing is allowed. The less
the individual consumes in period 1, the more he can consume
in period 2.

Figure
11.1

borrowing money, so that the most he can spend in period 1 is m_1. His
budget constraint will then look like the one depicted in Figure 11.1.

We see that there will be two possible kinds of choices. The consumer
could choose to consume at (m_1, m_2), which means that he just consumes
his income each period, or he can choose to consume less than his income
during the first period. In this latter case, the consumer is saving some of
his first period consumption for a later date.

Now, let us allow the consumer to borrow and lend money at some
interest rate r. Keeping the prices of consumption in each period at 1 for
convenience, let us derive the budget constraint. Suppose first that the
consumer decides to be a saver so his first period consumption, c_1, is less
than his first period income, m_1. In this case, he will earn interest on the
amount he saves, $m_1 - c_1$, at the interest rate r. The amount that he can
consume next period is given by

$$c_2 = m_2 + (m_1 - c_1) + r(m_1 - c_1)$$
$$= m_2 + (1 + r)(m_1 - c_1). \tag{11.1}$$

This says that the amount that the consumer can consume in period 2 is
his income plus the amount he saved from period 1, plus the interest that
he earned on his savings.

Now suppose that the consumer is a borrower so that his first period
consumption is greater than his first period income. The consumer is a
borrower if $c_1 > m_1$, and the interest he has to *pay* second period will

be $r(c_1 - m_1)$. Of course, he also has to pay back the amount that he borrowed, $c_1 - m_1$. This means his budget constraint is given by

$$c_2 = m_2 - r(c_1 - m_1) - (c_1 - m_1)$$
$$= m_2 + (1 + r)(m_1 - c_1)$$

which is just what we had before. If $m_1 - c_1$ is positive then the consumer earns interest on this savings; if $m_1 - c_1$ is negative, then the consumer pays interest on his borrowings.

If $c_1 = m_1$, then necessarily $c_2 = m_2$, and the consumer is neither a borrower nor a lender. We might say that this consumption position is the "Polonius point."[1]

We can rearrange the budget constraint for the consumer to get two alternative forms that are useful:

$$(1 + r)c_1 + c_2 = (1 + r)m_1 + m_2 \qquad (11.2)$$

and

$$c_1 + \frac{c_2}{1 + r} = m_1 + \frac{m_2}{1 + r}. \qquad (11.3)$$

Note that both equations have the form

$$p_1 x_1 + p_2 x_2 = p_1 m_1 + p_2 m_2.$$

In the equation (11.2), $p_1 = 1 + r$ and $p_2 = 1$. In equation (11.3), $p_1 = 1$ and $p_2 = 1/(1 + r)$.

We say that equation (11.2) expresses the budget constraint in terms of **future value**, and equation (11.3) expresses the budget constraint in terms of **present value**. The reason for this terminology is that the first budget constraint makes the price of future consumption equal to 1, while the second budget constraint makes the price of present consumption equal to 1. The first budget constraint measures the period 1 price *relative* to the period 2 price, while the second equation does the reverse.

The geometric interpretation of present value and future value is given in Figure 11.2. The present value of an endowment of money in two periods is the amount of money in period 1 that would generate the same budget set as the endowment. This is just the horizontal intercept of the budget line, which gives the maximum amount of first period consumption possible. Examining the budget constraint, this amount is $\bar{c}_1 = m_1 + m_2/(1 + r)$, which is the present value of the endowment.

Similarly, the vertical intercept is the maximum amount of second period consumption, which occurs when $c_1 = 0$. Again, from the budget

---

[1] "Neither a borrower, nor a lender be; For loan oft loses both itself and friend, And borrowing dulls the edge of husbandry." *Hamlet*, Act I, scene *ii*; Polonius giving advice to his son.

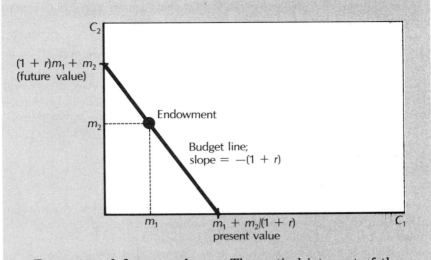

Present and future values. The vertical intercept of the budget line measures future value, and the horizontal intercept measures the present value.

Figure 11.2

constraint, we can solve for this amount $\bar{c}_2 = (1 + r)m_1 + m_2$, the future value of the endowment.

The present value form is the more important way to express the intertemporal budget constraint since it measures the future relative to the present, which is the way we naturally look at it.

It is easy from any of these equations to see the form of this budget constraint. The budget line passes through (m_1, m_2), since that is always an *affordable* consumption pattern, and the budget line has a slope of $-(1 + r)$.

11.2 Preferences for Consumption

Let us now consider the consumer's preferences, as represented by his indifference curves. The shape of the indifference curves indicates the consumer's tastes for consumption at different times. If we drew indifference curves with a constant slope of -1, for example, they would represent tastes of a consumer who didn't care whether he consumed today or tomorrow. His marginal rate of substitution between today and tomorrow is -1.

If we drew indifference curves for perfect complements, this would indicate that the consumer wanted to consume equal amounts today and tomorrow. Such a consumer would be unwilling to substitute consumption from one time period to the other, no matter what it might be worth to him to do so.

As usual, the intermediate case of well-behaved preferences is the more reasonable situation. The consumer is willing to substitute some amount of consumption today for consumption tomorrow, and how much he is willing to substitute depends on the particular pattern of consumption that he has.

Convexity of preferences is very natural in this context, since it says that the consumer would rather have an "average" amount of consumption each period rather than have a lot today and nothing tomorrow or vice versa.

11.3 Comparative Statics

Given a consumer's budget constraint and his preferences for consumption at the each of the two periods, we can examine the optimal choice of consumption (c_1, c_2). If the consumer chooses a point where $c_1 < m_1$, we will say that she is a **lender**, and if $c_1 > m_1$, we say that she is a **borrower**. In Figure 11.3A we have depicted a case where the consumer is a borrower, and in Figure 11.3B we have depicted a lender.

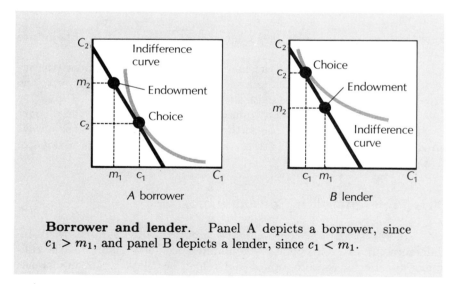

<table>
<tr><td>A borrower</td><td>B lender</td></tr>
</table>

Figure 11.3

Borrower and lender. Panel A depicts a borrower, since $c_1 > m_1$, and panel B depicts a lender, since $c_1 < m_1$.

Let us now consider how the consumer would react to a change in the interest rate. From equation (11.1) we see that increasing the rate of interest must tilt the budget line to a steeper position: for a given reduction in c_1 you will get more consumption in the second period if the interest rate is higher. Of course the endowment always remains affordable, so the tilt is really a pivot around the endowment.

We can also say something about how the choice of being a borrower or a lender changes as the interest rate changes. There are two cases, depending on whether the consumer is initially a borrower or initially a lender. Suppose first that he is a lender. Then it turns out that if the interest rate increases, the consumer must remain a lender.

This argument is illustrated in Figure 11.4. If the consumer is initially a lender then his consumption bundle is to the left of the endowment point. Now let the interest rate increase. Is it possible that the consumer shifts to a new consumption point to the *right* of the endowment?

No, because that would violate the principle of revealed preference: choices to the right of the endowment point were available to the consumer when he faced the original budget set and were rejected in favor of the chosen point. Since the original optimal bundle is still available at the new budget line, the new optimal bundle must be a point *outside* the old budget set—which means it must be to the left of the endowment. The consumer must remain a lender when the interest rate increases.

There is a similar effect for borrowers: if the consumer is initially a borrower and the interest rate declines, he or she will remain a borrower. (You might sketch a diagram similar to Figure 11.4 and see if you can spell out the argument.)

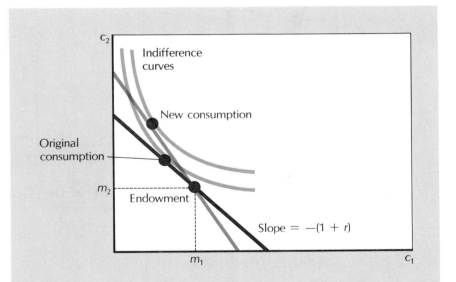

If a person is a lender and the interest rate rises, he or she will remain a lender. Increasing the interest rate pivots the budget line around the endowment to a steeper position; revealed preference implies that the new consumption bundle must lie to the left of the endowment.

Figure
11.4

Thus if a person is a lender and the interest rate increases, he will remain a lender. If a person is a borrower and the interest rate decreases, he will remain a borrower. On the other hand, if a person is a lender and the interest rate decreases, he may well decide to switch to being a borrower; similarly, an increase in the interest rate may induce a borrower to become a lender. Revealed preference tells us nothing about these last two cases.

Revealed preference can also be used to make judgments about how the consumer's welfare changes as the interest rate changes. If the consumer is initially a borrower, and the interest rate rises, but he decides to remain a borrower, then he must be worse off at the new interest rate. This argument is illustrated in Figure 11.5; if the consumer remains a borrower, he must be operating at a point that was affordable under the old budget set but was rejected, which implies that he must be worse off.

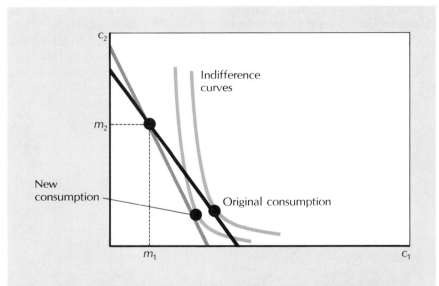

Figure
11.5

A borrower is made worse off by an increase in the interest rate. When the interest rate facing a borrower increases, and the consumer chooses to remain a borrower he or she is certainly worse off.

11.4 The Slutsky Equation and Intertemporal Choice

The Slutsky equation can be used to decompose the change in demand due to an interest rate change into income effects and substitution effects, just as in Chapter 9. Suppose that the interest rate rises. What will be the effect on consumption in each period?

This is a case that is easier to analyze using the future value budget constraint, rather than the present value constraint. In terms of the future value budget constraint, raising the interest rate is just like raising the price of consumption today as compared to consumption tomorrow. Writing out the Slutsky equation we have

$$\frac{\Delta c_1^t}{\Delta p_1} = \frac{\Delta c_1^s}{\Delta p_1} + (m_1 - c_1)\frac{\Delta c_1^m}{\Delta m}.$$
$$(?) \qquad (-) \qquad (?) \qquad (+)$$

The substitution effect, as always, works opposite the direction of price. In this case the price of period one consumption goes up, so the substitution effect says the consumer should consume less first period. This is the meaning of the minus sign under the substitution effect. Let's assume that consumption this period is a normal good, so that the very last term—how consumption changes as income changes—will be positive. So we put a plus sign under the last term. Now the sign of the whole expression will depend on the sign of $(m_1 - c_1)$. If the person is a borrower, this term will be negative and the whole expression will therefore unambiguously be negative—for a borrower, an increase in the interest rate must lower today's consumption.

Why does this happen? When the interest rate rises, there is always a substitution effect towards consuming less today. For a borrower, an increase in the interest rate means he will have to pay more interest tomorrow. This effect induces him to borrow less, and thus consume less, in the first period.

For a lender the effect is ambiguous. The total effect is the sum of a negative substitution effect and a positive income effect. From the viewpoint of a lender an increase in the interest rate may give him so much extra income that he will want to consume even more first period.

The effects of changing interest rates are not terribly mysterious. There is an income effect and a substitution effect as in any other price change. But without a tool like the Slutsky equation to separate out the various effects, the changes may be hard to disentangle. With such a tool, the sorting out of the effects is quite straightforward.

11.5 Inflation

The above analysis has all been conducted in terms of a general "consumption" good. Giving up Δc units of consumption today buys you $(1 + r)\Delta c$ units of consumption tomorrow. Implicit in this analysis is the assumption that the "price" of consumption doesn't change—there is no inflation or deflation.

However, the analysis is not hard to modify to deal with the case of inflation. Let us suppose that the consumption good now has a different price in each period. It is convenient to choose today's price of consumption as 1 and to let p_2 be the price of consumption tomorrow. It is also convenient to think of the endowment as being measured in units of the consumption goods as well, so that the monetary value of the endowment in period 2 is $p_2 m_2$. Then the amount of money the consumer can spend in the second period is given by

$$p_2 c_2 = p_2 m_2 + (1 + r)(m_1 - c_1)$$

and the amount of consumption available second period is

$$c_2 = m_2 + \frac{1 + r}{p_2}(m_1 - c_1).$$

Note that this equation is very similar to the equation given earlier—we just use $(1 + r)/p_2$ rather than $1 + r$.

Let us express this budget constraint in terms of the rate of inflation. The inflation rate, π, is just the rate at which prices grow. Recalling that $p_1 = 1$, we have

$$p_2 = 1 + \pi$$

which gives us

$$c_2 = m_2 + \frac{1 + r}{1 + \pi}(m_1 - c_1).$$

Let's create a new variable ρ, the **real interest rate**, and define it by[2]

$$1 + \rho = \frac{1 + r}{1 + \pi}$$

so that the budget constraint becomes

$$c_2 = m_2 + (1 + \rho)(m_1 - c_1).$$

One plus the real interest rate, ρ, measures how much extra *consumption* you can get in period 2 if you give up some *consumption* in period 1. That is why it is called the *real* rate of interest: it tells you how much extra consumption you can get, not how many extra dollars you can get.

The interest rate on dollars is called the **nominal** rate of interest. As we've seen above, the relationship between the two is given by

$$1 + \rho = \frac{1 + r}{1 + \pi}.$$

---

[2] The Greek letter ρ, rho, is pronounced "row."

In order to get an explicit expression for ρ, we write this equation as

$$\rho = \frac{1+r}{1+\pi} - 1 = \frac{1+r}{1+\pi} - \frac{1+\pi}{1+\pi}$$
$$= \frac{r-\pi}{1+\pi}.$$

This is an exact expression for the real interest rate, but it is common to use an approximation. If the inflation rate isn't too large, the denominator of the fraction will be only slightly larger than 1. Thus the real rate of interest will be approximately given by

$$\rho \approx r - \pi$$

which says that the real rate of interest is just the nominal rate minus the rate of inflation. (The symbol $\approx$ means "approximately equal to.") This makes perfectly good sense: if the interest rate is 18 percent, but prices are rising at 10 percent, then the real interest rate—the extra consumption you can buy next period if you give up some consumption now—will be roughly 8 percent.

Of course, we are always looking into the future when making consumption plans. Typically we know the nominal rate of interest for the next period, but the rate of inflation for next period is unknown. The real interest rate is usually taken to be the current interest rate minus the *expected* rate of inflation. To the extent that people have different estimates about what the next year's rate of inflation will be, they will have different estimates of the real interest rate. If inflation can be reasonably well forecast, these differences may not be too large.

11.6 Present Value: A Closer Look

Let us return now to the two forms of the budget constraint described earlier in section 11.1 in equations (11.2) and (11.3):

$$(1+r)c_1 + c_2 = (1+r)m_1 + m_2$$

and

$$c_1 + \frac{c_2}{1+r} = m_1 + \frac{m_2}{1+r}.$$

Consider just the right-hand sides of these two equations. We said that the first one expresses the value of the endowment in terms of future value and the second one expresses it in terms of present value.

Let us examine the concept of future value first. If we can borrow and lend at an interest rate of r, what is the future equivalent of one dollar today? The answer is $(1+r)$ dollars. That is, one dollar today can be turned into $(1 + r)$ dollars next period simply by lending it to the bank at interest rate r. In other words $(1 + r)$ dollars next period is equivalent to one dollar today since that is how much you would have to pay next period to purchase—that is, borrow—one dollar today. The value $(1 + r)$ is just the price of a dollar today, relative to a dollar next period. This can be easily seen from the first budget constraint: it is expressed in terms of future dollars—the second-period dollars have a price of 1, and first-period dollars are measured relative to them.

What about present value? This is just the reverse: everything is measured in terms of today's dollars. How much is a dollar next period worth in terms of a dollar today? The answer is $1/(1+r)$ dollars. This is because $1/(1 + r)$ dollars can be turned into a dollar next period simply by saving it at the rate of interest r. The *present value* of a dollar to be delivered next period is $1/(1 + r)$.

The concept of present value gives us another way to express the budget for a two-period consumption problem: a consumption plan is affordable if *the present value of consumption equals the present value of income.*

The idea of present value has an important implication that is closely related to a point made in Chapter 9: if the consumer can freely buy and sell goods at constant prices, then the consumer would always prefer a higher valued endowment to a lower valued one. In the case of intertemporal decisions, this principle implies that *if a consumer can freely borrow and lend at a constant interest rate, then the consumer would always prefer a pattern of income with a higher present value to a pattern with a lower present value.*

This is true for the same reason that the statement in Chapter 9 was true: an endowment with a higher value gives rise to a budget line that is farther out. The new budget set contains the old budget set, which means that the consumer would have all the consumption opportunities she had with the old budget set plus some more. Economists sometimes say that an endowment with a higher present value **dominates** one with a lower present value in the sense that the consumer can have larger consumption in *every* period by selling the endowment with the higher present value that she could get by selling the endowment with the lower present value.

Of course, if the present value of one endowment is higher than another, then the future value will be higher as well. However, it turns out that the present value is a more convenient way to measure the purchasing power of an endowment of money over time, and it is the measure to which we will devote the most attention.

11.7 Analyzing Present Value for Several Periods

Let us consider a three-period model. We suppose that we can borrow or lend money at an interest rate r each period and that this interest rate will remain constant over the three periods. Thus the price of consumption in period 2 in terms of period 1 consumption will be $1/(1+r)$, just as before.

What will the price of period 3 consumption be? Well, if I invest one dollar today it will grow into $(1+r)$ dollars next period, and if I leave this money invested, it will grow into $(1+r)^2$ dollars by the third period. Thus if I start with $1/(1+r)^2$ dollars today, I can turn this into 1 dollar in period 3. The price of period 3 consumption relative to period 1 consumption is therefore $1/(1+r)^2$. Each extra dollar's worth of consumption in period 3 costs me $1/(1+r)^2$ dollars today. This implies that the budget constraint will have the form

$$c_1 + \frac{c_2}{1+r} + \frac{c_3}{(1+r)^2} = m_1 + \frac{m_2}{1+r} + \frac{m_3}{(1+r)^2}.$$

This is just like the budget constraints we've seen before, where the price of period t consumption in terms of today's consumption is given by

$$p_t = \frac{1}{(1+r)^{t-1}}.$$

As before, moving to an endowment that has a higher present value at these prices will be preferred by any consumer, since such a change will necessarily shift the budget set farther out.

We have derived this budget constraint under the assumption of constant interest rates, but it is easy to generalize to the case of changing interest rates. Suppose, for example, that the interest earned on savings from period 1 to 2 is r_1, while savings from period 2 to 3 earn r_2. Then a dollar in period 1 will grow to $(1+r_1)(1+r_2)$ dollars in period 3. The present value of a dollar in period 3 is therefore $1/(1+r_1)(1+r_2)$. This implies that the correct form of the budget constraint is

$$c_1 + \frac{c_2}{1+r_1} + \frac{c_3}{(1+r_1)(1+r_2)} = m_1 + \frac{m_2}{1+r_1} + \frac{m_3}{(1+r_1)(1+r_2)}.$$

This expression is not so hard to deal with, but we will typically be content to examine the case of constant interest rates.

Table 11.1 contains some examples of the present value of a dollar T years in the future at different interest rates. The notable fact about this table is how quickly the present value goes down for "reasonable" interest rates. For example, at an interest rate of 10 percent, the value of a dollar 20 years from now is only 15 cents.

11.8 Use of Present Value

Let us start by stating an important general principle: *present value is the only correct way to convert a stream of payments into today's dollars*. This

Table 11.1

The present value of a dollar t years in the future.

Rate	1	2	5	10	15	20	25	30
.05	.95	.91	.78	.61	.48	.37	.30	.23
.10	.91	.83	.62	.39	.24	.15	.09	.06
.15	.87	.76	.50	.25	.12	.06	.03	.02
.20	.83	.69	.40	.16	.06	.03	.01	.00

principle follows directly from the definition of present value: the present value measures the value of a consumer's endowment of money. As long as the consumer can borrow and lend freely at a constant interest rate, an endowment with higher present value can always generate *more* consumption in every period than an endowment with lower present value. Regardless of your own tastes for consumption in different periods, you should always prefer a stream of money that has a higher present value to one with lower present value—since that always gives you more consumption possibilities in every period.

This argument is illustrated in Figure 11.6. In this figure, (m'_1, m'_2) is a worse consumption bundle than the consumer's original endowment, (m_1, m_2), since it lies beneath the indifference curve through her endowment. Nevertheless the consumer would prefer (m'_1, m'_2) to (m_1, m_2) if she is able to borrow and lend at the interest rate r. This is true since with the endowment (m'_1, m'_2) she can afford to consume a bundle such as (c_1, c_2) which is unambiguously better than her current consumption bundle.

One very useful application of present value is in valuing different kinds of investments. If you want to compare two different investments that yield different streams of payments to see which is better, you simply compute the two present values and choose the larger one. The investment with the larger present value always gives you more consumption possibilities.

EXAMPLE: Valuing a Stream of Payments

Suppose that we are considering two investments, A and B. Investment A pays $100 now and will also pay $200 next year. Investment B pays $0 now, and will generate $310 next year. Which is the better investment?

The answer is: it depends on the interest rate. If the interest rate is 0, the answer is clear—just add up the payments. For if the interest rate is 0, then the present value calculation boils down to summing up the payments.

If the interest rate is zero the present value of investment A is

$$PV_A = 100 + 200 = 300$$

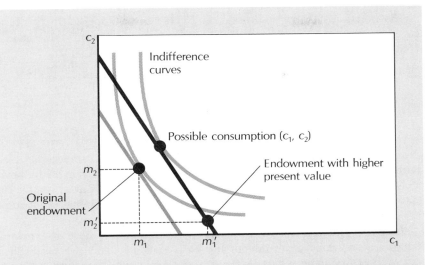

Higher present value.   An endowment with higher present value gives the consumer more consumption possibilities in each period if she can borrow and lend at the market interest rates.

**Figure
11.6**

and the present value of investment B is

$$PV_B = 0 + 310 = 310$$

so B is the preferred investment.

But we get the opposite answer if the interest rate is high enough. Suppose, for example, that the interest rate is 20 percent. Then the present value calculation becomes

$$PV_A = 100 + \frac{200}{1.20} = 266.67$$
$$PV_B = 0 + \frac{310}{1.20} = 258.33.$$

Now A is the better investment. The fact that A pays back more money earlier means that it will have a higher present value when the interest rate is large enough.

EXAMPLE: How Much Is Winning the Lottery Really Worth?

Newspapers love large numbers. When someone wins a lottery we usually see headlines telling how so-and-so has won a MILLION DOLLARS FOR LIFE! What the articles typically omit is the fact that the million dollars is paid out over a relatively long period. For example, suppose that the million dollar lottery prize is paid as \$50,000 a year for 20 years. It is true that this totals up to a million dollars, but the present value of this stream of payments at a 10 percent interest rate is only \$425,678. Nothing to sneeze at, but that's a long way from getting a million dollars today.

11.9 Bonds

Securities are financial instruments that promise certain patterns of payment schedules. There are many kinds of financial instruments because there are many kinds of payment schedules that people want. Financial markets give people the opportunity to trade different patterns of cash flows over time. These cash flows are typically used to finance consumption at some time or other.

The particular kind of security that we will examine here is a **bond.** Bonds are issued by governments and corporations. They are basically a way to borrow money. The borrower—the agent who issues the bond— promises to pay a fixed number of dollars x (the **coupon**) each period until a certain date T (the **maturity date**), at which point the borrower will pay an amount F (the **face value**) to the holder of the bond.

Thus the payment stream of a bond looks like $(x, x, x, \ldots, F)$. If the interest rate is constant, the present discounted value of such a bond is easy to compute. It is given by

$$ PV = \frac{x}{(1+r)} + \frac{x}{(1+r)^2} + \cdots + \frac{F}{(1+r)^T}. $$

Note that the present value of a bond will decline if the interest rate increases. Why is this? When the interest rate goes up the price now for a dollar delivered in the future goes down. So the future payments of the bond will be worth less now.

There is a large and developed market for bonds. The market value of outstanding bonds will fluctuate as the interest rate fluctuates since the present value of the stream of payments represented by the bond will change.

An interesting special kind of a bond is a bond that makes payments forever. These are called **consols** or **perpetuities**. Suppose that we consider a consol that promises to pay \$$x$ a year forever. To compute the value of this consol we have to compute the infinite sum:

$$ PV = \frac{x}{1+r} + \frac{x}{(1+r)^2} + \cdots . $$

The trick to computing this is to factor out $1/(1+r)$ to get

$$ PV = \frac{1}{1+r} \left[x + \frac{x}{(1+r)} + \frac{x}{(1+r)^2} + \cdots \right] . $$

But the term in the brackets is just x plus the present value! Substituting and solving for PV:

$$PV = \frac{1}{(1+r)} \left[x + PV \right]$$
$$= \frac{x}{r}.$$

This wasn't hard to do, but there is an easy way to get the answer right off. How much money, V, would you need at an interest rate r to get x dollars forever? Just write down the equation:

$$Vr = x$$

which says that the interest on V must equal x. But then the value of such an investment is given by

$$V = \frac{x}{r}.$$

Thus it must be that the present value of a consol that promises to pay x dollars forever must be given by x/r.

For a consol it is easy to see directly how increasing the interest rate reduces the value of a bond. Suppose, for example, that a consol is issued when the interest rate is 10 percent. Then if it promises to pay \$10 a year forever, it will be worth \$100 now—since \$100 would generate \$10 a year in interest income.

Now suppose that the interest rate goes up to 20 percent. The value of the consol must fall to \$50, since it only takes \$50 to earn \$10 a year at a 20 percent interest rate.

The formula for the consol can be used to calculate an approximate value of a long-term bond. If the interest rate is 10 percent, for example, the value of a dollar 30 years from now is only 6 cents. For the size of interest rates we usually encounter, 30 years might as well be infinity.

EXAMPLE: Installment Loans

Suppose that you borrow \$1000 that you promise to pay back in 12 monthly installments of \$100 each. What rate of interest are you paying?

At first glance it seems that your interest rate is 20 percent: you have borrowed \$1000 and you are paying back \$1200. But this analysis is wrong. For you haven't really borrowed \$1000 for an entire year. You have borrowed \$1000 for a month, and then you pay back \$100. Then you only have borrowed \$900, and you owe only a month's interest on the \$900. You borrow that for a month and then pay back another \$100. And so on.

The stream of payments that we want to value is

$$(1000, -100, -100, \ldots, -100).$$

We can find the interest rate that makes the present value of this stream equal to 0 by using a calculator or a computer. The actual interest rate that you are paying on the installment loan is about 35 percent!

11.10 Taxes

In the U.S. economy, interest payments are taxed as ordinary income. Thus you pay the same rate on income interest as on income from labor. Suppose that your marginal tax bracket is t, so that each *extra* dollar of income, Δm, increases your tax liability by $t\Delta m$.

Then if you invest X dollars in an asset, you'll receive an interest payment of rX. But you'll also have to pay taxes of trX on this income, which will leave you with only $(1-t)rX$ dollars of after-tax income. We call the rate $(1-t)r$ the **after-tax rate of interest**.

What if you decide to borrow X dollars, rather than lend it? Then you'll have to pay an interest payment of rX on the money you borrowed. In the U.S., interest payments are tax deductible. If you itemize deductions, you can subtract your interest payments from your other income and only pay taxes on what's left. Thus the rX dollars you pay in interest will reduce your tax payments by trX. The total cost of the X dollars you borrowed will be $rX - trX = (1-t)rX$.

Thus the after-tax interest rate is same whether you are borrowing or lending, for people in the same tax bracket. The tax on saving will reduce the amount of money that people want to save, but the subsidy on borrowing will increase the amount of money that people want to borrow.

11.11 Choice of the Interest Rate

In the above discussion, we've talked about "the interest rate." In real life there are many interest rates: there are nominal rates, real rates, before-tax rates, after-tax rates, short-term rates, long-term rates, and so on. Which is the "right" rate to use in doing present value analysis?

The way to answer this question is to think about the fundamentals. The idea of present discounted value arose because we wanted to be able to convert money at one point in time to an equivalent amount at another point in time. "The interest rate" is the return on an investment that allows us to transfer funds in this way.

If we want to apply this analysis when there are a variety of interest rates available, we need to ask which one has the properties most like the stream of payments we are trying to value. If the stream of payments is not taxed, we should use an after-tax interest rate. If the stream of payments will continue for 30 years, we should use a long-term interest rate. If the stream of payments is risky, we should use the interest rate on an investment with similar risk characteristics. (We'll have more to say later about what this last statement actually means.)

The interest rate measures the *opportunity cost* of funds—what else you could be doing with your money. So every stream of payments should be compared to your best alternative that has similar characteristics in terms of tax treatment, risk, and liquidity.

EXAMPLE: The Tax Advantage of an IRA

In the U.S. it is now possible for certain individuals to save up to $2,000 a year tax free in an Individual Retirement Account (IRA). The entire amount of money (up to the $2,000 limit) that you invest in an IRA account can be deducted from your income taxes. Also, you don't have to pay taxes on any of the interest earned from your IRA.[3]

The catch is that you have to pay taxes on the money when you withdraw it—presumably when you are retired and possibly in a lower tax bracket. Sometimes it is argued that an IRA isn't that good of a deal since you might well end up in the same tax bracket or higher when you retire. This is a faulty argument.

Even if you aren't in a lower tax bracket when you cash in your IRA, the IRA is still a good deal; but not for the reason most people think. The usual story is that you benefit from deferring your taxes on your IRA deposit. It is true that you benefit by doing this, but of course the amount of money that you have to pay in taxes also increases. These two effects just cancel each other out. The real advantage of the IRA is that you get to accumulate interest tax-free.

Suppose, for example, that the interest rate is r, your tax bracket is t, and you have X dollars of extra income this year that you want to save for T years. First consider what happens if you invest your money without the benefit of an IRA. Then when you receive the X dollars of income, the first thing you have to do is to pay tX dollars in tax, which leaves you with $(1 - t)X$ dollars to invest. The first year you will earn interest at rate r, but then you have to pay taxes on that interest income at a rate of t. So if the interest rate is r, the after-tax interest rate will be $(1 - t)r$.

This means that the amount of money that you will have after T years is

$$(1 - t)X[1 + (1 - t)r]^T. \tag{11.4}$$

This is how your principal of $(1-t)X$ will grow at an interest rate of $(1-t)r$.

Now what happens if you use an IRA? This time you get to invest the entire X dollars, and it will accumulate at a *before-tax* interest rate of r. This means that you'll have $X(1 + r)^T$ in your IRA account in T years. But then, when you take the money out, you'll have to pay taxes on it at rate t—the tax rate is the same by assumption.

This leaves you with

$$(1 - t)X[1 + r]^T \tag{11.5}$$

---

[3] Under recent tax proposals, the tax status of the IRA may change.

of after-tax income. Comparing equations (11.4) and (11.5), we see that the difference comes in the interest term, not in the principal term: the real tax advantage of the IRA is that it allows you to compound interest tax-free. This effect can be substantial. If you are in a 40 percent tax bracket and you put $2,000 now in an IRA and leave it there for 10 years at interest rate of 10 percent, you will have $5,138 dollars at the end of that 10 years. If you invest the money outside of an IRA at 10 percent, your after-tax interest rate will be 6 percent $((1 - .40) \times 10)$. In 10 years, you will only have $3,582. Quite a difference!

Summary

1. The budget constraint for intertemporal consumption can be expressed in terms of present value or future value.

2. The comparative statics results derived earlier for general choice problems can be applied to intertemporal consumption as well.

3. The real rate of interest measures the extra consumption that you can get in the future by giving up some consumption today.

4. A consumer who can borrow and lend at a constant interest rate should always prefer an endowment with a higher present value to one with a lower present value.

Review Questions

1. How much is a million dollars to be delivered 20 years in the future worth today if the interest rate is 20 percent?

2. As the interest rate rises, does the intertemporal budget constraint become steeper or flatter?

3. Would the assumption that goods are perfect substitutes be valid in a study of intertemporal food purchases?

4. A consumer, who is initially a lender, remains a lender even after a decline in interest rates. Is this consumer better off or worse off after the change in interest rates? If the consumer becomes a borrower after the change is he better off or worse off?

5. What is the present value of $100 one year from now if the interest rate is 10%? What is the present value if the interest rate is 5%?

ASSET MARKETS

Assets are goods that provide a flow of services over time. Assets can provide a flow of consumption services, like housing services, or can provide a flow of money that can be used to purchase consumption. Assets that provide a monetary flow are called **financial assets**.

The bonds that we discussed in the last chapter are examples of financial assets. The flow of services they provide is the flow of interest payments. Other sorts of financial assets such as corporate stock provide different patterns of cash flows. In this chapter we will examine the functioning of asset markets under conditions of complete certainty about future flow of services provided by the asset.

12.1 Rates of Return

Under this admittedly extreme hypothesis, we have a simple principle relating asset rates of return: if there is no uncertainty about the cash flow provided by assets, then all assets have to have the same rate of return. The reason is obvious: if one asset had a higher rate of return than another, and both assets were otherwise identical, then no one would want to buy the asset with the lower rate of return. So in equilibrium, all assets that are actually held must pay the same rate of return.

Let us consider the process by which these rates of return adjust. Consider an asset A that has current price p_0 and is expected to have a price of p_1 tomorrow. Everyone is certain about what today's price of the asset is, and everyone is certain about what tomorrow's price will be. We suppose for simplicity that there are no dividends or other cash payments between periods 0 and 1. Suppose furthermore that there is another investment, B, that one can hold between periods 0 and 1 that will pay an interest rate of r. Now consider two possible investments: invest one dollar in asset A and cash it in next period, or invest one dollar in asset B and earn interest of r dollars over the period.

What are the values of these two investment plans at the end of the first period? In order to invest one dollar in asset A we need to buy x units of it first period where x satisfies

$$p_0 x = 1$$

or

$$x = \frac{1}{p_0}.$$

Thus the future value of one dollar's worth of this asset next period will be

$$FV = p_1 x = \frac{p_1}{p_0}.$$

On the other hand, if we invest one dollar in asset B, we will have $1 + r$ dollars next period. If assets A and B are both held in equilibrium, then a dollar invested in either one of them must be worth the same amount second period. Thus we have an equilibrium condition:

$$1 + r = \frac{p_1}{p_0}.$$

What happens if this equality is not satisfied? Then there is a sure way to make money. For example, if

$$1 + r > \frac{p_1}{p_0}$$

people who own asset A can sell one unit for p_0 dollars in the first period and invest the money in asset B. Next period their investment in asset B will be worth $p_0(1 + r)$, which is greater than p_1 by the above equation. This will guarantee that second period they will have enough money to repurchase asset A, and be back where they started from, but now with extra money.

This kind of operation—buying some of one asset and selling some of another to realize a sure return—is known as **riskless arbitrage**, or **arbitrage** for short. As long as there are people around looking for "sure things" we would expect that well-functioning markets should quickly eliminate any opportunities for arbitrage. Thus another way to state our equilibrium condition is to say that in equilibrium *there should be no opportunities for arbitrage*. We'll refer to this as the **no arbitrage condition**.

But how does arbitrage actually work to eliminate the inequality? In the example given above, we argued that if $1 + r > p_1/p_0$, then anyone who held asset A would want to sell it first period, since they were guaranteed enough money to repurchase it second period. But who would they sell it to? Who would want to buy it? There would be plenty of people willing to supply asset A at p_0, but there wouldn't be anyone foolish enough to demand it at that price.

This means that supply would exceed demand and therefore the price will fall. How far will it fall? Just enough to satisfy the arbitrage condition: until $1 + r = p_1/p_0$.

12.2 Arbitrage and Present Value

We can rewrite the arbitrage condition in a useful way by cross multiplying to get

$$p_0 = \frac{p_1}{1 + r}.$$

This says that the current price of an asset must be its present value. Essentially we have converted the future value comparison in the arbitrage condition to a present value comparison. So if the no arbitrage condition is satisfied then we are assured that assets must sell for their present values. Any deviation from present value pricing leaves a sure way to make money.

12.3 Adjustments for Differences Among Assets

The no arbitrage rule assumes that the asset services provided by the two assets are identical, except for the purely monetary difference. If the services provided by the assets have different characteristics, then we would want to adjust for those differences before we blandly assert that the two assets must have the same equilibrium rate of return.

For example, one asset might be easier to sell than the other. We sometimes express this by saying that one asset is more **liquid** than another. In this case, we might want to adjust the rate of return to take account of the difficulty involved in finding a buyer for the asset. Thus a house that is worth \$100,000 is probably a less liquid asset than \$100,000 in Treasury bills.

Similarly, one asset might be riskier than another. The rate of return on one asset may be guaranteed, while the rate of return on another asset may be highly risky. We'll examine ways to adjust for risk differences in Chapter 14.

Here we want to consider two other types of adjustment we might make. One is adjustment for assets that have some return in consumption value, and the other is for assets that have different tax characteristics.

12.4 Assets with Consumption Returns

Many assets pay off only in money. But there are other assets that pay off in terms of consumption as well. The prime example of this is housing. If you own a house that you live in, then you don't have to rent living quarters; thus part of the "return" to owning the house is the fact that you get to live in the house without paying rent. Or, put another way, you get to pay the rent for your house to yourself. This latter way of putting it sounds peculiar, but it contains an important insight.

It is true that you don't make an *explicit* rental payment to yourself for the privilege of living in your house, but it turns out to be fruitful to think of a homeowner as *implicitly* making such a payment. The **implicit rental rate** on your house is the rate at which you could rent a similar house. Or, equivalently, it is the rate at which you could rent your house to someone else on the open market. By choosing to "rent your house to yourself" you are forgoing the opportunity of earning rental payments from someone else, and thus incurring an opportunity cost.

Suppose that the implicit rental payment on your house would work out to T per year. Then part of the return to owning your house is the fact that it generates for you an implicit income of T per year—the money that you would otherwise have to pay to live in the same circumstances as you do now.

But that is not the entire return on your house. As real estate agents never tire of telling us, a house is also an *investment*. When you buy a house you pay a significant amount of money for it, and you might reasonably expect to earn a monetary return on this investment as well, through an increase in the value of your house. This increase in the value of an asset is known as **appreciation**.

Let us use A to represent the expected appreciation in the dollar value of your house over a year. The total return to owning your house is the sum of the rental return, T, and the investment return, A. If your house initially cost P, then the *total* rate of return on your initial investment in housing is

$$h = \frac{T + A}{P}.$$

This total rate of return is composed of the consumption rate of return, T/P, and the investment rate of return, A/P.

Let us use r to represent the rate of return on other financial assets. Then the total rate of return on housing should, in equilibrium, be equal to r:

$$r = \frac{T + A}{P}.$$

Think about it this way. At the beginning of the year, you can invest P in a bank and earn rP, or you can invest P in a house and save T of rent and earn A of money by the end of the year. The total return from these two investments has to be the same. If $T + A < rP$ you would be better off investing your money in the bank and paying T in rent. You would then have $rP - T > A$ dollars at the end of the year. If $T + A > rP$, then housing would be the better choice. (Of course, this is ignoring the real estate agent's commission and other transactions costs associated with the purchase and sale.)

Since the total return should rise at the rate of interest, the financial rate of return A/P will generally be less than the rate of interest. Thus in general, assets that pay off in consumption will in equilibrium have a lower financial rate of return than purely financial assets. This means that buying houses, or paintings, or jewelry *solely* as a financial investment is probably not a good idea since the rate of return on these assets will probably be lower than the rate of return on purely financial assets, because part of the price of the asset reflects the consumption return that people receive from owning such assets. On the other hand if you place a sufficiently high value on the consumption return on such assets, it may well make sense to buy them. The *total* return on such assets may well make this a sensible choice.

12.5 Taxation on Asset Returns

The Internal Revenue Service distinguishes two different kinds of asset returns for purposes of taxation. The first kind is the **dividend** or **interest** return. These are returns that are paid periodically—each year or each month—over the life of the asset. You pay taxes on interest and dividend income at your ordinary tax rate, the same rate that you pay on your labor income.[1]

The second kind of returns are called **capital gains**. Capital gains occur when you sell an asset at a price higher than the price at which you bought it. Capital gains are taxed only when you actually sell the asset, and even then, you are taxed on only 40 percent of your actual capital gain. Thus

---

[1] Actually, you can exclude the first $100 of dividend income from being taxed, but we will ignore this feature of the tax code.

capital gains are favored in two ways: they are taxed at a lower rate, and they are only taxed when you sell the asset, not each year like dividends.[2]

Suppose that you intend to hold an asset for a year and that it will pay D dollars of dividends that year and be worth K dollars more than your original price P_0. If your marginal tax rate is t, then the after-tax return on this asset during that year will be

$$\frac{(1-t)D + (1-.4t)K}{P_0}.$$
(12.1)

If you hold the asset for more than a year, the capital gains part of the tax becomes less important, since you don't have to pay it until you actually want to sell the asset. The **effective tax on capital gains** is the amount of money that you would have to set aside each year in order to pay the capital gains tax when you actually sell the asset. Assets are held on the average about 7 years in the U.S., and it can be shown that the effective tax rate on capital gains is about $0.05t$. Capital gains are hardly taxed at all compared to other types of returns.

The consumption part of an asset's payment is also tax exempt. In the case of a house, for example, the capital gains component of the total return is taxed, albeit at a very light rate, but the consumption returns are hardly taxed at all. An asset that pays $R a year and is taxed at a rate t, gives an after-tax income of $\$(1-t)R$. A house that pays $R in implicit rent gives an (implicit) after-tax income of $R, since the implicit rent isn't taxed. So from the viewpoint of after-tax returns, assets that pay off in consumption might not be so bad after all—if you value the consumption that the assets provide.

The fact that different assets are taxed differently means that the arbitrage rule must adjust for the tax differences in comparing rates of return. Suppose that one asset pays a before-tax interest rate, r_b, and another asset pays a return that is tax exempt, r_e. Then if both assets are held by individuals who pay taxes on income at rate t, we must have

$$(1-t)r_b = r_e.$$

That is, the after-tax return on each asset must be the same. Otherwise, individuals would not want to hold both assets—it would always pay them to switch exclusively to holding the asset that gave them the higher after-tax return. (Abstracting away from differences in liquidity, risk, etc.)

In the case of a house, we claimed above that the capital gains component and the consumption component of the return were effectively tax exempt.

---

[2] In order to get the favorable capital gains tax treatment, you have to hold an asset for a minimum length of time. Currently, the minimum time is six months.

Thus individuals who hold a house along with other taxable assets earning an interest rate of r must satisfy the no arbitrage condition that

$$\frac{T + A}{P} = (1 - t)r.$$

This equation states that the untaxed consumption rate of return (T/P) plus the (almost untaxed) appreciation rate of return (A/P) has to equal the after-tax return on other assets.

12.6 Applications

The fact that all riskless assets must earn the same return is obvious, but very important. It has surprisingly powerful implications for the functioning of asset markets.

Depletable Resources

Let us study the market equilibrium for a depletable resource like oil. Consider a competitive oil market, with many suppliers, and suppose for simplicity that there are zero costs to extract oil from the ground. Then how will the price of oil change over time?

It turns out that the price of oil must rise at the rate of interest. For oil in the ground is an asset like any other asset. If it is worthwhile for a producer to hold it from one period to the next, it must provide a return to him equivalent to the financial return he could get elsewhere. If we let p_{t+1} and p_t be the prices at times $t + 1$ and t, then we have

$$p_{t+1} = (1 + r)p_t$$

as our intertemporal arbitrage condition.

The argument boils down to this simple idea: oil in the ground is like money in the bank. If money in the bank earns a rate of return of r, then oil in the ground must earn the same rate of return. If oil in the ground earned a higher return than money in the bank, then no one would take oil out of the ground, preferring to wait till later to extract it, thus pushing the current price of oil up. If oil in the ground earned a lower return than money in the bank, then the owners of oil wells would try to pump their oil out immediately in order to put the money in the bank, thereby depressing the current price of oil.

This argument tells us how the price of oil changes. But what determines the price level itself? The price level turns out to be determined by the demand for oil. Let us consider a very simple model of the demand side of the market.

Suppose that the demand for oil is constant at D barrels a year and that there is a total world supply of S barrels. Thus we have a total of $T = S/D$ years of oil left. When the oil has been depleted we will have to use an alternative technology, say liquefied coal, which can be produced at a constant cost of C dollars per barrel. We suppose that liquefied coal is a perfect substitute for oil in all applications.

Now, T years from now, when the oil is just being exhausted, how much must it sell for? Clearly it must sell for C dollars a barrel, the price of its perfect substitute, liquefied coal. This means that the price today of a barrel of oil, p_0, must grow at the rate of interest r over the next T years to be equal to C. This gives us the equation

$$p_0(1+r)^T = C$$

or

$$p_0 = \frac{C}{(1+r)^T}.$$

This expression gives us the current price of oil as a function of the other variables in the problem. We can now ask interesting comparative statics questions. For example, what happens if there is an unforeseen new discovery of oil? This means that T, the number of years remaining of oil, will increase, and thus $(1+r)^T$ will increase, thereby decreasing p_0. So an increase in the supply of oil will, not surprisingly, decrease its current price.

What if there is a technological breakthrough that decreases the value of C? Then the above equation shows that p_0 must decrease. The price of oil has to be equal to the price of its perfect substitute, liquefied coal, when liquefied coal is the only alternative.

When to Cut a Forest

Suppose that the size of a forest—measured in terms of the lumber that you can get from it—is some function of time, $F(t)$. Suppose further that the price of lumber is constant and that the rate of growth of the tree starts high and gradually declines. If there is a competitive market for lumber, when should the forest be cut for timber?

Answer: when the rate of growth of the forest equals the interest rate. Before that, the forest is earning a higher rate of return than money in the bank, and after that point it is earning less than money in the bank. The optimal time to cut a forest is when its growth rate just equals the interest rate.

We can express this more formally by looking at the present value of cutting the forest at time T. This will be

$$PV = \frac{F(T)}{(1+r)^T}.$$

We want to find the choice of T that maximizes the present value—that is, that makes the value of the forest as large as possible. If we choose a very small value of T, the rate of growth of the forest will exceed the interest rate, which means that the PV would be increasing so it would pay to wait a little longer. On the other hand, if we consider a very large value of T, the forest would be growing more slowly than the interest rate, so the PV would be decreasing. The choice of T that maximizes present value occurs when the rate of growth of the forest just equals the interest rate.

This argument is illustrated in Figure 12.1. In Figure 12.1A we have plotted the *rate* of growth of the forest and the *rate* of growth of a dollar invested in a bank. If we want to have the largest amount of money at some unspecified point in the future, we should always invest our money in the asset with the highest return available at each point in time. When the forest is young, it is the asset with the highest return. As it matures, its rate of growth declines, and eventually the bank offers a higher return.

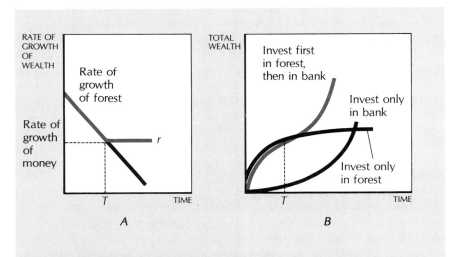

Harvesting a forest. The optimal time to cut a forest is when the rate of growth of the forest equals the interest rate.

Figure 12.1

The effect on total wealth is illustrated in Figure 12.1B. Before T wealth grows most rapidly when invested in the forest. After T it grows most rapidly when invested in the bank. Therefore, the optimal strategy is to invest in the forest up until time T, then harvest the forest, and invest the proceeds in the bank.

12.7 Financial Institutions

Asset markets allow people to change their pattern of consumption over time. Consider, for example, two people A and B who have different endowments of wealth. A might have $100 today and nothing tomorrow, while B might have $100 tomorrow and nothing today. It might well happen that each would rather have $50 today and $50 tomorrow. But they can reach this pattern of consumption simply by trading: A gives B $50 today, and B gives A $50 tomorrow.

In this particular case, the interest rate is zero: A lends B $50 and only gets $50 in return the next day. If people have convex preferences over consumption today and tomorrow, they would like to smooth their consumption over time, rather than consume everything in one period, even if the interest rate were 0.

We can repeat the same kind of story for other patterns of asset endowments. One individual might have an endowment that provides a steady stream of payments and prefer to have a lump sum, while another might have a lump sum and prefer a steady stream. For example, a twenty-year-old individual might want to have a lump sum of money now to buy a house, while a sixty-year-old might want to have a steady stream of money to finance his retirement. It is clear that both of these individuals could gain by trading their endowments with each other.

In a modern economy financial institutions exist to facilitate these trades. In the case described above, the sixty-year-old can put his lump sum of money in the bank, and the bank can then lend it to the twenty-year-old. The twenty-year-old then makes mortgage payments to the bank, which are, in turn, transferred to the sixty-year-old as interest payments. Of course, the bank takes its cut for arranging the trade, but if the banking industry is sufficiently competitive, this cut should end up pretty close to the actual costs of doing business.

Banks aren't the only kind of financial institution that allow one to reallocate consumption over time. Another important example is the stock market. Suppose that an entrepreneur starts a company that becomes successful. In order to start the company, the entrepreneur probably had some financial backers who put up money to help him get started—to pay the bills until the revenues started rolling in. Once the company has been established, the owners of the company have a claim to the profits that the company will generate in the future: they have a claim to a stream of payments.

But it may well be that they prefer a lump sum reward for their efforts now. In this case, the owners can decide to sell the firm to other people via the stock market. They issue shares in the company that entitle the shareholders to a cut of the future profits of the firm in exchange for a lump sum payment now. People who want to purchase part of the stream of profits of the firm pay the original owners for these shares. In this way, both sides of the market can reallocate their wealth over time.

There are a variety of other institutions and markets that help facilitate intertemporal trade. But what happens when the buyers and sellers aren't evenly matched? What happens if more people want to sell consumption tomorrow than want to buy it? Just as in any market, if the supply of something exceeds the demand, the price will fall. In this case, the price of consumption tomorrow will fall. We saw earlier that the price of consumption tomorrow was given by

$$p = \frac{1}{1+r}$$

so this means that the interest rate must rise. The increase in the interest rate induces people to save more and to demand less consumption now, and thus tends to equate demand and supply.

Summary

1. In equilibrium, all assets with certain payoffs must earn the same rate of return. Otherwise there would be a riskless arbitrage opportunity.

2. The fact that all assets must earn the same return implies that all assets will sell for their present value.

3. If assets are taxed differently, or have different risk characteristics, then we must compare their after-tax rates of return, or their risk adjusted rates of return.

Review Questions

1. Suppose asset A can be sold for $11 next period. If assets similar to A are paying a rate of return of 10%, what must be asset A's current price?

2. A house, which you could rent for $10,000 a year and sell for $110,000 a year from now, can be purchased for $100,000. What is the rate of return on this house?

3. The payments of certain types of bonds (e.g., municipal bonds) are not taxable. If similar taxable bonds are paying 10% and everyone faces a marginal tax rate of 40%, what rate of return must the nontaxable bonds pay?

4. Suppose that a scarce resource, facing a constant demand, will be exhausted in 10 years. If an alternative resource will be available at a price of $40 and if the interest rate is 10%, what must the price of the scarce resource be today?

APPENDIX

Suppose that you invest a dollar in an asset yielding an interest rate r where the interest is paid once a year. Then after T years you will have $(1 + r)^T$ dollars. Suppose now that the interest is paid monthly. This means that the monthly interest rate will be $T/12$, and there will be $12T$ payments, so that after T years you will have $(1 + r/12)^{12T}$ dollars. If the interest rate is paid daily, you will have $(1 + r/365)^{365T}$ and so on.

In general, if the interest is paid n times a year, you will have $(1 + r/n)^{nT}$ dollars after T years. It is natural to ask how much money you will have if the interest is paid *continuously*. That is, we ask what is the limit of this expression as n goes to infinity. It turns out that this is given by the following expression:

$$e^{rT} = \lim_{n \to \infty} (1 + r/n)^{nT}$$

where e is $2.7183\ldots$, the base of natural logarithms.

This expression for continuous compounding is very convenient for calculations. For example, let us verify the claim in the text that the optimal time to harvest the forest is when the rate of growth of the forest equals the interest rate. Since the forest will be worth $F(T)$ at time T, the present value of the forest harvested at time T is

$$V(T) = \frac{F(T)}{e^{rT}} = e^{-rT} F(T).$$

In order to maximize the present value, we differentiate this with respect to T and set the resulting expression equal to zero. This yields

$$V'(T) = e^{-rT} F'(T) - re^{-rT} F(T) = 0$$

or

$$F'(T) - rF(T) = 0.$$

This can be rearranged to establish the result:

$$r = \frac{F'(T)}{F(T)}.$$

13

UNCERTAINTY

Uncertainty is a fact of life. People face risks every time they take a shower, walk across the street, or make an investment. But there are financial institutions such as insurance markets and the stock market that can mitigate at least some of these risks. We will study the functioning of these markets in the next chapter, but first we must study individual behavior with respect to choices involving uncertainty.

13.1 Contingent Consumption

Since we now know all about the standard theory of consumer choice, let's try to use what we know to understand choice under uncertainty. The first question to ask is what is the basic "thing" that is being chosen?

The consumer is presumably concerned with the **probability distribution** of getting different consumption bundles of goods. A probability distribution consists of a list of different outcomes—in this case, consumption bundles—and the probability associated with each outcome. When a consumer decides how much automobile insurance to buy, or how much to invest in the stock market, he is in effect deciding on a pattern of getting different amounts of consumption with different probabilities.

For example, suppose that you have $100 now, and you are contemplating buying lottery ticket number 13. If number 13 is drawn in the lottery, the holder will be paid $200. This ticket costs, say, $5. The two outcomes that are of interest are the event that the ticket is drawn and the event that it isn't.

Your original endowment of wealth—the amount that you would have if you did not purchase the lottery ticket—is $100 if 13 is drawn, and $100 if it isn't drawn. But if you buy the lottery ticket for $5, you will have a wealth distribution consisting of $295 if the ticket is a winner, and $95 if it is not a winner. The original endowment of probabilities of wealth in different circumstances has been changed by the purchase of the lottery ticket. Let us examine this point in more detail.

In this discussion we'll restrict ourselves to examining monetary gambles for convenience of exposition. Of course, it is not money alone that matters; it is the consumption goods that money can buy that are the ultimate "good" that is being chosen. The same principles apply to gambles over goods, but restricting ourselves to monetary outcomes makes things simpler. Second, we will restrict ourselves to very simple situations where there are only a few possible outcomes. Again, this is only for reasons of simplicity.

Above we described the case of gambling in a lottery; here we'll consider the case of insurance. Suppose that an individual initially has $35,000 worth of assets, but there is a possibility that he may lose $10,000. For example, his car may be stolen, or a storm may damage his house. Suppose that the probability of this event happening is $p = .01$. Then the probability distribution the person is facing is a 1 percent probability of having $25,000 of assets, and a 99 percent probability of having $35,000.

Insurance offers a way to change this probability distribution. Suppose that there is an insurance contract that will pay the person $100 if the loss occurs in exchange for a $1 premium. Of course the premium must be paid whether or not the loss occurs. If the person decides to purchase $10,000 dollars of insurance, it will cost him $100. In this case he will have a 1 percent chance of having $34,900 ($35,000 of other assets − $10,000 loss + $10,000 payment from the insurance payment − $100 insurance premium) and a 99 percent chance of having $34,900 ($35,000 of assets − $100 insurance premium). Thus the consumer ends up with the same wealth no matter what happens. He is now fully insured against loss.

In general, if this person purchases K dollars of insurance and has to pay a premium γK, then he will face the gamble:[1]

probability .01 of getting $\$25,000 + K - \gamma K$

---

[1] The Greek letter γ, gamma, is pronounced "gam-ma."

and

probability .99 of getting $\$35,000 - \gamma K$.

What kind of insurance will this person choose? Well, that depends on his preferences. He might be very conservative and choose to purchase a lot of insurance, or he might like to take risks and not purchase any insurance at all. People have different preferences over probability distributions in the same way that they have different preferences over the consumption of ordinary goods.

In fact, one very fruitful way to look at decision making under uncertainty is just to think of the money available under different circumstances as different goods. A thousand dollars after a large loss has occurred may mean a very different thing than a thousand dollars when it hasn't. Of course, we don't have to apply this idea just to money: an ice cream cone if it happens to be hot and sunny tomorrow is a very different good than an ice cream cone if it is rainy and cold. In general, consumption goods will be of different value to a person depending upon the circumstances under which they become available.

Let us think of the different outcomes of some random event as being different **states of nature**. In the insurance example given above there were two states of nature: the loss occurs or it doesn't. But in general there could be many different states of nature. We can then think of a **contingent consumption plan** as being a specification of what will be consumed in each different state of nature—each different outcome of the random process. *Contingent* means depending on something not yet certain, so a contingent consumption plan means a plan that depends on the outcome of some event. In the case of insurance purchases, the contingent consumption was described by the terms of the insurance contract: how much money you would have if a loss occurred and how much you would have if it didn't. In the case of the rainy and sunny days, the contingent consumption would just be the *plan* of what would be consumed given the various outcomes of the weather.

People have preferences over different plans of consumption, just like they have preferences over actual consumption. It certainly might make you feel better now to know that you are fully insured. People make choices that reflect their preferences over consumption in different circumstances, and we can use the theory of choice that we have developed to analyze those choices.

If we think about a contingent consumption plan as being just an ordinary consumption bundle, we are right back in the framework described in the previous chapters. We can think of preferences as being defined over different consumption plans, the "terms of trade" as given by the budget constraint, and we can model the consumer as choosing the best consumption plan he or she can afford, just as we have done all along.

Let's describe the insurance purchase in terms of the indifference curve analysis we've been using. The two states of nature are the event that the loss occurs and the event that it doesn't. The contingent consumptions are the values of how much money you would have in each circumstance. We can plot this on a graph as in Figure 13.1.

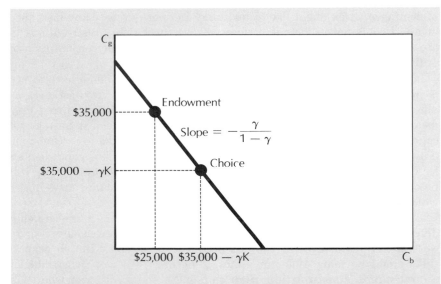

**Figure
13.1** **Insurance.** The budget line associated with the purchase of insurance. The insurance premium γ allows us to give up some consumption in the good outcome (C_g) in order to have more consumption in the bad outcome (C_b).

Your endowment of contingent consumption is $25,000 in the "bad" state—if the loss occurs—and $35,000 in the "good" state—if it doesn't occur. Insurance offers you a way to move away from this endowment point. If you purchase K dollars worth of insurance, you give up γK dollars of consumption possibilities in the good state in exchange for $K - \gamma K$ dollars of consumption possibilities in the bad state. Thus the extra consumption you can get in the bad state, divided by the extra consumption you lose in the good state, is

$$\frac{\Delta C_g}{\Delta C_b} = -\frac{\gamma K}{K - \gamma K} = -\frac{\gamma}{1 - \gamma}.$$

This is the slope of the budget line through your endowment. It is just as if the price of consumption in the good state is $1 - \gamma$ and the price in the bad state is γ.

We can draw in the indifference curves that a person might have for contingent consumption. Here again it is very natural for indifference curves to have a convex shape: this means that the person would rather have a constant amount of consumption in each state than a large amount in one state and a low amount in the other.

Given the indifference curves for consumption in each state of nature, we can look at the choice of how much insurance to purchase. As usual, this will be characterized by a tangency condition: the marginal rate of substitution between consumption in each state of nature should be equal to the price at which you can trade off consumption in those states.

Of course, once we have a model of optimal choice, we can apply all of the machinery developed in early chapters to its analysis. We can examine how the demand for insurance changes as the price of insurance changes, as the wealth of the consumer changes, and so on. The theory of consumer behavior is perfectly adequate to model behavior under uncertainty as well as certainty.

13.2 Utility Functions and Probabilities

If the consumer has reasonable preferences about consumption in different circumstances, then we will be able to use a utility function to describe these preferences, just as we have done in other contexts. However, the fact that we are considering choice under uncertainty does add a special structure to the choice problem. In general, how a person values consumption in one state as compared to another will depend on the *probability* that the state in question will actually occur. In other words, the rate at which I am willing to substitute consumption if it rains for consumption if it doesn't should have something to do with how likely I think rain is. The preferences for consumption in different states of nature will depend on the beliefs of the individual about how likely those states are.

For this reason, we will write the utility function as depending on the probabilities as well as on the consumption levels. Suppose that we are considering two mutually exclusive states such as rain and shine, loss or no loss, or whatever. Let c_1 and c_2 represent consumption in states 1 and 2, and let π_1 and π_2 be the probabilities that state 1 or state 2 actually occurs.

If the two states are really mutually exclusive, so that only one of them can happen, then $\pi_2 = 1 - \pi_1$. But we'll generally write out both probabilities just to keep things looking symmetric.

Given this notation, we can write the utility function for consumption in states 1 and 2 as $u(c_1, c_2, \pi_1, \pi_2)$. This is the function that represents the individual's preference over consumption in each state.

EXAMPLE: Some Examples of Utility Functions

We can use nearly any of the examples of utility functions that we've seen up until now in the context of choice under uncertainty. For example, one nice case is the case of perfect substitutes where we weight each consumption by the probability that it will occur. This gives us a utility function of the form

$$u(c_1, c_2, \pi_1, \pi_2) = \pi_1 c_1 + \pi_2 c_2.$$

In the context of uncertainty, this kind of expression is known as the **expected value**. It is just the average level of consumption that you would get.

Another example of a utility function that might be used to examine choice under uncertainty is the Cobb–Douglas utility function:

$$u(c_1, c_2, \pi, 1 - \pi) = c_1^\pi c_2^{1-\pi}.$$

Here the utility attached to any combination of consumption bundles depends on the pattern of consumption in a nonlinear way.

As usual, we can take a monotonic transformation of utility and still represent the same preferences. It turns out that the logarithm of the Cobb-Douglas utility will be very convenient in what follows. This will give us a utility function of the form

$$\ln u(c_1, c_2, \pi_1, \pi_2) = \pi_1 \ln c_1 + \pi_2 \ln c_2.$$

13.3 Expected Utility

One particularly convenient form that the utility function might take is the following:

$$u(c_1, c_2, \pi_1, \pi_2) = \pi_1 v(c_1) + \pi_2 v(c_2).$$

This says that utility can be written as a weighted sum of some function of consumption in each state, $v(c_1)$ and $v(c_2)$, where the weights are given by the probabilities.

Two examples of this were given above. The perfect substitutes, or expected value utility function, had this form where $v(c) = c$. The Cobb-Douglas didn't have this form originally, but when we expressed it in terms of logs it had the linear form with $v(c) = \ln c$.

If one of the states is certain, so that $\pi_1 = 1$, say, then $v(c_1)$ is the utility of certain consumption in state 1. Similarly, if $\pi_2 = 1$, $v(c_2)$ is the utility of consumption in state 2. Thus the expression

$$\pi_1 v(c_1) + \pi_2 v(c_2)$$

represents the average utility, or the expected utility, of the pattern of consumption (c_1, c_2).

For this reason, we refer to a utility function with the particular form described here as an **expected utility function**, or, sometimes, a **von Neumann–Morgenstern utility function.**[2]

When we say that a consumer's preferences can be represented by an expected utility function, or that the consumer's preferences have the expected utility property, we mean that we can choose a utility function that has the additive form described above. Of course we could also choose a different form; any monotonic transformation of an expected utility function is a utility function that describes the same preferences. But the additive form representation turns out to be especially convenient. If the consumer's preferences are described by $\pi_1 \ln c_1 + \pi_2 \ln c_2$ they will also be described by $c_1^{\pi_1} c_2^{\pi_2}$. But the latter representation does not have the expected utility property, while the former does.

On the other hand, the expected utility function can be subjected to some kinds of monotonic transformation and still have the expected utility property. We say that a function $v(u)$ is a **positive affine transformation** if it can be written in the form: $v(u) = au + b$ where $a > 0$. A positive affine transformation is simply multiplying by a positive number and adding a constant. It turns out that if you subject an expected utility function to a positive affine transformation it not only represents the same preferences (this is obvious since an affine transformation is just a special kind of monotonic transformation), but it also still has the expected utility property.

Economists say that an expected utility function is "unique up to an affine transformation." This just means that you can apply an affine transformation to it and get another expected utility function that represents the same preferences. But any other kind of transformation will destroy the expected utility property.

13.4 Why Expected Utility Is Reasonable

The expected utility representation is a convenient one, but is it a reasonable one? Why would we think that preferences over uncertain choices would have the particular structure implied by the expected utility function? As it turns out there are compelling reasons why expected utility is a reasonable objective for choice problems in the face of uncertainty.

The fact that outcomes of the random choice are consumption goods that will be consumed in different circumstances means that ultimately

---

[2] John von Neumann was one of the major figures in mathematics in the twentieth century. He also contributed several important insights to physics, computer science, and economic theory. Oscar Morgenstern was an economist at Princeton who, along with von Neumann, helped to develop mathematical game theory.

only one of those outcomes is actually going to occur. Either your house will burn down or it won't; either it will be a rainy day or a sunny day. The way we have set up the choice problem means that only one of the many possible outcomes is going to occur, and hence only one of the contingent consumption plans will actually be realized.

This turns out to have a very interesting implication. Suppose you are considering purchasing fire insurance on your house for the coming year. In making this choice you will be concerned about wealth in three situations: your wealth now (c_0), your wealth if your house burns down (c_1), and your wealth if it doesn't (c_2). (Of course, what you really care about are your consumption possibilities in each outcome, but we are simply using wealth as a proxy for consumption here.) If π_1 is the probability that your house burns down and π_2 is the probability that it doesn't, then your preferences over these three different consumptions can generally be represented by a utility function $u(\pi_1, \pi_2, c_0, c_1, c_2)$.

Suppose that we are considering the tradeoff between wealth now and one of the possible outcomes—say, how much money we would be willing to sacrifice now to get a little more money if the house burns down. *Then this decision should be independent of how much consumption you will have in the other state of nature—how much wealth you will have if the house is not destroyed.* For the house will either burn down or it won't. If it happens to burn down then the value of extra wealth shouldn't depend on how much wealth you would have if it *didn't* burn down. Bygones are bygones—so what *doesn't* happen shouldn't affect the value of consumption in the outcome that *does* happen.

Note that this is an *assumption* about an individual's preferences. It may be violated. When people are considering a choice between two things, the amount of a third thing they have typically matters. The choice between coffee and tea may well depend on how much cream you have. But this is because you consume coffee together with cream. If you considered a choice where you rolled a dice and got either coffee, *or* tea, *or* cream, then the amount of cream that you might get shouldn't affect your preferences between coffee and tea. Why? Because you are either getting one thing or the other: if you end up with cream, the fact that you might have gotten either coffee or tea is irrelevant.

Thus in choice under uncertainty there is a natural kind of "independence" between the different outcomes because they must be consumed separately—in different states of nature. The choices that people plan to make in one state of nature should be independent from the choices that they plan to make in other states of nature. This assumption is known as the **independence assumption**. It turns out that this implies that the utility function for contingent consumption will take a very special structure: it has to be additive across the different contingent consumption bundles.

That is, if c_1, c_2, and c_3 are the consumptions in different states of nature, and π_1, π_2, and π_3 are the probabilities that these three different states of nature materialize, then if the independence assumption alluded to above is satisfied, the utility function must take the form

$$U(c_1, c_2, c_3) = \pi_1 u(c_1) + \pi_2 u(c_2) + \pi_3 u(c_3).$$

This is what we have called an expected utility function. Note that the expected utility function does indeed satisfy the property that the marginal rate of substitution between two goods is independent of how much there is of the third good. The marginal rate of substitution between goods 1 and 2, say, takes the form

$$\begin{aligned}
\mathrm{MRS}_{12} &= \frac{\Delta U(c_1, c_2, c_3)/\Delta c_1}{\Delta U(c_1, c_2, c_3)/\Delta c_2} \\
&= \frac{\pi_1 \Delta u(c_1)/\Delta c_1}{\pi_2 \Delta u(c_2)/\Delta c_2}.
\end{aligned}$$

This MRS depends only on how much you have of goods 1 and 2, not how much you have of good 3.

13.5 Risk Aversion

We claimed above that the expected utility function had some very convenient properties for analyzing choice under uncertainty. In this section we'll give an example of this.

Let's apply the expected utility framework to a simple choice problem. Suppose that a consumer currently has \$10 of wealth and is contemplating a gamble that gives him a 50 percent probability of winning \$5 and a 50 percent probability of losing \$5. The *expected value* of this gamble is \$10, and the expected utility is

$$\frac{1}{2} u(\$15) + \frac{1}{2} u(\$5).$$

This is depicted in Figure 13.2. The expected utility of the gamble is the average of the two numbers $u(\$15)$ and $u(\$5)$, labeled $.5u(5) + .5u(15)$ in the graph. We have also depicted the utility of the expected value of the gamble, which is labeled $u(\$10)$. Note that in this diagram the expected utility of the gamble is less than the utility of the expected value. That is:

$$u\left(\frac{1}{2}15 + \frac{1}{2}5\right) = u(10) > \frac{1}{2}u(15) + \frac{1}{2}u(5).$$

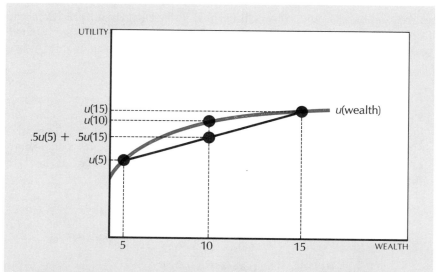

Figure
13.2

Risk aversion. For a risk averse consumer the utility of the expected value of this gamble, $u(10)$, is greater than the expected utility of the gamble, $.5u(5) + .5u(15)$.

In this case we say that the consumer is **risk averse** since he prefers to have the expected value of a gamble rather than face the gamble itself. Of course, it could happen that the preferences of the consumer were such that he prefers a gamble to its expected value, in which case we say that the consumer is a **risk lover**. An example is given in Figure 13.3.

Note the difference between Figures 13.2 and 13.3. The risk averse consumer has a *concave* utility function—its slope gets flatter as wealth is increased. The risk loving consumer has a *convex* utility function—its slope gets steeper as wealth increases. Thus the curvature of the utility function measures the consumer's attitude towards risk. In general, the more concave the utility function, the more risk averse the consumer will be, and the more convex the utility function, the more risk loving the consumer will be.

The intermediate case is that of a linear utility function. Here the consumer is **risk neutral**: the expected utility of a gamble is just its expected value. This is the case of perfect substitutes we described earlier. For this kind of utility function the consumer doesn't care about the riskiness of the gamble at all—only about its expected value.

EXAMPLE: The Demand for Insurance

Let's apply the expected utility structure to the demand for insurance that we considered earlier. Recall in that example that the person had a wealth

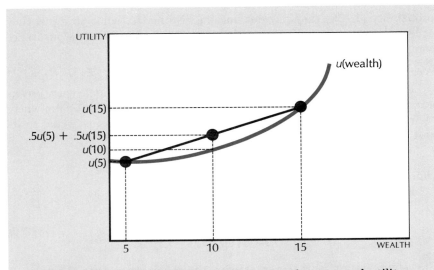

Risk loving. For a risk loving consumer the expected utility of the gamble, $.5u(5) + .5u(15)$, is greater than the utility of the expected value of the gamble, $u(10)$.

Figure
13.3

of \$35,000 and that he might incur a loss of \$10,000. The probability of the loss was 1 percent, and it cost him γK to purchase K dollars of insurance. By examining this using indifference curves, we saw that the optimal choice of insurance was determined by the condition that the marginal rate of substitution between consumption in the two outcomes—loss or no loss— was equal to $-\gamma/(1 - \gamma)$. Let π be the probability that the loss will occur, and $1 - \pi$ be the probability that it won't occur.

Let state 1 be the situation involving no loss, so that his wealth in that state is

$$c_1 = \$35,000 - \gamma K$$

and let state 2 be the loss situation with wealth

$$c_2 = \$35,000 - \$10,000 + K - \gamma K.$$

Then the consumer's optimal choice of insurance is determined by the condition that his marginal rate of substitution between consumption in the two outcomes is equal to the price ratio:

$$\text{MRS} = -\frac{\pi \Delta u(c_2)/\Delta c_2}{(1 - \pi)\Delta u(c_1)/\Delta c_1} = -\frac{\gamma}{1 - \gamma}. \qquad (13.1)$$

Now let us look at the insurance contract from the viewpoint of the insurance company. With probability π they must pay out K and with probability $(1 - \pi)$ they pay out nothing. No matter what happens, they collect the premium γK. Then the expected profit, P, of the insurance company is

$$P = \gamma K - \pi K - (1 - \pi) \cdot 0 = \gamma K - \pi K.$$

Let us suppose that on the average the insurance company just breaks even on the contract. That is, they offer insurance at a "fair" rate, where "fair" means that the expected value of the insurance is just equal to its cost. Then we have

$$P = \gamma K - \pi K = 0$$

which implies that $\gamma = \pi$.

Inserting this into equation (13.1) we have

$$\frac{\pi \Delta u(c_2)/\Delta c_2}{(1 - \pi)\Delta u(c_1)/\Delta c_1} = \frac{\pi}{1 - \pi}.$$

Canceling the π's, this leaves us with the requirement that the optimal amount of insurance must satisfy

$$\frac{\Delta u(c_1)}{\Delta c_1} = \frac{\Delta u(c_2)}{\Delta c_2}. \tag{13.2}$$

This equation says that the *marginal utility of an extra dollar of income if the loss occurs should be equal to the marginal utility of an extra dollar of income if the loss doesn't occur.*

Let us suppose that the consumer is risk averse so that his marginal utility of money is declining as the amount of money he has increases. Then if $c_1 > c_2$, the marginal utility at c_1 would be less than the marginal utility at c_2, and vice versa. Furthermore if the marginal utilities of income are equal at c_1 and c_2, as they are in equation (13.2), then we must have $c_1 = c_2$. Applying the formulas for c_1 and c_2:

$$35,000 - \gamma K = 25,000 + K - \gamma K$$

which implies that $K = \$10,000$. This means that when given a chance to buy insurance at a "fair" premium, a risk averse consumer will always choose to fully insure.

This happens because the utility of wealth in each state depends only on the total amount of wealth the consumer has in that state—and not what he *might* have in some other state—so that if the total amounts of wealth the consumer has in each state are equal, the marginal utilities of wealth must be equal as well.

To sum up: if the consumer is a risk averse expected utility maximizer, and if he is offered fair insurance against a loss, then he will optimally choose to fully insure.

13.6 Diversification

Let us turn now to a different topic involving uncertainty—the benefits of diversification. Suppose that you are considering investing $100 in two different companies, one that makes sunglasses and one that makes raincoats. The long-range weather forecasters have told you that next summer is equally likely to be rainy or sunny. How should you invest your money?

Wouldn't it make sense to hedge your bets and put some money in each? By diversifying your holdings of the two investments, you can get a return on your investment that is more certain, and therefore more desirable to a risk averse person.

Suppose, for example, that shares of the raincoat company and the sunglasses company currently sell for $10 apiece. If it is a rainy summer, the raincoat company will be worth $20 and the sunglasses company will be worth $5. If it is a sunny summer, the payoffs are reversed: the sunglasses company will be worth $20 and the raincoat company will be worth $5. If you invest your entire $100 in the sunglasses company, you are taking a gamble that has a 50 percent chance of giving you $200, and a 50 percent chance of giving you $50. The same magnitude of payoffs results if you invest all your money in the sunglasses company: in either case you have an expected payoff of $125.

But look what happens if you put half of your money in each. Then, if it is sunny you get $100 from the sunglasses investment and $25 from the raincoat investment. But if it is rainy, you get $100 from the raincoat investment and $25 from the sunglasses investment. Either way, you end up with $125 for sure. By diversifying your investment in the two companies, you have managed to reduce the overall risk of your investment, while keeping the expected payoff the same.

Diversification was quite easy in this example: the two assets were perfectly negatively correlated—when one went up, the other went down. Pairs of assets like this can be extremely valuable because they can reduce risk so dramatically. But, alas, they are also very hard to find. Most asset values move together: when GM stock is high, so is Ford stock, and so is Goodrich stock. But as long as asset price movements are not *perfectly* correlated, there will be some gains from diversification.

13.7 Risk Spreading

Let us return now to the example of insurance. There we considered the situation of an individual who had $35,000 and faced a .01 probability of a $10,000 loss. Suppose that there were 1,000 such individuals. Then, on average, there would be 10 losses incurred, and thus $100,000 lost each year. Each of the 1,000 people would face an *expected loss* of .01 times

$10,000, or $100 a year. Let us suppose that the probability that any person incurs a loss doesn't affect the probability that any of the others incur losses. That is, let us suppose that the risks are *independent*.

Then each individual will have an expected wealth of $.99 \times \$35,000 + .01 \times \$25,000 = \$34,900$. But each individual also bears a large amount of risk: each person has a 1 percent probability of losing $10,000.

Suppose that each consumer decides to *diversify* the risk that he or she faces. How can they do this? Answer: by selling some of their risk to other individuals. Suppose that the 1,000 consumers decide to insure each other. If anybody incurs the $10,000 loss, each of the 1.000 consumers will contribute $10 to that person. This way, the poor person whose house burns down is compensated for his loss, and the other consumers have the peace of mind that they will be compensated, if that poor soul happens to be themselves! This is an example of **risk spreading**: each consumer spreads his risk over all of the other consumers and thereby reduces the amount of risk he bears.

Now on the average, 10 houses will burn down a year, so on the average, each of the 1000 individuals will be paying out $100 a year. But this is just on the average. Some years there might be 12 losses, and other years there might be 8 losses. The probability is very small that an individual would actually have to pay out more than $200, say, in any one year, but even so, the risk is there.

But there is even a way to diversify this risk. Suppose that the homeowners agree to pay $100 a year for certain, whether or not there are any losses. Then they can build up a cash reserve fund that can be used in those years when there are multiple fires. They are paying $100 a year for certain, and on average that money will be sufficient to compensate homeowners for fires.

As you can see, we now have something very much like a cooperative insurance company. We could add a few more features: the insurance company gets to invest its cash reserve fund and earn interest on its assets, and so on, but the essence of the insurance company is clearly present.

13.8 Role of the Stock Market

The stock market plays a role similar to that of the insurance market in that it allows for risk spreading. Recall from Chapter 12 that we argued that the stock market allowed the original owners of firms to convert their stream of returns over time to a lump sum. Well, the stock market also allows them to convert their risky position of having all of their wealth tied up in one enterprise to a situation where they have a lump sum that they can invest in a variety of assets. The original owners of the firm have an incentive to issue shares in their company so that they can spread the risk of that single company over a large number of shareholders.

Similarly, the later shareholders of a company can use the stock market to reallocate their risks. If a company you hold shares in is adopting a policy that is too risky for your taste—or too conservative—you can sell those shares and purchase others.

In the case of insurance, an individual was able to reduce his risk to zero by purchasing insurance. For a flat fee of $100, the individual could purchase full insurance against the $10,000 loss. This was true because there was basically no risk in the aggregate: if the probability of the loss occurring was 1 percent, then on average 10 of the 1000 people would face a loss—we just didn't know which ones.

In the case of the stock market, there is risk in the aggregate. One year the stock market as a whole might do well and another year it might do poorly. Somebody has to bear that kind of risk. The stock market offers a way to transfer risky investments from people who don't want to bear risk to people who are willing to bear risk.

Of course, few people outside of Las Vegas *like* to bear risk: most people are risk averse. Thus the stock market allows people to transfer risk from people who don't want to bear it to people who are willing to bear it if they are sufficiently compensated for it. We'll explore this idea further in the next chapter.

Summary

1. Consumption in different states of nature can be viewed as consumption goods, and all the analysis of previous chapters can be applied to choice under uncertainty.

2. However, the utility function that summarizes choice behavior under uncertainty may have a special structure. In particular, if the utility function is linear in the probabilities, then the utility assigned to a gamble will just be the expected utility of the various outcomes.

3. The curvature of the expected utility function describes the consumer's attitudes towards risk. If it is concave, the consumer is a risk averter, and if it is convex, the consumer is a risk lover.

4. Financial institutions such as insurance markets and the stock market provide ways for consumers to diversify and spread risks.

Review Questions

1. Which of the following utility functions have the expected utility property? (a) $u(c_1, c_2, \pi_1, \pi_2) = a(\pi_1 c_1 + \pi_2 c_2)$, (b) $u(c_1, c_2, \pi_1, \pi_2) = \pi_1 c_1 + \pi_2 c_2^2$, (c) $u(c_1, c_2, \pi_1, \pi_2) = \ln c_1 + (\pi_2/\pi_1) \ln c_2$.

2. A risk averse individual is offered a choice between a gamble that pays $1000 with a probability of 25% and $100 with a probability of 75%, or a payment of $325. Which would he choose?

3. What if the payment was $320?

4. Draw a utility function that exhibits risk loving behavior for small gambles and risk averse behavior for larger gambles.

5. Why might a neighborhood group have a harder time self-insuring for flood damage versus fire damage?

APPENDIX

Let us examine a simple problem to demonstrate the principles of expected utility maximization. Suppose that the consumer has some wealth w and is considering investing some amount x in a risky asset. This asset could earn a return of r_g in the "good" outcome or it could earn a return of r_b in the "bad" outcome. You should think of r_g as being a positive return—the asset increases in value, and r_b being a negative return—a decrease in asset value.

Thus the consumer's wealth in the good and bad outcomes will be

$$W_g = (w - x) + x(1 + r_g) = w + xr_g$$
$$W_b = (w - x) + x(1 + r_b) = w + xr_b.$$

Suppose that the good outcome occurs with probability π and the bad outcome with probability $(1 - \pi)$. Then the expected utility if the consumer decides to invest x dollars is

$$EU(x) = \pi u(w + xr_g) + (1 - \pi)u(w + xr_b).$$

The consumer wants to choose x so as to maximize this expression.

Differentiating with respect to x, we find the way in which utility changes as x changes:

$$EU'(x) = \pi u'(w + xr_g)r_g + (1 - \pi)u'(w + xr_b)r_b. \tag{13.3}$$

The second derivative of utility with respect to x is

$$EU''(x) = \pi u''(w + xr_g)r_g^2 + (1 - \pi)u''(w + xr_b)r_b^2. \tag{13.4}$$

If the consumer is risk averse his utility function will be concave, which implies that $u''(w) < 0$ for every level of wealth. Thus the second derivative of expected utility is unambiguously negative. Expected utility will be a concave function of x.

Consider the change in expected utility for the first dollar invested in the risky asset. This is just equation (13.3) with the derivative evaluated at $x = 0$:

$$EU'(0) = \pi u'(w)r_g + (1 - \pi)u'(w)r_b$$
$$= u'(w)[\pi r_g + (1 - \pi)r_b].$$

The expression inside the brackets is the **expected return** on the asset. If the expected return on the asset is negative, then expected utility must decrease when the first dollar is invested in the asset. But since the second derivative of expected utility is negative due to concavity, then utility must continue to decrease as additional dollars are invested.

Hence we have found that if the *expected value* of a gamble is negative, a risk averter will have the highest *expected utility* at $x^* = 0$: he will want no part of a losing proposition.

On the other hand, if the expected return on the asset is positive, then increasing x from zero will increase expected utility. Thus he will always want to invest a little bit in the risky asset, no matter how risk averse he is.

Expected utility as a function of x is illustrated in Figure 13.4. In Figure 13.4A, the expected return is negative and the optimal choice is $x^* = 0$. In Figure 13.4B, the expected return is positive over some range, so the consumer wants to invest some positive amount x^* in the risky asset.

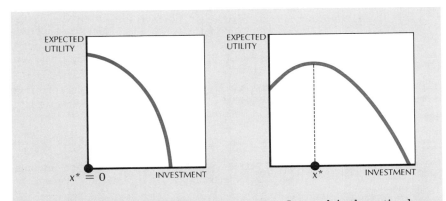

How much to invest in the risky asset. In panel A, the optimal investment is zero, but in panel B the consumer wants to invest a positive amount.

Figure 13.4

The optimal amount for the consumer to invest will be determined by the condition that the derivative of expected utility with respect to x be equal to zero. Since the second derivative of utility is automatically negative, due to concavity, this will be a global maximum.

Setting (13.3) equal to zero we have

$$EU'(x) = \pi u'(w + xr_g)r_g + (1 - \pi)u'(w + xr_b)r_b = 0. \qquad (13.5)$$

This equation determines the optimal choice of x for the consumer in question.

EXAMPLE: The Effect of Taxation on Investment in Risky Assets

How does the level of investment in a risky asset behave when you tax its return? If the individual pays taxes at rate t, then the after-tax returns will be $(1 - t)r_g$

and $(1-t)r_b$. Thus the first-order condition determining his optimal investment, x, will be

$$EU'(x) = \pi u'(w + x(1-t)r_g)(1-t)r_g + (1-\pi)u'(w + x(1-t)r_b)(1-t)r_b = 0.$$

Canceling the $(1-t)$ terms, we have

$$EU'(x) = \pi u'(w + x(1-t)r_g)r_g + (1-\pi)u'(w + x(1-t)r_b)r_b = 0. \qquad (13.6)$$

Let us denote the solution to the maximization problem without taxes—when $t = 0$—by x^* and denote the solution to the maximization problem with taxes by $\hat{x}$. What is the relationship between x^* and $\hat{x}$?

Your first impulse is probably to think that $x^* > \hat{x}$—that taxation of a risky asset will tend to discourage investment in it. But that turns out to be exactly wrong! Taxing a risky asset in the way we described will actually *encourage* investment in it!

In fact, there is an exact relation between x^* and $\hat{x}$. It must be the case that

$$\hat{x} = \frac{x^*}{1-t}.$$

The proof is simply to note that this value of $\hat{x}$ satisfies the first-order condition for the optimal choice in the presence of the tax. Substituting this choice into equation (13.6) we have

$$EU'(\hat{x}) = \pi u'\left(w + \frac{x^*}{1-t}(1-t)r_g\right)r_g$$
$$+ (1-\pi)u'\left(w + \frac{x^*}{1-t}(1-t)r_b\right)r_b$$
$$= \pi u'(w + x^*r_g)r_g + (1-\pi)u'(w + x^*r_b)r_b = 0$$

where the last equality follows from the fact that x^* is the optimal solution when there is no tax.

What is going on here? How can imposing a tax increase the amount of investment in the risky asset? Here is what is happening. When the tax is imposed, the individual will have less of a gain in the good state, but he will also have *less of a loss in the bad state*. By scaling his original investment up by $1/(1-t)$ the consumer can reproduce the same *after-tax* returns that he had before the tax was put in place. The tax reduces his expected return, but it also reduces his risk: by increasing his investment the consumer can get exactly the same pattern of returns he had before, and thus completely offset the effect of the tax. A tax on a risky investment represents a tax on the gain when the return is positive—but it represents a subsidy on the loss when the return is negative.

RISKY ASSETS

In the last chapter we examined a model of individual behavior under uncertainty and the role of two economic institutions for dealing with uncertainty: insurance markets and stock markets. In this chapter we will further explore how stock markets serve to allocate risk. In order to do this, it is convenient to consider a simplified model of behavior under uncertainty.

14.1 Mean-Variance Utility

In the last chapter we examined the expected utility model of choice under uncertainty. Another approach to choice under uncertainty is to describe the probability distributions that are the objects of choice by a few parameters and think of the utility function as being defined over those parameters. The most popular example of this approach is the **mean–variance model**. Instead of thinking that a consumer's preferences depend on the entire probability distribution of his wealth over every possible outcome, we suppose that his preferences can be well described by considering just a few summary statistics about the probability distribution of his wealth.

Let us suppose that a random variable w takes on the values w_s for $s = 1, \ldots, S$ with probability π_s. The **mean** of a probability distribution is simply its average value:

$$\mu_w = \sum_{s=1}^{S} \pi_s w_s.$$

This is the formula for an average: take each outcome w_s, weight it by the probability that it occurs, and sum it up over all outcomes.[1]

The **variance** of a probability distribution is the average value of $(w - \mu_w)^2$:

$$\sigma_w^2 = \sum_{s=1}^{S} \pi_s (w_s - \mu_w)^2.$$

The variance measures the "spread" of the distribution and is a reasonable measure of the riskiness involved. A closely related measure is the **standard deviation**, denoted by σ_w, which is the square root of the variance: $\sigma_w = \sqrt{\sigma_w^2}$.

The mean of a probability distribution measures its average value— what the distribution is centered around. The variance of the distribution measures the "spread" of the distribution — how spread out it is around the mean. See Figure 14.1 for a graphical depiction of probability distributions with different means and variances.

The mean–variance model assumes that the utility of a probability distribution that gives the investor wealth w_s with a probability of π_s can be expressed as a function of the mean and variance of that distribution, $u(\mu_w, \sigma_w^2)$. Or, if it is more convenient, the utility can be expressed as a function of the mean and standard deviation, $u(\mu_w, \sigma_w)$. Since both variance and standard deviation are measures of the riskiness of the wealth distribution, we can think of utility as depending on either one.

This model can be thought of as a simplification of the expected utility model described in the last chapter. If the choices that are being made can be completely characterized in terms of their mean and variance, then a utility function for mean and variance will be able to rank choices in the same way that an expected utility function will rank them. Furthermore, even if the probability distributions cannot be completely characterized by their means and variances, the mean–variance model may well serve as a reasonable approximation to the expected utility model.

We will make the natural assumption that a higher expected return is good, other things being equal, and that a higher variance is bad. This is simply another way to state the assumption that people are typically averse to risk.

---

[1] The Greek letter μ, mu, is pronounced "mew." The Greek letter σ, sigma, is pronounced "sig-ma."

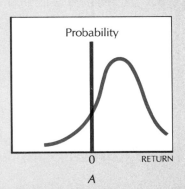
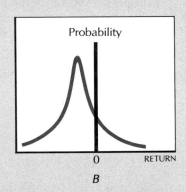

Mean and variance. The probability distribution depicted in panel A has a positive mean, while that depicted in panel B has a negative mean. The distribution in panel A is more "spread out" that the one in panel B which means that it has a larger variance.

Figure 14.1

Let us use the mean–variance model to analyze a simple portfolio problem. Suppose that you can invest in two different assets. One of them, the **risk-free asset**, always pays a fixed rate of return, r_f. This would be something like a Treasury bill that pays a fixed rate of interest regardless of what happens.

The other asset is a **risky asset**. Think of this asset as being an investment in a large mutual fund that buys stocks. If the stock market does well, then your investment will do well. If the stock market does poorly, your investment will do poorly. Let m_s be the return on this asset if state s occurs, and let π_s be the probability that state s will occur. We'll use r_m to denote the expected return of the risky asset and σ_m to denote the standard deviation of its return.

Of course you don't have to choose one or the other of these assets; typically you'll be able to divide your wealth between the two. If you hold a fraction of your wealth x in the risky asset, and a fraction $(1 - x)$ in the risk-free asset, the average return on your portfolio will be given by

$$r_x = \sum_{s=1}^{S}(xm_s + (1 - x)r_f)\pi_s$$

$$= x\sum_{s=1}^{S} m_s\pi_s + (1 - x)r_f \sum_{s=1}^{S} \pi_s.$$

Since $\sum \pi_s = 1$, we have

$$r_x = xr_m + (1 - x)r_f.$$

Thus the expected return on the portfolio is a weighted average of the two expected returns.

The variance of your portfolio return will be given by

$$\sigma_x^2 = +\sum_{s=1}^{S}(xm_s + (1-x)r_f - r_x)^2\pi_s.$$

Substituting for r_x, this becomes

$$\sigma_x^2 = \sum_{s=1}^{S}(xm_s - xr_m)^2\pi_s$$
$$= \sum_{s=1}^{S}x^2(m_s - r_m)^2\pi_s$$
$$= x^2\sigma_m^2.$$

Thus the standard deviation of the portfolio return is given by

$$\sigma_x = \sqrt{x^2\sigma_m^2} = x\sigma_m.$$

As you choose to devote a higher fraction of your wealth to the risky asset, you will get a higher expected return, but you will also incur higher risk. This is depicted in Figure 14.2.

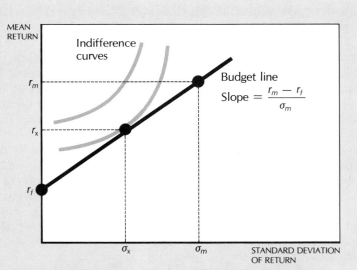

Figure 14.2

Risk and return. The budget line measures the cost of achieving a larger expected return in terms of the increased standard deviation of the return. At the optimal choice the indifference curve must be tangent to this budget line.

If you set $x = 1$ you will be putting all of your money in the risky asset and you have an expected return and standard deviation of (r_m, σ_m). If you set $x = 0$ you have all of your wealth in the sure asset and you have an expected return and standard deviation of $(r_f, 0)$. And if you set x somewhere between 0 and 1 you end up somewhere in the middle of that line. This line gives us a budget line describing the market tradeoff between risk and return.

Since we are assuming that peoples' preferences depend only on the mean and variance of their wealth, we can draw indifference curves that illustrate an individual's preferences for risk and return. If people are risk averse, then a higher expected return makes them better off and a higher standard deviation makes them worse off. This means that standard deviation is a "bad" which implies that the indifference curves will have a positive slope, as shown in Figure 14.2.

At the optimal choice of risk and return the slope of the indifference curve has to equal the slope of the budget line in Figure 14.2. We might call this slope the **price of risk** since it measures how risk and return can be traded off in making portfolio choices. From inspection of Figure 14.2 the price of risk is given by

$$p = \frac{r_m - r_f}{\sigma_m}. \tag{14.1}$$

So our optimal portfolio choice between the sure and the risky asset could be characterized by saying that the marginal rate of substitution between risk and return must be equal to the price of risk:

$$\text{MRS} = -\frac{\Delta U/\Delta \sigma}{\Delta U/\Delta \mu} = \frac{r_m - r_f}{\sigma_m}. \tag{14.2}$$

Now suppose that there are many individuals who are choosing between these two assets. Each one of them has to have his marginal rate of substitution equal to the price of risk. Thus in equilibrium all of the individuals' MRSs will be equal: when people are given sufficient opportunities to trade risks, the equilibrium price of risk will be equal across individuals. Risk is like any other good in this respect.

We can use the ideas that we have developed in earlier chapters to examine how choices change as the parameters of the problem change. All of the framework of normal goods, inferior goods, revealed preference, and so on can be brought to bear on this model. For example, suppose that an individual is offered a choice of a new risky asset y that has a mean return of r_y, say, and a standard deviation of σ_y, as illustrated in Figure 14.3.

If offered the choice between investing in x and investing in y, which will the consumer choose? The original budget set and the new budget set are both depicted in Figure 14.3. Note that every choice of risk and return that was possible in the original budget set is possible with the new budget

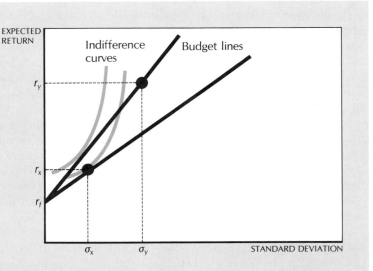

EXPECTED RETURN

Indifference curves

Budget lines

r_y

r_x

r_f

σ_x σ_y

STANDARD DEVIATION

Figure
14.3

Preferences between risk and return. The asset with risk-return combination y is preferred to the one with combination x.

set since the new budget set contains the old one. Thus investing in the asset y and the risk-free asset is definitely better to investing in x and the risk-free asset, since the consumer can choose a better final portfolio.

The fact that the consumer can choose how much of the risk and return to take of the risky asset is very important for this argument. If this were an "all or nothing" choice where the consumer were compelled to invest all of his money in either x or y, we would get a very different outcome. In the example depicted in Figure 14.3, the consumer would prefer investing all of his money in x to investing all of his money in y, since x lies on a higher indifference curve than y. But if he can mix the risky asset with the risk-free asset, he would always prefer to mix with y rather than to mix with x.

14.2 Measuring Risk

We have a model above that describes the price of risk ... but how do we measure the *amount* of risk in an asset? The first thing that you would probably think of is the standard deviation of an asset's return. After all, we are assuming that utility depends on the mean and variance of wealth, aren't we?

In the above example, where there is only one risky asset, that is exactly right: the amount of risk in the risky asset is its standard deviation. But if there are many risky assets, the standard deviation is not an appropriate measure for the amount of risk in an asset.

This is because a consumer's utility depends on the mean and variance of total wealth—not the mean and variance of any single asset that he might hold. What matters is how the returns of the various assets a consumer holds *interact* to create a mean and variance of his wealth. As in the rest of economics, it is the marginal impact of a given asset on total utility that determines its value, not the value of that asset held alone. Just as the value of an extra cup of coffee may depend on how much cream is available, the amount that someone would be willing to pay for an extra share of a risky asset will depend on how it interacts with other assets in his portfolio.

Suppose, for example, that you are considering purchasing two assets, and you know that there are only two possible outcomes that can happen. Asset A will be worth either $10 or −$5 and asset B will be worth either −$5 or $10. But when asset A is worth $10, asset B will be worth −$5 and vice versa. In other words the values of the two assets will be *negatively correlated:* when one has a large value, the other will have a small value.

Suppose that the two outcomes are equally likely, so that the average value of each asset will be $2.50. Then if you don't care about risk at all and you must hold one asset or the other, the most that you would be willing to pay for either one would be $2.50—the expected value of each asset. If you are averse to risk, you would be willing to pay even less than $2.50.

But what if you can hold both assets? Then if you hold one share of each asset, you will get $5 whichever outcome arises. Whenever one asset is worth $10, the other is worth −$5. Thus, if you can hold both assets, the amount that you would be willing to pay to purchase *both* assets would be $5.

This example shows in a vivid way that the value of an asset will depend in general on how it is correlated with other assets. Assets that move in opposite directions—that are negatively correlated with each other—are very valuable because they reduce overall risk. In general the value of an asset tends to depend much more on the correlation of its return with other assets than with its own variation. Thus the amount of risk in an asset depends on its correlation with other assets.

It is convenient to measure the risk in an asset relative to the risk in the stock market as a whole. We call the riskiness of a stock relative to the risk of the market the **beta** of a stock, and denote it by the Greek letter β. Thus, if i represents some particular stock, we write β_i for its riskiness relative to the market as a whole. Roughly speaking:

$$\beta_i = \frac{\text{how risky asset } i \text{ is}}{\text{how risky the stock market is}}.$$

If a stock has a beta of 1, then it is just as risky as the market as a whole;

when the market moves up by 10 percent, this stock will, on the average, move up by 10 percent. If a stock has a beta of less than 1, then when the market moves up by 10 percent, the stock will move up by less than 10 percent. The beta of a stock can be estimated by statistical methods to determine how sensitive the movements of one variable are relative to another, and there are many investment advisory services that can provide you with estimates of the beta of a stock.[2]

14.3 Equilibrium in a Market for Risky Assets

We are now in a position to state the equilibrium condition for a market with risky assets. Recall that in a market with only certain returns, we saw that all assets had to earn the same rate of return. Here we have a similar principle: all assets, after adjusting for risk, have to earn the same rate of return.

The catch is about adjusting for risk. How do we do that? The answer comes from the analysis of optimal choice given earlier. Recall that we considered the choice of an optimal portfolio that contained a riskless asset and a risky asset. The risky asset was interpreted as being a mutual fund— a diversified portfolio including many risky assets. In this section we'll suppose that this portfolio consists of *all* risky assets.

Then we can identify the expected return on this market portfolio of risky assets with the market expected return, r_m, and identify the standard deviation of the market return with the market risk, σ_m. The return on the safe asset is r_f, the risk-free return.

We saw in equation (14.1) that the price of risk, p, is given by

$$p = \frac{r_m - r_f}{\sigma_m}.$$

We said above that the amount of risk in a given asset i relative to the total risk in the market is denoted by β_i. This means that to measure the *total* amount of risk in asset i, we have to multiply by the market risk, σ_m. Thus the total risk in asset i is given by $\beta_i \sigma_m$.

What is the cost of this risk? Just multiply the total amount of risk, $\beta_i \sigma_m$, by the price of risk. This gives us the *risk adjustment:*

$$\text{risk adjustment} = \beta_i \sigma_m p$$
$$= \beta_i \sigma_m \frac{r_m - r_f}{\sigma_m}$$
$$= \beta_i (r_m - r_f).$$

---

[2] The Greek letter β, beta, is pronounced "bait-uh." For those of you who know some statistics, the beta of a stock is defined to be $\beta_i = \text{cov}(\tilde{r}_i, \tilde{r}_m)/\text{var}(\tilde{r}_m)$. That is, β_i is the covariance of the return on the stock with the market return divided by the variance of the market return.

Now we can state the equilibrium condition in markets for risky assets: in equilibrium all assets should have the same risk-adjusted rate of return. The logic is just like the logic used in Chapter 13: if one asset had a higher risk-adjusted rate of return than another, everyone would want to hold the asset with the higher risk-adjusted rate. Thus in equilibrium the risk-adjusted rates of return must be equalized.

If there are two assets i and j that have expected returns r_i and r_j, and betas of β_i and β_j, we must have the following equation satisfied in equilibrium:

$$r_i - \beta_i(r_m - r_f) = r_j - \beta_j(r_m - r_f).$$

This equation says that in equilibrium the risk-adjusted returns on the two assets must be the same—where the risk adjustment comes from multiplying the total risk of the asset times the price of risk.

Another way to express this condition is to note the following. The risk-free asset, by definition, must have $\beta_f = 0$. This is because it has zero risk, and β measures the amount of risk in an asset. Thus for any asset i we must have

$$r_i - \beta_i(r_m - r_f) = r_f - \beta_f(r_m - r_f) = r_f.$$

Rearranging, this equation says

$$r_i = r_f + \beta_i(r_m - r_f)$$

or that the expected return on any asset must be the risk-free return plus the risk adjustment. This latter term reflects the extra return that people demand in order to bear the risk that the asset embodies. This equation is the main result of the **Capital Asset Pricing Model (CAPM)**, which has many uses in the study of financial markets.

14.4 How Returns Adjust

In studying asset markets under certainty, we showed how prices of assets adjust to equalize returns. Let's look at the same adjustment process here.

According to the model sketched out above, the expected return on any asset should be the risk-free return plus the risk premium:

$$r_i = r_f + \beta_i(r_m - r_f).$$

In Figure 14.4 we have illustrated this line in a graph with the different values of beta plotted along the horizontal axis, and different expected returns on the vertical axis. According to our model, all assets that are

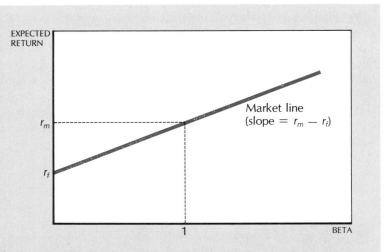

Figure
14.4
The market line. The market line depicts the combinations
of expected return and beta for assets held in equilibrium.

held in equilibrium have to lie along this line. This line is called the **market
line**.

What if some asset's expected return and beta didn't lie on the market
line? What would happen?

The expected return on the asset is the expected change in its price
divided by its current price:

$$r_i = \text{ expected value of } \frac{p_1 - p_0}{p_0}.$$

This is just like the definition we had before, with the addition of the word
"expected." We have to include "expected" now since the price of the asset
tomorrow is uncertain.

Suppose that you found an asset whose expected return, adjusted for
risk, was higher than the risk-free rate:

$$r_i - \beta_i(r_m - r_f) > r_f.$$

Then this asset is a very good deal. It is giving a higher risk-adjusted
return than the risk-free rate.

When people discover that this asset exists, they will want to buy it.
They might want to keep it for themselves, or they might want to buy it
and sell it to others, but since it is offering a better tradeoff between risk
and return than existing assets, there is certainly a market for it.

But as people attempt to buy this asset they will bid up today's price:
p_0 will rise. This means that the expected return $r_i = (p_1 - p_0)/p_0$ will

fall. How far will it fall? Just enough to lower the expected rate of return back down to the market line.

Thus it is a good deal to buy an asset that lies above the market line. For when people discover that it has a higher return given its risk than assets they currently hold, they will bid up the price of that asset.

This is all dependent on the hypothesis that people agree about the amount of risk in various assets. If they disagree about the expected returns or the betas of different assets, the model becomes much more complicated.

EXAMPLE: Ranking Mutual Funds

The Capital Asset Pricing Model described above can be used to compare different investments with respect to their risk and their return. One popular kind of investment is a mutual fund. These are large organizations that accept money from individual investors and use this money to buy and sell stocks of companies. The profits made by such investments are then paid out to the individual investors.

The advantage of a mutual fund is that you have professionals managing your money. The disadvantage is they charge you for managing it. These fees are usually not terribly large, however, and most small investors are probably well advised to use a mutual fund.

But how do you choose a mutual fund in which to invest? You want one with a high expected return of course, but you also probably want one with a minimum amount of risk. The question is, how much risk are you willing to tolerate to get that high expected return?

One thing that you might do is to look at the historical performance of various mutual funds and calculate the average yearly return and the beta—the amount of risk—of each mutual fund you are considering. Since we haven't discussed the precise definition of beta, you might find it hard to calculate. But there are books where you can look up the historical betas of mutual funds.

If you plotted the expected returns versus the betas, you would get a diagram similar to that depicted in Figure 14.5.[3] Note that the mutual funds with high expected returns will generally have high risk. The high expected returns are there to compensate people for bearing risk.

One interesting thing you can do with the mutual fund diagram is to compare investing with professional managers to a very simple strategy like investing part of your money in an **index fund.** There are several

[3] See Michael Jensen, "The Performance of Mutual Funds in the Period 1945–1964," *Journal of Finance*, 23 (May 1968), 389–416, for a more detailed discussion of how to examine mutual fund performance using the tools we have sketched out in this chapter. For an extensive and readable discussion of these ideas, see Burton Malkiel, *A Random Walk Down Wall Street*, 4th ed. (New York: Norton, 1985).

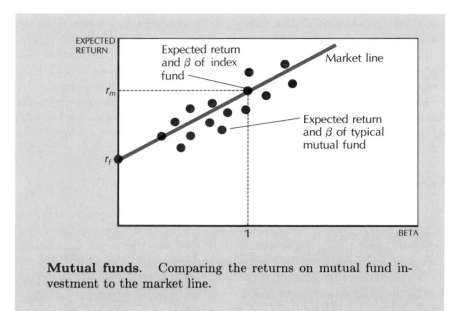

**Figure
14.5**   **Mutual funds.**   Comparing the returns on mutual fund investment to the market line.

indices of stock market activity like the Dow–Jones Index, or the Standard and Poor's index, and so on. The indices are typically the average returns on a given day of a certain group of stocks. The Standard and Poor's index, for example, is based on the average performance of 500 stocks traded on the New York Stock Exchange.

An **index fund** is a mutual fund that holds the stocks that make up such an index. This means that you are guaranteed to get the average performance of the stocks in the index, virtually by definition. Since holding the average is not a very difficult thing to do—at least compared to trying to beat the average—index funds typically have low management fees. Since an index fund holds a very broad base of risky assets, it will have a beta that is very close to 1—it will be just as risky as the market as a whole, because the index fund holds nearly all the stocks in the market as a whole.

How does an index fund do as compared to the typical mutual fund? Remember the comparison has to be made with respect to both risk and return of the investment. One way to do this is to plot the expected return and the beta of the Standard and Poor's index fund, say, and draw the line connecting it to the risk-free rate, as in Figure 14.5. You can get any combination of risk and return on this line that you want just by deciding how much money you want to invest in the risk-free asset and how much you want to invest in the index fund.

Now let's count the number of mutual funds that plot below this line. These are mutual funds that offer risk and return combinations that are dominated by those available by the index fund/risk-free asset combinations. When this is done it typically turns out that about 85 percent of the mutual funds are below the line! So much for the benefits of professional management!

But seen another way, this finding might not be too surprising. The stock market is an incredibly competitive environment. People are always trying to find undervalued stocks in order to purchase them. This means that on average, stocks are usually trading for what they're really worth. If that is the case, then betting the averages is a pretty reasonable strategy—since beating the averages is almost impossible.

Summary

1. We can use the budget set and indifference curve apparatus developed earlier to examine the choice of how much money to invest in risky and riskless assets.

2. The marginal rate of substitution between risk and return will have to equal the slope of the budget line. This slope is known as the price of risk.

3. The amount of risk present in an asset depends to a large extent on its correlation with other assets. An asset that moves opposite the direction of other assets helps to reduce the overall risk of your portfolio.

4. The amount of risk in an asset relative to that of the market as a whole is called the **beta** of the asset.

5. The fundamental equilibrium condition in asset markets is that risk-adjusted returns have to be the same.

Review Questions

1. If the risk-free rate of return is 6% and if a risky asset is available with a return of 9% and a standard deviation of 3%, what is the maximum rate of return you can achieve if you are willing to accept a standard deviation of 2%? What percent of your wealth would have to be invested in the risky asset?

2. What is the price of risk in the above exercise?

3. If a stock has a β of 1.5, the return on the market is 10%, and the risk-free rate of return is 5%, what expected rate of return should this stock offer according to the Capital Asset Pricing Model? If the expected value of the stock is $100, what price should the stock be selling for today?

15

CONSUMER'S SURPLUS

In the preceding chapters we have shown how to derive a consumer's demand function from the underlying preferences or utility function. In Chapter 7 we discussed one aspect of the reverse problem: how to use revealed preference to derive preferences from observations on demand behavior. In this chapter we will consider another aspect of this problem: how to derive a measure of utility from observing demand behavior. The resulting measure turns out to have many applications in economics that we will discuss later in the book. It is particularly useful for evaluating the impact on consumer welfare of various kinds of economic policies.

At the most fundamental level of analysis, it is only the consumer's preferences that matter for measuring how well-off a consumer is. If a consumer prefers bundle (x_1, x_2) to bundle (y_1, y_2)—in the sense that he or she would choose (x_1, x_2) over (y_1, y_2)—then it seems reasonable to conclude that the consumer is better off having (x_1, x_2) than (y_1, y_2). Of course, one can think up extreme examples involving addiction or psychosis for which this is problematic, but for the kinds of choices economists usually examine, this seems like a reasonable starting point.

The trouble with just using consumer preferences to measure consumer welfare is that the comparisons may be difficult to interpret in many practical circumstances. It is often more useful to consider a *numeric* measure of consumer welfare such as the consumer's utility.

In Chapter 4 we suggested that there was no unique way to measure a consumer's utility—as long as we have a way to assign numbers to bundles of goods that rank the bundles in the same way as the consumer's preferences, we have a utility function. Despite this, there are some standard ways to assign utilities that are convenient for analysis of economic policy.

The general sort of measure that we want to discuss might be called measures of the "willingness to pay." Given two situations represented by the consumption bundles (x_1, x_2) and (y_1, y_2), we want to measure how much the consumer would be willing to pay (or be paid) to be in one situation rather than the other. The resulting number turns out to be closely related to certain ways of measuring utility and is useful for evaluating proposed policy changes.

15.1 The Basic Idea of Consumer's Surplus

Since the subsequent discussion becomes somewhat involved, it is worthwhile laying out the basic idea before delving into the details. The goal is to use the consumer's observed demand function to estimate the "total value" to the consumer of some consumption bundle.

The key insight is to recognize that the price of a good measures the *marginal value* of the good to a consumer: how much a consumer would be willing to pay for the *last* unit of consumption purchased. Let x_1 measure the amount of consumption of the good in which we are interested, and let x_2 measure the amount of money that the consumer has left to consume on all other goods. Thus the price of good 2 is automatically 1 since it costs a dollar to buy a dollar. In this framework, we know that the marginal rate of substitution equals the price of good 1:

$$\text{MRS} = p_1.$$

Recall that the marginal rate of substitution measures how much of good 2 the consumer must be given to compensate her for reducing her consumption of good 1. Since the market price equals the MRS at the optimal level of consumption, it therefore measures the amount of money necessary to compensate the consumer for a small reduction in good 1.

In Figure 15.1A the height of the demand curve at x_1 measures the marginal rate of substitution at that level of consumption. If we want to determine how much money the consumer would needs to be compensated for giving up his or her *entire* consumption of good 1, we need to add the amounts of money necessary to compensate the consumer for *each* unit of consumption that is given up.

Suppose that the consumer is initially consuming $x_1 = 50$ units of some good per month, and that Figure 15.1A represents the monthly demand curve for that good. Then if we reduce the consumption of the good by 1

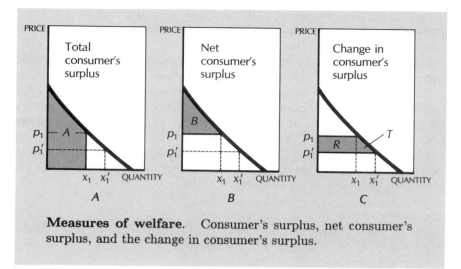

Figure
15.1

Measures of welfare. Consumer's surplus, net consumer's surplus, and the change in consumer's surplus.

unit, and give the consumer back the money spent on that last unit, $p(50)$, the consumer would be just about as well-off as he or she was originally.

But now we can do the same thing again. The consumer has 49 units of good 1, so if we take away another unit of the good and give the consumer $p(49)$ dollars, the consumer would still be just about as well-off as before.

Continuing in this way, we can reduce the consumption of good 1 to zero and give the consumer $A = \sum_{i=1}^{50} p(i)$ dollars in compensation. This amount is the area under the demand curve depicted in Figure 15.1A. It is known as the **total consumer's surplus**. It measures the total value of consumption of good 1 to the consumer in the sense that it is how much money the consumer would need to compensate him or her for reducing the consumption of good 1 to zero. The price of good 1 at each level of consumption measures how the consumer values a marginal unit of the good at that level of consumption. So the sum of the prices at each different level of consumption measures the total value of the good to the consumer.

Suppose now that the consumer was originally purchasing x_1 units of the good at the market price p_1. Then we have argued that she needs the area A as the total compensation for reducing the consumption of the good to zero. However, some amount of this compensation is offset by the fact that the consumer will have the extra $p_1 x_1$ dollars that were being spent on good 1 in the first place. The total value of good 1 to the consumer is the area under the demand curve, but the consumer has to spend $p_1 x_1$ to acquire that value, so the **net consumer's surplus** is $B = A - p_1 x_1$. The total consumer's surplus measures the total value of good 1; the net consumer's surplus measures the net value of good 1, subtracting from the total surplus the amount that is actually spent to acquire the good.[1] The net consumer's surplus is depicted in Figure 15.1B by the area B. It is the area under the demand curve minus the expenditure on the good.

Finally we have the idea of the **change in consumer's surplus**. If the price of a good changes from p_1 to p'_1, and the consumption changes from x_1 to x'_1, then the change in consumer's surplus will change as depicted in Figure 15.1C. This roughly trapezoidal shape measures the value to the consumer of the change in consumption. It is composed of the (exactly) rectangular area indicated by R and the (roughly) triangular area indicated by T. (If the demand curve were a straight line, then this latter area would be exactly triangular.)

The rectangular area is given by $(p_1 - p'_1)x_1$. It measures the benefit to the consumer from paying the lower price p'_1 for the units of the good that he or she was originally consuming. The roughly triangular area measures the value of the *additional* consumption that the consumer chooses to purchase at the lower price p'_1. Thus the change in consumer's surplus measures the value to the consumer of facing the price p'_1 rather than p_1.

The idea of using an area under the demand curve to measure the total value that a good provides is really quite intuitive. Certainly you would be willing to pay a lot more for nearly any good if the consumption of that good was an all or nothing proposition. Think how much you might be willing to pay for a cup of coffee on Monday morning if that were the only cup you were allowed to have all week! And compare that to what you actually pay for an extra cup of coffee. The price of coffee—or any other good—measures its marginal value: how much money a consumer is willing to sacrifice to get one more unit of the good. The total value of coffee to the consumer is very different: it is the sum of all those marginal values at each different level of consumption.

The marginal value of the first cup of coffee in the morning may be very high. The marginal value of the next cup at 10 o'clock is probably somewhat less. Perhaps the value of a nice cup after dinner is even less. And the value of the "marginal" cup of coffee—the one you could just about take or leave—should be just equal to its price. The total value of your daily consumption of coffee is the sum of all these marginal values.

15.2 A Closer Look

The intuitive discussion of consumer's surplus given in the last section is a useful introduction, but upon closer examination, it raises some difficult questions. First, and most important, the concept of "value" is awfully

---

[1] Warning: economists tend to be somewhat sloppy about their use of this terminology and often drop the words "total" and "net" and let meaning be determined by the context.

vague. We said in the introduction to this chapter that the fundamental measure of how well-off the consumer was had to be the consumer's utility function. What is the relation between the concept of utility and the concept of consumer's surplus?

Second, there is a problem in the construction of consumer's surplus. As we reduce the consumption of good 1, we are giving money to the consumer to compensate him or her for the reduced consumption if good 1. In other words, we are increasing the consumer's money income to compensate for the lower consumption of good 1. But this increase in money income will likely have some effect on the demand curve. Remember, the demand curve for a good is drawn for *fixed* values of other prices and income. In this case there is no problem with the other prices—we've assumed that the price of the other good is fixed at 1—but if we are giving the consumer money to compensate for reduced consumption, then the money income will definitely change. This means that the process we have described to measure consumer's surplus will be *exactly* correct only in rather special circumstances. However, it turns out to be *approximately* correct in a wider variety of cases.

Because of these difficulties with the intuitive derivation of consumer's surplus, we will provide a more careful derivation in the rest of this chapter. First, we will derive two exact monetary measures of consumer welfare in terms of the utility function, so that the relationship between utility and monetary measures of consumer welfare will be clear. Then we will show how we can calculate values for these measures from examination of the demand function in a special case. This latter calculation turns out to be equivalent to the consumer's surplus calculations described above.

15.3 Money Metric Utility

It is most convenient to proceed graphically. Suppose that we have a consumption bundle (x_1, x_2) as depicted in Figure 15.2. We can ask how much money the consumer would need at some set of prices (p_1, p_2) to be as well-off as he would be with the consumption bundle (x_1, x_2). That is, we ask how much money would the consumer need at prices (p_1, p_2) to purchase a bundle that is just indifferent to the bundle (x_1, x_2).

The answer is depicted in the diagram—we draw the budget line that just touches the indifference curve through (x_1, x_2) and has a slope of $-p_1/p_2$. We want to know what amount of income, m, goes with this budget line. The vertical intercept is m/p_2 and the horizontal intercept is m/p_1—so p_2 times the vertical intercept, or p_1 times the horizontal intercept, is the amount we want.

To make things easy, let us suppose that p_2 is 1, so that the vertical intercept itself measures the amount of money that we need to make the

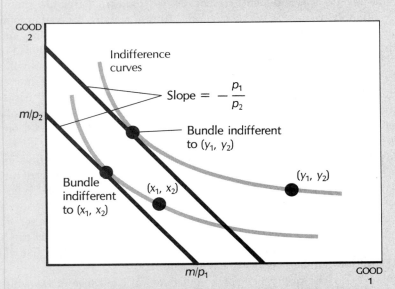

The money metric utility function. The vertical intercept times p_2 measures the amount of money necessary at prices (p_1, p_2) to purchase a bundle that is just as good as (x_1, x_2) according to this consumer's preferences.

Figure
15.2

consumer as well-off at the prices $(p_1, 1)$ as he would be with consumption bundle (x_1, x_2).

Now suppose that we consider a consumption bundle on a higher indifference curve, say bundle (y_1, y_2), as in Figure 15.2. It is clear that the consumer would now need *more* money at prices $(p_1, 1)$ to get to the indifference curve through (y_1, y_2). In fact, the consumer would need more and more money to get to bundles on higher and higher indifference curves. So if we assign amounts of money in this way, we are certain to label higher indifference curves with larger numbers.

But this is just what it takes to be a utility function. And in fact, this is one of the most convenient ways to construct a utility function—it is called a **money metric utility function**.

Of course, this way of assigning monetary measures to consumption bundles is not a unique way to measure utility. We could square it, or take the logarithm, or use any other increasing function and we would still have a utility function. But the money metric utility function we have defined does have some convenient properties and seems like a very natural way to label indifference curves.

But even if we restrict ourselves to money metric utilities, we have some ambiguities. For in general, the money metric utility assigned to some bundle of goods will depend on the prices (p_1, p_2). After all, money is only valuable because it will buy goods. And how much a given amount of money is worth will depend on what prices prevail. Thus the money metric utility function will in general depend on the prices (p_1, p_2). We'll call these prices the **reference prices**. Each different set of reference prices will give us a different money metric utility function since the value of money in terms of purchasing consumption will depend on the prevailing prices. In terms of the diagram, this simply says that the height of the tangent line to an indifference curve at the vertical axis will typically depend on the slope of the tangent line.

We will denote the money metric utility function by an expression of the form $m(p_1, p_2, x_1, x_2)$. The notation reminds us that in general the money metric utility of a bundle (x_1, x_2) will depend on the reference prices that prevail, (p_1, p_2). According to the definition of money metric utility, $m(p_1, p_2, x_1, x_2)$ is the amount of money that a consumer would need at prices (p_1, p_2) to be as well-off as he would be consuming the bundle (x_1, x_2). Thus it represents, in some sense, the monetary value of the consumption bundle (x_1, x_2) to the consumer.

If we know the preferences of a consumer, in the sense of knowing his indifference curves or his utility function, it will generally be possible to compute his money metric utility function. There are very general ways to do this that are studied in advanced courses, but in this chapter we need only concern ourselves with the geometry of the situation, and a particular special case that we will discuss later.

EXAMPLE: Examples of Money Metric Utility

Question: Suppose that a consumer's preferences are represented by the utility function $u(x_1, x_2) = \min\{x_1, x_2\}$. How much money would she need at prices $(1, 1)$ to purchase a bundle that leaves her indifferent to $(5, 8)$? What is this consumer's money metric utility function?

Answer: Since the consumer's preferences are of the perfect complement variety, the cheapest bundle indifferent to $(5, 8)$ will be the bundle $(5, 5)$. This bundle will cost \$10 at prices $(1, 1)$.

To compute the money metric utility, we proceed as follows. First, given an arbitrary bundle (x_1, x_2), let x be the smaller of the two numbers x_1 and x_2; that is, $x = \min\{x_1, x_2\}$. Then the cheapest bundle that will yield the same utility as (x_1, x_2) for this consumer will be the bundle (x, x), and this bundle will cost $p_1 x + p_2 x = (p_1 + p_2)x = (p_1 + p_2)\min\{x_1, x_2\}$. Thus the money metric utility function for perfect complement preferences is given by

$$m(p_1, p_2, x_1, x_2) = (p_1 + p_2)\min\{x_1, x_2\}.$$

Note that this is a monotonic transformation of the original utility function. Since the money metric utility function represents the same preferences as the original utility function, it *has* to be a monotonic transformation.

Question: What is the money metric utility representation for a Cobb-Douglas utility function, $u(x_1, x_2) = x_1^a x_2^{1-a}$?

Answer: We have seen in Chapter 6 that the demand functions for Cobb-Douglas preferences are given by the formulas $x_1(p_1, p_2, m) = am/p_1$ and $x_2(p_1, p_2, m) = (1 - a)m/p_2$. Given an arbitrary bundle (x_1, x_2), and the prices (p_1, p_2), we want to find the level of income such that the optimal choice at those prices and income has the same utility as the bundle (x_1, x_2). In order to do this we write down the equation that says the optimal choice has the same utility as the bundle (x_1, x_2):

$$\left(\frac{am}{p_1}\right)^a \left(\frac{(1-a)m}{p_2}\right)^{1-a} = x_1^a x_2^{1-a}$$

and solve this equation for m to get

$$m(p_1, p_2, x_1, x_2) = \left(\frac{p_1}{a}\right)^a \left(\frac{p_2}{1-a}\right)^{1-a} x_1^a x_2^{1-a}.$$

This gives us the minimum amount of money necessary at prices (p_1, p_2) to purchase a bundle on the same indifference curve as (x_1, x_2). It is easily seen that this is a monotonic transformation of the original utility function.

15.4 Compensating and Equivalent Variations

Let's use the money metric utility function to measure the monetary impact on the consumer of imposing a tax. We'll let $p_2 = 1$ for convenience, and write $m(p_1, x_1, x_2)$ for the money metric utility function. Suppose that initially the consumer faces price p_1^*, has income m^*, and chooses to consume some bundle (x_1^*, x_2^*). Now suppose that the government imposes a tax on good 1 so that its price rises to $\hat{p}_1$. At this new budget, we denote the consumer's optimal choice by $(\hat{x}_1, \hat{x}_2)$, as depicted in Figure 15.3. In general, we would expect that the consumer would reduce his consumption of good 1 when it is taxed and will certainly be worse off facing the tax. But *how* much worse off has the tax made the consumer? How much "harm" does this tax inflict?

One way to answer this question is to ask how much money the consumer would pay to avoid the tax. We can use the money metric utility function to measure this amount. How much money would the consumer need at the original price p_1^* to be as well-off as he would be at the taxed situation,

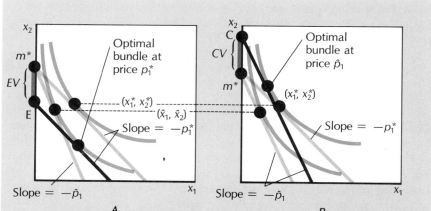

Figure
15.3
The compensating and equivalent variation in income.
Panel A shows the equivalent variation and panel B shows the
compensating variation.

facing the price $\hat{p}_1$ and choosing to consume $(\hat{x}_1, \hat{x}_2)$? In terms of money
metric utility, this amount of money is denoted by $m(p_1^*, \hat{x}_1, \hat{x}_2)$. If the
consumer had this much income and faced the price p_1^*, he would be just
as well-off as if he had income m^* and faced the price $\hat{p}_1$. Having the
income $m(p_1^*, \hat{x}_1, \hat{x}_2)$ and facing the original price p_1^* allows the consumer
to purchase a bundle that is *equivalent* to the bundle $(\hat{x}_1, \hat{x}_2)$ in the sense
that it is on the same indifference curve as $(\hat{x}_1, \hat{x}_2)$.

The **equivalent income** is depicted in Figure 15.3A by E. It is that
amount of income such that a budget line drawn at the original prices and
income E just touches the indifference curve through $(\hat{x}_1, \hat{x}_2)$.

We define the **equivalent variation** in income to be the maximum
amount that the consumer would pay to avoid the tax. That is:

$$EV = m^* - E = m^* - m(p_1^*, \hat{x}_1, \hat{x}_2).$$

The equivalent variation in income is the difference between m^* and E in
Figure 15.3A: this is the amount of money the consumer would be willing
to pay to keep the price at p_1^*, rather than having it changed to $\hat{p}_1$.

The equivalent variation measures how much harm the tax imposes on
the consumer in the sense that it measures how much money he would pay
to avoid it. But this isn't the only measure of the harm of the tax that we
might want to use. Another measure of the harm of a tax would be how
much money we would have to give the consumer to *compensate* him for
imposing the tax in the first place: how much money would the consumer
need at the *new* price to be as well-off as he was originally?

This amount is labeled C in Figure 15.3B. The budget line at the price

$\hat{p}_1$ and income C just touches the indifference curve through the original bundle (x_1^*, x_2^*). In terms of the money metric utility function, $C = m(\hat{p}_1, x_1^*, x_2^*)$.

The **compensating variation** in income is defined to be how much extra income the consumer would need to be as well-off after the tax is imposed as he was originally. It is the difference between C and m^* and is explicitly defined by

$$CV = C - m^* = m(\hat{p}_1, x_1^*, x_2^*) - m^*.$$

Now we have two measures of the "harm" imposed by a tax—the equivalent variation and the compensating variation. The first measures how much the consumer would pay to avoid the tax, and the second measures how much the consumer would have to be paid to compensate him for having to pay the tax. In general these two measures will differ because the value of a dollar will be different at the different prices—the before-tax and the after-tax price. Both measures are equally valid; which one is the more appropriate will depend on the use to which the numbers are being put.

In geometric terms, the compensating and equivalent variations are just two different ways to measure "how far apart" two indifference curves are. In each case we are measuring the distance between two indifference curves by seeing how far apart their tangent lines are. In general this measure of distance will depend on the slope of the tangent lines—that is, on the prices that we choose to determine the budget lines.

15.5 Quasilinear Preferences

We saw above that in general the compensating and equivalent variations will be different, since they measure the value of money at different prices. Geometrically, this is because they are measuring how far apart two indifference curves are by how far apart their tangent lines are, and in general this will depend on the slope of the tangent line. But in one special case the compensating and equivalent variations turn out to be the same. This is the case of quasilinear preferences. Recall from Chapter 4 that preferences are quasilinear if all the indifference curves are vertically parallel to each other. Thus the slope of the indifference curve depends only on x_1 and is independent of x_2. If this is so, then the compensating and equivalent variations will be equal to each other. The argument is depicted in Figure 15.4. Since the indifference curves are all vertically parallel to each other it doesn't matter if we measure how far they are apart using one set of prices or another: the distance between two indifference curves is independent of where we measure it. Thus the compensating variation and the equivalent variation will be the same.

We said earlier that quasilinear preferences are pretty unrealistic, and we would think it unlikely that people would have the same shape of in-

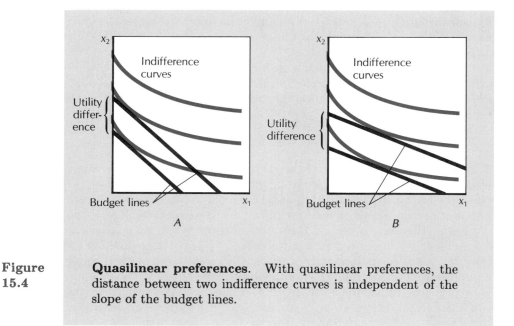

Figure 15.4

Quasilinear preferences. With quasilinear preferences, the distance between two indifference curves is independent of the slope of the budget lines.

difference curves at low levels of consumption as at high levels. But the assumption of quasilinear preferences is often taken as a first approximation for small changes in the levels of consumption.

In this book we are going to work with this approximation because it is easy to handle and provides good intuition. Once the fundamentals of this approximation are mastered, you can turn to more advanced treatments that allow one to measure money metric utilities without the need for this kind of approximation. For most goods, approximating the compensating and equivalent variations by the consumer's surplus turns out to be reasonably accurate.

To verify this point, it is instructive to reexamine Figure 15.3. The indifference curves illustrated there are not vertically parallel, but the slope doesn't change too drastically as x_2 increases. Thus the compensating and equivalent variations are about the same size. If the indifference curves were parallel, then the compensating and equivalent variations would be exactly the same, but in the case depicted in Figure 15.3 the difference between the two numbers is hardly significant.

15.6 Money Metric Utility and the Demand Curve

In previous chapters we saw how to go from a utility function to a demand curve—simply maximize utility at each set of prices and income. This will work for any utility function, and in particular it will work for the money metric utility. In this section we want to explore the *reverse* problem—given the demand curve, how can we figure out the utility function that generated that demand curve? In particular, how can we figure out the money metric utility function?

This question can be answered in general, but the mathematical techniques used are quite advanced. However, if we restrict ourselves to the special case of quasilinear preferences, we can calculate the money metric utility relatively easily. The methods used for this special case can be extended to general analysis through the use of more advanced mathematics, and, more importantly, the special case of quasilinear preferences can often serve as a good approximation to more general forms of preferences.

The best way to think about the indifference curves in this problem is to think of the good on the vertical axis as "money"—that is, money that can be spent on all sorts of other goods to generate utility. Under this interpretation it is natural to think of the price of good 2 as being 1 dollar; as noted before, a dollar bill will cost you one dollar to purchase.

It is convenient to depart from our standard terminology, and refer to the two goods as the x-good and the y-good. The x-good is a particular consumption good, and the y-good is the amount of money that the consumer can use to spend on other consumption goods. If the y-good is measured in money, then one money metric labeling of the indifference curves is pretty easy: we just label each indifference curve according to its height at the vertical axis. Each indifference curve will then have a label that measures how many dollars—to be spent on other goods—it would take to be indifferent to each other combination of the x-good and the y-good on the indifference curve. This will be the money metric utility associated with the reference prices that induce the consumer to demand zero units of the x-good.

Note that for the special case of quasilinear preferences the difference between the money metric utility assigned to any two indifference curves won't depend on the reference prices. Since the indifference curves are all parallel, the distance between any two of them won't depend on the slope of the tangent lines that we use to define the money metric utility function. Measuring the difference on the vertical axis is simply a convenient choice.

Thus assigning a money metric utility is easy in the case of quasilinear preferences, if we know the *indifference curves*. We just label each indifference curve with its height as measured along the vertical axis. The question we pose now is: how can we determine the height of the indifference curve from just knowing the *demand curve*?

Consider the indifference curve depicted in Figure 15.5A. The consumer is initially consuming the bundle (x_1, y_1), and we want to determine the value y_5—the vertical intercept of the indifference curve through (x_1, y_1). In order to do this, we think of breaking the x good up into several small pieces, each of size Δx. In Figure 15.5 there are four small pieces, but that is only for purposes of illustration; in principle there could be many more pieces.

Now start at (x_1, y_1), and take Δx units of the x-good away from the consumer, but compensate him by giving him enough y-good, Δy, to just get back on the indifference curve. In Figure 15.5A, the amount of the y-good necessary to put the consumer back on the indifference curve when we take away the first Δx of the x-good is labeled Δy_1. If we do this, the ratio of the extra y-good to the diminished x-good will be the slope of the indifference curve—the marginal rate of substitution:

$$\frac{\Delta y_1}{\Delta x} = \text{MRS}.$$

Or, turning this equation around, the extra y-good that we have to give the consumer to compensate him for the first small reduction in the x-good is simply

$$\Delta y_1 = \text{MRS}\Delta x. \tag{15.1}$$

Now consider what this means in terms of the demand curve depicted in Figure 15.5B. Let us represent this curve by the (inverse) demand function, $p(x)$. Recall that the inverse demand function measures the price that the consumer is willing to pay to purchase x units of the good. Because of our assumption of quasilinear preferences, the price at which the consumer will demand x units of the x-good will be independent of how much of the y-good he has—since the slope of the indifference curve only depends on x, but not on y. The MRS at (x_1, y_1) is therefore simply the price at which the consumer demands (x_1, y_1), which is given by the inverse demand curve $p(x_1)$. Thus the amount of extra money that we have to give the consumer to compensate him for the first small reduction in his consumption of the x-good, Δx, is

$$\Delta y_1 = p(x_1)\Delta x. \tag{15.2}$$

This is the area of a rectangle with height $p(x_1)$ and width Δx in Figure 15.5B. This box tells us how much money we need to give the consumer to compensate him for the first marginal reduction in his consumption of the x-good.

The consumer now has $y_2 = y_1 + p(x_1)\Delta x$ dollars, and he is at a new consumption level $x_2 = x_1 - \Delta x$. At this point, the slope of his indifference curve—his MRS—is $p(x_2)$. We can repeat the same operation again: take another Δx away from him and compensate him with $p(x_2)\Delta x$ units of good 2—as illustrated in Figure 15.5.

Continuing in this manner, we trace our way up the staircase in 15.5A and take away $\Delta x + \Delta x + \Delta x + \Delta x$ units of good 1 from the consumer and compensate him with $p(x_1)\Delta x + p(x_2)\Delta x + p(x_3)\Delta x + p(x_4)\Delta x$ dollars. All the way along, the consumer remains indifferent to the original starting point (x_1, y_1).

After we have taken away all of good 1, we can look to see how much of good 2 we had to give the consumer in total to keep him or her indifferent

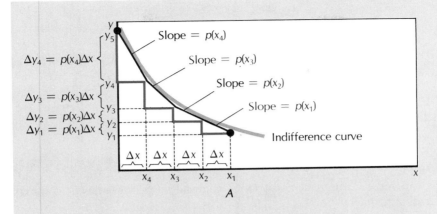

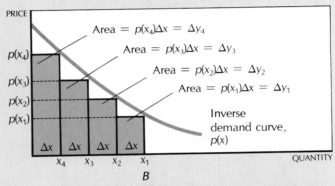

Using the demand curve to measure money metric utility. Panel A shows the movement along the staircase, moving up the indifference curve, and panel B interprets this as the area under the demand curve.

Figure
15.5

to this transaction. The answer is $p(x_1)\Delta x + p(x_2)\Delta x + p(x_3)\Delta x + p(x_4)\Delta x$ dollars. The consumer started out with y_1 dollars originally, so the total amount of money that the consumer has to have to make him willing to give up his entire consumption of good 1 is

$$y_5 = y_1 + p(x_1)\Delta x + p(x_2)\Delta x + p(x_3)\Delta x)\Delta x + p(x_4)\Delta x.$$

This sum represents the sum of the areas of the rectangles in Figure 15.5B. If we think of Δx as getting smaller and smaller, the areas of these rectangles approaches the area under the demand curve. Thus, for small values of Δx we have

$$y_5 = y_1 + \text{the area under the demand curve.}$$

15.7 An Algebraic Treatment

To really derive consumer's surplus correctly, we need to use calculus, as is done in the Appendix to this chapter. But we can go a long way with just a little algebra. Here is how it works.

First we consider the consumer choice problem in the case of quasilinear utility:

$$\max_{x,y} v(x) + y$$

such that $px + y = m$.

We can solve the budget constraint for y and write the equivalent maximization problem:

$$\max_x v(x) + m - px. \tag{15.3}$$

In this form it is easy to see the condition that characterizes the optimal choice of x: the marginal utility from a small change in the consumption of good x must equal its price. If this condition were not met, the consumer could get more utility by changing his or her consumption of the good. We write this condition as

$$\frac{\Delta v(x)}{\Delta x} = p$$

or, using the definition of marginal utility:

$$\frac{v(x) - v(x - \Delta x)}{\Delta x} = p. \tag{15.4}$$

This equation says that the marginal utility from changing the consumption of the x–good must be equal to its price.

Equation (15.4) gives us an expression for the inverse demand curve $p(x)$: at any level of consumption x, the price that it would take to get the consumer to demand x is given by

$$p(x) = \frac{v(x) - v(x - \Delta x)}{\Delta x} \tag{15.5}$$

We'll use equation (15.5) in a little while. Now let's consider what we are trying to measure. As explained in the last section, we want to calculate the vertical intercept of an indifference curve: that is, we want to find how much of good y the consumer would need to make him indifferent to giving up all of good x.

In terms of the utility function, we are trying to find y^* such that

$$v(x) + y = v(0) + y^*.$$

Solving this equation, we need to find y^* such that

$$y^* = v(x) - v(0) + y. \tag{15.6}$$

Let us divide x into n small pieces of size Δx, so that

$$x = \Delta x + \ldots + \Delta x.$$

Note that it is identically true that

$$
\begin{aligned}
v(x) - v(0) = {} & v(x) - v(x - \Delta x) \\
& + v(x - \Delta x) - v(x - 2\Delta x) \\
& + v(x - 2\Delta x) - v(x - 3\Delta x) \\
& + \ldots \\
& + v(x - n\Delta x) - v(0)
\end{aligned}
$$

since all the terms on the right-hand side except for the first and the last cancel out.

If we divide and multiply this expression by Δx we have another identity:

$$
\begin{aligned}
v(x) - v(0) = {} & \frac{v(x) - v(x - \Delta x)}{\Delta x} \Delta x \\
& + \frac{v(x - \Delta x) - v(x - 2\Delta x)}{\Delta x} \Delta x \\
& + \ldots \\
& + \frac{v(x - n\Delta x) - v(0)}{\Delta x} \Delta x. \tag{15.7}
\end{aligned}
$$

Now look at equations (15.5) and (15.7). Each of the fractions on the right-hand side of equation (15.7) is the price of good x at different levels of demand. Substituting equation (15.5) into equation (15.7) we have

$$
\begin{aligned}
v(x) - v(0) = {} & p(x)\Delta x + p(x - \Delta x)\Delta x + \ldots \\
& + p(x - n\Delta x)\Delta x + p(0)\Delta x. \tag{15.8}
\end{aligned}
$$

The sum on the right-hand side is just the area of a number of small rectangles; as Δx becomes smaller and smaller, this area will approach the area under the demand curve. Combining equations (15.8) and (15.6) we have the final expression for y^*:

$$
\begin{aligned}
y^* = {} & y + p(x)\Delta x + p(x - \Delta x)\Delta x + \ldots + p(x - n\Delta x)\Delta x + p(0)\Delta x \\
= {} & y + \text{the area under the demand curve.}
\end{aligned}
$$

This is what we wanted to show: the utility function for quasilinear preferences can be taken to be the amount of the y-good plus the area under the demand curve for the x-good:

$$u(x, y) = y + \text{area under the demand curve for } x.$$

It is worthwhile asking what goes wrong with this sort of argument when preferences aren't quasilinear. If preferences are not quasilinear, the inverse demand curve will in general depend on the amount of money that the consumer has as well as the amount of the x-good. Thus, as we take the x–good away from the consumer and give him some money in compensation, the rate at which he is willing to give up the *next* unit of the good will change. But the market demand curve is drawn holding money income fixed, so it will not reflect this change in demand due to the change in income—the income effect.

With quasilinear preferences, the change in the demand for the x–good as income changes is zero, so there is no distortion in measuring the true willingness to pay. As it turns out, the magnitude of the income effect is not all that large for most goods, and the change in the area under the demand curve usually gives a pretty good approximation to the true change in money metric utility.

15.8 Net Consumer's Surplus

Suppose that the consumer is purchasing the bundle (x, y) at the prices $(p(x), 1)$. Then he is getting a money metric utility of $y^* = y + A$, where A is the area under the demand curve as described above. Thus the bundle (x, y) is *equivalent* in terms of the consumer's preferences to the bundle $(0, y^*)$, which means it is equivalent to y^* dollars alone.

But the consumer only has to spend $p(x)x$ dollars to get this bundle of goods. The difference between how much the consumer would be *willing to pay* to consume x units of the good minus how much he *actually has to pay* to get x units of the good is illustrated in Figure 15.6A. This area is the difference between the amount that the consumer would be willing to pay to consume x—the area under the demand curve—and the amount that the consumer actually has to pay to consume x, which is $p(x)x$. As we saw earlier in this chapter, this area is known as the net consumer's surplus.

One way to think of net consumer's surplus is to think of it as how much money the consumer would need for him to agree to reduce his consumption of the x-good to zero if he was currently purchasing x units of the x-good. In terms of his preferences, the bundle (x, y) is equivalent to the bundle $(0, y^*)$. But the cost of the bundle (x, y) is $px + y$, and the cost of the bundle $(0, y^*)$ is just y^*. Thus the *extra* money the consumer would need to agree to reduce his consumption of the x-good to zero is $y^* - y - px$. We've already seen that $y^* - y$ is the area under the demand curve for the

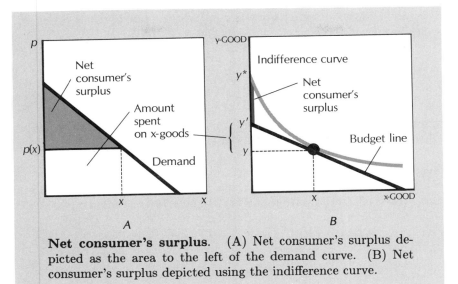

Net consumer's surplus.   (A) Net consumer's surplus depicted as the area to the left of the demand curve. (B) Net consumer's surplus depicted using the indifference curve.

Figure 15.6

x-good, denoted by A, so this formula reduces to the one given above: the net consumer's surplus is $A - px$.

In terms of the indifference curve diagram in Figure 15.6B, the consumer's surplus is the difference between the point where the indifference curve intercepts the vertical axis, $y*$, and the point where the budget line intercepts the vertical axis, $y' = px + y$. If the consumer were not allowed to purchase any of the x-good, he would have to be given y^* dollars to make him as well-off as he would be at (x, y). But if he is allowed to purchase the x-good at a constant price given by the budget line, then he would only have to be given y' dollars. The difference, $y^* - y' = A - px$, measures the surplus that the consumer is enjoying from being able to consume the x-good at the market price p.

Yet another way to think about consumer's surplus is to imagine somebody selling the x-good to the consumer in dribs and drabs. Suppose the consumer starts with 0 units of the x-good and y^* units of the y-good. Now he is just willing to pay $p(1)$ dollars for the first unit of the x-good—in the sense that he is just indifferent between having it and not having it at that price. Then he is just willing to pay $p(2)$ dollars for the next unit of the x-good, $p(3)$ dollars for the next unit, and so on.

By the time we get down to x units, he has paid out a total of $A = p(1) + p(2) + p(3) + \ldots + p(x)$ dollars and is now consuming a bundle $(x, y^* - A)$. But if he were allowed to purchase all the units of the good at the *same* price $p(x)$, he would be consuming the bundle $(x, y^* - p(x)x)$. So the surplus or the extra dollars of the y-good that he enjoys by being able to purchase all the units of the x–good at the same price is $A - p(x)x$, which is the area illustrated in Figure 15.6A.

EXAMPLE: Consumer's Surplus with a Linear Demand Curve

Question: Suppose that the demand curve for the x-good is given by $D(p) = 20 - 2p$. At the price $p = 4$, what is the consumer's surplus?

Answer: When $p = 10$, demand is zero; when $p = 4$, demand is 12. Thus the consumer's surplus is the area of a triangle with height of $h = 10 - 4 = 6$ and a base of $b = 12$. Applying the formula for the area of a triangle, $A = bh/2$, we find that the consumer's surplus is 36.

15.9 The Change in Consumer's Surplus

We are usually not terribly interested in the absolute level of consumer's surplus. We are generally much more interested in the change in consumer's surplus that results from some policy change. For example, suppose the price of a good changes from p' to p''. How does the consumer's surplus change?

In Figure 15.7 we have illustrated the change in consumer's surplus associated with a change in price. The change in consumer's surplus is the difference between two roughly triangular regions, and will therefore have a roughly trapezoidal shape. The trapezoid is further composed of two subregions, the rectangle indicated by R and the roughly triangular region indicated by T.

The rectangle measures the loss in surplus due to the fact that the consumer is now paying more for all the units he continues to consume. He is still consuming x'' units of the good, and each unit of the good is now more expensive by $p'' - p'$, so he has lost that much money that he was previously spending on other goods.

The triangle measures the value of the *lost* consumption of the x-good. Because the price is higher, the consumer has decided to forgo some of his consumption of it, and the triangle measures how much that consumption was worth to the consumer. The first marginal unit he gave up was worth $p' = p(x')$ dollars to him, and that's how much he was paying for it, so there was basically no loss from that unit. The next unit was worth $p(x' - \Delta x)$, and he was only paying p' for it. Similarly the third unit was worth $p(x' - 2\Delta x)$ and he was paying p' for it, and so on. The total loss to the consumer from the change in consumption induced by the price change is the sum of all these areas, which, in the limit, is the area T in Figure 15.7.

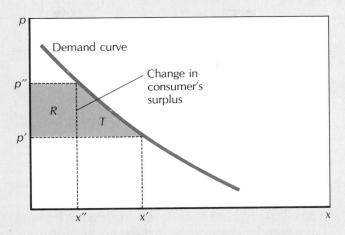

Change in consumer's surplus. The change in consumer's surplus will be the difference between two roughly triangular areas, and thus will have a roughly trapezoidal shape.

Figure 15.7

EXAMPLE: The Change in Consumer's Surplus

Question: Consider the same linear demand curve given above, $D(p) = 20 - 2p$. When the price changes from 2 to 3 what is the associated change in consumer's surplus?

Answer: When $p = 2$, $D(2) = 16$, and when $p = 3$, $D(3) = 14$. Thus we want to compute the area of a trapezoid with a height of 1 and bases of 14 and 16. This is equivalent to a rectangle with height 1 and base 14 (having area 14), plus a triangle of height 1 and base 2 (having area of 1). The total area will therefore be 15.

15.10 Variations and Surplus

We started this chapter by describing two measures of utility change known as the compensating and equivalent variations. What is the relationship of these measures to consumer's surplus? In the case of quasilinear preferences—the case where consumer's surplus is a valid measure of utility—all three concepts come down to the same thing.

If preferences are quasilinear, the distance between any two indifference curves is independent of where you measure it. The distance measured at the after-tax prices is the compensating variation, the distance measured at the before-tax prices is the equivalent variation, and the distance measured along the vertical axis is the change in consumer's surplus.

With other sorts of preferences, the compensating variation, the equivalent variation, and consumer's surplus will generally differ. Given sufficient data on consumer choices it will usually be possible to estimate the consumer's preferences and actually calculate all three numbers. However, since consumer's surplus is so easy to calculate, it is often used as an approximation to the other two "exact" measures. In this book, we will use consumer's surplus in this fashion.

15.11 Producer's Surplus

The demand curve measures the amount that will be demanded at each price; the **supply curve** measures the amount that will be supplied at each price. Just as the area *under* the demand curve measures the surplus enjoyed by the demanders of a good, the area *above* the supply curve measures the surplus enjoyed by the suppliers of a good.

We've referred to the area under the demand curve as consumer's surplus. By analogy, the area above the supply curve is known as **producer's surplus**. The terms consumer's surplus and producer's surplus are somewhat misleading, since who is doing the consuming and who is doing the producing really doesn't matter. It would be better to use the terms "demander's surplus" and "supplier's surplus," but we'll have to bow to tradition and use the standard terminology.

So suppose that we have a supply curve for a good. This simply measures the amount of a good that will be supplied at each different price. The good could be supplied by an individual who owns the good in question, or it could be supplied by a firm that produces the good. We'll take the latter interpretation so as to stick with the traditional terminology, and depict the producer's supply curve in Figure 15.8. If the producer is able to sell x^* units of his product in a market at a price p^*, what is the surplus he enjoys?

It is most convenient to conduct the analysis in terms of the producer's *inverse* supply curve, $p_s(x)$. This function measures what the price would have to be to get the producer to supply x units of the good. In terms of this function, the producer is willing to sell the first unit of the good at price $p_s(\Delta x)$, but he actually gets the market price p^* for it. Similarly, he is willing to sell the second unit for $p_s(2\Delta x)$, but he gets p^* for it. Continuing until we get to the last unit he sells, he is just willing to sell that for $p_s(x^*) = p^*$.

The difference between the minimum amount he would be willing to sell the x^* units for and the amount he actually sells the units for is the **net producer's surplus**. It is the triangular area depicted in Figure 15.8A.

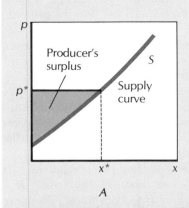
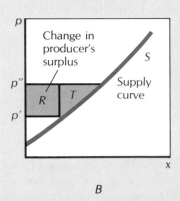

Producer's surplus. The net producer's surplus is the triangular area to the left of the supply curve in panel A, and the change in producer's surplus is the trapezoidal area in panel B.

Figure
15.8

Just as in the case of consumer's surplus, we can ask how producer's surplus changes when the price increases from p' to p''. In general, the change in producer's surplus will be the difference between two triangular regions and will therefore generally have the roughly trapezoidal shape depicted in Figure 15.8B. As in the case of consumer's surplus, the roughly trapezoidal region will be composed of a rectangular region R and a roughly triangular region T. The rectangle measures the gain from selling the units previously sold anyway at p' at the higher price p''. The roughly triangular region measures the gain from selling the extra units at the price p''. This is entirely analogous to the change in consumer's surplus considered earlier.

Although it is very common to refer to this kind of change as an increase in producer's surplus, in a deeper sense it really represents an increase in consumer's surplus in the sense that it is an amount of money paid to some individual, or group of individuals, who own the firm that generated the supply curve. Producer's surplus is closely related to the idea of profit, but we'll have to wait until we study firm behavior in more detail to spell out the relationship.

15.12 Calculating Gains and Losses

If we have estimates of the market demand and supply curves for a good, it is not difficult to calculate the loss in consumer's surplus due to different kinds of government policies. For example, suppose the government decides to change its tax treatment of some good. This will result in a change in the prices facing consumers and therefore a change in the amount of the good that they choose to consume. We can calculate the consumer's surplus associated with different tax proposals and see which tax reforms generate the smallest loss.

This is often useful information for judging various methods of taxation, but it suffers from two defects. First, as we've indicated earlier, the consumer's surplus calculation is only valid for special forms of preferences—namely, preferences representable by a quasilinear utility function. We argued earlier that this kind of utility function may be a reasonable approximation for goods for which changes in income lead to small changes in demand, but for goods whose consumption is closely tied to income the use of consumer surplus may be inappropriate.

Second, the calculation of this loss effectively lumps together all the consumers and producers and generates an estimate of the "cost" of a social policy only for some mythical "representative consumer." In many cases it is desirable to know not only the average cost across the population, but who bears the costs. The political success or failure of policies often depends more on the *distribution* of gains and losses than on the average gain or loss.

Consumer's surplus may be easy to calculate, but it is not that much more difficult to calculate the true money metric utility associated with a price change, although this calculation does require more advanced methods. If we have estimates of the demands and supplies of each household—or at least the demand functions for a sample of representative households—we can calculate the impact of a policy change on each household in terms of money metric utility. Thus we will have a measure of the "benefits" or "costs" imposed on each household by the proposed policy change.

Mervyn King has described a nice example of this approach to analyzing the implications of reforming the tax treatment of housing in Britain.[2] He first examined the housing expenditures of 5,895 households and estimated a demand function that best described their purchases of housing services. Next, he used this demand function to calculate the money metric utility function for each household. This calculation is similar in spirit to calculating the area under the demand curve in the consumer's surplus calculation described above, but is somewhat more complex.

Finally, he used the estimated money metric utility function to calculate how much each household would gain or lose under certain changes in the taxation of housing in Britain. The basic nature of the tax reform he studied was to eliminate tax concessions to owner-occupied housing and to raise rents in public housing. The revenues generated by these changes would be handed back to the households in the form of transfers proportional to household income.

King found that 4,888 of the 5,895 households would benefit from this

---

[2] See Mervyn King, "Welfare Analysis of Tax Reforms Using Household Data," *Journal of Public Economics*, 21 (1983), 183–214.

kind of reform. More importantly he could identify explicitly those households that would have significant losses from the tax reform. King found, for example, that 94 percent of the highest income households gained from the reform, while only 58 percent of the lowest income households gained. This kind of information would allow special measures to be undertaken which might help in designing the tax reform in away that would harm the fewest people.

Summary

1. The money metric utility function measures how much money a consumer would need at some reference prices to be as well-off as he would be at a given consumption bundle.

2. The money metric utility can be used to define the compensating and equivalent variations, which measure the monetary equivalent of a change in the consumption bundle.

3. In general the compensating and equivalent variations will depend on the reference prices, but in the case of quasilinear utility, they will be independent of the reference prices.

4. In the case of quasilinear utility, the money metric utility function is given by the area under the demand curve plus the consumer's income.

5. The consumer's surplus is the difference between how much the consumer would be willing to pay to consume some good and how much he or she actually has to pay. It will generally be an area to the left of the demand curve.

Review Questions

1. Which would a consumer prefer: a bundle (x, y), or the amount of money given by the level of money metric utility for that bundle at the prevailing prices?

2. Consider the utility function for perfect substitutes, $u(x_1, x_2) = x_1 + x_2$. What is the associated money metric utility?

3. Suppose the demand curve is given by $D(p) = 10 - p$. What is the total consumer's surplus from consuming 6 units of the good?

4. In the above example, if the price changes from 4 to 6, what is the change in consumer's surplus?

APPENDIX

Let's use some calculus to treat consumer's surplus rigorously. Start with the maximization problem in equation (15.3). The first-order condition for this problem is

$$v'(x) = p.$$

This means that the inverse demand function $p(x)$ is defined by

$$p(x) = v'(x). \tag{15.9}$$

Now look at equation (15.6). We can use the Fundamental Theorem of Calculus to write this as

$$y^* = \int_0^x v'(t)\,dt + y = v(x) - v(0) + y. \tag{15.10}$$

Substituting from (15.9) into (15.10) we have

$$y^* = \int_0^x p(t)\,dt + y$$

which says that y^* is just y plus the area under the demand curve.

16

MARKET DEMAND

We have seen in earlier chapters how to model individual consumer choice. Here we see how to add up individual choices to get total **market demand**. Once we have derived the market demand curve, we will examine some of its properties, such as the relationship between demand and revenue.

16.1 From Individual to Market Demand

Let us use $x_i^1(p_1, p_2, m_i)$ to represent consumer i's demand function for good 1 and $x_i^2(p_1, p_2, m_i)$ for consumer i's demand function for good 2. Suppose that there are n consumers. Then the **market demand** for good 1, also called the **aggregate demand** for good 1, is the sum over the consumers of these individual demands:

$$X^1(p_1, p_2, m_1, \ldots, m_n) = \sum_{i=1}^{n} x_i^1(p_1, p_2, m_i).$$

The analogous equation holds for good 2.

Since each individual's demand for each good depends on prices and his or her money income, the aggregate demand will generally depend on prices and the *distribution* of incomes. However, it is sometimes convenient to think of the aggregate demand as the demand of some "representative consumer" who has an income that is just the sum of all individual incomes. The conditions under which this can be done are rather stringent, but a discussion of this issue is beyond the scope of this book.

If we do make the representative consumer assumption, the aggregate demand function will have the form $X^1(p_1, p_2, M)$, where M is the sum of the incomes of the individual consumers. Under this assumption, the aggregate demand in the economy is just like the demand of some individual who faces prices (p_1, p_2) and has income M.

If we fix all the money incomes and the price of good 2, we can illustrate the relation between the aggregate demand for good 1 and its price, as in Figure 16.1. Note that this curve is drawn holding all other prices and incomes fixed. If these other prices and incomes change, the aggregate demand curve will shift.

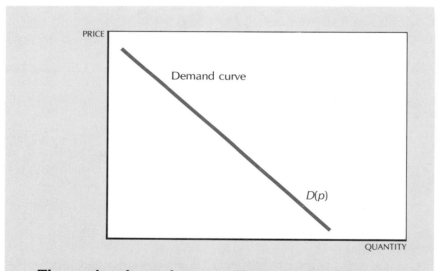

Figure 16.1

The market demand curve. The market demand curve is the sum of the individual demand curves.

For example, if goods 1 and 2 are substitutes, then we know that increasing the price of good 2 will tend to increase the demand for good 1 whatever its price. This means that increasing the price of good 2 will tend to shift the aggregate demand curve for good 1 outward. Similarly, if goods 1 and 2 are complements, increasing the price of good 2 will shift the aggregate demand curve for good 1 inward.

If good 1 is a normal good for some individual, then increasing that individual's money income, holding everything else fixed, would tend to increase that individual's demand, and therefore shift the aggregate demand curve outward. If we adopt the representative consumer model, and suppose that good 1 is a normal good for the representative consumer, then any economic change that increases aggregate income will increase the demand for good 1.

16.2 The Inverse Demand Curve

We can look at the aggregate demand curve as giving us quantity as a function of price, or giving us price as a function of quantity. When we want to emphasize this latter view, we will sometimes refer to the **inverse demand curve**, $P(X)$. This function measures what the market price for good 1 would have to be for X units of it to be demanded.

We've seen earlier that the price of a good measures the marginal rate of substitution between it and all other goods; that is, the price of a good represents the marginal willingness to pay for an extra unit of the good by anyone who is demanding that good. If all consumers are facing the same prices for goods, then all consumers will have the same marginal rate of substitution at their optimal choices. Thus the inverse demand curve, $P(X)$, measures the marginal rate of substitution, or the marginal willingness to pay, of *every* consumer who is purchasing the good.

The geometric interpretation of this summing operation is pretty obvious. Note that we are summing the demand or supply curves *horizontally*: for any given price, we add up the individuals' quantities demanded which, of course, are measured on the horizontal axis.

EXAMPLE: Adding up "Linear" Demand Curves

Suppose that one individual's demand curve is $D_1(p) = 20 - p$ and another individual's is $D_2(p) = 10 - 2p$. What is the market demand function? We have to be a little careful here about what we mean by "linear" demand functions. Since a negative amount of a good usually has no meaning, we *really* mean that the individual demand functions have the form

$$D_1(p) = \max\{20 - p, 0\}$$
$$D_2(p) = \max\{10 - 2p, 0\}.$$

What economists call "linear" demand curves actually aren't linear functions! The sum of the two demand curves looks like the curve depicted in Figure 16.2. Note the kink at $p = 5$.

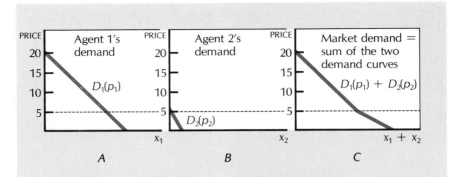

Figure
16.2

The sum of two "linear" demand curves. Since the demand curves are only linear for positive quantities, there will typically be a kink in the market demand curve.

16.3 The Reservation Price Model

We encountered the reservation price of a consumer in Chapter 1. It is that price at which the consumer is just willing to purchase a unit of a good—any higher price and he would decide not to purchase. Usually the reservation price model is used when goods come in large discrete units, like houses and cars. How does this kind of behavior fit in with the budget constraint and indifference curve analysis described earlier?

Suppose that good 1 is some good that comes in discrete units and that good 2 is money to be spent on all other goods. Think of good 1 as being something like a washing machine, so that the consumer will want either 0 or 1 washing machines, depending on their price.

Since the good 2 is measured in dollars it's price is automatically 1. Thus the budget constraint takes the form

$$p_1 x_1 + x_2 = m.$$

Since x_1 must be either 0 or 1, we have only two interesting consumption bundles:

$$(x_1 = 0, x_2 = m)$$

and

$$(x_1 = 1, x_2 = m - p_1).$$

Which one of these has the largest utility? Let us compare $u(0, m)$ to $u(1, m - p_1)$.

If p_1 is small enough, the consumer will obviously prefer to purchase good 1. If p_1 is high enough, he would prefer not to purchase good 1. Thus there will generally be some price p_1^* where the two alternatives are equally valued by the consumer:

$$u(0, m) = u(1, m - p_1^*).$$

The price p_1^* is the consumer's reservation price: where he is just indifferent between purchasing and not purchasing the discrete good.

In terms of demand functions, we have the situation depicted in Figure 16.3: the demand for the discrete good is zero if p_1 is greater than p_1^*, and the demand is 1 if p_1 is less than p_1^*.

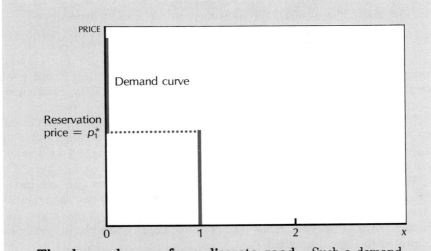

The demand curve for a discrete good. Such a demand curve will be zero for price greater than the reservation price, and 1 for prices at or below the reservation price.

Figure
16.3

The market demand curve is just the sum of demand curves like the one depicted in Figure 16.3. Note that the market demand curve in this case must slope downward, since a decrease in the market price must increase the number of consumers who are willing to pay at least that price. An example with two consumers is depicted in Figure 16.4.

16.4 The Extensive and the Intensive Margin

In previous chapters we have concentrated on consumer choice in which the consumer was consuming positive amounts of each good. When the

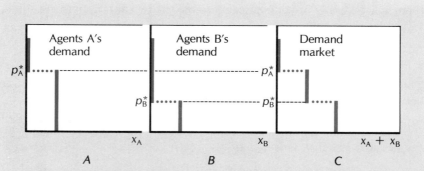

Figure
16.4
Market demand. The market demand curve in the reservation price model. The market demand curve is the sum of the
demand curves of all the consumers in the market, here represented by the two consumers A and B.

price changes the consumer decides to consume more or less of one good
or the other, but still ends up consuming some of both goods. Economists
sometimes say that this is an adjustment on the **intensive margin**.

In the reservation price model, the consumers are deciding whether or not
to enter the market for one good or the other. This is sometimes called an
adjustment on the **extensive margin**. The slope of the aggregate demand
curve will be affected by both sorts of decisions.

We saw earlier that the adjustment on the intensive margin was in the
"right" direction for normal goods: when the price went up, the quantity
demanded went down. The adjustment on the extensive margin also works
in the "right" direction. Thus aggregate demand curves can generally be
expected to slope downward.

16.5 Elasticity

In Chapter 6 we saw how to derive a demand curve from a consumer's
underlying preferences. It is often of interest to have a measure of how
"responsive" demand is to some change in price or income. Now the first
measure that springs to mind is using the slope of a demand curve as a
measure of responsiveness. After all, the definition of the slope of a demand
curve is the change in quantity demanded divided by the change in price:

$$\text{slope of demand curve} = \frac{\Delta q}{\Delta p}$$

and that certainly looks like a measure of responsiveness.

Well, it is a measure of responsiveness—but it has some problems. The
most important problem is that the slope of a demand curve depends on the

units in which you measure demand and price. If you measure demand in gallons rather than quarts, the slope becomes four times steeper. Rather than specify units all the time, it is convenient to consider a unit-free measure of responsiveness. Economists have chosen to use a measure known as **elasticity**, which we first encountered in Chapter 6.

The **price elasticity of demand**, ϵ, is defined to be the percent change in quantity divided by the percent change in price.[1] A ten percent increase in price represents the same size increase whether the price is measured in American dollars or English pounds; thus measuring increases in percentage terms keeps the definition of elasticity unit-free.

In symbols the definition of elasticity is

$$\epsilon = \frac{\Delta q/q}{\Delta p/p}.$$

Rearranging this definition we have the more common expression:

$$\epsilon = \frac{p}{q}\frac{\Delta q}{\Delta p}.$$

The elasticity of demand is the slope of the demand curve multiplied by the price and divided by the quantity. The sign of the elasticity of demand is generally negative, since demand curves invariably have a negative slope. However, it is tedious to keep referring to an elasticity of *minus* something-or-other, so it is common in verbal discussion to refer to elasticities of 2 or 3, rather than -2 or -3. We will try to keep the signs straight in the text by referring to the absolute value of elasticity, but you should be aware that verbal treatments tend to drop the minus sign.

Another problem with negative numbers arises when we compare magnitudes. Is an elasticity of -3 greater or less than an elasticity of -2? From an algebraic point of view -3 is smaller than -2, but economists tend to say that the demand with the elasticity of -3 is "more elastic" than the one with -2. In this book we will make comparisons in terms of absolute value so as to avoid this kind of ambiguity.

EXAMPLE: The Elasticity of a Linear Demand Curve

Consider the linear demand curve, $q = a - bp$, depicted in Figure 16.5. The slope of this demand curve is a constant, $-b$. Plugging this into the formula for elasticity we have

$$\epsilon = \frac{-bp}{q} = \frac{-bp}{a - bp}.$$

[1] The Greek letter ϵ, epsilon, is pronounced "eps-i-lon."

When $p = 0$, the elasticity of demand is 0. When $q = 0$, the elasticity of demand is (negative) infinity. At what value of price is the elasticity of demand equal to -1?

To find such a price, we write down the equation

$$\frac{-bp}{a - bp} = -1$$

and solve it for p. This gives

$$p = \frac{a}{2b}$$

which, as we see in Figure 16.5, is just halfway down the demand curve.

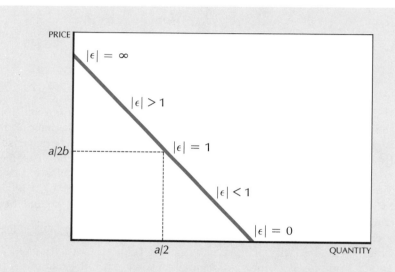

Figure
16.5

The elasticity of a linear demand curve. Elasticity is infinite at the vertical intercept, one halfway down the curve, and zero at the horizontal intercept.

16.6 Elasticity and Demand

If a good has an elasticity of demand greater than 1 in absolute value we say that it has an **elastic demand**. If the elasticity is less than 1 in absolute value we say that it has an **inelastic demand**. And if it has an elasticity of exactly -1, we say it has **unit elastic demand**.

An elastic demand curve is one for which the quantity demanded is very responsive to price: if you increase the price by 1 percent, the quantity demanded decreases by more than 1 percent. So think of elasticity as the responsiveness of the quantity demanded to price, and it will be easy to remember what elastic and inelastic mean.

In general the elasticity of demand for a good depends to a large extent on how many close substitutes it has. Take an extreme case—our old friend, the red pencils and blue pencils example. Suppose that everyone regards these goods as perfect substitutes. Then if some of each of them are bought, they must sell for the same price. Now think what would happen to the demand for red pencils if their price rose, and the price of blue pencils stayed constant. Clearly it would drop to zero—the demand for red pencils is very elastic since it has a perfect substitute.

If a good has many close substitutes, we would expect that its demand curve would be very responsive to its price changes. On the other hand, if there are few close substitutes for a good, it can exhibit a quite inelastic demand.

16.7 Elasticity and Revenue

Revenue is just the price of a good times the quantity sold of that good. If the price of a good increases, then the quantity sold decreases, so revenue may increase or decrease. Which way it goes obviously depends on how responsive demand is to the price change. If demand drops a lot when the price increases, then revenue will fall. If demand drops only a little when the price increases, then revenue will increase. This suggests that the direction of the change in revenue has something to do with the elasticity of demand.

Indeed, there is a very useful relationship between price elasticity and revenue change. The definition of revenue is

$$R = pq.$$

If we let the price change to $p + \Delta p$ and the quantity change to $q + \Delta q$, we have a new revenue of

$$R' = (p + \Delta p)(q + \Delta q)$$
$$= pq + q\Delta p + p\Delta q + \Delta p\Delta q.$$

Subtracting R from R' we have

$$\Delta R = q\Delta p + p\Delta q + \Delta p\Delta q.$$

For small values of Δp and Δq, the last term can safely be neglected, leaving us with an expression for the change in revenue of the form

$$\Delta R = q\Delta p + p\Delta q.$$

That is, the change in revenue is roughly equal to the quantity times the change in price plus the price times the change in quantity. If we want an expression for the rate of change of revenue per change in price, we just divide this expression by Δp to get

$$\frac{\Delta R}{\Delta p} = q + p\frac{\Delta q}{\Delta p}.$$

This is treated geometrically in Figure 16.6. The revenue is just the area of the box: price times quantity. When the price increases, we add a rectangular area on the top of the box, which is approximately $q\Delta p$, but we subtract an area on the side of the box, which is approximately $p\Delta q$. For small changes, this is exactly the expression given above. (The leftover part, $\Delta p\Delta q$, is the little square in the corner of the box, which will be very small relative to the other magnitudes.)

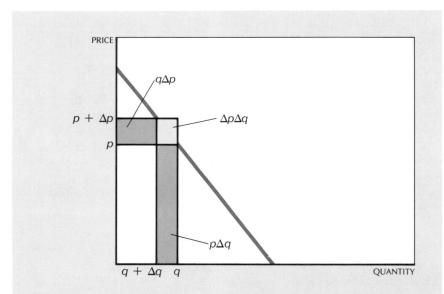

Figure
16.6

How revenue changes when price changes. The change in revenue is the sum of the box on the top minus the box on the side.

When will the net result of these two effects be positive? That is, when do we satisfy the following inequality:

$$\frac{\Delta R}{\Delta p} = p\frac{\Delta q}{\Delta p} + q(p) > 0?$$

Rearranging we have

$$\frac{p}{q}\frac{\Delta q}{\Delta p} > -1.$$

The left-hand side of this expression is $\epsilon(p)$, which is a negative number. Multiplying through by -1 reverses the sense of the inequality to give us:

$$|\epsilon(p)| < 1.$$

Thus revenue increases when price increases if the elasticity of demand is less than one in absolute value. Similarly, revenue decreases when price increases if the elasticity of demand is greater than one in absolute value.

Another way to see this is to write the revenue change as we did above:

$$\Delta R = p\Delta q + q\Delta p > 0$$

and rearrange this to get

$$-\frac{p}{q}\frac{\Delta q}{\Delta p} = |\epsilon(p)| < 1.$$

Yet a third way to see this is to take the formula for $\Delta R/\Delta p$ and rearrange it as follows:

$$\frac{\Delta R}{\Delta p} = q + p\frac{\Delta q}{\Delta p}$$

$$= q\left[1 + \frac{p}{q}\frac{\Delta q}{\Delta p}\right]$$

$$= q\left[1 + \epsilon(p)\right].$$

Since demand elasticity is naturally negative, we can also write this expression as

$$\frac{\Delta R}{\Delta p} = q\left[1 - |\epsilon(p)|\right].$$

In this formula it is easy to see how revenue responds to a change in price: if the absolute value of elasticity is greater than 1, then $\Delta R/\Delta p$ must be negative and vice versa.

The intuitive content of these mathematical facts is not hard to remember. If demand is very responsive to price—that is, it is very elastic—then an increase in price will reduce demand so much that revenue will fall. If demand is very unresponsive to price—it is very inelastic—then an increase in price will not change demand very much and overall revenue will increase. The dividing line happens to be an elasticity of -1. At this point if the price increases by 1 percent, the quantity will decrease by 1 percent, so overall revenue doesn't change at all.

16.8 Constant Elasticity Demands

What kind of demand curve gives us a constant elasticity of demand? In a linear demand curve the elasticity of demand goes from zero to infinity, which is not exactly what you would call constant, so that's not the answer.

We can use the above revenue calculation to get an example. We know that if the elasticity is 1 at price p, then the revenue will not change when the price changes by a small amount. So if the revenue remains constant for all changes in price, we must have a demand curve that has an elasticity of -1 everywhere.

But this is easy. We just want price and quantity to be related by the formula

$$pq = R$$

which means that

$$q = \frac{R}{p}$$

is the formula for a demand function with constant elasticity of -1. The graph of the function $q = R/p$ is given in Figure 16.7. Note that price times quantity is constant along the demand curve.

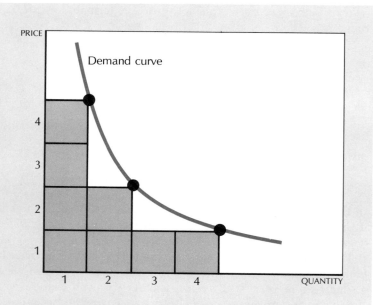

Figure 16.7

Unit elastic demand. For this demand curve price times quantity is constant at every point. Thus the demand curve has a constant elasticity of -1.

The general formula for a demand with an elasticity of ϵ turns out to be

$$q = Ap^\epsilon$$

where A is an arbitrary positive constant and ϵ, being an elasticity, will typically be negative. This formula will be useful in some examples later on.

A convenient way to express a constant elasticity demand curve is to take logarithms and write

$$\ln q = \ln A + \epsilon \ln p.$$

In this expression, the logarithm of q depends in a linear way on the logarithm of p.

16.9 Elasticity and Marginal Revenue

In section 16.7 we examined how revenue changes when you change the price of a good, but it is often of interest to consider how revenue changes when you change the quantity of a good. This is especially useful when we are considering production decisions by firms.

We saw earlier that for small changes in price and quantity, the change in revenue is given by

$$\Delta R = p\Delta q + q\Delta p.$$

If we divide both sides of this expression by Δq, we get the expression for **marginal revenue**:

$$\text{MR} = \frac{\Delta R}{\Delta q} = p + q\frac{\Delta p}{\Delta q}.$$

There is a useful way to rearrange this formula. Note that we can also write this as

$$\frac{\Delta R}{\Delta q} = p\left[1 + \frac{q\Delta p}{p\Delta q}\right].$$

What is the second term inside the brackets? Nope, it's not elasticity, but you're close. It is the reciprocal of elasticity:

$$\frac{1}{\epsilon} = \frac{1}{\dfrac{p\Delta q}{q\Delta p}} = \frac{q\Delta p}{p\Delta q}.$$

Thus the expression for marginal revenue becomes

$$\frac{\Delta R}{\Delta q} = p(q)\left[1 + \frac{1}{\epsilon(q)}\right].$$

(Here we've written $p(q)$ and $\epsilon(q)$ to remind ourselves that both price and elasticity will typically depend on the level of output.)

When there is a danger of confusion due to the fact that elasticity is a negative number we will sometimes write this expression as

$$\frac{\Delta R}{\Delta q} = p(q) \left[1 - \frac{1}{|\epsilon(q)|} \right].$$

This means that if elasticity of demand is -1 then marginal revenue is 0—revenue doesn't change when you increase output. If demand is inelastic then $|\epsilon|$ is less than 1, which means $1/|\epsilon|$ is greater than 1. Thus $1 - 1/|\epsilon|$ is negative, so that revenue will decrease when you increase output.

This is quite intuitive. If demand isn't very responsive to price then you have to cut prices a lot to increase output: so revenue goes down. This is all completely consistent with the earlier discussion about how revenue changes as we change price, since an increase in quantity means a decrease in price and vice versa.

EXAMPLE: Setting a Price

Suppose that you were in charge of setting a price for some product that you were producing and that you had a good estimate of the demand curve for that product. Let us suppose that your goal is to set a price that maximizes profits—revenue minus costs. Then you would never want to set it where the elasticity of demand was less than 1—you would never want to set a price where demand was inelastic.

Why? Consider what would happen if you raised your price. Then your revenues would increase—since demand was inelastic—and the quantity you were selling would decrease. But if the quantity sold decreases, then your production costs must also decrease, or at least, they can't increase. So your overall profit must rise, which shows that operating at an inelastic part of the demand curve cannot yield maximal profits.

16.10 Marginal Revenue Curves

We saw in the last section that marginal revenue is given by

$$\frac{\Delta R}{\Delta q} = p(q) + \frac{\Delta p(q)}{\Delta q} q$$

or

$$\frac{\Delta R}{\Delta q} = p(q) \left[1 - \frac{1}{|\epsilon(q)|} \right].$$

We will find it useful to plot these marginal revenue curves. First, note that when quantity is zero, marginal revenue is just equal to the price. For the first unit of the good sold, the extra revenue you get is just the price. But after that, the marginal revenue will be less than the price, since $\Delta p / \Delta q$ is negative.

Think about it. If you decide to sell one more unit of output, you will have to decrease the price. But this reduction in price reduces the revenue you receive on all the units of output that you were selling already. Thus the extra revenue you receive will be less than the price that you get for selling the extra unit.

Let's consider the special case of the linear (inverse) demand curve:

$$p(q) = a - bq.$$

Here it is easy to see that the slope of the inverse demand curve is constant:

$$\frac{\Delta p}{\Delta q} = -b.$$

Thus the formula for marginal revenue becomes

$$
\begin{aligned}
\frac{\Delta R}{\Delta q} &= p(q) + \frac{\Delta p(q)}{\Delta q} q \\
&= p(q) - bq \\
&= a - bq - bq \\
&= a - 2bq.
\end{aligned}
$$

This MR curve is depicted in Figure 16.8A. The marginal revenue curve has the same vertical intercept as the demand curve, but has twice the slope. Marginal revenue is negative when $q > a/2b$. The quantity $a/2b$ is the quantity at which the elasticity is equal to -1. At any larger quantity demand will be inelastic, which implies that marginal revenue is negative.

The constant elasticity demand curve provides another special case of the marginal revenue curve. If the elasticity of demand is constant at $\epsilon(q) = \epsilon$, then the marginal revenue curve will have the form

$$MR = p(q) \left[1 - \frac{1}{|\epsilon|} \right].$$

Since the term in brackets is constant, the marginal revenue curve is some constant fraction of the inverse demand curve. When $|\epsilon| = 1$, the marginal revenue curve is constant at zero. When $|\epsilon| > 1$, the marginal revenue curve lies below the inverse demand curve, as depicted. When $|\epsilon| < 1$, marginal revenue is negative.

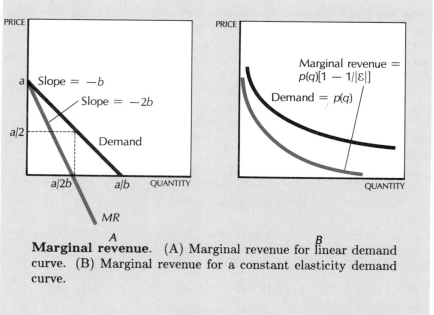

Figure 16.8

Marginal revenue. (A) Marginal revenue for linear demand curve. (B) Marginal revenue for a constant elasticity demand curve.

Summary

1. The market demand curve is simply the sum of the individual demand curves.

2. The reservation price measures the price at which a consumer is just indifferent between purchasing or not purchasing a good.

3. The demand function measures quantity demanded as a function of price. The inverse demand function measures price as a function of quantity. A given demand curve can be described in either way.

4. The elasticity of demand measures the responsiveness of the quantity demanded to price. It is formally defined as the percent change in quantity divided by the percent change in price.

5. If the absolute value of the elasticity of demand is less than 1 at some point, we say that demand is *inelastic* at that point. If the absolute value of elasticity is greater than 1 at some point, we say demand is *elastic* at that point. If the absolute value of the elasticity of demand at some point is exactly 1, we say that the demand has *unit* elasticity at that point.

6. If demand is inelastic at some point, then an increase in quantity will

result in a reduction in revenue. If demand is elastic, then an increase in quantity will result in an increase in revenue.

7. The marginal revenue is the extra revenue one gets from increasing the quantity sold. The formula relating marginal revenue and elasticity is $\text{MR} = p[1 + 1/\epsilon] = p[1 - 1/|\epsilon|]$.

8. If the inverse demand curve is a linear function $p(y) = a - by$, then the marginal revenue is given by $\text{MR} = a - 2by$.

Review Questions

1. If the market demand curve is $D(p) = 100 - .5p$, what is the inverse demand curve?

2. If a consumer has a utility function $u(x_1, x_2) = x_1 + x_2$, and $p_2 = 1$, what is his reservation price for good 1 as a function of p_1 and m?

3. If a consumer has a utility function $u(x_1, x_2) = ax_1 + x_2$, and $p_2 = 1$, what is his reservation price for good 1 as a function of p_1 and m?

4. An addict's demand function for a drug may be very inelastic, but the market demand function might be quite elastic. How can this be?

5. If $D(p) = 12 - 2p$, what price will maximize revenue?

6. Suppose that the demand curve for a good is given by $D(p) = 100/p$. What price will maximize revenue?

APPENDIX

In terms of derivatives the price elasticity of demand is defined by

$$\epsilon = \frac{p}{q}\frac{dq}{dp}.$$

In the text we claimed that the formula for a constant elasticity demand curve was $q = Ap^\epsilon$. To verify that this is correct, we can just differentiate it with respect to price:

$$\frac{dq}{dp} = \epsilon Ap^{\epsilon-1}$$

and multiply by price over quantity:

$$\frac{p}{q}\frac{dq}{dp} = \frac{p}{Ap^\epsilon}\epsilon Ap^{\epsilon-1} = \epsilon.$$

Everything conveniently cancels, leaving us with ϵ as required.

EXAMPLE: The Laffer Curve

In this section, we'll consider some simple elasticity calculations that can be used to examine an issue of considerable policy interest, namely how tax revenue changes when the tax rate changes.

Suppose that we graph tax revenue versus the tax rate. If the tax rate is zero, then tax revenues are zero; if the tax rate is 1, nobody will want to demand or supply the good in question, so the tax revenue is also zero. Thus revenue as a function of the tax rate must first increase and eventually decrease. (Of course, it can go up and down several times between 0 and 1, but we'll ignore this possibility to keep things simple.) The curve that relates tax rates and tax revenues is known as the **Laffer curve**, depicted in Figure 16.9.

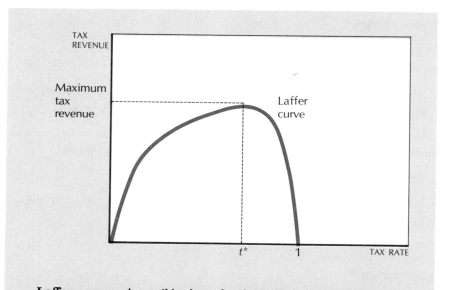

Figure 16.9

Laffer curve. A possible shape for the Laffer curve, which relates tax rates and tax revenues.

The interesting feature of the Laffer curve is that it suggests that when the tax rate is high enough, an increase in the tax rate will end up *reducing* the revenues collected. The reduction in supply of the good will reduce the tax revenues so much that the higher tax rate doesn't make up for the reduction. This is called the **Laffer effect**, after the economist who popularized this diagram a few years ago. It has been said that the virtue of the Laffer curve is that you can explain it to a congressman in half an hour and he can talk about it for six months. Indeed, the Laffer curve figured prominently in the debate over the effect of the 1980 tax cuts. The catch in the above argument is the phrase "high enough." Just how high does the tax rate have to be for the Laffer effect to work?

To answer this question let's consider the following simple model of the labor market. Suppose that firms will demand zero labor if the wage is greater than $\overline{w}$ and an arbitrarily large amount of labor if the wage is exactly $\overline{w}$. This means that the demand curve for labor is flat at some wage $\overline{w}$. Suppose that the supply curve of labor, $S(p)$, has a conventional upward slope. The equilibrium in the labor market is depicted in Figure 16.10.

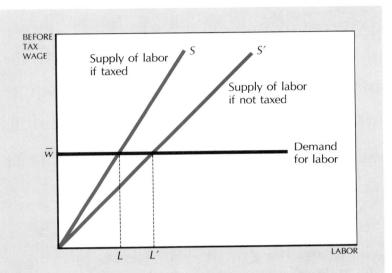

Labor market. Equilibrium in the labor market with a horizontal demand curve for labor. When labor income is taxed, less will be supplied at each wage rate.

Figure 16.10

If we put a tax on labor at the rate t, then if the firm pays $\overline{w}$, the worker only gets $w = (1-t)\overline{w}$. Thus the supply curve of labor tilts to the left and the amount of labor sold drops, as in Figure 16.10. The after–tax wage has gone down and this has discouraged the sale of labor. So far so good.

Tax revenue, T, is therefore given by the formula

$$T = tS(w)\overline{w}$$

where $w = (1 - t)\overline{w}$ and $S(w)$ is the supply of labor.

In order to see how tax revenue changes as we change the tax rate we differentiate this formula with respect to t to find

$$\frac{dT}{dt} = \left[-t\frac{dS(w)}{dw}\overline{w} + S(w) \right]\overline{w}. \tag{16.1}$$

(Note the use of the chain rule, and the fact that $dw/dt = -\overline{w}$.)

The Laffer effect occurs when revenues decline when t increases—that is, when this expression is negative. Now this clearly means that the supply of labor is going to have to be quite elastic—it has to drop a lot when the tax increases. So let's try to see what values of elasticity will make this expression negative.

In order for equation (16.1) to be negative, we must have

$$-t\frac{dS(w)}{dw}\overline{w} + S(w) < 0.$$

Transposing yields

$$t\frac{dS(w)}{dw}\overline{w} > S(w)$$

and dividing both sides by $tS(w)$ gives

$$\frac{dS(w)}{dw}\frac{\overline{w}}{S(w)} > \frac{1}{t}.$$

Multiplying both sides by $(1-t)$ and using the fact that $w = (1-t)\overline{w}$ gives us

$$\frac{dS}{dw}\frac{w}{S} > \frac{1-t}{t}.$$

The left-hand side of this expression is the elasticity of labor supply. We have shown that the Laffer effect can only occur if the elasticity of labor supply is greater than $(1-t)/t$.

Let us take an extreme case and suppose that the tax rate on labor income is 50 percent. Then the Laffer effect can occur only when the elasticity of labor supply is greater than 1. This means a one percent reduction in the wage would lead to more than a one percent reduction in the labor supply. This is a very large response.

Econometricians have often estimated labor supply elasticities, and about the largest value anyone has ever found has been around 0.2. So the Laffer effect seems pretty unlikely for the kinds of tax rates that we have in the United States. However, in other countries, such as Sweden, tax rates go much higher, and there is some evidence that the Laffer phenomenon may have occurred.[2]

EXAMPLE: Another Expression for Elasticity

Here is another expression for elasticity that is sometimes useful. It turns out that elasticity can also be expressed as

$$\frac{d\ln Q}{d\ln P}.$$

---

[2] See Charles E. Stuart, "Swedish Tax Rates, Labor Supply, and Tax Revenues," *Journal of Political Economy*, 89, 5 (October 1981), 1020–38.

The proof involves repeated application of the chain rule. We start by noting that

$$\frac{d\ln Q}{d\ln P} = \frac{d\ln Q}{dQ}\frac{dQ}{d\ln P}$$

$$= \frac{1}{Q}\frac{dQ}{d\ln P}. \tag{16.2}$$

We also note that

$$\frac{dQ}{dP} = \frac{dQ}{d\ln P}\frac{d\ln P}{dP}$$

$$= \frac{dQ}{d\ln P}\frac{1}{P}$$

which implies that

$$\frac{dQ}{d\ln P} = P\frac{dQ}{dP}.$$

Substituting this into equation (16.2), we have

$$\frac{d\ln Q}{d\ln P} = \frac{1}{Q}\frac{dQ}{dP}P = \epsilon$$

which is what we wanted to establish.

Thus elasticity measures the slope of the demand curve plotted on log–log paper: how the log of the quantity changes as the log of the price changes.

17

EQUILIBRIUM

In previous chapters we have seen how to construct individual demand curves using information about preferences and prices. In Chapter 16 we added up these individual demand curves to construct market demand curves. In this chapter we will describe how to use these market demand curves to determine the equilibrium market price.

Recall that we said in Chapter 1 that there were two fundamental principles of microeconomic analysis. These were the optimization principle and the equilibrium principle. Up until now we have been studying examples of the optimization principle: what follows from the assumption that people choose their consumption optimally from their budget sets. In later chapters we will study the profit maximization behavior of firms, and then combine the behavior of consumers and firms to study the equilibrium outcomes.

But before undertaking that study it seems worthwhile to give some examples of equilibrium analysis—how the prices adjust so as to make the demand and supply decisions of economic agents compatible. To do so, we will have to briefly consider the other side of the market—the supply side.

17.1 Supply

We have already seen a few examples of supply curves. In Chapter 1 we looked at a vertical supply curve for apartments. In Chapter 9 we considered situations where consumers would choose to be net suppliers or demanders of goods that they owned. In Chapter 10 we examined the labor supply decision.

In all of these cases the supply curve simply measured how much the consumer was willing to supply of a good at each possible market price. Indeed, this is the definition of the supply curve: for each p, we determine how much of the good will be supplied, $S(p)$. In the next few chapters we will discuss the supply behavior of firms. However, for many purposes, it is not really necessary to know where the supply curve or the demand curve comes from in terms of the optimizing behavior that generates the curves. For many problems the fact that there is a functional relationship between the price and the quantity that consumers want to demand or supply at that price is enough to establish important insights.

17.2 Market Equilibrium

Suppose that we have a number of consumers of a good. Given their individual demand curves we can add them up to get a market demand curve. Similarly, if we have a number of independent suppliers of this good, we can add up their individual supply curves to get the **market supply curve**.

The individual demanders and suppliers are assumed to take prices as given—outside of their control—and simply determine the best thing to do given those market prices. A market where each economic agent takes the market price as outside of his or her control is called a **competitive market.**

The usual justification for the competitive market assumption is that each consumer or producer is a small part of the market as a whole and thus has a negligible effect on the market price. For example, each supplier of wheat takes the market price to be more or less independent of his actions when he determines how much wheat he wants to produce and supply to the market.

Although the market price may be independent of any *one* agent's actions in a competitive market, it is the actions of all the agents together that determine the market price. The **equilibrium price** of a good is that price where the supply of the good equals the demand. Geometrically, this is the price where the demand and the supply curves cross.

If we let $D(p)$ be the market demand curve and $S(p)$ the market supply curve, the equilibrium price is the price p^* which solves the equation

$$D(p^*) = S(p^*).$$

The solution to this equation, p^*, is the price where market demand equals market supply.

Why should this be an equilibrium price? An economic equilibrium is a situation where all agents are choosing the best possible action for themselves, and each person's behavior is consistent with that of the others. At any price other than an equilibrium price, some agents' behaviors would be infeasible, and there would therefore be a reason for their behavior to change. Thus a price that is not an equilibrium price cannot be expected to persist.

The demand and supply curves represent the optimal choices of the agents involved, and the fact that they are equal at some price p^* indicates that the behaviors of the demanders and suppliers are compatible. At any price *other* than the price where demand equals supply these two conditions will *not* be met.

For example, suppose that we consider some price p' where demand is greater than supply. Then some suppliers will realize that they can sell their goods at more than the going price p' to the disappointed demanders. As more and more suppliers realize this, the market price will be pushed up to the point where demand and supply are equal.

Similarly if demand is less than supply, then some suppliers will not be able to sell the amount that they expected to sell. The only way in which they will be able to sell more output will be to offer it at a lower price. But if all suppliers are selling the identical goods, and if some supplier offers to sell at a lower price, the other suppliers must match that price. Thus excess supply exerts a downward pressure on the market price. Only when the amount that people want to buy at a given price equals the amount that people want to sell at that price will the market be in equilibrium.

17.3 Two Special Cases

There are two special cases of market equilibrium that are worth mentioning since they come up fairly often. The first is the case of fixed supply. Here the amount supplied is some given number and is independent of price; that is, the supply curve is vertical. In this case the equilibrium *quantity* is determined entirely by the supply conditions and the equilibrium *price* is determined entirely by demand conditions.

The opposite case is the case where the supply curve is completely horizontal. If an industry has a perfectly horizontal supply curve, it means that the industry will supply any amount desired of a good at a constant price. In this situation the equilibrium *price* is determined by the supply conditions while the equilibrium *quantity* is determined by the demand curve.

The two cases are depicted in Figure 17.1. In these two special cases the determination of price and quantities can be separated; but in the

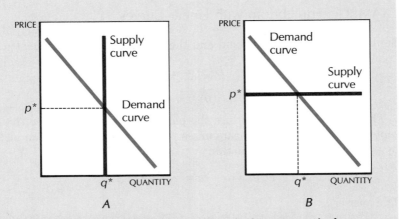

Special cases of equilibrium. Case A shows a vertical supply curve so that the equilibrium price is determined solely by
demand. Case B depicts a horizontal supply curve so that the
equilibrium price is determined solely by the supply curve.

Figure
17.1

general case the equilibrium price and the equilibrium quantity are jointly
determined by the demand and supply curves.

17.4 Inverse Demand Curves

We can look at market equilibrium in a slightly different way that is often
useful. As indicated earlier, individual demand curves are normally viewed
as giving the optimal quantities as a function of the price charged. But
we can also view them as inverse demand functions that measure the *price*
that someone is willing to pay in order to acquire some given amount of
a good. The same thing holds for supply curves. They can be viewed as
measuring the quantity supplied as a function of the price. But we can also
view them as measuring the *price* that must prevail in order to call forth
a given amount of supply.

These same constructions can be used with *market* demand and supply
curves, and the interpretations are just those given above. In this framework an equilibrium price is determined by finding that quantity at which
the amount the demanders are willing to pay to consume that quantity is
the same as the price that suppliers must receive in order to supply that
quantity.

Thus, if we let $P_S(q)$ be the inverse supply curve and $P_D(q)$ be the inverse
demand curve, equilibrium is determined by the condition

$$P_S(q*) = P_D(q*).$$

EXAMPLE: Equilibrium with Linear Curves

Suppose that both the demand and the supply curves are linear:

$$D(p) = a - bp$$

$$S(p) = c + dp.$$

The coefficients (a, b, c, d) are the parameters that determine the intercepts and slopes of these linear curves. The equilibrium price can be found by solving the following equation:

$$D(p) = a - bp = c + dp = S(p).$$

The answer is

$$p^* = \frac{a - c}{d + b}.$$

The equilibrium quantity demanded (and supplied) is

$$D(p^*) = a - bp^*$$
$$= a - b\frac{a - c}{b + d}$$
$$= \frac{ad + cb}{b + d}.$$

We can also solve this problem using the inverse demand and supply curves. First we need to find the inverse demand curve. At what price is some quantity q demanded? Simply substitute q for $D(p)$ and solve for p. We have

$$q = a - bp$$

so

$$P_D(q) = \frac{a - q}{b}.$$

In the same manner we find

$$P_S(q) = \frac{q - c}{d}.$$

Setting the demand price equal to the supply price and solving for the equilibrium quantity we have

$$P_D(q) = \frac{a - q}{b} = \frac{q - c}{d} = P_S(q)$$

$$q^* = \frac{ad + cb}{b + d}.$$

Note that this gives the same answer as in the original problem for both the equilibrium price and the equilibrium quantity.

17.5 Comparative Statics

After we have found an equilibrium by using the demand equals supply condition (or the demand price equals the supply price condition) we can see how it will change as the demand and supply curves change. For example, it is easy to see that if the demand curve shifts to the right in a parallel way—some fixed amount more is demanded at every price—the equilibrium price and quantity must both rise. On the other hand, if the supply curve shifts to the right, the equilibrium quantity rises but the equilibrium price must fall.

What if both curves shift to the right? Then the quantity will definitely increase while the change in price is ambiguous—it could increase or it could decrease.

EXAMPLE: Shifting Both Curves

Question: Consider the market for apartments described in Chapter 1. Let the equilibrium price in that market be p^* and the equilibrium quantity be q^*. Suppose that a developer converts m of the apartments to condominiums, which are bought by the people who are currently living in the apartments. What happens to the equilibrium price?

Answer: The situation is depicted in Figure 17.2. The demand and supply curves both shift to the left by the *same* amount. Hence the price is unchanged and the quantity sold simply drops by m.

Algebraically the new equilibrium price is determined by

$$D(p) - m = S(p) - m$$

which clearly has the same solution as the original demand equals supply condition.

17.6 Taxes

Describing a market before and after taxes are imposed presents a very nice exercise in comparative statics, as well as being of considerable interest in the conduct of economic policy. Let us see how it is done.

The fundamental thing to understand about taxes is that when a tax is present in a market, there are *two* prices of interest: the price the demander pays and the price the supplier gets. These two prices—the demand price and the supply price—differ by the amount of the tax.

There are several different kinds of taxes that one might impose. Two examples we will consider here are **quantity taxes** and **value** taxes (also called **ad valorem** taxes).

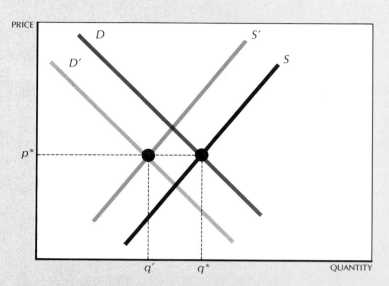

Figure
17.2

Shifting both curves. Both demand and supply curves shift to the left, which implies the equilibrium price will remain unchanged.

A quantity tax is a tax levied per unit of quantity bought or sold. Gasoline taxes are a good example of this. The gasoline tax is roughly 12 cents a gallon. If the demander is paying $P_D = \$1.50$ per gallon of gasoline, the supplier is getting $P_S = \$1.50 - .12 = \$1.38$ per gallon. In general, if t is the amount of the quantity tax per unit sold, then

$$P_D = P_S + t.$$

A value tax is a tax expressed in percentage units. State sales taxes are the most common example of value taxes. If your state has a 5 percent sales tax, then when you pay $1.05 for something (including the tax), the supplier gets $1.00. In general, if the tax rate is given by τ, then

$$P_D = (1 + \tau)P_S.$$

Let us consider what happens in a market when a quantity tax is imposed. For our first case we suppose that the supplier is required to pay the tax, as in the case of the gasoline tax. Then the amount supplied will depend on the supply price—the amount the supplier actually gets after paying the tax—and the amount demanded will depend on the demand price—the amount that the demander pays. The amount that the supplier gets will be the amount the demander pays minus the amount of the tax. This gives us two equations:

$$D(P_D) = S(P_S)$$

$$P_S = P_D - t.$$

Substituting the second equation into the first, we have the equilibrium condition:

$$D(P_D) = S(P_D - t).$$

Alternatively we could also rearrange the second equation to get $P_D = P_S + t$ and then substitute to find

$$D(P_S + t) = S(P_S).$$

Either way is equally valid; which one you use will depend on convenience in a particular case.

Now suppose that instead of the supplier paying the tax, the demander has to pay the tax. Then we write

$$P_D - t = P_S$$

which says that the amount paid by the demander minus the tax equals the price received by the supplier. Substituting this into the demand equals supply condition we find

$$D(P_D) = S(P_D - t).$$

Note that this is the same equation as in the case where the supplier pays the tax. As far as the equilibrium price facing the demanders and the suppliers is concerned, it really doesn't matter who is responsible for paying the tax—it just matters that the tax must be paid by someone.

This really isn't so mysterious. Think of the gasoline tax. There the tax is included in the posted price. But if the price were instead listed as the before-tax price and the gasoline tax were added on as a separate item to be paid by the demanders, then do you think that the amount of gasoline demanded would change? After all, the final price to the consumers would be the same whichever way the tax was charged. Insofar as the consumers can recognize the net cost to them of goods they purchase, it really doesn't matter which way the tax is levied.

There is an even simpler way to show this using the inverse demand and supply functions. The equilibrium quantity traded is that quantity q^* such that the demand price at q^* *minus the tax being paid* is just equal to the supply price at q^*. In symbols:

$$P_D(q^*) - t = P_S(q^*).$$

If the tax is being imposed on the suppliers, then the condition is that the supply price *plus the amount of the tax* must equal the demand price:

$$P_D(q^*) = P_S(q^*) + t.$$

But of course these are the same equations so the same equilibrium prices and quantities must result.

Finally, we consider the geometry of the situation. This is most easily seen by using the inverse demand and supply curves discussed above. We want to find the quantity where the curve $P_D(q) - t$ crosses the curve $P_S(q)$. In order to locate this point we simply shift the demand curve down by t and see where this shifted demand curve intersects the original supply curve. Alternatively we can find the quantity where $P_D(q)$ equals $P_S(q) + t$. To do this, we simply shift the supply curve up by the amount of the tax. Either way gives us the correct answer for the equilibrium quantity. The picture is given in Figure 17.3.

From this diagram we can easily see the qualitative effects of the tax. The quantity sold must decrease, the price paid by the demanders must go up, and the price received by the suppliers must go down.

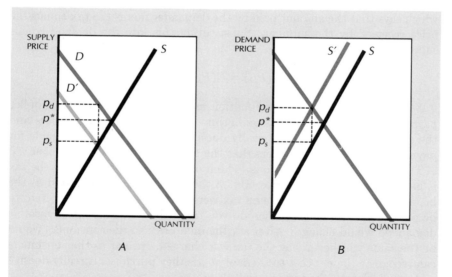

Figure 17.3

The imposition of a tax. In order to study the impact of a tax, we can either shift the demand curve down, as in panel A, or shift the supply curve up, as in panel B. The equilibrium prices paid by the demanders and received by the suppliers will be the same either way.

Figure 17.4 depicts another way to determine the impact of a tax. Think about the definition of equilibrium in this market. We want to find a quantity q^* such that when the supplier faces the price p_s and the demander faces the price $p_d = p_s + t$, the quantity q^* is demanded by the demander and supplied by the supplier. Let us represent the tax t by a vertical line segment and slide it along the supply curve until it just touches the demand curve. That point is our equilibrium quantity!

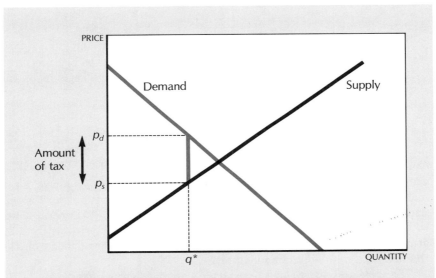

Another way to determine the impact of a tax. Slide the line segment along the supply curve until it hits the demand curve.

Figure
17.4

EXAMPLE: Taxation with Linear Demand and Supply

Suppose that the demand and supply curves are both linear. Then if we impose a tax in this market, the equilibrium is determined by the equations

$$a - bp_D = c + dp_S$$

and

$$p_D = p_S + t.$$

Substituting from the second equation into the first, we have

$$a - b(p_S + t) = c + dp_S.$$

Solving for the equilibrium supply price, p_S, gives

$$p_S^* = \frac{a - c - bt}{d + b}.$$

The equilibrium demand price, p_D^*, is then given by $p_S^* + t$:

$$p_D^* = \frac{a - c - bt}{d + b} + t$$
$$= \frac{a - c + dt}{d + b}.$$

Note that the price paid by the demander decreases and the price received by the supplier increases. The amount of the price change depends on the slope of the demand and supply curves.

17.7 Passing Along a Tax

One often hears about how a tax on producers doesn't hurt profits, since firms can simply pass along a tax to consumers. As we've seen above, a tax really shouldn't be regarded as a tax on firms or on consumers. Rather, taxes are on transactions *between* firms and consumers. In general a tax will both raise the price paid by consumers and lower the price received by firms. How much of a tax gets passed along will therefore depend on the characteristics of demand and supply.

This is easiest to see in the extreme cases: when we have a perfectly horizontal supply curve or a perfectly vertical supply curve. These are also known as the case of **perfectly elastic** and **perfectly inelastic** supply.

We've already encountered these two special cases earlier in this chapter. If an industry has a horizontal supply curve, it means that the industry will supply any amount desired of the good at some given price, and zero units of the good at any lower price. In this case the price is entirely determined by the supply curve and the quantity sold is determined by demand. If an industry has a vertical supply curve, it means that the quantity of the good is fixed. The equilibrium price of the good is determined entirely by demand.

Let's consider the imposition of a tax in a market with a perfectly elastic supply curve. As we've seen above, imposing a tax is just like shifting the supply curve up by the amount of the tax, as illustrated in Figure 17.5A.

In this case it is easy to see that the price to the consumers goes up by exactly the amount of the tax. The supply price is exactly the same as it was before the tax, and the demanders end up paying the entire tax. When you think about the meaning of the horizontal supply curve, this is not hard to understand. The horizontal supply curve means that the industry is willing to supply any amount of the good at some particular

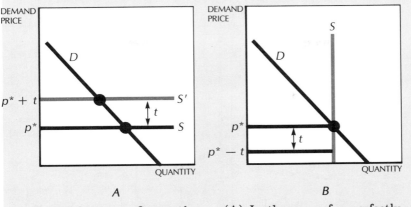

Special cases of taxation.   (A) In the case of a perfectly elastic supply curve the tax gets completely passed along to the consumers. (B) In the case of a perfectly inelastic supply none of the tax gets passed along.

Figure 17.5

price, p^*, and zero amount at any lower price. Thus, if any amount of the good is going to be sold at all in equilibrium, the suppliers must receive p^* for selling it. This effectively determines the equilibrium supply price, and the demand price is $p^* + t$.

The opposite case is illustrated in Figure 17.5B. If the supply curve is vertical, and we "shift the supply curve up," we don't change anything in the diagram. The supply curve just slides along itself and we still have the same amount of the good supplied, with or without the tax. In this case, it is the demanders who are determining the equilibrium price of the good, and they are willing to pay a certain amount, p^*, for the supply of the good that is available, tax or no tax. Thus they end up paying p^*, and the suppliers end up receiving $p^* - t$. The entire amount of the tax is paid by the suppliers.

This case often strikes people as paradoxical, but it really isn't. If the suppliers could raise their prices when the tax is imposed, and still sell their entire fixed supply, they would have raised their prices before the tax was imposed and made more money! If the demand curve doesn't move, then the only way a price can increase is if the supply is reduced. If a policy doesn't change either supply or demand, it certainly can't affect price.

Now that we understand the special cases, we can examine the in between case where the supply curve has an upward slope, but is not perfectly vertical. In this situation, the amount of the tax that gets passed along will depend on the steepness of the supply curve relative to the demand curve. If the supply curve is nearly horizontal, nearly all of the tax gets passed along, while if the supply curve is nearly vertical, almost none of the tax gets passed along. See Figure 17.6 for some examples.

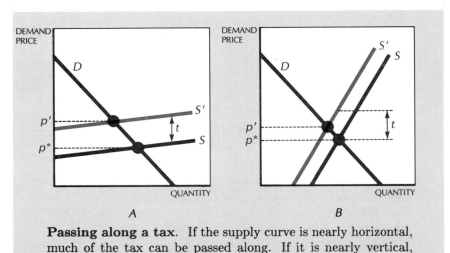

Figure
17.6

Passing along a tax. If the supply curve is nearly horizontal, much of the tax can be passed along. If it is nearly vertical, very little of the tax can be passed along.

17.8 The Deadweight Loss of a Tax

We've seen that taxing a good will typically increase the price paid by the demanders and decrease the price received by the suppliers. This certainly represents a cost to the demanders and suppliers, but from the economist's viewpoint the real cost of the tax is that the output has been reduced.

The lost output is the social cost of the tax. Let us explore the social cost of a tax using the consumer's and producer's surplus tools developed in Chapter 15. We start with the diagram given in Figure 17.7. This depicts the equilibrium demand price and supply price after a tax, t, has been imposed.

Output has been decreased by this tax and we can use the tools of consumer's and producer's surplus to value the social loss. The loss in consumer's surplus is given by the areas $A + B$ and the loss in producer's surplus is given in areas $C + D$. These are the same kind of losses that we examined in Chapter 15.

Since we're after an expression for the social cost of the tax, it seems sensible to add the areas $A + B$ and $C + D$ to each other to get the total loss to the consumers and the producers of the good in question. However, we've still left out one party—namely, the government.

The government *gains* revenue from the tax. And of course the consumers who benefit from the government services provided with these tax

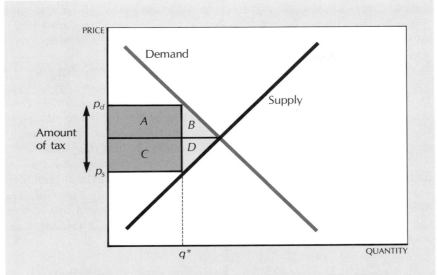

The deadweight loss of a tax. The area $B + D$ measures the deadweight loss of the tax.

Figure
17.7

revenues also gain from the tax. We can't really say how much they gain until we know what the tax revenues will be spent on.

Let us make the assumption that the tax revenues will just be handed back to the consumers and the producers, or equivalently that the services provided by the government revenues will be just equal in value to the revenues spent on them.

Then the net benefit to the government is the area $A + C$—the total revenue from the tax. Since the loss of producer's and consumer's surpluses are net costs, and the tax revenue to the government is a net benefit, the total net cost of the tax is the algebraic sum of the these areas: the loss in consumer's surplus, $-(A + B)$, the loss in producer's surplus, $-(C + D)$, and the gain in government revenue, $+(A + C)$.

The net result is the area $-(B + D)$. This area is known as the **deadweight loss** of the tax or the **excess burden** of the tax. This latter phrase is especially descriptive.

Recall the interpretation of the loss of consumers' surplus. It is how much the consumers would pay to avoid the tax. In terms of this diagram the consumers are willing to pay $A + B$ to avoid the tax. Similarly, the producers are willing to pay $C + D$ to avoid the tax. Together they are willing to pay $A + B + C + D$ to avoid a tax that raises $A + C$ dollars of revenue. The *excess burden* of the tax is therefore $B + D$.

What is the source of this excess burden? Basically it is the lost value to the consumers and producers due to the reduction in the sales of the good. You can't tax what isn't there.[1] So the government doesn't get any revenue on the reduction in sales of the good. From the viewpoint of society, it is a pure loss—a deadweight loss.

We could also derive the deadweight loss directly from its definition, by just measuring the social value of the lost output. Suppose that we start at the old equilibrium and start moving to the left. The first unit lost was one where the price that someone was willing to pay for it was just equal to the price that someone was willing to sell it for. Here there is hardly any social loss since this unit was the marginal unit that was sold.

Now move a little farther to the left. The demand price measures how much someone was willing to pay to receive the good and the supply price measures the price at which someone was willing to supply the good. The difference is the lost value on that unit of the good. If we add this up over the units of the good that are not produced and consumed because of the presence of the tax, we get the deadweight loss.

EXAMPLE: The Market for Loans

The amount of borrowing or lending in an economy is influenced to a large degree by the interest rate charged. The interest rate serves as a price in the market for loans.

We can let $D(r)$ be the demand for loans by borrowers and $S(r)$ be the supply of loans by lenders. The equilibrium interest rate, r^*, is then determined by the condition that demand equals supply:

$$D(r^*) = S(r^*). \tag{17.1}$$

Suppose we consider adding taxes to this model. What will happen to the equilibrium interest rate?

In the U.S. economy individuals have to pay income tax on the interest they earn from lending money. If everyone is in the same tax bracket t, the after-tax interest rate facing lenders will be $(1 - t)r$. Thus the supply of loans, which depends on the after-tax interest rate, will be $S((1 - t)r)$.

On the other hand, the Internal Revenue code allows borrowers to deduct their interest charges, so if the borrowers are in the same tax bracket as the lenders, the after-tax interest rate they pay will be $(1 - t)r$. Hence the demand for loans will be $D((1 - t)r)$. The equation for interest rate determination with taxes present is then

$$D((1 - t)r') = S((1 - t)r'). \tag{17.2}$$

---

[1] At least the government hasn't figured out how to do this yet. But they're working on it.

Now observe that if r^* solves equation (17.1), then $r^* = (1-t)r'$ must solve equation (17.2) so that

$$r^* = (1-t)r'.$$

Or

$$r' = \frac{r^*}{(1-t)}.$$

Thus the interest rate in the presence of the tax will be higher by $1/(1-t)$. The *after-tax* interest rate $(1-t)r'$ will be r^*, just as it was before the tax was imposed!

Figure 17.8 may make things clearer. Making interest income taxable will tilt the supply curve for loans up by a factor of $1/(1-t)$; but making interest payments tax deductible will also tilt the demand curve for loans up by $1/(1-t)$. The net result is that the market interest rate rises by precisely $1/(1-t)$.

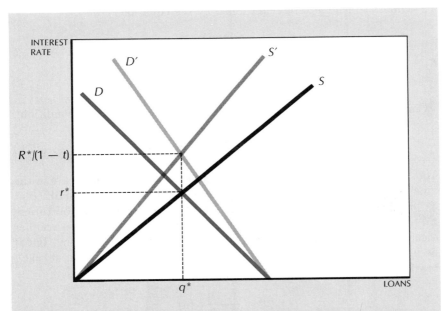

Equilibrium in the loan market. If borrowers and lenders are in the same tax bracket, the after-tax interest rate and the amount borrowed are unchanged.

Figure 17.8

Inverse demand and supply functions provide another way to look at this problem. Let $r_b(q)$ be the inverse demand function for borrowers. This tells us what the after-tax interest rate would have to be to induce people to borrow q. Similarly, let $r_l(q)$ be the inverse supply function for lenders. The equilibrium amount lent will then be determined by the condition

$$r_b(q^*) = r_l(q^*). \tag{17.3}$$

Now introduce taxes into the situation. To make things more interesting, we'll allow borrowers and lenders to be in different tax brackets, denoted by t_b and t_l. If the market interest rate is r, then the after-tax rate facing borrowers will be $(1 - t_b)r$, and the quantity they choose to borrow will be determined by the equation

$$(1 - t_b)r = r_b(q)$$

or

$$r = \frac{r_b(q)}{1 - t_b}. \tag{17.4}$$

Similarly, the after-tax rate facing lenders will be $(1 - t_l)r$, and the amount they choose to lend will be determined by the equation

$$(1 - t_l)r = r_l(q)$$

or

$$r = \frac{r_l(q)}{1 - t_l}. \tag{17.5}$$

Combining equations (17.4) and (17.5) gives the equilibrium condition:

$$r = \frac{r_b(\hat{q})}{1 - t_b} = \frac{r_l(\hat{q})}{1 - t_l}. \tag{17.6}$$

From this equation it is easy to see that if borrowers and lenders are in the same tax bracket, so that $t_b = t_l$, then $\hat{q} = q^*$. What if they are in different tax brackets? It is not hard to see that the tax law is subsidizing borrowers and taxing lenders, but what is the net effect? If the borrowers face a higher price than the lenders, then the system is a net tax on borrowing, but if the borrowers face a lower price than the lenders, then it is a net subsidy. Rewriting the equilibrium condition, equation (17.6), we have

$$r_b(\hat{q}) = \frac{1 - t_b}{1 - t_l} r_l(\hat{q}).$$

Thus borrowers will face a higher price than lenders if

$$\frac{1 - t_b}{1 - t_l} > 1$$

which means that $t_l > t_b$. So if the tax bracket of lenders is greater than the tax bracket of borrowers, the system is a net tax on borrowing, but if $t_l < t_b$ it is a net subsidy.

EXAMPLE: Food Subsidies

In years when there were bad harvests in nineteenth-century England the rich would provide charitable assistance to the poor by buying up the harvest, consuming a fixed amount of the grain, and selling the remainder to the poor at half the price they paid for it. At first thought this seems like it would provide significant benefits to the poor, but on second thought, doubts begin to arise.

The only way that the poor can be made better off is if they end up consuming more grain. But there is a fixed amount of grain available after the harvest. So how can the poor be better off because of this policy?

As a matter of fact they are not; the poor end up paying exactly the same price for the grain with or without the policy. To see why, we will model the equilibrium with and without this program. Let $D(p)$ be the demand curve for the poor, K the amount demanded by the rich, and S the fixed amount supplied in a year with a bad harvest. By assumption the supply of grain and the demand by the rich are fixed. Without the charity provided by the rich, the equilibrium price is determined by total demand equals total supply:

$$D(p^*) + K = S.$$

With the program in place, the equilibrium price is determined by

$$D(\hat{p}/2) + K = S.$$

But now observe: if p^* solves the first equation, then $\hat{p} = 2p^*$ solves the second equation. So when the rich offer to buy the grain and distribute it to the poor, the market price is simply bid up to twice the original price—and the poor pay the same price they did before!

When you think about it this isn't too surprising. If the demand of the rich is fixed and the supply of grain is fixed then the amount that the poor can consume is fixed. Thus the equilibrium price facing the poor is determined entirely by their own demand curve; the equilibrium price will be the same, regardless of how the grain is provided to the poor.

17.9 Pareto Efficiency

An economic situation is **Pareto efficient** if there is no way to make any person better off without hurting anybody else. Pareto efficiency is a desirable thing—if there is some way to make some group of people better off why not do it?—but efficiency is not the only goal of economic policy.

However, it is an important goal, and it is worth asking how well a competitive market does in achieving Pareto efficiency. A competitive market, or any economic mechanism, has to determine two things. First, how much is produced, and second, who gets it. A competitive market determines how much is produced based on how much people are willing to pay to purchase the good as compared to how much people must be paid to supply the good.

Consider Figure 17.9. At any amount of output less than the competitive amount q^*, there is someone who is willing to supply an extra unit of the good at a price that is less than the price that someone is willing to pay for an extra unit of the good. If the good were produced and exchanged between these two people, for any price between the demand price and the supply price, they would both be made better off. Thus any amount less than the equilibrium amount cannot be Pareto efficient, since there will be at least two people who could be made better off.

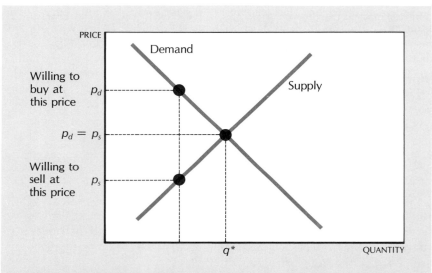

Figure 17.9

Pareto efficiency. The competitive market determines a Pareto efficient amount of output because at q^* the price that someone is willing to pay to buy an extra unit of the good is equal to the price that someone must be paid to sell an extra unit of the good.

Similarly, at any output larger than q^*, the amount someone would be willing to pay for an extra unit of the good is less than the price that it would take to get it supplied. Only at the market equilibrium q^* would we have a Pareto efficient amount of output supplied—an amount such that the willingness to pay for an extra unit is just equal to the willingness to be paid to supply an extra unit.

Thus the competitive market produces a Pareto efficient amount of output. What about the way in which the good is allocated among the consumers? In a competitive market everyone pays the same price for a good—the marginal rate of substitution between the good and "all other goods" is equal to the price of the good. Everyone who is willing to pay this price is able to purchase the good, and everyone who is not willing to pay this price cannot purchase the good.

What would happen if there were an allocation of the good where the marginal rates of substitution between the good and "all other goods" were not the same? Then there must be at least two people who value a marginal unit of the good differently. Maybe one values a marginal unit at $5 and one values it at $4. Then if the one with the lower value sells a bit of the good to the one with the higher value at any price between $4 and $5, both people would be made better off. Thus any allocation with different marginal rates of substitution—different marginal willingness to pay—cannot be Pareto efficient.

Summary

1. The supply curve measures how much people will be willing to supply of some good at each price.

2. An equilibrium price is one where the quantity that people are willing to supply equals the quantity that people are willing to demand.

3. The study of how the equilibrium price and quantity change when the underlying demand and supply curves change is another example of comparative statics.

4. When a good is taxed, there will always be two prices: the price paid by the demanders and the price received by the suppliers. The difference between the two represents the amount of the tax.

5. How much of a tax gets passed along to consumers depends on the relative steepness of the demand and supply curves. If the supply curve is horizontal, all of the tax gets passed along to consumers; if the supply curve is vertical, none of the tax gets passed along.

6. The deadweight loss of a tax is the net loss in consumer's plus producer's surplus that arises from imposing the tax. It measures the value of the output that is not sold due to the presence of the tax.

7. A situation is Pareto efficient if there is no way to make some group of people better off without making some other group worse off.

8. The Pareto efficient amount of output to supply in a single market is that amount where the demand and supply curve cross, since this is the

only point where the amount that demanders are willing to pay for an extra unit of output equals the price at which suppliers are willing to supply an extra unit of output.

Review Questions

1. What is the effect of a subsidy in a market with a horizontal supply curve? With a vertical supply curve?

2. Suppose that the demand curve is vertical while the supply curve slopes upward. If a tax is imposed in this market who ends up paying it?

3. Suppose that all consumers view red pencils and blue pencils as perfect substitutes. Suppose that the supply curve for red pencils is upward sloping. Let the price of red pencils and blue pencils be p_r and p_b. What would happen if the government put a tax only on red pencils?

4. The U.S. imports about half of its petroleum needs. Suppose that the rest of the oil producers are willing to supply as much oil as the U.S. wants at a constant price of \$25 a barrel. What would happen to the price of domestic oil if a tax of \$5 a barrel was placed on foreign oil?

5. Suppose that the supply curve is vertical. What is the deadweight loss of a tax in this market?

6. How much revenue does a tax system on loans like that described in the text raise if borrowers and lenders are in the same tax bracket?

7. Does a tax system on loans like that described in the text raise a positive or negative amount of revenue when $t_l < t_b$?

18

TECHNOLOGY

In this chapter we begin our study of firm behavior. The first thing to do is to examine the constraints on a firm's behavior. When a firm makes choices it faces many constraints. These constraints are imposed by its customers, by its competitors, and by nature. In this chapter we're going to consider the latter source of constraints: nature. Nature imposes the constraint that there are only certain feasible ways to produce outputs from inputs: there are only certain kinds of technological choices that are possible. Here we will study how economists describe these technological constraints.

18.1 Inputs and Outputs

Inputs to production are called **factors of production**. Factors of production are often classified into broad categories such as land, labor, capital, and raw materials. It is pretty apparent what labor, land, and raw materials mean, but capital may be a new concept. **Capital goods** are those inputs to production that are themselves produced goods. Basically capital goods are machines of one sort or another: tractors, buildings, computers, or whatever.

Sometimes capital is used to describe the money used to start up or maintain a business. We will always use the term **financial capital** for this concept, and use the term capital goods, or **physical capital**, for produced factors of production.

We will usually want to think of inputs and outputs as being measured in *flow* units: a certain amount of labor per week and a certain number of machine hours per week will produce a certain amount of output a week.

We won't find it necessary to use the classifications given above very often. Most of what we want to describe about technology can be done without reference to the *kind* of inputs and outputs involved—just with the amounts of inputs and outputs.

18.2 Describing Technological Constraints

Nature imposes **technological constraints** on firms: only certain combinations of inputs are feasible ways to produce a given amount of output, and the firm must limit itself to technologically feasible production plans.

The easiest way to describe feasible production plans is to list them. That is, we can list all combinations of inputs and outputs that are technologically feasible. The set of all combinations of inputs and outputs that comprise a technologically feasible way to produce is called a **production set.**

Suppose, for example, that we have only one input, measured by x, and one output, measured by y. Then a production set might have the shape indicated in Figure 18.1. To say that some point (x, y) is in the production set is just to say that it is technologically possible to produce y amount of output if you have x amount of input. The production set shows the *possible* technological choices facing a firm.

As long as the inputs to the firm are costly it makes sense to limit ourselves to examining the *maximum possible output* for a given level of input. This is the boundary of the production set depicted in Figure 18.1. The function determined by this boundary is known as the **production function.** It measures the maximum possible output that you can get from a given amount of input.

Of course, the concept of a production function applies equally well if there are several inputs. If, for example, we consider the case of two inputs, the production function $f(x_1, x_2)$ would measure the maximum amount of output y that we could get if we had x_1 units of good 1 and x_2 units of good 2.

In the two input case there is a convenient way to depict production relations known as the **isoquant.** An isoquant is the set of all possible combinations of inputs 1 and 2 that are just sufficient to produce a given amount of output.

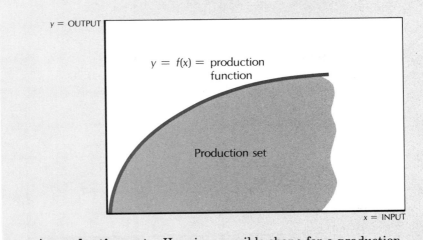

y = OUTPUT

$y = f(x) =$ production function

Production set

x = INPUT

A production set. Here is a possible shape for a production set.

Figure
18.1

Isoquants are similar to indifference curves. As we've seen earlier, an indifference curve depicts the different consumption bundles that are just sufficient to produce a certain level of utility. But there is one important difference between indifference curves and isoquants. Isoquants are labeled with the amount of output they can produce, not with a utility level. Thus the labeling of isoquants is fixed by the technology and doesn't have the kind of arbitrary nature that the utility labeling has.

18.3 Examples of Technology

Since we already know a lot about indifference curves, it is easy to understand how isoquants work. Let's consider a few examples of technologies and their isoquants.

Fixed Proportions

Suppose that we are producing holes and that the only way to get a hole is to use one man and one shovel. Extra shovels aren't worth anything, and neither are extra men. Thus the total number of holes that you can get will be the minimum of the number of men that you have and the number of shovels that you have. We write the production function as $f(x_1, x_2) = \min\{x_1, x_2\}$. The isoquants look like those depicted in Figure 18.2. Note that these isoquants are just like the case of perfect complements in consumer theory.

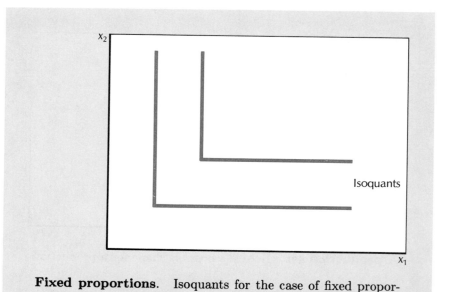

Figure
18.2   **Fixed proportions.** Isoquants for the case of fixed proportions.

Perfect Substitutes

Suppose now that we are producing homework and the inputs are red
pencils and blue pencils. The amount of homework produced depends only
on the total number of pencils, so we write the production function as
$f(x_1, x_2) = x_1 + x_2$. The resulting isoquants are just like the case of perfect
substitutes in consumer theory, as depicted in Figure 18.3.

Cobb-Douglas

If the production function has the form $f(x_1, x_2) = A x_1^a x_2^b$ then we say
that it is a **Cobb-Douglas production function**. This is just like the
functional form for Cobb-Douglas preferences that we studied earlier. The
magnitude of the utility function was not important so we had $A = 1$ and
$a + b = 1$. But the magnitude of the production function does matter so
we have to allow these parameters to take arbitrary values. The parameter
A measures, roughly speaking, the scale of production: how much output
we would get if we used one unit of each input. The parameters a and b
measure how the amount of output responds to changes in the inputs. We'll
examine their impact in more detail later on. In some of the examples, we
will choose to set $A = 1$ in order to simplify the calculations.

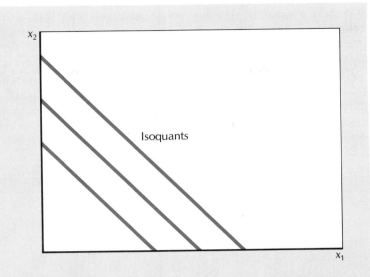

Perfect substitutes. Isoquants for the case of perfect substitutes.

Figure
18.3

The Cobb-Douglas isoquants have the same nice well-behaved shape that the Cobb-Douglas indifference curves have; as in the case of utility functions, the Cobb-Douglas production function is about the simplest example of well-behaved isoquants.

18.4 Properties of Technology

As in the case of consumers, it is common to assume certain properties about technology. First we will generally assume that technologies are **monotonic**: if you have at least as much of both inputs, it should be possible to produce at least as much output. This is sometimes referred to as the property of **free disposal**, since if the firm can costlessly dispose of any inputs, having extra inputs around can't hurt it.

Second, we will often assume that the technology is **convex**. This means that if you have two ways to produce y units of output, (x_1, x_2) and (z_1, z_2), then their weighted average will produce *at least* y units of output.

One argument for convex technologies goes as follows. Suppose that you have a way to produce 1 unit of output using a_1 units of good 1 and a_2 units of good 2, and you have another way to produce 1 unit of output using b_1 units of good 1 and b_2 units of good 2. We call these two ways to produce output **production techniques**.

Furthermore, let us suppose that you are free to scale the output up by arbitrary amounts so that $(100a_1, 100a_2)$ and $(100b_1, 100b_2)$ will produce

100 units of output. But now note that if you have $25a_1 + 75b_1$ units of good 1 and $25a_2 + 75b_2$ units of good 2 you can still produce 100 units of output: just produce 25 units of the output using the "a" technique and 75 units of the output using the "b" technique.

This is depicted in Figure 18.4. By choosing the level at which you operate each of the two activities, you can produce a given amount of output in a variety of different ways. In particular, every input combination along the line connecting (a_1, a_2) and (b_1, b_2) will be a feasible way to produce y units of output.

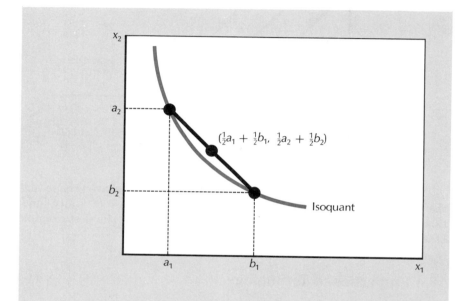

Figure 18.4

Convexity. If you can operate production activities independently, then weighted averages of production plans will also be feasible. Thus the isoquants will have a convex shape.

In this kind of technology, where you can scale the production process up and down easily and where separate production processes don't interfere with each other, convexity is a very natural assumption.

18.5 The Marginal Product

Suppose that we are operating at some point (x_1, x_2) and we consider using a little bit more of factor 1 while keeping factor 2 fixed at the level x_2. How much more output will we get per unit of factor 1? We have to look at the change in output per unit change of factor 1:

$$\frac{\Delta y}{\Delta x_1} = \frac{f(x_1 + \Delta x_1, x_2) - f(x_1, x_2)}{\Delta x_1}.$$

We call this the **marginal product of factor 1**. The marginal product of factor 2 is defined in a similar way, and we denote them by $MP_1(x_1, x_2)$ and $MP_2(x_1, x_2)$, respectively.

Sometimes we will be a bit sloppy about the concept of marginal product and describe it as the extra output we get from having "one" more unit of good 1. As long as "one" is small relative to the total amount of good 1 that we are using, this will be satisfactory. But we should remember that a marginal product is a *rate*: the extra amount of output per unit of extra input.

The concept of marginal product is just like the concept of marginal utility that we described in our discussion of consumer theory, except for the ordinal nature of utility. Here, we are discussing physical output: the marginal product of a factor is a specific number, which can, in principle, be observed.

18.6 The Technical Rate of Substitution

Suppose that we are operating at some point (x_1, x_2) and we consider giving up a little bit of good 1 and using just enough more of good 2 to produce the same amount of output y. How much extra of good 2, Δx_2, do we need if we are going to give up a little bit of good 1, Δx_1? This is just the slope of the isoquant; we refer to it as the **technical rate of substitution**, and denote it by $\mathrm{TRS}(x_1, x_2)$.

The technical rate of substitution measures the tradeoff between two inputs in production. It measures the rate at which the firm will have to substitute one input for another in order to keep output constant.

To derive a formula for the TRS, we can use the same idea that we used to determine the slope of the indifference curve. Consider a change in our use of factors 1 and 2 that keeps output fixed. Then we have

$$\Delta y = MP_1(x_1, x_2)\Delta x_1 + MP_2(x_1, x_2)\Delta x_2 = 0$$

which we can solve to get

$$\mathrm{TRS}(x_1, x_2) = \frac{\Delta x_2}{\Delta x_1} = -\frac{MP_1(x_1, x_2)}{MP_2(x_1, x_2)}.$$

Note the similarity with the definition of the marginal rate of substitution.

18.7 Diminishing Marginal Product

Suppose that we have certain amounts of factors 1 and 2 and we consider adding more of factor 1 while holding factor 2 fixed at a given level. What might happen to the marginal product of factor 1?

As long as we have a monotonic technology, we know that the total output will go up as we increase the amount of factor 1. But it is natural to expect that it will go up at a decreasing rate. Let's consider a specific example, the case of farming.

One man on one acre of land might produce 100 bushels of corn. If we add another man and keep the same amount of land, we might get 200 bushels of corn, so in this case the marginal product of an extra worker is 100. Now keep adding workers to this acre of land. Each worker may produce more output, but eventually the extra amount of corn produced by an extra worker will be less than 100 bushels. After 4 or 5 people are added the additional output per worker will drop to 90, 80, 70 ... or even fewer bushels of corn. If we get hundreds of workers crowded together on this one acre of land, an extra worker may even cause output to go down! As in the making of broth, extra cooks *can* make things worse.

Thus we would typically expect that the marginal product of a good will diminish as we get more and more of that good. This is called the **law of diminishing marginal product.** It isn't really a "law"; it's just a common feature of most kinds of production processes.

It is important to emphasize that the law of diminishing marginal product applies only when all *other* inputs are being held fixed. In the farming example, we considered changing only the labor input, holding the land and raw materials fixed.

18.8 Diminishing Technical Rate of Substitution

Another closely related assumption about technology is that of **diminishing technical rate of substitution.** This says that as we increase the amount of factor 1, and adjust factor 2 so as to stay on the same isoquant, the technical rate of substitution declines. Roughly speaking, the assumption of diminishing TRS means that the slope of an isoquant must decrease in absolute value as we move along the isoquant in the direction of increasing x_1, and it must increase as we move in the direction of increasing x_2. This means that the isoquants will have the same sort of convex shape that well-behaved indifference curves have.

The assumptions of a diminishing technical rate of substitution and diminishing marginal product are closely related but are not exactly the same. Diminishing marginal product is an assumption about how the marginal product changes as we increase the amount of one good, *holding the other good fixed.* Diminishing TRS is about how the *ratio* of the marginal products—the slope of the isoquant—changes as we increase one good and *adjust the other good so as to stay on the same isoquant.*

18.9 Long and Short Runs

Let us return now to the original idea of a technology as being just a list of the feasible production plans. We may want to distinguish between the production plans that are *immediately* feasible and those that are *eventually* feasible.

In the **short run**, there will be some factors of production that are fixed at predetermined levels. Our farmer described above might only consider production plans that involve a fixed amount of land, if that is all he has access to. It may be true that if he had more land, he could produce more corn, but in the short run he is stuck with the amount of land that he has.

On the other hand, in the long run the farmer is free to purchase more land, or to sell some of the land he now owns. He can adjust the level of the land input so as to maximize his profits.

The economist's distinction between the long run and the short run is this: in the short run there are some factors of production that are fixed: a fixed amount of land, a fixed plant size, a fixed number of machines, or whatever. In the **long run**, *all* the factors of production can be varied.

There is no specific time interval implied here. What is the long run and what is the short run depends on what kinds of choices we are examining. In the short run at least some factors are fixed at given levels, but in the long run the amount used of these factors can be changed.

Let's suppose that factor 2, say, is fixed at $\bar{x}_2$ in the short run. Then the relevant production function for the short run is $f(x_1, \bar{x}_2)$. We can plot the functional relation between output and x_1 in a diagram like Figure 18.5.

Note that we have drawn the short-run production function as getting flatter and flatter as the amount of good 1 increases. This is just the law of diminishing marginal product in action again. Of course it can easily happen that there is an initial region of increasing marginal returns where the marginal product of factor 1 increases as we add more of it. In the case of the farmer adding labor, it might be that the first few workers added increase output more and more because they would be able to divide up jobs efficiently, and so on. But given the fixed amount of land, eventually the marginal product of labor will decline.

18.10 Returns to Scale

Now let's consider a different kind of experiment. Instead of increasing the amount of one input while holding the other input fixed, let's increase the

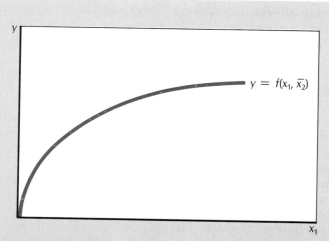

Figure
18.5

Production function. This is a possible shape for a short-run production function.

amount of *all* inputs to the production function. In other words, let's scale the amount of all inputs up by some constant factor: for example, use twice as much of both good 1 and good 2.

If we use twice as much of each good how much output will we get? The most likely outcome is that we will get twice as much output. This is called the case of **constant returns to scale.** In terms of the production function, this means that two times as much of each input gives two times as much output. In the case of two inputs we can express this mathematically by

$$2f(x_1, x_2) = f(2x_1, 2x_2).$$

In general if we scale all of the inputs up by some amount t, constant returns to scale implies that we should get t times as much output:

$$tf(x_1, x_2) = f(tx_1, tx_2).$$

We say that this is the likely outcome for the following reason: it should typically be possible for the firm to *replicate* what it was doing before. If the firm has twice as much of each input, it can just set up two plants side by side and thereby get twice as much output. With three times as much of each input, it can set up three plants, and so on.

Note that it is perfectly possible for a technology to exhibit constant returns to scale and diminishing marginal product to each factor. **Returns to scale** describes what happens when you increase *all* inputs, while diminishing marginal product describes what happens when you increase *one* of the inputs and hold the others fixed.

Constant returns to scale is the most "natural" case because of the replication argument, but that isn't to say that other things might not happen. For example, it could happen that if we scale up both inputs by some factor t we get *more* than t times as much output. This is called the case of **increasing returns to scale**. Mathematically, increasing returns to scale means that

$$f(tx_1, tx_2) > tf(x_1, x_2).$$

What would be an example of a technology that had increasing returns to scale? One nice example is that of an oil pipeline. If we double the diameter of a pipe we use twice as much materials, but the cross section of the pipe goes up by a factor of four. Thus we will likely be able to pump more than twice as much oil through it.

(Of course, we can't push this example too far. If we keep doubling the diameter of the pipe, it will eventually collapse of its own weight. Increasing returns to scale usually just applies over some range of output.)

The other case to consider is that of **decreasing returns to scale**, where

$$f(tx_1, tx_2) < tf(x_1, x_2).$$

for all $t > 0$.

This case is somewhat peculiar. If we get less than twice as much output from having twice as much of each input we must be doing something wrong. After all, we could just replicate what we were doing before!

The usual way in which diminishing returns to scale arises is because we forgot to account for some input. If we have twice as much of every input but one, we won't be able to exactly replicate what we were doing before, so there is no reason that we have to get twice as much output. Diminishing returns to scale is really a short-run phenomenon, with something being held fixed.

Of course a technology can exhibit different kinds of returns to scale at different levels of production. It may well happen that for low levels of production, the technology exhibits increasing returns to scale—as you scale all the inputs by some small amount t, the output increases by *more* that t. Later on, for larger levels of output, increasing scale by t may just increase output by the same factor t.

Summary

1. The technological constraints of the firm are described by the production set, which depicts all the technologically feasible combinations of inputs and outputs, and by the production function, which gives the maximum amount of output associated with a given amount of the inputs.

2. Another way to describe the technological constraints facing a firm is through the use of isoquants—curves that indicate all the combinations of inputs capable of producing a given level of output.

3. We generally assume that isoquants are convex and monotonic, just like well–behaved preferences.

4. The marginal product measures the extra output per extra unit of an input, holding all other inputs fixed. We typically assume that the marginal product of an input diminishes as we use more and more of that input.

5. The technical rate of substitution measures the slope of an isoquant. We generally assume that the TRS diminishes as we move out along an isoquants—which is another way of saying that the isoquants have a convex shape.

6. In the short run some inputs are fixed, while in the long run all inputs are variable.

7. Returns to scale refers to the way that output changes as we change the *scale* of production. If we scale all inputs up by some amount t and output goes up by the same factor, then we have constant returns to scale. If output scales up by more that t we have increasing returns to scale, and if it scales up by less than t we have decreasing returns to scale.

Review Questions

1. Consider the production function $f(x_1, x_2) = x_1^2 x_2^2$. Does this exhibit constant, increasing, or decreasing returns to scale?

2. Consider the production function $f(x_1, x_2) = x_1^3 x_2^7$. Does this exhibit constant, increasing, or decreasing returns to scale?

3. The Cobb–Douglas production function is given by $f(x_1, x_2) = Ax_1^a x_2^b$. It turns out that the type of returns to scale of this function will depend on the magnitude of $a + b$. Which values of $a + b$ will be associated with the different kinds of returns to scale?

4. The technical rate of substitution between factors x_2 and x_1 is -4. If you desire to produce the same amount of output, but cut your use of x_1 by 3 units, how many more units of x_2 will you need?

5. True or false? If the law of diminishing marginal product did not hold, the world's food supply could be grown in a flowerpot.

6. In a production process is it possible to have decreasing marginal product in an input and yet increasing returns to scale?

PROFIT
MAXIMIZATION

In the last chapter we discussed ways to describe the technological choices facing the firm. In this chapter we describe a model of how the firm chooses the amount to produce and how to produce it. The model that we will use is that the firm chooses a production plan that maximizes profits.

In this chapter we will assume that the firm faces fixed prices for its inputs and outputs. We said earlier that economists call a market where the individual producers take the prices as outside their control a **competitive market**. So in this chapter we want to study the profit maximization problem of a firm that faces competitive markets for the factors of production it uses and the output goods it produces.

19.1 Profits

Profits are defined as revenues minus costs. Suppose that the firm produces n outputs $(y_1, \ldots, y_n)$ and uses m inputs $(x_1, \ldots, x_m)$. Let the prices of the output goods be $(p_1, \ldots, p_n)$ and the prices of the inputs be $(w_1, \ldots, w_m)$.

The profits the firm receives, π, can be expressed as

$$\pi = \sum_{i=1}^{n} p_i y_i - \sum_{i=1}^{m} w_i x_i.$$

The first term is revenue, and the second term is costs.

In the expression for costs we should be sure to include *all* of the factors of production used by the firm, valued at their market price. Usually this is pretty obvious, but in cases where the firm is owned and operated by the same individual, it is possible to forget about some of the factors.

For example, if an individual works in his own firm, then his labor is an input and it should be counted as part of the costs. His wage rate is simply the market price of his labor—what he *would* be getting if he sold his labor on the open market. Similarly, if a farmer owns some land and uses it in his production, that land should be valued at its market value for purposes of computing the economic costs.

We have seen that economic costs like these are often referred to as **opportunity costs.** The name comes from the idea that if you are using your labor, for example, in one application, you forgo the opportunity of employing it elsewhere. Therefore those lost wages are part of the cost of production. Similarly with the land example. The farmer has the opportunity of renting his land to someone else, but he chooses to forgo that rental income in favor of renting it to himself. The lost rents are part of the opportunity cost of his production.

The economic definition of profit requires that we value all inputs and outputs at their opportunity cost. Profits as determined by accountants do not necessarily accurately measure economic profits, as they typically use historical costs—what a factor was purchased for originally—rather than economic costs—what a factor would cost if purchased now. There are many variations on the use of the term "profit," but we will always stick to the economic definition.

Another confusion that sometimes arises is due to getting time scales mixed up. We usually think of the factor inputs as being measured in terms of *flows*. So many labor hours per week and so many machine hours per week will produce so much output per week. Then the factor prices will be factor prices for the purchase of such flows. Wages are naturally expressed in terms of dollars per hour. The analog for machines would be the **rental rate**—the rate at which you can rent a machine for the given time period.

In many cases there isn't a very well developed market for the rental of machines, since firms will typically buy their capital equipment. In this case, we have to compute the implicit rental rate by seeing how much it would cost to buy a machine at the beginning of the period and sell it at the end of the period.

19.2 The Organization of Firms

In a capitalist economy, firms are owned by individuals. Firms are only legal entities; ultimately it is the owners of firms who are responsible for the behavior of the firm, and it is the owners who reap the rewards or pay the costs of that behavior.

Generally speaking, firms can be organized as proprietorships, partnerships, or corporations. A **proprietorship** is a firm that is owned by a single individual. A **partnership** is owned by two or more individuals. A **corporation** is usually owned by several individuals as well, but under the law has an existence separate from that of its owners. Thus a partnership will last only as long as both partners are alive and agree to maintain its existence. A corporation can last longer than the lifetimes of any of its owners. For this reason, most large firms are organized as corporations.

The owners of each of these different types of firms may have different goals with respect to managing the operation of the firm. In a proprietorship or a partnership the owners of the firm usually take a direct role in actually managing the day-to-day operations of the firm, so they are in a position to carry out whatever objectives they have in operating the firm. Typically the owners would be interested in maximizing the profits of their firm, but, if they have nonprofit goals, they can certainly indulge in these goals instead.

In a corporation, the owners of the corporation are often distinct from the managers of the corporation. Thus there is a separation of ownership and control. The owners of the corporation must define an objective for the managers to follow in their running of the firm, and then do their best to see that they actually pursue the goals the owners have in mind. Again, profit maximization is a common goal. As we'll see below, this goal, properly interpreted, is likely to lead the managers of the firm to choose actions that are in the interests of the owners of the firm.

19.3 Profits and Stock Market Value

Often the production process that a firm uses goes on for many periods. Inputs put in place at time t pay off with a whole flow of services at later times. For example, a factory building erected by a firm could last for 50 or 100 years. In this case an input at one point in time helps to produce output at other times in the future.

In this case we have to value a flow of costs and a flow of revenues over time. As we've seen in Chapter 11, the appropriate way to do this is to use the concept of present value. When people can borrow and lend in financial markets, the interest rate can be used to define a natural price of consumption at different times. Firms have access to the same sorts of financial markets, and the interest rate can be used to value investment decisions in exactly the same way.

Consider a world of perfect certainty where a firm's flow of future profits is publicly known. Then the present value of those profits would be the **present value of the firm**. It would be how much someone would be willing to pay to purchase the firm.

As we indicated above, most large firms are organized as corporations, which means that they are jointly owned by a number of individuals. The corporation issues stock certificates to represent ownership of shares in the corporation. At certain times the corporation issues dividends on these shares, which represent a share of the profits of the firm. The shares of ownership in the corporation are bought and sold in the **stock market**. The price of a share represents the present value of the stream of dividends that people expect to receive from the corporation. The total stock market value of a firm represents the present value of the stream of profits that the firm is expected to generate. Thus the objective of the firm—maximizing the present value of the stream of profits the firm generates—could also be described as the goal of maximizing stock market value. In a world of certainty, these two goals are the same thing.

The owners of the firm will generally want the firm to choose production plans that maximize the stock market value of the firm, since that will make the value of the shares they hold as large as possible. We saw in Chapter 11 that whatever an individual's tastes for consumption at different times, he or she will always prefer an endowment with a higher present value to one with a lower present value. By maximizing stock market value, a firm makes its shareholders' budget sets as large as possible, and thereby acts in the best interests of all of its shareholders.

If there is uncertainty about a firm's stream of profits, then instructing managers to maximize profits has no meaning. Should they maximize expected profits? Should they maximize the expected utility of profits? What attitude towards risky investments should the managers have? It is difficult to assign a meaning to profit maximization when there is uncertainty present. However, in a world of uncertainty, maximizing *stock market value* still has meaning. If the managers of a firm attempt to make the value of the firm's shares as large as possible, then they make the firm's owners—the shareholders—as well-off as possible. Thus maximizing stock market value gives a well-defined objective function to the firm in nearly all economic environments.

Despite these remarks about time and uncertainty, we will generally limit ourselves to the examination of much simpler profit maximization problems, namely those in which there is a single, certain output and a single point in time. This simple story still generates significant insights and builds the proper intuition to study more general models of firm behavior. Most of the ideas that we will examine carry over in a natural way to these more general models.

19.4 Fixed and Variable Factors

In a given time period, it may be very difficult to adjust some of the inputs. Typically a firm may have contractual obligations to employ certain inputs at certain levels. An example of this would be a lease on a building, where the firm is legally obligated to purchase a certain amount of space over the period under examination. We refer to a factor of production that is in a fixed amount for the firm as a **fixed factor**. If a factor can be used in different amounts, we refer to it as a **variable factor**.

As we saw in Chapter 18, the short run is defined as that period of time in which there are some fixed factors—factors that can only be used in fixed amounts. In the long run, on the other hand, the firm is free to vary all of the factors of production: all factors are variable factors.

There is no rigid boundary between the short run and the long run. The exact time period involved depends on the problem under examination. The important thing is that some of the factors of production are fixed in the short run and variable in the long run. Since all factors are variable in the long run, a firm is always free to decide to use zero inputs and produce zero output—that is, to go out of business. Thus the least profits a firm can make in the long run are zero profits.

In the short run, the firm is obligated to employ some factors, even if it decides to produce zero output. Therefore it is perfectly possible that the firm could make *negative* profits in the short run.

By definition, fixed factors are factors of production that must be paid for even if the firm decides to produce zero output: if a firm has a long-term lease on a building, it must make its lease payments each period whether or not it decides to produce anything that period. But there is another category of factors that only need to be paid for if the firm decides to produce a positive amount of output. One example is electricity used for lighting. If the firm produces zero output, it doesn't have to provide any lighting; but if it produces any positive amount of output, it has to purchase a fixed amount of electricity to use for lighting.

Factors such as these are called **quasi–fixed factors**. They are factors of production that must be used in a fixed amount, independent of the output of the firm, as long as the output is positive. The distinction between fixed factors and quasi–fixed factors is sometimes useful in analyzing the economic behavior of the firm.

19.5 Short-Run Profit Maximization

Let's consider the short-run profit maximization problem when input 2 is fixed at some level $\overline{x}_2$. Let $f(x_1, x_2)$ be the production function for the firm. Then the profit maximization problem facing the firm can be written as

$$\max_{x_1} \ pf(x_1, \overline{x}_2) - w_1 x_1 - w_2 \overline{x}_2.$$

The condition for the optimal choice of factor 1 is not difficult to discover.

If x_1^* is the profit maximizing choice of factor 1, then it must be the case that the output price times the marginal product of factor 1 should equal the factor price. In symbols:

$$pMP_1(x_1^*, \overline{x}_2) = w_1.$$

In other words, the *value of the marginal product of a factor should equal its price.*

In order to understand this rule, think about the decision to employ a little more of factor 1. As you add a little more of it, Δx_1, you produce $\Delta y = MP_1 \Delta x_1$ more output that is worth $pMP_1 \Delta x_1$. But this marginal output costs $w_1 \Delta x_1$ to produce. If the value of marginal product exceeds its cost, then profits can be increased by increasing input 1. If the value of marginal product is less than its cost, then profits can be increased by *decreasing* the level of input 1.

If the profits of the firm are as large as possible, then profits should not increase when we increase or decrease input 1. This means that at a profit maximizing choice of inputs and outputs, the value of the marginal product, $pMP_1(x_1^*, \overline{x}_2)$, should equal the factor price, w_1.

We can derive the same condition graphically. Consider Figure 19.1. The curved line represents the production function holding factor 2 fixed at $\overline{x}_2$. Using y to denote the output of the firm, profits are given by

$$\pi = py - w_1 x_1 - w_2 \overline{x}_2.$$

This expression can be solved for y to express output as a function of x_1:

$$y = \frac{\pi}{p} + \frac{w_2}{p} \overline{x}_2 + \frac{w_1}{p} x_1. \tag{19.1}$$

This equation describes **isoprofit lines**. As π varies we get a family of parallel straight lines each with a slope of w_1/p and each having a vertical intercept of $\pi/p + w_2 \overline{x}_2/p$, which measures the profits plus the fixed costs of the firm.

The fixed costs are fixed, so the only thing that really varies as we move from one isoprofit line to another is the level of profits. Thus higher levels of profit will be associated with isoprofit lines with higher vertical intercepts.

The profit maximization problem is then to find the point on the production function that has the highest associated isoprofit line. Such a point is illustrated in Figure 19.1. As usual it is characterized by a tangency condition: the slope of the production function should equal the slope of

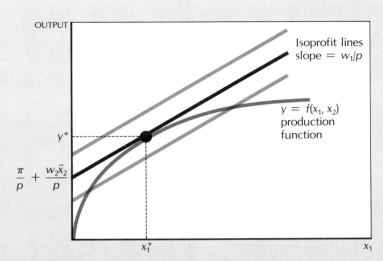

Profit maximization. The firm chooses the input and output combination that lies on the highest isoprofit line. In this case the profit maximizing point is (x_1^*, y^*).

Figure
19.1

the isoprofit line. Since the slope of the production function is the marginal product, and the slope of the isoprofit line is w_1/p, this condition can also be written as

$$MP_1 = \frac{w_1}{p}$$

which is precisely the condition we derived above.

19.6 Comparative Statics

We can use the geometry depicted in Figure 19.1 to analyze how a firm's choice of inputs and outputs varies as the prices of inputs and outputs vary; that is, we can analyze the **comparative statics** of firm behavior.

For example: how does the optimal choice of factor 1 vary as we vary its factor price w_1? Referring to equation (19.1), which defines the isoprofit line, we see that increasing w_1 will make the isoprofit line steeper, as shown in Figure 19.2A. When the isoprofit line is steeper, the tangency must occur further to the left. Thus the optimal level of factor 1 must decrease. This simply means that as the price of factor 1 increases, the demand for factor 1 must decrease: factor demand curves must slope downward.

Similarly, if the output price decreases the isoprofit line must become steeper, as shown in Figure 19.2B. By the same argument as given in the last paragraph the profit maximizing choice of factor 1 will decrease. If the

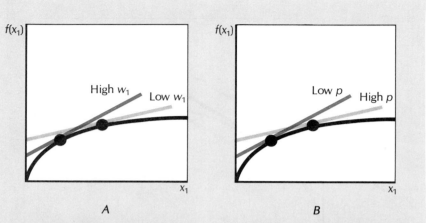

Figure
19.2

Comparative statics. Panel A shows that increasing w_1 will reduce the demand for factor 1. Panel B shows that increasing the price of output will increase the demand for factor 1 and therefore increase the supply of output.

amount of factor 1 decreases, and the level of factor 2 is fixed in the short run by assumption, then the supply of output must decrease. This gives us another comparative statics result: a reduction in the output price must decrease the supply of output. In other words, the supply function must slope upwards.

Finally we can ask what will happen if the price of factor 2 changes? Because this is a short-run analysis, changing the price of factor 2 will not change the firm's choice of factor 2—in the short run, the level of factor 2 is fixed at $\overline{x}_2$. Changing the price of factor 2 has no effect on the *slope* of the isoprofit line. Thus the optimal choice of factor 1 will not change, nor will the supply of output. All that changes are the profits that the firm makes.

19.7 Profit Maximization in the Long Run

In the long run the firm is free to choose the level of all of its inputs. Thus the long-run profit maximization problem can be posed as

$$\max_{x_1, x_2} \ pf(x_1, x_2) - w_1 x_1 - w_2 x_2.$$

This is basically the same as the short-run problem described above, but now both factors are free to vary.

The condition describing the optimal choices is essentially the same as before, but now we have to apply it to *each* factor. Before we saw that the value of the marginal product of factor 1 must be equal to its price, whatever the level of factor 2. The same sort of condition must now hold for *each* factor choice:

$$pMP_1(x_1^*, x_2^*) = w_1$$

$$pMP_2(x_1^*, x_2^*) = w_2.$$

If the firm has made the optimal choices of factors 1 and 2, the value of the marginal product of each factor should equal its price. At the optimal choice, the firm's profits cannot increase by changing the level of either input.

The argument is the same as used for the short-run profit maximizing decisions. If the value of the marginal product of factor 1, for example, exceeded the price of factor 1, then using a little more of factor 1 would produce MP_1 more output, which would sell for pMP_1 dollars. If the value of this output exceeds the cost of the factor used to produce it, it clearly pays to expand the use of this factor.

These two conditions give us two equations in two unknowns, x_1^* and x_2^*. If we know how the marginal products behave as a function of x_1 and x_2, we will be able to solve for the optimal choice of each factor as a function of the prices. The resulting equations are known as the **factor demand curves**.

19.8 Inverse Factor Demand Curves

The **factor demand curves** of a firm measure the relationship between the price of a factor and the profit maximizing choice of that factor. We saw above how to find the profit maximizing choices: for any prices (p, w_1, w_2) we just find those factor demands (x_1^*, x_2^*) such that the value of the marginal product of each factor equals its price.

The **inverse factor demand curve** measures the same relationship, but from a different point of view. It measures what the factor prices must be for some given quantity of inputs to be demanded. Given the optimal choice of factor 2, we can draw the relationship between the optimal choice of factor 1 and its price in a diagram like that depicted in Figure 19.3. This is simply a graph of the equation

$$pMP_1(x_1, x_2^*) = w_1.$$

This curve will be downward sloping by the assumption of diminishing marginal product. For any level of x_1, this curve depicts what the factor price must be in order to induce the firm to demand that level of x_1, holding factor 2 fixed at x_2^*.

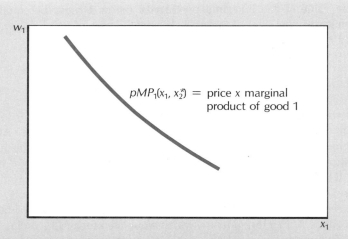

Figure
19.3
The inverse factor demand curve. This measures what the price of factor 1 must be to get x_1 units demanded, if the level of the other factor is held fixed at x_2^*.

19.9 Profit Maximization and Returns to Scale

There is an important relationship between competitive profit maximization and returns to scale. Suppose that a firm has chosen a long-run profit maximizing output $y^* = f(x_1^*, x_2^*)$, which it is producing using input levels (x_1^*, x_2^*).

Then its profits are given by

$$\pi^* = py^* - w_1 x_1^* - w_2 x_2^*.$$

Suppose that this firm's production function exhibits constant returns to scale and that it is making positive profits in equilibrium. Then consider what would happen if it doubled the level of its input usage. According to the constant returns to scale hypothesis, it would double its output level. What would happen to profits?

It is not hard to see that its profits would also double. But this contradicts the assumption that its original choice was profit maximizing! We derived this contradiction by assuming that the original profit level was positive; if the original level of profits were 0 there would be no problem: two times zero is still zero.

This argument shows that the only reasonable long-run level of profits for a competitive firm that has constant returns to scale at all levels of output is a zero level of profits. (Of course if a firm has negative profits in the long run, it should go out of business.)

Most people find this to be a surprising statement. Firms are out to maximize profits aren't they? How can it be that they can only get zero profits in the long run?

Think about what would happen to a firm that did try to expand indefinitely. Three things might occur. First, the firm could get so large that it could not really operate effectively. This is just saying that the firm *really* doesn't have constant returns to scale at all levels of output. Eventually, due to coordination problems, it might enter a region of decreasing returns to scale.

Second, the firm might get so large that it would totally dominate the market for its product. In this case there is no reason for it to behave competitively—to take the price of output as given. Instead, it would make sense for such a firm to try to use its size to influence the market price. The model of competitive profit maximization would no longer be a sensible way for the firm to behave, since it would effectively have no competitors. We'll investigate more appropriate models of firm behavior in this situation when we discuss monopoly.

Third, if one firm can make positive profits with a constant returns to scale technology, so can any other firm with access to the same technology. If one firm wants to expand its output, so would other firms. But if all firms expand their outputs, this will certainly push down the price of output and lower the profits of all the firms in the industry.

19.10 Revealed Profitability

When a profit maximizing firm makes its choice of inputs and outputs it reveals two things: first, that the inputs and outputs used represent a *feasible* production plan, and second, that these choices are more profitable than other feasible choices that the firm could have made. Let us examine these points in more detail.

Suppose that we observe two choices that the firm makes at two different sets of prices. At time t, it faces prices (p^t, w_1^t, w_2^t) and makes choices (y^t, x_1^t, x_2^t). At time s, it faces prices (p^s, w_1^s, w_2^s) and makes choices (y^s, x_1^s, x_2^s). If the production function of the firm hasn't changed between times s and t, and the firm is a profit maximizer, then we must have

$$p^t y^t - w_1^t x_1^t - w_2^t x_2^t \geq p^t y^s - w_1^t x_1^s - w_2^t x_2^s \qquad (19.2)$$

and

$$p^s y^s - w_1^s x_1^s - w_2^s x_2^s \geq p^s y^t - w_1^s x_1^t - w_2^s x_2^t. \qquad (19.3)$$

That is, the profits that the firm achieved facing the t period prices must be larger than if they used the s period plan and vice versa. If either of these inequalities were violated, the firm could not have been a profit maximizing firm (with an unchanging technology).

Thus if we ever observe two time periods where these inequalities are violated we would know that the firm was not maximizing profits. The satisfaction of these inequalities is virtually an axiom of profit maximizing behavior, so it might be referred to as the **Weak Axiom of Profit Maximizing Behavior (WAPM)**.

If the firm's choices satisfy WAPM we can derive a useful comparative statics statement about the behavior of factor demands and output supplies when prices change. Transpose the two sides of equation (19.3) to get

$$-p^s y^t + w_1^s x_1^t + w_2^s x_1^t \geq -p^s y^s + w_1^s x_1^s + w_2^s x_2^s \qquad (19.4)$$

and add equation (19.4) to equation (19.2) to get

$$(p^t - p^s)y^t - (w_1^t - w_1^s)x_1^t - (w_2^t - w_2^s)x_2^t$$
$$\geq (p^t - p^s)y^s - (w_1^t - w_1^s)x_1^s - (w_2^t - w_2^s)x_2^s. \qquad (19.5)$$

Now rearrange this equation to yield

$$(p^t - p^s)(y^t - y^s) - (w_1^t - w_1^s)(x_1^t - x_1^s) - (w_2^t - w_2^s)(x_2^t - x_2^s) \geq 0. \quad (19.6)$$

Finally define the change in prices, $\Delta p = (p^t - p^s)$, the change in output, $\Delta y = (y^t - y^s)$, and so on to get

$$\Delta p \Delta y - \Delta w_1 \Delta x_1 - \Delta w_2 \Delta x_2 \geq 0 \qquad (19.7)$$

This equation is our final result. It says that the change in the price of output times the change in output minus the change in each factor price times the change in that factor must be nonnegative. This equation comes solely from the definition of profit maximization. Yet it contains all of the comparative statics results about profit maximizing choices!

For example, suppose that we consider a situation where the price of output changes, but the price of each factor stays constant. If $\Delta w_1 = \Delta w_2 = 0$ then equation (19.7) reduces to

$$\Delta p \Delta y \geq 0.$$

Thus, if the price of output goes up, so that $\Delta p > 0$, then the change in output must be nonnegative as well, $\Delta y \geq 0$. This says that the profit maximizing supply curve of a competitive firm must have a positive (or at least a zero) slope.

Similarly, if the price of output and of factor 2 remain constant, equation (19.7) becomes

$$-\Delta w_1 \Delta x_1 \geq 0$$

which is to say

$$\Delta w_1 \Delta x_1 \leq 0.$$

Thus, if the price of factor 1 goes up, so that $\Delta w_1 > 0$, then equation (19.7) implies that the demand for factor 1 will go down (or at worst stay the same), so that $\Delta x_1 \leq 0$.

The simple inequality in WAPM, and its implication in equation (19.7), give us strong observable restrictions about how a firm will behave. It is natural to ask whether these are all of the restrictions that the model of profit maximization imposes on firm behavior. Said another way, if we observe a firm's choices, and these choices satisfy WAPM, can we construct an estimate of the technology for which the observed choices are profit maximizing choices? It turns out that the answer is yes. Figure 19.4 shows how to construct such a technology.

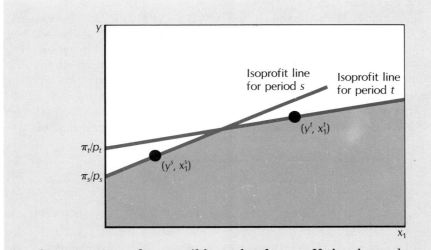

Construction of a possible technology. If the observed choices are maximal profit choices at each set of prices, then we can estimate the shape of the technology that generated those choices by using the isoprofit lines.

Figure 19.4

In order to illustrate the argument graphically, we suppose that there is one input and one output. Suppose that we are given an observed choice in period t and in period s, which we indicate by (p^t, w_1^t, y^t, x_1^t) and (p^s, w_1^s, y^s, x_1^s). In each period we can calculate the profits π_s and π_t and plot all the combinations of y and x_1 that yield these profits.

That is, we plot the two isoprofit lines

$$\pi_t = p^t y - w_1^t x_1$$

and

$$\pi_s = p^s y - w_1^s x_1.$$

The points above the isoprofit line for period t have higher profits than π_t at period t prices, and the points above the isoprofit line for period s have higher profits than π_s at period s prices. WAPM requires that the choice in period t must lie below the period s isoprofit line, and that the choice in period s must lie below the period t isoprofit line.

If this condition is satisfied it is not hard to generate a technology for which (y^t, x_1^t) and (y^s, x_1^s) are profit maximizing choices. Just take the shaded area beneath the two lines. These are all of the choices that yield lower profits than the observed choices at both sets of prices.

The proof that this technology will generate the observed choices as profit maximizing choices is clear geometrically. At the prices (p^t, w_1^t), the choice (y^t, x_1^t) is on the highest isoprofit line possible, and the same goes for the period s choice.

Thus, when the observed choices satisfy WAPM, we can "reconstruct" an estimate of a technology that might have generated the observations. In this sense, any observed choices consistent with WAPM could be profit maximizing choices. If we observe more and more choices that the firm makes, we can get a tighter and tighter estimate of the production function, as illustrated in Figure 19.5.

This estimate of the production function can be used to forecast firm behavior in other environments or for other uses in economic analysis.

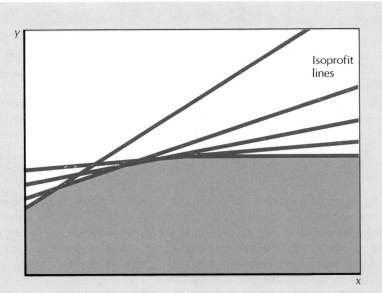

Figure 19.5

Estimating the technology. As we observe more choices we get a tighter estimate of the production function.

EXAMPLE: How Do Farmers React to Price Supports?

The U.S. government currently spends between $40 and $60 billion a year in aid to farmers. A large fraction of this amount is used to subsidize the production of various products including milk, wheat, corn, soybeans, and cotton. Occasionally, attempts are made to reduce or eliminate these subsidies. The effect of elimination of these subsidies would be to reduce the price of the product received by the farmers.

Farmers sometimes argue that eliminating the subsidies to milk, for example, would not reduce the total supply of milk, since dairy farmers would choose to *increase* their herds and their supply of milk so as to keep their standard of living constant.

If farmers are behaving so as to maximize profits, this is impossible. As we've seen above, the logic of profit maximization *requires* that a decrease in the price of an output leads to a reduction in its supply: if Δp is negative, then Δy must be negative as well.

It is certainly possible that small family farms have goals other than simple maximization of profits, but larger "agribusiness" farms are more likely to be profit maximizers. Thus the perverse response to the elimination of subsidies alluded to above could only occur on a limited scale, if at all.

19.11 Cost Minimization

If a firm is maximizing profits and it chooses to supply some output y, then it must be minimizing the cost of producing y. If this were not so, then there would be some cheaper way of producing y units of output, which would mean that the firm was not maximizing profits in the first place.

This simple observation turns out to be quite useful in examining firm behavior. It turns out to be convenient to break the profit maximization problem up into two stages: first we figure out how to minimize the costs of producing any desired level of output y, then we figure out which level of output is indeed a profit maximizing level of output. We begin this task in the next chapter.

Summary

1. Profits are the difference between revenues and costs. In this definition it is important that all costs are measured at their appropriate market prices.

2. Fixed factors are factors whose amount is independent of the level of output; variable factors are factors whose amount used changes as the level of output changes.

3. In the short run, some factors must be used in predetermined amounts. In the long run, all factors are free to vary.

4. If the firm is maximizing profits, then the value of the marginal product of each factor that it is free to vary must equal its factor price.

5. The logic of profit maximization implies that the supply function of a competitive firm must be an increasing function of the price of output and that each factor demand function must be a decreasing function of its price.

6. If a firm exhibits constant returns to scale, then its long-run maximum profits must be zero.

Review Questions

1. In the short run, if the price of the fixed factor is increased, what will happen to profits?

2. If a firm had everywhere increasing returns to scale, what would happen to its profits if prices remained fixed and it doubled its scale of operation?

3. If a firm had decreasing returns to scale at all levels of output, and it divided up into two equal sized smaller firms, what would happen to its overall profits?

4. A gardener exclaims: "For only $1.00 in seeds I've grown over $20.00 in produce!" Besides the fact that most of the produce is in the form of zucchini, what other observations would a cynical economist make about this situation?

5. Is maximizing a firm's profits always identical to maximizing the firm's stock market value?

6. If $pMP_1 > w_1$ then should the firm increase or decrease the amount of factor 1 in order to increase profits?

7. Suppose a firm is maximizing profits in the short run with variable factor x_1 and fixed factor x_2. If the price of x_2 goes down, what happens to the firm's use of x_1? What happens to the firm's level of profits?

8. A profit maximizing competitive firm that is making positive profits in long-run equilibrium (may/may not) have a technology with constant returns to scale.

APPENDIX

The profit maximization problem of the firm is

$$\max_{x_1,x_2} pf(x_1,x_2) - w_1 x_1 - w_2 x_2$$

which has first-order conditions

$$p\frac{\partial f(x_1^*, x_2^*)}{\partial x_1} - w_1 = 0$$

$$p\frac{\partial f(x_1^*, x_2^*)}{\partial x_2} - w_2 = 0.$$

These are just the same as the marginal product conditions given in the text. Let's see how profit maximizing behavior looks using the Cobb–Douglas production function.

Suppose the Cobb-Douglas function is given by $f(x_1, x_2) = x_1^a x_2^b$. Then the two first-order conditions become

$$pax_1^{a-1}x_2^b - w_1 = 0$$

$$pbx_1^a x_2^{b-1} - w_2 = 0.$$

Multiply the first equation by x_1 and the second equation by x_2 to get

$$pax_1^a x_2^b - w_1 x_1 = 0$$

$$pbx_1^a x_2^b - w_2 x_2 = 0.$$

Using $y = x_1^a x_2^b$ to denote the level of output of this firm we can rewrite these expressions as

$$pay = w_1 x_1$$

$$pby = w_2 x_2.$$

Solving for x_1 and x_2 we have

$$x_1^* = \frac{apy}{w_1}$$

$$x_2^* = \frac{bpy}{w_2}.$$

This gives us the demands for the two factors as a function of the optimal output choice. But we still have to solve for the optimal choice of output. Inserting the optimal factor demands into the Cobb–Douglas production function we have the expression

$$\left(\frac{pay}{w_1}\right)^a \left(\frac{pby}{w_2}\right)^b = y.$$

Factoring out the y gives

$$\left(\frac{pa}{w_1}\right)^a \left(\frac{pb}{w_2}\right)^b y^{a+b} = y.$$

Or

$$y = \left(\frac{pa}{w_1}\right)^{\frac{a}{1-a-b}} \left(\frac{pb}{w_2}\right)^{\frac{b}{1-a-b}}$$

This gives us the supply function of the Cobb–Douglas firm. Along with the factor demand functions derived above it gives us a complete solution to the profit maximization problem.

Note that when the firm exhibits constant returns to scale—when $a + b = 1$—this supply function is not well defined. As long as the output and input prices are consistent with zero profits, a firm with a Cobb–Douglas technology is indifferent about its level of supply.

COST
MINIMIZATION

Our goal is to study the behavior of profit maximizing firms in competitive and noncompetitive market environments. In the last chapter we began our investigation of profit maximizing behavior in a competitive environment by examining the profit maximization problem directly.

However, it turns out that there is insight to be had from taking a more indirect approach. Our strategy will be to break up the profit maximization problem into two pieces. First we will look at the problem of how to minimize the costs of producing any given level of output and then we will look at how to choose the most profitable level of output. In this chapter we'll look at the first step—minimizing the costs of producing a given level of output.

20.1 Cost Minimization

Suppose that we have two factors of production x_1 and x_2 that have prices w_1 and w_2, and we want to figure out the cheapest way to produce a given level of output, y. If we let $f(x_1, x_2)$ be the production function for the firm, we can write this problem as

$$\min_{x_1, x_2} w_1 x_1 + w_2 x_2$$

such that $f(x_1, x_2) = y$.

The same warnings apply as in the last chapter concerning this sort of analysis: make sure that you have included *all* costs of production in the calculation of costs, and make sure that everything is being measured on a compatible time scale.

The solution to this cost minimization problem—the minimum costs necessary to achieve the desired level of output—will depend on w_1, w_2, and y, so we write it as $c(w_1, w_2, y)$. This function is known as the **cost function** and will be of considerable interest to us. The cost function $c(w_1, w_2, y)$ measures the minimal costs of producing y units of output when factor prices are (w_1, w_2).

In order to understand the solution to this problem, let us depict the costs and the technological constraints facing the firm on the same diagram. The isoquants give us the technological constraints—all the combinations of x_1 and x_2 that can produce y.

Suppose that we want to plot all of the combinations of inputs that have some given level of cost, C. We can write this as

$$w_1 x_1 + w_2 x_2 = C$$

which can be rearranged to give

$$x_2 = \frac{C}{w_2} - \frac{w_1}{w_2} x_1.$$

It is easy to see that this is a straight line with a slope of $-w_1/w_2$ and a vertical intercept of C/w_2. As we let the number C vary we get a whole family of **isocost lines**. Every point on an isocost curve has the same cost, C, and higher isocost lines are associated with higher costs.

Thus our cost minimization problem can be rephrased as: find the point on the isoquant that has the lowest possible isocost line associated with it. Such a point is illustrated in Figure 20.1.

Note that if the optimal solution involves using some of each factor, and if the isoquant is a nice smooth curve, then the cost minimizing point will be characterized by a tangency condition: the slope of the isoquant must be equal to the slope of the isocost curve. Or, using the terminology of Chapter 18, the *technical rate of substitution must equal the factor price ratio:*

$$-\frac{MP_1(x_1^*, x_2^*)}{MP_2(x_1^*, x_2^*)} = \text{TRS}(x_1^*, x_2^*) = -\frac{w_1}{w_2}. \tag{20.1}$$

(If we have a boundary solution where one of the two factors isn't used, this tangency condition need not be met. Similarly, if the production function has "kinks" the tangency condition has no meaning. This is just like the situation with the consumer, so we won't emphasize these cases in this chapter.)

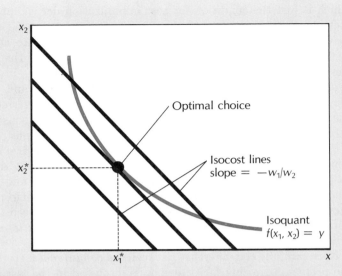

Cost minimization. The choice of factors that minimize production costs can be determined by finding the point on the isoquant that has the lowest associated isocost curve.

Figure
20.1

The algebra that lies behind equation (20.1) is not difficult. Consider any change in the pattern of production $(\Delta x_1, \Delta x_2)$ that keeps output constant. Such a change must satisfy

$$MP_1(x_1^*, x_2^*)\Delta x_1 + MP_2(x_1^*, x_2^*)\Delta x_2 = 0. \qquad (20.2)$$

If we are at the cost minimum then this change cannot lower costs, so we have

$$w_1\Delta x_1 + w_2\Delta x_2 \geq 0. \qquad (20.3)$$

Now consider the change $(-\Delta x_1, -\Delta x_2)$. This also produces a constant level of output and it too cannot lower costs. This implies that

$$-w_1\Delta x_1 - w_2\Delta x_2 \geq 0. \qquad (20.4)$$

Putting equations (20.3) and (20.4) together gives us

$$w_1\Delta x_1 + w_2\Delta x_2 = 0. \qquad (20.5)$$

Solving equations (20.2) and (20.5) for $\Delta x_1/\Delta x_2$ gives

$$\frac{\Delta x_2}{\Delta x_1} = -\frac{w_1}{w_2} = -\frac{MP_1(x_1^*, x_2^*)}{MP_2(x_1^*, x_2^*)}$$

which is just the condition for cost minimization derived above by a geometric argument.

Note that Figure 20.1 bears a certain resemblance to the solution to the consumer choice problem depicted earlier. Although the solutions look the same, they really aren't the same kind of problem. In the consumer problem, the straight line was the budget constraint, and the consumer moved along the budget constraint to find the most preferred position. In the producer problem, the isoquant is the technological constraint and the producer moves along the isoquant to find the optimal position.

The choices of inputs that yield minimal costs for the firm will in general depend on the input prices and the level of output that the firm wants to produce, so we write these choices as $x_1(w_1, w_2, y)$ and $x_2(w_1, w_2, y)$. These are called the **conditional factor demand functions**, or **derived factor demands**. They measure the relationship between the prices and output and the optimal factor choice of the firm, *conditional* on the firm producing a given level of output, y.

Note carefully the difference between the *conditional* factor demands and the profit maximizing factor demands discussed in the last chapter. The conditional factor demands give the cost minimizing choices for a given *level* of output; the profit maximizing factor demands give the profit maximizing choices for a given *price* of output.

EXAMPLE: Minimizing Costs for Specific Technologies

Suppose that we consider a technology where the goods are perfect complements, so that $f(x_1, x_2) = \min\{x_1, x_2\}$. Then if we want to produce y units of output, we clearly need y units of x_1 and y units of x_2. Thus the minimal costs of production will be

$$c(w_1, w_2, y) = w_1 y + w_2 y = (w_1 + w_2)y.$$

What about the perfect substitutes technology, $f(x_1, x_2) = x_1 + x_2$? Since goods 1 and 2 are perfect substitutes in production it is clear that the firm will use whichever is cheaper. Thus the minimum cost of producing y units of output will be $w_1 y$ or $w_2 y$, whichever is less. In other words:

$$c(w_1, w_2, y) = \min\{w_1 y, w_2 y\} = \min\{w_1, w_2\}y.$$

Finally, we consider the Cobb-Douglas technology, which is described by the formula $f(x_1, x_2) = A x_1^a x_2^b$. In this case we can use calculus techniques to show that the cost function will have the form

$$c(w_1, w_2, y) = K w_1^{\frac{a}{a+b}} w_2^{\frac{b}{a+b}} y^{\frac{1}{a+b}}$$

where K is a constant that depends on a, b, and A.

20.2 Revealed Cost Minimization

The assumption that the firm chooses factors to minimize the cost of producing output will have implications for how the observed choices change as factor prices change.

Suppose that we observe two sets of prices, (w_1^t, w_2^t) and (w_1^s, w_2^s), and the associated choices of the firm, (x_1^t, x_2^t) and (x_1^s, x_2^s). Suppose that each of these choices produces the same output level y. Then if each choice is a cost minimizing choice at its associated prices, we must have

$$w_1^t x_1^t + w_2^t x_2^t \leq w_1^t x_1^s + w_2^t x_2^s$$

and

$$w_1^s x_1^s + w_2^s x_2^s \leq w_1^s x_1^t + w_2^s x_2^t.$$

If the firm is always choosing the cost minimizing way to produce y units of output, then its choices at times t and s must satisfy these inequalities. We will refer to these inequalities as the **Weak Axiom of Cost Minimization (WACM)**.

Write the second equation as

$$-w_1^s x_1^t - w_2^s x_2^t \leq -w_1^s x_1^s - w_2^s x_2^s$$

and add it to the first equation to get

$$(w_1^t - w_1^s)x_1^t + (w_2^t - w_2^s)x_2^t \leq (w_1^t - w_1^s)x_1^s + (w_2^t - w_2^s)x_2^s$$

which can be rearranged to give us

$$(w_1^t - w_1^s)(x_1^t - x_1^s) + (w_2^t - w_2^s)(x_2^t - x_2^s) \leq 0.$$

Using the delta notation to depict the *changes* in the two factor demands, we have

$$\Delta w_1 \Delta x_1 + \Delta w_2 \Delta x_2 \leq 0.$$

This equation follows solely from the assumption of cost minimizing behavior. It implies restrictions on how the firm's behavior can change when input prices change and output remains constant.

For example, if the price of the first good increases and the price of the second good stays constant, then $\Delta w_2 = 0$, so the inequality becomes

$$\Delta w_1 \Delta x_1 \leq 0.$$

If the price of factor 1 increases, then this inequality implies that the demand for factor 1 must decrease; thus the conditional factor demand functions must slope down.

What can we say about how the minimal costs change as we change the parameters of the problem? It is easy to see that costs must increase if either factor price increases: if one good becomes more expensive and the other stays the same, the minimal costs cannot go down and in general will increase. Similarly, if the firm chooses to produce more output, its costs will have to increase.

20.3 Returns to Scale and the Cost Function

In Chapter 18 we discussed the idea of returns to scale for the production function. Recall that a technology is said to have increasing, decreasing, or constant returns to scale as $f(tx_1, tx_2)$ is greater, less than, or equal to $tf(x_1, x_2)$ for all $t > 0$. It turns out that there is a nice relation between the kind of returns to scale exhibited by the production function and the behavior of the cost function.

Suppose first that we have the natural case of constant returns to scale. Imagine that we have solved the cost minimization problem to produce 1 unit of output, so that we know the **unit cost function**, $c(w_1, w_2, 1)$. Now what is the cheapest way to produce y units of output? Simple: we just use y times as much of every input as we were using to produce 1 unit of output. This would mean that the minimal cost to produce y units of output would just be $c(w_1, w_2, 1)y$. In the case of constant returns to scale, the cost function is linear in output.

What if we have increasing returns to scale? In this case it turns out that costs increase less than linearly in output. If the firm decides to produce twice as much output, it can do so at *less* than twice the cost, as long as the factor prices remain fixed. This is a natural implication of the idea of increasing returns to scale: if the firm doubles its inputs it will more than double its output. Thus if it wants to produce double the output it will be able to do so by using less than twice as much of every input.

But using twice as much of every input will exactly double costs. So using less than twice as much of every input will make costs go up by less than twice as much: this is just saying that the cost function will increase less than linearly in output. Similarly, if the technology exhibits decreasing returns to scale, the cost function will increase more than linearly in output. If output doubles, costs will more than double.

These facts can be expressed in terms of the behavior of the **average cost function.** The average cost function is simply the cost *per unit* to produce y units of output:

$$AC(y) = \frac{c(w_1, w_2, y)}{y}.$$

If the technology exhibits constant returns to scale, then we saw above that the cost function had the form $c(w_1, w_2, y) = c(w_1, w_2, 1)y$. This means that the average cost function will be

$$AC(w_1, w_2, y) = \frac{c(w_1, w_2, 1)y}{y} = c(w_1, w_2, 1).$$

That is, the cost per unit of output will be constant no matter what level of output the firm wants to produce.

If the technology exhibits increasing returns to scale, then the costs will increase less than linearly with respect to output, so the average costs will be declining in output: as output increases, the average costs of production will tend to fall.

Similarly, if the technology exhibits decreasing returns to scale, then average costs will be rising as output increases.

As we remarked earlier, a given technology can have regions of increasing, constant, or decreasing returns to scale—output can increase more rapidly, equally rapidly, or less rapidly than the scale of operation of the firm. Similarly, the cost function can increase less rapidly, equally rapidly, or more rapidly than output. This implies that the average cost function may decrease, remain constant, or increase over different levels of output. In the next chapter we will explore these possibilities in more detail.

From now on we will be most concerned with the behavior of the cost function with respect to the output variable. For the most part we will regard the factor prices as being fixed at some predetermined levels and only think of costs as depending on the output choice of the firm. Thus for the remainder of the book we will write the cost function as a function of output alone: $c(y)$.

20.4 Long-Run and Short-Run Costs

The cost function is defined as the minimum cost of achieving a given level of output. Often it is important to distinguish the minimum costs if the firm is allowed to adjust all of its factors of production from the minimum costs if the firm is only allowed to adjust some its factors.

We have defined the short run to be a time period where some of the factors of production must be used in a fixed amount. In the long run, all factors are free to vary. The **short-run cost function** is defined as the minimum cost to produce a given level of output, only adjusting the variable factors of production. The **long-run cost function** gives the minimum cost of producing a given level of output, adjusting *all* of the factors of production.

Suppose that in the short run factor 2 is fixed at some predetermined level $\overline{x}_2$, but in the long run it is free to vary. Then the short-run cost function is defined by

$$c_s(y, \overline{x}_2) = \min_{x_1} w_1 x_1 + w_2 \overline{x}_2$$

such that $f(x_1, \overline{x}_2) = y$.

Note that in general the minimum cost to produce y units of output in the short run will depend on the amount of the fixed factor that is available.

The short-run factor demand function for factor 1 is the amount of factor 1 that minimizes costs. In general it will depend on the factor prices and on the levels of the fixed factors as well, so we write the short-run factor demands as

$$x_1 = x_1^s(w_1, w_2, \overline{x}_2, y)$$
$$x_2 = \overline{x}_2.$$

These equations just say, for example, that if the building size is fixed in the short run, then the number of workers that a firm wants to hire at any given set of prices and output choice will typically depend on the size of the building.

Note that by definition of the short-run cost function

$$c_s(y, \overline{x}_2) = w_1 x_1(w_1, w_2, \overline{x}_2, y) + w_2 \overline{x}_2.$$

This just says that the minimum cost of producing output y is the cost associated with using the cost minimizing choice of inputs. This is true by definition, but turns out to be useful nevertheless.

The long-run cost function in this example is defined by

$$c(y) = \min_{x_1, x_2} w_1 x_1 + w_2 x_2$$

such that $f(x_1, x_2) = y$.

Here both factors are free to vary. Long-run costs depend only on the level of output that the firm wants to produce along with factor prices. We write the long-run cost function as $c(y)$, and write the long-run factor demands as

$$x_1 = x_1(w_1, w_2, y)$$
$$x_2 = x_2(w_1, w_2, y).$$

We can also write the long-run cost function as

$$c(y) = w_1 x_1(w_1, w_2, y) + w_2 x_2(w_1, w_2, y).$$

Just as before, this simply says that the minimum costs are the costs that the firm gets by using the cost minimizing choice of factors.

There is an interesting relation between the short-run and the long-run cost functions that we will use in the next chapter. For simplicity, let us suppose that factor prices are fixed at some predetermined levels, and write the long-run factor demands as

$$x_1 = x_1(y)$$
$$x_2 = x_2(y).$$

Then the long-run cost function can also be written as

$$c(y) = c_s(y, x_2(y)).$$

To see why this is true, just think about what it means. The equation says that the minimum costs when all factors are variable is just the minimum cost when factor 2 is fixed *at the level that minimizes long-run costs.* It follows that the long-run demand for the variable factor—the cost minimizing choice—is given by

$$x_1(w_1, w_2, y) = x_1^s(w_1, w_2, x_2(y), y).$$

This equation says that the cost minimizing amount of the variable factor in the long run is that amount that the firm would choose in the short run—if it happened to have the long-run cost minimizing amount of the fixed factor.

20.5 Fixed and Quasi-Fixed Costs

In Chapter 19 we made the distinction between fixed factors and quasi–fixed factors. Fixed factors are factors that must receive payment whether or not any output is produced. Quasi-fixed factors must be paid only if the firm decides to produce a positive amount of output.

It is natural to define fixed costs and quasi–fixed costs in a similar manner. **Fixed costs** are costs associated with the fixed factors: they are independent of the level of output, and, in particular, they must be paid whether or not the firm produces output. **Quasi-fixed costs** are costs that are also independent of the level of output, but only need to be paid if the firm produces a positive amount of output.

There are no fixed costs in the long run, by definition of the long run. However, there may easily be quasi-fixed costs in the long run. If it is necessary to spend a fixed amount of money before any output at all can be produced, then quasi-fixed costs will be present.

Summary

1. The cost function, $c(w_1, w_2, y)$, measures the minimum costs of producing a given level of output at given factor prices.

2. Cost minimizing behavior imposes certain observable restrictions on choices that firms make. In particular, conditional factor demand functions will be negatively sloped.

3. There is an intimate relationship between the returns to scale exhibited by the technology and the behavior of the cost function. *Increasing* returns to scale implies *decreasing* average cost, *decreasing* returns to scale implies *increasing* average cost, and *constant* returns to scale implies *constant* average cost.

Review Questions

1. Prove that a profit maximizing firm will always minimize costs.

2. If a firm is producing where $MP_1/w_1 > MP_2/w_2$, what can it do to reduce costs but maintain the same output?

3. Suppose that a cost minimizing firm uses two inputs that are perfect substitutes. If the two inputs are priced the same, what do the conditional factor demands look like for the inputs?

4. If a cost minimizing firm increases the use of one input while not changing the level of output or the amount of other inputs used, what does the theory of revealed cost minimization imply about this situation?

5. If a firm uses n inputs $(n > 2)$ what inequality does the theory of revealed cost minimization imply about changes in factor prices (Δw_i) and the changes in factor demands (Δx_i) for a given level of output?

APPENDIX

Let us study the cost minimization problem posed in the text using the optimization techniques introduced in Chapter 5. The problem is a constrained minimization problem of the form

$$\min_{x_1, x_2} w_1 x_1 + w_2 x_2$$

such that $f(x_1, x_2) = y$.

Recall that we had several techniques to solve this kind of problem. One way was to substitute the constraint into the objective function. This can still be used when we have a specific functional form for $f(x_1, x_2)$, but isn't much use in the general case.

The second method was the method of Lagrange multipliers and that works fine. To apply this method we set up the Lagrangian

$$L = w_1 x_1 + w_2 x_2 - \lambda(f(x_1, x_2) - y)$$

and differentiate with respect to x_1, x_2, and λ. This gives us the first-order conditions:

$$w_1 - \lambda \frac{\partial f(x_1, x_2)}{\partial x_1} = 0$$

$$w_2 - \lambda \frac{\partial f(x_1, x_2)}{\partial x_2} = 0$$

$$f(x_1, x_2) - y = 0.$$

The last condition is simply the constraint. We can rearrange the first two equations and divide the first equation by the second equation to get

$$\frac{w_1}{w_2} = \frac{\partial f(x_1, x_2)/\partial x_1}{\partial f(x_1, x_2)/\partial x_2}.$$

Note that this is the same first-order condition that we derived in the text: the technical rate of substitution must equal the factor price ratio.

Let's apply this method to the Cobb-Douglas production function:

$$f(x_1, x_2) = x_1^a x_2^b.$$

The cost minimization problem is then

$$\min_{x_1, x_2} w_1 x_1 + w_2 x_2$$

such that $x_1^a x_2^b = y$.

Here we have a specific functional form and we can solve it using either the substitution method or the Lagrangian method. The substitution method would involve first solving the constraint for x_2 as a function of x_1:

$$x_2 = \left(y x_1^{-a}\right)^{1/b}$$

and then substituting this into the objective function to get the unconstrained maximization problem

$$\min_{x_1} w_1 x_1 + w_2 \left(y x_1^{-a}\right)^{1/b}.$$

We could now differentiate with respect to x_1 and set resulting derivative equal to zero, as usual. The resulting equation can be solved to get x_1 as a function of w_1, w_2, and y, to get the conditional factor demand for x_1. This isn't hard to do but the algebra is messy, so we won't write down the details.

We will, however, solve the Lagrangian problem. The three first-order conditions are

$$w_1 = \lambda a x_1^{a-1} x_2^b$$
$$w_2 = \lambda b x_1^a x_2^{b-1}$$
$$x_1^a x_2^b - y = 0.$$

Multiply the first equation by x_1 and the second equation by x_2 to get

$$w_1 x_1 = \lambda a x_1^a x_2^b = \lambda a y$$

$$w_2 x_2 = \lambda b x_1^a x_2^b = \lambda b y$$

so that

$$x_1 = \lambda \frac{ay}{w_1} \tag{20.6}$$

$$x_2 = \lambda \frac{by}{w_2}. \tag{20.7}$$

Now we use the third equation to solve for λ. Substituting the solutions for x_1 and x_2 into the third first-order condition, we have

$$\left(\frac{\lambda ay}{w_1}\right)^a \left(\frac{\lambda by}{w_2}\right)^b = y.$$

We can solve this equation for λ to get the rather formidable expression

$$\lambda = (a^{-a}b^{-b}w_1^a w_2^b y^{1-a-b})^{\frac{1}{a+b}}$$

which, along with equations (20.6) and (20.7), gives us our final solutions for x_1 and x_2. These factor demand functions will take the form

$$x_1(w_1, w_2, y) = \left(\frac{a}{b}\right)^{\frac{b}{a+b}} w_1^{\frac{-b}{a+b}} w_2^{\frac{b}{a+b}} y^{\frac{1}{a+b}}$$

$$x_2(w_1, w_2, y) = \left(\frac{a}{b}\right)^{-\frac{a}{a+b}} w_1^{\frac{a}{a+b}} w_2^{\frac{-a}{a+b}} y^{\frac{1}{a+b}}.$$

The cost function can be found by writing down the costs when the firm makes the cost minimizing choices. That is:

$$c(w_1, w_2, y) = w_1 x_1(w_1, w_2, y) + w_2 x_2(w_1, w_2, y).$$

Some tedious algebra shows that

$$c(w_1, w_2, y) = \left[\left(\frac{a}{b}\right)^{\frac{b}{a+b}} + \left(\frac{a}{b}\right)^{\frac{-a}{a+b}}\right] w_1^{\frac{a}{a+b}} w_2^{\frac{b}{a+b}} y^{\frac{1}{a+b}}.$$

(Don't worry, this formula won't be on the final exam. It is presented only to demonstrate how to get an explicit solution to the cost minimization problem by applying the method of Lagrange multipliers.)

Note that costs will increase more than, equal to, or less than linearly with output as $a + b$ is less than, equal to, or greater than 1. This makes sense since the Cobb-Douglas technology exhibits decreasing, constant, or increasing returns to scale depending on the value of $a + b$.

21

COST
CURVES

In the last chapter we described the cost minimizing behavior of a firm. Here we continue that investigation through the use of an important geometric construction, the **cost curve**. Cost curves can be used to depict graphically the cost function of a firm and are important in studying the determination of optimal output choices.

21.1 Average Costs

Consider the cost function described in the last chapter. This is the function $c(w_1, w_2, y)$ that gives the minimum cost of producing output level y when factor prices are (w_1, w_2). In the rest of this chapter we will take the factor prices to be fixed so that we can write output as a function of y alone, $c(y)$.

Some of the costs of the firm are independent of the level of output of the firm. As we've seen in Chapter 20, these are the fixed costs. Fixed costs are the costs that must be paid regardless of what level of output the firm produces. For example, the firm might have mortgage payments that are required no matter what its level of output.

Other costs change when output changes: these are the variable costs. The total costs of the firm can always be written as the sum of the variable costs, $c_v(y)$, and the fixed costs, F:

$$c(y) = c_v(y) + F.$$

The **average cost function** measures the cost per unit of output. The **average variable cost function** measures the variable costs per unit of output, and the **average fixed cost function** measures the fixed costs per unit output. By the above equation:

$$AC(y) = \frac{c(y)}{y} = \frac{c_v(y)}{y} + \frac{F}{y} = AVC(y) + AFC(y)$$

where $AVC(y)$ stands for average variable costs and $AFC(y)$ stands for average fixed costs. What do these functions look like? The easiest one is certainly the average fixed cost function: when $y = 0$ it is infinite and as y gets larger and larger the average fixed costs approach 0. This is depicted in Figure 21.1A.

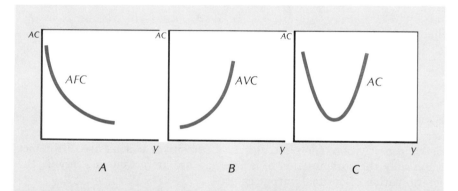

Figure 21.1

Construction of the average cost curve. The average fixed costs decrease as output is increased. The average variable costs eventually increase as output is increased. The combination of these two effects produces a U-shaped average cost curve.

Consider the variable cost function. Start at a zero level of output and consider producing one unit. Then the average variable costs at $y = 1$ is just the cost of producing this one unit. Now increase the level of production to 2 units. We would expect that, at worst, variable costs would double, so that average variable costs would remain constant. If we can organize production in a more efficient way as the scale of output is increased, the average variable costs might even decrease initially. But eventually we would expect the average variable costs to rise. Why? If fixed factors are present, they will eventually constrain the production process.

For example, suppose that the fixed costs are due to the rent or mortgage payments on a building of fixed size. Then as production increases, average variable costs—the per unit production costs—may remain constant for a while. But as the capacity of the building is reached, these costs will rise sharply, producing an average variable cost curve of the form depicted in Figure 21.1B.

The average cost curve is the sum of these two curves; thus it will have the U shape indicated in Figure 21.1C. The initial decline in average costs is due to the decline in average fixed costs; the eventual increase in average costs is due to the increase in average variable costs. The combination of these two effects yields the U shape depicted in the diagram.

21.2 Marginal Costs

There is one more cost curve of interest: the **marginal cost curve**. The marginal cost curve measures the *change* in costs for a given change in output. That is, at any given level of output y, we can ask how costs will change if we change output by some amount Δy:

$$MC(y) = \frac{\Delta c(y)}{\Delta y} = \frac{c(y + \Delta y) - c(y)}{\Delta y}.$$

We could just as well write the definition of marginal costs in terms of the variable cost function:

$$MC(y) = \frac{\Delta c_v(y)}{\Delta y} = \frac{c_v(y + \Delta y) - c_v(y)}{\Delta y}.$$

This is equivalent to the first definition, since $c(y) = c_v(y) + F$ and the fixed costs, F, don't change as y changes.

Often we think of Δy as being one unit of output, so that marginal cost indicates the change in our costs if we consider producing another unit of output. This is convenient for discussion, but is sometimes misleading. Remember, marginal cost measures a *rate of change*: the change in costs divided by a change in output.

How can we put this marginal cost curve on the diagram presented above? First we note the following. The variable costs are zero when zero units of output are produced, by definition. Thus for the first Δy units of output produced

$$MC(\Delta y) = \frac{c_v(\Delta y) + F - c_v(0) - F}{\Delta y} = c_v(\Delta y)/\Delta y = AVC(\Delta y).$$

Thus the marginal cost for the first small amount of output equals the average variable cost for that output.

Now suppose that we are producing in a range of output where *average* variable costs are decreasing. Then it must be that the *marginal* costs are less than the average variable costs in this range. For the way that you push an average down is to add in numbers that are less than the average.

Think about a sequence of numbers representing average costs at different levels of output. If the average is decreasing, it must be that the cost of each additional unit produced is less than average up to that point. To make the average go down, you have to be adding additional units that are less than the average.

Similarly, if we are in a region where average variable costs are rising, then it must be the case that the marginal costs are greater than the average variable costs—it is the high marginal costs that are pushing the average up.

Thus we know that the marginal cost curve must lie below the average variable cost curve to the left of its minimum point and above it to the right. This implies that the marginal cost curve must intersect the average variable cost curve at its minimum point.

Exactly the same kind of argument applies for the average cost curve. If average costs are falling, then it must be that the marginal costs are less than the average costs, and if average costs are rising it must be the high marginal costs that are pushing average costs up. These observations allow us to draw in the marginal cost curve as in Figure 21.2.

To review the important points:

• The average variable cost curve may initially slope down, but need not. However, it will eventually rise, as long as there are any fixed factors.

• The average cost curve will initially fall due to declining fixed costs but then rise due to the increasing average variable costs.

• The marginal cost and average variable cost are the same at the first unit of output.

• The marginal cost curve passes through the minimum point of both the average variable cost and the average cost curves.

21.3 Marginal Costs and Variable Costs

There are also some other relationships between the various curves. Here is one that is not so obvious: it turns out that the area beneath the marginal cost curve up to y gives us the variable cost of producing y units of output. Why is that?

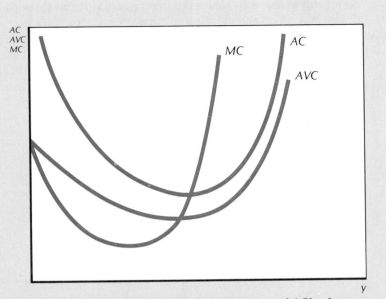

Cost curves. Here are the average cost curve (AC), the average variable cost curve (AVC), and the marginal cost curve (MC).

Figure
21.2

Think about it. The marginal cost curve measures the cost of producing each additional unit of output. If we add up the cost of producing each unit of output we will get the total costs of production—except for fixed costs.

More rigorously we can note that

$$c_v(y) = [c_v(y) - c_v(y - \Delta y)] + [c_v(y - \Delta y) - c_v(y - 2\Delta y)] +$$
$$\ldots + [c_v(\Delta y) - c_v(0)]$$

since $c_v(0) = 0$ and all the middle terms cancel out; that is, the second term cancels the third term, the fourth term cancels the fifth term, and so on. Now multiply each term of this sum by $\Delta y / \Delta y$ to get

$$c_v(y) = \frac{c_v(y) - c_v(y - \Delta y)}{\Delta y} \Delta y + \frac{c_v(y - \Delta y) - c_v(y - 2\Delta y)}{\Delta y} \Delta y + \ldots$$
$$+ \frac{c_v(\Delta y) - c_v(0)}{\Delta y} \Delta y.$$

Each term in this sum is the marginal cost at a different level of output times Δy. That is:

$$c_v(y) = MC(y)\Delta y + MC(y - \Delta y)\Delta y + \ldots + MC(0)\Delta y.$$

Thus each term in the sum represents the area of a rectangle with height $MC(y)$ and base Δy. Summing up all these rectangles gives us the area under the marginal cost curve as depicted in Figure 21.3.

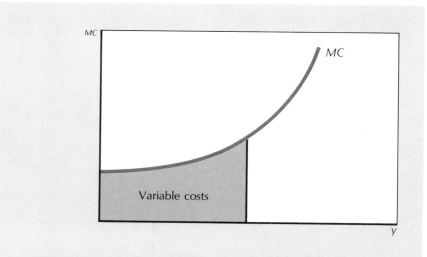

Figure
21.3

Marginal cost and average variable costs. The area under the marginal cost curve gives the variable costs.

EXAMPLE: Specific Cost Curves

Let's consider the cost function $c(y) = y^2 + 1$. We have the following derived cost curves:

- variable costs: $c_v(y) = y^2$

- fixed costs: $c_f(y) = 1$

- average variable costs: $AVC(y) = y^2/y = y$

- average fixed costs: $AFC(y) = 1/y$

- average costs: $AC(y) = \dfrac{y^2 + 1}{y} = y + \dfrac{1}{y}$

- marginal costs: $MC(y) = 2y$.

These are all obvious except for the last one, which is also obvious if you know calculus. If the cost function is $c(y) = y^2 + F$, then the marginal cost function is given by $MC(y) = 2y$. If you don't know this fact already, memorize it, since you'll use it in the exercises.

What do these cost curves look like? The easiest way to draw them is first to draw the average variable cost curve, which is a straight line with slope 1. Then it is also simple to draw the marginal cost curve, which is a straight line with slope 2.

The average cost curve reaches its minimum where average cost equals marginal cost, which says

$$y + \frac{1}{y} = 2y$$

which can be solved to give $y_{\min} = 1$. The average cost at $y = 1$ is 2, which is also the marginal cost. The final picture is given in Figure 21.4.

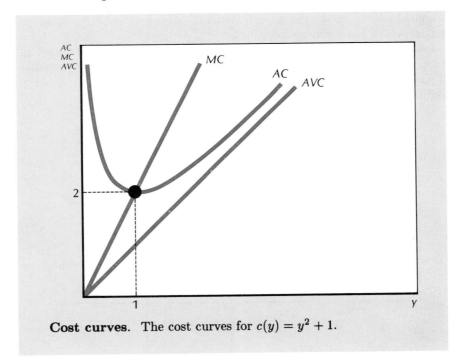

Cost curves. The cost curves for $c(y) = y^2 + 1$.

Figure
21.4

EXAMPLE: Marginal Cost Curves for Two Plants

Suppose that you have two plants that have two different cost functions, $c_1(y_1)$ and $c_2(y_2)$. You want to produce y units of output in the cheapest way. In general, you will want to produce some amount of output in each plant. The question is, how much should you produce in each plant?

Set up the minimization problem:

$$\min_{y_1, y_2} c_1(y_1) + c_2(y_2)$$

such that $y_1 + y_2 = y$.

Now how do you solve it? It turns out that at the optimal division of output between the two plants we must have the marginal cost of producing output at plant 1 equal to the marginal cost of producing output at plant 2. In order to prove this, suppose the marginal costs were not equal; then it would pay to shift a small amount of output from the plant with higher marginal costs to the plant with lower marginal costs. If the output division is optimal, then switching output from one plant to the other can't lower costs.

Let $c(y)$ be the cost function that gives the cheapest way to produce y units of output—that is, the cost of producing y units of output given that you have divided output in the best way between the two plants. The marginal cost of producing an extra unit of output must be the same no matter which plant you produce it in.

Let us depict the two marginal cost curves $MC_1(y_1)$ and $MC_2(y_2)$ in Figure 21.5. The marginal cost curve for the two plants taken together is just the horizontal sum of the two marginal cost curves, as depicted in Figure 21.5C.

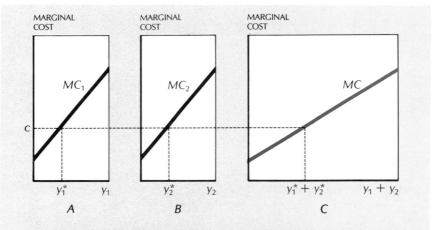

Figure 21.5

Marginal costs for a firm with two plants. The overall marginal cost curve on the right is the horizontal sum of the marginal cost curves for the two plants shown on the left.

For any fixed level of marginal costs, say c, we will produce y_1^* and y_2^* such that $MC_1(y_1^*) = MC(y_2^*) = c$ and we will thus have $y_1^* + y_2^*$ units of output produced. Thus the amount of output produced at any marginal cost c is just the sum of the outputs where the marginal costs of firm 1 equals c and the marginal costs of firm 2 equals c: the horizontal sum of the marginal costs.

21.4 Long-Run Costs

In the above analysis, we have described the firm's fixed costs as being the costs that involve payments to factors that it is unable to adjust in the short run. In the long run a firm can choose the level of its "fixed" factors—they are no longer fixed.

Of course there may still be quasi-fixed factors in the long run. That is, it may be a feature of the technology that some costs have to be paid to produce any positive level of output. But in the long run there are no fixed costs, in the sense that it is always possible to produce zero units of output at zero costs—that is, it is always possible to go out of business. If quasi-fixed factors are present in the long run, then the average cost curve will tend to have a U-shape, just as in the short run. But in the long run it will always be possible to produce zero units of output at a zero cost, by definition of the long run.

Of course, what constitutes the long run depends on the problem we are analyzing. If we are considering the fixed factor to be the size of the plant, then the long run will be how long it would take the firm to change the size of its plant. If we are considering the fixed factor to be the contractual obligations to pay salaries, then the long run would be how long it would take the firm to change the size of its work force.

Just to be specific, let's think of the fixed factor as being plant size and denote it by k. The firm's short-run cost function, given that it has a plant of k square feet, will be denoted by $c_s(y, k)$, where the s subscript stands for "short run." (Here k is playing the role of $\bar{x}_2$ in Chapter 20.)

For any given level of output, there will be some plant size that is the optimal size to produce that level of output. Let us denote this plant size by $k(y)$. This is the firm's conditional factor demand for plant size as a function of output. (Of course it also depends on the prices of plant size and other factors of production, but we have suppressed these arguments.) Then, as we've seen in Chapter 20, the long-run cost function of the firm will be given by $c_s(y, k(y))$. This is the total cost of producing an output level y, given that the firm is allowed to adjust its plant size optimally. The long-run cost function of the firm is just the short-run cost function evaluated at the optimal choice of the fixed factors:

$$c(y) = c_s(y, k(y)).$$

Let us see how this looks graphically. Pick some level of output y^*, and let $k^* = k(y^*)$ be the optimal plant size for that level of output. The short-run cost function for a plant of size k^* will be given by $c_s(y, k^*)$, and the long-run cost function will be given by $c(y) = c_s(y, k(y))$, just as above.

Now, note the important fact that the short-run cost to produce output y must always be at least as large as the long-run cost to produce y. Why? In the short run the firm has a fixed plant size, while in the long run the firm is free to adjust its plant size. Since one of its long-run choices is always to choose the plant size k^*, its optimal choice to produce y units of output must have costs at least as small as $c(y, k^*)$. This means that the firm must be able to do at least as well by adjusting plant size as by having it fixed. Thus

$$c(y) \le c_s(y, k^*)$$

for all levels of y.

In fact, at one particular level of y, namely y^*, we know that

$$c(y^*) = c_s(y^*, k^*).$$

Why? Because at y^* the *optimal* choice of plant size is k^*. So at y^*, the long-run costs and the short-run costs are the same.

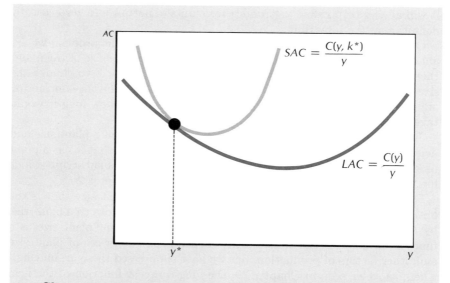

Figure
21.6

Short-run and long-run average costs. The short-run average cost curve must be tangent to the long-run average cost curve.

If the short-run cost is always greater than the long-run cost and they are equal at one level of output, then this means that the short-run and the long-run average costs have the same property:

$$AC(y) \le AC_s(y, k^*)$$

and

$$AC(y^*) = AC_s(y^*, k^*).$$

This implies that the short-run average cost curve always lies above the long-run average cost curve and that they touch at one point, y^*. Thus the long-run average cost curve (LAC) and the short-run average cost curve (SAC) must be tangent at that point, as depicted in Figure 21.6.

We can do the same sort of construction for levels of output other than y^*. Suppose we pick outputs $y_1, y_2, \ldots, y_n$ and associated plant sizes $k_1 = k(y_1), k_2 = k(y_2), \ldots, k_n = k(y_n)$. Then we get a picture like that in Figure 21.7. We summarize Figure 21.7 by saying that the long-run average cost curve is the **lower envelope** of the short-run average cost curves.

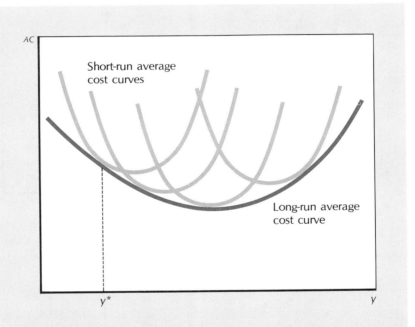

Short-run and long-run average costs. The long-run average cost curve is the envelope of the short-run average cost curve.

Figure
21.7

21.5 Discrete Levels of Plant Size

In the above discussion we have implicitly assumed that we can choose a continuous number of different plant sizes. Thus each different level of output has a unique optimal plant size associated with it. But we can also consider what happens if there are only a few different levels of plant size to choose from.

Suppose, for example, that we have only three different choices, k_1, k_2, and k_3. We can draw the three different average cost curves associated with these plant sizes as in Figure 21.8.

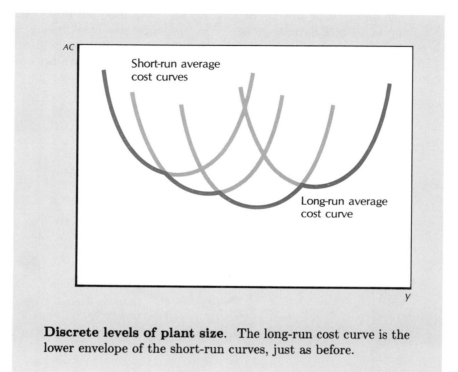

Figure 21.8

Discrete levels of plant size. The long-run cost curve is the lower envelope of the short-run curves, just as before.

How can we construct the long-run average cost curve? Well, remember the long-run average cost curve is the cost curve you get by adjusting k optimally. In this case that isn't hard to do: since there are only three different plant sizes, we just see which one has the lowest costs associated with it and pick that plant size. That is, for any level of output y, we just choose the plant size that gives us the minimum cost of producing that output level.

Thus the long-run average cost curve will be the lower envelope of the short-run average costs, as depicted in Figure 21.8. Note that this figure has qualitatively the same implications as Figure 21.7: the short-run average costs always are at least as large as the long-run average costs and they are the same at the level of output where the long-run demand for the fixed factor equals the amount of the fixed factor that you have.

21.6 Long-Run Marginal Costs

We've seen in the last section that the long-run average cost curve is the lower envelope of the short-run average cost curves. What are the implications of this for marginal costs? Let's first consider the case where there are discrete levels of plant size. In this situation the long-run marginal cost curve consists of the appropriate pieces of the short-run marginal cost curves, as depicted in Figure 21.9. For each level of output, we see which short-run average cost curve we are operating on and then look at the marginal cost associated with that curve.

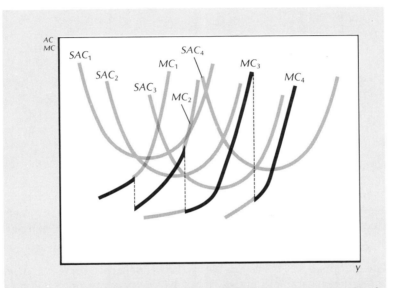

Long-run marginal costs. When there are discrete levels of the fixed factor, the firm will choose the amount of the fixed factor to minimize average costs. Thus the long-run marginal cost curve will consist of the various segments of the short-run marginal cost curves associated with each different level of the fixed factor.

Figure
21.9

This has to hold true no matter how many different plant sizes there are, so the picture for the continuous case looks like Figure 21.10. The long-run marginal cost at any output level y has to equal the short-run marginal cost associated with the optimal level of plant size to produce y.

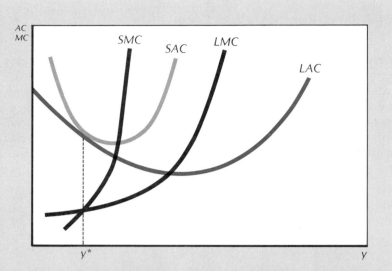

Figure
21.10

Long-run marginal costs. The relationship between the long-run and the short-run marginal costs with continuous levels of the fixed factor.

Summary

1. Average costs are composed of average variable costs plus average fixed costs. Average fixed costs always decline with output, while average variable costs tend to increase. The net result is a U-shaped average cost curve.

2. The marginal cost curve lies below the average cost curve when average costs are decreasing, and above when they are increasing. Thus marginal costs must equal average costs at the point of minimum average costs.

3. The area under the marginal cost curve measures the variable costs.

4. The long-run average cost curve is the lower envelope of the short-run average cost curves.

Review Questions

1. Which of the following are true? (1) Average fixed costs never increase with output; (2) average total costs are always greater than or equal to average variable costs; (3) average cost can never rise while marginal costs are declining.

2. A firm produces identical outputs at two different plants. If the marginal cost at the first plant exceeds the marginal cost at the second plant, how can the firm reduce costs and maintain the same level of output?

3. True or false? In the long run a firm always operates at the minimum level of average costs for the optimally sized plant to produce a given amount of output.

APPENDIX

In the text we claimed that average variable cost equals marginal cost for the first unit of output. In calculus terms this translates to

$$\lim_{y \to 0} \frac{c_v(y)}{y} = \lim_{y \to 0} c'(y).$$

The left-hand side of this expression is not defined at $y = 0$. But its limit is defined, and we can compute it using l'Hôpital's rule, which states that the limit of a fraction whose numerator and denominator both approach zero is given by the limit of the derivatives of the numerator and the denominator. Applying this rule, we have

$$\lim_{y \to 0} \frac{c_v(y)}{y} = \frac{\lim_{y \to 0} dc_v(y)/dy}{\lim_{y \to 0} dy/dy} = \frac{c'(0)}{1}$$

which establishes the claim.

We also claimed that the area under the marginal cost curve gave us variable cost. This is easy to show using the fundamental theorem of calculus. Since

$$MC(y) = \frac{dc_v(y)}{dy}$$

we know that the area under the marginal cost curve is

$$c_v(y) = \int_0^y \frac{dc_v(x)}{dx} \, dx = c_v(y) - c_v(0) = c_v(y).$$

The discussion of long-run and short-run marginal cost curves is all pretty clear geometrically, but what does it mean economically? It turns out that the calculus argument gives the nicest intuition. The argument is simple. The marginal cost of production is just the change in cost that arises from changing output. In the short run we have to keep plant size (or whatever) fixed, while in the long-run we are free to adjust it. So the long-run marginal cost will consist of two pieces: how marginal costs change holding plant size fixed plus how marginal costs change when plant size adjusts. But if the plant size is chosen optimally, this last term has to be zero! Thus the long-run and the short-run marginal costs have to be the same.

The mathematical proof involves the chain rule. Using the definition from the text:

$$c(y) \equiv c_s(y, k(y)).$$

Differentiating with respect to y gives

$$\frac{dc(y)}{dy} = \frac{\partial c_s(y, k)}{\partial y} + \frac{\partial c_s(y, k)}{\partial k}\frac{\partial k(y)}{\partial y}.$$

If we evaluate this at a specific level of output y^* and its associated optimal plant size $k^* = k(y^*)$ we know that

$$\frac{\partial c_s(y^*, k^*)}{\partial k} = 0$$

because that is the necessary first-order condition for k^* to be the cost minimizing plant size at y^*. Thus the second term in the expression cancels out and all that we have left is the short-run marginal cost:

$$\frac{dc(y^*)}{dy} = \frac{\partial c_s(y^*, k^*)}{\partial y}.$$

FIRM
SUPPLY

In this chapter we will see how to derive the supply curve of a competitive firm from its cost function using the model of profit maximization. The first thing we have to do is to describe the market environment in which the firm operates.

22.1 Market Environments

Every firm faces two important decisions: choosing how much it should produce, and choosing what price it should set. If there were no constraints on a profit maximizing firm, it would set an arbitrarily high price and produce an arbitrarily large amount of output. But no firm exists in such an unconstrained environment. In general the firm faces two sorts of constraints on its actions.

First, it faces the **technological constraints** summarized by the production function. There are only certain feasible combinations of inputs and outputs, and even the most profit hungry firm has to respect the realities of the physical world. We have already discussed how we can summarize the technological constraints, and we've seen how the technological constraints lead to the **economic constraints** summarized by the cost function.

But now we bring in a new constraint—or at least an old constraint from a different perspective. This is the **market constraint**. A firm can produce whatever is physically feasible, and it can set whatever price it wants ... but it can only sell as much as people are willing to buy.

If it sets a certain price p it will sell a certain amount of output x. We call the relationship between the price a firm sets and the amount that it sells *the demand curve facing the firm.*

If there were only one firm in the market, the demand curve facing the firm is very simple to describe: it is just the market demand curve described in earlier chapters on consumer behavior. For the market demand curve measures how much of the good people want to buy at each price. Thus the demand curve summarizes the market constraints facing a firm that has a market all to itself.

But if there are other firms in the market, the constraints facing the firm will be different. In this case, the firm has to guess how the *other* firms in the market will behave when it chooses its price and output.

This is not an easy problem to solve, either for firms or for economists. There are a lot of different possibilities, and we will try to examine them in a systematic way. We'll use the term **market environment** to describe the ways that firms respond to each other when they make their pricing and output decisions.

In this chapter we'll examine the simplest market environment, that of **pure competition**. This is a good comparison point for many other environments and it is of considerable interest in its own right. First let's give the economist's definition of pure competition, and then we'll try to justify it.

22.2 Pure Competition

To a lay person, "competition" has the connotation of intense rivalry. That's why students are often surprised that the economist's definition of competition seems so passive: we say that a market is **purely competitive** if each firm assumes that the market price is independent of its own level of output. Thus, in a competitive market, each firm only has to worry about how much output it wants to produce. Whatever it produces can only be sold at one price: the going market price.

In what sort of environment might this be a reasonable assumption for a firm to make? Well, suppose that we have an industry composed of many firms that produce an identical product, and that each firm is a small part of the market. A good example would be the market for wheat. There are thousands of wheat farmers in the U.S., and even the largest of them produces only an infinitesimal fraction of the total. It is reasonable in this case for any one firm in the industry to take the market price as being predetermined. A wheat farmer doesn't have to worry about what price to set for his wheat—if he wants to sell any at all, he has to sell it at the market price. He is a **price-taker**: the price is given as far as he is concerned; all he has to worry about is how much to produce.

This kind of situation—an identical product and many small firms—is a classic example of a situation where price taking behavior is sensible. But it is not the only case where price taking behavior is possible. Even if there are only a few firms in the market, they may still treat the market price as being outside their control.

Think of a case where there is a fixed supply of a perishable good: say fresh fish or cut flowers in a marketplace. Even if there are only 3 or 4 firms in the market, each firm may have to take the *other* firms' prices as given. If the customers in the market only buy at the lowest price, then the lowest price being offered is the market price. If one of the other firms wants to sell anything at all, it will have to sell at the market price. So in this sort of situation competitive behavior—taking the market price as outside of your control—seems plausible as well.

We can describe the relationship between price and quantity perceived by a competitive firm in terms of a diagram as in Figure 22.1. As you can see, this demand curve is very simple. A competitive firm believes that it will sell nothing if it charges a price higher than the market price. If it sells at the market price, it can sell whatever amount it wants, and if it sells below the market price, it will get the entire market demand at that price.

As usual we can think of this kind of demand curve in two ways. If we think of quantity as a function of price, this curve says that you can sell any amount you want at or below the market price. If we think of price as a function of quantity, it says that no matter how much you sell, the market price will be independent of your sales.

(Of course, this doesn't have to be true for literally *any* amount. Price has to be independent of your output for any amount you might consider selling. In the case of the cut flower seller, the price has to be independent of how much she sells for any amount up to her stock on hand—the maximum that she could consider selling.)

It is important to understand the difference between the "demand curve facing a firm" and the "market demand curve." The market demand curve measures the relationship between the market price and the total amount of output sold. The demand curve facing a firm measures the relationship between the market price and the output of *that particular firm*.

The market demand curve depends on consumers' behavior. The demand curve facing a firm not only depends on consumers' behavior, but it also depends on the behavior of the other firms. The usual justification for the competitive model is that when there are many small firms in the market, each one faces a demand curve that is essentially flat. But even if there are only two firms in the market, and one insists on charging a fixed price no matter what, then the other firm in the market will face a competitive demand curve like the one depicted in Figure 22.1. Thus the competitive model may hold in a wider variety of circumstances than is apparent at first glance.

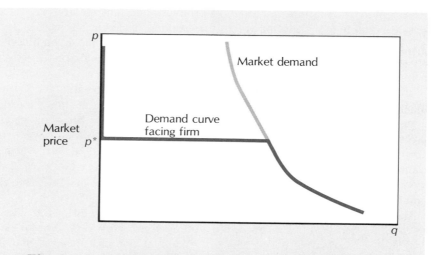

Figure 22.1   **The demand curve facing a competitive firm.** The firm's demand is horizontal at the market price. At higher prices, the firm sells nothing, and below the market price it faces the entire market demand curve.

22.3 The Supply Decision of a Competitive Firm

Let us use the facts we have discovered about cost curves to figure out the supply curve of a competitive firm. By definition a competitive firm ignores its influence on the market price. Thus the maximization problem facing a competitive firm is

$$\max_{y} py - c(y).$$

This just says that the competitive firm wants to maximize its profits: the difference between its revenue, py, and its costs, $c(y)$.

What level of output will a competitive firm choose to produce? Answer: it will operate where marginal revenue equals marginal cost—where the extra revenue gained by one more unit of output just equals the extra cost of producing another unit. If this condition did not hold the firm could always increase its profits by changing its level of output.

In the case of a competitive firm, marginal revenue is simply the price. To see this, ask how much extra revenue a competitive firm gets when it increases its output by Δy. We have

$$\Delta R = p\Delta y$$

since by hypothesis p doesn't change. Thus the extra revenue per unit of output is given by

$$\frac{\Delta R}{\Delta y} = p$$

which is the expression for marginal revenue.

Thus a competitive firm will choose a level of output y where the marginal cost that it faces at y is just equal to the market price. In symbols:

$$p = MC(y).$$

For a given market price, p, we want to find the level of output where profits are maximal. If price is greater than marginal cost at some level of output y, then the firm can increase its profits by producing a little more output. For price greater than marginal costs means

$$p - \frac{\Delta c}{\Delta y} > 0.$$

So increasing output by Δy means that

$$p\Delta y - \frac{\Delta c}{\Delta y}\Delta y > 0.$$

Simplifying we find that

$$p\Delta y - \Delta c > 0$$

which means that the increase in revenues from the extra output exceeds the increase in costs. Thus profits must increase.

A similar argument can be made when price is less than marginal cost. Then reducing output will increase profits, since the lost revenues are more than compensated for by the reduced costs.

So at the optimal level of output, a firm must be producing where price equals marginal costs. Whatever the level of the market price p, the firm will choose a level of output y where $p = MC(y)$. Thus the marginal cost curve of a competitive firm is precisely its supply curve. Or put another way, the market price is precisely marginal cost—as long as each firm is producing at its profit maximizing level.

22.4 An Exception

Well ... maybe not *precisely*. There are two troublesome cases. The first case is when there are several levels of output where price equals marginal cost, such as the case depicted in Figure 22.2. Here there are two levels of output where price equals marginal cost. Which one will the firm choose?

It is not hard to see the answer. Consider the first intersection, where the marginal cost curve is sloping down. Now if we increase output a little bit here, the costs of each additional unit of output will decrease. That's what it means to say that the marginal cost curve is decreasing. But the market price will stay the same. Thus profits must definitely go up.

So we can rule out levels of output where the marginal cost curve slopes downward. At those points an increase in output must always increase profits. The supply curve of a competitive firm must lie along the upward sloping part of the marginal cost curve. This means that the supply curve itself must always be upward sloping. The "Giffen good" phenomenon cannot arise for supply curves.

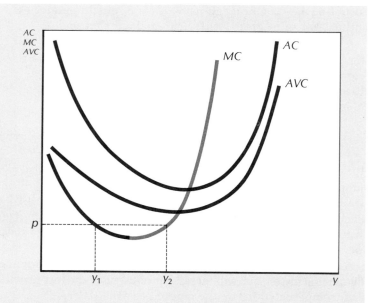

Figure
22.2

Marginal cost and supply. Although there are two levels of output where price equals marginal cost, the profit maximizing quantity supplied can lie only on the upward sloping part of the marginal cost curve.

Price equals marginal cost is a *necessary* condition for profit maximization. It is not in general a *sufficient* condition. Just because we find a point where price equals marginal cost doesn't mean that we've found the maximum profit point. But if we find the maximum profit point, we know that price must equal marginal cost.

22.5 Another Exception

This discussion is assuming that it is profitable to produce something. After all it could be that the best thing for a firm to do is to produce zero output. Since it is always possible to produce a zero level of output, we have to compare our candidate for profit maximization with the choice of doing nothing at all.

If a firm produces zero output it still has to pay its fixed costs, F. Thus the profits from producing zero units of output are just $-F$. The profits from producing a level of output y are $py - c_v(y) - F$. The firm is better off going out of business when

$$-F > py - c_v(y) - F$$

that is when the profits from producing nothing, and just paying the fixed costs, exceed the profits from producing where price equals marginal cost. Rearranging this equation gives us the **shutdown condition:**

$$AVC(y) = \frac{c_v(y)}{y} > p.$$

If average variable costs are greater than p, the firm would be better off producing zero units of output. This makes good sense, since it says that the revenues from selling the output y don't even cover the *variable* costs of production, $c_v(y)$. In this case the firm might as well go out of business. It would lose its fixed costs, but it would lose even more if it continued to produce.

This discussion indicates that only the portions of the marginal cost curve that lie above the average variable cost curve are possible points on the supply curve. If a point where price equals marginal cost is beneath the average variable cost curve, the firm would optimally choose to produce zero units of output.

We now have a picture for the supply curve like that in Figure 22.3. The competitive firm produces along the part of the marginal cost curve that is upward sloping and lies above the average variable cost curve.

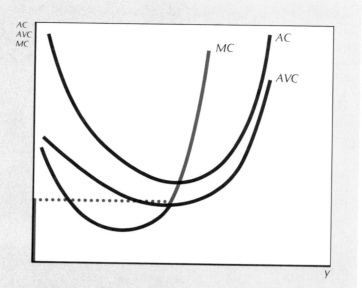

Figure
22.3
Average variable cost and supply. The supply curve is the upward sloping part of the marginal cost curve that lies above the average variable cost curve. The firm will not operate on those points on the marginal cost curve below the average cost curve since it could have greater profits (less losses) by shutting down.

22.6 The Inverse Supply Curve

We have seen that the supply curve of a competitive firm is determined by the condition that price equals marginal cost. As before we can express this relation between price and output in two ways: we can either think of output as a function of price, as we usually do, or we can think of the "inverse supply curve" that gives price as a function of output. There is a certain insight to be had by looking at it in the latter way. Since price equals marginal cost at each point on the supply curve, the market price must be a measure of marginal cost for every firm operating in the industry. A firm that produces a lot of output and a firm that produces only a little output must have the *same* marginal cost, if they are both maximizing profits. The total cost picture of each firm can be very different, but the marginal cost picture must be the same.

The equation $p = MC(y)$ gives us the inverse supply curve directly: price as a function of output. This way of expressing the supply curve can be very useful.

22.7 Profits and Producer's Surplus

Given the market price we can now compute the optimal operating position for the firm from the condition that $p = MC(y)$. Given the optimal operating position we can compute the profits of the firm. In Figure 22.4 the area of the box is just p^*y^*, or total revenue. The area $y^*AC(y^*)$ is total costs since

$$yAC(y) = y\frac{c(y)}{y} = c(y).$$

Profits are simply the difference between these two areas.

Recall our discussion of **producer's surplus** in Chapter 17. We defined producer's surplus to be the area to the left of the supply curve, in analogy to consumer's surplus which was the area to the left of the demand curve. It turns out that producer's surplus is closely related to the profits of a firm. More precisely, producer's surplus is equal to revenues minus variable costs, or equivalently, profits plus the fixed costs:

profits $= py - c_v(y) - F$

producer's surplus $= py - c_v(y).$

We can measure producer's surplus by looking at the difference between the revenue box and the box $y^*AVC(y^*)$, as in Figure 22.5. But there is a

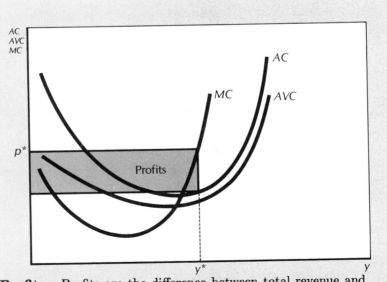

Profits.   Profits are the difference between total revenue and total costs, as shown by the colored rectangle.

Figure
22.4

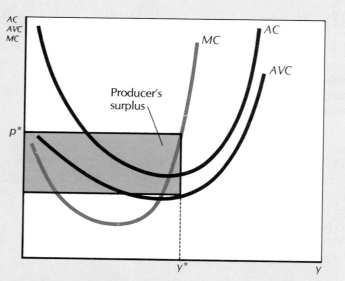

Figure
22.5

Producer's surplus. Producer's surplus is the difference between revenue and variable costs, as show by the colored rectangle.

more useful way to measure producer's surplus by using the marginal cost curve itself.

We know from Chapter 20 that the area under the marginal cost curve measures the total variable costs. This is true because the area under the marginal cost curve is the cost of producing the first unit plus the cost of producing the second unit, and so on. So to get producer's surplus, we can subtract the area under the marginal cost curve from the revenue box and get the area depicted in Figure 22.6. Hence producer's surplus is given by the area to the left of the marginal cost curve. But since the supply curve of the firm coincides with the upward sloping part of the marginal cost curve, the area to the left of the marginal cost curve will generally be the same as the area to the left of the supply curve. This argument justifies the original definition of producer surplus, at least when the marginal cost curve is upward sloping at all levels of output.

We are seldom interested in the *total* amount of producer's surplus; more often it is the *change* in producer's surplus that is of interest. The change in producer's surplus when the firm moves from output y^* to output y' will generally be a trapezoidal shaped region like that depicted in Figure 22.7.

Note that the change in producer's surplus in moving from y^* to y' is just the change in profits in moving from y^* to y', since by definition the fixed costs don't change. Thus we can measure the impact on profits of

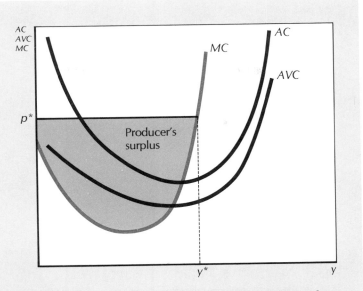

Producer's surplus and marginal cost. Producer's surplus can also be measured by the revenue box minus the area beneath the marginal cost curve.

Figure
22.6

a change in output from the information contained in the marginal cost curve, without having to refer to the average cost curve at all.

EXAMPLE: The Supply Curve for a Specific Cost Function

What does the supply curve look like for the example given in the last chapter where $c(y) = y^2 + 1$? In that example the marginal cost curve was always above the average cost curve, and it always sloped upwards. So "price equals marginal costs" gives us the supply curve directly. Substituting $2y$ for marginal cost we get the formula

$$p = 2y.$$

This gives us the inverse supply curve, or price as a function of output. Solving for output as a function of price we have

$$S(p) = y = \frac{p}{2}$$

as our formula for the supply curve. This is depicted in Figure 22.8.

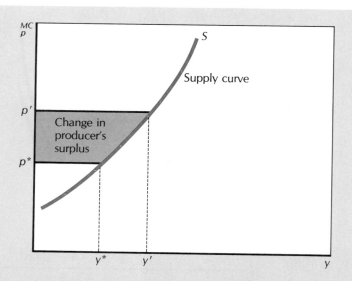

Figure
22.7

The change in producer's surplus. Since the supply curve coincides with the upward sloping part of the marginal cost curve, the change in producer's surplus will typically have a roughly trapezoidal shape.

If we substitute this supply function into the definition of profits we can calculate the maximum profits for each price p. Performing the calculation we have:

$$\pi(p) = py - c(y)$$
$$= p\frac{p}{2} - \left(\frac{p}{2}\right)^2 - 1$$
$$= \frac{p^2}{4} - 1.$$

How do the maximum profits relate to producer's surplus? In Figure 22.8 we see that producer's surplus—the area to the left of the supply curve—will be a triangle with a base of $y = p/2$ and a height of p. The area of this triangle is

$$A = \left(\frac{1}{2}\right)\left(\frac{p}{2}\right)p = \frac{p^2}{4}.$$

Comparing this with the profits expression, we see that producer's surplus equals profits plus fixed costs, as claimed.

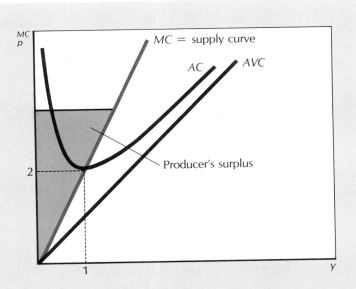

A specific example of a supply curve. The supply curve and producer's surplus for the cost function $c(y) = y^2 + 1$.

Figure 22.8

22.8 The Long-Run Supply Curve of a Firm

The long-run supply function for the firm measures how much the firm would optimally produce when it is allowed to adjust plant size (or whatever factors are fixed in the short run). That is, the long-run supply curve will be given by

$$p = MC_l(y) = MC(y, k(y)).$$

The short-run supply curve is given by price equals marginal cost at some fixed level of k:

$$p = MC(y, k).$$

Note the difference between the two expressions. The short-run supply curve involves the marginal cost of output holding k fixed at a given level of output, while the long-run supply curve involves the marginal cost of output when you adjust k optimally.

Now, we know something about the relationship between short-run and long-run marginal costs: the short-run and the long-run marginal costs coincide at the level of output y^* where the fixed factor choice associated with the short-run marginal cost is the optimal choice, k^*. Thus the short-run and the long-run supply curves of the firm coincide at y^*, as in Figure 22.9.

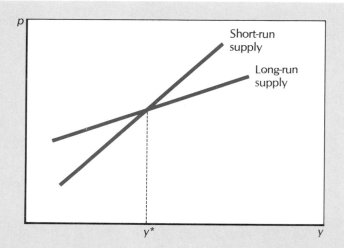

Figure
22.9
The short-run and long-run supply curves. Typically the long-run supply curve will be more elastic than the short-run supply curve.

In the short run the firm has some factors in fixed supply; in the long run these factors are variable. Thus, when the price of output changes, the firm has more choices to adjust in the long run than in the short run. This suggests that the long-run supply curve will be more responsive to price—more elastic—than the short-run supply curve, as illustrated in Figure 22.9.

What else can we say about the long-run supply curve? The long run is defined to be that time period in which the firm is free to adjust all of its inputs. One choice that the firm has is the choice of whether to remain in business. Since in the long run the firm can always get zero profits by going out of business, the profits that the firm makes in long-run equilibrium have to be at least zero:

$$py - c(y) \geq 0$$

which means

$$p \geq \frac{c(y)}{y}.$$

This says that in the long run price has to be at least as large as average cost. Thus the relevant part of the long-run supply curve is the upward sloping part of the marginal cost curve that lies above the long-run average cost curve, as depicted in Figure 22.10.

This is completely consistent with the short-run story. In the long run all costs are variable costs, so the short-run condition of having price above

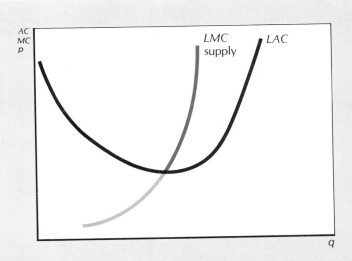

The long-run supply curve. The long-run supply curve will be the upward sloping part of the long-run marginal cost curve that lies above the average cost curve.

Figure
22.10

average variable cost is equivalent to the long-run condition of having price above average cost.

22.9 Long-Run Constant Average Costs

One particular case of interest is that in which the long-run technology of the firm exhibits constant returns to scale. In this case the long-run supply curve will be the long-run marginal cost curve, which, in the case of constant average cost, coincides with the long-run average cost curve. Thus we have the situation depicted in Figure 22.11 where the long-run supply curve is a horizontal line at c_{min}, the level of constant average cost.

This supply curve means that the firm is willing to supply any amount of output at $p = c_{min}$, an arbitrarily large amount of output at $p > c_{min}$, and zero output at $p < c_{min}$. When we think about the replication argument for constant returns to scale this makes perfect sense. Constant returns to scale implies that if you can produce 1 unit for c_{min} dollars, you can produce n units for nc_{min} dollars. Therefore you will be willing to supply any amount of output at a price equal to c_{min}, and an arbitrarily large amount of output at any price greater than c_{min}.

On the other hand, if $p < c_{min}$, so that you cannot break supplying even one unit of output, you will certainly not be able to break even supplying

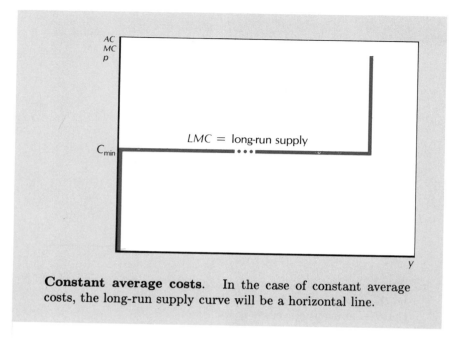

Figure 22.11

Constant average costs. In the case of constant average costs, the long-run supply curve will be a horizontal line.

n units of output. Hence, for any price less than c_{min}, you will want to supply zero units of output.

Summary

1. The relationship between the price a firm charges and the output that it sells is known as the demand curve facing the firm. By definition, a competitive firm faces a horizontal demand curve whose height is determined by the market price—the price charged by the other firms in the market.

2. The (short-run) supply curve of a competitive firm is that portion of its (short-run) marginal cost curve that is upward sloping and lies above the average variable cost curve.

3. The change in producer's surplus when the market price changes from p_1 to p_2 is the area to the left of the marginal cost curve between p_1 and p_2. It also measures the firm's change in profits.

4. The long-run supply curve of a firm is that portion of its long-run marginal cost curve that is upward sloping and that lies above its long-run average cost curve.

Review Questions

1. A firm has a cost function given by $c(y) = 10y^2 + 1000$. What is its supply curve?

2. A firm has a cost function given by $c(y) = 10y^2 + 1000$. At what output is average cost minimized?

3. If the supply curve is given by $S(p) = 100 + 20p$, what is the formula for the inverse supply curve?

4. A firm has a supply function given by $S(p) = 4p$. Its fixed costs are 100. If the price changes from 10 to 20, what is the change in its profits?

5. If $c(y) = y^2 + 1$, what is the long-run supply curve of the firm?

6. Classify each of the following as either technological or market constraints: the price of inputs, the number of other firms in the market, the quantity of output produced, and the ability to produce more given the current input levels.

7. What is the major assumption that characterizes a purely competitive market?

8. In a purely competitive market a firm's marginal revenue is always equal to what? A profit maximizing firm in such a market will operate at what level of output?

9. If average variable costs exceed the market price what level of output should the firm produce? What if there are no fixed costs?

10. Is it ever better for a perfectly competitive firm to produce output even though it is losing money? If so, when?

11. In a perfectly competitive market what is the relationship between the market price and the cost of production for all firms in the industry?

APPENDIX

The discussion in this chapter is very simple if you speak calculus. The profit maximization problem is

$$\max_{y} \ py - c(y)$$

such that $y \geq 0$.

The necessary conditions for the optimal supply, y^*, are the first-order condition

$$p - c'(y^*) = 0$$

and the second-order condition

$$-c''(y^*) \leq 0.$$

The first-order condition says price equals marginal cost, and the second-order condition says that the marginal cost must be increasing. Of course this is presuming that $y^* > 0$. If price is less than average variable cost at y^*, it will pay the firm to produce a zero level of output. To determine the supply curve of a competitive firm, we must find all the points where the first- and second-order conditions are satisfied and compare them to each other—and to $y = 0$—and pick the one with the largest profits. That's the profit maximizing supply.

23

INDUSTRY SUPPLY

We have seen how to derive a firm's supply curve from its marginal cost curve. But in a competitive market there will typically be many firms, so the supply curve presented to the market will be the sum of the supplies of all the individual firms. In this chapter we will investigate the **industry supply curve**.

23.1 Short-Run Industry Supply

We begin by studying an industry with a fixed number of firms, n. We let $S_i(p)$ be the supply curve of firm i, so that the **industry supply curve**, or the **market supply curve** is

$$S(p) = \sum_{i=1}^{n} S_i(p)$$

which is the sum of the individual supply curves. Geometrically we take the sum of the quantities supplied by each firm at each price, which gives us a *horizontal* sum of supply curves, as in Figure 23.1.

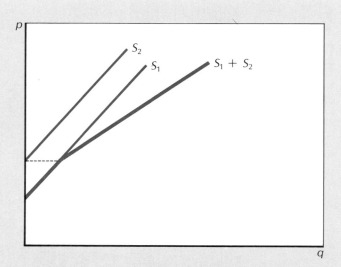

**Figure
23.1**

The industry supply curve. The industry supply curve $(S_1 + S_2)$ is the sum of the individual supply curves (S_1 and S_2).

23.2 Industry Equilibrium in the Short Run

In order to find the industry equilibrium we take this market supply curve and find the intersection with the market demand curve. This gives us an equilibrium price, p^*.

Given this equilibrium price, we can go back to look at the individual firms and examine their output levels and profits. A typical configuration with three firms, A, B, and C, is illustrated in Figure 23.2. In this example, firm A is operating at a price and output combination that lies on its average cost curve. This means that

$$p = \frac{c(y)}{y}.$$

Cross multiplying and rearranging, we have

$$py - c(y) = 0.$$

Thus firm A is making zero profits.

Firm B is operating at a point where price is greater than average cost: $p > c(y)/y$, which means it is making a profit in this short-run equilibrium. Firm C is operating where price is less than average cost, so it is making negative profits, that is, making a loss.

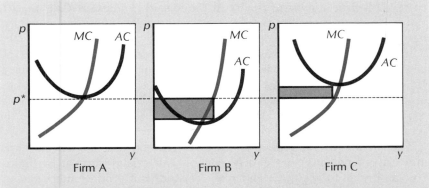

Short-run equilibrium.   Here is an example of a short-run equilibrium with three firms. Firm A is making zero profits, firm B is making positive profits, and firm C is making negative profits, that is, making a loss.

Figure
23.2

In general, combinations of price and output that lie above the average cost curve represent positive profits, and combinations that lie below represent negative profits. Even if a firm is making negative profits it will still be better for it to stay in business in the short run if the price and output combination lie above the average *variable* cost curve. For in this case, it will make less of a loss by remaining in business than by producing a zero level of output.

23.3 Industry Equilibrium in the Long Run

In the long run, firms are able to adjust their fixed factors. They can choose the plant size, or the capital equipment, or whatever to maximize their long-run profits. This just means that they will move from their short-run to their long-run cost curves, and this adds no new analytical difficulties: we simply use the long-run supply curves as determined by the long-run marginal cost curve.

However, there is an additional long-run effect that may occur. If a firm is making losses in the long run, there is no reason to stay in the industry, so we would expect to see such a firm *exit* the industry, since by exiting from the industry, the firm could reduce its losses to zero. This is just another way of saying that the only relevant part of a firm's supply curve in the long run is that part that lies *on or above* the average cost curve—since these are locations that correspond to nonnegative profits.

Similarly, if a firm is making profits we would expect *entry* to occur. After all, the cost curve is supposed to include the cost of all factors necessary to produce output, measured at their market price (i.e., their opportunity cost). If a firm is making profits in the long run it means that *anybody* can go to market, acquire those factors, and produce the same amount of output at the same cost.

In most competitive industries there are no restrictions against new firms entering the industry; in this case we say the industry exhibits **free entry**. However, in some industries there are **barriers to entry**, such as licenses or legal restrictions on how many firms can be in the industry. For example, regulations on the sales of alcohol in many states prevent free entry to the retail liquor industry.

The two long-run effects—acquiring different fixed factors and the entry and exit phenomena—are closely related. An existing firm in an industry can decide to acquire a new plant or store and produce more output. Or a new firm may enter the industry by acquiring a new plant and producing output. The only difference is in who owns the new production facilities.

Of course as more firms enter the industry—and firms that are losing money exit the industry—the total amount produced will change and lead to a change in the market price. This in turn will affect profits and the incentives to exit and enter. What will the final equilibrium look like in an industry with free entry?

Let's examine a case where all firms have identical long-run cost functions, say, $c(y)$. Given the cost function we can compute the level of output where average costs are minimized, which we denote by y^*. We let $p^* = c(y^*)$, the minimum value of average cost. This cost is significant because it is the lowest price that could be charged in the market and still allow firms to break even.

We can now graph the industry supply curves for each different number of firms that can be in the market. Figure 23.3 illustrates the industry supply curves if there are $1, \ldots, 4$ firms in the market. (We are using 4 firms only for purposes of an example; in reality, one would expect there to be many more firms in a competitive industry.) Note that since all firms have the same supply curve, the total amount supplied if 2 firms are in the market is just twice as much as when 1 firm is the market, the supply when 3 firms are in the market is just three times as much, and so on.

Now add two more lines to the diagram: a horizontal line at p^*, the minimum price consistent with nonnegative profits, and the market demand curve. Consider the intersections of the demand curve and the supply curves for $n = 1, 2, \ldots$ firms. If firms enter the industry when positive profits are being made, then the relevant intersection is the *lowest price consistent with nonnegative profits*. This is denoted by p' in Figure 23.3, and it happens to occur when there are three firms in the market. If one more firm enters the market, profits are pushed to be negative. In this case, the maximum number of competitive firms this industry can support is three.

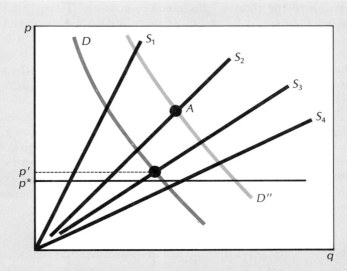

Supply curves with free entry. Supply curves for $1, 2, \ldots, 4$
firms. The equilibrium price, p', occurs at the lowest possible
intersection of demand and supply such that $p' \geq p^*$.

Figure
23.3

23.4 The Long-Run Supply Curve

The construction given in the last section—draw the industry supply curves
for each possible number of firms that could be in the market and then look
for the largest number of firms consistent with nonnegative profits—is perfectly rigorous and easy to apply. However, there is a useful approximation
that usually gives something very close to the right answer.

Let's see if there is some way to construct *one* industry supply curve out
of the n curves we have above. The first thing to note is that we can rule
out all of the points on the supply curve that are below p^*, since those can
never be long-run operating positions. But we can also rule out some of
the points on the supply curves *above* p^*.

We typically assume that the market demand curve is downward sloping. The steepest possible demand curve is therefore a vertical line. This
implies that points like A in Figure 23.3 would never be observed—for any
downward sloping demand curve that passed through A would also have to
intersect a supply curve associated with a larger number of firms, as shown
by the hypothetical supply curve D'' passing through the point A in Figure
23.3.

Thus we can eliminate a portion of each supply curve from being a possible long-run equilibrium position. Every point on the 1–firm supply curve

that lies to the right of the intersection of the 2–firm supply curve and the line determined by p^* cannot be consistent with long-run equilibrium. Similarly, every point on the 2–firm supply curve that lies to the right of the intersection of the 3–firm supply curve with the p^* line cannot be consistent with long-run equilibrium ... and every point on the n-firm supply curve that lies to the right of the intersection of the $n+1$-firm supply curve with the p^* line cannot be consistent with equilibrium.

The parts of the supply curves on which the long-run equilibrium can actually occur are indicated by the colored lines in Figure 23.4. The nth colored line segment shows all the combinations of prices and industry output that are consistent with having n firms in long-run equilibrium. Note that these line segments get flatter and flatter as we consider larger and larger levels of industry output, involving more and more firms in the industry.

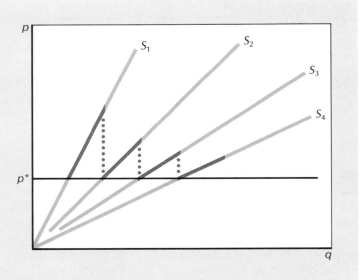

Figure 23.4

The long-run supply curve. We can eliminate portions of the supply curves that can never be intersections with a downward sloping market demand curve in the long run, such as the points on each supply curve to the right of the dotted lines.

Why do these curves get flatter? Think about it. If there is one firm in the market and the price goes up by Δp, it will produce, say, Δy more output. If there are n firms in the market and the price goes up by Δp, *each* firm will produce Δy more output, so we will get $n\Delta y$ more output in total. This means that the supply curve will be getting flatter and flatter as there are more and more firms in the market, since the supply of output will be more and more sensitive to price.

By the time we get a reasonable number of firms in the market, the slope of the supply curve will be very flat indeed. Flat enough so that it is reasonable to take it as having a slope of zero—that is, as taking the long-run industry supply curve to be a flat line at price equals minimum average cost. This will be a poor approximation if there are only a few firms in the industry in the long run. But the assumption that a small number of firms behave competitively will also probably be a poor approximation! If there are a reasonable number of firms in the long run, the equilibrium price cannot get far from minimum average cost. This is depicted in Figure 23.5.

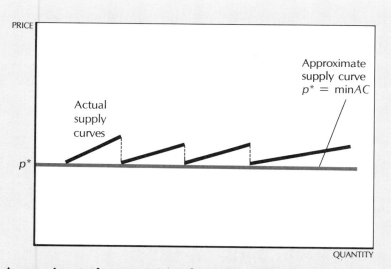

Approximate long-run supply curve. The long-run supply curve will be approximately flat at price equals minimum
average cost.

Figure
23.5

This has the important implication that in a competitive industry with free entry, profits cannot get very far from zero. If there are significant levels of profits in an industry with free entry, it will induce other firms to enter that industry, and thereby push profits towards zero.

Remember, the correct calculation of economic costs involves measuring all factors of production at their market prices. As long as *all* factors are being measured and properly priced, a firm earning positive profits can be exactly duplicated by anyone. Anyone can go to the open market and purchase the factors of production necessary to produce the same output in the same way as the firm in question.

In an industry with free entry and exit, the long-run average cost curve should be essentially flat at a price equal to the minimum average cost. This is just the kind of long-run supply curve that a firm with constant returns to scale would have. This is no accident. We argued that constant returns to scale was a reasonable assumption since a firm could always replicate what it was doing before. But another firm could replicate it as well! Expanding output by building a duplicate plant is just like a new firm entering the market with duplicate production facilities. Thus the long-run supply curve of a competitive industry with free entry will look like the long-run supply curve of a firm with constant returns to scale: a flat line at price equals minimum average cost.

EXAMPLE: Taxation in the Long Run and the Short Run

Consider an industry that has free entry and exit. Suppose that initially it is in a long-run equilibrium with a fixed number of firms, and zero profits, as depicted in Figure 23.6. In the short run, with a fixed number of firms, the supply curve of the industry is upward sloping, while in the long run, with a variable number of firms, the supply curve is flat at price equals minimum average cost.

What happens when we put a tax on this industry? We use the geometric analysis discussed in Chapter 16: in order to find the new price paid by the demanders, we shift the supply curve up by the amount of the tax.

In general, the consumer will face a higher price and the producers will receive a lower price after the tax is imposed. But the producers were just breaking even before the tax was imposed; thus they must be losing money at any lower price. These economic losses will encourage some firms to leave the industry. Thus the supply of output will be reduced and the price to the consumers will rise even further.

In the long run, the industry will supply along the horizontal long-run supply curve. In order to supply along this curve, the firms will have to receive a price equal to minimum average cost—just what they were receiving before the tax was imposed. Thus the price to the consumers will have to rise by the entire amount of the tax.

In Figure 23.6, the equilibrium is initially at $P_D = P_S$. Then the tax is imposed, shifting the short-run supply curve up by the amount of the tax, and the equilibrium price paid by the demanders increases to P_D'. The equilibrium price paid by the suppliers falls to $P_S' = P_D' - t$. But this is only in the short run—when there are a fixed number of firms in the industry. Because of free entry and exit, the *long-run* supply curve in the industry is horizontal at $P_D = P_S$ = minimum average cost. Hence, in the long run,

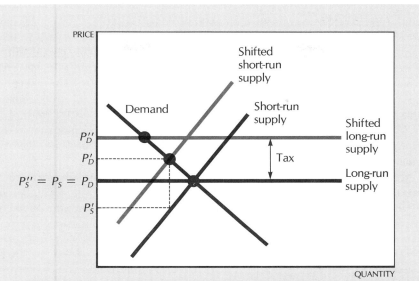

PRICE

Shifted
short-run
supply

Demand   Short-run
supply

Shifted
long-run
supply

P_D''

P_D' Tax

Long-run
supply

$P_S'' = P_S = P_D$

P_S'

QUANTITY

Taxation in the short run and long run. In the short run,   Figure
with a fixed number of firms, the industry supply curve will have   23.6
an upward slope so that part of the tax falls on the consumers
and part on the firms. In the long run, the industry supply curve
will be horizontal so all of the tax falls on the consumers.

shifting up the supply curve implies that the entire amount of the tax gets
passed along to the consumers.

To sum up: in an industry with free entry, a tax will initially raise the
price to the consumers by less than the amount of the tax, since some of
the incidence of the tax will fall on the producers. But in the long run the
tax will induce firms to exit from the industry, thereby reducing supply, so
that consumers will eventually end up paying the entire burden of the tax.

23.5 The Meaning of Zero Profits

In an industry with free entry, profits will be driven to zero by new entrants:
whenever profits are positive, there will be an incentive for a new firm to
come in to acquire some of those profits. When profits are zero it doesn't
mean that the industry disappears; it just means that it stops growing,
since there is no longer an inducement to enter.

In a long-run equilibrium with zero profits, all of the factors of production
are being paid their market price—the same market price that these factors
could earn elsewhere. The owner of the firm, for example, is still collecting

a payment for her labor time, or for the amount of money she invested in the firm, or for whatever she contributes to the operation of the firm. The same goes for all other factors of production. The firm is still making money—it is just that all the money that it makes is being paid out to purchase the inputs that it uses. Each factor of production is earning the same amount in this industry that it could earn elsewhere, so there are no extra rewards—no pure profits—to attract new factors of production to this industry. But there is nothing to cause them to leave either. Industries in long-run equilibrium with zero profits are mature industries; they're not likely to appear as the cover story on *Business Week*, but they form the backbone of the economy.

Remember, economic profits are defined using the market prices of all factors of production. The market prices measure the opportunity cost of those factors—what they could earn elsewhere. Any amount of money earned in excess of the payments to the factors of production is a pure economic profit. But whenever someone finds a pure economic profit, other people will try to enter the industry and acquire some of that profit for themselves. It is this attempt to capture economic profits that eventually drives them to zero in a competitive industry with free entry.

In some quarters, the profit motive is regarded with some disdain. But when you think about it purely on economic grounds, profits are providing exactly the right signals as far as resource allocation is concerned. If a firm is making positive profits, it means that people value the output of the firm more highly than they value the inputs. Doesn't it make sense to have more firms producing that kind of output?

23.6 Fixed Factors and Economic Rent

If there is free entry, profits are driven to zero in the long run. But not every industry has free entry. In some industries the number of firms in the industry is fixed.

A common reason for this is that there are some factors of production that are available in fixed supply. We said that in the long run the fixed factors could be bought or sold by an individual firm. But there are some factors that are fixed for the *economy as a whole* even in the long run.

The most obvious example of this is in resource extraction industries: oil in the ground is a necessary input to the oil extraction industry, and there is only so much oil around to be extracted. A similar statement could be made for coal, gas, precious metals, or any other such resource. Agriculture gives another example. There is only a certain amount of land that is suitable for agriculture.

A more exotic example of such a fixed factor is talent. There are only a certain number of people who possess the necessary level of talent to be a professional athlete or entertainer. There may be "free entry" into such fields—but only for those who are good enough to get in!

There are other cases where the fixed factor is fixed not by nature, but by law. In many industries it is necessary to have a license or permit, and the number of these permits may be fixed by law. The taxicab industry in many cities is regulated in this way. Liquor licenses are another example.

If there are restrictions such as the above on the number of firms in the industry, so that firms cannot enter the industry freely, it may appear that it is possible to have an industry with positive profits in the long run, with no economic forces to drive those profits to zero.

This appearance is wrong. There is an economic force that pushes profits to zero. If a firm is operating at a point where its profits appear to be positive in the long run, it is probably because we are not appropriately measuring the market value of whatever it is that is preventing entry.

Here it is important to remember the economic definition of costs: we should value each factor of production at its *market price*—its opportunity cost. If it appears that a farmer is making positive profits after we have subtracted his costs of production, it is probably because we have forgotten to subtract the cost of his land.

Suppose that we manage to value all of the inputs to farming except for the land cost, and we end up with some figure π dollars per year for profits. How much would the land be worth on a free market? How much would someone pay to rent that land for a year?

The answer is: they would be willing to rent it for π dollars per year, the "profits" that it brings in. You wouldn't even have to know anything about farming to rent this land and earn π dollars—after all, we valued the farmer's labor at its market price as well, and that means that you can hire a farmer and still make π dollars of profit. So the market value of that land—its competitive rent—is just π. The economic profits to farming are zero.

Note that the rental rate determined by this procedure may have nothing whatsoever to do with the historical cost of the farm. What matters is not what you bought it for, but what you can sell it for—that's what determines opportunity cost.

Whenever there is some fixed factor that is preventing entry into an industry, there will be an equilibrium rental rate for that factor. Even with fixed factors, you can always enter an industry by buying out the position of a firm that is currently in the industry. Every firm in the industry has the option of selling out—and the opportunity cost of not doing so is a cost of production that it has to consider.

Thus in one sense it is always the *possibility* of entry that drives profits to zero. After all, there are two ways to enter an industry: you can form a new firm, or you can buy out an existing firm that is currently in the industry. If a new firm can buy everything necessary to produce in an industry and still make a profit, it will do so. But if there are some factors that are in fixed supply, then competition for those factors among potential entrants will bid the prices of these factors up to a point where the profit disappears.

23.7 Economic Rent

The examples in the last section are instances of **economic rent**. Economic rent is defined as those payments to a factor of production that are in excess of the minimum payment necessary to have that factor supplied.

Consider, for example, the case of oil discussed earlier. In order to produce oil you need some labor, some machinery, and, most importantly, some oil in the ground! Suppose that it costs $1 a barrel to pump oil out of the ground from an existing well. Then any price in excess of $1 a barrel will induce firms to supply oil from existing wells. But the actual price of oil is much higher than $1 a barrel. People want oil for various reasons and they are willing to pay more than its cost of production to get it. The excess of the price of oil over its cost of production is economic rent.

Why don't firms enter this industry? Well, they try. But there is only a certain amount of oil available. Oil will sell for more than its cost of production because of the limited supply.

Now consider taxicab licenses. Viewed as pieces of paper, these cost almost nothing to produce. But in New York City a taxicab license can sell for $100,000! Why don't people enter this industry and produce more taxicab licenses? The reason is that entry is illegal—the supply of taxicab licenses is controlled by the city.

Farmland is yet another example of economic rent. In the aggregate, the total amount of land is fixed. There would be just as much land supplied at zero dollars an acre as at $1000 an acre. Thus, in the aggregate, the payments to land constitute economic rent.

From the viewpoint of the economy as a whole, it is the price of agricultural products that determines the value of agricultural land. But from the viewpoint of the individual farmer, the value of his land is a cost of production that enters into the pricing of his product.

This is depicted in Figure 23.7. Here AVC represents the average cost curve for all factors of production *excluding* land costs. (We are assuming that land is the only fixed factor.) If the price of the crop grown on this land is p^*, then the "profits" attributable to the land are measured by the area of the box: these are the economic rents. This is how much the land would rent for in a competitive market—whatever it took to drive the profits to zero.

The average cost curve *including* the value of the land is labeled AC. If we measure the value of the land correctly, the economic profits to operating the farm will be exactly zero. Since the equilibrium rent for the land will

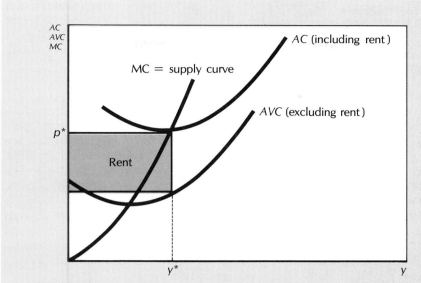

Economic rent for land. The area of the box represents the economic rent on the land.

Figure
23.7

be whatever it takes to drive profits to zero, we have

$$p^* y^* - c_v(y^*) - \text{rent} = 0$$

or

$$\text{rent} = p^* y^* - c_v(y^*). \tag{23.1}$$

This is precisely what we referred to as producer's surplus earlier. Indeed, it is the same concept, simply viewed in a different light. Thus we can also measure rent by taking the area to the left of the marginal cost curve, as we saw earlier.

Given the definition of rent in equation (23.1), it is now easy to see the truth of what we said earlier: it is the equilibrium price that determines rent, not the reverse. The firm supplies along its marginal cost curve—which is independent of the expenditures on the fixed factors. The rent will adjust to drive profits to zero.

23.8 Rental Rates and Prices

Since we are measuring output in flow units—so much output per unit of time, we should be careful to measure profits and rents in dollars per unit of time. Thus in the above discussion we talked about the rent per year for land, or for a taxicab license.

If the land or the license is to be sold outright, rather than rented, the equilibrium price would be the present value of the stream of rental payments. This is a simple consequence of the usual argument that assets generating a stream of payments should sell for their present values in a competitive market.

23.9 The Politics of Rent

In many cases, economic rent exists because of legal restrictions on entry into the industry. We mentioned two examples above: taxicab licenses and liquor licenses. In each of these cases the number of licenses is fixed by law, thus restricting entry to the industry and creating economic rents.

Suppose that the New York City government wants to increase the number of operating taxicabs. What will happen to the market value of the existing taxicab licenses? Obviously they will fall in value. This reduction in value hits the industry right in the pocketbook, and is a sure way to create a lobbying force to oppose any such move.

The federal government also artificially restricts output of some products in such a way as to create a rent. For example, the federal government has declared that tobacco can only be grown on certain lands. The value of this land is then determined by the demand for tobacco products. Any attempt to eliminate this licensing system has to contend with a serious lobby. Once the government creates artificial scarcity, it is very hard to eliminate it. The beneficiaries of the artificial scarcity—the people who have acquired the right to operate in the industry—will vigorously oppose any attempts to enlarge the industry.

The incumbents in a legally restricted industry may well devote considerable resources to maintaining their favored position. Lobbying expenses, public relations costs, and so on can be substantial. From the viewpoint of society these kinds of expenses represent pure social waste. They aren't true costs of production; they don't lead to any *more* output being produced. Lobbying and public relations efforts just determine who gets the money associated with existing output.

Efforts directed at keeping or acquiring claims to factors in fixed supplies are sometimes referred to as **rent seeking**. From the viewpoint of society they represent a pure deadweight loss since they don't create any more output, they just change who owns factors of production.

EXAMPLE: Taxation in an Industry with Fixed Factors

In an earlier example we investigated the impact of a tax in an industry with free entry. Let's look at the same analysis now in an industry in which there are some economic rents. To be specific, let's look at the farming industry.

Suppose that there is a fixed amount of land suitable for growing grapes to produce wine. Initially the industry is in long-run equilibrium. The price of wine determines in part the price of grapes, and therefore the rent on grape growing land, as depicted in Figure 23.8.

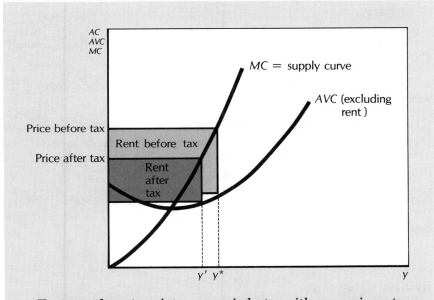

Taxes and rents. A tax on an industry with economic rents will typically fall primarily on the rents.

Figure 23.8

Now suppose that the government puts a tax on wine. This will reduce the demand for wine, and thereby lower the price of grapes received by the grower. The net effect will be to reduce the revenue received by a typical grower, as depicted in Figure 23.8. Hence, the rent on the wine growing land must fall. The end result of the tax on wine will be to reduce the value of land used for growing grapes.

The producers of grapes are presumably aware of the connection between wine taxation and the value of their land. If an increase in the wine tax is proposed then the grape growers will find it in their interest to lobby against the increase. They could devote a considerable amount of money and time to try to prevent this tax from being imposed. Resources that could be used to produce new wealth will be directed instead to struggling over the division of existing wealth.

When we attempt to measure the total deadweight loss of the tax we may want to count not only the deadweight loss due the reduced production and consumption of wine, but also the costs due to rent seeking. The amount that growers will be willing to pay to avoid a tax increase will be at most equal to the reduction in the value of their land due to the additional taxes, so this plus the ordinary deadweight loss serves as an upper bound on the total social cost of the tax.

Summary

1. The short-run supply curve of an industry is just the horizontal sum of the supply curves of the individual firms in that industry.

2. The long-run supply curve of an industry must take into account the exit and entry of firms in the industry.

3. If there is free entry and exit, then the long-run equilibrium will involve the maximum number of firms consistent with nonnegative profits. This means that the long-run supply curve will be essentially horizontal at a price equal to the minimum average cost.

4. If there are forces preventing the entry of firms into a profitable industry, the factors that prevent entry will earn economic rents. The rent earned is determined by the price of the output of the industry.

Review Questions

1. If $S_1(p) = p - 10$ and $S_2(p) = p - 15$, then at what price does the industry supply curve have a kink in it?

2. In the short run the demand for cigarettes is totally inelastic. In the long run, suppose that it is perfectly elastic. What is the impact of a cigarette tax on the price that consumers pay in the short run and in the long run?

3. True or false? Convenience stores near the campus have high prices because they have to pay high rents.

4. True or false? In long-run industry equilibrium no firm will be losing money.

5. According to the model presented in this chapter, what determines the amount of entry or exit a given industry experiences?

6. The model of entry presented in this chapter implies that the more firms in a given industry, the (steeper, flatter) is the long-run industry supply curve.

7. A New York City cab driver appears to be making positive profits in the long run after carefully accounting for the operating and labor costs. Does this violate the competitive model? Why or why not?

24

MARKETS

Now that we understand the relationship between costs and supply, we can enter into a more detailed analysis of supply and demand equilibrium. The last several chapters have outlined a systematic way to examine the behavior of competitive markets. First we examine the profit maximization problem of a representative firm, and model the incentives it faces in its attempt to maximize profits. Next we use the price equals marginal cost rule to calculate the supply function of the firm, and add up all of the supply functions of the individual firms to get the market supply function. Given the market demand curve of the consumers, we can find the price that clears the market. We can then examine the comparative statics properties of the price and output in order to see how various policies will affect these variables, calculate the profit positions of the firms in the market, or discuss other variations in the underlying model. This chapter will describe some examples of this kind of analysis.

24.1 Oil Markets

We start with a very famous example about U.S. energy policy. In 1974 the Organization of Petroleum Exporting Countries, OPEC, levied a significant increase in the price of oil. Countries that had no domestically produced petroleum had little choice about energy policy—the price of oil and goods produced using oil had to rise.

At that time the United States produced about half of its domestic oil consumption, and Congress felt that it was unfair that the domestic producers should receive "windfall profits" from an uncontrolled increase in price. (The term windfall profits refers to an increase in profits due to some outside event, as opposed to an increase in profits due to production decisions.) Consequently Congress devised a bizarre plan to attempt to hold down the price of products that used oil. The most prominent of these products is gasoline, so we will analyze the effect of the program for that market.

The policy adopted by Congress was known as "two-tiered" oil pricing, and it went something like this. Imported oil would sell for whatever its market price was, but domestic oil—oil produced from wells that were in place before 1974—would sell for its old price: the price that it sold for before OPEC. Roughly speaking, we'll say that imported oil sold for about $15 a barrel, while domestic oil sold for around $5. The idea was that the average price of oil would then be about $10 a barrel and this would help hold down the price of gasoline.

Could such a scheme work? Let's think about it from the viewpoint of the gasoline producers. What would the supply curve of gasoline look like? In order to answer this question we have to ask what the marginal cost curve for gasoline looked like.

What would you do if you were a gasoline refiner? Obviously you would try to use the cheap domestic oil first. Only after you had exhausted your supplies of domestic oil would you turn to the more expensive imported oil. Thus the aggregate marginal cost curve—the industry supply curve—for gasoline would have to look something like that depicted in Figure 24.1. The curve takes a jump at the point where the U.S. production of domestic oil is exhausted and the imported oil begins to be used. Before that point, the domestic price of oil measures the relevant factor price for producing gasoline. After that point, it is the price of foreign oil that is the relevant factor price.

Figure 24.1 depicts the supply curve for gasoline if all oil were to sell for the world price of $15 a barrel, and if all oil were to sell for the domestic price of $5 a barrel. If domestic oil actually sells for $5 a barrel and foreign sells for $15 a barrel, then the supply curve for gasoline will coincide with the $5 a barrel supply curve until the cheaper domestic oil is used up, and then coincide with the $15 a barrel supply curve.

Now let's find the intersection of this supply curve with the market demand curve to find the equilibrium price in Figure 24.1. The diagram reveals an interesting fact: the price of gasoline is exactly the same in the two-tiered system as it would be if all oil sold at the foreign oil price! The

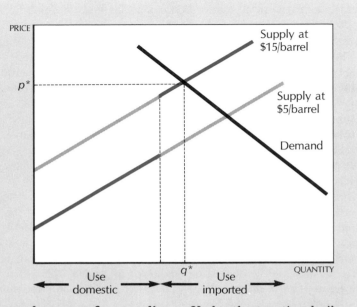

PRICE

Supply at
$15/barrel

p^*

Supply at
$5/barrel

Demand

q^*

Use
domestic

Use
imported

QUANTITY

**Figure
24.1**

The supply curve for gasoline. Under the two-tiered oil
pricing policy, the supply curve of gasoline would be discontinuous, jumping from the lower supply curve to the upper supply
curve when the cheaper oil was exhausted.

price of gasoline is determined by the *marginal* cost of production, and the
marginal cost is determined by the cost of the imported oil.

If you think about it a minute this makes perfectly good sense. The
gasoline companies will sell their product at the price the market will bear.
Just because you were lucky enough to get some cheap oil doesn't mean
you won't sell your gasoline for the same price that other firms are selling
theirs for.

Suppose for the moment that all oil did sell for one price, and that
equilibrium was reached at the price p^*. Then the government comes along
and lowers the price of the first 100 barrels of oil that each refiner used.
Will this affect their supply decision? No way—in order to affect supply
you have to change the incentives at the margin. The only way to get a
lower price of gasoline is to increase the supply, and that means that you
have to make the marginal cost of oil cheaper.

The two-tiered oil pricing policy was simply a transfer from the domestic
oil producers to the domestic oil refiners. The domestic producers got $5.00
less for their oil, and the profits they would have gotten went to the gasoline
refiners. It had no effect on the supply of gasoline, and thus it could have
no effect on the price of gasoline.

24.2 Price Controls

The economic forces inherent in this argument didn't take long to make themselves felt. The Department of Energy soon realized that it couldn't allow market forces to determine the price of gasoline under the two-tiered system—since market forces alone would imply one price of gasoline, and that would be the same price that would prevail in the absence of the two-tiered system.

So they instituted price controls on gasoline. Each refiner was required to charge a price for gasoline that was based on the costs of producing the gasoline—which in turn was primarily determined by the cost of the oil that the refiner was able to purchase.

The availability of cheap domestic oil varied with location. In Texas the refiners were close to the major source of production and thus were able to purchase large supplies of cheap oil. Due to the price controls, the price of Texas gasoline was relatively cheap. In New England, virtually all oil had to be imported, and thus the price of gasoline in New England was quite high.

When you have different prices for the same product, it is natural for firms to try to sell at the higher price. Again, the Department of Energy had to intervene to prevent the uncontrolled shipping of gasoline from low price regions to high price regions. The result of this intervention was the famous gasoline shortages of the mid-seventies. Periodically, the supply of gasoline in a region of the country would dry up, and there would be little available at any price. The free market system of supplying petroleum products had never exhibited such behavior; the shortages were entirely due to the two-tiered oil pricing system coupled with price controls.

Economists pointed this out at the time, but it didn't have much effect on policy. What did have an effect was lobbying by the gasoline refiners. Much of the domestic oil was sold on long-term contracts, and some refiners were able to buy a lot of it, while others could only buy the expensive foreign oil. Naturally they objected that this was unfair, so Congress figured out another scheme to allocate the cheap domestic oil more equitably.

This program was known as the "entitlement program," and it went something like this. Each time a refiner bought a barrel of expensive foreign oil he got a coupon that allowed him to buy a certain amount of cheap domestic oil. The amount that the refiner was allowed to buy depended on supply conditions, but let's say that it was one for one: each barrel of foreign oil that he bought for $15 allowed him to buy one barrel of domestic oil for $5.

What did this do to the marginal price of oil? Now the marginal price of oil was just a weighted average of the domestic price and the foreign price of oil; in the one-for-one case described above, the price would be $10. The effect on the supply curve of gasoline is depicted in Figure 24.2.

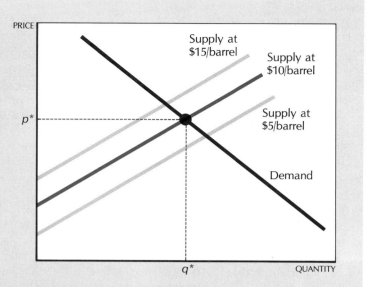

Figure
24.2

The entitlement program. Under the entitlement program the supply curve of gasoline would lie between the supply curve if all oil were provided at the imported price and the supply curve if all oil were provided at the domestic price.

The marginal cost of oil was reduced all right, and that meant that the price of gasoline was reduced as well. But look who is paying for it: the domestic oil producers! The U.S. was buying foreign oil that cost $15 a barrel in real dollars and pretending that it only cost $10. The domestic oil producers were required to sell their oil for less than the market price on the world oil market. We were subsidizing the importation of foreign oil and forcing the domestic oil producers to pay the subsidy!

Eventually this program was abandoned as well, and the U.S. went in for a windfall profits tax that allowed all oil to sell for the same price but taxed the production of domestic oil so that the domestic oil producers wouldn't reap windfall profits due to OPEC's action. Of course, such a tax would discourage production of domestic oil, and thereby increase the price of gasoline, but this was apparently acceptable to Congress at the time.

24.3 The Payment–in–Kind Program

In 1984, the Reagan administration adopted a new program to deal with the mounting government surplus of agricultural products. For many years the government had been guaranteeing farmers price floors for their products by buying up surplus amounts at legally fixed prices. This imposed two costs on the government: the cost of buying the products in the first place and the cost of storing the surplus. The Reagan administration decided to deal with both of these problems at once by using the agricultural surpluses to pay farmers *not* to grow further amounts. Hence the name, *Payment in Kind* (PIK). In this section, we will model the effects of the PIK program.[1]

Suppose that for every bushel of corn that a farmer decides *not* to grow the government gives him a units of corn from their stores. Note that this has two effects on supply: it reduces the supply when farmers decide not to grow as much corn, but it increases the supply since some of the surplus corn from the government stockpiles is given to the farmers to sell on the open market.

Let's look at the individual farmer's decision. Suppose that p is the price of corn, y is the amount he grows, $c(y)$ is the cost function for growing corn, and $\hat{y}$ is how much he would have grown in the absence of this program.

The farmer's profit maximization problem is then

$$\max_{y} \ py - c(y) + pa(\hat{y} - y).$$

The last term in this expression is the value of the payment in kind, or PIK payment. Rewriting the profit maximization problem we have

$$\max_{y} \ (1 - a)py - c(y) + pa\hat{y}.$$

From this expression we can see that the PIK program simply provides a lump sum subsidy to the farmer in the amount of $ap\hat{y}$ and changes the price the farmer faces to $(1 - a)p$. The profit maximization condition of price equals marginal cost becomes

$$p(1 - a) = MC(y)$$

or

$$p = \frac{MC(y)}{1 - a}.$$

This is illustrated in Figure 24.3. The supply curve of each individual farmer tilts up by the fraction $1/(1 - a)$.

But this isn't the end of the story. All that corn that was distributed to the farmers by the government is also sold on the market: if y units of corn are produced by the farmer in question, then the total amount supplied by this farmer will be $y + a(\hat{y} - y)$. Let's plot this on the graph so we can get the total supply of corn. In the case we've depicted, the supply curve is

---

[1] This model is based on an exposition by University of Michigan economist Richard Porter published in *The Free Lunch*, an underground economics journal that many people claim does not exist.

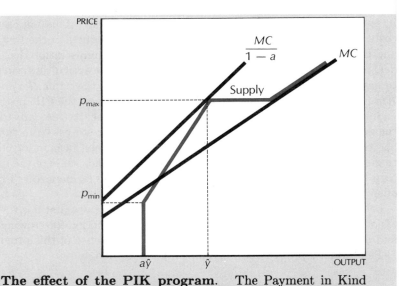

Figure 24.3

The effect of the PIK program. The Payment in Kind program generates a kinked supply curve.

linear, so we only need to get two points on the supply curve to draw the whole thing. This isn't too hard.

First, consider the price $p_{\max}$. Here the price is so high that the farmer finds it optimal to produce $\hat{y}$ amount of corn, and thus not get any PIK payments at all. So at this price—and at any higher price—the total supply curve is just the original marginal cost curve.

Next, consider the price $p_{\min}$. At this price, or any lower price, the farmers find it optimal to produce zero corn. Thus they will get the maximum PIK payment, $pa\hat{y}$. This gives us two points on the supply curve, and we can connect them to get the entire curve, as depicted in Figure 24.3.

However, this is still not the end of the story. We have illustrated the supply curve for a farmer who has decided to participate in the PIK program at all prices up to $p_{\max}$. But is this the most profitable decision for the farmer? If the price of corn is high, it might make sense to produce a lot of corn rather than accept the relatively small amount of the PIK payment.

Therefore we have to compare the profits from participating in the PIK program to the profits from not participating in it. We can do this by looking at the producer's surplus in each case; the argument is illustrated in Figure 24.4.

If the farmer decides to produce y^* amount of corn at a price of p^*, he will receive a PIK payment of $p^*a(\hat{y} - y^*)$. This PIK payment will be worth the area of the box in Figure 24.4A.

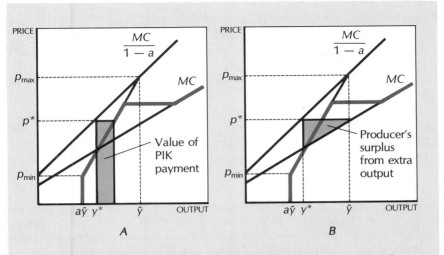

The producer's surplus from participating or not participating in the PIK program. By comparing the producer's surplus in these two situations, we can determine whether the farmer is better off participating in the program or not.

Figure
24.4

If the farmer decides to get out of the PIK program, he will produce y^* amount of output and get a producer's surplus—an increase in profits—represented by the area of the triangle in Figure 24.4B. If the area of the triangle in Figure 24.4B is larger than the area of the rectangle in Figure 24.4A, the farmer will choose not to participate in the PIK program. In the particular case illustrated, the area of the triangle appears to be somewhat less than the area of the rectangle. But at a slightly higher price for corn, the area of the rectangle will be smaller—since the value of the PIK payment will be less—and the area of the triangle will be greater since the value of the extra output will be greater. Thus at *some* price less than p_{max} it will pay the farmer not to participate in the PIK program—to produce the profit maximizing amount of output and sell it at the market price.

The net result is a supply curve like the colored line depicted in Figure 24.4A and B. The farmer will participate in the PIK program for lower prices, but exit from the program at higher prices, and supply along his original supply curve.

24.4 Parrot Smuggling

Rare species of parrots can sell for up to $6,000. Not surprisingly, such high prices have created an active market in birds from the wilds of South

America, Africa, and Asia. The World Wildlife Fund estimates that at least 100,000 contraband birds are sold each year. Several parrot species are in danger of becoming extinct because of their popularity as pets.[2]

Efforts by conservationists have led to bans on exports and imports of several species of birds. In 1975, 87 nations signed a Convention on International Trade in Endangered Species of Wild Fauna and Flora. This convention has encouraged many countries to make the transportation of endangered bird species illegal. Unfortunately, the fact that transporting parrots is illegal has induced smugglers to hide the birds in small enclosed places when crossing the borders, and the birds often die from such mistreatment. Thousands of birds have died due to attempts to hide them from the law.

Note that there are two effects going on here: the penalty tends to decrease the number of parrots smuggled out, but the smuggling technology results in such losses that an even larger number of birds must be caught in order to get a given number of live birds to market. If the goal is one of preserving the largest number of birds in the wild as possible, it may be that the penalties are counterproductive. Let's try to model these two conflicting effects.

Suppose that the number of birds exported is x, the fine is F per bird, and the probability of getting caught is πx. Then if a smuggler exports x birds, he faces an *expected* fine of $\pi x F$. But if he exports x birds, on the average only kx of them will survive, where k is some number less than one. And of the ones that survive, only $(1 - \pi)$ of them will get past the customs guards. Summing this up, if x birds are caught, $(1 - \pi)kx$ make it to market, and the smuggler pays an expected fine of $\pi F x$.

The profit maximization problem facing the bird smuggler is

$$\max_{x} \ p(1 - \pi)kx - c(x) - \pi F x.$$

The first term is the revenue received for the surviving birds, the second term is the cost of collecting the birds, and the last term is the expected cost of the fine that the smuggler has to pay. We can rearrange this expression for profits to get

$$\max_{x} \ [p(1 - \pi)k - \pi F]x - c(x).$$

This makes it clear that the "price" of a bird, from the viewpoint of a smuggler, is given by the bracketed term.

Setting this price equal to marginal cost yields

$$p(1 - \pi)k - \pi F = MC(x)$$

---

[2] For a discussion of the parrot smuggling industry, see D. Jackson, "Pirates Are Pushing Parrots out on a Limb," *Smithsonian*, April 1985, pp. 58–67. The discussion here follows that of University of Michigan economist Theodore Bergstrom in an article in *The Free Lunch*.

or

$$p = \frac{MC(x)}{(1-\pi)k} + \frac{\pi F}{(1-\pi)k}.$$

Geometrically, this means that the marginal cost curve is first shifted up by πF, and then tilted up by the amount $1/(1-\pi)k$, as depicted in Figure 24.5. This curve gives us the relationship between the market price and the number of birds caught.

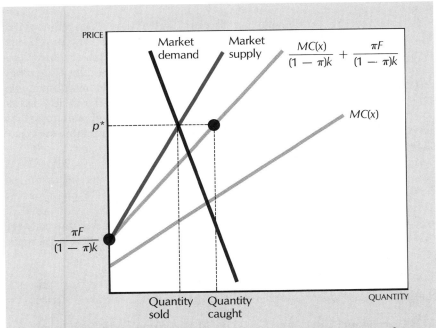

The supply curve for parrots. There are two relevant supply curves: the amount of parrots caught by the poachers and the amount sold to the market.

Figure 24.5

Now what is the appropriate equilibrium condition? If there are $S(p)$ birds caught, then only $(1-\pi)kS(p)$ actually make it to market. Thus the equilibrium condition is

$$D(p) = (1-\pi)kS(p).$$

This says that to get the final number of birds supplied to the market we have to tilt the supply curve once more. Referring to Figure 24.5, we find the intersection of the market demand and supply curves to determine final equilibrium price. The intersection of the market demand and supply curves gives the equilibrium number of birds sold, and we can look at the shifted marginal cost curve to find the number of birds caught.

In the case depicted in Figure 24.5, more birds are caught than if there were no penalty for export at all. The effect of making the birds illegal has had a perverse effect on the incentives of the bird smugglers: making the sales of birds illegal has induced the smugglers to use an inferior technology for transporting birds and has raised the market price. The net effect is for the bird suppliers to capture *more* wild birds than if there were no penalties at all.

It does not have to be this way. It could well happen that fewer birds would get caught. Which way it goes depends on the actual shapes of the supply curves and the actual magnitudes of the probabilities, the fines, and so on. Nonetheless, the possibility of this kind of perverse consequence is disturbing. Governments often want to use tax policy to discourage the consumption or production of different goods. But anything that raises the price of a good will tend to *encourage* the production of that good—so the net effects of such policies should be examined with care to ensure that they really have the desired effect.

Summary

1. This chapter has described several examples of the use of economic tools to analyze the functioning of competitive markets. There is a systematic procedure that can be used to do this kind of analysis.

2. First, write down the profit maximization problem of the firm, and use the price equals marginal cost condition to derive the supply function.

3. If there is more than one firm, add up the supply functions to get the industry supply function.

4. Write down the relationship between the amount of output produced by the firms and the amount actually supplied to the market.

5. Find the price and quantities where the amount of output demanded in the market equals the amount of output supplied to the market.

Review Questions

1. Suppose that the foreign price of oil was $20 a barrel, the domestic price of oil was $10 a barrel, and each barrel of foreign oil that a refiner purchased allowed it to purchase one barrel of domestic oil under the entitlement program. What was the dollar subsidy per barrel of foreign oil?

2. Suppose that Kenya wants to discourage the poaching of elephants for their ivory. When the poachers who have contraband ivory are captured, what should the government do with the confiscated ivory?

3. The government is considering two plans to reduce the production of moonshine. The first plan is to make the production of moonshine legal, but put a 50% tax on it, which all firms will pay. The second plan is to make moonshine illegal and destroy any that is discovered. The authorities estimate that they can find half of the moonshine produced. Compare the effects of these two plans on the production decisions of firms.

25

MONOPOLY

In the previous chapters we have analyzed the behavior of a competitive industry, a market structure that is most likely when there are a large number of small firms. In this chapter we turn to the opposite extreme and consider an industry structure when there is only *one* firm in the industry—a **monopoly**.

When there is only one firm in a market, it is very unlikely to take the market price as given. Instead, a monopoly would recognize its influence over the market price, and choose that level of price and output that maximized its overall profits.

Of course, it can't choose price and output independently; for any given price, the monopoly will be able to sell only what the market will bear. If it chooses a high price, it will be able to sell only a small quantity. The demand behavior of the consumers will constrain the monopolist's choice of price and quantity.

We can view the monopolist as choosing the price, and letting the consumers choose how much they wish to buy at that price, or we can think of the monopolist as choosing the quantity, and letting the consumers decide what price they will pay for that quantity. The first approach is probably more natural, but the second turns out to be analytically more convenient. Of course, both approaches are equivalent when done correctly.

25.1 Maximizing Profits

We begin by studying the monopolist's profit maximization problem. Let us use $p(y)$ to denote the market inverse demand curve, and $c(y)$ to denote the cost function. Let $r(y) = p(y)y$ denote the revenue function of the monopolist. The monopolist's profit maximization problem then takes the form

$$\max_{y} \ r(y) - c(y).$$

The optimality condition for this problem is straightforward: at the optimal choice of output we must have marginal revenue equal to marginal cost. If marginal revenue were less than marginal cost it would pay the firm to decrease output, since the savings in cost would more than make up for the loss in revenue. If the marginal revenue were greater than the marginal cost, it would pay the firm to increase output. The only point where the firm has no incentive to change output is where marginal revenue equals marginal cost.

In terms of algebra, we can write the optimization condition as

$$MR = MC$$

or

$$\frac{\Delta r}{\Delta y} = \frac{\Delta c}{\Delta y}.$$

The same $MR = MC$ condition has to hold in the case of a competitive firm; in that case, marginal revenue is equal to the price and the condition reduces to price equals marginal cost.

In the case of a monopolist, the marginal revenue term is slightly more complicated. If the monopolist decides to increase his output by Δy, there are two effects on profits. First he sells more output, and gets a revenue of $p\Delta y$ from that. But second, he pushes the price down by Δp and he gets this lower price on *all* the output he has been selling.

Thus the total effect on revenues of changing output by Δy will be

$$\Delta r = p\Delta y + y\Delta p$$

so that the change in revenue divided by the change in output—the marginal revenue—is

$$\frac{\Delta r}{\Delta y} = p + \frac{\Delta p}{\Delta y}y.$$

(This is exactly the same derivation we went through in our discussion of marginal revenue in Chapter 16. You might want to review that material before proceeding.)

Another way to think about this is to think of the monopolist as choosing his output and price simultaneously—recognizing, of course, the constraint imposed by the demand curve. If the monopolist wants to sell more output he has to lower his price. But this lower price will mean a lower price for all of the units he is selling, not just the new units. Hence the term $y\Delta p$.

In the competitive case, a firm that could lower its price below the price charged by other firms would immediately capture the entire market from its competitors. But in the monopolistic case, the monopoly already has the entire market; when it lowers its price, it has to take into account the effect of the price reduction on all the units it sells.

Following the discussion in Chapter 16, we can also express marginal revenue in terms of elasticity via the formula

$$MR(y) = p(y)\left[1 + \frac{1}{\epsilon(y)}\right]$$

and write the "marginal revenue equals marginal costs" optimality condition as

$$p(y)\left[1 + \frac{1}{\epsilon(y)}\right] = MC(y). \tag{25.1}$$

Since elasticity is naturally negative, we could also write this expression as

$$p(y)\left[1 - \frac{1}{|\epsilon(y)|}\right] = MC(y).$$

From these equations it is easy to see the connection with the competitive case: in the competitive case, the firm faces a flat demand curve—an infinitely elastic demand curve. This means that $1/\epsilon = 1/\infty = 0$, so the appropriate version of this equation for a competitive firm is simply price equals marginal cost.

Note that a monopolist will never choose to operate where the demand curve is *inelastic*. For if $|\epsilon| < 1$, then $1/|\epsilon| > 1$ and the marginal revenue is negative, so it can't possibly equal marginal cost. The meaning of this becomes clear when we think of what is implied by an inelastic demand curve: if $|\epsilon| < 1$, then reducing output will increase revenues, and reducing output must reduce total cost, so profits will necessarily increase. Thus any point where $|\epsilon| < 1$ cannot be a profit maximum for a monopolist, since it could increase its profits by producing less output. It follows that a point that yields maximum profits can only occur where $|\epsilon| \geq 1$.

25.2 Linear Demand Curve and Monopoly

Suppose that the monopolist faces a linear demand curve:

$$p(y) = a - by.$$

Then the revenue function is

$$r(y) = p(y)y = ay - by^2$$

and the marginal revenue function is

$$MR(y) = a - 2by.$$

(This follows from the formula given at the end of Chapter 16. It is easy to derive using simple calculus. If you don't know calculus, just memorize the formula, since we will use it quite a bit.)

Note that the marginal revenue function has the same vertical intercept, a, as the demand curve, but it is twice as steep. This gives us an easy way to draw the marginal revenue curve. We know that the vertical intercept is a. To get the horizontal intercept, just take half of the horizontal intercept of the demand curve. Then connect the two intercepts with a straight line. We have illustrated the demand curve and the marginal revenue curve in Figure 25.1.

The optimal output, y^*, is where the marginal revenue curve intersects the marginal cost curve. The monopolist will then charge the maximum

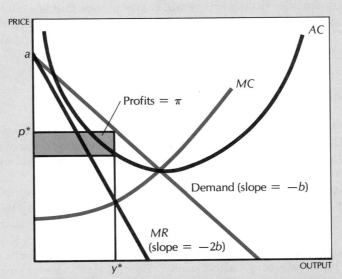

Monopoly with a linear demand curve. The monopolist's profit maximizing output occurs where marginal revenue equals marginal cost.

Figure 25.1

price he can get at this output, $p(y^*)$. This gives him a revenue of $p(y*)y^*$ from which we subtract the total cost $c(y^*) = AC(y^*)y^*$, leaving a profit area as illustrated.

25.3 Markup Pricing

We can use the elasticity formula for the monopolist to express his optimal pricing policy in another way. Rearranging equation (25.1) we have

$$p(y) = \frac{MC(y^*)}{1 - 1/|\epsilon(y)|}. \tag{25.2}$$

This formulation indicates that the market price is a markup over marginal cost, where the amount of the markup depends on the elasticity of demand. The markup is given by

$$\frac{1}{1 - 1/|\epsilon(y)|}.$$

Since the monopolist always operates where the demand curve is elastic, we are assured that $\epsilon > 1$ and thus the markup is greater than 1.

In the case of a constant elasticity demand curve, this formula is especially simple since $\epsilon(y)$ is a constant. A monopolist who faces a constant elasticity demand curve will charge a price that is a *constant* markup on marginal cost. This is illustrated in Figure 25.2. The curve labeled $MC/(1 - 1/|\epsilon|)$ is a constant fraction higher than the marginal cost curve; the optimal level of output occurs where $p = MC/(1 - 1/|\epsilon|)$.

EXAMPLE: The Impact of Taxes on a Monopolist

Let us consider a firm with constant marginal costs and ask what happens to the price charged when a quantity tax is imposed. Clearly the marginal costs go up by the amount of the tax, but what happens to the market price?

Let's first consider the case of a linear demand curve, as depicted in Figure 25.3. When the marginal cost curve, MC, shifts up by the amount of the tax to $MC+t$, the intersection of marginal revenue and marginal cost moves to the left. Since the demand curve is half as steep as the marginal revenue curve, the price goes up by half the amount of the tax.

This is easy to see algebraically. The marginal revenue equals marginal cost plus the tax condition is

$$a - 2by = c + t.$$

Solving for y yields

$$y = \frac{a - c - t}{2b}.$$

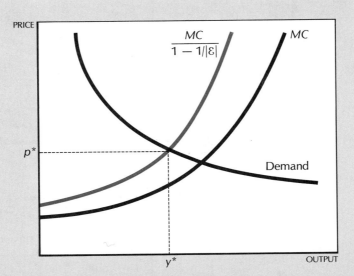

Monopoly with constant elasticity demand. To locate the profit maximizing output level we find the output level where the curve $MC/(1 - 1/|\epsilon|)$ crosses the demand curve.

Figure
25.2

Thus the change in output is given by

$$\frac{\Delta y}{\Delta t} = -\frac{1}{2b}.$$

The demand curve is

$$p(y) = a - by$$

so price will change by $-b$ times the change in output:

$$\frac{\Delta p}{\Delta t} = -b \times -\frac{1}{2b} = \frac{1}{2}.$$

In this calculation the factor $1/2$ occurs because of the linear demand curve, but the interesting feature is that the price rises by less than the tax increase. Is this likely to be true in general?

The answer is no—in general a tax may increase the price by more or less than the amount of the tax. For an easy example, consider the case of a monopolist facing a constant elasticity demand curve. Then we have:

$$p = \frac{c + t}{1 - 1/|\epsilon|}$$

so that

$$\frac{\Delta p}{\Delta t} = \frac{1}{1 - 1/|\epsilon|}$$

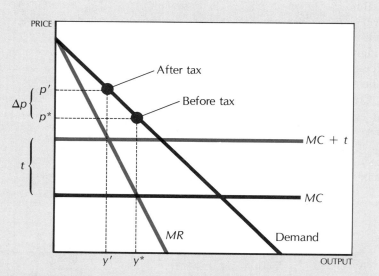

Figure 25.3

Linear demand and taxation. Imposition of a tax on a monopolist facing a linear demand. Note that the price will rise by half the amount of the tax.

which is certainly bigger than 1. In this case, the monopolist passes on *more* than the amount of the tax.

Another kind of tax that we might consider is the case of a profits tax. In this case the monopolist is required to pay some fraction τ of his profits to the government. The maximization problem that he faces is then

$$\max_{y} (1 - \tau)[p(y)y - c(y)].$$

But the value of y that maximizes profits will also maximize $(1 - \tau)$ times profits. Thus a pure profits tax will have no effect on a monopolist's choice of output.

25.4 Inefficiency of Monopoly

A competitive industry operates at a point where price equals marginal cost. A monopolized industry operates where price is greater than marginal cost. Thus in general the price will be higher and the output lower if a firm behaves monopolistically rather than competitively. For this reason, consumers will typically be worse off in an industry organized as a monopoly than one organized competitively.

But, by the same token, the firm will be better off! Counting both the firm and the consumer, it is not clear whether competition or monopoly will be a "better" arrangement. It appears that one must make a value judgment about the relative welfare of consumers and the owners of firms. However, we will see that one can argue against monopoly on grounds of efficiency alone.

Consider a monopoly situation, as depicted in Figure 25.4. Suppose that we could somehow costlessly force this firm to behave as a competitor and take the market price as being set exogenously. Then we would have (p_c, y_c) for the competitive price and output. Alternatively, if the firm recognized its influence on the market price and chose its level of output so as to maximize profits, we would see the monopoly price and output (p_m, y_m).

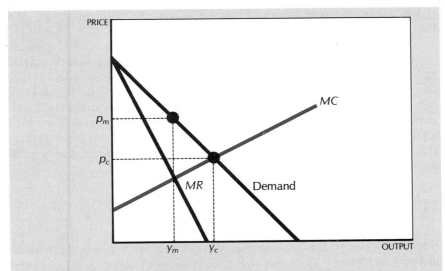

Inefficiency of monopoly. A monopolist produces less than the competitive amount of output, and is therefore Pareto inefficient.

Figure 25.4

Recall that an economic arrangement is Pareto efficient if there is no way to make anyone better off without making somebody else worse off. Is the monopoly level of output Pareto efficient?

Remember the definition of the inverse demand curve. At each level of output, $p(y)$ measures how much people are willing to pay for an additional unit of the good. Since $p(y)$ is greater than $MC(y)$ for all the output levels between y_m and y_c, there is a whole range of output where people are willing to pay more for a unit of output than it costs to produce it. Clearly there is a potential for Pareto improvement here!

For example, consider the situation at the monopoly level of output y_m. Since $p(y_m) > MC(y_m)$ we know that there is someone who is willing to pay more for an extra unit of output than it costs to produce that extra unit. Suppose that the firm produces this extra output and sells it to this person at any price p where $p(y_m) > p > MC(y_m)$. Then this consumer is made better off since he or she was just willing to pay $p(y_m)$ for that unit of consumption and it was sold for $p < p(y_m)$. Similarly, it cost the monopolist $MC(y_m)$ to produce that extra unit of output and he sold it for $p > MC(y_m)$. All the other units of output are being sold for the same price as before, so nothing has changed there. But in the sale of the extra unit of output, each side of the market gets some extra surplus—each side of the market is made better off and no one else is made worse off. We have found a Pareto improvement.

It is worthwhile considering the reason for this inefficiency. The efficient level of output is when the willingness to pay for an extra unit of output just equals the cost of producing this extra unit. A competitive firm makes this comparison. But a monopolist also looks at the effect of increasing output on the revenue received from the **inframarginal** units, and these inframarginal units have nothing to do with efficiency. A monopolist would always be ready to sell an additional unit at a lower price than it is currently charging if it did not have to lower the prices of all the other inframarginal units it is currently selling.

25.5 Deadweight Loss of Monopoly

Now that we know that a monopoly is inefficient, we might want to know just how inefficient it is. Is there a way to measure the total loss in efficiency due to a monopoly? We know how to measure the loss to the consumers from having to pay p_m rather than p_c—we just look at the change in consumers' surplus. Similarly, for the firm we know how to measure the gain in profits from charging p_m rather than p_c—we just use the change in producer's surplus.

The most natural way to combine these two numbers is to treat the firm—or, more properly, the owners of the firm—and the consumers of the firm's output symmetrically and add together the profits of the firm and the consumers' surplus. The change in the profits of the firm—the change in producer's surplus—measures how much the owners would be willing to pay to get the higher price under monopoly, and the change in consumers' surplus measures how much the consumers would have to be paid to compensate them for the higher price. Thus the difference between these two numbers should give a sensible measure of the net benefit or cost of the monopoly.

The changes in the producer's and consumers' surplus from a movement from monopolistic to competitive output are illustrated in Figure 25.5. The monopolist's surplus goes down by A due to the lower price on the units he was already selling. It goes up by D due to the profits on the extra units he is now selling.

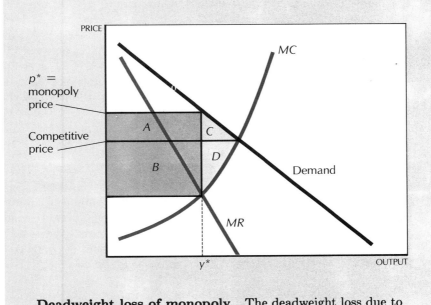

Deadweight loss of monopoly. The deadweight loss due to the monopoly is given by the area $C + D$.

Figure
25.5

The consumers' surplus goes up by A, since the consumers are now getting all the units they were buying before at a cheaper price, and it goes up by C since they get some surplus on the extra units that are being sold. The area A is just a transfer from the monopolist to the consumer; one side of the market is made better off and one side is made worse off, but the total surplus doesn't change. The area $C + D$ does represent a true increase in surplus—this area measures the value that the consumers and the producers place on the extra output that has been produced.

The area $C + D$ is known as the *deadweight loss due to the monopoly*. It provides a measure of how much worse off people are paying the monopoly price than paying the competitive price. The deadweight loss due to monopoly, like the deadweight loss due to a tax, measures the value of the lost output by valuing each unit of lost output at the price that people are willing to pay for that unit.

To see that the deadweight loss measures the value of the lost output, just think about starting at the monopoly point and providing one more unit of output. The value of that marginal unit of output is just the market price—what someone is willing to pay for the last unit of output. The cost of producing the additional unit of output is the marginal cost. Thus the "social value" of producing an extra unit will be simply the price minus the marginal cost. Now consider the value of the next unit of output; again its social value will be the gap between price and marginal cost at that level of output. And so it goes. As we move from the monopoly level of output to the competitive level of output, we "sum up" the distances between the demand curve and the marginal cost curve to generate the value of the lost output due to the monopoly behavior. The total area between the two curves from the monopoly output to the competitive output is the deadweight loss.

25.6 The Optimal Life of a Patent

A **patent** offers inventors the exclusive right to benefit from their inventions for a limited period of time. Thus a patent offers a kind of limited monopoly. The reason for offering such patent protection is to encourage innovation. In the absence of a patent system, it is likely that individuals and firms would be unwilling to invest much in research and development, since any new discoveries that they would make could be copied by competitors.

In the United States the life of a patent is 17 years. During that period, the holders of the patent have a monopoly on the invention; after the patent expires, anyone is free to utilize the technology described in the patent. Other countries have different patent terms. In the English patent system of 1624, the term was 14 years, which was apparently based on the 7-year term of apprentices.

The longer the life of a patent, the more gains can be accrued by the inventors, and thus the more incentive they have to invest in research and development. However, the longer the monopoly is allowed to exist, the more deadweight loss will be generated. The benefit from a long patent life is that it encourages innovation; the cost is that it encourages monopoly. The "optimal" patent life is the period that balances these two conflicting effects.

The problem of determining the optimal patent life has been examined by William Nordhaus of Yale University.[1] As Nordhaus indicates, the problem is very complex and there are many unknown relationships involved. Nevertheless, some simple calculations can give some insight as to whether

---

[1] William Nordhaus, *Invention, Growth, and Welfare* (Cambridge, MA: M.I.T. Press, 1969).

the current patent life is wildly out of line with the estimated benefits and costs described above.

If one assumes that the average invention reduces costs by about one percent and assumes a constant elasticity demand curve for the product, then it is possible to calculate the present discounted value of the surplus attributable to the invention, and compare it to the present discounted value of the deadweight loss. If the invention reduces costs by one percent, and the elasticity of demand is relatively small, it turns out that the optimal life of a patent is almost exactly 17 years.

However, Nordhaus finds that other choices of parameters give quite different estimates. If the elasticity of demand for the product is relatively large and the invention reduces costs by 5 percent, the optimal life turns out to be 8.7 years. For the range of parameter values that Nordhaus considers, the optimal life of a patent ranges between 1 and 34 years.

Nordhaus also computed the total consumer's surplus associated with the different parameter values. Somewhat surprisingly, it turned out that total surplus was relatively insensitive to the exact values of the parameters chosen. According to Nordhaus: "The welfare index is insensitive to the life of the patent once a life of between six and ten years has been reached. This conclusion holds for all parameter values examined." Even though the *optimal life* of the patent was sensitive to variations in the unknown parameters, the *total surplus* was relatively insensitive. For "run of the mill" inventions of the sort Nordhaus was considering, a patent system with a 17 year life was roughly 90 percent efficient—meaning that it achieved 90 percent of the maximum possible consumers' surplus. On the basis of these figures, it does not seem like there is a compelling reason to make drastic changes in the patent system.

25.7 Natural Monopoly

We have seen earlier that the Pareto efficient amount of output in an industry occurs where price equals marginal cost. A monopolist produces where marginal revenue equals marginal cost and thus produces too little output. It would seem that regulating a monopoly to eliminate the inefficiency is pretty easy—all the regulator has to do is to set price equal to marginal cost, and profit maximization will do the rest. Unfortunately this analysis leaves out one important aspect of the problem: it may be that the monopolist would make negative profits at such a price.

An example of this is shown in Figure 25.6. Here the minimum point of the average cost curve is to the right of the demand curve, and the intersection of demand and marginal cost lies underneath the average cost curve. Even though the level of output y_{MC} is efficient, it is not profitable. If a regulator set this level of output, the monopolist would prefer to go out of business.

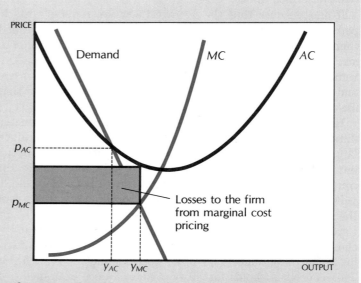

Figure 25.6

A natural monopoly. If a natural monopolist operates where price equals marginal cost, then it will produce an efficient level of output, y_{MC}, but it will be unable to cover its costs. If it is required to produce an output where price equals average cost, y_{AC}, then it will cover its costs, but will produce too little output relative to the efficient amount.

This kind of situation often arises with public utilities. Think of a gas company, for example. Here the technology involves very large fixed costs—creating and maintaining the gas delivery pipes—and a very small marginal cost to providing extra units of gas—once the pipe is laid, it costs very little to pump more gas down the pipe. Similarly a local telephone company involves very large fixed costs for providing the wires and switching network, while the marginal costs of an extra unit of telephone service is very low. When there are large fixed costs and small marginal costs, you can easily get the kind of situation described in Figure 25.6. Such a situation is referred to as a **natural monopoly**.

If allowing a natural monopolist to set the monopoly price is undesirable due to the Pareto inefficiency, and forcing the natural monopoly to produce at the competitive price is infeasible due to negative profits, what is left? For the most part natural monopolies are regulated or operated by governments. Different countries have adopted different approaches. In some countries the telephone service is provided by the government and in others it is provided by private firms that are regulated by the government. Both of these approaches have their advantages and disadvantages.

For example, let us consider the case of government regulation of a natural monopoly. If the regulated firm is to require no subsidy, it must make nonnegative profits, which means it must operate on or above the average cost curve. If it is to provide service to all who are willing to pay for it, it must also operate on the demand curve. Thus the natural operating position for a regulated firm is a point like (p_{AC}, y_{AC}) in Figure 25.6. Here the firm is selling its product at the average cost of production, so it covers its costs, but it is producing too little output relative to the efficient level of output.

This solution is often adopted as a kind of second-best pricing policy for a natural monopolist. Government regulators set the prices that the public utility is allowed to charge. Ideally these prices are supposed to be prices that just allow the firm to break even—produce at a point where price equals average costs.

The problem facing the regulators is determining just what the true costs of the firm are. Usually there is a public utility commission that investigates the costs of the monopoly in an attempt to determine the true average cost, and then sets a price that will cover costs. (Of course one of these costs is the payment that the firm has to make to its shareholders and other creditors in exchange for the money they have loaned to the firm.)

In the United States these regulatory boards operate at the state and local level. Typically electricity, natural gas, and telephone service operate in this way. Other natural monopolies like cable TV are usually regulated at the local level.

The other solution to the problem of natural monopoly is to let the government operate it. The ideal solution here in this case is to operate the service at price equals marginal cost and provide a lump sum subsidy to keep the firm in operation. This is often the practice for local public transportation systems such as buses and subways. The lump sum subsidies may not reflect inefficient operation *per se*, but rather just reflect the large fixed costs associated with such public utilities.

Then again, the subsidies may just represent inefficiency! The problem with government run monopolies is that it is almost as difficult to measure their costs as it is to measure the costs of regulated public utilities. Government regulatory commissions that oversee the operations of public utilities often subject them to probing hearings to require them to justify cost data whereas an internal government bureaucracy may escape such intense scrutiny. The government bureaucrats who run such government monopolies may turn out to be less accountable to the public than those who run the regulated monopolies.

25.8 What Causes Monopolies?

Given information on costs and demand, when would we predict that an industry would be competitive and when would we predict that it would be monopolized? In general the answer depends on the relationship between the average cost curve and the demand curve. The crucial factor is the size of the **minimum efficient scale (MES)**, the level of output that minimizes average cost, relative to the size of demand.

Consider Figure 25.7 where we have illustrated the average cost curve and the market demand curves for two goods. In the first market there is room in the market for many firms, each charging a price close to p^* and each operating at a relatively small scale. In the second market, only one firm can make positive profits. We would expect that the first market might well operate as a competitive market, and the second would operate as a monopolist.

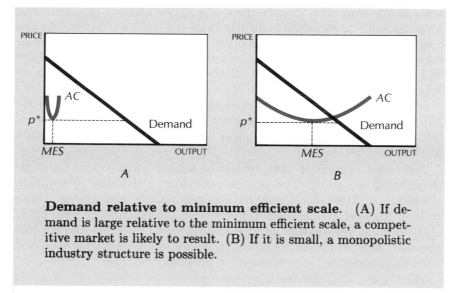

Figure
25.7

Demand relative to minimum efficient scale. (A) If demand is large relative to the minimum efficient scale, a competitive market is likely to result. (B) If it is small, a monopolistic industry structure is possible.

Thus the shape of the average cost curve, which in turn is determined by the underlying technology, is therefore one important aspect that determines whether a market will operate competitively or monopolistically. If the minimum efficient scale of production—the level of output that minimizes average costs—is small relative to the size of the market, we might expect that competitive conditions will prevail.

Note that this is a *relative* statement: what matters is the scale relative to the market size. We can't do too much about the minimum efficient scale—that is determined by the technology. But economic policy can influence the size of the market. If a country chooses nonrestrictive foreign trade policies, so that domestic firms face foreign competition, then the domestic firms' ability to influence prices will be much less. Conversely, if a country adopts restrictive trade policies, so that the size of the market is limited only to that country, then monopolistic practices are more likely to take hold.

If monopolies arise because the minimum efficient scale is large relative to the size of the market, and it is infeasible to increase the size of the market, then the industry is a candidate for regulation or other sorts of government intervention. Of course such regulation and intervention are costly too. Regulatory boards cost money, and the efforts of the firm to satisfy the regulatory boards can be quite expensive. From society's point of view, the question should be whether the deadweight costs of the monopoly exceed the costs of regulation.

A second reason why monopoly might occur is that several different firms in an industry might be able to collude and restrict output in order to raise prices and thereby increase their profits. When firms collude in this way and attempt to reduce output and increase price, we say the industry is organized as a **cartel**.

Cartels are illegal. The Antitrust Division of the Justice Department is charged with searching for evidence of noncompetitive behavior on the part of firms. If the government can establish that a group of firms attempted to restrict output or engaged in certain other anticompetitive practices, the firms in question can be forced to pay heavy fines.

On the other hand, an industry may have one dominant firm purely by historical accident. If one firm is first to enter some market, it may have enough of a cost advantage to be able to discourage other firms from entering the industry. Suppose, for example, that there are very large "tooling up" costs to entering an industry. Then the incumbent—the firm already in the industry—may under certain conditions be able to convince potential entrants that it will cut its prices drastically if they attempt to enter the industry. By preventing entry in this manner, a firm can eventually dominate a market. We will study an example of pricing to prevent entry in Chapter 27.

25.9 Price Discrimination

We have argued earlier that a monopoly operates at an inefficient level of output since it restricts output to a point where people are willing to pay more for extra output than it costs to produce it. The monopolist doesn't want to produce this *extra* output, because it would force down the price that he would be able to get for *all* of its output.

But if the monopolist could sell different units of output at different prices, then we have another story. Selling different units of output at different prices is called **price discrimination**. Economists generally consider three kinds of price discrimination:

First-degree price discrimination means that the monopolist sells different units of output for different prices *and* these prices may differ from person to person. This is sometimes known as the case of **perfect price discrimination**.

Second-degree price discrimination means that the monopolist sells different units of output for different prices, but every individual who buys the same amount of the good pays the same price. Thus prices differ across the units of the good, but not across people. The most common example of this is bulk discounts.

Third-degree price discrimination occurs when the monopolist sells output to different people for different prices, but every unit of output sold to a given person sells for the same price. This is the most common form of price discrimination, and examples include senior citizens' discounts, student discounts, and so on.

Let us look at each of these to see what economics can say about how price discrimination works.

25.10 Second-Degree Price Discrimination

Second-degree price discrimination is also known as the case of **nonlinear pricing**, since it means that the price per unit of output is not constant, but depends on how much you buy. This form of price discrimination is commonly used by public utilities; for example, the price of electricity often depends on how much is bought. In other industries bulk discounts for large purchases are sometimes available.

How might a firm decide how to set a nonlinear pricing schedule? What can we say about the economic significance of the prices being charged? In general the problem of nonlinear pricing is quite complicated, and a complete analysis is beyond the scope of this book. However, there is one nice result that can be described here.

Suppose that a regulated monopolist (or the regulating board) is trying to pick a schedule of pricing that maximizes total consumers' surplus subject to the constraint that it cover costs. Then it turns out that the *largest* purchaser must face a price equal to marginal cost for the last unit that it buys.

The argument goes like this. Suppose, contrary to the claim, that the largest purchaser faced a price p^* greater than marginal cost, and was purchasing y^* units of output. Now consider what would happen if we lowered the price of the next unit of output greater than y^* to some price p' where p' is less than p^* and greater than marginal cost. The largest purchaser will purchase this extra unit, since its price is now lower, making him better off, and the seller will sell this extra unit at a price exceeding marginal cost, so it too will be better off. Since this kind of adjustment can be done whenever the price facing the largest purchaser exceeds marginal cost, a Pareto efficient price schedule must involve the largest purchaser paying marginal cost.

Note the similarity of this argument to the argument establishing that an ordinary monopolist's choice of output was Pareto inefficient. The reasoning is much the same: whenever price is greater than marginal cost, there is some way to make all parties better off. The trick is just to find it.

The same sort of argument applies to a profit maximizing monopolist. It should choose a price schedule for which the largest purchaser faces a "marginal price" equal to marginal cost. Any higher price for the last unit sold represents lost profits, since producing extra output and selling it for a lower price, without changing any other prices, would necessarily increase profits.

25.11 First-Degree Price Discrimination

Under first-degree price discrimination, or perfect price discrimination, each unit is sold to that individual who values it most highly, at the maximum price that this individual is willing to pay for it. Thus there is no consumer's surplus generated in such a market—all of the surplus goes to the producer. In turns out that perfect price discrimination produces an efficient level of output. To prove this, note that a perfectly price discriminating monopolist must produce at an output level where price equals marginal cost: if price were greater than marginal cost, that would mean that there is someone who is willing to pay more than it costs to produce an extra unit of output—so why not produce that extra unit and sell it to that person?

Perfect price discrimination by a monopolist leads to a Pareto efficient outcome. Just as in the case of a competitive market, the sum of producer's and consumer's surplus is maximized. However, the producer ends up getting *all* of the surplus generated in the market! If the producer really can charge each consumer a different price for each different unit, he will choose a price that makes each consumer just indifferent between consuming or not consuming the good.

Perfect price discrimination is an idealized concept—as the word "perfect" might suggest—but it is interesting theoretically since it gives us an example of a resource allocation mechanism other than a competitive market that achieves Pareto efficiency. There are very few real-life examples of perfect price discrimination. The closest example would be something like a small-town doctor who charges his patients different prices, based on their ability to pay.

25.12 Third-Degree Price Discrimination

Recall that this means that the monopolist sells to different people at different prices, but every unit of the good sold to a given group is sold at the same price. Third-degree price discrimination is the most common form of price discrimination. Examples of this might be student discounts at the movies, or senior citizens' discounts at the drugstore. How does the monopolist determine the optimal prices to charge in each market?

Let us suppose that the monopolist is able to identify two groups of people and can sell an item to each group at a different price. We suppose that the consumers in each market are not able to resell the good. Let us use $p_1(y_1)$ and $p_2(y_2)$ to denote the inverse demand curves of groups 1 and 2, respectively, and let $c(y_1 + y_2)$ be the cost of producing output. Then the profit maximization problem facing the monopolist is

$$\max_{y_1,y_2} \; p_1(y_1)y_1 + p_2(y_2)y_2 - c(y_1 + y_2).$$

The optimal solution must have

$$MR_1(y_1) = MC(y_1 + y_2)$$

$$MR_2(y_2) = MC(y_1 + y_2).$$

That is, the marginal cost of producing an extra unit of output must be equal to the marginal revenue in *each* market. If the marginal revenue in market 1 exceeded marginal cost, it would pay to expand output in market 1, and similarly for market 2. Since marginal cost is the same in each market, this means of course that marginal revenue in each market must also be the same. Thus a good should bring the same increase in revenue whether it is sold in market 1 or in market 2.

We can use the standard elasticity formula for marginal revenue and write the profit maximization conditions as

$$p_1(y_1) \left[1 - \frac{1}{|\epsilon_1(y_1)|} \right] = MC(y_1 + y_2)$$

$$p_2(y_2) \left[1 - \frac{1}{|\epsilon_2(y_2)|} \right] = MC(y_1 + y_2)$$

where $\epsilon_1(y_1)$ and $\epsilon_2(y_2)$ represent the elasticities of demand in the respective markets, evaluated at the profit maximizing choices of output.

Now note the following. If $p_1 > p_2$, then we must have

$$1 - \frac{1}{|\epsilon_1(y_1)|} < 1 - \frac{1}{|\epsilon_2(y_2)|}$$

which in turn implies that

$$\frac{1}{|\epsilon_1(y_1)|} > \frac{1}{|\epsilon_2(y_2)|}.$$

This means that

$$|\epsilon_2(y_2)| > |\epsilon_1(y_1)|.$$

Thus the market with the higher price must have the lower elasticity of demand. Upon reflection, this is quite sensible. An elastic demand is a price sensitive demand. A firm that price discriminates will therefore set a low price for the price sensitive group and a high price for the group that is relatively price insensitive. In this way it maximizes its overall profits.

We suggested that senior citizens' discounts and student discounts were good examples of third-degree price discrimination. Now we can see why they have discounts. It is likely that students and senior citizens are more sensitive to price than the average consumer, and thus have more elastic demands for the relevant region of prices. Therefore a profit maximizing firm will price discriminate in their favor.

EXAMPLE: Linear Demand Curves

Let's consider a problem where the firm faces two markets with linear demand curves, $x_1 = a - bp_1$ and $x_2 = c - dp_2$. Suppose for simplicity that marginal costs are zero. If the firm is allowed to price discriminate it will produce where marginal revenue equals zero in each market—at a price and output combination that is halfway down each demand curve, with outputs $x_1^* = a/2$ and $x_2^* = c/2$, and prices $p_1^* = a/2b$ and $p_2^* = c/2d$.

Suppose that the firm were forced to sell in both markets at the same price. Then it would face a demand curve of $x = (a + c) - (b + d)p$ and would produce halfway down this demand curve, resulting in an output of $x^* = (a + c)/2$, and price of $p^* = (a + c)/2(b + d)$. Note that the total output is the same whether or not price discrimination is allowed. (This is a special feature of the linear demand curve and does not hold in general.)

However, there is an important exception to this statement. We have assumed that when the monopolist chooses the optimal single price it will sell a positive amount of output in each market. It may very well happen that at the profit maximizing price, the monopolist will sell output to only one of the markets, as illustrated in Figure 25.8.

Here we have two linear demand curves; since marginal cost is assumed to be zero, the monopolist will want to operate at a point where the elasticity of demand is zero, which we know to be halfway down the market demand curve. Thus the price p_1^* is a profit maximizing price—lowering the price any further would reduce revenues. The demand is so small in market 2 that the monopolist won't want to set a price low enough to sell to anyone in this market. Instead, it will sell only to the high demand market 1.

In this case, allowing price discrimination will unambiguously increase total output, since the monopolist will find it in its interest to sell to both markets if it can charge a different price in each one.

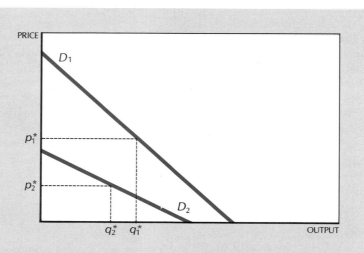

Figure 25.8

Price discrimination with linear demands. If the monopolist can charge only one price, it will charge p_1^*, and sell only to market 1. But if price discrimination is allowed, it will also sell at price p_2^* to market 2.

EXAMPLE: Calculating Optimal Price Discrimination

Suppose that a monopolist faces two markets with demand curves given by

$$D_1(p_1) = 100 - p_1$$
$$D_2(p_2) = 100 - 2p_2.$$

Assume that the monopolist's marginal cost is constant at \$20 a unit. If it can price discriminate, what price should it charge in each market in order to maximize profits? What if it can't price discriminate? Then what price should it charge?

To solve the price discrimination problem, we first calculate the inverse demand functions:

$$p_1(y_1) = 100 - y_1$$
$$p_2(y_2) = 50 - y_2/2.$$

Marginal revenue equals marginal cost in each market yields the two equations:

$$100 - 2y_1 = 20$$
$$50 - y_2 = 20.$$

Solving we have $y_1^* = 40$ and $y_2^* = 30$. Substituting back into the inverse demand functions gives us the prices $p_1^* = 60$ and $p_2^* = 35$.

If the monopolist must charge the same price in each market, we first calculate the total demand:

$$D(p) = D_1(p_1) + D_2(p_2) = 200 - 3p.$$

The inverse demand curve is

$$p(y) = \frac{200}{3} - \frac{y}{3}.$$

Marginal revenue equals marginal cost gives us

$$\frac{200}{3} - \frac{2}{3}y = 20$$

which can be solved to give $y^* = 70$ and $p^* = 43\frac{1}{3}$.

EXAMPLE: Price Discrimination in Academic Journals

Most written scholarly communication takes place in academic journals. These journals are sold by subscription to libraries and to individual scholars. It is very common to see different subscription prices being charged to libraries and individuals. In general, we would expect that the demand by libraries would be much more inelastic than demand by individuals, and, just as economic analysis would predict, the prices for library subscriptions are typically much higher than the prices for individual subscriptions. Often library subscriptions are 2 to 3 times more expensive than subscriptions to individuals.

More recently, some publishers have begun to price discriminate by geography. During 1984, when the U.S. dollar was at an all-time high as compared to the English pound, many British publishers began to charge different prices to U.S. subscribers than to European subscribers. It would be expected that the U.S. demand would be more inelastic. Since the dollar price of British journals was rather low due to the exchange rate, a 10 percent increase in the U.S. price would result in a smaller percentage drop in demand than a similar increase in the British price. Thus, on grounds of profit maximization, it made sense for the British publishers to raise the prices of their journals to the group with the lower elasticity of demand—the U.S. subscribers. According to a 1984 study, North American libraries were charged an average of 67 percent more for their journals than U.K. libraries, and 34 percent more than anyone else in the world.[2]

Further evidence for price discrimination can be found by examining the pattern of price increases. According to a study by the University of Michigan Library, "... publishers have carefully considered their new pricing strategy. There seems to be a direct correlation ... between patterns of library usage and the magnitude of the pricing differential. The greater the use, the larger the differential."[3]

By 1986 the exchange rate had turned in favor of the pound, and the dollar prices of the British journals had increased significantly. Along with the price increase came some serious resistance to the higher prices. The concluding sentences of the Michigan report are illustrative: "One expects that a vendor with a monopoly on a product will charge according to demand. What the campus as a customer must determine is whether it will continue to pay up to 114% more than its British counterparts for the identical product."

25.13 Monopolistic Competition

We have described a monopolistic industry as being one in which there is a single large producer. But we've been somewhat vague about exactly what comprises an industry. One definition of an industry is that it consists of all firms that produce a given product. But then what do we mean by product? After all, there is only one firm that produces Coca–Cola—does that mean that this firm is a monopolist?

Clearly the answer is no. The Coca–Cola firm has to compete with other producers of soft drinks. We should really think of an industry as being the set of firms that produce products that are viewed as close substitutes by consumers. Each firm in the industry can produce a unique product—a unique brand name, say—but consumers view each of the brands as being substitutes to some degree.

Even though a firm may have a legal monopoly on its trademarks, and brand names, so that other firms can't produce *exactly* the same product, it is usually possible for other firms to produce *similar* products. From the viewpoint of a given firm, the production decisions of its competitors will be a very important consideration in deciding exactly how much it will produce and what price it can charge.

Thus the demand curve facing a firm will usually depend on the output decisions and the prices charged by other firms that produce similar

---

[2] Hamaker, C. and Astle, D., "Recent Pricing Patterns in British Journal Publishing," *Library Acquisitions: Practice and Theory*, 8, 4 (Spring 1984), 225–32.

[3] The study was conducted by Robert Houbeck for the University of Michigan Library, and published in Vol. 2, No. 1 of the *University Library Update*, April, 1986.

products. The slope of the demand curve facing the firm will depend on how similar the other firms' products are. If a large number of the firms in the industry produce *identical* products, then the demand curve facing any one of them will be essentially flat. Each firm must sell its product for whatever price the other firms are charging. Any firm that tried to raise its price above the prices of the other firms selling identical product would soon lose all of its customers.

On the other hand, if one firm has the exclusive rights to sell a particular product, then it may be able to raise its price without losing all of its customers. Some of its customers may switch to competitors' products, but not all. How many customers switch depends on how close a substitute the products are in the minds of the consumers.

If a firm is making a profit selling a product in an industry, and other firms are not allowed to perfectly reproduce that product, they still may find it profitable to enter that industry and produce a similar but distinctive product. Economists refer to this phenomenon as **product differentiation**—each firm attempts to differentiate its product from the other firms in the industry. The more successful it is at differentiating its product from other firms selling similar products, the more monopoly power it has—that is, the less elastic is the demand curve for the product.

An industry structure such as that described above shares elements of both competition and monopoly; it is therefore referred to as **monopolistic competition**. The industry structure is monopolistic in that each firm faces a downward sloping demand curve for its product. It therefore has some market power in the sense that it can set its own price, rather than passively accept the market price as does a competitive firm. On the other hand the firms must compete for customers in terms of both price and the kinds of products they sell. Furthermore, there are no restrictions against new firms entering into a monopolistically competitive industry. In these aspects the industry is like a competitive industry.

Monopolistic competition is probably the most prevalent form of industry structure. Unfortunately, it is also the most difficult form to analyze. The extreme cases of pure monopoly and pure competition are much simpler, and can often be used as first approximations to more elaborate models of monopolistic competition. In a detailed model of a monopolistically competitive industry, much depends on the specific details of the products and technology, as well as on the nature of the strategic choices available to firms. It is unreasonable to model a monopolistically competitive industry in the abstract, as we have done with the simpler cases of pure competition and pure monopoly. Rather, the institutional details of the particular industry under consideration must be examined. We will describe some ways that economists use to analyze strategic choice in the next two chapters, but a detailed study of monopolistic competition will have to wait for more advanced courses.

We can, however, describe an interesting feature of the free entry aspect of monopolistic competition. As more and more firms enter the industry for a particular kind of product, how would we expect the demand curve of an incumbent firm to change? First, we would expect the demand curve to shift inward since we would expect that at each price, it would sell fewer units of output as more firms enter the industry. Second, we would expect that the demand curve facing a given firm would become more elastic as more firms produced more and more similar products. Thus entry into an industry by new firms with similar products will tend to shift the demand curves facing existing firms to the left and make them flatter.

If firms continue to enter the industry as long as they expect to make a profit, we can describe the equilibrium of the industry in the following way:

1. Each firm is selling at a price and output combination on its demand curve.

2. Each firm is maximizing its profits, given the demand curve facing it.

3. Entry has forced each firm down to zero profits.

These facts imply a very particular geometrical relationship between the demand curve and the average cost curve: the demand curve and the average cost curve must be tangent to each other.

The argument is illustrated in Figure 25.9. Fact 1 says that the output and price combination must be somewhere on the demand curve, and fact 3 says that the output and price combination must also be on the average cost curve. Thus the operating position of the firm must be at a point that lies on both curves. Could the demand curve cross the average cost curve? No, because then there would be some point on the demand curve above the average cost curve—but this would be a point yielding *positive* profits.[4] And by fact 2, the zero profit point is a profit maximum.

Another way to see this is to examine what would happen if the firm depicted in Figure 25.9 charged any price other than the break-even price. At any other price, higher or lower, the firm would lose money, while at the break-even price, the firm makes zero profits. Thus the break-even price is the profit maximizing price.

There are two worthwhile observations about the monopolistically competitive equilibrium. First, although profits are zero, the situation is still Pareto inefficient. Profits have nothing to do with the efficiency question: when price is greater than marginal cost, there is an efficiency argument for expanding output.

Second, it is clear that firms will typically be operating to the left of the level of output where average cost is minimized. This has sometimes

---

[4] If $p > c(y)/y$, then simple algebra shows that $py - c(y) > 0$.

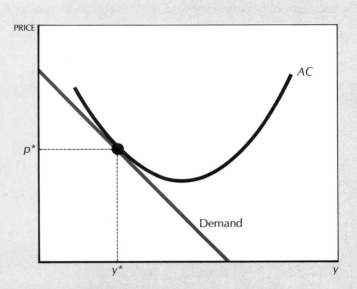

PRICE

AC

p^*

Demand

y^* y

Monopolistic competition. In a monopolistically competitive equilibrium with zero profits, the demand curve and the
average cost curve must be tangent.

Figure
25.9

been interpreted as saying that in monopolistic competition there is "excess
capacity." If there were fewer firms, each could operate at a more efficient
scale of operation, which would be better for consumers. However, if there
were fewer firms there would also be less product variety, and this would
tend to make consumers worse off. Which of these effects dominates is a
difficult question to answer.

25.14 Monopsony

In a monopoly there is a single seller of a commodity. In a **monopsony**
there is a single buyer. The analysis of a monopsonist is very similar to
that of a monopolist, so we won't spend much time on it.

   Suppose we consider a labor market where there is only one large employer in a given area. The employer faces an inverse supply curve of labor
denoted by $w(L)$; that is, if it wants to hire L units of labor it has to pay a
wage of $w(L)$. Let $f(L)$ be the production function of output as a function
of labor input. Then the profit maximization problem is

$$\max_{L} \ pf(L) - w(L)L.$$

   The condition for profit maximization is that the extra revenue from
hiring an extra unit of labor should equal the marginal cost of that unit.

The marginal revenue is easy—that is pMP_L. What about the marginal cost?

The total change in costs from hiring ΔL more labor will be

$$\Delta c = w\Delta L + L\Delta w$$

so that the change in costs per unit change in ΔL is

$$\frac{\Delta c}{\Delta L} = MC = w + \frac{\Delta w}{\Delta L}L.$$

The interpretation of this expression is similar to the interpretation of the marginal revenue expression: when the firm increases employment it has to pay $w\Delta L$ to the new workers. But the increased demand for labor will push the wage rate up by Δw and the firm has to pay this higher wage to all of its existing workers.

We can also write marginal cost as

$$MC = w\left[1 + \frac{L}{w}\frac{\Delta w}{\Delta L}\right]$$

$$= w\left[1 + \frac{1}{\epsilon}\right]$$

where ϵ now represents the *supply* elasticity of labor. Note the similarity with the analogous condition for a monopolist.

Let's analyze the case of a monopolist facing a linear supply curve for labor. The inverse supply curve has the form

$$w(L) = a + bL$$

so that total costs have the form

$$C(L) = w(L)L = aL + bL^2$$

and thus marginal costs have the form

$$MC(L) = a + 2bL.$$

The construction of the monopsony solution is given in Figure 25.10. We find the position where marginal revenue equals marginal cost to determine L^*, and then see what the wage rate is at that level of employment.

Since the marginal cost exceeds the wage rate, the wage rate will be lower than if the firm had no market power in the labor market and had to pay a competitively determined wage. Too little labor will be hired relative to the competitive labor market. Just as in the case of the monopoly, a monopolist operates at a Pareto inefficient point. But the inefficiency now lies in the factor market, rather than the output market.

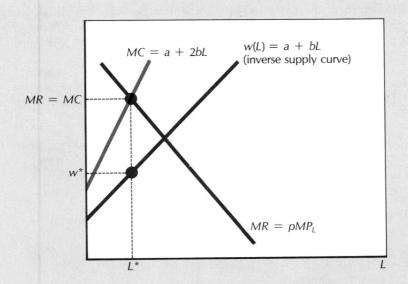

Monopsony. The monopsony solution in the case of a linear supply curve. The firm operates where the marginal revenue from hiring extra unit of labor equals the marginal cost of that extra labor.

Figure
25.10

Summary

1. When there is only a single firm in an industry, we say that it is a monopoly.

2. A monopolist operates at a point where marginal revenue equals marginal cost. Hence a monopolist charges a price that is a markup on marginal cost, where the size of the markup depends on the elasticity of demand.

3. Since a monopolist charges a price in excess of marginal cost, it will produce an inefficient amount of output. The size of the inefficiency can be measured by the deadweight loss—the net loss of consumers' and the producer's surplus.

4. A natural monopoly occurs when a firm cannot operate at an efficient level of output without losing money. Many public utilities are natural monopolies of this sort, and are therefore regulated by the government.

5. Whether an industry is competitive or monopolized depends in part on the nature of technology. If the minimum efficient scale is large relative to

demand, then the market is likely to be monopolized. But if the minimum efficient scale is small relative to demand, there is room for many firms in the industry, and there is a hope for a competitive market structure.

6. There will typically be an incentive for a monopolist to engage in price discrimination of some sort. If the firm can charge different prices in two different markets it will tend to charge the lower price in the market with the more elastic demand.

7. The industry structure known as monopolistic competition refers to a situation in which there is product differentiation, so each firm has some degree of monopoly power, but there is also free entry so that profits are driven to zero.

8. Just as a monopoly consists of a market with a single seller, a monopsony consists of a market with a single buyer.

Review Questions

1. The market demand curve for heroin is said to be highly inelastic. Heroin supply is also said to be monopolized by the mafia, which we assume is a profit maximizer. Are these two views consistent?

2. The monopolist faces a demand curve given by $D(p) = 100 - 2p$. Its cost function is $c(y) = 2y$. What is its optimal level of output and price?

3. The monopolist faces a demand curve given by $D(p) = 10p^{-3}$. Its cost function is $c(y) = 2y$. What is its optimal level of output and price?

4. If $D(p) = 100/p$ and $c(y) = y^2$, what is the optimal level of output of the monopolist? (Be careful.)

5. A monopolist is operating at an output level where $|\epsilon| = 3$. The government imposes a quantity tax of $6 per unit of output. If the demand curve facing the monopolist is linear, how much does the price rise?

6. What is the answer to the above question if the demand curve facing the monopolist has constant elasticity?

7. If the demand curve facing the monopolist has a constant elasticity of 2, then what will be the monopolist's markup on marginal cost?

8. The government is considering subsidizing the marginal costs of the monopolist described in the question above. What level of subsidy should they choose if they want the monopolist to produce the socially optimal amount of output?

9. Suppose that a monopolist sells to two groups that have constant elasticity demand curves, with elasticity ϵ_1 and ϵ_2. The marginal cost of production is constant at c. What price is charged to each group?

10. Show mathematically that a monopolist always sets its price above marginal cost.

11. True or false? Imposing a quantity tax on a monopolist will always cause the market price to increase by the amount of the tax.

12. What problems face a regulatory agency attempting to force a monopolist to charge the perfectly competitive price?

13. What kinds of economic and technological conditions are conducive to the formation of monopolies?

14. Will a monopoly ever provide a Pareto efficient level of output on its own?

APPENDIX

Define the revenue function by $r(y) = p(y)y$. Then the monopolist's profit maximization problem is

$$\max \; r(y) - c(y).$$

The first-order condition for this problem is simply

$$r'(y) - c'(y) = 0$$

which implies that marginal revenue should equal marginal cost at the optimal choice of output.

Differentiating the definition of the revenue function gives $r'(y) = p(y) + p'(y)y$, and substituting this into the monopolist's first-order condition yields the alternative form

$$p(y) + p'(y)y = c'(y).$$

The second-order condition for the monopolist's profit maximization problem is

$$r''(y) - c''(y) \leq 0.$$

This implies that

$$c''(y) \geq r''(y)$$

or that the slope of the marginal cost curve exceeds the slope of the marginal revenue curve.

EXAMPLE: Value Taxes and Quantity Taxes

Let's use the first-order conditions for the monopolist to prove a nice result that compares the revenue raised by a quantity tax and a value tax; namely, *if a quantity tax and a value tax affect output produced by a monopolist in the same way, then the value tax will always raise more revenue.*

Recall the distinction between the two kinds of taxes. Let $P_D(y)$ be the inverse demand curve: that is, $P_D(y)$ is the price paid by the demanders of the good when y units are demanded. Let $P_S(y)$ be the price received by the supplier of the good—the monopolist—when y units are demanded. (Note: this is *not* an inverse supply curve! A monopolist doesn't have a supply curve.)

In the case of a quantity tax, P_S and P_D are related by

$$P_D(y) = P_S(y) + t. \qquad (25.3)$$

That is, the price paid by the demanders is the price received by the supplier plus the amount of the tax. In the case of a value tax, P_S and P_D are related by

$$P_D(y) = (1 + \tau)P_S(y). \qquad (25.4)$$

This equation says that the price paid by the demanders is the price received by the suppliers times 1 plus the tax rate.

The monopolist's profit depends only on the price it receives. Thus the monopolist wants to solve the profit maximization problem

$$\max\ P_S(y)y - c(y). \qquad (25.5)$$

In the case of the quantity tax, we use equation (25.3) to rewrite this problem as

$$\max\ [P_D(y) - t]y - c(y).$$

Or

$$\max\ P_D(y)y - ty - c(y). \qquad (25.6)$$

Let $r(y) = P_D(y)y$ denote the revenue function—the amount of money paid by the demanders of the good. Then we can rewrite equation (25.6) as

$$\max\ r(y) - ty - c(y).$$

Let y_q be the output level that maximizes the monopolist's profits. At this point we must satisfy the optimality condition that marginal revenue equals marginal cost, or

$$r'(y_q) - t - c'(y_q) = 0.$$

Solving for marginal revenue, we have

$$r'(y_q) = c'(y_q) + t. \qquad (25.7)$$

In the case of the value tax, the profit maximization problem comes from combining equations (25.4) and (25.5) to get

$$\max \frac{P_D(y)}{1+\tau} y - c(y).$$

Using the definition of $r(y) = P_D(y)y$, we can write this expression as

$$\max \frac{r(y)}{1+\tau} - c(y).$$

Letting y_p be the level of output that solves this problem, we have

$$\frac{r'(y_p)}{1+\tau} - c'(y_p) = 0.$$

Again solving for marginal revenue gives us

$$r'(y_p) = (1+\tau)c'(y_p). \tag{25.8}$$

Now we want to compare the two equations (25.7) and (25.8) that characterize the optimal choices under the quantity tax and the value tax. Suppose that we adjust the two taxes so that the output levels y_p and y_q are the same: $y_p = y_q = y$, say. This implies that $r'(y_p) = r'(y_q) = r'(y)$ and $c'(y_p) = c'(y_q) = c'(y)$.

Setting equation (25.7) equal to equation (25.8) and canceling marginal cost from each side gives us

$$\tau = \frac{t}{c'(y)}. \tag{25.9}$$

This equation gives us the relationship between the value tax rate, τ, and the quantity tax rate, t, that must hold if they are to have the same effect on output.

We are almost done. All we need now is an expression for the tax revenue. By definition of the two kinds of taxes, the tax revenue for the value tax is $TR_p = \tau p y$ and the tax revenue for the quantity tax is $TR_q = ty$.

Multiply both sides of equation (25.9) by py to get

$$\tau p y = \frac{tpy}{c'(y)}$$

and use the definition of tax revenue to write

$$TR_p = \frac{p}{c'(y)} TR_q.$$

But we know that for a monopolist $p > c'(y)$. Hence, the last equation implies $TR_p > TR_q$, which is what we wanted to show: the revenue raised by a value tax will exceed the revenue raised from a quantity tax, if they have the same effect on output.

OLIGOPOLY

We have now investigated two forms of market structure: pure competition, where there are typically many small competitors, and pure monopoly, where there is only one large firm in the market. However, much of the world fits in between these two extremes. Often there are a number of competitors in the market, but not so many as to regard each of them as having an infinitesimal share of the market. This is the situation known as **oligopoly.**

The model of monopolistic competition described in Chapter 25 is a form of oligopoly. However, monopolistic competition emphasizes issues of product differentiation and entry, whereas the more general models of oligopoly are more concerned with strategic interaction.

In this chapter we will describe some models of this sort. There are several models that are relevant since there are several different ways for firms to behave in an oligopolistic environment. It is unreasonable to expect one grand model since many different behavior patterns can be observed in the real world. What we want is a guide to some of the possible patterns of behavior, and some indication of what factors might be important in deciding when the various models are applicable.

For simplicity, we will usually restrict ourselves to the case of two firms; this is called a situation of **duopoly**. The duopoly case allows us to capture many of the important features of firms engaged in strategic interaction without the notational complications involved in models with a larger number of firms.

26.1 Cournot Equilibrium

When a firm in a competitive market makes its decisions, it has only to examine the market price. A competitive firm by definition is such a small part of the market that it views itself as being unable to influence the market price by its own actions, so it can ignore the impact of its own decisions on the market price.

When a monopoly firm makes its output and pricing decisions, it has only to take into account the demand curve of its customers. Since a monopoly is by definition a single firm that dominates a market, it has no competitors to worry about.

However, when a firm in a duopoly decides how much output to produce, it must take into account its rival's behavior. In a duopoly, each firm has to forecast the other firm's output choice in order to make sensible decisions about its own output choice.

In this section we will examine a one-period model in which each firm has to forecast the other firm's output choice. Given its forecast, each firm then chooses a profit maximizing output for itself. We then seek an equilibrium in forecasts—a situation where each firm finds its beliefs about the other firm to be confirmed. This model is known as the **Cournot model**, after the nineteenth-century French mathematician who first examined its implications.[1]

Let us begin by assuming that firm 1 expects that firm 2 will produce y_2^e units of output. (The e stands for *expected* output.) Then if firm 1 decides to produce y_1 units of output, the total output it expects to be sold is $Y = y_1 + y_2^e$, which will yield a market price of $p(Y) = p(y_1 + y_2^e)$. The profit maximization problem of firm 1 then is

$$\max_{y_1} p(y_1 + y_2^e)y_1 - c(y_1).$$

If firm 1 chooses its optimal level of output, y_1^*, then it must satisfy the now familiar "marginal revenue equals marginal cost" condition:

$$p(y_1^* + y_2^e) + \frac{\Delta p}{\Delta Y}y_1^* = MC(y_1^*).$$

---

[1] Augustin Cournot (pronounced "core-no") was born in 1801. His influential book, *Researches into the Mathematical Principles of the Theory of Wealth*, was published in 1838.

This has the usual interpretation: when the firm increases its output by Δy_1 it raises its profits by selling more output at the price p, but it also increases industry output by ΔY, pushing the price down and thereby reducing its profits on all the other units it is selling. The sum of these two effects gives us marginal revenue—which has to be equal to marginal cost at the maximum profit output.

For any given belief about the output of firm 2, y_2^e, there will be some optimal choice of output for firm 1, y_1^*. Let us write this functional relationship between the *expected output* of firm 2 and the *optimal choice* of firm 1 as

$$y_1^* = f_1(y_2^e).$$

This function is known as firm 1's **reaction curve**. It shows how firm 1's choice of output varies depending on the different beliefs it might have about the output choice of firm 2.

Similarly, we can derive firm 2's reaction curve:

$$y_2^* = f_2(y_1^e)$$

which gives firm 2's optimal choice of output for a given expectation about firm 1's output, y_1^e.

Now, recall that each firm is choosing its output level *assuming* that the other firm's output will be at y_1^e or y_2^e. For arbitrary values of y_1^e and y_2^e this won't happen—in general firm 1's *optimal* level of output, y_1^*, will be different from what firm 2 expects it to do, y_1^e.

Let us seek an output combination $(\hat{y}_1, \hat{y}_2)$ such that the optimal output level for firm 1, assuming firm 2 produces $\hat{y}_2$, is $\hat{y}_1$, and the optimal output level for firm 2, assuming that firm 1 stays at $\hat{y}_1$, is $\hat{y}_2$. In other words, the output choices $(\hat{y}_1, \hat{y}_2)$ satisfy

$$\hat{y}_1 = f_1(\hat{y}_2)$$

$$\hat{y}_2 = f_2(\hat{y}_1).$$

Such a combination of output levels is known as a **Cournot equilibrium**. In a Cournot equilibrium, each firm is maximizing its profits, given its beliefs about the other firm's output choice, and, furthermore, those beliefs are confirmed in equilibrium: each firm optimally chooses to produce the amount of output that the other firm expects it to produce. In a Cournot equilibrium neither firm will find it profitable to change its output once it discovers the choice actually made by the other firm.

26.2 An Example of Cournot Equilibrium

In order to understand how a Cournot equilibrium works, it is convenient to calculate an example. We'll work an algebraic example for the case of a linear demand curve, and then illustrate it graphically.

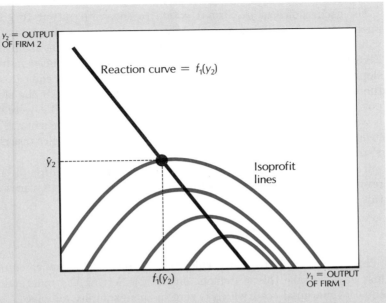

**Figure
26.1** **Derivation of a reaction curve.** This reaction curve gives
the profit maximizing output for firm 1 for each value of the
expected output choice of firm 2.

Let's suppose that the market demand curve is linear, so that we can
write $p(y_1 + y_2) = a - b(y_1 + y_2)$. For convenience we'll take marginal costs
to be zero, and we'll drop the e superscript to distinguish the expected
output from the actual output since we'll be looking for the point where
they coincide.

Then the profit function for firm 1 is

$$\pi_1(y_1, y_2) = [a - b(y_1 + y_2)]y_1$$

or

$$\pi_1(y_1, y_2) = ay_1 - by_1^2 - by_1y_2.$$

We can use this expression to draw the **isoprofit** lines in Figure 26.1.
These are lines depicting those combinations of y_1 and y_2 that yield a
constant level of profit. What do these isoprofit lines look like? To get a
formula for them, solve the above equation for y_2 as a function of y_1 to get

$$y_2 = \frac{a}{b} - y_1 - \frac{\pi_1}{by_1}.$$

This equation gives us a curve describing all combinations of (y_1, y_2) that
yield profits of π_1. Note that profits to firm 1 will increase as we move to
lower isoprofit lines—for any fixed value of y_1, firm 1's profits will become
larger as firm 2's output decreases.

For each choice of y_2, firm 1 wants to chose its output to give it the maximum profits. This means that for each choice of y_2, firm 1 will pick the value of y_1 that puts it on the lowest possible isoprofit line, as illustrated in Figure 26.1. This point will satisfy the usual sort of tangency condition: the slope of the isoprofit line must equal zero at the optimal choice: otherwise there would be a way for firm 1 to increase its profits. If the slope were positive, then it would pay firm 1 to increase its output; if it were negative, it would pay firm 1 to decrease its output. Only when the slope is zero will firm 1 be content to stay put. The locus of these tangencies describes firm 1's reaction curve, $f_1(y_2)$.

To see this result algebraically, we need the expression for the marginal revenue for the profit/revenue function described above. It turns out that this expression is given by

$$MR_1(y_1, y_2) = a - by_2 - 2by_1.$$

(This is easy to derive using calculus. If you don't know calculus, you'll just have to take this statement on faith.) Setting the marginal revenue equal to marginal cost, which is zero in this example, we have

$$a - by_2 - 2by_1 = 0$$

which we can solve to derive firm 1's reaction curve:

$$y_1 = \frac{a - by_2}{2b}.$$

This is the straight line depicted in Figure 26.1.

Since in this example firm 2 is exactly the same as firm 1, its reaction curve has the same form:

$$y_2 = \frac{a - by_1}{2b}.$$

Figure 26.2 depicts this pair of reaction curves. The intersection of the two lines gives us the Cournot equilibrium. At the Cournot equilibrium each firm's choice is the profit maximizing choice, given its beliefs about the other firm's behavior, and each firm's beliefs about the other firm's behavior are confirmed by its *actual* behavior.

In order to calculate the Cournot equilibrium algebraically, we have to solve the following two equations in two unknowns:

$$y_1 = \frac{a - by_2}{2b}$$

$$y_2 = \frac{a - by_1}{2b}.$$

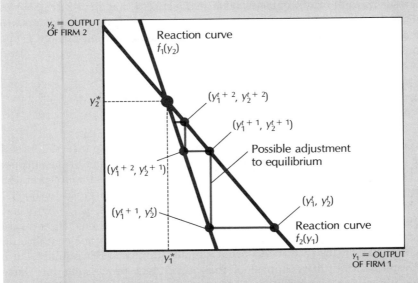

y_2 = OUTPUT OF FIRM 2

Reaction curve $f_1(y_2)$

$(y_1^t + 2, y_2^t + 2)$

$(y_1^t + 1, y_2^t + 1)$

Possible adjustment to equilibrium

$(y_1^t + 2, y_2^t + 1)$

$(y_1^t + 1, y_2^t)$

(y_1^t, y_2^t)

Reaction curve $f_2(y_1)$

y_1^*

y_1 = OUTPUT OF FIRM 1

y_2^*

Cournot equilibrium. Each firm is maximizing its profits, given its beliefs about the other firm's output decision. The Cournot equilibrium is at (y_1^*, y_2^*), where the two reaction curves cross.

Figure 26.2

In this example, both firms are identical, so each will produce the same level of output in equilibrium. Hence we can substitute $y_1 = y_2$ into the above equation to get

$$y_1 = \frac{a - by_1}{2b}.$$

Solving for $\hat{y}_1$, we get

$$\hat{y}_1 = \frac{a}{3b}.$$

Since the two firms are identical, this implies that

$$\hat{y}_2 = \frac{a}{3b}$$

as well, and the total industry output is

$$\hat{y}_1 + \hat{y}_2 = \frac{2a}{3b}.$$

26.3 Adjustment to Equilibrium

We can use Figure 26.2 to describe a process of adjustment to equilibrium. Suppose at time t the firms are producing outputs (y_1^t, y_2^t), which are not necessarily equilibrium outputs. If firm 1 expects that firm 2 is going to continue to keep its output at y_2^t, then next period firm 1 would want to choose the profit maximizing output given that expectation, namely $f(y_2^t)$. Thus firm 1's choice in period $t+1$ will be given by

$$y_1^{t+1} = f_1(y_2^t).$$

Firm 2 can reason the same way, so firm 2's choice next period will be

$$y_2^{t+1} = f_2(y_1^t).$$

These equations describe how each firm adjusts its output in the face of the other firm's choice. Figure 26.2 illustrates the movement of the outputs of the firms implied by this behavior. Here is the way to interpret the diagram. Start with some value for y_1^t, and then move up to $y_2^{t+1} = f_2(y_1^t)$ to find firm 2's optimal response. Given firm 2's choice, y_2^{t+1}, move left to find firm 1's optimal response to that, y_1^{t+2}, and so on. In the case illustrated, this adjustment process converges to the Cournot equilibrium. We say that in this case the Cournot equilibrium is a stable equilibrium.

Despite the intuitive appeal of this adjustment process, it does have some difficulties. Each firm is assuming the other's output will be fixed from one period to the next, but as it turns out, both firms keep changing their output. Only in equilibrium is one firm's expectation about the other firm's output choice actually satisfied. For this reason, we will generally beg the question of how the equilibrium is reached, and focus only on the issue of how the firms behave in the equilibrium.

26.4 Many Firms in Cournot Equilibrium

Suppose now that we have several firms involved in a Cournot equilibrium, not just 2. In this case, we suppose that each firm has an expectation about the output choices of the other firms in the industry and seek to describe the equilibrium output.

Suppose that there are n firms and let $Y = y_1 + \ldots + y_n$ be the total industry output. Then the "marginal revenue equals marginal cost condition" for firm i is

$$p(Y) + \frac{\Delta p}{\Delta Y} y_i = MC(y_i).$$

If we multiply the second term by Y/Y, we can write this equation as

$$p(Y) \left[1 + \frac{\Delta p}{\Delta Y} \frac{Y}{p(Y)} \frac{y_i}{Y} \right] = MC(y_i).$$

Using the definition of elasticity of the aggregate demand curve and letting $s_i = y_i/Y$ be firm i's share of total market output, this reduces to

$$p(Y) \left[1 - \frac{s_i}{|\epsilon(Y)|} \right] = MC(y_i). \tag{26.1}$$

We can also write this expression as

$$p(Y) \left[1 - \frac{1}{|\epsilon(Y)|/s_i} \right] = MC(y_i).$$

This looks just like the expression for the monopolist except for the s_i term. We can think of $\epsilon(Y)/s_i$ as being the elasticity of the demand curve facing the firm: the smaller the market share of the firm, the more elastic the demand curve it faces.

If its market share is 1—the firm is a monopolist—the demand curve facing the firm is the market demand curve, so the condition just reduces to that of the monopolist. If the firm is a very small part of a large market, its market share is effectively zero, and the demand curve facing the firm is effectively infinite. Thus the condition reduces to that of the pure competitor: price equals marginal cost.

This is one justification for the competitive model described in Chapter 22. If there are a large number of firms, then each firm's influence on the market price is negligible, and the Cournot equilibrium is effectively the same as pure competition.

EXAMPLE: Calculating Price in a Cournot Equilibrium

Suppose that there are three identical firms in a Cournot industry, each having constant marginal costs of 1. The elasticity of the market demand curve is constant at -2. What is the equilibrium price?

To solve this problem, we apply equation (26.1). Since the firms are identical, they will each have a constant market share of $1/3$. Thus we have

$$p(Y) \left[1 + \frac{s_i}{\epsilon(Y)} \right] = MC(y_i)$$

$$p(Y) \left[1 - \frac{1/3}{2} \right] = 1.$$

Solving for the price gives

$$p(Y) = 1.2.$$

What happens to the price as more firms enter the industry and the share of each firm declines to zero? As the share of each firm goes to zero, we must have price approaching marginal cost, which, in this example, is 1.

EXAMPLE: Taxation in a Cournot Industry

Consider a Cournot industry in which firm i has a constant marginal cost c_i and faces a constant quantity tax t_i. In this case, the tax simply increases the marginal costs of each firm. Each firm's profit maximization condition can be written as

$$p(Y) + \frac{\Delta p}{\Delta Y} y_i = c_i + t_i.$$

We want to find out the effect of this tax on total industry output, Y. To do this, sum this equation over all n firms to get

$$np(Y) + \frac{\Delta p}{\Delta Y} \sum_{i=1}^{n} y_i = \sum_{i=1}^{n} c_i + \sum_{i=1}^{n} t_i.$$

Since by definition $Y = \sum_{i=1}^{n} y_i$, we can also write

$$np(Y) + \frac{\Delta p}{\Delta Y} Y = \sum_{i=1}^{n} c_i + \sum_{i=1}^{n} t_i.$$

Here is the interesting fact about this equation: the right-hand side only depends on the *sum* of the tax rates. Therefore, the left-hand side can only depend on the sum of the tax rates. Hence total industry output and total industry price will only depend on the sum of the taxes—the distribution of taxes among the firms has no impact on the output of the Cournot industry, as long as all n firms remain in the industry.

26.5 Collusion

The Cournot equilibrium is only one possible duopoly solution. If each firm acts independently, it is a reasonable one. But if the firms collude so as to jointly determine their output, it is not very reasonable. If collusion is possible, the firms would do better to choose the output that maximizes total industry profits and then divide up the profits between them. When firms get together and attempt to set prices and outputs so as to maximize total industry profits, they are known as a cartel. As we saw in Chapter 25, a cartel is simply a group of firms that jointly collude to behave like a single monopolist and maximize the sum of their profits.

Thus profit maximization problem facing the two firms is to choose their outputs y_1 and y_2 so as to maximize total industry profits:

$$\max_{y_1, y_2} p(y_1 + y_2)[y_1 + y_2] - c_1(y_1) - c_2(y_2).$$

This will have the optimality conditions

$$p(y_1^* + y_2^*) + \frac{\Delta p}{\Delta Y} [y_1^* + y_2^*] = MC_1(y_1^*)$$

$$p(y_1^* + y_2^*) + \frac{\Delta p}{\Delta Y} [y_1^* + y_2^*] = MC_2(y_2^*).$$

The interpretation of these conditions is interesting. When firm 1 considers expanding its output by Δy_1, it will contemplate the usual two effects: the extra profits from selling more output at price p and the effect from reducing the price. But in the second effect, it now counts both its own output and the output of the other firm. This is because it is now interested in maximizing total industry profits, not just its own profits.

The optimality conditions imply that the marginal revenue of an extra unit of output must be the same no matter where it is produced. It follows that $MC_1(y_1^*) = MC_2(y_2^*)$, so that the two marginal costs will be equal in equilibrium. If one firm has a cost advantage, so that its marginal cost curve always lies below that of the other firm, then it will necessarily produce more output in equilibrium in the cartel solution.

The problem with agreeing to a cartel in real life is that there is always a temptation to cheat. Suppose, for example, that the two firms are operating at the outputs that maximize industry profits (y_1^*, y_2^*) and firm 1 considers producing a little more output, Δy_1. The marginal profits accruing to firm 1 will be

$$\frac{\Delta \pi_1}{\Delta y_1} = p(y_1^* + y_2^*) + \frac{\Delta p}{\Delta Y} y_1^* - MC_1(y_1^*). \qquad (26.2)$$

We saw earlier that the optimality condition for the cartel solution is

$$p(y_1^* + y_2^*) + \frac{\Delta p}{\Delta Y} y_1^* + \frac{\Delta p}{\Delta Y} y_2^* - MC_1(y_1^*) = 0.$$

Rearranging this equation gives us

$$p(y_1^* + y_2^*) + \frac{\Delta p}{\Delta Y} y_1^* - MC_1(y_1^*) = -\frac{\Delta p}{\Delta Y} y_2^* > 0. \qquad (26.3)$$

The last inequality follows since $\Delta p / \Delta Y$ is negative (that is, the market demand curve has a negative slope.)

Inspecting equations (26.2) and (26.3) we see that

$$\frac{\Delta \pi_1}{\Delta y_1} > 0.$$

Thus, if firm 1 believes that firm 2 will keep its output fixed, then it will believe that it can make a profit by increasing its own production. In the cartel solution, the firms act together to restrict output so as not to "spoil" the market. They recognize the effect on joint profits from producing more output in either firm. But if each firm believes that the other firms will stick to their output quota, then each firm will be tempted to increase its own profits by unilaterally expanding its output. At the output levels that maximize joint profits, it will always be profitable for each firm to unilaterally increase its output—if it believes that the other firm will keep its output fixed.

The situation is even worse than that. If firm 1 believes that firm 2 will keep its output fixed, then it will find it profitable to increase its own output. But if it thinks that firm 2 will increase its output, then firm 1 would want increase its output first and make its profits while it can!

Thus, in order to maintain an effective cartel, the firms need a way to detect and punish cheating. If they have no way to observe each other's output, the temptation to cheat may break the cartel. We'll return to this point a little later.

To make sure that we understand the cartel solution, let's calculate it for the case of zero marginal costs and the linear demand curve we used in the Cournot case.

The aggregate profit function will be

$$\pi(y_1, y_2) = a(y_1 + y_2) - b(y_1 + y_2)^2$$

so the marginal revenue equals marginal cost conditions will be

$$a - 2b(y_1^* + y_2^*) = 0$$

which implies that

$$y_1^* + y_2^* = \frac{a}{2b}.$$

Since marginal costs are zero, the division of output between the two firms doesn't matter. All that is determined is the total level of industry output.

This solution is shown in Figure 26.3. Here we have illustrated the isoprofit curves for each of the firms, and have highlighted the locus of common tangents. Why is this line of interest? Since the cartel is trying to maximize total industry profits, it follows that the marginal profits from having either firm produce more output must be the same—otherwise it would pay to have the more profitable firm produce more output. This in turn implies that the slopes of the isoprofit curves must be the same for each firm. Hence the output combinations that maximize total industry profits—the cartel solution—are those that lie along the line illustrated in Figure 26.3.

Figure 26.3 also illustrates the temptation to cheat that is present at the cartel solution. Consider, for example, the point where the two firms split the market equally. Think about what would happen if firm 1 believed that firm 2 would keep its output constant. If firm 1 increased its output and firm 2 kept constant output, then firm 1 would move to a lower isoprofit line—which means that firm 1 would increase its profits. This is exactly the story told in the algebra above. If one firm thinks that the other's output will remain constant, it will be tempted to increase its own output and thereby make higher profits.

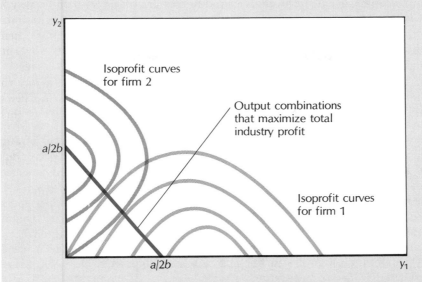

A cartel. If industry profits are maximized, then the marginal profit from producing more output in either firm must be the same. This implies that the isoprofit curves must be tangent to each other at the profit maximizing levels of output.

Figure
26.3

EXAMPLE: Agricultural Marketing Committees

The Agricultural Marketing Act of 1937 allowed for the establishment of marketing committees that legally regulate sales of certain agricultural products for the benefit of the producers of such products. These committees are exempt from standard antitrust penalties. As it happens, more than half of the fruit and nut trees and 15 percent of the vegetables produced in the United States are regulated by such committees.

One of the most effective of these marketing committees is the one composed to regulate the production of California navel oranges. This group is composed of representatives of growers and packing houses and it has the legal power to set quotas on how much each producer can sell to the primary market for oranges.

So far this sounds very much like the model of a cartel described above. However, there is one important difference. We argued above that the producers could always agree on the output level that maximized total industry profits, and then divide up the profits among themselves.

In the case of the California orange producers, there are significant size differences among the participants and there seems to be no effective way to make side payments from one producer to another. Thus the decision of how much to produce is a contentious one. Small producers, who have little effect on the market price, want to produce a lot. Larger producers, who have significant effects on the market price, want to produce less. The conflicts between the two are very real. Consider the following passage:

"[One of the orange growers] also criticized the level at which their weekly allotments were placed by the committee, holding that they always had customers who were willing to buy more of their oranges, if only the level of volume proration had not been set so low. From the viewpoint of any shipper who controls such a small part of the total supply, the amount he ships does not have any effect on the price he receives. This was the position of [this grower] and the independents. Thus their criticisms of the committee in this matter were understandable. Had all the small shippers been permitted to ship what they wanted each week, these incremental supplies would probably have had a substantial price reducing effect... The program would fail if for no other reason than that which caused the voluntary programs to fail—those whose shipments were not being restricted gained disproportionately."[2]

This is precisely the kind of cheating described in the last section: if the cartel is successful in maximizing the total industry profits, each firm will find it in its private interest to unilaterally increase its own level of output. But if all firms attempt to do this, the cartel will certainly fail.

26.6 Stackelberg Behavior

In the Cournot case, each firm took the other firm's output as determined independently of its own decisions. This is sensible given that both firms have to make their output decisions at the same time. However, if firm 1, say, gets to act before firm 2, then firm 1 may realize that it can influence firm 2's behavior through its choice of output. In this case, we say that firm 1 is behaving as a **leader** in a **Stackelberg industry** and firm 2 is behaving as a **follower**.[3]

The Stackelberg model is often used to describe industries in which there is a dominant firm, or a natural leader. For example, IBM is often taken to be a dominant firm in the computer industry. A commonly observed pattern of behavior is for smaller firms in the computer industry to wait for

---

[2] Robert Clodius, *An Analysis of Statutory Marketing Control Programs in the California–Arizona Orange Industry*, University of California at Berkeley, Ph.D. dissertation, p. 327.

[3] Heinrich von Stackelberg was a German economist who published his influential work on market organization, *Marktform und Gleichgewicht*, in 1934.

IBM's announcements of new products, and then adjust their own product decisions accordingly. In this case, we might want to model the computer industry with IBM playing the role of a Stackelberg leader, and the other firms in the industry being Stackelberg followers.

Let us turn now to the details of the theoretical model. We know how a follower behaves: according to its reaction function $f_2(y_1)$. For each value of y_1, $f_2(y_1)$ gives the optimal choice of firm 2. Then the problem facing the leader is

$$\max_{y_1} \; p(y_1 + f_2(y_1))y_1 - c_1(y_1).$$

Firm 1 wants to maximize profits, as always, but now it recognizes that its own choice of output, y_1, will influence firm 2's choice of output via the reaction function $f_2(y_1)$.

As always the optimality condition for this problem will be "marginal revenue equals marginal cost," but now it will have an extra twist. When firm 1 considers increasing its output it will realize the indirect effect that it will have on firm 2's output and will take that into account as well. Let's try to figure out how this works.

The fundamental "marginal revenue equals marginal cost" condition is

$$p(y_1^* + y_2^*) + \frac{\Delta p}{\Delta y_1} y_1^* = MC_1(y_1^*). \tag{26.4}$$

This has the standard interpretation: when the firm increases its output by Δy_1, it changes the price by $\Delta p/\Delta y_1$ and this lower price will apply to its entire output y_1^*.

We can write the slope term, $\Delta p/\Delta y_1$, as

$$\frac{\Delta p}{\Delta y_1} = \frac{\Delta p}{\Delta Y} \frac{\Delta Y}{\Delta y_1}. \tag{26.5}$$

This equation says that the change in price when firm 1 changes its output is the product of the change in price when total industry output changes times how industry output changes when firm 1's output changes. The first term, $\Delta p/\Delta Y$, is the slope of the industry demand curve.

In order to interpret the second term, we write the change in industry output as

$$\Delta Y = \Delta y_1 + \Delta y_2.$$

Hence the change in industry output per unit change in Δy_1 is

$$\frac{\Delta Y}{\Delta y_1} = 1 + \frac{\Delta y_2}{\Delta y_1}. \tag{26.6}$$

That is, if firm 1 contemplates increasing its output by 1 unit, industry output will increase by 1 unit directly. But the increase in firm 1's output will also induce firm 2 to change its output by $\Delta y_2 / \Delta y_1$, and the total effect on industry output is the sum of these two changes.

If we substitute equations (26.6) and (26.5) into equation (26.4) we have

$$p(y_1^* + y_2^*) + \frac{\Delta p}{\Delta Y} \left[1 + \frac{\Delta y_2}{\Delta y_1} \right] y_1^* = MC_1(y_1^*). \tag{26.7}$$

This equation still just says that marginal revenue equals marginal cost. But now we have a more detailed expression for marginal revenue. The second term is the interesting one. When firm 1 increases its output by Δy_1, industry output goes up by

$$\Delta Y = \Delta y_1 + \frac{\Delta y_2}{\Delta y_1} \Delta y_1$$

and the resulting increase in output will tend to reduce the price. Firm 1 has to worry about the impact of this price reduction on the output it is selling, y_1^*.

In the case of the linear demand curve and zero marginal cost, we can get an explicit solution for the Stackelberg equilibrium. The reaction function for firm 2 is given by

$$y_2 = \frac{a - by_1}{2b}.$$

This means that when firm 1 changes its output by Δy_1, firm 2 will respond by changing its output by $\Delta y_2 = -\Delta y_1 / 2$. Thus $\Delta y_2 / \Delta y_1 = -1/2$. Substituting this into equation (26.4) we have

$$MR(y_1) = a - b \left[y_1 + \frac{a - by_1}{2b} \right] - b \left[1 - \frac{1}{2} \right] y_1 = 0 = MC(y_1).$$

Solving this equation for y_1 yields

$$y_1^* = \frac{a}{2b}.$$

Substituting back into firm 2's reaction function gives us

$$y_2^* = \frac{a}{4b}.$$

These two equations give a total industry output of $y_1^* + y_2^* = 3a/4b$.

The Stackelberg solution can also be illustrated graphically using the isoprofit curves depicted in Figure 26.4. In this diagram we have illustrated both reaction curves, but have only drawn in the isoprofit lines for firm 1. Firm 2 is behaving as a follower, which means that it will choose an output along its reaction curve, $f_2(y_1)$. Thus firm 1 wants to choose an output combination on the reaction curve that gives it the highest possible profits. But the highest possible profits means picking that point on the reaction curve that touches the *lowest* isoprofit line, as illustrated in Figure 26.4.

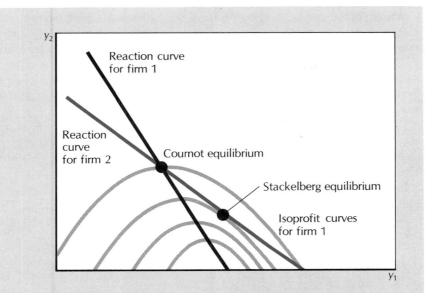

Stackelberg equilibrium. Firm 1, the leader, chooses the point on firm 2's reaction curve that touches firm 1's lowest possible isoprofit line, thus yielding the highest possible profits for firm 1.

Figure
26.4

26.7 Bertrand Equilibrium

In the oligopoly models described above we have assumed that firms were choosing their quantities and letting the market determine the price. Another approach is to think of firms as setting their prices and letting the market determine the quantity sold. When firms choose their prices, they have to make an assumption about how the other firms in the industry are going to behave. One possibility is that they will not respond at all; that is, the other firms will keep their prices fixed at their current levels. This kind of behavior is known as **Bertrand competition.**[4]

Bertrand behavior is similar to Cournot behavior described above, but there we thought of the other firms as keeping their *outputs* fixed while in the Bertrand case we think of the other firms as keeping their *prices* fixed.

What does a Bertrand equilibrium look like? When firms are selling identical products, the Bertrand equilibrium has a very simple structure indeed. It turns out to be the competitive equilibrium, where price equals marginal cost!

---

[4] Joseph Bertrand, also a French mathematician, presented his model in a review of Cournot's work that appeared forty-five years after its publication.

We will prove this by showing that any price that is greater than marginal cost cannot be an equilibrium. Suppose that both firms are selling output at some price $\hat{p}$ greater than marginal cost. Consider the position of firm 1. If it lowers its price by any small amount Δp, and the other firm keeps its price fixed at $\hat{p}$, firm 1 will gain the whole market. By cutting its price by an arbitrarily small amount, it can steal all of the customers from firm 2.

If firm 1 really believes that firm 2 is going to keep charging $\hat{p}$, it will always pay it to cut its price to $\hat{p} - \Delta p$. But firm 2 can make the same argument! Thus any price higher than marginal cost cannot be an equilibrium. The only equilibrium is the competitive equilibrium.

In the case of linear demand and zero marginal cost, the competitive equilibrium has to have price equal to marginal cost—which is zero. This means that total industry output will be a/b, and that each firm will produce $a/2b$ if they equally divide the market.

26.8 Comparison of the Solutions

We have now examined four models of duopoly behavior: Cournot, cartel, Stackelberg, and Bertrand. How do they compare? Table 26.1 gives the equilibrium output and price for each model in the special case of linear demand and zero marginal cost with two firms in the industry. Note that competition and Bertrand give the most output, then Stackelberg, Cournot, and the cartel solution. This would be the order one would expect in general, but odd shaped demand curves can change the ranking a bit.

Table 26.1

Comparison of oligopoly models with linear demand curve.

Behavior	$\Delta y_1/\Delta y_2$	y_1	$\Delta y_2/\Delta y_1$	y_2	Y	P
Competition	-1	$a/2b$	-1	$a/2b$	a/b	0
Cournot	0	$a/3b$	0	$a/3b$	$2a/3b$	$a/3$
Cartel	y_1/y_2	$a/4b$	y_2/y_1	$a/4b$	$a/2b$	$a/2$
Stackelberg	$-1/2$	$a/2b$	0	$a/4b$	$3a/4b$	$a/4$
Bertrand	N/A	$a/2b$	N/A	$a/2b$	a/b	0

In each of these models the defining characteristic is how each firm believes the other firm will respond to its output choice. We can classify these models to some extent by listing the various assumptions about the other firm's behavior. A useful tool for cataloging these possibilities is the **conjectural variation**.

We have seen that the condition characterizing profit maximization for a Stackelberg oligopolist can be written as

$$p(y_1 + y_2) + \frac{\Delta p}{\Delta Y} \left[1 + \frac{\Delta y_2}{\Delta y_1} \right] y_1 = MC(y_1). \qquad (26.8)$$

The term $\Delta y_2/\Delta y_1$ was firm 1's belief about how firm 2 would respond to changes in firm 1's output. In the Stackelberg case it was assumed the be the slope of firm 2's reaction function—since firm 2 was supposed to behave as a passive Cournot competitor.

But we don't have to think of $\Delta y_2/\Delta y_1$ in such limited terms. We can examine the implications of *arbitrary* beliefs about how firm 2 will respond to changes in firm 1's output. The **conjectural variation** describes how firm 1 conjectures firm 2 will vary its output when firm 1 makes a small change in output, Δy_1.

Each of the cases we have described above corresponds to some assumption about the conjectural variation. In the Cournot case, the conjectural variation is zero—each firm thinks that the other won't respond to its output change. In the Stackelberg case, one firm, the follower, behaves passively and takes the other firm's output choice as fixed, while the other firm, the leader, recognizes the influence of its output choices on the follower.

The conjectural variation that yields the competitive equilibrium is -1. This is clear formally, since setting $\Delta y_2/\Delta y_1 = -1$ will automatically make price equal to marginal costs. We can also see this by thinking about the economics of the matter. The defining feature of competition is that when each firm considers changes in its output, it assumes that the market price will stay fixed. Formally this means that when a firm considers cutting its output by Δy_1, it assumes that the other firm will *increase* its output by the same amount so that the market price will remain constant.

The conjectural variation that gives rise to the cartel solution turns out to be y_2/y_1. To see this just substitute y_2/y_1 for $\Delta y_2/\Delta y_1$ in equation (26.8) and note that it reduces to the equation for the cartel solution.

The conjectural variation for a cartel has an interesting interpretation. Remember we said that one of the problems facing a cartel was in policing the behavior of its members to ensure that they don't cheat on the cartel agreement. The temptation to cheat comes from the fact that at the cartel solution, it will always pay a firm to sell more output than it agreed to, *if it assumes that the other firm won't respond.*

But what if the other firm does respond? Depending on how much the other firm responds, it may or not be profitable to cheat. If the other firm responds by dumping a lot of output onto the market, so that the price is driven way down, then the cheating may be rendered unprofitable. How much does the other firm have to change its output in order to render cheating by firm 1 unprofitable? The answer is just that conjectural variation that supports the cartel solution: $\Delta y_2/\Delta y_1 = y_2/y_1$. For this is the belief about the other firm's response that makes it appear profitable for firm 1 to stay at the cartel output.

If firm 2 is large relative to firm 1 then y_2/y_1 will be large, and firm 1 has to believe that firm 2 will have a large response to any changes in its output, in order for the cartel solution to remain viable. By the same token, firm 2 will have to believe that firm 1 will have a small response. If each firm can convince the other that it will indeed respond to increases in the other's output in this way, the cartel can be stabilized.

Summary

1. An oligopoly is characterized by a market with a few firms that recognize their strategic interdependence. There are several possible ways for oligopolies to behave depending on the exact nature of their interaction.

2. In the Cournot model, each firm chooses its output so as to maximize its profits given its beliefs about the other firm's choice, and in equilibrium each firm finds that its expectation about the other firm's choice is confirmed.

3. A Cournot equilibrium in which each firm has a small market share implies that price will be very close to marginal cost—that is, the industry will be nearly competitive.

4. A cartel involves a number of firms colluding to restrict output and maximize industry profits. A cartel will typically be unstable in the sense that each firm will be tempted to sell more than its agreed upon output, if it believes that the other firms will not respond.

5. In a Stackelberg equilibrium, the Stackelberg leader chooses an output that the follower takes as given. The leader takes into account its influence on the choice of the follower when setting its own level of output.

6. Conjectural variations are the conjectured beliefs about how the other firm in the industry will respond to changes in a given firm's output. They can be used to summarize the different models described above.

Review Questions

1. Suppose that we have two firms that face a linear demand curve $p(Y) = a - bY$ and have constant marginal costs, c, for each firm. Solve for the Cournot equilibrium output.

2. Consider a cartel in which each firm has identical and constant marginal costs. If the cartel maximizes total industry profits, what does this imply about the division of output between the firms?

3. Can the leader ever get a lower profit in a Stackelberg equilibrium than he would get in the Cournot equilibrium?

4. Suppose there are n identical firms in a Cournot equilibrium. Show that the elasticity of the market demand curve must be greater than $1/n$. (Hint: in the case of a monopolist, $n = 1$, and this simply says that a monopolist operates at an elastic part of the demand curve. Apply the logic that we used to establish that fact to this problem.)

5. Draw a set of reaction curves that result in an unstable equilibrium.

6. Do oligopolies produce an efficient level of output?

GAME THEORY

The previous chapter on oligopoly theory presented the classical economic theory of strategic interaction among firms. But that is really just the tip of the iceberg. Economic agents can interact strategically in a variety of ways, and many of these have been studied by using the apparatus of **game theory.** Game theory is concerned with the general analysis of strategic interaction. It can be used to study parlor games, political negotiation, and economic behavior. In this chapter we will briefly explore this fascinating subject to give you a flavor of how it works, and how it can be used to study economic behavior in oligopolistic markets.

27.1 The Payoff Matrix of a Game

Strategic interaction can involve many players and many strategies, but we'll limit ourselves to two-person games with a finite number of strategies. This will allow us to depict the game easily in a **payoff matrix.** It is simplest to examine this in the context of a specific example.

Suppose that two people are playing a simple game. Person A will write one of two words on a piece of paper, "top" or "bottom." Simultaneously, person B will independently write "left" or "right" on a piece of paper. After they do this, the papers will be examined and they will each get the payoff depicted in Table 27.1. If A says top and B says left then we examine the top left-hand corner of the matrix. In this matrix the payoff to A is the first entry in the box, 1, and the payoff to B is the second entry, 2. Similarly, if A says bottom and B says right, then A will get a payoff of 1 and B will get a payoff of 0.

Person A has two strategies: he can choose top or he can choose bottom. These strategies could represent economic choices like "raise price" or "lower price." Or they could represent political choices like "declare war" or "don't declare war." The payoff matrix of a game simply depicts the payoffs to each player for each combination of strategies that are chosen.

What will be the outcome of this sort of game? The game depicted in Table 27.1 has a very simple solution. From the viewpoint of person A, it is always better for him to say bottom since his payoffs from that choice (2 or 1) are always greater than their corresponding entries in top (1 or 0). Similarly, it is always better for B to say left since 2 and 1 dominate 1 and 0. Thus we would expect that the equilibrium strategy is for A to play bottom and B to play left.

In this case, we have a **dominant strategy**. There is one optimal choice of strategy for each player no matter what the other player does. Whichever choice B makes, player A will get a higher payoff if he plays bottom, so it makes sense for A to play bottom. And whichever choice A makes, B will get a higher payoff if he plays left. Hence, these choices dominate the alternatives, and we have an equilibrium in dominant strategies.

A payoff matrix of a game.

Table 27.1

		Player B	
		Left	Right
Player A	Top	1, 2	0, 1
	Bottom	2, 1	1, 0

If there is a dominant strategy for each player in some game, then we would predict that it would be the equilibrium outcome of the game. For a dominant strategy is a strategy that is best no matter what the other player does. In this example, we would expect an equilibrium outcome in which A plays bottom, receiving an equilibrium payoff of 2, and B plays left, receiving an equilibrium payoff of 1.

27.2 Nash Equilibrium

Dominant strategy equilibria are nice when they happen, but they don't happen all that often. For example, the game depicted in Table 27.2 doesn't have a dominant strategy equilibrium. Here when B chooses left the payoffs to A are 2 or 0. When B chooses right, the payoffs to A are 0 or 1. This means that when B chooses left, A would want to choose top and when B chooses right, A would want to choose bottom. Thus A's optimal choice depends on what he thinks B will do.

Table 27.2

A Nash equilibrium.

		Player B	
		Left	Right
Player A	Top	2, 1	0, 0
	Bottom	0, 0	1, 2

However, perhaps the dominant strategy equilibrium is too demanding. Rather than require that A's choice be optimal for *all* choices of B, we can just require that it be optimal for the *optimal* choices of B. For if B is a well-informed intelligent player, he will only want to choose optimal strategies. (Although, what is optimal for B will depend on A's choice as well!)

We will say that a pair of strategies is a **Nash equilibrium** if A's choice is optimal, given B's choice, *and* B's choice is optimal given A's choice.[1] Remember that neither person knows what the other person will do when he has to make his own choice of strategy. But each person may have some expectation about what the other person's choice will be. A Nash equilibrium can be interpreted as a pair of expectations about each person's choice such that, when the other person's choice is revealed, neither individual wants to change his behavior.

In the case of Table 27.2, the strategy (top, left) is a Nash equilibrium. To prove this note that if A chooses top, then the best thing for B to do is to choose left, since the payoff to B from choosing left is 1 and from choosing right is 0. And if B chooses left then the best thing for A to do is to choose top since then A will get a payoff of 2 rather than of 0.

[1] John Nash is an American mathematician who formulated this fundamental concept of game theory in 1951.

Thus if A chooses top the optimal choice for B is to choose left, and if B chooses left then the optimal choice for A is top. So we have a Nash equilibrium: each person is making the optimal choice, *given* the other person's choice.

The Nash equilibrium is a generalization of the Cournot equilibrium described in the last chapter. There the choices were output levels, and each firm chose its output level taking the other firm's choice as being fixed. Each firm was supposed to do the best for itself, assuming that the other firm continued to produce the output level it had chosen—that is, it continued to play the strategy it had chosen. A Cournot equilibrium occurs when each firm is maximizing profits given the other firm's behavior; this is precisely the definition of a Nash equilibrium.

The Nash equilibrium notion has a certain logic. Unfortunately, it also has some problems. First, a game may have more than one Nash equilibrium. In fact in Table 27.2 the choices (bottom, right) also comprise a Nash equilibrium. You can either verify this by the kind of argument used above, or just note that the structure of the game is symmetric: B's payoffs are the same in one outcome as A's payoffs are in the other, so that our proof that (top, left) is an equilibrium is also a proof that (bottom, right) is an equilibrium.

The second problem with the concept of a Nash equilibrium is that there are games that have no Nash equilibrium of the sort we have been describing at all. Consider, for example, the case depicted in Table 27.3. Here a Nash equilibrium of the sort we have been examining does not exist. If player A plays top, then player B wants to play left. But if player B plays left, then player A wants bottom. Similarly, if player A plays bottom, then player B will play right. But if player B plays right, then player A will play top.

A game with no Nash equilibrium (in pure strategies).   Table 27.3

		Player B	
		Left	Right
Player A	Top	0, 0	0, −1
	Bottom	1, 0	−1, 3

27.3 Mixed Strategies

However, if we enlarge our definition of strategies, we can find a new sort of Nash equilibrium for this game. We have been thinking of each agent as choosing a strategy once and for all. That is, each agent is making one choice and sticking to it. This is called a **pure strategy**.

Another way to think about it is to allow the agents to *randomize* their strategies—to assign a probability to each choice and to play their choices according to those probabilities. For example, A might choose to play top 50 percent of the time and bottom 50 percent of the time, while B might choose to play left 50 percent of the time and right 50 percent of the time. This kind of strategy is called a **mixed strategy**.

If A and B follow the mixed strategies given above, of playing each of their choices half the time, then they will have a probability of 1/4 of ending up in each of the four cells in the payoff matrix. Thus the average payoff to A will be 0, and the average payoff to B will be 1/2.

A Nash equilibrium in mixed strategies refers to an equilibrium in which each agent chooses the optimal frequency with which to play his strategies given the frequency choices of the other agent.

It can be shown that for the sort of games we are analyzing in this chapter, there will always exist a Nash equilibrium in mixed strategies. Because a Nash equilibrium in mixed strategies always exists, and because the concept has a certain inherent plausibility, it is a very popular equilibrium notion in analyzing game behavior. In the example in Table 27.3 it can be shown that if player A plays top with probability 3/4 and bottom with probability 1/4, and player B plays left with probability 1/2 and right with probability 1/2 this will constitute a Nash equilibrium.

27.4 The Prisoner's Dilemma

Another problem with the Nash equilibrium of a game is that it does not necessarily lead to Pareto efficient outcomes. Consider, for example, the game depicted in Table 27.4. This game is known as the **prisoner's dilemma**. The original discussion of the game considered a situation where two prisoners who were partners in a crime were being questioned in separate rooms. Each prisoner had a choice of confessing to the crime, and thereby implicating the other, or denying that he had participated in the crime. If only one prisoner confessed, then he would go free, and the authorities would throw the book at the other prisoner, requiring him to spend 6 months in prison. If both prisoners denied being involved, then both would be held for 1 month on a technicality, and if both players confessed they would both be held for 3 months. The payoff matrix for this game is given in Table 27.4. The entries in each cell in the matrix represent the utility that each of the agents assigns to the various prison terms, which for simplicity we take to be the negative of the length of their prison terms.

Put yourself in the position of player A. If player B decides to deny committing the crime, then you are certainly better off confessing, since then you'll get off free. Similarly, if player B confesses, then you'll be

The prisoner's dilemma.

Table
27.4

		Player B	
		Confess	Deny
Player A	Confess	$-3, -3$	$0, -6$
	Deny	$-6, 0$	$-1, -1$

better off confessing, since then you get a sentence of 3 months rather than a sentence of 6 months. Thus *whatever* player B does, player A is better off confessing.

The same thing goes for player B—he is better of confessing as well. Thus the unique Nash equilibrium for this game is for both players to confess. In fact, both players confessing is not only a Nash equilibrium, it is a dominant strategy equilibrium, since each player has the same optimal choice independent of the other player.

But if they could both just hang tight, they would both be better off! If they both could be sure the other would hold out, and both could agree to hold out themselves, they would each get a payoff of -1 which would make them both better off. The strategy (deny, deny) is Pareto efficient—there is no other strategy choice that makes both players better off—while the strategy (confess, confess) is Pareto inefficient.

The problem is that there is no way for the two prisoners to coordinate their actions. If each could trust the other, then they could both be made better off.

The prisoner's dilemma applies to a wide range of economic and political phenomena. Consider, for example, the problem of arms control. Interpret the strategy of "confess" as "deploy a new missile" and the strategy of "deny" as "don't deploy." Note that the payoffs are reasonable. If my opponent deploys his missiles, I certainly want to deploy, even though the best strategy for both of us is to agree not to deploy. But if there is no way to make a binding agreement, we each end up deploying the missile and are both made worse off.

Another good example is the problem of cheating in a cartel. Now interpret confess as "produce more than your quota of output" and interpret deny as "stick to the original quota." If you think the other firm is going to stick to its quota, it will pay you to produce more than your own quota. And if you think that the other firm will overproduce, then you might as well, too!

The prisoner's dilemma has provoked a lot of controversy as to what is the "correct" way to play the game—or, more precisely, what is a reasonable way to play the game. The answer seems to depend on whether you are playing a one–shot game or whether the game is to be repeated an indefinite number of times.

If the game is going to be played just one time, the strategy of defecting—in this example, confessing—seems to be a reasonable one. After all, whatever the other fellow does, you are better off, and you have no way of influencing the other person's behavior.

27.5 Repeated Games

In the previous section, the players met only once and played the prisoner's dilemma game a single time. However, the situation is different if the game is to be played repeatedly by the same players. In this case there are new strategic possibilities open to each player. If the other player chooses to defect on one round, then you can choose to defect on the next round. Thus your opponent can be "punished" for "bad" behavior. In a repeated game, each player has the opportunity to establish a reputation for cooperation, and thereby encourage the other player to do the same.

Whether this kind of strategy will be viable depends on whether the game is going to be played a *fixed* number of times or an *indefinite* number of times.

Let us consider the first case, where both players know that the game is going to be played 10 times, say. What will the outcome be? Suppose we consider round 10. This is the last time the game will be played, by assumption. In this case, it seems likely that each player will choose the dominant strategy equilibrium, and defect. After all, playing the game for the last time is just like playing it once, so we should expect the same outcome.

Now consider what will happen on round 9. We have just concluded that each player will defect on round 10. So why cooperate on round 9? If you cooperate, the other player might as well defect now and exploit your good nature. Each player can reason the same way, and thus each will defect.

Now consider round 8. If the other person is going to defect on round 9 ... and so it goes. If the game has a known, fixed number of rounds, then each player will defect on every round. If there is no way to enforce cooperation on the last round, there will be no way to enforce cooperation on the next to the last round, and so on.

Players cooperate because they hope that cooperation will induce further cooperation in the future. But this requires that there will always be the possibility of future play. Since there is no possibility of future play in the last round, no one will cooperate then. But then why should anyone cooperate on the next to the last round? Or the one before that? And so it goes—the cooperative solution "unravels" from the end in a prisoner's dilemma with a known, fixed number of plays.

But if the game is going to be repeated an indefinite number of times, then you *do* have a way of influencing your opponent's behavior: if he refuses to cooperate this time, you can refuse to cooperate next time. As long as both parties care enough about future payoffs, the threat of non-cooperation in the future may be sufficient to convince people to play the Pareto efficient strategy.

This has been demonstrated in a convincing way in an experiment run recently by Robert Axelrod.[2] He asked dozens of experts on game theory to submit their favorite strategies for the prisoner's dilemma and then ran a "tournament" on a computer to pit these strategies against each other. Every strategy was played against every other strategy on the computer and the computer kept track of the total payoffs.

The winning strategy—the one with the highest overall payoff—turned out to be the simplest strategy. It is called "tit–for–tat" and goes like this. On the first round, you cooperate—play the "deny" strategy. On every round thereafter, if your opponent cooperated on the previous round you cooperate. If your opponent defected on the previous round, you defect. In other words, whatever your opponent did the last round, you do on this round. That's all there is to it.

The tit–for–tat strategy does very well because it offers an immediate punishment for defection. It is also a forgiving strategy: it punishes the other player only once for each defection. If he falls into line and starts to cooperate, then tit–for–tat will reward the other player with cooperation. It appears to be a remarkably good mechanism for achieving the efficient outcome in a prisoner's dilemma that will be played an indefinite number of times.

27.6 Enforcing a Cartel

In Chapter 26 we discussed the behavior of duopolists playing a price set-ting game. We argued there that if each duopolist could choose his price, then the equilibrium outcome would be the competitive equilibrium. If each firm thought that the other firm would keep its price fixed, then each firm would find it profitable to undercut the other. The only place where this would not be true was if each firm were charging the lowest possible price, which in the case we examined was a price of zero, since the marginal costs were zero. In the terminology of this chapter, each firm charging a zero price is a Nash equilibrium in pricing strategies—what we called a Bertrand equilibrium in Chapter 26.

The payoff matrix for the duopoly game in pricing strategies has the same structure as the prisoner's dilemma. If each firm charges a high price, then they both get large profits. This is the situation where they are both

---

[2] Robert Axelrod is a political scientist from the University of Michigan. For an ex-tended discussion, see his book *The Evolution of Cooperation* (New York: Basic Books, 1984).

cooperating to maintain the monopoly outcome. But if one firm is charging a high price, then it will pay the other firm to cut its price a little, capture the other fellow's market, and thereby get even higher profits. But if both firms cut their prices, they both end up making lower profits. Whatever price the other fellow is charging, it will always pay you to shave your price a little bit. The Nash equilibrium occurs when each fellow is charging the lowest possible price.

However, if the game is repeated an indefinite number of times, there may be other possible outcomes. Suppose that you decide to play tit–for–tat. If the other fellow cuts his price this week, you will cut yours next week. If each player knows that the other player is playing tit–for–tat, then each player would be fearful of cutting his price and starting a price war. The threat implicit in tit–for–tat may allow the firms to maintain high prices.

It has been argued that real life cartels sometimes try to employ such strategies. Robert Porter has described an example of this in a recent paper.[3] The Joint Executive Committee was a famous cartel that set the price of railroad freight in the U.S. in the late 1800s. The formation of this cartel preceded the antitrust regulation in the U.S., and at the time it was perfectly legal.

The cartel determined what market share each railroad could have of the freight shipped. Each firm set its rates individually, and the JEC kept track of how much freight each firm shipped. However, there were several occasions during 1881, 1884, and 1885 where some members of the cartel thought that other member firms were cutting rates so as to increase their market share, despite their agreement. During these periods, there were often price wars. When one firm tried to cheat, all firms would cut their prices so as to "punish" the defectors. This kind of tit–for–tat strategy was apparently able to support the cartel arrangement for some time.

27.7 Sequential Games

Up until now we have been thinking about games in which both players act simultaneously. But in many situations one player gets to move first, and the other player responds. An example of this is the Stackelberg model described in Chapter 26, where one player is a leader and the other player is a follower.

Let's describe a game like this. In the first round, player A gets to choose top or bottom. Player B gets to observe the first player's choice and then chooses left or right. The payoffs are illustrated in a game matrix in Table 27.5.

---

[3] Robert Porter, "A Study of Cartel Stability: the Joint Executive Committee, 1880–1886," *The Bell Journal of Economics*, 14, 2 (Autumn 1983), 301–25.

The payoff matrix of a sequential game.

Table
27.5

		Player B	
		Left	Right
Player A	Top	1, 9	1, 9
	Bottom	0, 0	2, 1

Note that when the game is presented in this form it has two Nash equilibria: (top, left) and (bottom, right). However, we'll show below that one of these equilibria isn't really reasonable. The payoff matrix hides the fact that one player gets to know what the other player has chosen before he makes his choice. In this case it is more useful to consider a diagram that illustrates the asymmetric nature of the game.

Table 27.6 is a picture of the game in **extensive form**—a way to represent the game that shows the time pattern of the choices. First, player A has to choose top or bottom and then player B has to choose left or right. But when B makes his choice, he will know what A has done.

A game in extensive form.

Table
27.6

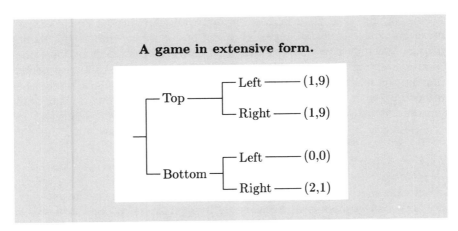

The way to analyze this game is to go to the end and work backwards. Suppose that player A has already made his choice and we are sitting in one branch of the game tree. If player A has chosen top, then it doesn't matter what player B does and the payoff is (1,9). If player A has chosen bottom, then the sensible thing for player B to do is to choose right and the payoff is (2,1).

Now think about player A's initial choice. If he chooses top, the outcome will be (1,9) and thus he will get a payoff of 1. But if he chooses bottom he gets a payoff of 2. So the sensible thing for him to do is to choose bottom.

Thus the equilibrium choices in the game will be (bottom, right), so that the payoff to player A will be 2 and to player B will be 1.

The strategies (top, left) are not a reasonable equilibrium in this sequential game. That is, they are not an equilibrium given the order in which the players actually get to make their choices. It is true that if player A chooses top, player B could choose left—but it would be silly for player A to ever choose top!

From player B's point of view this is rather unfortunate, since he ends up with a payoff of 1 rather than 9! What might he do about it?

Well, he can *threaten* to play left if player A plays bottom. If player A thought that player B would actually carry out this threat he would be well advised to play top. For top gives him 1, while bottom—if player B carries out his threat—will only give him 0.

But is this threat credible? After all, once player A makes his choice, that's it. Player B can get either 0 or 1, and he might as well get 1. Unless player B can somehow convince player A that he will really carry out his threat—even when it hurts him to do so—he will just have to settle for the lower payoff.

Player B's problem is that once player A has made his choice, player A expects player B to do the rational thing. Player B would be better off if he could *commit* himself to play left if player A plays bottom.

One way for B to make such a commitment is to allow someone else to make his choices. For example, B might hire a lawyer and instruct him to play left if A plays bottom. If A is aware of these instructions, the situation is radically different from his point of view. If he knows about B's instructions to his lawyer, then he knows that if he plays bottom he will end up with a payoff of 0. So the sensible thing for him to do is to play top. In this case B has done better for himself by *limiting* his choices.

27.8 A Game of Entry Deterrence

In our examination of oligopoly we took the number of firms in the industry as fixed. But in many situations, entry is possible. Of course, it is in the interest of the firms in the industry to try to prevent such entry. Since they are already in the industry, they get to move first and thus have an advantage in choosing ways to keep their opponents out.

Suppose, for example, that we have a monopolist who is facing a threat of entry by another firm. The entrant decides whether or not to come into the market, and then the incumbent decides whether or not to cut its price in response. If the entrant decides to stay out, it gets a payoff of 1 and the incumbent gets a payoff of 9.

If the entrant decides to come in, then its payoff depends on whether the incumbent fights—by competing vigorously—or not. If the incumbent fights, then we suppose that both players end up with 0. If the incumbent decides not to fight, we suppose that the entrant gets 2 and the incumbent gets 1.

Note that this is exactly the structure of the sequential game we studied earlier, and thus has a structure identical to that depicted in Table 27.6. The incumbent is player B, while the potential entrant is player A. The top strategy is stay out and the bottom strategy is enter. The left strategy is fight and the right strategy is don't fight. As we've seen in this game, the equilibrium outcome is for the potential entrant to enter and the incumbent *not* to fight.

The incumbent's problem is that he cannot precommit himself to fighting if the other firm enters. If the other firm enters, the damage is done and the rational thing for the incumbent to do is to live and let live. Insofar as the potential entrant recognizes this, he will correctly view any threats to fight as empty.

But now suppose that the incumbent can purchase some extra production capacity that will allow him to produce more output at the same marginal cost he currently has. Of course, if he remains a monopolist, he won't want to actually use this capacity since he is already producing the profit maximizing monopoly output.

But, if the other firm enters, the incumbent will now be able to produce so much output that he may well be able to compete much more successfully against the new entrant. By investing in the extra capacity, he will lower his costs of fighting if the other firm tries to enter. Let us assume that if he purchases the extra capacity and if he chooses to fight that he will make a profit of 2. This changes the game tree to the form depicted in Table 27.7.

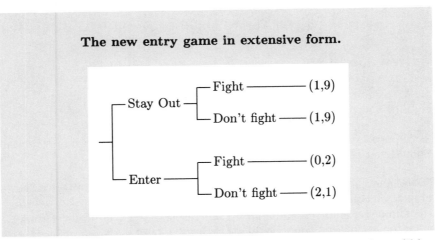

The new entry game in extensive form.   Table
                                                             27.7

Now, because of the increased capacity, the threat of fighting is credible. If the potential entrant comes into the market, the incumbent will get a payoff of 2 if he fights and 1 if he doesn't; thus the incumbent will rationally choose to fight. The entrant will therefore get a payoff of 0 if he enters, and if he stays out he will get a payoff of 1. The sensible thing to do is to stay out. But this means that the incumbent will remain a monopolist and never use his extra capacity! Despite this, it is worthwhile for the monopolist to have the extra capacity to make credible the threat of fighting if a new firm tries to enter the market.

Summary

1. A game can be described by indicating the payoffs to each of the players for each configuration of strategic choices they make.

2. A dominant strategy equilibrium is a set of choices for which each player's choices are optimal *regardless* of what the other players choose.

3. A Nash equilibrium is a set of choices for which each player's choice is optimal, given the choices of the other players.

4. The prisoner's dilemma is a particular game in which the Pareto efficient outcome is strategically dominated by an inefficient outcome.

5. If a prisoner's dilemma is repeated an indefinite number of times, then it is possible that the Pareto efficient outcome may result from rational play.

6. In a sequential game, the time pattern of choices is important. In these games, it can often be advantageous to find a way to precommit to a particular line of play.

Review Questions

1. Are dominant strategy equilibria always Nash equilibria? Are Nash equilibria always dominant strategy equilibria?

2. Suppose your opponent is *not* playing her Nash equilibrium strategy. Should you play your Nash equilibrium strategy?

3. We know that the single-shot prisoner's dilemma game results in a dominant Nash equilibrium strategy that is Pareto inefficient. Suppose we allow the two prisoners to retaliate after their respective prison terms. Formally, what aspect of the game would this affect? Could a Pareto efficient outcome result?

4. What is the dominant Nash equilibrium strategy for the repeated prisoner's dilemma game for the case where both players know that the game

will end after one million repetitions? If you were going to run an experiment with human players for such a scenario, would you predict that players would use this strategy?

5. Suppose that player B rather than player A gets to move first in the sequential game described in this chapter. Draw the extensive form of the new game. What is the equilibrium for this game? Does player B prefer to move first or second?

28

EXCHANGE

Up until now we have generally considered the market for a single good in isolation. We have viewed the demand and supply functions for a good as depending on its price alone, disregarding the prices of other goods. But in general the prices of other goods *will* affect people's demands and supplies for a particular good. Certainly the prices of substitutes and complements for a good will influence the demand for it, and, more subtly, the prices of goods that people sell will affect the amount of income they have and thereby influence how much of other goods they will be able to buy.

Up until now we have been ignoring the effect of these other prices on the market equilibrium. When we discussed the equilibrium conditions in a particular market, we only looked at part of the problem: how demand and supply were affected by the price of the particular good we were examining. This is called **partial equilibrium** analysis.

In this chapter we will begin our study of **general equilibrium** analysis: how demand and supply conditions interact in several markets to determine the prices of many goods. As you might suspect, this is a complex problem, and we will have to adopt several simplifications in order to deal with it.

First, we will limit our discussion to the behavior of competitive markets, so that each consumer or producer will take prices as given, and optimize accordingly. The study of general equilibrium with imperfect competition is very interesting but too difficult to examine at this point.

Second, we will adopt our usual simplifying assumption of looking at the smallest number of goods and consumers that we possibly can. In this case, it turns out that many interesting phenomena can be depicted using only two goods and two consumers. All of the aspects of general equilibrium analysis that we will discuss can be generalized to arbitrary numbers of consumers and goods, but the exposition is simpler with two of each.

Third, we will look at the general equilibrium problem in two stages. We will start with an economy where people have fixed endowments of goods and examine how they might trade these goods among themselves; no production will be involved. This case is naturally known as the case of **pure exchange**. Once we have a clear understanding of pure exchange markets we will examine production behavior in the general equilibrium model.

28.1 The Edgeworth Box

There is a convenient graphical tool known as the **Edgeworth box** that can be used to analyze the exchange of two goods between two people.[1] The Edgeworth box allows us to depict the endowments and preferences of two individuals in one convenient diagram, which can be used to study various outcomes of the trading process. In order to understand the construction of an Edgeworth box it is necessary to examine the indifference curves and the endowments of the people involved.

Let us call the two people involved A and B, and the two goods involved 1 and 2. We will indicate A's consumption bundle by $X_A = (x_A^1, x_A^2)$, where x_A^1 represents A's consumption of good 1 and x_A^2 represents A's consumption of good 2. Then B's consumption bundle is denoted by $X_B = (x_B^1, x_B^2)$. A *pair* of consumption bundles, X_A and X_B, is called an **allocation**. An allocation is a **feasible allocation** if the total amount of each good used is equal to the total amount available:

$$x_A^1 + x_B^1 = \omega_A^1 + \omega_B^1$$

$$x_B^2 + x_B^2 = \omega_B^2 + \omega_B^2.$$

A particular feasible allocation that is of interest is the **initial endowment allocation**, (ω_A^1, ω_A^2) and (ω_B^1, ω_B^2). This is the allocation that the consumers start with. It consists of the amount of each good that consumers bring to the market. They will exchange some of these goods with each other in the course of tra le to end up at a **final allocation**.

---

[1]   The Edgeworth box is named in honor of Francis Ysidro Edgeworth (1845–1926), an English economist who was one of the first to use this analytical tool.

The Edgeworth box shown in Figure 28.1 can be used to illustrate these concepts graphically. We first use a standard consumer theory diagram to illustrate the endowment and preferences of consumer A. We can also mark off on these axes the *total* amount of each good in the economy—the amount that A has plus the amount that B has of each good. Since we will only be interested in feasible allocations of goods between the two consumers, we can draw a box that contains the set of possible bundles of the two goods that A can hold.

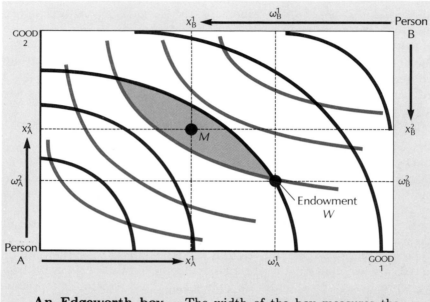

Figure
28.1

An Edgeworth box. The width of the box measures the total amount of good 1 in the economy and the height measures the total amount of good 2. Person A's consumption choices are measured from the lower left-hand corner while person B's choices are measured from the upper right.

Note that the bundles in this box also indicate the amount of the goods that B can hold. If there are 10 units of good 1 and 20 units of good 2, then if A holds (7,12), B must be holding (3,8). We can depict how much A holds of good 1 by the distance along the horizontal axis from the origin in the lower left-hand corner of the box, and the amount B holds of good 1 by measuring the distance along the horizontal axis from the upper right-hand corner. Similarly, distances along the vertical axes give the amounts of good 2 that A and B hold. Thus the points in this box give us both the bundles that A can hold and the bundles that B can hold—just measured from different origins. The points in the Edgeworth box can represent all feasible allocations in this simple economy.

We can depict A's indifference curves in the usual manner, but B's indifference curves take a somewhat different form. To construct them we take a standard diagram for B's indifference curves, turn it upside down, and "overlay" it on the Edgeworth box. This gives us B's indifference curves on the diagram. If we start at A's origin in the lower left hand corner and move up and to the right, we will be moving to allocations that are more preferred by A. As we move down and to the left we will be moving to allocations that are more preferred by B. (If you rotate your book and look at the diagram, this discussion may seem clearer.)

The Edgeworth box allows us to depict the possible consumption bundles for both consumers—the feasible allocations—and the preferences of both consumers. It thereby gives a complete description of the economically relevant characteristics of the two consumers.

28.2 Trade

Now that we have both sets of preferences and endowments depicted we can begin to analyze the question of how trade takes place. We start at the original endowment of goods, denoted by the point W in Figure 28.1. Consider the indifference curves of A and B that pass through this allocation. The region where A is better off than at his endowment consists of all the bundles above his indifference curve through W. The region where B is better off than at his endowment consists of all the allocations that are above—from his point of view—*his* indifference curve through W. (This is *below* his indifference curve from *our* point of view.)

Where is the region of the box where A and B are *both* made better off? Clearly it is in the intersection of these two regions. This is the lens-shaped region illustrated in Figure 28.1. Presumably in the course of their negotiations the two people involved will find some mutually advantageous trade—some trade that will move them to some point inside the lens-shaped area such as the point M in Figure 28.1.

The particular movement to M depicted in Figure 28.1 involves person A giving up $|x_A^1 - \omega_A^1|$ units of good 1 and acquiring in exchange $|x_A^2 - \omega_A^2|$ units of good 2. This means that B acquires $|x_B^1 - \omega_B^1|$ units of good 1 and gives up $|x_B^2 - \omega_B^2|$ units of good 2.

There is nothing particularly special about the allocation M. Any allocation inside the lens-shaped region would be possible—for every allocation of goods in this region is an allocation that makes each consumer better off than he or she was at the original endowment. We only need to suppose that the consumers trade to *some* point in this region.

Now we can repeat the same analysis at the point M. We can draw the two indifference curves through M, construct a new lens shaped "region of mutual advantage," and imagine the traders moving to some new point N in this region. And so it goes ... the trade will continue until there are no more trades that are preferred by both parties. What does such a position look like?

28.3 Pareto Efficient Allocations

The answer is given in Figure 28.2. At the point M in this diagram the set of points above A's indifference curve doesn't intersect the set of points above B's indifference curve. The region where A is made better off is disjoint from the region where B is made better off. This means that any movement that makes one of the parties better off necessarily makes the other party worse off. Thus there are no exchanges that are advantageous for both parties. There are no mutually improving trades at such an allocation.

An allocation such as this is known as a **Pareto efficient** allocation. The idea of Pareto efficiency is a very important concept in economics that arises in various guises.

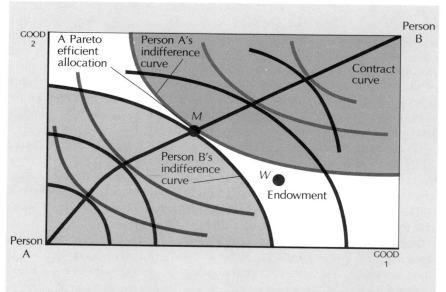

**Figure
28.2**   **A Pareto efficient allocation.** At a Pareto efficient allocation such as M, each person is on his highest possible indifference curve, given the indifference curve of the other person. The line connecting such points is known as the contract curve.

A Pareto efficient allocation can be described as an allocation where:

1. There is no way to make all the people involved better off; or

2. there is no way to make some individual better off without making someone else worse off; or

3. all of the gains from trade have been exhausted; or

4. there are no mutually advantageous trades to be made, and so on.

Indeed we have mentioned the concept of Pareto efficiency several times already in the context of a single market: we spoke of the Pareto efficient level of output in a single market as being that amount of output where the marginal willingness to buy equaled the marginal willingness to sell. At any level of output where these two numbers differed, there would be a way to make both sides of the market better off by carrying out a trade. In this chapter we will examine more deeply the idea of Pareto efficiency involving many goods and many traders.

Note the following simple geometry of Pareto efficient allocations: the indifference curves of the two agents must be tangent at any Pareto efficient allocation in the interior of the box. It is easy to see why. If the two indifference curves are not tangent at an allocation in the interior of the box, then they must cross. But if they cross, then there must be some mutually advantageous region—so that point cannot be Pareto efficient. (It is possible to have Pareto efficient allocations on the sides of the box—where one consumer has zero consumption of some good—in which the indifference curves are not tangent. These boundary cases are not important for the current discussion.)

From the tangency condition it is easy to see that there are a lot of Pareto efficient allocations in the Edgeworth box. In fact, given any indifference curve for person A, for example, there is an easy way to find a Pareto efficient allocation. Simply move along A's indifference curve until we find the point that is the best point for B. This will be a Pareto efficient point, and thus both indifference curves must be tangent at this point.

The set of *all* Pareto efficient points in the Edgeworth box is known as the **Pareto set**, or the **contract curve**. The latter name comes from the idea that all "final contracts" for trade must lie on the Pareto set—otherwise they wouldn't be final because there would be some improvement that could be made!

In a typical case the contract curve will stretch from A's origin to B's origin across the Edgeworth box, as shown in Figure 28.2. If we start at A's origin, A has none of either good and B holds everything. This is Pareto efficient since the only way A can be made better off is to take something away from B. As we move up the contract curve A is getting more and more well-off until we finally get to B's origin.

The Pareto set describes all the possible outcomes of mutually advantageous trade from starting anywhere in the box. If we are given the starting point—the initial endowments for each consumer—we can look at the subset of the Pareto set that each consumer prefers to his initial endowment. This is simply the subset of the Pareto set that lies in the lens-shaped region depicted in Figure 28.1. The allocations in this lens-shaped region are the possible outcomes of mutual trade starting from the particular initial endowment depicted in that diagram. But the Pareto set itself doesn't depend on the initial endowment, except insofar as the endowment determines the total amounts of both goods that are available, and thereby determines the dimensions of the box.

28.4 Market Trade

The equilibrium of the trading process described above—the set of Pareto efficient allocations—is very important, but it still leaves a lot of ambiguity about where the agents end up. The reason is that the trading process we have described is very general. Essentially we have only assumed that the two parties will move to *some* allocation where they are both made better off.

If we have a *particular* trading process, we will have a more precise description of equilibrium. Let's try to describe a trading process that mimics the outcome of a competitive market.

Suppose that we have a third party who is willing to act as an "auctioneer" for the two agents A and B. The auctioneer chooses a price for good 1 and a price for good 2 and presents these prices to the agents A and B. Each agent then sees how much his or her endowment is worth at the prices (p_1, p_2) and decides how much of each good he or she would want to buy at those prices.

One warning is in order here. If there are really only two people involved in the transaction, then it doesn't make much sense for them to behave in a competitive manner. Instead they would probably attempt to bargain over the terms of trade. One way around this difficulty is to think of the Edgeworth box as depicting the average demands in an economy with only two *types* of consumers, but with many consumers of each type. Another way to deal with this is to point out that the behavior is implausible in the two-person case, but it makes perfect sense in the many-person case, which is what we are really concerned with.

Either way, we know how to analyze the consumer choice problem in this framework—it is just the standard consumer choice problem we described in Chapter 5. In Figure 28.3 we illustrate the two demanded bundles of the two agents.

As in Chapter 9 there are two relevant concepts of "demand" in this framework. The **gross demand** of agent A for good 1, say, is the total

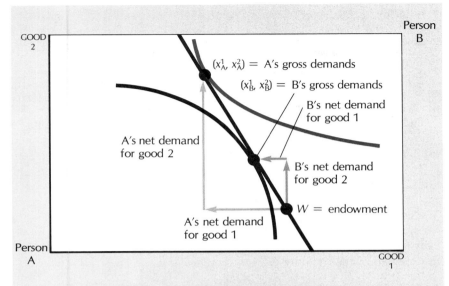

Gross demands and net demands.   Gross demands are
the amount the person wants to consume; net demands are the
amount the person wants to purchase.

Figure
28.3

amount of good 1 that he wants at the going prices. The **net demand**
of agent A for good 1 is the difference between this total demand and
the initial endowment of good 1 that agent A holds. In the context of
general equilibrium analysis, net demands are sometimes called **excess
demands**. We will denote the excess demand of agent A for good 1 by
e_A^1. By definition, if A's gross demand is x_A^1, and his endowment is ω_A^1, we
have

$$e_A^1 = x_A^1 - \omega_A^1.$$

The concept of excess demand is probably more natural but the concept
of gross demand is generally more useful. We will typically use the word
"demand" to mean gross demand, and specifically say "net demand" or
"excess demand" if that is what we mean.

For arbitrary prices (p_1, p_2) there is no guarantee that supply will equal
demand—in either sense of demand. In terms of net demand, this means
that the amount that A will want to buy (or sell) will not necessarily equal
the amount that B will want to sell (or buy). In terms of gross demand this
means that the total amount that A wants to hold of one of the goods plus
the total amount that B wants to hold is not equal to the total amount of
that good available. Indeed, this is true in the example depicted in Figure
28.3.

We say that in this case the market is in **disequilibrium**. In such a situation, it is natural to suppose that the auctioneer will change the prices of the goods. If there is excess demand for one of the goods, the auctioneer will raise the price of that good, and if there is excess supply for one of the goods, the auctioneer will lower its price.

Suppose that this adjustment process continues until the demand for each of the goods equals the supply. What will the final configuration look like?

The answer is given in Figure 28.4. Here the amount that A wants to buy of good 1 just equals the amount that B wants to sell of good 1, and similarly for good 2. Said another way, the total amount that each person wants to buy of each good at the current prices is equal to the total amount available. We say that the market is in **equilibrium**. More precisely, this is called a **market equilibrium**, a **competitive equilibrium**, or a **Walrasian equilibrium**.[2] Each of these terms refers to the same thing: a set of prices such that each consumer is choosing his or her most preferred affordable bundle, and all consumer's choices are compatible in the sense that demand equals supply in every market.

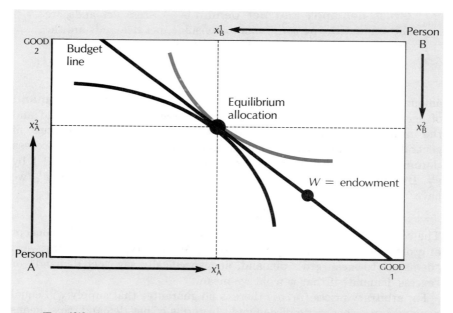

Figure
28.4

Equilibrium in the Edgeworth box. In equilibrium, each person is choosing the most preferred bundle in his budget set, and the choices exhaust the available supply.

[2] Leon Walras (1834–1910) was a French economist at Lausanne who was an early investigator of general equilibrium theory.

In equilibrium, each agent is choosing the best bundle that he can afford, and the choices of all the agents are compatible in the sense that the total demand for each good equals the total supply. We know that if each agent is choosing the best bundle that he can afford, then his marginal rate of substitution between the two goods must be equal to the ratio of the prices.

But if all consumers are facing the same prices, then all consumers will have to have the *same* marginal rate of substitution between each of the two goods. In terms of Figure 28.4, an equilibrium has the property that each agent's indifference curve is tangent to his budget line. But since each agent's budget line has the slope $-p_1/p_2$, this means that the two agents' indifference curves must be tangent to each other.

28.5 The Algebra of Equilibrium

If we let $x_A^1(p_1,p_2)$ be agent A's demand function for good 1 and $x_B^1(p_1,p_2)$ be agent B's demand function for good 1, and define the analogous expressions for good 2, we can describe this equilibrium as a set of prices (p_1,p_2) such that

$$x_A^1(p_1,p_2) + x_B^1(p_1,p_2) = \omega_A^1 + \omega_B^1$$
$$x_A^2(p_1,p_2) + x_B^2(p_1,p_2) = \omega_A^2 + \omega_B^2.$$

These equations say that in equilibrium the total demand for each good should be equal to the total supply.

Another way to describe the equilibrium is to rearrange these two equations to get

$$[x_A^1(p_1,p_2) - \omega_A^1] + [x_B^1(p_1,p_2) - \omega_B^1] = 0$$
$$[x_A^2(p_1,p_2) - \omega_A^2] + [x_B^2(p_1,p_2) - \omega_B^2] = 0.$$

These equations say that the sum of *net demands* of each agent for each good should be zero. Or, in other words, the net amount that A chooses to demand or supply must be equal to the net amount that B chooses to supply or demand.

Yet another formulation of these equilibrium equations comes from the concept of the **aggregate excess demand function**. Let us denote the net demand function for good 1 by agent A by

$$e_A^1(p_1,p_2) = x_A^1(p_1,p_2) - \omega_A^1$$

and define $e_B^1(p_1,p_2)$ in a similar manner.

The function $e_A^1(p_1,p_2)$ measures agent A's **net demand** or his **excess demand**—the difference between what he wants to consume of good 1 and what he initially has of good 1. Now let us add together agent A's net demand for good 1 and agent B's net demand for good 1. We get

$$z_1(p_1,p_2) = e_A^1(p_1,p_2) + e_B^1(p_1,p_2)$$
$$= x_A^1(p_1,p_2) + x_B^1(p_1,p_2) - \omega_A^1 - \omega_B^1$$

which we call the **aggregate excess demand** for good 1. There is a similar aggregate excess demand for good 2, which we denote by $z_2(p_1, p_2)$.

Then we can describe an equilibrium (p_1^*, p_2^*) by saying that the aggregate excess demand for each good is zero:

$$z_1(p_1^*, p_2^*) = 0$$
$$z_2(p_1^*, p_2^*) = 0.$$

Actually, this definition is stronger than necessary. It turns out that if the aggregate excess demand for good 1 is zero then the aggregate excess demand for good 2 must necessarily be zero. In order to prove this, it is convenient to first establish a property of the aggregate excess demand function known as **Walras' law**.

28.6 Walras' Law

Using the notation established above, Walras' law states that

$$p_1 z_1(p_1, p_2) + p_2 z_2(p_1, p_2) \equiv 0.$$

That is, *the value of aggregate excess demand is identically zero.* To say that the value of aggregate demand is identically zero means that it is zero for *all* possible choices of prices, not just equilibrium prices.

The proof of this follows from adding up the two agents' budget constraints. Consider first agent A. Since his demand for each good satisfies his budget constraint, we have

$$p_1 x_A^1(p_1, p_2) + p_2 x_A^2(p_1, p_2) \equiv p_1 \omega_A^1 + p_2 \omega_A^2$$

or

$$p_1 [x_A^1(p_1, p_2) - \omega_A^1] + p_2 [x_A^2(p_1, p_2) - \omega_A^2] \equiv 0$$
$$p_1 e_A^1(p_1, p_2) + p_2 e_A^2(p_1, p_2) \equiv 0.$$

This equation says that the *value of agent A's net demand is zero.* That is, the value of how much A wants to buy of good 1 plus the value of how much he wants to buy of good 2 must equal zero. (Of course the amount that he wants to buy of *one* of the goods must be negative—that is, he intends to sell some of one of the goods to buy more of the other.)

We have a similar equation for agent B:

$$p_1 [x_B^1(p_1, p_2) - \omega_B^1] + p_2 [x_B^2(p_1, p_2) - \omega_B^2] \equiv 0$$
$$p_1 e_B^1(p_1, p_2) + p_2 e_B^2(p_1, p_2) \equiv 0.$$

Adding the equations for agent A and agent B together and using the definition of aggregate demand, $z_1(p_1, p_2)$ and $z_2(p_1, p_2)$, we have

$$p_1 [e_A^1(p_1, p_2) + e_B^1(p_1, p_2)] + p_2 [e_A^2(p_1, p_2) + e_B^2(p_1, p_2)] \equiv 0$$
$$p_1 z_1(p_1, p_2) + p_2 z_2(p_1, p_2) \equiv 0.$$

Now we can see where Walras' law comes from: since the value of each agent's excess demand equals zero, the value of the sum of the agents' excess demands must equal zero.

We can now demonstrate that if demand equals supply in one market, demand must also equal supply in the other market. Note that Walras' law must hold for all prices, since each agent must satisfy his or her budget constraint for all prices. Since Walras' law holds for all prices, in particular, it holds for a set of prices where the excess demand for good 1 is zero:

$$z_1(p_1^*, p_2^*) = 0.$$

According to Walras' law it must also be true that

$$p_1 z_1(p_1^*, p_2^*) + p_2 z_2(p_1^*, p_2^*) = 0.$$

It easily follows from these two equations that if $p_2 > 0$ then we must have

$$z_2(p_1^*, p_2^*) = 0.$$

Thus, as asserted above, if we find a set of prices (p_1, p_2) where the demand for good 1 equals the supply of good 1, we are guaranteed that the demand for good 2 must equal the supply of good 2. Alternatively, if we find a set of prices where the demand for good 2 equals the supply of good 2, we are guaranteed that market 1 will be in equilibrium.

In general, if there are markets for k goods, then we only need to find a set of prices where $k - 1$ of the markets are in equilibrium. Walras' law then implies that the market for good k will automatically have demand equal to supply.

28.7 Relative Prices

As we've seen above, Walras' law implies that there are only $k - 1$ independent equations in a k-good general equilibrium model: if demand equals supply in $k - 1$ markets, demand must equal supply in the final market. But if there are k goods, there will be k prices to be determined. How can you solve for k prices with only $k - 1$ equations?

The answer is that there are really only $k - 1$ *independent* prices. We saw in Chapter 2 that if we multiplied all prices and income by a positive number t, then the budget set wouldn't change, and thus the demanded bundle wouldn't change either. In the general equilibrium model, each consumer's income is just the value of his or her endowment at the market prices. If we multiply all prices by $t > 0$ we will automatically multiply each consumer's income by t. Thus, if we find some equilibrium set of prices (p_1^*, p_2^*), then (tp_1^*, tp_2^*) are equilibrium prices as well, for any $t > 0$.

This means that we are free to choose one of the prices and set it equal to a constant. In particular it is often convenient to set one of the prices equal to 1 so that all of the other prices can be interpreted as being measured relative to it. As we saw in Chapter 2 such a price is called a **numeraire** price. If we choose the first price as the numeraire price, then it is just like multiplying all prices by the constant $t = 1/p_1$.

The requirement that demand equal supply in every market can only be expected to determine the equilibrium relative prices, since multiplying all prices by a positive number will not change anybody's demand and supply behavior.

EXAMPLE: An Algebraic Example of Equilibrium

The Cobb-Douglas utility function described in Chapter 6 has the form $u_A(x_A^1, x_A^2) = (x_A^1)^a (x_A^2)^{1-a}$ for person A, and a similar form for person B. We saw there that this utility function gave rise to the following demand functions:

$$x_A^1(p_1, p_2, m_A) = a \frac{m_A}{p_1}$$

$$x_A^2(p_1, p_2, m_A) = (1-a) \frac{m_A}{p_2}$$

$$x_B^1(p_1, p_2, m_B) = b \frac{m_B}{p_1}$$

$$x_B^2(p_1, p_2, m_B) = (1-b) \frac{m_B}{p_2}$$

where a and b are the parameters of the two consumers' utility functions.

We know that in equilibrium, the money income of each individual is given by the value of his or her endowment:

$$m_A = p_1 \omega_A^1 + p_2 \omega_A^2$$

$$m_B = p_1 \omega_B^1 + p_2 \omega_B^2.$$

Thus the aggregate excess demands for the two goods are

$$z_1(p_1, p_2) = a \frac{m_A}{p_1} + b \frac{m_B}{p_1} - \omega_A^1 - \omega_B^1$$

$$= a \frac{p_1 \omega_A^1 + p_2 \omega_A^2}{p_1} + b \frac{p_1 \omega_B^1 + p_2 \omega_B^2}{p_1} - \omega_A^1 - \omega_B^1$$

and

$$z_2(p_1, p_2) = (1-a) \frac{m_A}{p_2} + (1-b) \frac{m_B}{p_2} - \omega_A^2 - \omega_B^2$$

$$= (1-a) \frac{p_1 \omega_A^1 + p_2 \omega_A^2}{p_2} + (1-b) \frac{p_1 \omega_B^1 + p_2 \omega_B^2}{p_2} - \omega_A^2 - \omega_B^2.$$

You should verify that these aggregate demand functions satisfy Walras' law.

Let us choose p_2 as the numeraire price, so that these equations become

$$z_1(p_1, 1) = a\frac{p_1\omega_A^1 + \omega_A^2}{p_1} + b\frac{p_1\omega_B^1 + \omega_B^2}{p_1} - \omega_A^1 - \omega_B^1$$

$$z_2(p_1, 1) = (1 - a)(p_1\omega_A^1 + \omega_A^2) + (1 - b)(p_1\omega_B^1 + \omega_B^2) - \omega_A^2 - \omega_B^2.$$

All we've done here is set $p_2 = 1$.

We now have an equation for the excess demand for good 1, $z_1(p_1, 1)$, and an equation for the excess demand for good 2, $z_2(p_1, 1)$, with each equation expressed as a function of the relative price of good 1, p_1. In order to find the *equilibrium* price, we set either of these equations equal to zero and solve for p_1. According to Walras' law, we should get the same equilibrium price, no matter which equation we solve.

The equilibrium price turns out to be

$$p_1^* = \frac{a\omega_A^2 + b\omega_B^2}{(1 - a)\omega_A^1 + (1 - b)\omega_B^1}.$$

(Skeptics may want to insert this value of p_1 into the demand equals supply equations to verify that the equations are satisfied.)

28.8 The Existence of Equilibrium

In the example given above, we had specific equations for each consumer's demand function and we could explicitly solve for the equilibrium prices. But in general, we don't have explicit algebraic formulas for each consumer's demands. We might well ask how do we know that there is *any* set of prices such that demand equals supply in every market? This is known as the question of the **existence of a competitive equilibrium**.

The existence of a competitive equilibrium is important insofar as it serves as a "consistency check" for the various models that we have examined in previous chapters. What use would it be to build up elaborate theories of the workings of a competitive equilibrium if such an equilibrium commonly did not exist?

Early economists noted that in a market with k goods there were $k - 1$ relative prices to be determined, and there were $k - 1$ equilibrium equations stating that demand should equal supply in each market. Since the number of equations equaled the number of unknowns, they asserted that there would be a solution where all of the equations were satisfied.

Economists soon discovered that such arguments were fallacious. Merely counting the number of equations and unknowns is not sufficient to prove that an equilibrium solution will exist. However, there are mathematical tools that can be used to establish the existence of a competitive equilibrium. The crucial assumption turns out to be that the aggregate excess demand function is a **continuous function**. This means, roughly speaking, that small changes in prices should result in only small changes in aggregate demand: a small change in prices should not result in a big jump in the quantity demanded.

Under what conditions will the aggregate demand functions be continuous? Essentially there are two kinds of conditions that will guarantee continuity. One is that each individual's demand function be continuous—that small changes in prices will lead to only small changes in demand. This turns out to require that each consumer have convex preferences, which we discussed in Chapter 3. The other condition is more general. Even if consumers themselves have discontinuous demand behavior, as long as all consumers are small relative to the size of the market, the aggregate demand function will be continuous.

This latter condition is quite nice. After all, the assumption of competitive behavior only makes sense when there are a lot of consumers who are small relative to the size of the market. This is exactly the condition that we need in order to get the aggregate demand functions to be continuous. And continuity is just the ticket to ensure that a competitive equilibrium exists. Thus the very assumptions that make the postulated behavior reasonable will ensure that the equilibrium theory will have content.

28.9 Equilibrium and Efficiency

We have now analyzed market trade in a pure exchange model. This gives us a specific model of trade that we can compare to the general model of trade that we discussed in the beginning of this chapter. One question that might arise about the use of a competitive market is whether this mechanism can really exhaust all of the gains from trade. After we have traded to a competitive equilibrium where demand equals supply in every market, will there be any more trades that people will desire to carry out? This is just another way to ask whether the market equilibrium is Pareto efficient: will the agents desire to make any more trades after they have traded at the competitive prices?

We can see the answer by inspecting Figure 28.4: it turns out that the market equilibrium allocation *is* Pareto efficient. The proof is this: an allocation in the Edgeworth box is Pareto efficient if the set of bundles that A prefers doesn't intersect the set of bundles that B prefers. But at the market equilibrium, the set of bundles preferred by A must lie above his budget set, and the same thing holds for B, where "above" means "above from B's point of view." Thus the two sets of preferred allocations can't intersect. This means that there are no allocations that both agents prefer to the equilibrium allocation, so the equilibrium is Pareto efficient.

28.10 The Algebra of Efficiency

We can also show this algebraically. Suppose that we have a market equilibrium that is *not* Pareto efficient. We will show that this assumption leads to logical contradiction.

To say that the market equilibrium is not Pareto efficient means that there is some other feasible allocation $(y_A^1, y_A^2, y_B^1, y_B^2)$ such that

$$y_A^1 + y_B^1 = \omega_A^1 + \omega_B^1 \tag{28.1}$$

$$y_A^2 + y_B^2 = \omega_A^2 + \omega_B^2 \tag{28.2}$$

and

$$(y_A^1, y_A^2) \succ_A (x_A^1, x_A^2) \tag{28.3}$$

$$(y_B^1, y_B^2) \succ_B (x_B^1, x_B^2). \tag{28.4}$$

The first two equations say that the y–allocation is feasible and the next two equations say that it is preferred by each agent to the x–allocation.

But by hypothesis, we have a market equilibrium where each agent is purchasing the best bundle he or she can afford. If (y_A^1, y_A^2) is better than the bundle that A is choosing, then it must cost more than A can afford, and similarly for B:

$$p_1 y_A^1 + p_2 y_A^2 > p_1 \omega_A^1 + p_2 \omega_A^2$$

$$p_1 y_B^1 + p_2 y_B^2 > p_1 \omega_B^1 + p_2 \omega_B^2.$$

Now add these two equations together to get

$$p_1(y_A^1 + y_B^1) + p_2(y_A^2 + y_B^2) > p_1(\omega_A^1 + \omega_B^1) + p_2(\omega_A^2 + \omega_B^2).$$

Substitute from equations (28.1) and (28.2) to get

$$p_1(\omega_A^1 + \omega_B^1) + p_2(\omega_A^2 + \omega_B^2) > p_1(\omega_A^1 + \omega_B^1) + p_2(\omega_A^2 + \omega_B^2)$$

which is clearly a contradiction, since the left-hand side and the right-hand side are the same.

We derived this contradiction by assuming that the market equilibrium was not Pareto efficient. Therefore, this assumption must be wrong. It follows that all market equilibria are Pareto efficient: a result known as the **First Theorem of Welfare Economics.**

The First Welfare Theorem guarantees that a competitive market will exhaust all of the gains from trade: an equilibrium allocation achieved by a set of competitive markets will necessarily be Pareto efficient. Such an allocation may not have any other desirable properties, but it will necessarily be efficient.

In particular, the First Welfare Theorem says nothing about the distribution of economic benefits. The market equilibrium might not be a "just" allocation—if person A owned everything to begin with, then he would own everything after trade. That would be efficient, but it would probably not be very fair. But, after all, efficiency does count for something, and it is reassuring to know that a simple market mechanism like the one we have described is capable of achieving an efficient allocation.

EXAMPLE: Monopoly in the Edgeworth Box

In order to understand the First Welfare Theorem better, it is useful to consider another resource allocation mechanism that does not lead to efficient outcomes. A nice example of this occurs when one consumer attempts to behave as a monopolist. Suppose now that there is no auctioneer, and that instead, agent A is going to quote prices to agent B, and agent B will decide how much he or she wants to trade at the quoted prices. Suppose further that A knows B's "demand curve" and will attempt to choose the set of prices that makes A as well-off as possible, given the demand behavior of B.

In order to examine the equilibrium in this process, it is appropriate to recall the definition of a consumer's **price offer curve**. The price offer curve, which we discussed in Chapter 6, represents all of the optimal choices of the consumer at different prices. B's offer curve represents the bundles that he will purchase at different prices; that is, it describes B's demand behavior. If we draw a budget line for B, then the point where that budget line intersects his offer curve represents B's optimal consumption.

Thus, if agent A wants to choose the prices to offer to B that make A as well-off as possible, he should find that point on B's offer curve where A has the highest utility. Such a choice is depicted in Figure 28.5.

This optimal choice will be characterized by a tangency condition as usual: A's indifference curve will be tangent to B's offer curve. If B's offer curve cut A's indifference curve there would be some point on B's offer curve that A preferred—so we couldn't be at the optimal point for A.

Once we have identified this point—denoted by X in Figure 28.5—we just draw a budget line to that point from the endowment. At the prices that generate this budget line, B will choose the bundle X, and A will be as well-off as possible.

Is this allocation Pareto efficient? In general the answer is no. To see this simply note that A's indifference curve will not be tangent to the budget line at X, and therefore will not be tangent to B's indifference curve. A's indifference curve is tangent to B's offer curve, and therefore will *not* be tangent to B's indifference curve. The monopoly allocation is Pareto inefficient.

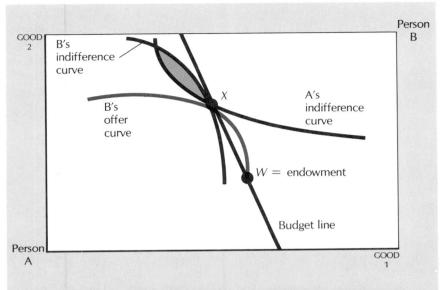

Monopoly in the Edgeworth box. A chooses the point on B's offer curve that gives him the highest utility.

Figure
28.5

In fact, it is Pareto inefficient in exactly the same way that we described in our discussion of monopoly in Chapter 25. At the margin A would like to sell more at the equilibrium prices, but he can only do so by lowering the price at which he sells—and this will lower his income received from all his inframarginal sales.

We saw in Chapter 25 that a perfectly discriminating monopolist would end up producing an efficient level of output. Recall that a discriminating monopolist was one who was able to sell each unit of a good to the person who was willing to pay the most for that unit. What does a perfectly discriminating monopolist look like in the Edgeworth box?

The answer is depicted in Figure 28.6. Let us start at the initial endowment, W, and imagine A selling each unit of good 1 to B at a different price—the price at which B is just indifferent between buying or not buying that unit of the good. Thus, after A sells the first unit, B will remain on the same indifference curve. Then A sells the second unit of good 1 to B for the maximum price he is willing to pay. This means that the allocation moves further to the left, but remains on B's indifference curve. Agent A continues to sell units to B in this manner, thereby moving up B's indifference curve to find his—A's—most preferred point, denoted by an X in Figure 28.6.

It is easy to see that such a point must be Pareto efficient. Agent A will be as well-off as possible given B's indifference curve. At such a point, A

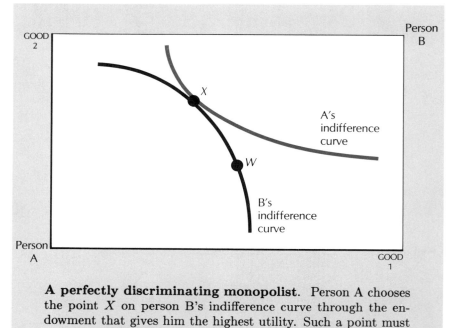

Figure
28.6
A perfectly discriminating monopolist. Person A chooses the point X on person B's indifference curve through the endowment that gives him the highest utility. Such a point must be Pareto efficient.

has managed to extract all of B's consumer's surplus: B is no better off than he was at his endowment.

These two examples provide useful benchmarks with which to think about the First Welfare Theorem. The ordinary monopolist gives an example of a resource allocation mechanism that results in inefficient equilibria, and the discriminating monopolist gives another example of a mechanism that results in efficient equilibria.

28.11 Efficiency and Equilibrium

The First Welfare Theorem says that the equilibrium in a set of competitive markets is Pareto efficient. What about the other way around? Given a Pareto efficient allocation, can we find prices such that it is a market equilibrium? It turns out that the answer is yes, under certain conditions. The argument is illustrated in Figure 28.7.

Let us pick a Pareto efficient allocation. Then we know that the set of allocations that A prefers to his current assignment is disjoint from the set that B prefers. This implies of course that the two indifference curves are tangent at the Pareto efficient allocation. So let us draw in the straight line that is their common tangent, as in Figure 28.7.

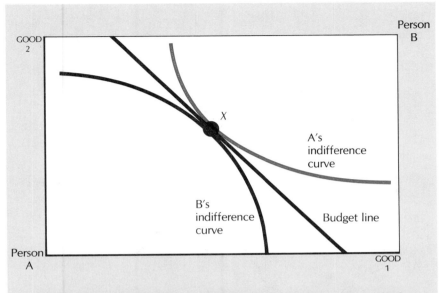

The Second Theorem of Welfare Economics. When preferences are convex, a Pareto efficient allocation is an equilibrium for some set of prices.

Figure
28.7

Suppose that the straight line represents the agents' budget sets. Then if each agent chooses the best bundle on his or her budget set, the resulting equilibrium will be the original Pareto efficient allocation.

Thus the fact that the original allocation is efficient automatically determines the equilibrium prices. The endowments can be any bundles that give rise to the appropriate budget set—that is, bundles that lie somewhere on the constructed budget line.

Can the construction of such a budget line always be carried out? Unfortunately, the answer is no. Figure 28.8 gives an example. Here the illustrated point X is Pareto efficient, but there are no prices that will make it a market equilibrium. The most obvious candidate is drawn in the diagram, but the optimal demands of agents A and B don't coincide for that budget. Agent A wants to demand the bundle Y, but agent B wants the bundle X—demand does not equal supply at these prices.

The difference between Figure 28.7 and Figure 28.8 is that the preferences in Figure 28.7 are convex while the ones in Figure 28.8 are not. If the preferences of both agents are convex, then the common tangent will not intersect either indifference curve more than once and everything will work out fine. This observation gives us the **Second Theorem of Welfare Economics:** if all agents have convex preferences, then there will always be a set of prices such that each Pareto efficient allocation is a market

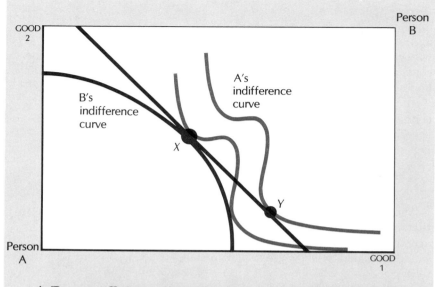

Figure
28.8

A Pareto efficient allocation that is not an equilibrium.
It is possible to find Pareto efficient allocations such as X in
this diagram that cannot be achieved by competitive markets if
preference are nonconvex.

equilibrium for an appropriate assignment of endowments.

The proof is essentially the geometric argument we gave above. At a
Pareto efficient allocation, the bundles preferred by agent A and by agent
B must be disjoint. Thus if both agents have convex preferences we can
draw a straight line between the two sets of preferred bundles that separates
one from the other. The slope of this line gives us the relative prices, and
any endowment that puts the two agents on this line will lead to the final
market equilibrium being the original Pareto efficient allocation.

28.12 Implications of the First Welfare Theorem

The two theorems of welfare economics are among the most fundamental
results in economics. We have demonstrated the theorems only in the simple Edgeworth box case, but they are true for much more complex models
with arbitrary numbers of consumers and goods. The welfare theorems
have profound implications for the design of ways to allocate resources.

Let us consider the First Welfare Theorem. This says that any competitive equilibrium is Pareto efficient. There are hardly any explicit assumptions in this theorem—it follows almost entirely from the definitions. But

there are some implicit assumptions. One major assumption is that agents only care about their own consumption of goods, and not about what other agents consume. If one agent does care about another agent's consumption, we say that there is a **consumption externality**. We shall see that when consumption externalities are present, a competitive equilibrium need not be Pareto efficient.

To take a simple example, suppose that agent A cares about agent B's consumption of cigars. Then there is no particular reason why each agent choosing his own consumption bundle at the market prices will result in a Pareto efficient allocation. After each person has purchased the best bundle they can afford, there may still be ways to make both of them better off—such as A paying B to smoke fewer cigars. We will discuss externalities in more detail in Chapter 31.

Another important implicit assumption in the First Welfare Theorem is that agents actually behave competitively. If there really were only two agents, as in the Edgeworth box example, then it is unlikely that they would each take price as given. One or both of the agents would probably recognize the market power that they have and might attempt to use that market power to improve their own positions. The concept of competitive equilibrium only makes sense when there are enough agents to ensure that each behaves competitively.

Finally, the First Welfare Theorem is only of interest if a competitive equilibrium actually exists. As we have argued above, this will be the case if the consumers are sufficiently small relative to the size of the market.

Given these provisos, the First Welfare Theorem is a pretty strong result: a private market, with each agent seeking to maximize his or her own utility, will result in an allocation that achieves Pareto efficiency.

The importance of the First Welfare Theorem is that it gives a general mechanism—the competitive market—that we can use to ensure Pareto efficient outcomes. If there are only two agents involved, this doesn't matter very much; it is easy for two people to get together and examine the possibilities for mutual trades. But if there are thousands, or even millions, of people involved there must be some kind of structure imposed on the trading process. The First Welfare Theorem shows that the particular structure of competitive markets has the desirable property of achieving a Pareto efficient allocation.

If we are dealing with a resource problem involving many people, it is important to note that the use of competitive markets economizes on the information that any one agent needs to possess. The only things that a consumer needs to know to make his consumption decisions are the prices of the goods he is considering consuming. Consumers don't need to know anything about how the goods are produced, or who owns what goods, or where the goods come from in a competitive market. If each consumer knows only the prices of the goods, he can determine his demands, and if the market functions well enough to determine the competitive prices, we are guaranteed an efficient outcome. The fact that competitive markets economize on information in this way is a strong argument in favor of their use as a way to allocate resources.

28.13 Implications of the Second Welfare Theorem

The Second Theorem of Welfare Economics asserts that under certain conditions, every Pareto efficient allocation can be achieved as a competitive equilibrium.

What is the meaning of this result? The Second Welfare Theorem implies that the problems of distribution and efficiency can be separated. Whatever Pareto efficient allocation you want can be supported by the market mechanism. The market mechanism is distributionally neutral; whatever your criteria for a good or a just distribution of welfare, you can use competitive markets to achieve it.

Prices play two roles in the market system: an *allocative* role and a *distributive* role. The allocative role of prices is to indicate relative scarcity; the distributive role is to determine how much of different goods different agents can purchase. The Second Welfare Theorem says that these two roles can be separated: we can redistribute endowments of goods to determine how much wealth agents have, and then use prices to indicate relative scarcity.

Policy discussions often become confused on this point. One often hears arguments for intervening in pricing decisions on grounds of distributional equity. However, such intervention is typically misguided. As we have seen above, a convenient way to achieve efficient allocations is for each agent to face the true social costs of his or her actions, and make choices that reflect those costs. Thus in a perfectly competitive market the marginal decision of whether to consume more or less of some good will depend on the price—which measures how everyone else values this good on the margin. The considerations of efficiency are inherently marginal decisions—each person should face the correct marginal tradeoff in making his or her consumption decisions.

The decision about *how much* different agents should consume is a totally different issue. In a competitive market this is determined by the value of the resources that a person has to sell. From the viewpoint of the pure theory, there is no reason why the state can't transfer purchasing power—endowments—among consumers in any way that is seen fit.

In fact the state doesn't need to transfer the physical endowments themselves. All that is necessary is to transfer the purchasing power of the endowment. The state could tax one consumer on the basis of the value of his endowment and transfer this money to another. As long as the taxes are based on the value of the consumer's *endowment* of goods there will be no loss of efficiency. It is only when taxes depend on the *choices* that a consumer makes that inefficiencies result, since in this case, the taxes will affect the consumer's marginal choices.

It is true that a tax on endowments will generally change people's behavior. But, according to the First Welfare Theorem, trade from any initial endowments will result in a Pareto efficient allocation. Thus no matter how one redistributes endowments, the equilibrium allocation as determined by market forces will still be Pareto efficient.

However, there are practical matters involved. It would be easy to have a lump sum tax on consumers. We could tax all consumers with blue eyes, and redistribute the proceeds to consumers with brown eyes. As long as eye color can't be changed, there would be no loss in efficiency. Or we could tax consumers with high IQs and redistribute the funds to consumers with low IQs. Again, as long as IQ can be measured, there is no efficiency loss in this kind of tax.

But there's the problem. How do we measure people's endowments of goods? For most people, the bulk of their endowment consists of their own labor power. People's endowments of labor consist of the labor that they *could* consider selling, not the amount of labor that they actually end up selling. Taxing labor that people decide to sell to the market is distortionary—taxing sales of labor will generally result in less labor being sold. Taxing the potential value of labor—the endowment of labor—is not distortionary. The potential value of labor is, by definition, something that is not changed by taxation per se. Taxing the value of the endowment sounds easy until we realize that it involves identifying and taxing something that *might* be sold, rather than taxing something that is sold.

We could *imagine* a mechanism for levying this kind of tax. Suppose that we considered a society where each consumer was required to give the money earned in 10 hours of his labor time to the state each week. This kind of tax would be independent of how much the person actually worked—it would only depend on the endowment of labor, not on how much was actually sold. Such a tax is basically transferring some part of each consumer's endowment of labor time to the state. The state could then use these funds to provide various goods, or it could simply transfer these funds to other agents.

According to the Second Welfare Theorem, this kind of lump sum taxation would be nondistortionary. Essentially any Pareto efficient allocation could be achieved by such lump sum redistribution.

However, no one is advocating such a radical restructuring of the tax system. Most people's labor supply decisions are relatively insensitive to variations in the wage rate, so the efficiency loss from taxing labor may not be too large anyway. But the message of the Second Welfare Theorem is important. Prices should be used to reflect scarcity. Lump sum transfers of wealth should be used to adjust for distributional goals. To a large degree, these two policy decisions can be separated.

People's concern about the distribution of welfare can lead them to advocate various forms of manipulation of prices. It has been argued, for example, that senior citizens should have access to less expensive telephone service, or that small users of electricity should pay lower rates than large users. These are basically attempts to redistribute income through the price system by offering some people lower prices than others.

When you think about it this is a terribly inefficient way to redistribute income. If you want to redistribute income, why don't you simply redistribute income? If you give me a lower price on electricity, then I will be better off only to the extent that I consume more electricity. If you give me an extra dollar, then I can choose to consume more of any of the goods that I want to consume—not necessarily just electricity. Thus lump sum redistribution will always be preferred to manipulating prices.

Summary

1. General equilibrium refers to the study of how the economy can adjust to have demand equal supply in all markets at the same time.

2. The Edgeworth box is a graphical tool to examine such a general equilibrium with 2 consumers and 2 goods.

3. A Pareto efficient allocation is one in which there is no feasible reallocation of the goods that would make all consumers at least as well-off and some consumers strictly better off.

4. Walras' law states that the value of aggregate excess demand is zero for all prices.

5. A general equilibrium allocation is one in which each agent chooses a most preferred bundle of goods from the set of goods that he or she can afford.

6. Only relative prices are determined in a general equilibrium system.

7. If the demand for each good varies continuously as prices vary, then there will always be some set of prices where demand equals supply in every market; that is, a competitive equilibrium.

8. The First Theorem of Welfare Economics states that a competitive equilibrium is Pareto efficient.

9. The Second Theorem of Welfare Economics states that as long as preferences are convex, then every Pareto efficient allocation can be supported as a competitive equilibrium.

Review Questions

1. Is it possible to have a Pareto efficient allocation where someone is worse off than he is at an allocation that is not Pareto efficient?

2. Is it possible to have a Pareto efficient allocation where everyone is worse off than they are at an allocation that is not Pareto efficient?

3. True or false? If we know the contract curve then we know the outcome of any trading.

4. Can some individual be made better off if we are at a Pareto efficient allocation?

5. If the value of excess demand in 8 out of 10 markets is equal to zero, what must be true about the remaining two markets?

6. Given a set of initial endowments, will a system of prices always allow the economy to achieve a Pareto efficient allocation?

APPENDIX

Let us examine the calculus conditions describing Pareto efficient allocations. By definition, a Pareto efficient allocation makes each agent as well-off as possible, given the utility of the other agent. So let us pick $\overline{u}$ as the utility level for agent B, say, and see how we can make agent A as well-off as possible.

The maximization problem is

$$\max_{x_A^1, x_A^2, x_B^1, x_B^2} u_A(x_A^1, x_A^2)$$

such that $u_B(x_B^1, x_B^2) = \overline{u}$

$$x_A^1 + x_B^1 = \omega^1$$

$$x_A^2 + x_B^2 = \omega^2.$$

Here $\omega^1 = \omega_A^1 + \omega_B^1$ is the total amount of good 1 available and $\omega^2 = \omega_A^1 + \omega_B^1$ is the total amount of good 2 available. This maximization problem asks us to find the allocation $(x_A^1, x_A^2, x_B^1, x_B^2)$ that makes person A's utility as large as possible, given a fixed level for person B's utility, and given that the total amount of each good used is equal to the amount available.

We can write the Lagrangian for this problem as

$$L = u_A(x_A^1, x_A^2) - \lambda(u_B(x_B^1, x_B^2) - \overline{u})$$
$$- \mu_1(x_A^1 + x_B^1 - \omega^1) - \mu_2(x_A^2 + x_B^2 - \omega^2).$$

Here λ is the Lagrange multiplier on the utility constraint, and the μ's are the Lagrange multipliers on the resource constraints. When we differentiate with respect to each of the goods, we have four first-order conditions that must hold at the optimal solution:

$$\frac{\partial L}{\partial x_A^1} = \frac{\partial u_A}{\partial x_A^1} - \mu_1 = 0$$

$$\frac{\partial L}{\partial x_A^2} = \frac{\partial u_A}{\partial x_A^2} - \mu_2 = 0$$

$$\frac{\partial L}{\partial x_B^1} = -\lambda\frac{\partial u_B}{\partial x_B^1} - \mu_1 = 0$$

$$\frac{\partial L}{\partial x_B^2} = -\lambda\frac{\partial u_B}{\partial x_B^2} - \mu_2 = 0.$$

If we divide the first equation by the second, and the third equation by the fourth, we have

$$MRS_A = \frac{\partial u_A/\partial x_A^1}{\partial u_A/\partial x_A^2} = \frac{\mu_1}{\mu_2} \tag{28.5}$$

$$MRS_B = \frac{\partial u_B/\partial x_B^1}{\partial u_B/\partial x_B^2} = \frac{\mu_1}{\mu_2}. \tag{28.6}$$

The interpretation of these conditions is given in the text: at a Pareto efficient allocation, the marginal rates of substitution between the two goods must be the same. Otherwise, there would be some trade that would make each consumer better off.

Let us recall the conditions that must hold for optimal choice by consumers. If consumer A is maximizing utility subject to her budget constraint and consumer B is maximizing utility subject to his budget constraint, and both consumers face the same prices for goods 1 and 2, we must have

$$\frac{\partial u_A/\partial x_A^1}{\partial u_A/\partial x_A^2} = \frac{p_1}{p_2} \tag{28.7}$$

$$\frac{\partial u_B/\partial x_B^1}{\partial u_B/\partial x_B^2} = \frac{p_1}{p_2}. \tag{28.8}$$

Note the similarity with the efficiency conditions. The Lagrange multipliers in the efficiency conditions, μ_1 and μ_2, are just like the prices p_1 and p_2 in the consumer choice conditions. In fact the Lagrange multipliers in this kind of problem are sometimes known as **shadow prices** or **efficiency prices**.

Every Pareto efficient allocation has to satisfy conditions like those in equations (28.5) and (28.6). Every competitive equilibrium has to satisfy conditions like those in equations (28.7) and (28.8). The conditions describing Pareto efficiency and the conditions describing individual maximization in a market environment are virtually the same.

29

PRODUCTION

In the last chapter we described a general equilibrium model of a pure exchange economy, and discussed issues of resource allocation when a fixed amount of each good was available. In this chapter we want to describe how production fits into the general equilibrium framework. When production is possible, the amounts of the goods are not fixed but will respond to market prices.

If you thought the two-consumer two-good assumption was a restrictive framework in which to examine trade, imagine what production is going to look like! The minimal set of players that we can have to make an interesting problem is one consumer, one firm, and two goods. The traditional name for this economic model is the **Robinson Crusoe economy**, after Defoe's shipwrecked hero.

29.1 The Robinson Crusoe Economy

In this economy Robinson Crusoe plays a dual role: he is both a consumer and a producer. Robinson can spend his time loafing on the beach thereby consuming leisure, or he can spend time gathering coconuts. The more coconuts he gathers the more he has to eat, but the less time he has to improve his tan.

Robinson's preferences for coconuts and leisure are depicted in Figure 29.1. They are just like the preferences for leisure and consumption depicted in Chapter 10, except we are measuring labor on the horizontal axis rather than leisure. So far nothing new has been added.

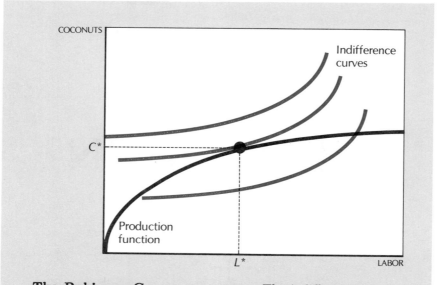

Figure 29.1

The Robinson Crusoe economy. The indifference curves depict Robinson's preferences for coconuts and leisure. The production function depicts the technological relationship between the amount that he works and the amount of coconuts he produces.

Now let's draw in the **production function:** the function that illustrates the relationship between how much Robinson works and how many coconuts he gets. This will typically have the shape depicted in Figure 29.1. The more Robinson works, the more coconuts he will get; but, due to diminishing returns to labor, the marginal product of his labor declines: the number of extra coconuts that he gets from an extra hour's labor decrease as the hours of labor increase.

How much does Robinson work and how much does he consume? To answer these questions, look for the highest indifference curve that just touches the production set. This will give the most preferred combination of labor and consumption that Robinson can get, given the technology for gathering coconuts that he is using.

At this point, the slope of the indifference curve must equal the slope of the production function by the standard argument: if they crossed, there would be some other feasible point that was preferred. This means that the marginal product of an extra hour of labor must equal the marginal rate of substitution between leisure and coconuts. If the marginal product were greater than the marginal rate of substitution, it would pay Robinson to give up a little leisure in order to get the extra coconuts. If the marginal product were less than the marginal rate of substitution, it would pay Robinson to work a little less.

29.2 Crusoe, Inc.

So far this story is only a slight extension of models we have already seen. But now let's add a new feature. Suppose that Robinson is tired of simultaneously being a producer and consumer, and he decides to alternate roles. One day he will behave entirely as a producer, and the next day he will behave entirely as a consumer. In order to coordinate these activities, he decides to set up a labor market and a coconut market.

He also sets up a firm, Crusoe, Inc., and becomes its sole shareholder. The firm is going to look at the prices for labor and coconuts and decide how much labor to hire and how many coconuts to produce, guided by the principle of profit maximization. Robinson, in his role as a worker, is going to collect income from working at the firm; in his role as shareholder in the firm he will collect profits; and, in his role as consumer he will decide how much to purchase of the firm's output. (No doubt this sounds peculiar, but there really isn't that much else to do on a desert island.)

In order to keep track of his transactions, Robinson invents a currency he calls "dollars," and he chooses, somewhat arbitrarily, to set the price of coconuts at one dollar apiece. Thus coconuts are the numeraire good for this economy; as we've seen in Chapter 2, a numeraire good is one whose price has been set to one. Since the price of coconuts is normalized at one, we have only to determine the wage rate. What should his wage rate be in order to make this market work?

We're going to think about this problem first from the viewpoint of Crusoe, Inc., and then from the viewpoint of Robinson, the consumer. The discussion is a little schizophrenic at times, but that's what you have to put up with if you want to have an economy with only one person. We're going to look at the economy after it has been running along for some time, and everything is in equilibrium. In equilibrium, the demand for coconuts will equal the supply of coconuts and the demand for labor will equal the supply of labor. Both Crusoe, Inc. and Robinson the consumer will be making optimal choices given the constraints they face.

29.3 The Firm

Each evening, Crusoe, Inc. decides how much labor it wants to hire the next day, and how many coconuts it wants to produce. Given a price of coconuts of 1 and a wage rate of labor of w we can solve the firm's profit maximization problem in Figure 29.2. We first consider all combinations of coconuts and labor that yield a constant level of profits, π. This means that

$$\pi = C - wL.$$

Solving for C, we have

$$C = \pi + wL.$$

Just as in Chapter 19, this formula describes the isoprofit lines—all combinations of labor and coconuts that yield profits of π. Crusoe, Inc. will choose a point where the profits are maximized. As usual, this implies a tangency condition: the slope of the production function—the marginal product of labor—must equal w, as illustrated in Figure 29.2.

Thus the vertical intercept of the isoprofit line measures the maximal level of profits measured in units of coconuts: if Robinson generates π^* dollars of profit, this money can buy π^* coconuts, since the price of coconuts

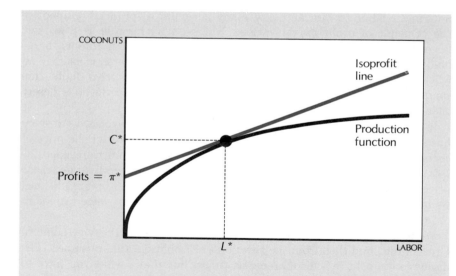

Figure 29.2

Profit maximization. Crusoe, Inc. chooses a profit maximizing production plan, which will be a point of tangency between the isoprofit line and the production function.

has been chosen to be 1. There we have it. Crusoe, Inc. has done its job. Given the wage w, it has determined how much labor it wants to hire, how many coconuts it wants to produce, and what profits it will generate by following this plan. So Crusoe, Inc. declares a stock dividend of π^* dollars and mails it off to its sole shareholder, Robinson.

29.4 Robinson's Problem

The next day Robinson wakes up and receives his dividend of π^* dollars. While eating his coconut breakfast, he contemplates how much he wants to work and consume. He may consider just consuming his endowment—spend his profits on π coconuts and consume his endowment of leisure. But listening to his stomach growl is not so pleasant, and it might make sense to work for a few hours instead. So Robinson trudges down to Crusoe, Inc. and starts to gather coconuts, just as he has done every other day.

We can describe Robinson's labor-consumption choice using standard indifference curve analysis. Plotting labor on the horizontal axis and coconuts on the vertical axis, we can draw in an indifference curve as illustrated in Figure 29.3. Since labor is a bad, by assumption, and coconuts are a good, the indifference curve has a positive slope as shown in the diagram.

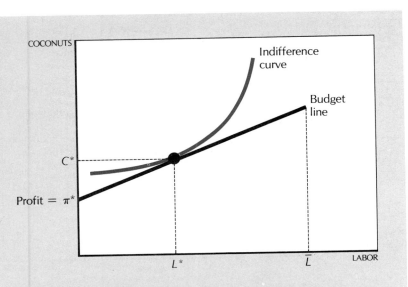

Robinson's maximization problem.   Robinson the consumer decides how much to work and consume given the prices and wages. The optimal point will occur where the indifference curve is tangent to the budget line.

Figure
29.3

If we indicate the maximum amount of labor by $\overline{L}$, then the distance from $\overline{L}$ to the chosen supply of labor gives Robinson's demand for leisure. This is just like the supply of labor model examined in Chapter 10, except we have reversed the origin on the horizontal axis.

Robinson's budget line is also illustrated in Figure 29.3. It has a slope of w and passes through his endowment point $(\pi^*, 0)$. (Robinson has a 0 endowment of labor and a π^* endowment of coconuts since that would be his bundle if he engaged in no market transactions.) Given the wage rate, Robinson chooses optimally how much he wants to work, and how many coconuts he wants to consume. At his optimal consumption, the marginal rate of substitution between consumption and leisure must equal the wage rate, just as in a standard consumer choice problem.

29.5 Putting Them Together

Now we superimpose Figures 29.2 and 29.3 to get Figure 29.4. Look at what has happened! Robinson's bizarre behavior has worked out all right after all. He ends up consuming at exactly the same point as he would have if he had made all the decisions at once. Using the market system results in the same outcome as choosing the consumption and production plans directly.

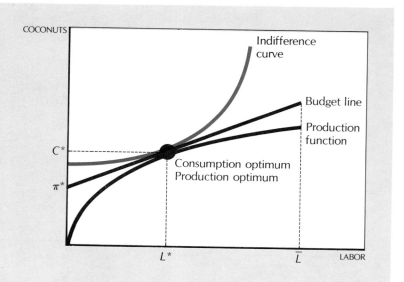

Figure 29.4

Equilibrium in both consumption and production. The amount of coconuts demanded by the consumer Robinson equals the amount of coconuts supplied by Crusoe, Inc.

Since the marginal rate of substitution between leisure and consumption equals the wage, and the marginal product of labor equals the wage, we are assured that the marginal rate of substitution between labor and consumption equals the marginal product—that is, that the slopes of the indifference curve and the production set are the same.

In the case of a one-person economy, using the market is pretty silly. Why should Robinson bother to break up his decision into two pieces? But in an economy with many people, breaking up decisions no longer seems so odd. If there are many firms, then questioning each person about how much they want of each good is simply impractical. In a market economy the firms simply have to look at the prices of goods in order to make their production decisions. For the prices of goods measure how much the consumers value *extra* units of consumption. And the decision that the firms face, for the most part, is whether they should produce more or less output.

The market prices reflect the marginal values of the goods that the firms use as inputs and outputs. If firms use the change in profits as a guide to production, where the profits are measured at market prices, then their decisions will reflect the marginal values that consumers place on the goods.

29.6 Different Technologies

In the above discussion we have assumed that the technology available to Robinson exhibited diminishing returns to labor. Since labor was the only input to production, this was equivalent to decreasing returns to scale. (This is not true if there is more than one input!)

It is useful to consider some other possibilities. Suppose, for example, that the technology exhibited constant returns to scale. Recall that constant returns to scale means that using twice as much of all inputs produces twice as much output. In the case of a one-input production function, this means that the production function must be a straight line through the origin as depicted in Figure 29.5.

Since the technology has constant returns to scale, the argument in Chapter 19 implies that the only reasonable operating position for a competitive firm is at zero profits. This is because if the profits were ever greater than zero, it would pay the firm to expand output indefinitely, and if profits were ever less than zero it would pay the firm to produce zero output.

Thus Robinson's endowment involves zero profits and $\overline{L}$, his initial endowment of labor time. His budget set coincides with the production set, and the story is much the same as before.

The situation is somewhat different with an increasing returns to scale technology, as depicted in Figure 29.6. There is no difficulty in this simple example in exhibiting the optimal choice of consumption and leisure for Robinson. The indifference curve will be tangent to the production set as usual. The problem arises in trying to support this point as a profit

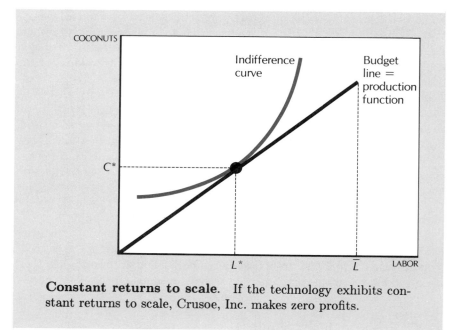

COCONUTS

Indifference curve

Budget line = production function

C^*

L^* $\overline{L}$ LABOR

Figure 29.5

Constant returns to scale. If the technology exhibits constant returns to scale, Crusoe, Inc. makes zero profits.

maximizing point. For if the firm were faced with the prices given by Robinson's marginal rate of substitution, it would want to produce more output than Robinson would demand.

If the firm exhibits increasing returns to scale at the optimal choice, then the average costs of production will exceed the marginal costs of production—and that means that the firm will be making negative profits. The goal of profit maximization would lead the firm to want to increase its output—but this would be incompatible with the demands for output and the supplies of inputs from the consumers. In the case depicted, there is *no* price at which the utility maximizing demand by the consumer will equal the profit maximizing supply from the firm.

Increasing returns to scale is an example of a **nonconvexity**. In this case the production set—the set of coconuts and labor that are feasible for the economy—is not a convex set. Thus the common tangent to the indifference curve and the production function at the point (L^*, C^*) in Figure 29.6 will not separate the preferred points from the feasible points as it does in Figure 29.4.

Nonconvexities such as this pose grave difficulties for the functioning of competitive markets. In a competitive market consumers and firms look at just one set of numbers—the market prices—to determine their consumption and production decisions. If the technology and the preferences are convex, then the only things that the economic agents need to know to make efficient decisions are the relationship between the prices and the

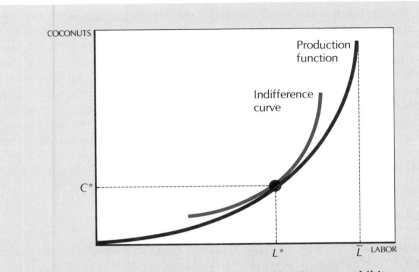

Increasing returns to scale.   The production set exhibits increasing returns to scale and the Pareto efficient allocation cannot be achieved by a competitive market.

Figure
29.6

marginal rates of substitution near the points where the economy is currently producing: the prices tell the agents everything that is necessary in order to determine an efficient allocation of resources.

But if the technology and/or the preferences are nonconvex, then the prices do not convey all the information necessary in order to choose an efficient allocation. Information about the slopes of the production function and indifference curves far away from the current operating position is also necessary.

However, these observations apply only when the returns to scale are large relative to the size of the market. Small regions of increasing returns to scale do not pose undue difficulties for a competitive market.

29.7 Production and the First Welfare Theorem

Recall that in the case of a pure exchange economy, a competitive equilibrium is Pareto efficient. This fact is known as the First Theorem of Welfare Economics. Does the same result hold in an economy with production? The diagrammatic approach used above is not adequate to answer this question, but a generalization of the algebraic argument we provided in Section 28.10 does nicely. It turns out that the answer is yes: if all firms act as competitive profit maximizers, then a competitive equilibrium will be Pareto efficient.

This result has the usual caveats. First, it has nothing to do with distribution. Profit maximization only ensures efficiency, not justice! Second, this result only makes sense when a competitive equilibrium actually exists. In particular, this will rule out large areas of increasing returns to scale. Third, the theorem implicitly assumes that the choices of any one firm do not affect the production possibilities of other firms. That is, it rules out the possibility of **production externalities**. Similarly, the theorem requires that firms' consumption decisions do not directly affect the consumption possibilities of consumers; that is, that there are no **consumption externalities.** More precise definitions of externalities will be given in Chapter 31, where we will examine their effect on efficient allocations in more detail.

29.8 Production and the Second Welfare Theorem

In the case of a pure exchange economy, every Pareto efficient allocation is a possible competitive equilibrium, as long as consumers exhibit convex preferences. In the case of an economy involving production, the same result is true, but now we require not only that consumers' preferences are convex, but also that firms' production sets are convex. As discussed above, this requirement effectively rules out the possibility of increasing returns to scale: if firms have increasing returns to scale at the equilibrium level of production, they would want to produce more output at the competitive prices.

However, with constant or decreasing returns to scale, the Second Welfare Theorem works fine. Any Pareto efficient allocation can be achieved through the use of competitive markets. Of course in general it will be necessary to redistribute endowments among the consumers to support different Pareto efficient allocations. In particular, both the income from endowments of labor and ownership shares of the firm will have to be redistributed. As indicated in the last chapter, there may be significant practical difficulties involved with this sort of redistribution.

29.9 Production Possibilities

We have now seen how production and consumption decisions can be made in a one-input, one-output economy. In this section we want to explore how this model can be generalized to an economy with several inputs and outputs. Although we will deal only with the two-good case, the concepts will generalize naturally to many goods.

So let us suppose that there is some other good that Robinson might produce—say fish. He can devote his time to gathering coconuts or to fishing. In Figure 29.7 we have depicted the various combinations of coconuts and fish that Robinson can produce from devoting different amounts of time to each activity. This set is known as a **production possibilities set**. The boundary of the production possibilities set is called the **production possibilities frontier**. This should be contrasted with the production function discussed earlier which depicts the relationship between the input good and the output good; the production possibilities set depicts only the set of *output* goods that is feasible. (In more advanced treatments, both inputs and outputs can be considered part of the production possibilities set, but these treatments cannot easily be handled with two-dimensional diagrams.)

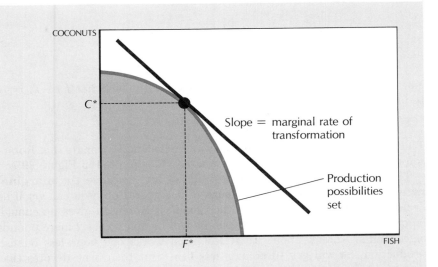

A production possibilities set. The production possibilities set measures the set of outputs that are feasible given the technology and the production functions.

Figure 29.7

The shape of the production possibilities set will depend on the nature of the underlying technologies. If the technology for producing coconuts and fish exhibit constant returns to scale the production possibilities set will take an especially simple form. Since by assumption there is only one input to production—Robinson's labor—the production functions for fish and coconuts will be simply *linear* functions of labor.

For example, suppose that Robinson can produce 10 pounds of fish per hour or 20 pounds of coconuts per hour. Then if he devotes L_c hours to coconut production, and L_f hours to fish production, he will produce $10L_f$ pounds of fish and $20L_c$ pounds of coconuts. Suppose that Robinson decides to work 10 hours a day. Then the production possibilities set will consist of all combinations of coconuts, C, and fish, F, such that

$$F = 10L_f$$
$$C = 20L_c$$
$$L_c + L_f = 10.$$

The first two equations measure the production relationships, and the third measures the resource constraint. To determine the production possibilities frontier solve the first two equations for L_f and L_c to get

$$L_f = \frac{F}{10}$$
$$L_c = \frac{C}{20}.$$

Now add these two equations together, and use the fact that $L_f + L_c = 10$ to find

$$\frac{F}{10} + \frac{C}{20} = 10.$$

This equation gives us all the combinations of fish and coconuts that Robinson can produce if he works 10 hours a day. It is plotted in Figure 29.7.

The slope of this production possibilities set measures the **marginal rate of transformation**—how much of one good Robinson can get if he decides to sacrifice some of the other good. If Robinson gives up enough labor to produce 1 less pound of fish, he will be able to get 2 more pounds of coconuts. Think about it: if Robinson works one hour less on fish production, he will get 10 pounds less fish. But then if he devotes that time to coconuts, he will get 20 pounds more coconuts. The tradeoff is at a ratio of 2 to 1.

29.10 Comparative Advantage

The construction of the production possibilities set given above was quite simple since there was only one way to produce fish and one way to produce coconuts. What if there is more than one way to produce each good? Suppose that we add another worker to our island economy, who has different skills in producing fish and coconuts.

To be specific, let us call the new worker Friday, and suppose that he can produce 20 pounds of fish per hour, or 10 pounds of coconuts per hour. Thus if Friday works for 10 hours, his production possibilities set will be determined by

$$F = 20L_f$$
$$C = 10L_c$$
$$L_c + L_f = 10.$$

Doing the same sort of calculations as we did for Robinson, Friday's production possibilities set is given by

$$\frac{F}{20} + \frac{C}{10} = 10.$$

Note that the marginal rate of transformation between coconuts and fish for Friday is $\Delta C / \Delta F = -1/2$, whereas for Robinson the marginal rate of transformation is -2. For every pound of coconuts that Friday gives up, he can get two pounds of fish; for every pound of fish that Robinson gives up he can get two pounds of coconuts. In this circumstance we say that Friday **has a comparative advantage** in fish production, and Robinson has a comparative advantage in coconut production. In Figure 29.8 we have depicted three production possibilities sets: Panel A shows Robinson's, panel B shows Friday's, and panel C depicts the joint production possibilities set—how much of each good could be produced in total by both people.

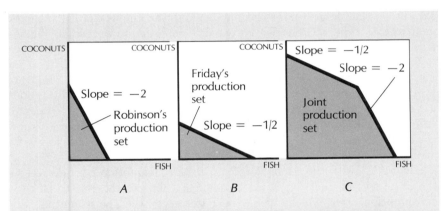

Joint production possibilities. Robinson's and Friday's production possibilities sets and the joint production possibilities set.

Figure 29.8

The joint production possibilities set combines the best of both workers. If both workers are used entirely to produce coconuts, we will get 300 coconuts—100 from Friday and 200 from Robinson. If we want to get more fish, it makes sense to shift the person who is most productive at fish—Friday—out of coconut production and into fish production. For each pound of coconuts that Friday doesn't produce we get 2 pounds of fish; thus the slope of the joint production possibilities set is $-1/2$—which is exactly Friday's marginal rate of transformation.

When Friday is producing 200 pounds of fish, he is fully occupied. If we want even more fish, we have to switch to using Robinson. From this point on the joint production possibilities set will have a slope of -2, since we will be operating along Robinson's production possibilities set. Finally, if we want to produce as much fish as possible, both Robinson and Friday concentrate on fish production and we get 300 pounds of fish, 200 from Friday and 100 from Robinson.

Since the workers each have a comparative advantage in different goods, the joint production possibilities set will have a "kink," as shown in Figure 29.8. There is only one kink in this example since there are just two different ways to produce output—Crusoe's way and Friday's way. If there are many different ways to produce output, the production possibilities set will have the more typical "rounded" structure, as depicted in Figure 29.7.

29.11 Pareto Efficiency

In the last two sections we saw how to construct the production possibilities set, the set that describes the feasible consumption bundles for the economy as a whole. Here we consider Pareto efficient ways to choose among the feasible consumption bundles.

We will indicate aggregate consumption bundles by (X^1, X^2). This indicates that there are X^1 units of good 1 and X^2 units of good 2 that are available for consumption. In the Crusoe/Friday economy, the two goods are coconuts and fish, but we will use the (X^1, X^2) notation in order to emphasize the similarities with the analysis in Chapter 28. Once we know the total amount of each good, we can draw an Edgeworth box as in Figure 29.9.

Given (X^1, X^2), the set of Pareto efficient consumption bundles will be the same sort as that examined in the last chapter: the Pareto efficient consumption levels will lie along the Pareto set—the line of mutual tangencies of the indifference curves, as illustrated in Figure 29.9. These are the allocations in which each consumer's marginal rate of substitution—the rate at which he or she is just willing to trade—equals that of the other.

These allocations are Pareto efficient as far as the consumption decisions are concerned. If people can simply trade one good for another, the Pareto set describes the set of bundles that exhausts the gains from trade. But in an economy with production, there is another way to "exchange" one good for another—namely, to produce less of one good and more of another.

The Pareto set describes the set of Pareto efficient bundles *given* the amounts of goods 1 and 2 available, but in an economy with production those amounts can themselves be chosen out of the production possibilities set. Which choices from the production possibilities set will be Pareto efficient choices?

Let us think about the logic underlying the marginal rate of substitution condition. We argued that in a Pareto efficient allocation, the MRS of consumer A had to be equal to the MRS of consumer B: the rate at which

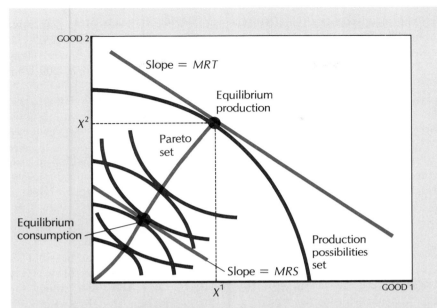

Production and the Edgeworth box. At each point on the production possibilities frontier, we can draw an Edgeworth box to illustrate the possible consumption allocations.

Figure
29.9

consumer A would just be willing to trade one good for the other should be equal to the rate at which consumer B would just be willing to trade one good for the other. If this were not true, then there would be some trade that would make both consumers better off.

Recall that the marginal rate of transformation (MRT) measures the rate at which one good can be "transformed" into the other. Of course, one good really isn't being literally *transformed* into the other. Rather the factors of production are being moved around so as to produce less of one good and more of the other.

Suppose that the economy were operating at a position where the marginal rate of substitution of one of the consumers was not equal to the marginal rate of transformation between the two goods. Then such a position cannot be Pareto efficient. Why? Because at this point, the rate at which the consumer is willing to trade good 1 for good 2 is different from the rate at which good 1 can be transformed into good 2—there is a way to make the consumer better off by rearranging the pattern of production.

Suppose, for example, that the consumer's MRS is 1; the consumer is just willing to substitute good 1 for good 2 on a one-to-one basis. Suppose that the MRT is 2, which means that giving up one unit of good 1 will allow society to produce two units of good 2. Then clearly it makes sense to reduce the production of good 1 by one unit; this will generate two extra units of good 2. Since the consumer was just indifferent between giving up one unit of good 1 and getting one unit of the other good in exchange, he or she will now certainly be better off by getting *two* extra units of good 2.

The same argument can be made whenever one of the consumers has a MRS that is different from the MRT—there will always be a rearrangement of consumption and production that will make that consumer better off. We have already seen that for Pareto efficiency each consumer's MRS should be the same, and the argument given above implies that each consumer's MRS should in fact be equal to the MRT.

Figure 29.9 illustrates a Pareto efficient allocation. The MRSs of each consumer are the same, since their indifference curves are tangent in the Edgeworth box. And each consumer's MRS is equal to the MRT—the slope of the production possibilities set.

29.12 Castaways, Inc.

In the last section we derived the necessary conditions for Pareto efficiency: the MRS of each consumer must equal the MRT. Any way of distributing resources that results in Pareto efficiency must satisfy this condition. Earlier in this chapter, we claimed that a competitive economy with profit maximizing firms and utility maximizing consumers would result in a Pareto efficient allocation. In this section we explore the details of how this works.

Our economy now contains two individuals, Robinson and Friday. There are four goods: two factors of production (Robinson's labor and Friday's labor) and two output goods (coconuts and fish). Let us suppose that Robinson and Friday are both shareholders of the firm, which we will now refer to as Castaways, Inc. Of course, they are also the sole employees and customers, but as usual we shall examine each role in turn, and not allow the participants to see the wider picture. After all, the object of the analysis is to understand how a *decentralized* resource allocation system works—one in which each person only has to determine his or her own decisions, without regard for the functioning of the economy as a whole.

Start first with Castaways, Inc., and consider the profit maximization problem. Castaways, Inc. produces two outputs, coconuts (C) and fish (F), and it uses two kinds of labor, Crusoe's labor (L_c) and Friday's labor (L_f). Given the price of coconuts (p_c), the price of fish (p_f), and the wage rates of Crusoe and Friday $(w_c$ and $w_f)$, the profit maximization problem is

$$\max_{C,F,L_f,L_c} p_c C + p_f F - w_c L_c - w_f L_f$$

subject to the technological constraints described by the production possibilities set.

Let us suppose that the firm finds it optimal in equilibrium to hire L_f^* units of Friday's labor and L_c^* units of Crusoe's labor. The question we want to focus on here is how profit maximization determines the pattern of output to produce. Let $L^* = w_c L_c^* + w_f L_f^*$ represent the labor costs of production, and write the profits of the firm, π, as

$$\pi = p_c C + p_f F - L^*.$$

This equation describes the **isoprofit lines** of the firm, as depicted in Figure 29.10. Rearranging the equation, we have

$$C = \frac{\pi + L^*}{p_c} + \frac{p_f F}{p_c}.$$

This shows that the isoprofit lines have slope of $-p_f/p_c$ and a vertical intercept of $(\pi + L^*)/p_c$. Since L^* is fixed by assumption, higher profits will be associated with isoprofit lines that have higher vertical intercepts.

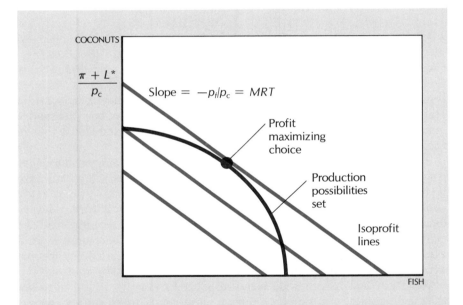

Profit maximization. At the point yielding maximum profits, the marginal rate of transformation must equal the slope of the isoprofit line, $-p_f/p_c$.

Figure 29.10

If the firm wants to maximize its profits, it will choose a point on the production possibilities set such that the isoprofit line through that point has the highest possible vertical intercept. By this stage, it should be clear that this implies that the isoprofit line must be tangent to the production possibilities set; that is,that the slope of the production possibilities set (the MRT) should be equal to the slope of the isoprofit line, p_f/p_c.

We've described this profit maximization problem in the case of one firm, but it holds for an arbitrary number of firms: each firm that chooses the most profitable way to produce coconuts and fish will operate where the marginal rate of transformation between any two goods that it produces equals the price ratio between those two goods. This holds true even if the firms have quite different production possibilities sets, as long as they face the same prices for the two goods.

This means that in equilibrium the prices of the two goods will measure the marginal rate of transformation—the opportunity cost of one good in terms of the other. If you want more coconuts, you will have to give up some fish. How much fish? Just look at the price ratio of fish to coconuts: the ratio of these economic variables tells us what the technological tradeoff must be.

29.13 Robinson and Friday as Consumers

We've seen how Castaways, Inc. determines its profit maximizing production plan. In order to do this, it must hire some labor and it may generate some profits. When it hires labor, it pays wages to the labor; when it makes profits, it pays dividends to its shareholders. Either way the money made by Castaways, Inc. gets paid back to Robinson and Friday, either in the form of wages or profits.

Since the firm pays out all of its receipts to its workers and its shareholders, this means that they must necessarily have enough income to purchase its output. This is just a variation on Walras' law discussed in Chapter 28: people get their income from selling their endowments, so they must always have enough income to purchase those endowments. Here people get income from selling their endowments and also receive profits from the firm. But since money never disappears from or is added to the system, people will always have exactly enough money to purchase what is produced.

What do the consumers do with the money from the firm? As usual, they use the money to purchase consumption goods. Each person chooses the best bundle of goods that he can afford at the prices p_f and p_c. As we've seen earlier, the optimal consumption bundle for each consumer must satisfy the condition that the marginal rate of substitution between the two goods must be equal to the common price ratio. But this price ratio is also equal to the marginal rate of transformation, due to the profit maximization behavior of the firm. Thus the necessary conditions for Pareto efficiency are met: the MRS of each consumer equals the MRT.

In this economy, the prices of the goods serve as a signal of relative scarcity. They indicate the technological scarcity—how much the production of one good must be reduced in order to produce more of the other;

and they indicate the consumption scarcity—how much people are willing to reduce their consumption of one good in order to acquire some of the other good.

29.14 Decentralized Resource Allocation

The Crusoe-Friday economy is a drastically simplified picture. In order to make a start on a larger model of the functioning of an economy, one needs to use substantially more elaborate mathematics. However, even this simple model contains some useful insights.

The most important of these is the relationship between individuals' *private* goals of utility maximization and the *social* goals of efficient use of resources. Under certain conditions, the individuals' pursuit of private goals will result in an allocation that is Pareto efficient overall. Furthermore, any Pareto efficient allocation can be supported as an outcome of a competitive market, if initial endowments—including the ownership of firms—can be suitably redistributed.

The great virtue of a competitive market is that each individual and each firm only has to worry about its own maximization problem. The only facts that need to be communicated among the firms and the consumers are the prices of the goods. Given those signals of relative scarcity, consumers and firms have enough information to make decisions that achieve an efficient allocation of resources. In this sense, the social problems involved in efficiently utilizing resources can be decentralized, and solved at the individual level.

Each individual can solve his or her own problem of what to consume. The firms face the prices of the goods the consumers consume and decide how much to produce of each of them. In making this decision, they are guided by profit signals. In this context, profits serve as exactly the right guide. To say that a production plan is profitable is to say that people are willing to pay more for some good than it costs to produce it—so it is natural to expand the production of such goods. If all firms pursue a competitive profit maximizing policy, and all consumers choose consumption bundles to maximize their own utility, then resulting competitive equilibrium must be a Pareto efficient allocation.

Summary

1. The general equilibrium framework can be extended by allowing competitive, profit maximizing firms to produce goods destined for exchange in the economy.

2. Under certain conditions there exists a set of prices for all of the input and output goods in the economy such that the profit maximizing actions

of firms along with the utility maximizing behavior of individuals results in the demand for each good equaling the supply in all markets—that is, a competitive equilibrium exists.

3. Under certain conditions the resulting competitive equilibrium will be Pareto efficient: the First Welfare Theorem holds in an economy with production.

4. With the addition of convex production sets, the Second Welfare Theorem also holds in the case of production.

5. When goods are being produced as efficiently as possible, the marginal rate of transformation between two goods indicates the number of units the economy must give up of one good to obtain additional units of the other good.

6. Pareto efficiency requires that each individual's marginal rate of substitution be equal to the marginal rate of transformation.

7. The virtue of competitive markets is that they provide a way to achieve an efficient allocation of resources by decentralizing production and consumption decisions.

Review Questions

1. The competitive price of coconuts is $6 per pound and the price of fish is $3 per pound. If society were to give up 1 pound of coconuts, how many more pounds of fish could be produced?

2. What would happen if the firm depicted in Figure 29.2 decided to pay a higher wage?

3. In what sense is a competitive equilibrium a good or bad thing for a given economy?

4. If Robinson's marginal rate of substitution between coconuts and fish is −2 and the marginal rate of transformation between the two goods is −1 what should he do if he wants to increase his utility?

5. Suppose that Robinson and Friday both want 60 pounds of fish and 60 pounds of coconuts per day. Using the production rates given in the chapter, how many hours must Robinson and Friday work per day if they don't help one another? Suppose they decide to work together in the most efficient manner possible. Now how many hours each day do they have to work? What is the economic explanation for the reduction in hours?

APPENDIX

Let us derive the calculus conditions for Pareto efficiency in an economy with production. We let X^1 and X^2 represent the total amount of good 1 and good 2 produced and consumed, as in the body of this chapter:

$$X^1 = x_A^1 + x_B^1$$
$$X^2 = x_A^2 + x_B^2.$$

The first thing we need is a convenient way to describe the production possibilities frontier—all the combinations of X^1 and X^2 that are technologically feasible. The most useful way to do this for our purposes is by use of the **transformation function**. This is a function of the aggregate amounts of the two goods $T(X^1, X^2)$, such that the combination (X^1, X^2) is on the production possibilities frontier (the boundary of the production possibilities set) if and only if

$$T(X^1, X^2) = 0.$$

Once we have described the technology, we can calculate the marginal rate of transformation: the rate at which we have to sacrifice good 2 in order to produce more of good 1. Although the name evokes an image of one good being "transformed" into another, that is a somewhat misleading picture. What really happens is that other resources are moved from producing good 2 to producing good 1. Thus, by devoting fewer resources to good 2 and more to good 1, we move from one point on the production possibilities frontier to another. The marginal rate of transformation is just the slope of the production possibilities set, which we denote by dX^2/dX^1.

Consider a small change in production (dX^1, dX^2) that remains feasible. Thus we have

$$\frac{\partial T(X^1, X^2)}{\partial X^1} dX^1 + \frac{\partial T(X^1, X^2)}{\partial X^2} dX^2 = 0.$$

Solving for the marginal rate of transformation:

$$\frac{dX^2}{dX^1} = -\frac{\partial T/\partial X^1}{\partial T/\partial X^2}.$$

We'll use this formula in a moment.

A Pareto efficient allocation is one that maximizes any one person's utility, given the level of the other peoples' utility. In the two-person case, we can write this maximization problem as

$$\max_{x_A^1, x_A^2, x_B^1, x_B^2} u_A(x_A^1, x_A^2)$$

$$u_B(x_B^1, x_B^2) = \overline{u}$$
$$T(X^1, X^2) = 0.$$

The Lagrangian for this problem is

$$L = u_A(x_A^1, x_A^2) - \lambda(u_B(x_B^1, x_B^2) - \bar{u})$$
$$- \mu(T(X_1, X_2) - 0)$$

and the first-order conditions are

$$\frac{\partial L}{\partial x_A^1} = \frac{\partial u_A}{\partial x_A^1} - \mu\frac{\partial T}{\partial X^1} = 0$$

$$\frac{\partial L}{\partial x_A^2} = \frac{\partial u_A}{\partial x_A^2} - \mu\frac{\partial T}{\partial X^2} = 0$$

$$\frac{\partial L}{\partial x_B^1} = -\lambda\frac{\partial u_B}{\partial x_B^1} - \mu\frac{\partial T}{\partial X^1} = 0$$

$$\frac{\partial L}{\partial x_B^2} = -\lambda\frac{\partial u_B}{\partial x_B^2} - \mu\frac{\partial T}{\partial X^2} = 0.$$

Rearranging and dividing the first equation by the second gives

$$\frac{\partial u_A/\partial x_A^1}{\partial u_A/\partial x_A^2} = \frac{\partial T/\partial X^1}{\partial T/\partial X^2}.$$

Performing the same operation on the third and fourth equations gives

$$\frac{\partial u_B/\partial x_B^1}{\partial u_B/\partial x_B^2} = \frac{\partial T/\partial X^1}{\partial T/\partial X^2}.$$

The left-hand sides of these equations are our old friends, the marginal rates of substitution. The right-hand side is the marginal rate of transformation. Thus the equations require that each person's marginal rate of substitution between the goods must equal the marginal rate of transformation: the rate at which each person is just willing to substitute one good for the other must be the same as the rate at which it is technologically feasible to transform one good into the other.

The intuition behind this result is straightforward. Suppose that the MRS for some individual was not equal to the MRT. Then the rate at which the individual would be willing to sacrifice one good to get more of the other would be different than the rate that was technologically feasible—but this means that there would be some way to increase that individual's utility while not affecting anyone else's consumption.

30

WELFARE

Up until now we have focused on considerations of Pareto efficiency in evaluating economic allocations. But there are other important considerations. It must be remembered that Pareto efficiency has nothing to say about the distribution of welfare across people; giving everything to one person will typically be Pareto efficient. But the rest of us might not consider this a reasonable allocation. In this chapter we will investigate some techniques that can be used to formalize ideas related to the distribution of welfare.

Pareto efficiency is in itself a desirable goal—if there is some way to make some group of people better off without hurting other people, why not do it? But there will usually be many Pareto efficient allocations; how can society choose among them?

The major focus of this chapter will be the idea of a **welfare function**, which provides a way to "add together" different consumer's utilities. More generally, a welfare function provides a way to rank different distributions of utility among consumers. Before we investigate the implications of this concept, it is worthwhile considering just how one might go about "adding together" the individual consumers' preferences to construct some kind of "social preferences."

30.1 Aggregation of Preferences

Let us return to our early discussion of consumer preferences. As usual, we will assume that these preferences are transitive. Originally, we thought of a consumer's preferences as being defined over his own bundle of goods, but now we want to expand on that concept and think of each consumer having preferences over the entire allocation of goods among the consumers. Of course, this includes the possibility that the consumer might not care about what other people have, just as we had originally assumed.

Let us use the symbol x to denote a particular allocation—a description of what every individual gets of every good. Then given two allocations, x and y, each individual i can say whether or not he or she prefers x to y.

Given the preferences of all the agents, we would like to have a way to "aggregate" them into one **social preference.** That is, if we know how all the individuals rank various allocations, we would like to be able to use this information to develop a social ranking of the various allocations. This is the problem of social decision making at its most general level. Let's consider a few examples.

One way to aggregate individual preferences is to use some kind of voting. We could agree that x is "socially preferred" to y if a majority of the individuals prefer x to y. However, there is a problem with this method—it may not generate a transitive social preference ordering. Consider, for example, the case illustrated in Table 30.1.

Table 30.1

Preferences that lead to intransitive voting.

Person A	Person B	Person C
x	y	z
y	z	x
z	x	y

Here we have listed the rankings for three alternatives, x, y, and z, by three people. Note that a majority of the people prefer x to y, a majority prefer y to z, and a majority prefer z to x. Thus aggregating individual preferences by majority vote won't work since, in general, the social preferences resulting from majority voting aren't well-behaved preferences, since they are not transitive. Since the preferences aren't transitive, there will be no "best" alternative from the set of alternatives (x, y, z). Which outcome society chooses will depend on the order in which the vote is taken.

To see this suppose that the three people depicted in Table 30.1 decide to vote first on **x** versus **y**, and then vote on the winner of this contest versus **z**. Since a majority prefer **x** to **y**, the second contest will be between **x** and **z**, which means that **z** will be the outcome.

But what if they decide to vote on **z** versus **x** and then pit the winner of this vote against **y**? Now **z** wins the first vote, but **y** beats **z** in the second vote. Which outcome is the overall winner depends crucially on the order in which the alternatives are presented to the voters.

Another kind of voting mechanism that we might consider is rank-order voting. Here each person ranks the goods according to his preferences and assigns a number that indicates its rank in his ordering: for example, a 1 for the best alternative, 2 for the second best, and so on. Then we sum up the scores of each alternative across the people to determine an aggregate score for each alternative, and say that one outcome is socially preferred to another if it has a lower score.

In Table 30.2 we have illustrated a possible preference ordering for three allocations **x**, **y**, and **z** by two people. Suppose first that only alternatives **x** and **y** were available. Then in this example **x** would be given a rank of 1 by person A and 2 by person B. The alternative **y** would be given just the reverse ranking. Thus the outcome of the voting would be a tie with each alternative having an aggregate rank of 3.

The choice between x and y depends on z.

Table 30.2

Person A	Person B
x	y
y	z
z	x

But now suppose that **z** is introduced to the ballot. Person A would give **x** a score of 1, **y** a score of 2, and **z** a rank of 3. Person B would give **y** a score of 1, **z** a score of 2, and **x** a score of 3. This means that **x** would now have an aggregate rank of 4, and **y** would have an aggregate rank of 3. In this case **y** would be preferred to **x** by rank-order voting.

The problem with both majority voting and rank-order voting is that their outcomes can be manipulated by astute agents. Majority voting can be manipulated by changing the order on which things are voted so as to yield the desired outcome. Rank-order voting can be manipulated by introducing new alternatives that change the final ranks of the relevant alternatives.

The question naturally arises as to whether there are social decision mechanisms—ways of aggregating preferences—that are immune to this kind of manipulation? Are there ways to "add up" preferences that don't have the undesirable properties described above?

Let's list some things that we would want our social decision mechanism to do:

1. Given any set of complete, reflexive, and transitive individual preferences, the social decision mechanism should result in social preferences that satisfy the same properties.

2. If everybody prefers alternative **x** to alternative **y**, then the social preferences should rank **x** ahead of **y**.

3. The preferences between **x** and **y** should depend only on how people rank **x** versus **y**, and not on how they rank other alternatives.

All three of these requirements seem eminently plausible. Yet it can be quite difficult to find a mechanism that satisfies all of them. In fact, Kenneth Arrow has proved the following remarkable result:[1]

Arrow's Impossibility Theorem. *If a social decision mechanism satisfies properties 1, 2, and 3, then it must be a dictatorship: all social rankings are the rankings of one individual.*

Arrow's Impossibility Theorem is quite surprising. It shows that three very plausible and desirable features of a social decision mechanism are inconsistent with democracy: there is no "perfect" way to make social decisions. There is no perfect way to "aggregate" individual preferences to make one social preference. If we want to find a way to aggregate individual preferences to form social preferences, we will have to give up one of the properties of a social decision mechanism described in Arrow's theorem.

30.2 Social Welfare Functions

If we were to drop any of the desired features of a social welfare function described above, it would probably be property 3—that the social preferences between two alternatives only depends on the ranking of those two alternatives. If we do that, certain kinds of rank-order voting become possibilities.

---

[1] See Kenneth Arrow, *Social Choice and Individual Values* (New York: Wiley, 1963). Arrow, a professor at Stanford University, was awarded the Nobel Prize in economics for his work in this area.

Given the preferences of each individual i over the allocations, we can construct utility functions, $u_i(\mathbf{x})$, that summarize the individuals' value judgments: person i prefers $\mathbf{x}$ to $\mathbf{y}$ if and only if $u_i(\mathbf{x}) > u_i(\mathbf{y})$. Of course, these are just like all utility functions—they can be scaled in any way that preserves the underlying preference ordering. There is no *unique* utility representation.

But let us pick some utility representation and stick with it. Then one way of getting social preferences from individuals' preferences is to add up the individual utilities and use the resulting number as a kind of social utility. That is, we will say that allocation $\mathbf{x}$ is socially preferred to allocation $\mathbf{y}$ if

$$\sum_{i=1}^{n} u_i(\mathbf{x}) > \sum_{i=1}^{n} u_i(\mathbf{y})$$

where n is the number of individuals in the society.

This works—but of course it is totally arbitrary, since our choice of utility representation is totally arbitrary. The choice of using the sum is also arbitrary. Why not use a weighted sum of utilities? Why not use the product of utilities, or the sum of the squares of utilities?

One reasonable restriction that we might place on the "aggregating function" is that it be increasing in each individual's utility. That way we are assured that if everybody prefers $\mathbf{x}$ to $\mathbf{y}$, then the social preferences will prefer $\mathbf{x}$ to $\mathbf{y}$.

There is a name for this kind of aggregating function; it is called a **social welfare function**. A social welfare function is just some function of the individual utility functions: $W(u_1(\mathbf{x}), \ldots, u_n(\mathbf{x}))$. It gives a way to rank different allocations that depends only on the individual preferences, and it is an increasing function of each individual's utility.

Let's look at some examples. One special case mentioned above is the *sum* of the individual utility functions

$$W(u_1, \ldots, u_n) = \sum_{i=1}^{n} u_i.$$

This is sometimes referred to as a **classical utilitarian** or **Benthamite** welfare function. [2] A slight generalization of this form is the **weighted-sum-of-utilities** welfare function:

$$W(u_1, \ldots, u_n) = \sum_{i=1}^{n} a_i u_i.$$

---

[2] Jeremy Bentham (1748–1832) was the founder of the utilitarian school of moral philosophy, a school that considers the highest good to be the greatest happiness for the greatest number.

Here the weights, $a_1, \ldots, a_n$, are supposed to be numbers indicating how important each agent's utility is to the overall social welfare. It is natural to take each a_i as being positive.

Another interesting welfare function is the **minimax** or **Rawlsian** social welfare function:

$$W(u_1, \ldots, u_n) = \min\{u_1, \ldots, u_n\}.$$

This welfare function says that the social welfare of an allocation depends only on the welfare of the worst off agent—the person with the minimal utility.[3]

Each of these is a possible way to compare individual utility functions. Each of them represents different ethical judgments about the comparison between different agents' welfares. About the only restriction that we will place on the structure of the welfare function at this point is that it be increasing in each consumer's utility.

30.3 Welfare Maximization

Once we have a welfare function we can examine the problem of welfare maximization. Let us use the notation x_i^j to indicate how much individual i has of good j, and suppose that there are n consumers and k goods. Then the allocation $\mathbf{x}$ consists of the list of how much each of the agents has of each of the goods.

If we have a total amount $X^1, \ldots, X^k$ of goods $1, \ldots, k$ to distribute among the consumers, we can pose the welfare maximization problem:

$$\max\ W(u_1(\mathbf{x}), \ldots, u_n(\mathbf{x}))$$

$$\text{such that } \sum_{i=1}^{n} x_i^1 = X^1$$

$$\vdots$$

$$\sum_{i=1}^{n} x_i^k = X^k.$$

Thus we are trying to find the feasible allocation that maximizes social welfare. What properties does such an allocation have?

The first thing that we should note is that a maximal welfare allocation must be a Pareto efficient allocation. The proof is easy: suppose that

---

[3] John Rawls is a contemporary moral philosopher at Harvard who has argued for this principle of justice.

it were not. Then there would be some other feasible allocation that gave everyone at least as large a utility, and someone strictly greater utility. But the welfare function is an increasing function of each agent's utility. Thus this new allocation would have to have higher welfare, which contradicts the assumption that we originally had a welfare maximum.

We can illustrate this situation in Figure 30.1, where the set U indicates the set of possible utilities in the case of two individuals. This set is known as the **utility possibilities set**. The boundary of this set—the **utility possibilities frontier**—is the set of utility levels associated with Pareto efficient allocations. If an allocation is on the boundary of the utility possibilities set, then there are no other feasible allocations that yield higher utilities for both agents.

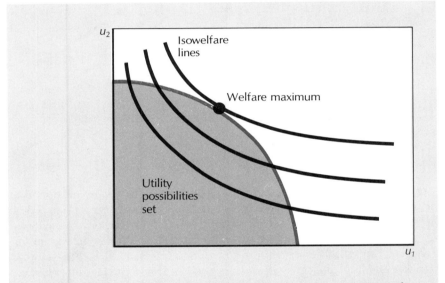

Welfare maximization. An allocation that maximizes a welfare function must be Pareto efficient.

Figure 30.1

The "indifference curves" in this diagram are called **isowelfare** lines since they depict those distributions of utility that have constant welfare. As usual, the optimal point is characterized by a tangency condition. But for our purposes, the notable thing about this maximal welfare point is that it is Pareto efficient—it must occur on the boundary of the utility possibilities set.

The next observation we can make from this diagram is that *any* Pareto efficient allocation must be a welfare maximum for some welfare function. An example is given in Figure 30.2.

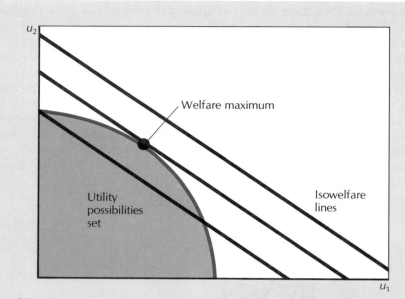

Figure
30.2
**Maximization of the weighted-sum-of-utilities welfare
function.** If the utility possibility set is convex, then every Pareto efficient point is a maximum for a weighted-sum-
of-utilities welfare function.

In Figure 30.2 we have picked a Pareto efficient allocation and found a
set of isowelfare curves for which it is maximal. Actually, we can say a
bit more than this. If the set of possible utility distributions is a convex
set, as illustrated, then every point on its frontier is a utility maximum for
a weighted-sum-of-utilities welfare function, as illustrated in Figure 30.2.
The welfare function thus provides a way to single out Pareto efficient
allocations: every welfare maximum is a Pareto efficient allocation, and
every Pareto efficient allocation is a welfare maximum.

30.4 Individualistic Social Welfare Functions

Up until now we have been thinking of individual preferences as being
defined over entire allocations rather than over each individual's bundle
of goods. But, as we remarked earlier, individuals might only care about
their own bundles. In this case, we can use x_i to denote individual $i's$
consumption bundle, and let $u_i(x_i)$ be individual $i's$ utility level using
some fixed representation of utility. Then a social welfare function will
have the form

$$W = W(u_1(x_1), \ldots, u_n(x_n)).$$

The welfare function is directly a function of the distribution of utilities, but it is indirectly a function of the individual agents consumption bundles. This special form of welfare function is known as an **individualistic welfare function** or a **Bergson-Samuelson welfare function**.[4]

If each agent's utility depends only on his or her own consumption, then there are no consumption externalities. Thus the standard results of Chapter 28 apply and we have an intimate relationship between Pareto efficient allocations and market equilibria: all competitive equilibria are Pareto efficient, and, under appropriate convexity assumptions, all Pareto efficient allocations are competitive equilibria.

Now we can carry this categorization one step further. Given the relationship between Pareto efficiency and welfare maxima described above, we can conclude that all welfare maxima are competitive equilibria, and all competitive equilibria are welfare maxima for some welfare function.

30.5 Fair Allocations

The welfare function approach is a very general way to describe social welfare. But because it is so general it can be used to summarize the properties of many kinds of moral judgments. On the other hand, it isn't much use in deciding what kinds of ethical judgments might be reasonable ones.

Another approach is to start with some specific moral judgments and then examine their implications for economic distribution. This is the approach taken in the study of **fair allocations.** We start with a definition of what might be considered a fair way to divide a bundle of goods, and then use our understanding of economic analysis to investigate its implications.

Suppose that you were given some goods to divide fairly among n equally deserving people. How would you do it? It is probably safe to say that in this problem most people would divide the goods equally among the n agents. Given that they are by hypothesis equally deserving, what else could you do?

What is appealing about this idea of equal division? One appealing feature is that it is *symmetric*. Each agent has the same bundle of goods; no agent prefers any other agent's bundle of goods to his or her own, since they all have exactly the same thing.

Unfortunately, an equal division will not necessarily be Pareto efficient. If agents have different tastes they will generally desire to trade away from equal division. Let us suppose that this trade takes place, and that it moves us to a Pareto efficient allocation.

---

[4] Abram Bergson and Paul Samuelson are contemporary economists who investigated properties of this kind of welfare function in the early 1940s. Samuelson was awarded a Nobel Prize in economics for his many contributions.

The question arises: is this Pareto efficient allocation still fair in any sense? Does trade from equal division inherit any of the symmetry of the starting point?

The answer is: not necessarily. Consider the following example. We have three people, A, B, and C. A and B have the same tastes, and C has different tastes. We start from an equal division and suppose that A and C get together and trade. Then they will typically both be made better off. Now B, who didn't have the opportunity to trade with C, will **envy** A—that is, he would prefer A's bundle to his own. Even though A and B started with the same allocation, A was luckier in her trading, and this destroyed the symmetry of the original allocation.

This means that arbitrary trading from an equal division will not necessarily preserve the symmetry of the starting point of equal division. We might well ask if there is any allocation that preserves this symmetry? Is there any way to get an allocation that is both Pareto efficient and equitable at the same time?

30.6 Envy and Equity

Let us now try to formalize some of these ideas. What do we mean by "symmetric" or "equitable" anyway? One possible set of definitions is as follows.

We say an allocation is **equitable** if no agent prefers any other agent's bundle of goods to his or her own. If some agent i does prefer some other agent $j's$ bundle of goods, we say that i **envies** j. Finally, if an allocation is both equitable and Pareto efficient, we will say that it is a **fair** allocation.

These are ways of formalizing the idea of symmetry alluded to above. An equal division allocation has the property that no agent envies any other agent—but there are many other allocations that have this same property.

Consider Figure 30.3. To determine whether any allocation is equitable or not, just look at the allocation that results if the two agents swap bundles. If this swapped allocation lies "below" each agent's indifference curve through the original allocation, then the original allocation is an equitable allocation. (Here "below" means below from the point of view of each agent; from our point of view the swapped allocation must lie between the two indifference curves.)

Note also that the allocation in Figure 30.3 is also Pareto efficient. Thus it is not only equitable, in the sense that we defined the term, but it is also efficient. By our definition, it is a fair allocation. Is this kind of allocation a fluke, or will fair allocations typically exist?

It turns out that fair allocations *will* generally exist, and there is an easy way to see that this is so. We start with the setup described in the last section, where we have an equal division allocation and consider trading to a Pareto efficient allocation. Instead of using just any old way to trade, let

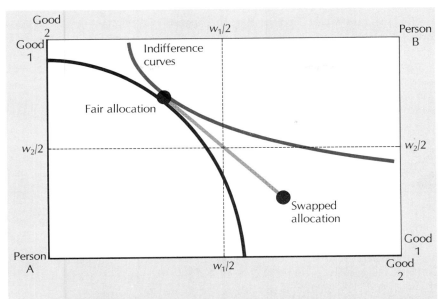

Fair allocations. A fair allocation in an Edgeworth box. Each person prefers the fair allocation to the swapped allocation.

Figure
30.3

us use the special mechanism of the competitive market. This will move us to a new allocation where each agent is choosing the best bundle of goods he or she can afford at the equilibrium prices (p_1, p_2), and we know from Chapter 28 that such an allocation must be Pareto efficient.

But is it still equitable? Well, suppose not. Suppose that one of the consumers, say consumer A, envies consumer B. This means that A prefers what B has to her own bundle. In symbols:

$$(x_A^1, x_A^2) \prec_A (x_B^1, x_B^2).$$

But, if A prefers B's bundle to her own, and her own bundle is the best bundle she can afford at the prices (p_1, p_2), this means that B's bundle must cost more than A can afford. In symbols:

$$p_1 \omega_A^1 + p_2 \omega_A^2 < p_1 x_B^1 + p_2 x_B^2.$$

But this is a contradiction! For by hypothesis, A and B started with exactly the same bundle, since they started from an equal division. If A can't afford B's bundle, then B can't afford it either.

Thus we can conclude that it is impossible for A to envy B in these circumstances. A competitive equilibrium from equal division must be a fair allocation. Thus the market mechanism will preserve certain kinds of equity: if the original allocation is equally divided, the final allocation must be fair.

Summary

1. Arrow's Impossibility Theorem shows that there is no ideal way to aggregate individual preferences into social preferences.

2. Nevertheless, economists often use welfare functions of one sort or another to represent distributional judgments about allocations.

3. As long as the welfare function is increasing in each individual's utility, a welfare maximum will be Pareto efficient. Furthermore, every Pareto efficient allocation can be thought of as maximizing some welfare function.

4. The idea of fair allocations provides an alternative way to make distributional judgments. This idea emphasizes the idea of symmetric treatment.

5. Even when the initial allocation is symmetric, arbitrary methods of trade will not necessarily produce a fair allocation. However, it turns out that the market mechanism will provide a fair allocation.

Review Questions

1. Suppose that we say that an allocation **x** is socially preferred to an allocation **y** only if *everyone* prefers **x** to **y**. (This is sometimes called the Pareto ordering, since it is closely related to the idea of Pareto efficiency.) What shortcoming does this have as a rule for making social decisions?

2. The opposite of the Rawlsian welfare function might be called the "Nietzschian" welfare function—a welfare function that says the value of an allocation depends only on the welfare of the *best off* agent. What mathematical form would the Nietzschian welfare function take?

3. Suppose that the utility possibilities set is a convex set, and that consumers care only about their own consumption. What kind of allocations represent welfare maxima of the Nietzschian welfare function?

4. Suppose that an allocation is Pareto efficient, and that each individual only cares about his own consumption. Prove that there must be some individual that envies no one, in the sense described in the text. (This puzzle requires some thought, but it is worth it.)

5. The ability to set the voting agenda can often be a powerful asset. Assuming that social preferences are decided by pair-wise majority voting and that the preferences given in Table 30.1 hold, demonstrate this fact by producing a voting agenda that results in allocation **y** winning. Find an

agenda that has **z** as the winner. What property of the social preferences is responsible for this agenda setting power?

APPENDIX

Here we consider the problem of welfare maximization, using an individualistic welfare function. Using the transformation function described in Chapter 29 to describe the production possibilities frontier, we write the welfare maximization problem as

$$\max_{x_A^1, x_A^2, x_B^1, x_B^2} W(u_A(x_A^1, x_A^2), u_B(x_B^1, x_B^2))$$

$$T(X^1, X^2) = 0$$

where we use X^1 and X^2 to denote the total amount of good 1 and good 2 produced and consumed.

The Lagrangian for this problem is

$$L = W(u_A(x_A^1, x_A^2), u_B(x_B^1, x_B^2)) - \lambda(T(X^1, X^2) - 0).$$

Differentiating with respect to each of the choice variables gives us the first-order conditions

$$\frac{\partial L}{\partial x_A^1} = \frac{\partial W}{\partial u_A} \frac{\partial u_A(x_A^1, x_A^2)}{\partial x_A^1} - \lambda \frac{\partial T(X^1, X^2)}{\partial X^1} = 0$$

$$\frac{\partial L}{\partial x_A^2} = \frac{\partial W}{\partial u_A} \frac{\partial u_A(x_A^1, x_A^2)}{\partial x_A^2} - \lambda \frac{\partial T(X^1, X^2)}{\partial X^2} = 0$$

$$\frac{\partial L}{\partial x_B^1} = \frac{\partial W}{\partial u_B} \frac{\partial u_B(x_B^1, x_B^2)}{\partial x_B^1} - \lambda \frac{\partial T(X^1, X^2)}{\partial X^1} = 0$$

$$\frac{\partial L}{\partial x_B^2} = \frac{\partial W}{\partial u_B} \frac{\partial u_B(x_B^1, x_B^2)}{\partial x_B^2} - \lambda \frac{\partial T(X^1, X^2)}{\partial X^2} = 0.$$

Rearranging and dividing the first equation by the second, and the third by the fourth, we have

$$\frac{\partial u_A/\partial x_A^1}{\partial u_A/\partial x_A^2} = \frac{\partial T/\partial X^1}{\partial T/\partial X^2}$$

$$\frac{\partial u_B/\partial x_B^1}{\partial u_B/\partial x_B^2} = \frac{\partial T/\partial X^1}{\partial T/\partial X^2}.$$

Note that these are exactly the same equations that we encountered in the Appendix to Chapter 29. Thus the welfare maximization problem gives us the same first-order conditions as the Pareto efficiency problem.

This is obviously no accident. According to the discussion in the text, the allocation resulting from the maximization of a Bergson-Samuelson welfare function is Pareto efficient, and every Pareto efficient allocation maximizes some welfare function. Thus welfare maxima and Pareto efficient allocations have to satisfy the same first-order conditions.

31

EXTERNALITIES

We say that an economic situation involves a **consumption externality** if one consumer cares directly about another agent's production or consumption. For example, I have definite preferences about my neighbor playing loud music at 3 in the morning, or the person next to me in a restaurant smoking a cheap cigar, or the amount of pollution produced by local automobiles. These are all examples of *negative* consumption externalities. On the other hand, I may get pleasure from observing my neighbor's flower garden—this is an example of a *positive* consumption externality.

Similarly, a **production externality** arises when the production possibilities of one firm are influenced by the choices of another firm or consumer. A classic example is that of an apple orchard located next to a bee keeper, where there are mutual positive production externalities—each firm's production positively affects the production possibilities of the other firm. Similarly, a fishery cares about the amount of pollutants dumped into its fishing area, since this will negatively influence its catch.

The crucial feature of externalities is that there are goods people care about that are not sold on markets. There is no market for loud music at 3 in the morning, or drifting smoke from cheap cigars, or a neighbor who keeps a beautiful flower garden. It is this lack of markets for externalities that causes problems.

Up until now we have implicitly assumed that each agent could make consumption or production decisions without worrying about what other agents were doing. All interactions between consumers and producers took place via the market, so that all the economic agents needed to know were the market prices and their own consumption or production possibilities. In this chapter we will relax this assumption and examine the economic consequences of externalities.

In earlier chapters we saw that the market mechanism was capable of achieving Pareto efficient allocations when externalities were *not* present. If externalities are present, the market will not necessarily result in a Pareto efficient provision of resources. However, there are other social institutions such as the legal system, or government intervention, that can "mimic" the market mechanism to some degree and thereby achieve Pareto efficiency. In this chapter we'll see how these institutions work.

31.1 Smokers and Nonsmokers

It is convenient to start with an example to illustrate some of the main considerations. We'll imagine two roommates, A and B, who have preferences over "money" and "smoke." We suppose that both consumers like money, but that A likes to smoke and B likes clean air.

We can depict the consumption possibilities for the two consumers in an Edgeworth box. The length of the horizontal axis will represent the total amount of money the two agents have, and the height of the vertical axis will represent the total amount of smoke that can be generated. The preferences of agent A are increasing in both money and smoke, while agent B's preferences are increasing in money and clean air—the absence of smoke. We'll measure smoke on a scale from 0 to 1, where 0 is no smoke at all, and 1 is the proverbial smoke filled room.

This setup gives us a diagram like that depicted in Figure 31.1. Note that the picture looks very much like the standard Edgeworth box, but the interpretation is quite different. The amount of smoke is a good for A and a bad for B, so that B is moved to a more preferred position as A consumes less smoke. Be sure to note the difference in the way things are measured on the horizontal and vertical axes. We measure A's money horizontally from the lower left-hand corner of the box, and B's money horizontally from the upper right-hand corner. But the total amount of smoke is measured vertically from the lower left-hand corner. The difference occurs because money can be divided between the two consumers, so there will always be two amounts of money to measure, but there is only one amount of smoke that they must both consume.

We've now illustrated the consumption possibilities of the two roommates and their preferences. What about their endowments? Let's assume that they both have the same amount of money, say $100 apiece, so that their endowments will lie somewhere on the vertical line in Figure 31.1. In order to determine exactly where on this line the endowments lie, we must determine the initial "endowment" of smoke/clean air.

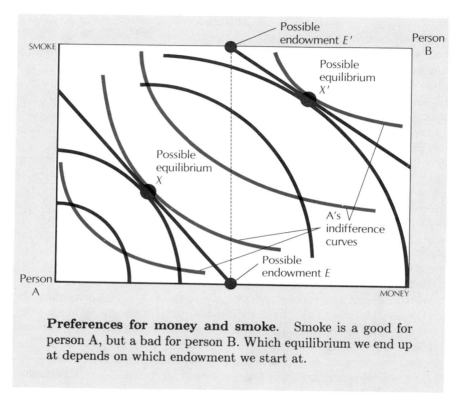

Figure 31.1

Preferences for money and smoke. Smoke is a good for person A, but a bad for person B. Which equilibrium we end up at depends on which endowment we start at.

The answer to this question depends on the legal rights of smokers and nonsmokers. It may be that A has a right to smoke as much as he wants, and B just has to put up with it. Or, it could be that B has a right to clean air. Or the legal right to smoke and clean air could be somewhere between these two extremes.

The initial endowment of smoke depends on the legal system. This is not so different from the initial endowment of ordinary sorts of goods. To say that A has an initial endowment of $100 means that A can decide to consume the $100 himself, or he can give it away or trade it to any other individual. There is a legal definition of property involved in saying that a person "owns" or "has a right to" $100. Similarly if a person has a property right to clean air, it means that he can consume clean air if he wants to, or he can give it away or sell that right to someone else. In this way, having a property right to clean air is no different from having a property right to $100.

Let's start by considering a legal situation where person B has a legal right to clean air. Then the initial endowment in Figure 31.1 is labeled E; it is where A has $(100, 0)$ and B has $(100, 0)$. This means that both A and B have $100, and that the initial endowment—what there would be in the absence of trade—is clean air.

Just as before, in the case with no externalities, there is no reason why the initial endowment is Pareto efficient. One of the aspects of having a property right to clean air is having the right to trade some of it away for other desirable goods—in this case, for money. It can easily happen that B would prefer to trade some of his right to clean air for some more money. The point labeled X in Figure 31.1 is an example of such a case.

As before, a Pareto efficient allocation is one where neither consumer can be made better off without the other being made worse off. Such an allocation will be characterized by the usual tangency condition that the marginal rates of substitution between smoke and money should be the same between the two agents, as illustrated in Figure 31.1. It is easy to imagine A and B trading to such a Pareto efficient point. In effect, B has the right to clean air, but he can allow himself to be "bribed" to consume some of A's smoke.

Of course, other assignments of property rights are possible. We could imagine a legal system where A had a right to smoke as much as he wanted, and B would have to bribe A to reduce his consumption of smoke. This would correspond to the endowment labeled E' in Figure 31.1. Just as before, this would typically not be Pareto efficient, so we could imagine the agents trading to a mutually preferred point such as the one labeled X'.

Both X and X' are Pareto efficient allocations; they just come from different initial endowments. Certainly the smoker, A, is better off at X' than at X, and the nonsmoker, B, is better off at X than at X'. The two points have different distributional consequences, but on grounds of efficiency they are equally satisfactory.

In fact, there is no reason to limit ourselves to just these two efficient points. As usual there will be a whole contract curve of Pareto efficient allocations of smoke and money. If agents are free to trade both of these goods, we know that they will end up somewhere on this contract curve. The exact position will depend on their property rights involving smoke and money and the precise mechanism that they use to trade.

One mechanism that they could use to trade is the price mechanism. Just as before we could imagine an auctioneer calling out prices and asking how much each agent would be willing to buy at those prices. If the initial endowment point gave A the property rights to smoke, he could consider selling some of his smoking rights to B in exchange for B's money. Similarly, if the property rights for clean air were given to B, he could sell some of his clean air to A.

When the auctioneer manages to find a set of prices where supply equals demand everything is fine: we have a nice Pareto efficient outcome. If there is a market for smoke, a competitive equilibrium will be Pareto efficient. Furthermore, the competitive prices will measure the marginal rate of substitution between the two goods, just as in the standard case.

This is just like the usual Edgeworth box analysis, but described in a slightly different framework. As long as we have well-defined property rights in the good involving the externality—no matter who holds the property rights—the agents can trade from their initial endowment to a Pareto efficient allocation. If we want to set up a market in the externality to encourage trade, that will work as well.

The only problem arises if the property rights are *not* well defined. If A believes that he has the right to smoke and B believes that he has the right to clean air, we have difficulties. *The practical problems with externalities generally arise because of poorly defined property rights.*

My neighbor may believe that he has the right to play his trumpet at 3 in the morning and I may believe that I have the right to silence. A firm may believe that it has the right to dump pollutants into the atmosphere that I breathe, while I may believe that it doesn't. Cases where property rights are poorly defined can lead to an inefficient production of externalities—which means that there would be ways to make both parties involved better off by changing the production of externalities. If property rights are well defined, and mechanisms are in place to allow for negotiation between people, then people can trade their rights to produce externalities in the same way that they trade rights to produce and consume ordinary goods.

31.2 Quasilinear Preferences and the Coase Theorem

We argued above that as long as property rights were well defined, trade between agents would result in an efficient allocation of the externality. In general, the amount of the externality that will be generated in the efficient solution will depend on the assignment of property rights. In the case of the two roommates, the amount of smoke generated will depend on whether the smoker has the property rights or the nonsmoker has them.

But there is a special case where the outcome of the externality is independent of the assignment of property rights. If the agents' preferences are **quasilinear**, then every efficient solution must have the same amount of the externality.

This case is illustrated in Figure 31.2 for the Edgeworth box case of the smoker versus the nonsmoker. Since the indifference curves are all horizontal translates of each other, the locus of mutual tangencies—the set of Pareto efficient allocations—will be a horizontal line. This means that

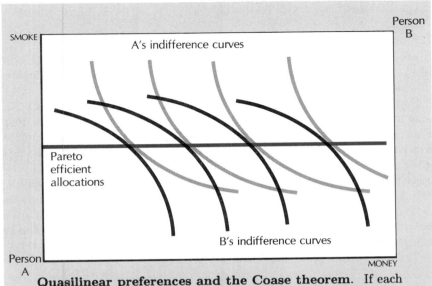

SMOKE

Person B

A's indifference curves

Pareto efficient allocations

B's indifference curves

Person A

MONEY

Quasilinear preferences and the Coase theorem. If each consumer's preferences are quasilinear, so that they are all horizontal translates of each other, the set of Pareto efficient allocations will be a horizontal line. Thus there will be a unique amount of the externality, in this case smoke, at each Pareto efficient allocation.

Figure 31.2

the amount of smoke is the same in every Pareto efficient allocation; only the dollar amounts held by the agents differ across the efficient allocations.

The result that under certain circumstances the efficient outcome is independent of the distribution of property rights is sometimes known as the **Coase Theorem.**[1] However, it should be emphasized just how special these circumstances are. Essentially, the quasilinear preference assumption requires that the demands for the good causing the externality are independent of the distribution of income—that there be no "income effects."

In this case, the Pareto efficient allocations will involve a unique amount of the externality being generated. The different Pareto efficient allocations will involve different amounts of money being held by the consumers; but the amount of the externality—the amount of smoke—will be independent of the distribution of wealth.

[1] Ronald Coase is an emeritus professor at the Chicago Law School. His famous paper, "The Problem of Social Costs," *The Journal of Law & Economics*, 3 (October 1960), has been given a variety of interpretations. Some authors suggest that Coase only asserted that costless bargaining over externalities achieves a Pareto efficient outcome, not that the outcome will be independent of the assignment of property rights.

31.3 Production Externalities

Let us now consider a situation involving production externalities. Firm S produces some amount of steel, s, and also produces a certain amount of pollution, x, which it dumps into a river. Firm F, a fishery, is located downstream and is adversely affected by S's pollution.

Suppose that firm S's cost function is given by $c_s(s, x)$, where s is the amount of steel produced and x is the amount of pollution produced. Firm F's cost function is given by $c_f(f, x)$, where f indicates the production of fish and x is the amount of pollution. Note that F's costs of producing a given amount of fish depend on the amount of pollution produced by the steel firm. We will suppose that pollution increases the cost of providing fish $\Delta c_f / \Delta x > 0$, and that pollution *decreases* the cost of steel production, $\Delta c_s / \Delta x \leq 0$. This last assumption says that increasing the amount of pollution will decrease the cost of producing steel—that reducing pollution will increase the cost of steel production, at least over some range.

The steel firm's profit maximization problem is

$$\max_{s,x} \ p_s s - c_s(s, x)$$

and the fishery's profit maximization problem is

$$\max_{f} \ p_f f - c_f(f, x).$$

Note that the steel mill gets to choose the amount of pollution that it generates, but the fishery must take the level of pollution as outside of its control.

The conditions characterizing profit maximization will be

$$p_s = \frac{\Delta c_s(s^*, x^*)}{\Delta s}$$

$$0 = \frac{\Delta c_s(s^*, x^*)}{\Delta x}$$

for the steel firm, and

$$p_f = \frac{\Delta c_f(f^*, x^*)}{\Delta f}$$

for the fishery. These conditions say that at the profit maximizing point, the price of increasing the output of each good—steel and pollution—should equal its marginal cost. In the case of the steel firm, one of its products is pollution which, by assumption, has a zero price. So the condition determining the profit maximizing supply of pollution says to produce pollution until the cost of an extra unit is zero.

It is not hard to see the externality here: the fishery cares about the production of pollution but has no control over it. The steel firm looks only at the cost of producing steel when it makes its profit maximizing calculation; it doesn't consider the cost it imposes on the fishery. The increase in the cost of fishing associated with an increase in pollution is part of the **social cost** of steel production, and it is being ignored by the steel firm. In general, we expect that the steel firm will produce too much pollution from a social point of view since it ignores the impact of that pollution on the fishery.

What does a Pareto efficient production plan for steel and fish look like? There is an easy way to see what it should be. Suppose that the fishery and the steel firm merged and formed one firm that produced both fish and steel (and possibly pollution). Then there is no externality! For a production externality only arises when one firm's actions affect another firm's production possibilities. If there is only one firm, then it will take the interactions between its different "divisions" into account when it chooses the profit maximizing production plan. We say that the externality has been **internalized** by this reassignment of property rights. Before the merger, each firm had the right to produce whatever amount of steel or fish or pollution that it wanted, regardless of what the other firm did. After the merger, the combined firm has the right to control the production of both the steel mill and the fishery.

The merged firm's profit maximization problem is

$$\max_{s,f,x} \ p_s s + p_f f - c_s(s,x) - c_f(f,x)$$

which yields optimality conditions of

$$p_s = \frac{\Delta c_s(\hat{s}, \hat{x})}{\Delta s}$$

$$p_f = \frac{\Delta c_f(\hat{f}, \hat{x})}{\Delta f}$$

$$0 = \frac{\Delta c_s(\hat{s}, \hat{x})}{\Delta x} + \frac{\Delta c_f(\hat{f}, \hat{x})}{\Delta x}.$$

The crucial term is the last one. This shows that the merged firm will take into account the effect of pollution on the marginal costs of both the steel firm and the fishery. When the steel division decides how much pollution to produce it considers the effect of this action on the profits of the fish division; that is, it takes the social cost of its production plan into account.

What does this imply about the amount of pollution produced? When the steel firm acted independently, the amount of pollution was determined by the condition

$$\frac{\Delta c_s(s^*, x^*)}{\Delta x} = 0. \tag{31.1}$$

That is, the steel mill produced pollution until the marginal cost was zero:

$$MC_S(s^*, x^*) = 0.$$

In the merged firm, the amount of pollution is determined by the condition

$$\frac{\Delta c_s(\hat{s}, \hat{x})}{\Delta x} + \frac{\Delta c_f(\hat{f}, \hat{x})}{\Delta x} = 0. \tag{31.2}$$

That is, the merged firm produces pollution until the *sum* of the marginal cost to the steel mill and the marginal cost to the fishery is zero. This condition can also be written as

$$-\frac{\Delta c_s(\hat{s}, \hat{x})}{\Delta x} = \frac{\Delta c_f(\hat{f}, \hat{x})}{\Delta x} > 0 \tag{31.3}$$

or

$$-MC_S(\hat{s}, \hat{x}) = MC_F(\hat{f}, \hat{x}).$$

In this latter expression $MC_F(\hat{f}, \hat{x})$ is positive, since more pollution increases the cost of producing a given amount of fish. Hence the merged firm will want to produce where $-MC_S(\hat{s}, \hat{x})$ is positive; that is, it will want to produce *less* pollution than the independent steel firm. When the true social cost of the externality involved in the steel production is taken into account, the optimal production of pollution will be reduced.

When the steel firm considers minimizing its **private costs** of producing steel, it produces where the marginal cost of extra pollution equals zero; but the Pareto efficient level of pollution requires minimizing the **social costs** of the pollution. At the Pareto efficient level of pollution, the *sum* of the two firm's marginal costs of pollution must be equal to zero.

This argument is illustrated in Figure 31.3. In this diagram $-MC_S$ measures the marginal cost to the steel firm from producing more pollution. The curve labeled MC_F measures the marginal cost to the fishery of more pollution. In the absence of any intervention, the steel firm produces pollution up to the point where its marginal costs from generating more pollution equals zero. In this case the steel firm is concerned only with its private costs of production. The amount of pollution generated by the steel firm is *privately optimal*, but not *socially optimal*.

But at the Pareto efficient level of pollution, the steel firm pollutes up to the point where the effect of a marginal increase in pollution is equal to the marginal social cost, which counts the impact of pollution on the costs of both firms. At the efficient level of pollution production, the amount that the steel firm is willing to pay for an extra unit of pollution should equal the social costs generated by that extra pollution—which include the costs it imposes on the fishery.

This is perfectly consistent with the efficiency arguments given in earlier chapters. There we assumed that there were no externalities, so that private costs and social costs coincided. In this case the free market will determine a Pareto efficient amount of output of each good. But if the private costs and the social costs diverge, the market alone may not be sufficient to achieve Pareto efficiency.

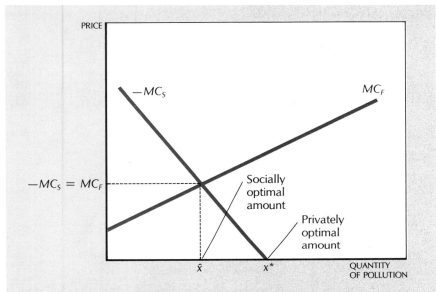

Social cost and private cost. The steel firm produces pollution up to the point where the marginal cost of extra pollution
equals zero. But the Pareto efficient production of pollution
is at the point where price equals marginal social cost, which
includes the cost of pollution borne by the fishery.

Figure
31.3

EXAMPLE: A Numerical Example

Let us plug some numbers into the steel/fishery example. Suppose that
the cost functions are given by

$$c_s(s, x) = s^2 + (x - 3)^2$$
$$c_f(f, x) = f^2 + 2x.$$

Note that increasing pollution will decrease the cost of producing steel over
some range, and will increase the cost of producing fish.

The steel firm will choose s and x so as to maximize profits

$$\max_{s,x} \ p_s s - s^2 - (x - 3)^2$$

which leads to the conditions

$$p_s - 2s = 0$$
$$-2(x - 3) = 0.$$

Solving, we have

$$s^* = \frac{p_s}{2}$$
$$x^* = 3.$$

The fishery will also attempt to maximize its profits:

$$\max \; p_f f - f^2 - 2x$$

which means

$$p_f - 2f = 0$$

or

$$f^* = \frac{p_f}{2}.$$

This gives us the supply of pollution, $x^* = 3$, and the supply functions of steel and fish when each firm acts independently.

In order to calculate the Pareto efficient levels of output, we maximize the sum of the two firms' profits:

$$\max_{s,x,f} \; p_s s + p_f f - s^2 - (x-3)^2 - f^2 - 2x.$$

This maximization problem yields the conditions

$$p_s - 2s = 0$$
$$p_f - 2f = 0$$
$$-2(x-3) - 2 = 0.$$

Solving, we have

$$\hat{s} = \frac{p_s}{2}$$
$$\hat{f} = \frac{p_f}{2}$$
$$\hat{x} = 2.$$

Note that the supply of pollution is less when the social cost of pollution is taken into account than when it is not.

In this example, the supply functions for each good remain the same, but the socially optimal amount of pollution is less than would be provided by the private market. In general the supply functions at the efficient solution would not be the same as the supply functions with independent operation. It occurs in this problem since the production of pollution does not affect the *marginal* costs of fish production.

EXAMPLE: Positive Externalities

Here we consider an example of a positive externality. Suppose that an apple orchard is located next to a bee keeper. If the orchard produces a apples, and the bee keeper produces h units of honey, the cost function for the apple orchard will be $c_a(a) = a^2$ and the cost function for the bee keeper will be $c_h(h) = h^2 - a$. Note that the more apples that are produced, the cheaper it will be to produce honey; this is an externality from the apple producer to the honey producer. Let p_a and p_h denote the prices of apples and honey, respectively.

If each producer operates independently, the inverse supply functions will be given by price equals marginal cost in each market:

$$p_a = 2a$$
$$p_h = 2h.$$

Thus the supply functions are

$$a = p_a/2$$
$$h = p_h/2.$$

But these supply decisions ignore the production externality between the two firms. The apple producer is concerned only with his own costs, not his influence on the costs of the honey producer. To solve for the socially efficient supply functions, we consider the *joint* profit maximization problem:

$$\max_{h,a} \; p_a a + p_h h - a^2 - (h^2 - a).$$

Now the price equals marginal cost equations become

$$p_a = 2a - 1$$
$$p_h = 2h.$$

So the supply curves are given by

$$a = p_a/2 + 1/2$$
$$h = p_h/2.$$

Note that the socially efficient supply decision involves the apple orchard producing more apples than it would if it only considered its own costs.

31.4 Interpretation of the Conditions

There are several useful interpretations of the conditions for Pareto efficiency derived above. Each of these interpretations suggests a scheme to correct the efficiency loss created by the production externality.

The first interpretation is that the steel firm faces the wrong price for pollution. As far as the steel firm is concerned, its production of pollution costs it nothing. But that neglects the costs that the pollution imposes on the fishery. According to this view, the situation can be rectified by making sure that the polluter faces the correct social cost of its actions.

One way to do this is to place a tax on the pollution generated by the steel firm. Suppose that we put a tax of t dollars per unit of pollution generated by the steel firm. Then the profit maximization problem of the steel firm becomes

$$\max_{s,x} p_s s - c_s(s, x) - tx.$$

The profit maximization conditions for this problem will be

$$p_s - \frac{\Delta c_s(s, x)}{\Delta s} = 0$$

$$-\frac{\Delta c_s(x, s)}{\Delta x} - t = 0.$$

Comparing these conditions to equation (31.3), we see that setting

$$t = \frac{\Delta c_f(\hat{s}, \hat{x})}{\Delta x}$$

will make these conditions the same as the conditions characterizing the Pareto efficient level of pollution.

This kind of a tax is known as a **Pigouvian tax**.[2] The problem with Pigouvian taxes is that we need to know the optimal level of pollution in order to impose the tax. But if we knew the optimal level of pollution we could just tell the steel firm to produce exactly that much and not have to mess with this taxation scheme at all.

Another interpretation of the problem is that there is a missing market—the market for the pollutant. The externality problem arises because the polluter faces a zero price for an output good that it produces, even though people would be willing to pay money to have that output level reduced. From a social point of view, the output of pollution should have a *negative* price.

---

[2] Arthur Pigou (1877–1959), an economist at Cambridge University, suggested such taxes in his influential book *The Economics of Welfare*.

We could imagine a world where the fishery had the right to clean water, but could sell the right to allow pollution. Let q be the price per unit of pollution and let x be the amount of pollution that the steel mill produces. Then the steel mill's profit maximization problem is

$$\max_{s,x} \; p_s s - qx - c_s(s, x)$$

and the fishery's profit maximization problem is

$$\max_{f,x} \; p_f f + qx - c_f(f, x).$$

The term qx enters with a negative sign in the profit expression for the steel firm since it represents a cost—the steel firm must buy the right to generate x units of pollution. But it enters with a positive sign in the expression for the profits of the fishery, since the fishery gets revenue from selling this right.

The profit maximization conditions are

$$p_s = \frac{\Delta c_s(s, x)}{\Delta s} \tag{31.4}$$

$$q = -\frac{\Delta c_s(s, x)}{\Delta x} \tag{31.5}$$

$$p_f = \frac{\Delta c_f(f, x)}{\Delta f} \tag{31.6}$$

$$q = \frac{\Delta c_f(f, x)}{\Delta x}. \tag{31.7}$$

Thus each firm is facing the social marginal cost of each of its actions when it chooses how much pollution to buy or sell. If the price of pollution is adjusted until the demand for pollution equals the supply of pollution we will have an efficient equilibrium, just as with any other good.

Note that at the optimal solution, equations (31.5) and (31.7) imply that

$$-\frac{\Delta c_s(s, x)}{\Delta x} = \frac{\Delta c_f(f, x)}{\Delta x}.$$

This says that the marginal cost to the steel firm of reducing pollution should equal the marginal benefit to the fishery of that pollution reduction. If this condition were not satisfied, we couldn't have the optimal level of pollution. This is, of course, the same condition we encountered in equation (31.3).

In analyzing this problem we have stated that the fishery had a right to clean water and the steel mill had to purchase the right to pollute. But we could have assigned the property rights in the opposite way: the steel mill could have the right to pollute and the fishery had to pay to induce it to not pollute as much. Just as in the case of the smoker and nonsmoker, this would also give an efficient outcome. In fact, it would give precisely the *same* outcome, since exactly the same equations would have to be satisfied.

To see this, we now suppose that the steel mill has the right to pollute up to some amount $\overline{x}$, say, but the fishery is willing to pay it to reduce its pollution. The profit maximization problem for the steel mill is then

$$p_s s + q(\overline{x} - x) - c_s(s, x).$$

Now the steel mill has two sources of income: it can sell steel, and it can sell pollution relief. The price equals marginal cost conditions become

$$p_s - \frac{\Delta c_s(s, x)}{\Delta s} = 0 \qquad (31.8)$$

$$-q - \frac{\Delta c_s(s, x)}{\Delta x} = 0. \qquad (31.9)$$

The fishery's maximization problem is now

$$\max_{f, x} p_f f - q(\overline{x} - x) - c_f(f, x)$$

which has optimality conditions

$$p_f - \frac{\Delta c_f(f, x)}{\Delta f} = 0 \qquad (31.10)$$

$$q - \frac{\Delta c_f(f, x)}{\Delta x} = 0. \qquad (31.11)$$

Now observe: the four equations (31.8) – (31.11) are precisely the same as the four equations (31.4) – (31.7). In the case of production externalities, the optimal pattern of production is independent of the assignment of property rights.

31.5 Market Signals

Finally we turn to the third interpretation of externalities, which in some respects is the most profound. In the case of the steel mill and the fishery there is no problem if both firms merge—so why don't they merge? In fact, when you think about it, there is a definite incentive for the two firms to merge: if the actions of one affect the other, then they can make higher profits together by coordinating their behavior than by each going alone. *The objective of profit maximization itself should encourage the internalization of production externalities.*

Said another way: if the joint profits of the firms with coordination exceed the sum of the profits without coordination, then the current owners could each be bought out for an amount equal to the present value of the stream of profits for their firm, the two firms could be coordinated, and the buyer could retain the excess profits. The new buyer could be either of the old firms, or anybody else for that matter.

The market itself provides a signal to internalize production externalities, which is one reason this kind of production externality is rarely observed. Most firms have *already* internalized the externalities between units that affect each other's production. The case of the apple orchard and the bee keeper mentioned earlier is a case in point. Here there *would* be an externality if the two firms ignored their interaction ... but why would they be so foolish as to do so? It is more likely that one or both of the firms would realize that more profits could be made by coordinating their activities, either by mutual agreement or by the sale of one of the firms to the other. Indeed, it is very common for apple orchards to keep honey bees for the purpose of fertilizing the trees. That particular externality is easily internalized.

31.6 The Tragedy of the Commons

We have argued above that if property rights are well defined, there will be no problem with production externalities. But if property rights are not well defined, the outcome of the economic interactions will undoubtedly involve inefficiencies.

In this section we will examine a particularly well-known inefficiency called "the tragedy of the commons."[3] We will pose this problem in the original context of a common grazing land, although there are many other possible illustrations.

Consider an agricultural village in which the villagers graze their cows on a common field. We want to compare two allocation mechanisms: the first is the private ownership solution where someone owns the field and decides how many cows should graze there; the second is the solution where the field is owned in common by the villagers and access to it is free and unrestricted.

Suppose that it costs a dollars to buy a cow. How much milk the cow produces will depends on how many other cows are grazed on the common land. We'll let $f(c)$ be the value of the milk produced if there are c cows grazed on the common. Thus the value of the milk per cow is just the average product, $f(c)/c$.

How many cows would be grazed on the common if we wanted to maximize the total wealth of the village? In order to maximize the total amount

[3] See G. Hardin, "The Tragedy of the Commons," *Science*, 1968, pp. 1243–47.

of wealth, we set up the following problem:

$$\max_{c} f(c) - ac.$$

It should be clear by now that the maximal production will occur when the marginal product of a cow equals its cost, a:

$$MP(c^*) = a.$$

If the marginal product of a cow were greater than a it would pay to put another cow on the commons, and if it were less than a, it would pay to take one off.

If the common grazing ground were owned by someone who could restrict access to it, this is indeed the solution that would result. For in this case, the owner of the grazing grounds would purchase just the right amount of cows to maximize his profits.

Now what would happen if the individual villagers decided whether or not to use the common field? Each villager has a choice of grazing a cow or not grazing one, and it will be profitable to graze a cow as long as the output generated by the cow is greater than the cost of a cow. Suppose that there are c cows currently being grazed, so that the current output per cow is $f(c)/c$. When a villager contemplates adding a cow, the total output will be $f(c+1)$, and the total number of cows will be $c+1$. Thus the revenue that the cow generates for the villager will be $f(c+1)/(c+1)$. He must compare this revenue to the cost of the cow, a. If $f(c+1)/(c+1) > a$, it is profitable to add the cow since the value of the output exceeds the cost. Hence the villagers will choose to graze cows until the average product of a cow is driven to zero; that is, the total number of cows grazed will be $\hat{c}$, where

$$\frac{f(\hat{c})}{\hat{c}} = a.$$

Another way to derive this result is to appeal to free entry. If it is profitable to graze a cow on the common field, villagers will purchase cows. They will stop adding cows to the common only when the profits have been driven to zero, that is, when

$$f(\hat{c}) - a\hat{c} = 0$$

which is just a rearrangement of the condition in the last paragraph.

When an individual decides whether or not to purchase a cow, he looks at the extra value he will get $f(c)/c$ and compares this to the cost of the cow, a. This is fine for him, but what has been left out of this calculation is the fact that his extra cow will reduce the output of milk from all the *other* cows. Since he is ignoring this **social cost** of his purchase, too many cows will be grazed on the common ground.

This argument is illustrated in Figure 31.4. Here we have depicted a falling average product curve, since it is reasonable to suppose that the output per cow declines as more and more cows are grazed on the common land. Since the average product is falling, it must be that the marginal product curve always lies below the average product curve. Thus the number of cows where the marginal product equals a must be less than where the average product equals a. The field will be overgrazed in the absence of a mechanism to restrict use.

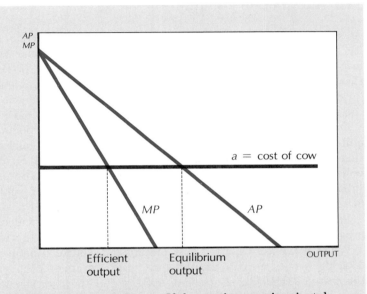

The tragedy of the commons. If the grazing area is privately owned, the number of cows will be chosen so that the marginal product of a cow equals its cost. But if grazing area is common property, cows will be grazed until the profits are driven to zero; thus the area will be overgrazed.

Figure
31.4

Private property provides such a mechanism. Indeed, we have seen that if everything that people care about is owned by someone who can control its use and, in particular, can exclude others from overusing it, then there are by definition no externalities. The market solution leads to a Pareto efficient outcome. Inefficiencies can only result from situations where there is no way to exclude others from using something, a topic that we will investigate in the next chapter.

Of course, private property is not the only social institution that can encourage efficient use of resources. For example, rules could be formulated about how many cows can be grazed on the village common. If there is a legal system to enforce those rules, this may be a cost effective solution to providing an efficient use of the common resource. However, in situations where the law is ambiguous or nonexistent, the tragedy of the commons can easily arise. Overfishing in international waters and the extermination of several species of animals due to overhunting are sobering examples of this phenomenon.

31.7 Automobile Pollution

As suggested above, pollution is a prime example of an economic externality. The activity of one consumer operating an automobile will typically lower the quality of the air that other consumers breathe. It seems unlikely that an unregulated free market would generate the optimal amount of pollution; more likely, if the consumer bears no cost in generating pollution, too much pollution would be produced.

One approach to controlling the amount of automobile pollution is to require that automobiles meet certain standards in the amount of pollution that they generate. This has been the basic thrust of U.S. antipollution policy since the Clean Air Act of 1963. That act, or, more properly, the subsequent amendments, set automobile emission standards for the manufacturers of vehicles in the United States.

Lawrence White has recently described the benefits and costs of this program; most of the following discussion is drawn from this work.[4]

White estimates that the cost of emission control equipment is about $600 per car, the extra maintenance costs are about $180 per car, and the costs of the reduced gasoline mileage and the necessity for unleaded gasoline come to about $670 per car. Thus the total cost per car of the emission control standards is about $1450 over the lifetime of the car. (All figures are in 1981 dollars.)

He argues that there are several problems with the current approach to the regulation of automobile emissions. First, it requires that all automobiles meet the same standards. (California is the only state with different standards for emission control.) This means that *everyone* who buys a car must pay an extra $1450 whether they live in a high pollution area or not. A National Academy of Sciences study in 1974 concluded that 63 percent of all U.S. cars did not require the stringent standards now in effect. According to White, "almost two–thirds of car buyers are spending . . . substantial sums for unnecessary systems."

Secondly, most of the responsibility for meeting the standards falls on the manufacturer, and little falls on the user. Owners of cars have little

---

[4] See Lawrence White, *The Regulation of Air Pollutant Emissions from Motor Vehicles* (Washington, D.C.: American Enterprise Institute for Public Policy Research, 1982).

incentive to keep their pollution control equipment in working order unless they live in a state with required inspections. Even then, they only have an incentive to have the equipment in working order at the time of the inspection.

More significantly, motorists have no incentive to economize on their driving. In cities such as Los Angeles, where pollution is a significant hazard, it makes good economic sense to encourage people to drive less. Under the current system, people who drive 2000 miles a year in North Dakota pay exactly the same amount for pollution control as people who drive 50,000 miles a year in Los Angeles. People who generate the costs of pollution do not face those costs under the current system.

An alternative solution to pollution would be *effluent fees*. As described by White, effluent fees would require an annual inspection of all vehicles along with an odometer reading and tests that would estimate the likely emissions of the vehicle during the past year. Different communities could then levy fees based on the estimated amount of pollution that had actually been generated by the operation of the vehicle. This method would ensure that people would face the true cost of generating pollution. Automobile pollution would be taxed at the source. If people faced the true social costs of their actions, they would optimally choose to generate the socially optimal amount of pollution.

Such a system of effluent fees would encourage the vehicle owners themselves to find low-cost ways of reducing their emissions—investing in pollution control equipment, changing their driving habits, and changing the kinds of vehicles that they operate. A system of effluent fees could impose even higher standards than are now in effect in communities where pollution is a serious problem. Any desired level of pollution control can be achieved by appropriate effluent fees ... and it can be achieved at a substantially lower cost than the current system of mandated standards.

Of course, there is no reason why there might not also be some federally mandated standards for the two–thirds of the vehicles that are operated in localities where pollution is not a serious problem. If it is cheaper to impose standards than to require inspections, then by all means that should be the proper choice. The appropriate method of pollution control for automobiles should depend on a rational analysis of benefits and costs—as should all social policies of this nature.

Summary

1. The First Theorem of Welfare Economics shows that a free, competitive market will provide an efficient outcome in the absence of externalities.

2. But if externalities are present, the outcome of a competitive market is unlikely to be Pareto efficient.

3. However, in this case, the state can sometimes "mimic" the role of the market by using prices to provide correct signals about the social cost of individual actions.

4. More importantly, the legal system can ensure that property rights are well defined, so that efficiency enhancing trades can be made.

5. If preferences are quasilinear the efficient amount of a consumption externality will be independent of the assignment of property rights.

6. Cures for production externalities include the use of Pigouvian taxes, setting up a market for the externality, simply allowing firms to merge, or transferring property rights in other ways.

7. The tragedy of the commons refers to the tendency for common property to be overused. This is a particularly prevalent form of externality.

Review Questions

1. True or false? The definition of property rights eliminates the problem of externalities.

2. True or false? The distributional consequences of the delineation of property rights are eliminated when preferences are quasilinear.

3. List some other examples of positive and negative consumption and production externalities.

4. Suppose the government wants to control the use of the commons, what methods exist for achieving the efficient level of use?

32

PUBLIC GOODS

In the last chapter we argued that for certain kinds of externalities, it was not difficult to eliminate the inefficiencies. In the case of a consumption externality between two people, for example, all one had to do was to ensure that initial property rights were clearly specified. People could then trade the right to generate the externality in the normal way. In the case of production externalities, the market itself provided profit signals to sort out the property rights in the most efficient way. In the case of common property, assigning property rights to someone would eliminate the inefficiency.

Unfortunately, not all externalities can be handled in that manner. As soon as there are more than two economic agents involved things become much more difficult. Suppose, for example, that instead of the two roommates examined in the last chapter, we had *three* roommates—one smoker and two nonsmokers. Then the amount of smoke would be a negative externality for both of the nonsmokers.

Let's suppose that property rights are well defined—say the nonsmokers have the right to demand clean air. Just as before, although they have the *right* to clean air, they also have the right to trade some of that clean air away in return for appropriate compensation. But now there is a problem involved—the nonsmokers have to agree between themselves how much smoke should be allowed and what the compensation should be.

Perhaps one of the nonsmokers is much more sensitive than the other, or one of them is much richer than the other. They may have very different preferences and resources, and yet they both have to reach some kind of agreement to allow for an efficient allocation of smoke.

Instead of roommates, we can think of inhabitants of a whole country. How much pollution should be allowed in the country? If you think that reaching an agreement is difficult with only three roommates, imagine what it is like with millions of people!

The smoke externality with three people is an example of a **public good**—a good that must be provided in the same amount to all the affected consumers. In this case the amount of smoke generated will be the same for all consumers—each person may value it differently, but they all have to consume the same amount.

Many public goods are provided by the government. For example, streets and sidewalks are provided by local municipalities. There are a certain number and quality of streets in a town and everyone has that number available to use. National defense is another good example; there is one level of national defense provided for all the inhabitants of a country. They may all value it differently—some may want more, some may want less—but they are all provided with the same amount.

Public goods are an example of a particular kind of consumption externality: everyone must consume the same amount of the good. They are a particularly troublesome kind of externality, for the decentralized market solutions that economists are fond of don't work very well in allocating public goods. People can't purchase different amounts of public defense; somehow they have to decide on a common amount.

The first issue to examine is what the ideal amount of the public good should be. Then we'll discuss some ways that might be used to make social decisions about public goods.

32.1 When to Provide a Public Good?

Let us start with a simple example. Suppose that there are two roommates, 1 and 2. They are trying to decide whether or not to purchase a TV. Given the size of their apartment, the TV will necessarily go in the living room and both roommates will be able to watch it. Thus it will be a public good, rather than a private good. The question is, is it worth it for them to acquire the TV?

Let's use w_1 and w_2 to denote each person's initial wealth, g_1 and g_2 to denote each person's contribution to the TV, and x_1 and x_2 to denote each person's money left over to spend on private consumption. The budget constraints are given by

$$x_1 + g_1 = w_1$$
$$x_2 + g_2 = w_2.$$

We also suppose that the TV costs c dollars, so that in order to purchase it, the sum of the two contributions must be at least c:

$$g_1 + g_2 \geq c.$$

This equation summarizes the technology available to provide the public good: the roommates can acquire one TV if together they pay the cost c.

The utility function of person 1 will depend on his or her private consumption, x_1, and the availability of the TV—the public good. We'll write person 1's utility function as $u_1(x_1, G)$, where G will either be a 0, indicating no TV, or 1, indicating that a TV is present. Person 2 will have utility function $u_2(x_2, G)$. Each person's private consumption has a subscript to indicate that the good is consumed by person 1 or person 2, but the public good has no subscript. It is "consumed" by both of the people. Of course it isn't really consumed in the sense of being "used up"; rather, it is the *services* of the TV that are consumed by the two roommates.

The roommates may value the services of the TV quite differently. We can measure the value that each person places on the TV by asking how much each person would be willing to pay to have the TV available. To do this, we'll use the concept of the **reservation price**, introduced in Chapter 16.

The reservation price of person 1 is the maximum amount that person 1 would be willing to pay to have the TV present. That is, it is that price, r_1, such that person 1 is just indifferent between paying r_1 and having the TV available, and not having the TV at all. If person 1 pays the reservation price and gets the TV, he will have $w_1 - r_1$ available for private consumption. If he doesn't get the TV, he will have w_1 available for private consumption. If he is to be just indifferent between these two alternatives, we must have

$$u_1(w_1 - r_1, 1) = u_1(w_1, 0).$$

This equation defines the reservation price for person 1—the maximum amount that he would be willing to pay to have the TV present. A similar equation defines the reservation price for person 2. Note that in general the reservation price of each person will depend each person's wealth: the maximum amount that an individual will be *willing* to pay will depend on how much that individual is *able* to pay.

Recall that an allocation is Pareto efficient if there is no way to make both people better off. An allocation is Pareto *inefficient* if there *is* some way to make both people better off; in this case, we say that a **Pareto improvement** is possible. In the TV problem there are only two sorts of allocations that are of interest. One is an allocation where the TV is not provided. This allocation takes the simple form $(w_1, w_2, 0)$; that is, each person spends his wealth only on his private consumption.

The other kind of allocation is the one where the public good is provided. This will be an allocation of the form $(x_1, x_2, 1)$, where

$$x_1 = w_1 - g_1$$

$$x_2 = w_2 - g_2.$$

These two equations come from rewriting the budget constraints. They say that each individual's private consumption is determined by the wealth that he has left over after making his contribution to the public good.

Under what conditions should the TV be provided? That is, when is there a payment scheme (g_1, g_2) such that both people will be better off having the TV and paying their share, than not having the TV? In the language of economics, when will it be a Pareto improvement to provide the TV?

It will be a Pareto improvement to provide the allocation (x_1, x_2, G) if both people would be better off having the TV provided than not having it provided. This means

$$u_1(w_1, 0) < u_1(x_1, 1)$$
$$u_2(w_2, 0) < u_2(x_2, 1).$$

Now use the definition of the reservation prices r_1 and r_2 and the budget constraint to write

$$u_1(w_1 - r_1, 1) = u_1(w_1, 0) < u_1(x_1, 1) = u_1(w_1 - g_1, 1)$$
$$u_2(w_2 - r_2, 1) = u_2(w_2, 0) < u_2(x_2, 1) = u_2(w_2 - g_2, 1).$$

Looking at the left- and the right-hand sides of this inequality, and remembering that more private consumption must increase utility, we can conclude that

$$w_1 - r_1 < w_1 - g_1$$
$$w_2 - r_2 < w_2 - g_2$$

which in turn implies

$$r_1 > g_1$$
$$r_2 > g_2.$$

This is a condition that must be satisfied if an allocation $(w_1, w_2, 0)$ is Pareto inefficient: it must be that the contribution that each person is making to the TV is less than his willingness to pay for the TV. If a consumer can acquire the good for less than the maximum that he would be willing to pay, then the acquisition would be to his benefit. Thus the condition that the reservation price exceeds the cost share simply says that a Pareto improvement will result when each roommate can acquire the services of the TV for less than the maximum that he would be willing to pay for it. This is clearly a *necessary* condition for provision of the TV to be a Pareto improvement over not having the TV.

If each roommate's willingness to pay exceeds his cost share, then the *sum* of the willingness to pay must be greater than the cost of the TV:

$$r_1 + r_2 > g_1 + g_2 = c. \tag{32.1}$$

This condition is a *sufficient* condition for it to be a Pareto improvement to provide the TV. If the condition is satisfied, then there will be some payment plan such that both people will be made better off by providing the public good. If $r_1 + r_2 \geq c$, then the total amount that the roommates will be willing to pay is at least as large as the cost of provision, so they can easily find a payment plan (g_1, g_2) such that $r_1 \geq g_1$, $r_2 \geq g_2$, and $g_1 + g_2 = c$. This condition is so simple that you might wonder why we went through all the detail in deriving it. Well, there are a few subtleties involved.

First, it is important to note that the condition describing when provision will be a Pareto improvement only depends on the *willingness* to pay and the total cost. If the sum of the reservation prices exceeds the cost of the TV, then there will always *exist* a payment scheme such that both people will be better off having the public good than not having it.

Second, whether or not it is Pareto efficient to provide the public good will, in general, depend on the initial distribution of wealth (w_1, w_2). This is true because, in general, the reservation prices r_1 and r_2 will depend on the distribution of wealth. It perfectly possible that for some distributions of wealth $r_1 + r_2 > c$, and for other distributions of wealth $r_1 + r_2 < c$.

To see how this can be, imagine a situation where one roommate really loves the TV and the other roommate is nearly indifferent about acquiring it. Then if the TV-loving roommate had all of the wealth, he would be willing to pay more than the cost of the TV all by himself. Thus it would be a Pareto improvement to provide the TV. But if the indifferent roommate had all of the wealth, then the TV lover wouldn't have much money to contribute towards the TV, and it would be Pareto efficient *not* to provide the TV.

Thus, in general, whether or not the public good should be provided will depend on the distribution of wealth. But in specific cases the provision of the public good may be independent of the distribution of wealth. For example, suppose that the preferences of the two roommates were quasilinear. This means that the utility functions take the form

$$u_1(x_1, G) = x_1 + v_1(G)$$
$$u_2(x_2, G) = x_2 + v_2(G)$$

where G will be 0 or 1, depending on whether or not the public good is available. For simplicity, suppose that $v_1(0) = v_2(0) = 0$. This says that no TV provides zero utility from watching TV.[1]

In this case the definition of the reservation price becomes

$$u_1(w_1 - r_1, 1) = w_1 - r_1 + v_1(1) = w_1 = u_1(w_1, 0)$$
$$u_2(w_2 - r_2, 1) = w_2 - r_2 + v_2(1) = w_2 = u_2(w_2, 0)$$

which implies that the reservation prices are given by

$$r_1 = v_1(1)$$
$$r_2 = v_2(1).$$

Thus the reservation prices are independent of the amount of wealth, and hence the optimal provision of the public good will be independent of wealth, at least over some range of wealths.[2]

32.2 Private Provision of the Public Good

We have seen above that acquiring the TV will be Pareto efficient for the two roommates if the sum of their willingness to pay exceeds the cost of providing the public good. This answers the question about efficient allocation of the good, but it does not necessarily follow that they will actually decide to acquire the TV. Whether they actually decide to acquire the TV depends on the particular method they adopt to make joint decisions.

If the two roommates cooperate and truthfully reveal how much they value the TV, then it should not be difficult for them to agree on whether or not they should buy the TV. But under some circumstances, they may not have incentives to tell the truth about their values.

For example, suppose that each person valued the TV the same, and that each person's reservation price was greater than the cost, so that $r_1 > c$ and $r_2 > c$. Then person 1 might think that if he said he had 0 value for the TV, the other person would acquire it anyway. But person 2 could reason the same way! One can imagine other situations where both people would refuse to contribute in the hopes that the other person would go out and unilaterally purchase the TV.

In this kind of situation, economists say that the people are attempting to **free ride** on each other: each person hopes that the other person will purchase the public good on his own. Since each person will have full use of the services of the TV if it is acquired, each person has an incentive to try to pay as little as possible toward the provision of the TV.

---

[1] Perhaps watching TV should be assigned a negative utility.

[2] Even this will only be true for some ranges of wealth, since we must always require that $r_1 \leq w_1$ and $r_2 \leq w_2$—i.e., the willingness to pay is less than the ability to pay.

32.3 Free Riding

Free riding is another example of the prisoner's dilemma that we examined in Chapter 27. To see this let us attach some numbers to the symbols used above. Suppose that each person has a wealth of $500, that each person values the TV at $300, and that the cost of the TV is $400. Since the sum of the values exceeds the cost, it is Pareto efficient to buy the TV.

Suppose that the roommates will decide whether or not to get the TV by the following procedure. Each person will write on a piece of paper whether or not he thinks the TV should be purchased. If both say yes, they buy the TV and split the cost evenly. If both say no, they don't buy the TV. If one says yes and the other says no, the person who says yes is obligated to buy the TV on his own. The payoff matrix for this game is given in Table 32.1.

Free riding and the prisoner's dilemma.

Table 32.1

		Player B	
		Buy	Don't buy
Player A	Buy	600, 600	400, 800
	Don't buy	800, 400	500, 500

Let's check a couple of entries in this payoff matrix. If they both decide to buy the TV, then they will each enjoy a value from the TV of $300, and each will have to pay $200 out of their $500 wealth, leaving each of them with $300 of wealth to spend on private consumption. Thus each has a net value of public and private consumption of $600. On the other hand if they both say no, they each just consume their private wealth of $500.

If one says yes, and the other says no, the no–sayer gets to enjoy his private wealth of $500 *and* he gets to watch the TV—which is worth $300 to him—thus his total payoff is $800. The yes–sayer, however, has to spend the entire $400 for the TV (which is only worth $300 to him) leaving him with a net position of $400.

It is not hard to see that this is an example of a prisoner's dilemma game. If player A decides to say yes, then it is in player B's interest to free ride. If player A decides to say no, then it is in player B's interest to say no as well, lest he be forced to pay for the whole TV. In the terminology of Chapter 27, it is a *dominant strategy* for both players to say no.

In the context of this example it may seem implausible that the two roommates could not find a better way to decide whether or not to buy a TV. But a lot of other problems can arise in the sharing of household public goods. For example, what about cleaning the living room? Each person may prefer to see the living room clean, and is willing to do his part. But each may also be tempted to free ride on the other—so that neither one ends up cleaning the room, with the usual untidy results.

The situation becomes even worse if there are more than just two people involved—since there are more people on whom to free ride! Letting the other guy do it may be optimal from an *individual* point of view, but it is Pareto inefficient from the viewpoint of society as a whole.

32.4 Different Levels of the Public Good

In the above example, we had an either/or decision: either provide the TV or not. But the same kind of phenomena occur when there is a choice of *how much* of the public good to provide. Suppose, for example, that the two roommates have to decide how much money to spend on the TV. The more money they decide to spend, the better the TV they can get.

As before we'll let x_1 and x_2 measure the private consumption of each person, and g_1 and g_2 their contributions to the TV. Let G now measure the "quality" of the TV they buy, and let the cost function for quality as a function of expenditure be given by $c(G)$. This means that if the two roommates want to purchase a TV of quality G, they have to spend $c(G)$ dollars to do so.

The constraint facing the roommates is that the total amount that they spend on their public and private consumption has to add up to how much money they have:

$$x_1 + x_2 + c(G) = w_1 + w_2.$$

A Pareto efficient allocation is one where consumer 1 is as well-off as possible given consumer 2's level of utility. If we fix the utility of consumer 2 at $\overline{u}_2$ we can write this problem as

$$\max_{x_1, x_2, G} u_1(x_1, G)$$

$$\text{s.t. } u_2(x_2, G) = \overline{u}_2$$

$$x_1 + x_2 + c(G) = w_1 + w_2.$$

It turns out that the appropriate optimality condition for this problem is that the *sum* of the marginal rates of substitution between the private good and the public good for the two consumers equals the marginal cost of providing an extra unit of the public good:

$$MRS_1 + MRS_2 = MC(G)$$

or, spelling out the definitions of the marginal rates of substitution,

$$\frac{\Delta x_1}{\Delta G} + \frac{\Delta x_2}{\Delta G} = \frac{MU_G}{MU_{x_1}} + \frac{MU_G}{MU_{x_2}} = MC(G).$$

In order to see why this must be the right efficiency condition, let us apply the usual trick and think about what would be the case if it were violated. Suppose, for example, that the sum of the marginal rates of substitution were less than the marginal cost; say $MC = 1$, $MRS_1 = 1/4$, and $MRS_2 = 1/2$. We need to show that there is some way to make both people better off.

Given his marginal rate of substitution we know that person 1 would be willing to accept 1/4 more dollars of the private good for the loss of 1 dollar of the public good (since both goods cost \$1 per unit). Similarly, person 2 would accept 1/2 more dollars of the private good for a 1 dollar decrease in the public good. Suppose we reduce the amount of the public good, and offer to compensate both individuals. When we reduce the public good by one unit we save a dollar. After we pay each individual the amount he requires to allow this change $(3/4 = 1/4 + 1/2)$ we find that we still have 1/4 of a dollar left over. This remaining money could be shared between the two individuals, thereby making them both better off.

Similarly, if the sum of the marginal rates of substitution were greater than 1, we could increase the amount of the public good to make them both better off. If $MRS_1 = 2/3$ and $MRS_2 = 1/2$, say, this means that person 1 would give up 2/3 dollars of private consumption to get 1 unit more of the public good and person 2 would give up 1/2 dollars of private consumption to get 1 unit more of the public good. But if person 1 gave up his 2/3 units, and person 2 gave up his 1/2 unit, we would have more than enough to produce the extra unit of the public good, since the marginal cost of providing the public good is 1. Thus we could give the left-over amount back to both people, thereby making them both better off.

What does the condition for Pareto efficiency mean? One way to interpret it is to think of the marginal rate of substitution as measuring the *marginal* willingness to pay for an extra unit of the public good. Then the efficiency condition just says that the *sum* of the marginal willingness to pay must equal the marginal cost of providing an extra unit of the public good. In the case of a discrete good that was either provided or not provided, we said that the efficiency condition was that the sum of the willingness to pay should be at least as large as the cost. In the case we're considering here, where the public good can be provided at different levels, the efficiency condition is that the sum of the *marginal* willingness to pay should *equal* the marginal cost at the optimal amount of the public good. For whenever the sum of the marginal willingness to pay for the public good exceeds the marginal cost, it is appropriate to provide more of the public good.

It is worthwhile to compare this efficiency condition for a public good to the efficiency condition we derived in the private good case. In the case of a private good each person's marginal rate of substitution, or marginal willingness to pay, equals the marginal cost; in the public good case, it is the sum of the marginal rates of substitution that must equal the marginal cost. In the case of private goods, each person can consume a different amount of the private good, but they all must value it the same at the margin—otherwise they would want to trade. In the case of public goods, each person must consume the same amount, but they can all value it differently at the margin. It is only the sum of their values that is relevant in determining the efficient provision of the public good.

We can illustrate the efficiency condition in Figure 32.1. We simply draw each person's MRS curve, and then add them vertically to get the sum of the MRS curves. The efficient allocation of the public good will occur where the sum of the MRSs equals the marginal cost, as illustrated in Figure 32.1.

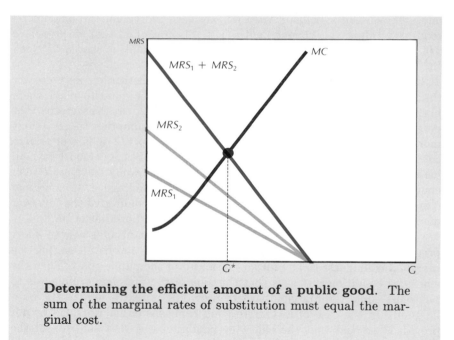

Figure 32.1

Determining the efficient amount of a public good. The sum of the marginal rates of substitution must equal the marginal cost.

32.5 Quasilinear Preferences and Public Goods

In general the optimal amount of the public good will be different at different allocations of the private good. But if the consumers have quasilinear preferences it turns out that there will be a unique amount of the public good supplied at every efficient allocation. The easiest way to see this is to think about the kind of utility function that represents quasilinear preferences.

As we saw in Chapter 4, quasilinear preferences have a utility representation of the form: $u_i(x_i, G) = x_i + v_i(G)$. This means that the marginal utility of the private good is always 1, and thus the marginal rate of substitution between the private and the public good—the ratio of the marginal utilities—will depend only on G. In particular:

$$MRS_1 = \frac{\Delta u_1(x_1, G)/\Delta G}{\Delta u_1/\Delta x_1} = \frac{\Delta v_1(G)}{\Delta G}$$

$$MRS_2 = \frac{\Delta u_2(x_2, G)/\Delta G}{\Delta u_2/\Delta x_2} = \frac{\Delta v_2(G)}{\Delta G}.$$

We already know that a Pareto efficient level of the public good must satisfy the condition

$$MRS_1 + MRS_2 = MC(G).$$

Using the special form of the MRSs in the case of quasilinear utility, we can write this condition as

$$\frac{\Delta v_1(G)}{\Delta G} + \frac{\Delta v_2(G)}{\Delta G} = MC(G).$$

Note that this equation determines G without any reference to x_1 or x_2. Thus there is a unique efficient level of provision of the public good.

Another way to see this is to think about the behavior of the indifference curves. In the case of quasilinear preferences, all of the indifference curves are just shifted versions of each other. This means, in particular, that the slope of the indifference curves—the marginal rate of substitution—doesn't change as we change the amount of the private good. Suppose that we find one efficient allocation of the public and private goods, where the sum of the MRSs equals $MC(G)$. Now if we take some amount of the private good away from one person and give it to another, the slopes of both indifference curves stay the same, so the sum of the MRSs is still equal to $MC(G)$ and we have another Pareto efficient allocation.

In the case of quasilinear preferences, all Pareto efficient allocations are found by just redistributing the private good. The amount of the public good stays fixed at the efficient level.

EXAMPLE: Pollution Revisited

Recall the model of the steel firm and the fishery described in Chapter 31. There we argued that the efficient provision of pollution was one which internalized the pollution costs borne by the steel firm and the fishery. Suppose now that there are two fisheries, and that the amount of pollution produced by the steel firm is a public good. (Or, perhaps more appropriately, is a public bad!)

Then the efficient provision of pollution will involve maximizing the sum of the profits of all three firms—that is, minimizing the total social cost of the pollution. Formally, let $c_s(s, x)$ be the cost to the steel firm of producing s units of steel and x units of pollution, and write $c_f^1(f_1, x)$ for the costs for firm 1 to catch f_1 fish when the pollution level is x, and $c_f^2(f_2, x)$ as the analogous expression for firm 2. Then to compute the Pareto efficient amount of pollution, we maximize the sum of the three firms' profits:

$$\max_{s, f_1, f_2, x} \; p_s s + p_f f_1 + p_f f_2 - c_s(s, x) - c_f^1(f_1, x) - c_f^2(f_2, x).$$

The interesting effect for our purposes is the effect on aggregate profits of increasing pollution. Increasing pollution lowers the cost of producing steel, but raises the costs of producing fish for each of the fisheries. The appropriate optimality condition from the profit maximization problem is

$$\frac{\Delta c_s(\hat{s}, \hat{x})}{\Delta x} + \frac{\Delta c_f^1(\hat{f}_1, \hat{x})}{\Delta x} + \frac{\Delta c_f^2(\hat{f}_2, \hat{x})}{\Delta x} = 0$$

which simply says that the *sum* of the marginal costs of pollution over the three firms should equal zero. Just as in the case of a public consumption good, it is the *sum* of the marginal benefits or costs over the economic agents that is relevant for determining the Pareto efficient provision of a public good.

32.6 The Free Rider Problem

Now that we know what the Pareto efficient allocations of public goods are, we can turn our attention to asking how to get there. In the case of private goods with no externalities we saw that the market mechanism will generate an efficient allocation. Will the market work in the case of public goods?

We can think of each person as having some endowment of a private good, w_i. Each person can spend some fraction of this private good on his own private consumption, or he or she can contribute some of it to purchase the public good. Let's use x_1 for 1's private consumption, and let g_1 denote the amount of the public good he buys, and similarly for person 2. Suppose for simplicity that $c(G) \equiv G$, which implies that the marginal cost of providing a unit of the public good is constant at 1. The total amount of the public good provided will be $G = g_1 + g_2$. Since each person cares about the *total* amount of the public good provided, the utility function of person i will have the form $u_i(x_i, g_i + g_i) = u_i(x_i, G)$.

In order for person 1 to decide how much he should contribute to the public good, he has to have some forecast of how much person 2 will contribute. The simplest thing to do here is to adopt the Nash equilibrium model described in Chapter 27, and suppose that person 1 will make some contribution $\bar{g}_2$. We make the same assumption about how person 2 behaves and look for an equilibrium where person 1 is making the optimal choice given person 2's behavior and vice versa.

Thus person 1's maximization problem takes the form

$$\max_{x_1, g_1} u_1(x_1, g_1 + \bar{g}_2)$$

such that $x_1 + g_1 = w_1$.

This is just like an ordinary consumer maximization problem. The optimization condition is therefore the same: if both people purchase both goods the marginal rate of substitution between the public and the private goods should be 1 for each consumer:

$$MRS_1 = 1$$

$$MRS_2 = 1.$$

However, we have to be careful here. It is true that if person 2 purchases any amount of the public good at all, he will purchase it until the marginal rate of substitution equals one. But it can easily happen that person 2 decides that the amount already contributed by person 1 is sufficient and that it would therefore be unnecessary for him to contribute anything towards the public good at all.

Formally, we are assuming that the individuals can only make positive contributions to the public good—they can put money into the collection plate, but they can't take money out. Thus there is an extra constraint on each person's contributions, namely, that $g_1 \geq 0$ and $g_2 \geq 0$. Each person can only decide whether or not he wants to *increase* the amount of the public good. But then it may well be that one person decides that the amount provided by the other is just fine, and would prefer to make no contribution at all.

A case like this is depicted in Figure 32.2. Here we have illustrated each person's private consumption on the horizontal axis and his or her public consumption on the vertical axis. The "endowment" of each person consists of his or her wealth, w_i, and the amount of the public good contribution of the *other* person—since this is how much of the public good will be available if the person in question decides not to contribute. Figure 32.2A shows a

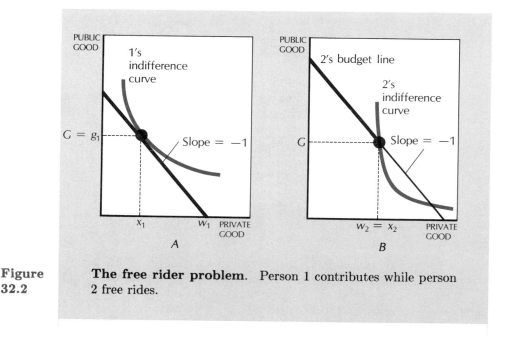

Figure
32.2
The free rider problem. Person 1 contributes while person 2 free rides.

case where person 1 is the only contributor to the public good, so that $g_1 = G$. If person 1 contributes G units to the public good, then person 2's endowment will consist of her private wealth, w_2, and the amount of the public good G—since person 2 gets to consume the public good whether or not she contributes to it. Since person 2 cannot reduce the amount of the public good, but can only increase it, her budget constraint is the bold line in Figure 32.2B. Given the shape of 2's indifference curve, it is optimal from her point of view to free ride on 1's contribution, and simply consume her endowment, as depicted.

This is an example where person 2 is free riding on person 1's contribution to the public good. Since public good is a good that everyone must consume in the same amount, the provision of a public good by any one person will tend to reduce the other peoples' provision. Thus in general there will be too little of the public good supplied in a voluntary equilibrium, relative to an efficient provision of the public good.

32.7 Comparison to Private Goods

In our discussion of private goods, we were able to show that a particular social institution—the competitive market—was capable of achieving a Pareto efficient allocation of private goods. Each consumer deciding for himself or herself how much to purchase of various goods would result in a pattern of consumption that was Pareto efficient. A major assumption in this analysis was that an individual's consumption did not affect other people's utility—that is, that there were no consumption externalities. Thus each person optimizing with respect to his or her own consumption was sufficient to achieve a kind of social optimum.

The situation is radically different with respect to public goods. In this case, the utilities of the individuals are inexorably linked since everyone is required to consume the same amount of the public good. In this case the market provision of *public* goods would be very unlikely to result in a Pareto efficient provision.

Indeed, for the most part we use *different* social institutions to determine the provision of public goods. Sometimes people use a **command mechanism**, where one person or small group of people determines the amount of various public goods that will be provided by the populace. Other times people use a **voting system** where individuals vote on the provision of public goods. One can well ask the same sorts of questions about voting, or other social mechanisms for decision making, that we asked about the private market: are they capable of achieving a Pareto efficient allocation of public goods? Can any Pareto efficient allocation of public goods be achieved by such mechanisms? A complete analysis of these questions is beyond the scope of this book, but we will be able to shed a little light on how some methods work below.

32.8 Voting

Private provision of a public good doesn't work very well, but there are several other mechanisms for social choice. One of the most common in democratic countries is **voting**. Let's examine how well it works for the provision of public goods.

Voting isn't very interesting in the case of two consumers, so we will suppose that we have n consumers. Furthermore, so as not to worry about ties, we'll suppose that n is an odd number. Let's imagine that the consumers are voting about the size of some public good—say the magnitude of expenditures on public defense. Each consumer has a most preferred level of expenditure and his valuation of other levels of expenditure depends on how close they are to his preferred level of expenditure.

The first problem with voting as a way of determining social outcomes has already been examined in Chapter 30. Suppose that we are considering three levels of expenditure, A, B, and C. It is perfectly possible that there is a majority of the consumers who prefer A to B, a majority who prefer B to C ... and a majority who prefer C to A!

Using the terminology of Chapter 30, the social preferences generated by these consumers are not transitive. This means that the outcome of voting on the level of public good may not be well defined—there is always a level of expenditure that beats every expenditure. If society is allowed to vote many times on an issue, this means that it may "cycle" around various choices. Or if society votes only once on an issue, the outcome depends on the order in which the choices are presented.

If first you vote on A versus B and then on A versus C, C will be the outcome. But if you vote on C versus A and then C versus B, B will be the outcome. You can get any of the three outcomes by choosing how the alternatives are presented!

The "paradox of voting" described above is disturbing. One natural thing to do is to ask what restrictions on preferences will allow us to rule it out; that is, what form must preferences have so as to ensure that the kinds of cycles described above cannot happen?

Let us depict the preferences of consumer i by a graph like those in Figure 32.3, where the height of the graph illustrates the value or the net utility of the level of different levels of the expenditure on the public good. The term "net utility" is appropriate since each person cares both about the level of the public good, and the amount that he has to contribute to it. Higher levels of expenditure mean more public goods, but also higher taxes in order to pay for those public goods. Thus it is reasonable to assume that the net utility of expenditure on the public good rises at first due to the benefits of the public good, but then eventually falls, due to the costs of providing it.

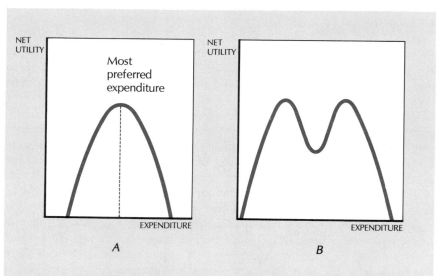

Figure 32.3

Shapes of preferences. Single-peaked preferences are shown in panel A and multiple peaked preferences in panel B.

One restriction on preferences of this sort is that they be **single-peaked**. This means that preferences must have the shape depicted in Figure 32.3A rather than that depicted in Figure 32.3B. With single-peaked preferences, the net utility of different levels of expenditure rises until the most preferred point and then falls, as it does in Figure 32.3A; it never goes up, down, and then up again, as it does in Figure 32.3B.

If each individual has single-peaked preferences, then it can be shown that the social preferences revealed by majority vote will never exhibit the kind of intransitivity we described above. Accepting this result for the moment, we can ask which level of expenditure will be chosen if everyone has single-peaked preferences. The answer turns out to be the **median expenditure**—that expenditure such that one-half of the population wants to spend more, and one-half wants to spend less. This result is reasonably intuitive: if more than one-half wanted more expenditure on the public good, they would vote for more, so the only possible equilibrium voting outcome is when the votes for increasing and decreasing expenditure on the public good are just balanced.

Will this be an efficient level of the public good? In general the answer is no. The median outcome just means that half the population wants more and half wants less; it doesn't say anything about *how much more* they want of the public good. Since efficiency takes this kind of information into account, voting will not in general lead to an efficient outcome.

Furthermore, even if peoples' true preferences are single-peaked, so that voting may lead to a reasonable outcome, individuals may choose to misrepresent their true preferences when they vote. In general people will have an incentive to vote differently than their true preferences would indicate in order to manipulate the final outcome.

32.9 Demand Revelation

We have seen above that majority voting, even if it leads to a well-defined outcome, will not necessarily provide the correct incentives for people to honestly reveal their true preferences. In general there will be an incentive to misrepresent preferences in order to manipulate the voting outcome.

This observation leads to the issue of what other methods there might be that would ensure that individuals have the proper incentives to correctly reveal their true preferences about a public good. Are there any procedures that provide the right incentives to tell the truth about the value of a public good?

It turns out that there is a way to ensure that people will correctly reveal their true value for a public good using a kind of market or "auction" process. Unfortunately this method also requires a special restriction on preferences, namely that they be quasilinear. As we've seen earlier, quasilinear preferences imply that we will have a unique optimal amount of the public good, and the issue is to discover what it is. In order to keep things simple, we'll just consider the case where there is one level of the public good to be supplied, and the question is whether to supply it or not.

We can think of a neighborhood association that is considering putting up a street light. The cost of providing the street light is known; say it is $100. Each person i places some value on the street light, which we denote by v_i. From our analysis of the public goods problem, we know that it is efficient to provide the street light if the *sum* of the values is greater than or equal to the cost:

$$\sum_{i=1}^{n} v_i \geq \$100.$$

One way to decide whether or not to put up the light is to ask each person how much they value the light, with the understanding that their share of the cost will be proportional to their stated value, if the street light gets built. The trouble with this mechanism is that people will have the incentive to free ride: if each person thinks that the other people are willing to pay enough to provide the street light, why should he contribute? It can easily happen that the street light may not get provided even though it would have been efficient to do so.

The problem with this mechanism is that the declaration of how much a person values the good affects how much he or she has to pay, so there is a natural incentive to shade the true value. Let's try to devise a scheme that doesn't have this fault. Suppose that we decide in advance that if the street light is built, everyone will pay a predetermined amount towards its construction, c_i. Then each person will announce his or her value and we'll see whether the sums of the values exceed the cost. It is convenient to define the term net value, n_i, as the difference between person i's value, v_i, and his or her cost, c_i:

$$n_i = v_i - c_i.$$

Using this definition, we can think of each person announcing his or her net value, and then we simply sum up the net values to see if the total is positive.

The problem with *this* decision mechanism is that it contains an incentive to exaggerate the statements of the true values. If you value the street light only a little more than your cost, you might as well say that you value it a million dollars more—that won't affect what you have to pay, and it will help to ensure that the sum of the values exceeds the cost. Similarly, if you value the light less than your cost, you might as well say it is worth zero to you. Again, that doesn't affect your payment, and it helps ensure that the street light *won't* get built.

The problem with both of these schemes is that there is no cost for deviating from the truth. And without some incentive to tell the truth about your true value of the public good, there is an incentive to understate or overstate your true value.

Let's think about a way to correct this. The first important idea is that exaggeration doesn't matter if it doesn't affect the social decision. If the sum of the values of everyone else already exceeds the cost, it doesn't matter if you state an exaggerated value. Similarly, if the sum of the values is already less than the cost, it doesn't matter what value you state, as long as the sum of everyone's values remains below the cost.

The only individuals that matter are those who *change* the sum of the values to be greater or less than the cost of the public good. These are called the **pivotal agents**. There might be no pivotal agents, or everyone might be pivotal. The importance of the pivotal agents is that they are the ones who have to have the right incentives to tell the truth; the nonpivotal people don't really matter. Of course, anybody *might* be pivotal, so in ensuring that the pivotal people have the right incentives, we are making sure that everyone has the right incentives in deciding whether or not to tell the truth.

So let's consider the situation of a pivotal person, one who changes the social decision. When the social decision is changed, there will be some harm imposed on the other agents. If the other agents wanted the street light, and this particular pivotal person voted it down, then the other agents have been made worse off by this agent's decision. Similarly, if the other agents didn't want the street light, and this agent cast the dollar vote that provided it, the other agents have been made worse off.

How much worse off are they? Well, if the sum of the net values was positive without person j, say, and person j made the sum go negative, then person j has imposed a total harm of

$$H_j = \sum_{i \neq j} n_i > 0$$

on the other people. This is because the other people wanted the street light, and person j has ensured that they won't get it.

Similarly, if everyone else didn't want the light on the average, so that the sum of their net values was negative, and j made it go positive, then the harm that j imposed is given by

$$H_j = -\sum_{i \neq j} n_i > 0.$$

In order to give person j the right incentives to decide whether or not to be pivotal, we'll just impose this social cost on him. By doing this we make sure that he faces the true social cost of his decision—namely, the harm that he imposes on the other people. This is much like the Pigouvian taxes we considered in regulating externalities; in the case of public good provision, the kind of tax is known as a **Clarke tax**.

We can now state the Clarke mechanism for making public goods decisions:

1. Assign a cost to each agent, c_i, which the individual will have to pay if it is decided that the public good will be provided.

2. Have each agent state a net value s_i. (This may or may not be his or her *true* net value n_i.)

3. If the sum of the stated net values is positive, the public good will be provided; if it is negative, it won't be.

4. Each pivotal person will be required to pay a tax. If person j changes the decision from provision to no provision, the tax on that person will be

$$H_j = \sum_{i \neq j} s_i.$$

If person j changes the decision from no provision to provision, the tax will be

$$H_j = -\sum_{i \neq j} s_i.$$

The tax is *not* paid to the other agents—it is paid to the state. It doesn't matter where the money goes, as long as it doesn't influence anybody else's decision; all that matters is that it be paid by the pivotal people so that they face the proper incentives.[3]

Optional

32.10 How the Clarke Tax Works

Now that we've described the Clarke tax, let's prove that it really works: that each agent will find it optimal to reveal his or her true net value so that the "right" social decision will be made. We want to show that it is optimal for each person to report $s_i = n_i$, his or her true net value, regardless of what the others do.

In order to do this we need to compare the payoffs to person i in various possible situations. There are two possibilities for the provision of the public good: it will be provided if the sum of the net bids is positive, and not provided if the sum is negative. There are also two possibilities with respect to the Clarke tax: a person must pay the tax if he changed the decision, but he doesn't have to pay if he didn't change the decision. Thus there are four possibilities in all:

---

[3] For a more detailed discussion of the Clarke tax, see N. Tideman and G. Tullock, "A New and Superior Process for Making Social Choices," *Journal of Political Economy*, 84, December 1976, pp. 1145–59.

Case	*Payoff to i*	*Verbal description*	*Math description*
1.	n_i	Good is provided i doesn't change decision	$s_i + \sum_{j \neq i} s_j > 0$ $\sum_{j \neq i} s_j > 0$
2.	$n_i + \sum_{j \neq i} s_j$	Good is provided i changes decision	$s_i + \sum_{j \neq i} s_j > 0$ $\sum_{j \neq i} s_j < 0$
3.	0	Good is not provided i doesn't change decision	$s_i + \sum_{j \neq i} s_j < 0$ $\sum_{j \neq i} s_j < 0$
4.	$-\sum_{j \neq i} s_j$	Good is not provided i changes decision	$s_i + \sum_{j \neq i} s_j < 0$ $\sum_{j \neq i} s_j > 0$

Just to check our understanding, let's make sure that we understand case 1. Here the good is provided, which means the sum of *all* the bids has to be positive; and i doesn't change the decision, which means the sum of everyone else *except* for i must be positive. In this case, i gets a net payoff of n_i, his net value for the public good. You should go through each of the other cases to make sure that you understand the payoffs before you proceed.

Now that we have the payoffs, let us argue that honesty is the best policy—at least when faced with the Clarke tax. Put yourself in the place of person i and consider what you should do. The first observation is that the only cases that really matter are the cases where you change the social decision. For if your bid doesn't change the decision, then it doesn't matter what you bid!

Suppose that your true net value is positive, and consider making some bid, s_i, that switches the decision from not providing the good to providing the good; that is, making a bid that changes the outcome from case 3 to case 2. You will want to do this if your payoff in case 2 is greater than your payoff in case 3, which means that

$$n_i + \sum_{j \neq i} s_j > 0.$$

But then reporting $s_i = n_i$ will ensure that $s_i + \sum_{j \neq i} s_j > 0$, so you are certain to end up having the good provided.

On the other hand, suppose that your net value is negative—you don't want the public good provided—and consider making a bid that switches the outcome from provision (case 1) to no provision (case 4). You will want to do this if

$$-\sum_{j \neq i} s_j > n_i$$

or

$$0 > n_i + \sum_{j \neq i} s_j.$$

But if this condition holds, you can ensure that the good will not be provided by reporting $s_i = n_i$.

Thus if your true net value is large enough or small enough to make it in your interest to switch the social decision, reporting the truth will be sufficient to switch the social decision, which shows that truth telling is the optimal strategy in this environment.

EXAMPLE: An Example of the Clarke Tax

It is convenient to consider a numerical example to see just how the Clarke tax works. Suppose that we have three roommates who have to decide whether or not to acquire a TV that costs $300. They agree in advance that if they jointly decide to get the TV, then they will each contribute $100 towards the cost. Persons A and B are willing to pay $50 each to have the TV present, while person C is willing to pay $250. This information is summarized in Table 32.2.

Table 32.2

Example of the Clarke tax

Person	Cost share	Value	Net value	Clarke tax
A	100	50	−50	0
B	100	50	−50	0
C	100	250	150	100

Note that the TV provides a positive net value only to person C. Thus if the roommates voted on whether or not to purchase the TV, a majority would be opposed. Nevertheless, it is Pareto efficient to provide the TV since the *sum* of the values ($350) exceeds the cost ($300).

Let us consider how the Clarke tax works in this example. Consider person A. The sum of the net values *excluding* person A is 100, and person A's net value is −50. Thus person A is not pivotal. Since person A is made worse off in the net by the provision of the public good, he might have a temptation to exaggerate his bid downwards. In order to ensure that the public good is *not* provided, A would have to bid −100 or below. But if he did this, then A would become pivotal, and he would have to pay a Clarke tax equal to the amount the other two people bid: −50 + 150 = 100. Thus exaggerating his bid down saves him $50 in net value, but costs him $100 in taxes—leaving him with a net loss of $50.

The same thing goes for person B. What about person C? In the example, person C is pivotal—without his bid the public good would not be supplied, and with his bid the good will be supplied. He receives a net value from the public good of $150, but pays a $100 tax, leaving him with a total value of his actions of $50. Would it be worth it for him to increase his bid over his true value? No, because that doesn't change any of his payoffs. Would it be worth it to lower his bid? No, because that lowers the chance that the public good will be supplied and doesn't change the amount of tax he has to pay. Thus it is in the interest of each of the parties to truthfully reveal his or her net value of the public good.

32.11 Problems with the Clarke Tax

Despite the nice features of the Clarke tax it does have some problems. The first problem is that it only works with quasilinear preferences. This is because we can't have the amount that you have to pay influence your demand for the public good. It is important that there is a unique optimal level of the public good.

The second problem is that the Clarke tax doesn't really generate a Pareto efficient outcome. The level of the public good will be optimal, but the private consumption could be greater. This is because of the tax collection. Remember that in order to have the correct incentives, the pivotal people must actually pay some taxes that reflect the harm that they do to the other people. And these taxes cannot go to anybody else involved in the decision process, since that might affect their decisions. The taxes have to disappear from the system. And that's the problem—if the taxes actually have to be paid, the private consumption will end up being lower than it could be otherwise, and therefore be Pareto inefficient.

However, the taxes only have to be paid if someone is pivotal. If there are many people involved in the decision, the probability that any one person is pivotal may not be very large; thus the tax collections might typically be expected to be rather small.

The final problem concerns the equity and efficiency tradeoff inherent in the Clarke tax. Since the payment scheme must be fixed in advance, there will generally be situations where some people will be made worse off by providing the public good, even though the Pareto efficient *amount* of the public good will be provided. To say that it is Pareto preferred to provide the public good is to say that there is *some* payment scheme for which everyone is better off having the public good provided than not having it. But this doesn't mean that for an *arbitrary* payment scheme everyone will be better off. The Clarke tax ensures that if everyone *could* be better off having the good provided, then it will be provided. But that doesn't imply that everyone will actually be better off.

It would be nice if there were a scheme that not only determined whether or not to provide the public good, but also the Pareto efficient way to pay for it—that is, a payment plan that makes everyone better off. However, it does not appear that such a general plan is available.

Summary

1. Public goods are goods for which everyone must "consume" the same amount, such as national defense, air pollution, and so on.

2. If a public good is to be provided in some fixed amount or not provided at all, then a necessary and sufficient condition for provision to be Pareto efficient is that the sum of the willingness to pay (the reservation price) exceeds the cost of the public good.

3. If a public good can be provided in a variable amount, then the necessary condition for a given amount to be Pareto efficient is that the sum of the marginal willingnesses to pay (the marginal rates of substitution) should equal the marginal cost.

4. The free rider problem refers to the temptation of individuals to let others provide the public goods. In general, purely individualistic mechanisms will not generate the optimal amount of a public good because of the free rider problem.

5. Various collective decision methods have been proposed to determine the supply of a public good. Such methods include the command mechanism, voting, and the Clarke tax.

Review Questions

1. Consider an auction in which people will bid in turn, where each bid has to be at least a dollar higher than the previous bid, and the item is sold to the person who bids the highest. If the value of the good to person i is v_i, what will be the winning bid? Which person will get the good?

2. Consider a sealed bid auction among n people for some good. Let v_i be the value of the good to person i. Prove that if the good is sold to the

highest bidder at the *second* highest price bid, it will be in each player's interest to tell the truth.

3. Suppose that 10 people live on a street and each of them is willing to pay \$2 for each extra streetlight, regardless of the number of streetlights provided. If the cost of providing x streetlights is given by $c(x) = x^2$, what is the Pareto efficient number of streetlights to provide?

APPENDIX

Let's solve the maximization problem that determines the Pareto efficient allocations of the public good:

$$\max_{x_1, x_2, G} u_1(x_1, G)$$

$$\text{such that } u_2(x_2, G) = \overline{u}_2$$

$$x_1 + x_2 + c(G) = w_1 + w_2.$$

We set up the Lagrangian:

$$L = u_1(x_1, G) - \lambda[u_2(x_2, G) - \overline{u}_2] - \mu[x_1 + x_2 + c(G) - w_1 - w_2]$$

and differentiate with respect to x_1, x_2, and G to get

$$\frac{\partial L}{\partial x_1} = \frac{\partial u_1(x_1, G)}{\partial x_1} - \mu = 0$$

$$\frac{\partial L}{\partial x_2} = -\lambda \frac{\partial u_2(x_2, G)}{\partial x_2} - \mu = 0$$

$$\frac{\partial L}{\partial G} = \frac{\partial u_1(x_1, G)}{\partial G} - \lambda \frac{\partial u_2(x_2, G)}{\partial G} - \mu \frac{\partial c(G)}{\partial G} = 0.$$

If we divide the third equation by μ and rearrange, we get

$$\frac{1}{\mu} \frac{\partial u_1(x_1, G)}{\partial G} - \frac{\lambda}{\mu} \frac{\partial u_2(x_2, G)}{\partial G} = \frac{\partial c(G)}{\partial G}. \qquad (32.2)$$

Now solve the first equation for μ to get

$$\mu = \frac{\partial u_1(x_1, G)}{\partial x_1}$$

and solve the second equation for μ/λ to get

$$\frac{\mu}{\lambda} = -\frac{\partial u_2(x_2, G)}{\partial x_2}.$$

Substitute these two equations into equation (32.2) to find

$$\frac{\partial u_1(x_1, G)/\partial G}{\partial u_1(x_1, G)/\partial x_1} + \frac{\partial u_2(x_2, G)/\partial G}{\partial u_2(x_2, G)/\partial x_2} = \frac{\partial c(G)}{\partial G}$$

which is just

$$MRS_1 + MRS_2 = MC(G)$$

as given in the text.

MATHEMATICAL APPENDIX

In this Appendix we will provide a brief review of some of the mathematical concepts that are used in the text. This material is meant to serve as a reminder of the definitions of various terms used in the text. It is emphatically not a tutorial in mathematics. The definitions given will generally be the simplest, not the most rigorous.

A.1 Functions

A **function** is a rule that describes a relationship between numbers. For each number x, a function assigns a *unique* number y according to some rule. Thus a function can be indicated by describing the rule, as "take a number and square it," or "take a number and multiply it by 2," and so on. We write these particular functions as $y = x^2$, $y = 2x$. Functions are sometimes referred to as **transformations**.

Often we want to indicate that some variable y depends on some other variable x, but we don't know the specific algebraic relationship between the two variables. In this case we write $y = f(x)$, which should be interpreted as saying that the variable y depends on x according to the rule f.

Given a function $y = f(x)$, the number x is often called the **independent variable**, and the number y is often called the **dependent variable**. The idea is that x varies independently, but the value of y *depends* on the value of x.

Often some variable y depends on several other variables x_1, x_2, and so on, so we write $y = f(x_1, x_2)$ to indicate that both variables together determine the value of y.

A.2 Graphs

A **graph** of a function depicts the behavior of a function pictorially. Figure A.1 shows two graphs of functions. In mathematics the independent variable is usually depicted on the horizontal axis, and the dependent variable is depicted on the vertical axis. The graph then indicates the relationship between the independent and the dependent variables.

However, in economics it is common to graph functions with the independent variable on the vertical axis and the dependent variable on the horizontal axis. Demand functions, for example, are usually depicted with the price on the vertical axis and the amount demanded on the horizontal axis.

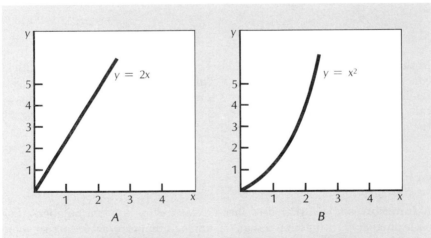

Figure A.1
Graphs of functions. Panel A denotes the graph of $y = 2x$ and panel B denotes the graph of $y = x^2$.

A.3 Properties of Functions

A **continuous** function is one that can be drawn without lifting a pencil from the paper: there are no jumps in a continuous function. A **smooth** function is on that has no "kinks" or corners. A **monotonic** function is one that is always increasing or always decreasing; a **positive monotonic** function is always increasing while **negative monotonic** function is always decreasing.

A.4 Inverse Functions

Recall that a function has the property that for each value of x there is a unique value of y associated with it and that a monotonic function is one that is always increasing or always decreasing. This implies that for a monotonic function there will be a unique value of x associated with each value of y.

We call the function that relates x to y in this way an **inverse function**. If you are given y as a function of x, you can calculate the inverse function just by solving for x as a function of y. If $y = 2x$, then the inverse function is $x = y/2$. If $y = x^2$, then there is no inverse function; given any y, both $x = +\sqrt{y}$ and $x = -\sqrt{y}$ have the property that their square is equal to y. Thus there is not a *unique* value of x associated with each value of y, as is required by the definition of a function.

A.5 Equations and Identities

An **equation** asks when a function is equal to some particular number. Examples of equations are

$$2x = 8$$
$$x^2 = 9$$
$$f(x) = 0.$$

The **solution** to an equation is a value of x that satisfies the equation. The first equation has a solution of $x = 4$. The second equation has two solutions, $x = 3$ and $x = -3$. The third equation is just a general equation. We don't know its solution until we know the actual rule that f stands for, but we can denote its solution by x^*. This simply means that x^* is a number such that $f(x^*) = 0$. We say that x^* **satisfies** the equation $f(x) = 0$.

An **identity** is a relationship between variables that holds for *all* values of the variables. Here are some examples of identities:

$$(x + y)^2 \equiv x^2 + 2xy + y^2$$
$$2(x + 1) \equiv 2x + 2.$$

The special symbol $\equiv$ means that the left-hand side and the right-hand side are equal for *all* values of the variables. An equation only holds for some values of the variables, whereas an identity is true for all values of the variables. Often an identity is true by the definition of the terms involved.

A.6 Linear Functions

A **linear function** is a function of the form

$$y = ax + b$$

where a and b are constants. Examples of linear functions are

$$y = 2x + 3$$
$$y = x - 99.$$

Strictly speaking, a function of the form $y = ax + b$ should be called an **affine function**, and only functions of the form $y = ax$ should be called linear functions. However, we will not insist on this distinction.

Linear functions can also be expressed implicitly in forms like $ax + by = c$. In such a case, we often like to solve for y as a function of x to convert this to the "standard" form:

$$y = \frac{c}{b} - \frac{a}{b}x.$$

A.7 Changes and Rates of Change

The notation Δx is read as "the change in x." It does *not* mean Δ times x. If x changes from x^* to x^{**}, then the change in x is just

$$\Delta x = x^{**} - x^*.$$

We can also write

$$x^{**} = x^* + \Delta x$$

to indicate that x^{**} is x^* plus a change in x.

Typically Δx will refer to a *small* change in x. We sometimes express this by saying that Δx represents a **marginal change.**

A **rate of change** is the ratio of two changes. If y is a function of x given by $y = f(x)$, then the rate of change of y with respect to x is denoted by

$$\frac{\Delta y}{\Delta x} = \frac{f(x + \Delta x) - f(x)}{\Delta x}.$$

The rate of change measures how y changes as x changes.

A linear function has the property that the rate of change of y with respect to x is constant. To prove this note that if $y = a + bx$, then

$$\frac{\Delta y}{\Delta x} = \frac{a + b(x + \Delta x) - a - bx}{\Delta x} = \frac{b\Delta x}{\Delta x} = b.$$

For nonlinear functions, the rate of change of the function will depend on the value of x. Consider, for example, the function $y = x^2$. For this function

$$\frac{\Delta y}{\Delta x} = \frac{(x + \Delta x)^2 - x^2}{\Delta x} = \frac{x^2 + 2x\Delta x + (\Delta x)^2 - x^2}{\Delta x} = 2x + \Delta x.$$

Here the rate of change from x to $x + \Delta x$ depends on the value of x and the size of the change, Δx. But if we consider very small changes in x, Δx will be nearly zero, so the rate of change of y with respect to x will be approximately $2x$.

A.8 Slopes and Intercepts

The rate of change of a function can be interpreted graphically as the **slope** of the function. In Figure A.2A we have depicted a linear function $y = -2x + 4$. The **vertical intercept** of this function is the value of y when $x = 0$, which is $y = 4$. The **horizontal intercept** is the value of x when $y = 0$, which is $x = 2$. The slope of the function is the rate of change of y as x changes. In this case, the slope of the function is -2.

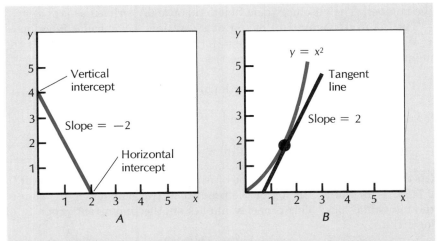

Slopes and intercepts. Panel A depicts the function $y = -2x + 4$ and panel B depicts the function $y = x^2$.

Figure
A.2

In general, if a linear function has the form $y = ax + b$, the vertical intercept will be $y^* = b$ and the horizontal intercept will be $x^* = -b/a$. If a linear function is expressed in the form

$$a_1 x_1 + a_2 x_2 = c$$

then the horizontal intercept will be the value of x_1 when $x_2 = 0$, which is $x_1^* = c/a_1$, and the vertical intercept will occur when $x_1 = 0$, which means $x_2^* = c/a_2$. The slope of this function is $-a_1/a_2$.

A nonlinear function has the property that its slope changes as x changes. A **tangent** to a function at some point x is a linear function that has the same slope. In Figure A.2B we have depicted the function x^2 and the tangent line at $x = 1$.

If y increases whenever x increases then Δy will always have the same sign as Δx, so that the slope of the function will be positive. If, on the other hand y decreases when x increases, or y increases when x decreases, Δy and Δx will have opposite signs so that the slope of the function will be negative.

A.9 Absolute Values and Logarithms

The **absolute value** of a number is a function $f(x)$ defined by the following rule:

$$f(x) = \begin{cases} x & \text{if } x \geq 0 \\ -x & \text{if } x < 0. \end{cases}$$

Thus the absolute value of a number can be found by dropping the sign of the number. The absolute value function is usually written as $|x|$.

The (natural) **logarithm** or **log** of x describes a particular function of x, which we write as $y = \ln x$ or $y = \ln(x)$. The logarithm function is the unique function that has the properties

$$\ln(xy) = \ln(x) + \ln(y)$$

for all positive numbers x and y and

$$\ln(e) = 1.$$

(In this last equation, e is the base of natural logarithms which is equal to $2.7183\ldots$) In words, the log of the product of two numbers is the sum of the individual logs. This property implies another important property of logarithms:

$$\ln(x^y) = y\ln(x)$$

which says that the log of x raised to the power y is equal to y times the log of x.

A.10 Derivatives

The derivative of a function $y = f(x)$ is defined to be

$$\frac{df(x)}{dx} = \lim_{\Delta x \to 0} \frac{f(x + \Delta x) - f(x)}{\Delta x}.$$

In words, the derivative is limit of the rate of change of y with respect to x as the change in x goes to zero. The derivative gives precise meaning to the phrase "the rate of change of y with respect to x for small changes in x." The derivative of $f(x)$ with respect to x is also denoted by $f'(x)$.

We have already seen that the rate of change of a linear function $y = ax + b$ is constant. Thus for this linear function

$$\frac{df(x)}{dx} = a.$$

For a nonlinear function the rate of change of y with respect to x will usually depend on x. We saw that in the case of $f(x) = x^2$, we had $\Delta y / \Delta x = 2x + \Delta x$. Applying the definition of the derivative

$$\frac{df(x)}{dx} = \lim_{\Delta x \to 0} 2x + \Delta x = 2x.$$

Thus the derivative of x^2 with respect to x is $2x$.

It can be shown by more advanced methods that if $y = \ln x$, then

$$\frac{df(x)}{dx} = \frac{1}{x}.$$

A.11 Second Derivatives

The **second derivative** of a function is the derivative of the derivative of that function. If $y = f(x)$, the second derivative of $f(x)$ with respect to x is written as $d^2 f(x)/dx^2$ or $f''(x)$. We know that

$$\frac{d(2x)}{dx} = 2$$

$$\frac{d(x^2)}{dx} = 2x.$$

Thus

$$\frac{d^2(2x)}{dx^2} = \frac{d(2)}{dx} = 0$$

$$\frac{d^2(x^2)}{dx^2} = \frac{d(2x)}{dx} = 2.$$

The second derivative measures the curvature of a function. A function with a negative second derivative at some point is concave near that point; its slope is decreasing. A function with a positive second derivative at a point is convex near that point; its slope is increasing. A function with a zero second derivative at a point is flat near that point.

A.12 The Product Rule and the Chain Rule

Suppose that $g(x)$ and $h(x)$ are both functions of x. We can define the function $f(x)$ that represents their product by $f(x) = g(x)h(x)$. Then the derivative of $f(x)$ is given by

$$\frac{df(x)}{dx} = g(x)\frac{dh(x)}{dx} + h(x)\frac{dg(x)}{dx}.$$

Given two functions $y = g(x)$ and $z = h(y)$, the **composite** function is

$$f(x) = h(g(x)).$$

For example, if $g(x) = x^2$ and $h(y) = 2y + 3$, then the composite function is

$$f(x) = 2x^2 + 3.$$

The **chain rule** says that the derivative of a composite function, $f(x)$, with respect to x is given by

$$\frac{df(x)}{dx} = \frac{dh(y)}{dy}\frac{dg(x)}{dx}.$$

In our example, $dh(y)/dy = 2$ and $dg(x)/dx = 2x$, so the chain rule says that $df(x)/dx = 2 \times 2x = 4x$. Direct calculation verifies that this is the derivative of the function $f(x) = 2x^2 + 3$.

A.13 Partial Derivatives

Suppose that y depends on both x_1 and x_2, so that $y = f(x_1, x_2)$. Then the **partial derivative** of $f(x_1, x_2)$ with respect to x_1 is defined by

$$\frac{\partial f(x_1, x_2)}{\partial x_1} = \lim_{\Delta x_1 \to 0} \frac{f(x_1 + \Delta x_1, x_2) - f(x_1, x_2)}{\Delta x_1}.$$

The partial derivative of $f(x_1, x_2)$ with respect to x_1 is just the derivative of the function with respect to x_1, *holding x_2 fixed.* Similarly, the partial derivative with respect to x_2 is

$$\frac{\partial f(x_1, x_2)}{\partial x_2} = \lim_{\Delta x_2 \to 0} \frac{f(x_1, x_2 + \Delta x_2) - f(x_1, x_2)}{\Delta x_2}.$$

Partial derivatives have exactly the same properties as ordinary derivatives; only the name has been changed to protect the innocent (that is, people who haven't seen the ∂ symbol).

In particular, partial derivatives obey the chain rule, but with an extra twist. Suppose that x_1 and x_2 both depend on some variable t, and we define the function $g(t)$ by

$$g(t) = f(x_1(t), x_2(t)).$$

Then the derivative of $g(t)$ with respect to t is given by

$$\frac{dg(t)}{dt} = \frac{\partial f(x_1, x_2)}{\partial x_1} \frac{dx_1(t)}{dt} + \frac{\partial f(x_1, x_2)}{\partial x_2} \frac{dx_2(t)}{dt}.$$

When t changes, it affects both $x_1(t)$ and $x_2(t)$. Therefore we need to calculate the derivative of $f(x_1, x_2)$ with respect to each of those changes.

A.14 Optimization

If $y = f(x)$, then $f(x)$ achieves a **maximum** at x^* if $f(x^*) \geq f(x)$ for all x. It can be shown that if $f(x)$ is a smooth function that achieves its maximum at x^*, then

$$\frac{df(x^*)}{dx} = 0$$

$$\frac{d^2 f(x^*)}{dx^2} \leq 0.$$

These expressions are referred to as the **first-order condition** and the **second-order condition** for a maximum. The first-order condition says that the function is flat at x^*, while the second-order condition says that the function is concave near x^*. Clearly both of these properties have to hold if x^* is indeed a maximum.

We say that $f(x)$ achieves its **minimum** value at x^* if $f(x^*) \leq f(x)$ for all x. If $f(x)$ is a smooth function that achieves its minimum at x^* then

$$\frac{df(x^*)}{dx} = 0$$

$$\frac{d^2 f(x^*)}{dx^2} \geq 0.$$

The first-order condition again says that the function is flat at x^*, while the second-order condition now says that the function is convex near x^*.

If $y = f(x_1, x_2)$ is a smooth function that achieves its maximum or minimum at some point (x_1, x_2), then we must satisfy

$$\frac{\partial f(x_1^*, x_2^*)}{\partial x_1} = 0$$

$$\frac{\partial f(x_1^*, x_2^*)}{\partial x_2} = 0.$$

These are referred to as the **first-order conditions**. There are also second-order conditions for this problem, but they are more difficult to describe.

A.15 Constrained Optimization

Often we want to consider the maximum or minimum of some function over some restricted values of (x_1, x_2). The notation

$$\max_{x_1, x_2} f(x_1, x_2)$$

$$\text{such that } g(x_1, x_2) = c.$$

means

find x_1^* and x_2^* such that $f(x_1^*, x_2^*) \geq f(x_1, x_2)$ for all values of x_1 and x_2 that satisfy the equation $g(x_1, x_2) = c$.

The function $f(x_1, x_2)$ is called the **objective function** and the equation $g(x_1, x_2) = c$ is called the **constraint**. Methods for solving this kind of constrained maximization problem are described in the Appendix to Chapter 5.

ANSWERS

1 The Market

1.1. It would be constant at \$500 for 25 apartments and then drop to \$200.

1.2. In the first case, \$500, and in the second case, \$200. In the third case, the equilibrium price would be any price between \$200 and \$500.

1.3. Because if we want to rent one more apartment, we have to offer a lower price. The number of people who have reservation prices greater than p must always increase as p decreases.

1.4. The price of apartments in the inner ring would go up since demand for apartments would not change but supply would decrease.

1.5. The price of apartments in the inner ring would rise.

1.6. A tax would undoubtedly reduce the number of apartments supplied in the long run.

1.7. Revenue would be $100p - 2p^2$. Differentiating this and setting the result equal to zero yields $p^* = 25$. Substitute into the demand curve to find $D(25) = 100 - 2 \times 25 = 50$.

1.8. He would set a price of 25 and rent 50 apartments. In the second case he would rent all 40 apartments at the maximum price the market would bear. This would be given by the solution to $D(p) = 100 - 2p = 40$, which is $p^* = 30$.

1.9. Everyone who had a reservation price higher than the equilibrium price in the competitive market, so that the final outcome would be Pareto efficient. (Of course in the long run there would probably be fewer new apartments built, which would lead to another kind of inefficiency.)

2 Budget Constraint

2.1. The new budget set is given by $2p_1 x_1 + 8p_2 x_2 = 4m$.

2.2. The vertical intercept (x_2 axis) decreases and the horizontal intercept (x_1 axis) stays the same. Thus the budget line becomes flatter.

2.3. Flatter. The slope is $-2p_1/3p_2$.

2.4. A good whose price has been set to 1; all other goods' prices are measured relative to the numeraire good's price.

2.5. A tax of 8 cents a gallon.

2.6. $(p_1 + t)x_1 + (p_2 - s)x_2 = m - u$.

2.7. Yes, since all of the bundles the consumer could afford before are affordable at the new prices and income.

3 Preferences

3.1. No. It might be that the consumer was indifferent between the two bundles. All we are justified in concluding is that $(x_1, x_2) \succeq (y_1, y_2)$.

3.2. Yes to both.

3.3. It is transitive, but it is not complete—two people might be the same height. It is not reflexive since it is false that a person is strictly taller than himself.

3.4. It is transitive, but not complete. What if A were bigger but slower than B? Which one would he prefer?

3.5. Yes. An indifference curve can cross itself, it just can't cross another distinct indifference curve.

3.6. No, because there are bundles on the indifference curve that have strictly more of both goods than other bundles on the (alleged) indifference curve.

3.7. A negative slope. If you give the consumer more anchovies, you've made him worse off, so you have to take away some pepperoni to get him back on his indifference curve.

3.8. Because the consumer weakly prefers the weighted average of two bundles to either bundle.

3.9. If you give up 1 $5 bill, how many $1 bills do you need to compensate you? Five one dollar bills will do nicely.

3.10. Zero—if you take away some of good 1, the consumer needs zero units of good 2 to compensate him for his loss.

3.11. Anchovies and peanut butter, scotch and Kool Aid, and other similar repulsive combinations.

4 Utility

4.1. The function $f(u) = u^2$ is a monotonic transformation for positive u, but not for negative u.

4.2. (1) Yes. (2) No (works for v positive). (3) No (works for v negative). (4) Yes (only defined for v positive). (5) Yes. (6) No. (7) Yes. (8) No.

4.3. Suppose that the diagonal intersected a given indifference curve at two points, say (x, x) and (y, y). Then either $x > y$ or $y > x$, which means that one of the bundles has more of *both* goods. But if preferences are monotonic, then one of the bundles would have to be preferred to the other.

4.4. Both represent perfect substitutes.

4.5. Quasilinear preferences. Yes.

4.6. The utility function represents Cobb-Douglas preferences. No. Yes.

4.7. Because the MRS is measured *along* an indifference curve, and utility remains constant along an indifference curve.

5 Choice

5.1. $x_2 = 0$ when $p_2 > p_1$, $x_2 = m/p_2$ when $p_2 < p_1$, and anything between 0 and m/p_2 when $p_1 = p_2$.

5.2. The optimal choices will be $x_1 = m/p_1$ and $x_2 = 0$ if $p_1/p_2 < b$, $x_1 = 0$ and $x_2 = m/p_2$ if $p_1/p_2 > b$, and any amount on the budget line if $p_1/p_2 = b$.

5.3. Let z be the number of cups of coffee the consumer buys. Then we know that $2z$ is the number of teaspoons of sugar he or she buys. We must satisfy the budget constraint

$$2p_1 z + p_2 z = m.$$

Solving for z we have

$$z = \frac{m}{2p_1 + p_2}.$$

5.4. We know that you'll either consume all ice cream or all olives. Thus the two choices for the optimal consumption bundles will be $x_1 = m/p_1$, $x_2 = 0$, or $x_1 = 0$, $x_2 = m/p_2$.

5.5. This is a Cobb-Douglas utility function, so she will spend $4/(1 + 4) = 4/5$ of her income on good 2.

5.6. For kinked preferences, such as perfect complements, where the change in price doesn't induce any change in demand.

6 Demand

6.1. No. If her income increases, and she spends it all, she must be purchasing more of at least one good.

6.2. The utility function for perfect substitutes is $u(x_1, x_2) = x_1 + x_2$. Thus if $u(x_1, x_2) > u(y_1, y_2)$, we have $x_1 + x_2 > y_1 + y_2$. It follows that $tx_1 + tx_2 > ty_1 + ty_2$, so that $u(tx_1, tx_2) > u(ty_1, ty_2)$.

6.3. The Cobb-Douglas utility function has the property that

$$u(tx_1, tx_2) = (tx_1)^a (tx_2)^{1-a} = t^a t^{1-a} x_1^a x_2^{1-a} = t x_1^a x_2^{1-a} = tu(x_1, x_2).$$

Thus if $u(x_1, x_2) > u(y_1, y_2)$ we know that $u(tx_1, tx_2) > u(ty_1, ty_2)$, so that Cobb-Douglas preferences are indeed homothetic.

6.4. The demand curve.

6.5. It looks just like the case of perfect substitutes.

6.6. We know that $x_1 = m/(p_1 + p_2)$. Solving for p_1 as a function of the other variables, we have

$$p_1 = \frac{m}{x_1} - p_2.$$

6.7. The answers are 1 and 0, respectively.

6.8. $1.133\ldots$

6.9. No—it violates the fact that the weighted sum of the price elasticities must be negative.

7 Revealed Preference

7.1. No. This consumer violates the Weak Axiom of Revealed Preference since when he bought (x_1, x_2) he could have bought (y_1, y_2) and vice versa. In symbols:

$$p_1 x_1 + p_2 x_2 = 1 \times 1 + 2 \times 2 = 5 > 4 = 1 \times 2 + 2 \times 1 = p_1 y_1 + p_2 y_2$$

and

$$q_1 y_1 + q_2 y_2 = 2 \times 2 + 1 \times 1 = 5 > 4 = 2 \times 1 + 1 \times 2 = q_1 x_1 + q_2 x_2.$$

7.2. Yes. No violations of WARP are present, since the y-bundle is not affordable when the x-bundle was purchased and vice versa.

7.3. Since the y-bundle was more expensive than the x-bundle when the x-bundle was purchased and vice versa, there is no way to tell which bundle is preferred.

7.4. If both prices changed by the same amount. Then the base year bundle would still be optimal.

7.5. Perfect complements.

8 Slutsky Equation

8.1. Yes.

8.2. Applying the formula in the text: $\epsilon_{11}^s = \epsilon_{11} + s_1\eta = -.2 + .05 = -.15$.

8.3. Then the income effect would cancel out. All that would be left would be the pure substitution effect, which would automatically be negative.

8.4. They are receiving tx' in revenues and paying out tx, so they are losing money.

8.5. Since their old consumption is affordable, the consumers would have to be at least as well-off. This happens because the government is giving them back *more* money than they are losing due to the higher price of gasoline.

9 Buying and Selling

9.1. Her gross demands are $(9, 1)$.

9.2. The bundle $(y_1, y_2) = (3, 5)$ costs more than the bundle $(4, 4)$ at the current prices. The consumer will not necessarily prefer consuming this bundle, but would certainly prefer to own it, since she could sell it and purchase a bundle that she would prefer.

9.3. Sure. It depends on whether she was a net buyer or a net seller of the good that became more expensive.

9.4. Yes, but only if the U.S. switched to being a net exporter of oil.

10 Labor Supply

10.1. The new budget line would shift outward and remain parallel to the old one, since the increase in the number of hours in the day is a pure endowment effect.

10.2. The slope will be positive.

10.3. Leisure must be a normal good over some range.

11 Intertemporal Choice

11.1. According to Table 11.1, a dollar 20 years from now is worth 3 cents today at a 15 percent interest rate. Thus a million dollars is worth $.03 \times 1,000,000 = \$30,000$ today.

11.2. The slope of the intertemporal budget constraint is equal to $-(1+r)$. Thus as r increases the slope becomes more negative (steeper).

11.3. If goods are perfect substitutes then consumers will only purchase the cheaper good. In the case of intertemporal food purchases, this implies that consumers only buy food in one period, which may not be very realistic.

11.4. In order to remain a lender after the change in interest rates, the consumer must be choosing a point that he could have chosen under the old interest rates, but decided not to. Thus the consumer must be worse off. If the consumer becomes a borrower after the change, then he is choosing a previously unavailable point that cannot be compared to the initial point (since the initial point is no longer available under the new budget constraint), and therefore the change in the consumer's welfare is unknown.

11.5. At an interest rate of 10%, the present value of $100 is $90.91. At a rate of 5% the present value is $95.24.

12 Asset Markets

12.1. Asset A must be selling for $11/(1 + .10) = \$10$.

12.2. The rate of return is equal to $(10,000 + 10,000)/100,000 = 20\%$.

12.3. We know that the rate of return on the nontaxable bonds, r, must be such that $(1 - t)r_t = r$, therefore $(1 - .40).10 = .06 = r$.

12.4. The price today must be $40/(1 + .10)^{10} = \$15.42$.

13 Uncertainty

13.1. Functions (a) and (b) have the expected utility property (they are affine transformations of the functions discussed in the chapter), while (c) does not.

13.2. Since they are risk averse, they prefer the expected value of the gamble, $325, to the gamble itself, and therefore they would take the single payment.

13.3. If the payment is $320 the decision will depend on the form of the utility function; we can't say anything in general.

13.4. Your picture should show a function that is initially convex, but then becomes concave.

13.5. In order to effectively self-insure the risks must be independent. However, this does not hold in the case of flood damage. If one house in the neighborhood is damaged by a flood it is likely that all of the houses will be damaged.

14 Risky Assets

14.1. To achieve a variance of 2% you will need to invest $x = \sigma_x/\sigma_m = 2/3$ of your wealth in the risky asset. This will result in a rate of return equal to $(2/3).09 + (1 - 2/3).06 = 8\%$.

14.2. The price of risk is equal to $(r_m - r_f)/\sigma_m = (9 - 6)/3 = 1$. That is, for every additional percent of standard deviation you can gain 1% of return.

14.3. According to the CAPM pricing equation, the stock should offer an expected rate of return of $r_f + \beta(r_m - r_f) = .05 + 1.5(.10 - .05) = .125$ or 12.5%. The stock should be selling for its expected present value, which is equal to $100/1.125 = \$88.89$.

15 Consumer's Surplus

15.1. By definition, their level of money metric utility for a bundle of goods is that amount of money that will make them indifferent between the bundle and the money.

15.2. In order to have the same utility as the bundle (x_1, x_2), the consumer will choose to consume the bundle $(x_1 + x_2, 0)$ or $(0, x_1 + x_2)$, whichever is cheaper. The cost of doing this will be $m(p_1, p_2, x_1, x_2) = \min\{p_1, p_2\}(x_1 + x_2)$.

15.3. We want to compute the area under the demand curve to the left of the quantity 6. Break this up into the area of a triangle with base of 6 and height of 6 and a rectangle with base 6 and height 4. Applying the formulas from high school geometry, the triangle has area 18 and the rectangle area 24. Thus the total consumer's surplus is 42.

15.4. When the price is 4, the net consumer's surplus is given by the area of a triangle with base of 6 and height of 6; i.e., the net consumer's surplus is 18. When the price is 6, the triangle has a base of 4 and a height of 4, giving an area of 8. Thus the price change has reduced consumer's surplus by $10.

16 Market Demand

16.1. The inverse demand curve is $P(q) = 200 - 2q$.

16.2. Set $u(0, m) = u(1, m - p_1)$ to find: $m = 1 + m - p_1$, or $p_1 = 1$.

16.3. Set $u(0, m) = u(1, m - p_1)$ to find: $m = a + m - p_1$, or $p_1 = a$.

16.4. The decision about whether to consume the drug at all could well be price sensitive so the adjustment of market demand on the extensive margin would contribute to the elasticity of the market demand.

16.5. Revenue is $R(p) = 12p - 2p^2$, which is maximized at $p = 3$.

16.6. Revenue is $pD(p) = 100$, regardless of the price, so all prices maximize revenue.

17 Equilibrium

17.1. The entire subsidy gets passed along to the consumers if the supply curve is flat, but the subsidy is totally received by the producers when the supply curve is vertical.

17.2. The consumer.

17.3. In this case the demand curve for red pencils is horizontal at the price p_b, since that is the most that they would be willing to pay for a red pencil. Thus, if a tax is imposed on blue pencils, consumers will end up paying p_b for them, so the entire amount of the tax will end up being borne by the producers (if any red pencils are sold at all—it could be that the tax would induce the producer to get out the red pencil business).

17.4. Here the supply curve of foreign oil is flat at $25. Thus the price to the consumers must rise by the $5 amount of the tax, so that the net price to the consumers becomes $30. Since foreign oil and domestic oil are perfect substitutes as far as the consumers are concerned, the domestic producers will sell their oil for $30 as well and get a windfall gain of $5 per barrel.

17.5. Zero. The deadweight loss measures the value of lost output. Since the same amount is supplied before and after the tax, there is no deadweight loss. Put another way: the suppliers are paying the entire amount of the tax, and everything they pay goes to the government. The amount that the suppliers would pay to avoid the tax is simply the tax revenue the government receives, so there is no excess burden of the tax.

17.6. Zero revenue.

17.7. It raises negative revenue, since in this case we have a net subsidy.

18 Technology

18.1. Increasing returns to scale.

18.2. Constant returns to scale.

18.3. If $a+b = 1$ we have constant returns to scale, $a+b < 1$ gives decreasing returns to scale, and $a + b > 1$ gives increasing returns to scale.

18.4. $4 \times 3 = 12$ units.

18.5. True.

18.6. Yes.

19 Profit Maximization

19.1. Profits will decrease.

19.2. Profit would increase, since output would go up more than the cost of the inputs.

19.3. If the firm really had decreasing returns to scale, dividing the scale of all inputs by 2 would produce more than half as much output. Thus the subdivided firm would make more profits than the big firm. This is one argument why having everywhere decreasing returns to scale is implausible.

19.4. The gardener has ignored opportunity costs. In order to accurately account for the true costs, the gardener must include the cost of her own time used in the production of the crop, even if no explicit wage was paid.

19.5. Not in general. For example, consider the case of uncertainty.

19.6. Increase.

19.7. The use of x_1 does not change, and profits will increase.

19.8. May not.

20 Cost Minimization

20.1. Since profit is equal to total revenue minus total costs, if a firm is not minimizing costs then there exists a way for the firm to increase profits; however, this contradicts the fact that the firm is a profit maximizer.

20.2. Increase the use of input 1.

20.3. Since the inputs are identically priced perfect substitutes the firm will be indifferent between which of the inputs it uses. Thus the firm will use any amounts of the two inputs such that $x_1 + x_2 = y$.

20.4. The price of the input that is used more must have fallen.

20.5. It implies that $\sum_{i=1}^{n} \Delta w_i \Delta x_i \leq 0$, where $\Delta w_i = w_i^t - w_i^s$ and $\Delta x_i = x_i^t - x_i^s$.

21 Cost Curves

21.1. True, true, false.

21.2. By simultaneously producing more output at the second plant and reducing production at the first plant the firm can reduce costs.

21.3. False.

22 Firm Supply

22.1. The inverse supply curve is $p = 20y$, so the supply curve is $y = p/20$.

22.2. Set $AC = MC$ to find $10y + 1000/y = 20y$. Solve to get $y^* = 10$.

22.3. Solve for p to get $P_s(y) = (y - 100)/20$.

22.4. At 10 the supply is 40 and at 20 the supply is 80. The producer's surplus is composed of a rectangle of area 10×40 plus a triangle of area $\frac{1}{2} \times 10 \times 40$, which gives a total change in producer's surplus of 600. This is the same as the change in profits, since the fixed costs don't change.

22.5. The supply curve is given by $y = p/2$ for all $p \geq 2$, and $y = 0$ for all $p \leq 2$. At $p = 2$ the firm is indifferent between supplying 1 unit of output or not supplying it.

22.6. Mostly technical (in more advanced models this could be market), market, could be either market or technical, technical.

22.7. That all firms in the industry take the market price as given.

22.8. The market price. A profit maximizing firm will set its output such that the marginal cost of producing the last unit of output is equal to its marginal revenue, which in the case of pure competition is equal to the market price.

22.9. The firm should produce zero output (with or without fixed costs).

22.10. In the short-run, if the market price is greater than the average variable cost, a firm should produce some output even though it is losing money. This is true because the firm would have lost more had it not produced since it must still pay fixed costs. However, in the long-run there are no fixed costs, and therefore any firm that is losing money can produce zero output and lose a maximum of zero dollars.

22.11. The market price must be equal to the marginal cost of production for all firms in the industry.

23 Industry Supply

23.1. The inverse supply curves are $P_1(y_1) = 10 + y_1$ and $P_2(y_2) = 15 + y_2$. When the price is below 10 neither firm supplies output. When the price is 15 firm 2 will enter the market, and at any price above 15, both firms are in the market. Thus the kink occurs at a price of 15.

23.2. In the short run, the consumers pay the entire amount of the tax. In the long run it is paid by the producers.

23.3. False. A better statement would be: convenience stores can charge high prices because they are near the campus. Because of the high prices the stores are able to charge, the landowners can in turn charge high rents for the use of the convenient location.

23.4. True.

23.5. The profits or losses of the firms that are currently operating in the industry.

23.6. Flatter.

23.7. No, it does not violate the model. In accounting for the costs we failed to value the rent on the license.

24 Markets

24.1. The marginal cost of a barrel of foreign oil to the refiner would be $15, but the cost to the U.S. was $20. Thus the net subsidy was $5.

24.2. If the government sells the ivory, it will depress the price of ivory and thereby reduce the incentives for the poachers to kill more elephants.

24.3. The two policies will have the same effect, since each one reduces the revenues received by the firms by a factor of one-half.

25 Monopoly

25.1. No. A profit maximizing monopolist would never operate where the demand for his product was inelastic.

25.2. First solve for the inverse demand curve to get $p(y) = 50 - y/2$. Thus the marginal revenue is given by $MR(y) = 50 - y$. Set this equal to marginal cost of 2, and solve to get $y = 48$. To determine the price, substitute into the inverse demand function, $p(48) = 50 - 48/2 = 26$.

25.3. The demand curve has a constant elasticity of -3. Using the formula $p[1 + 1/\epsilon] = MC$, we substitute to get $p[1 - 1/3] = 2$. Solving, we get $p = 3$. Substitute back into the demand function to get the quantity produced: $D(3) = 10 \times 3^{-3}$.

25.4. The demand curve has constant elasticity of 1. Thus marginal revenue is zero for all levels of output. Hence it can never be equal to marginal cost.

25.5. For a linear demand curve the price rises by $1/2$ the change in cost. In this case, the answer is $3.

25.6. In this case $p = kMC$, where $k = 1/(1 - 1/3) = 3/2$. Thus the price rises by $9.

25.7. Price will be two times marginal cost.

25.8. A subsidy of 50 percent, so the marginal costs facing the monopolist are $1/2$ the actual marginal costs. This will ensure that price equals marginal cost at the monopolist's choice of output.

25.9. $p_i = \epsilon_i c / (1 + \epsilon_i)$ for $i = 1, 2$.

25.10. A monopolist operates where $p(y) + y\Delta p / \Delta y = MC(y)$. Rearranging, we have $p(y) = MC(y) - y\Delta p / \Delta y$. Since demand curves have a negative slope, we know that $\Delta p / \Delta y < 0$ which proves that $p(y) > MC(y)$.

25.11. False. Imposing a tax on a monopolist may cause the market price to rise more than, the same as, or less than the amount of the tax.

25.12. A number of problems arise, including: determining the true marginal costs for the firm, making sure that all customers will be served, and ensuring that the monopolist will not make a loss at the new price and output level.

25.13. Some appropriate conditions are: large fixed costs and small marginal costs, large minimum efficient scale relative to the market, ease of collusion, etc.

25.14. Yes, if it is allowed to perfectly price discriminate.

26 Oligopoly

26.1. In equilibrium each firm will produce $(a - c)/3b$ so the total industry output is $2(a - c)/3b$.

26.2. Nothing. Since all firms have the same marginal cost, it doesn't matter which of them produces the output.

26.3. No, because one of the choices open to the Stackelberg leader is to choose the level of output it would have in the Cournot equilibrium. So it always has to be able to do at least this well.

26.4. We know from the text that we must have $p[1 - 1/n\epsilon] = MC$. Since $MC > 0$, and $p > 0$, we must have $1 - 1/n\epsilon > 0$. Rearranging this inequality gives the result.

26.5. Just switch the labels on the stable reaction curve diagram depicted in the text.

26.6. In general, no. In Table 26.1 we see that only in the Bertrand solution does the price equal the marginal cost.

27 Game Theory

27.1. Yes and no. A player prefers to play a dominant strategy regardless of the strategy of the opponent (even if the opponent plays her own dominant strategy). Thus, if all of the players are using dominant strategies then it is the case that they are all playing a strategy that is optimal given the strategy of their opponents, and therefore a Nash equilibrium exists. However, not all Nash equilibria are dominant strategy equilibria; for example, see Table 27.2.

27.2. Not necessarily. We know that your Nash equilibrium strategy is the best thing for you to do as long as your opponent is playing his Nash equilibrium strategy, but if he is not then perhaps there is a better strategy for you to pursue.

27.3. Formally, if the prisoners are allowed to retaliate the payoffs in the game may change. This could result in a Pareto efficient outcome for the game (for example, think of the case where the prisoners both agree that they will kill anyone who confesses, and assume death has a very low utility).

27.4. The dominant Nash equilibrium strategy is to defect in every round. This strategy is derived via the same backwards induction process that was used to derive the finite 10-round case. The experimental evidence using much smaller time periods seems to indicate that players rarely use this strategy.

27.5. The equilibrium has player B choosing left and player A choosing top. Player B prefers to move first since that results in a payoff of 9 verses a payoff of 1. (Note, however, that moving first is not always advantageous in a sequential game. Can you think of an example?)

28 Exchange

28.1. Yes. For example, consider the allocation where one person has everything. Then the other person is worse off at this allocation than he would be at an allocation where he had something.

28.2. No. For this would mean that at the allegedly Pareto efficient allocation there is some way to make everyone better off, contradicting the assumption of Pareto efficiency.

28.3. If we know the contract curve then any trading should end up somewhere on the curve; however, we don't know where.

28.4. Yes, but not without making someone else worse off.

28.5. The value of excess demand in the remaining two markets must sum to zero.

28.6. Yes, simply use the market mechanism to trade to a competitive equilibrium.

29 Production

29.1. Giving up 1 coconut frees up $6 worth of resources that could be used to produce 2 pounds (equals $6 worth) of fish.

29.2. A higher wage would produce a steeper isoprofit line, implying that the profit maximizing level for the firm would occur at a point to the left of the current equilibrium, entailing a lower level of labor demand. However, under this new budget constraint Robinson will want to supply more than the required level of labor (why?) and therefore the labor market will not be in equilibrium.

29.3. Given a few assumptions, an economy that is in competitive equilibrium is Pareto efficient. It is generally recognized that this is a good thing for a society since it implies that there are no opportunities to make any individual in the economy better off without hurting someone else. However, it may be the case that the society would prefer a different distribution of welfare; that is, it may be that society prefers making one group better off at the expense of another group.

29.4. He should produce more fish. His marginal rate of substitution indicates that he is willing to give up two coconuts for an additional fish. The marginal rate of transformation implies that he only has to give up one coconut to get an additional fish. Therefore, by giving up a single coconut (even though he would have been willing to give up two) he can have an additional fish.

29.5. Both would have to work 9 hours per day. If they both work for 6 hours per day (Robinson producing coconuts, and Friday catching fish) and give half of their total production to the other, they can produce the same output. The reduction in the hours of work from 9 to 6 hours per day is due to rearranging production based on each individual's comparative advantage.

30 Welfare

30.1. The major shortcoming is that there are many allocations that cannot be compared—there is no way to decide between any two Pareto efficient allocations.

30.2. It would have the form: $W(u_1, \ldots, u_n) = \max\{u_1, \ldots, u_n\}$.

30.3. Since the Nietzschian welfare function cares only about the best off individual, welfare maxima for this allocation would typically involve one person getting everything.

30.4. Suppose that this is not the case. Then each individual envies someone else. Let's construct a list of who envies whom. Person A envies someone—call him person B. Person B in turn envies someone—say person C. And so on. But eventually we will find someone who envies someone who came earlier in the list. Suppose the cycle is "C envies D envies E envies C." Then consider the following swap: C gets what D has, D gets what E has, and E gets what C has. Each person in the cycle gets a bundle that he prefers, and thus each person is made better off. But then the original allocation couldn't have been Pareto efficient!

30.5. First vote between **x** and **z**, and then vote between the winner (**z**) and **y**. First pair **x** and **y**, and then vote between the winner (**x**) and **z**. The fact that the social preferences are intransitive is responsible for this agenda-setting power.

31 Externalities

31.1. Usually, efficiency problems can be eliminated by the delineation of property rights. However, when we impose property rights we are also imposing an endowment, which may have important distributional consequences.

31.2. False.

31.3. Come on, your roommates aren't all bad . . ..

31.4. The government could just give away the optimal number of grazing rights. Another alternative would be to sell the grazing rights. (Question: how much would these rights sell for? Hint: think about rents.) The government could also impose a tax, t per cow, such that $f(c^*)/c^* + t = a$.

32 Public Goods

32.1. It will *not* be the highest value. Rather, it will be the *second* highest value plus a dollar. The person who is *willing* to bid the highest gets the good, but he only has to pay the price of the second highest bidder plus a small amount.

32.2. The argument is similar to the argument for the Clarke tax. Consider increasing your bid above your true value. If you were the high bidder anyway, you don't change your chances of getting the good. If you were not the high bidder, then if you increase your bid enough to exceed the actual high bidder, you will get the good, but have to pay the price bid by the second highest bidder—which is more than the value of the good to you. A similar argument can be made for underbidding.

32.3. We want the sum of the marginal rates of substitution to equal the marginal cost of providing the public good. The sum of the MRSs is 20 ($= 10 \times 2$), and the marginal cost is $2x$. Thus we have the equation $2x = 20$, which implies that $x = 10$. So the Pareto efficient number of streetlights is 10.

INDEX

—   —   —